Sports Illustrated for KIDS

YEAR IN SPORTS 2007

from the Editors of SPORTS ILLUSTRATED FOR KIDS

SCHOLASTIC REFERENCE

AN IMPRINT OF

SCHOLASTIC

CONTENTS

Cover photography credits
Dwyane Wade: Patrick Farrell/Miami Herald/KRT/ABACA
Maria Sharapova: Bob Martin
Paul Konerko: Kevork Djansezian/AP
LaDainian Tomlinson: Charles Baus/Icon SMI
Lyn-Z Adams Hawkins:Scott Pommier/Transworld Skateboarding
Lauryn Williams: Stu Forster/Getty Images
Tiger Woods: Robert Beck

Back-cover photography credits
Eddie Johnson: John Todd/ISI
Michelle Wie: Darren Carroll
Reggie Bush: Peter Read Miller

SPORTS ILLUSTRATED FOR KIDS Year in Sports 2007 is a production of SPORTS ILLUSTRATED FOR KIDS and SPORTS
ILLUSTRATED FOR KIDS Books: Neil Cohen, Project Editor; Edward Duarte, Designer; Ryan Schick,
Photo Editor; George Amores, Photo Assistant; André Carter, Nick Friedman, Gary Gramling, Ted Keith,
Ellen C. Labrecque, Shawn Nicholls, David Scott, Sachin Shenolikar, Contributors; Nate Herpich,
Reporter; Melissa Kong, Richard Zuckerman, Editorial Assistants; Neal C. O'Shea, Production Artist

Scholastic Reference staff: Andrea Pinkney, Vice President and Publisher;
Brenda Murray, Assistant Editor; Karyn Browne, Managing Editor; Susan Casel, Production Editor;
Becky Terhune, Art Director; Jess White, Manufacturing Coordinator

ISBN 13: 978-0-439-82767-6
ISBN 10: 0-439-82767-1

10 9 8 7 6 5 4 3 2   06 07 08 09 10

Printed in the U.S.A. 23
First printing, December 2006

For much of the 2005 NFL season, it looked as if the Indianapolis Colts would not only win Super Bowl XL, but that they would also become the first NFL team to finish a season undefeated since the Miami Dolphins went 17-0 in 1972.

But a funny thing happened on the Colts' way into the record book. First, they were beaten by the San Diego Chargers in their 14th game of the season. Then, in the second round of the playoffs, they ran into the surging Pittsburgh Steelers. Playing on Indy's home turf, Pittsburgh managed to stop the powerful Colts offense and squeeze out a 21-18 upset win.

The two-time defending Super Bowl champion New England Patriots suffered through a season of injuries. They wound up winning the AFC East and still had a chance for a championship "three-peat." But they fell to the Denver Broncos, 27-13, in the second round of the playoffs. Pittsburgh and Denver clashed in the AFC Championship game in Denver, which Pittsburgh won 34-17.

Meanwhile, in the NFC, Seattle rode league MVP, Shaun Alexander, to a 13-3 regular-season record and a Number 1 seed in the playoffs. Alexander and the Seahawks beat Washington (20-10) and Carolina (34-14) in the playoffs to advance to Super Bowl XL in Detroit, Michigan.

After taking a 3-0 lead in the game, Seattle suffered through a rash of penalties and missed opportunities. Pittsburgh scored 21 of the game's next 28 points for a 21-10 victory and the franchise's first Super Bowl win since 1980.

The game was a homecoming for Steeler running back Jerome ("The Bus") Bettis, who was born in Detroit. After the game, The Bus announced he was parking himself in the garage for good. "I'm a champion. I think the Bus' last stop is here in Detroit," Bettis said. "It's official, like the referee whistle."

Steeler receiver Hines Ward was named the game's Most Valuable Player after catching five passes for 123 yards and a touchdown in the title game.

Other highlights of the 2005 NFL season included:

• In the AFC, the Cincinnati Bengals made a major improvement, led by quarterback Carson Palmer. The third-year pro threw for 3,836 yards and 32 touchdowns on the season and finished fifth in MVP balloting. The Bengals, who finished at 8-8 in 2004, were 11-5 in '05 but lost in the first round of the playoffs to Pittsburgh.

• In the NFC, the once famous "Monsters of the Midway" seemed to return to Chicago. The Bears went 11-5 just a year after finishing 5-11. Chicago's defense allowed a league-lowest 12.6 points per game and finished second in total defense (281.8 yards per game) to Tampa Bay (277.8).

BILL FRAKES

Quarterback Ben Roethlisberger directed the Steelers on a late-season surge that led to the Super Bowl.

AFC TEAMS

Baltimore Ravens
Buffalo Bills
Cincinnati Bengals
Cleveland Browns
Denver Broncos
Houston Texans
Indianapolis Colts
Jacksonville Jaguars
Kansas City Chiefs
Miami Dolphins
New England Patriots
New York Jets
Oakland Raiders
Pittsburgh Steelers
San Diego Chargers
Tennessee Titans

Receiver Hines Ward was the MVP of Super Bowl XL.

NFC TEAMS

Arizona Cardinals
Atlanta Falcons
Carolina Panthers
Chicago Bears
Dallas Cowboys
Detroit Lions
Green Bay Packers
Minnesota Vikings
New Orleans Saints
New York Giants
Philadelphia Eagles
San Francisco 49ers
Seattle Seahawks
St. Louis Rams
Tampa Bay Buccaneers
Washington Redskins

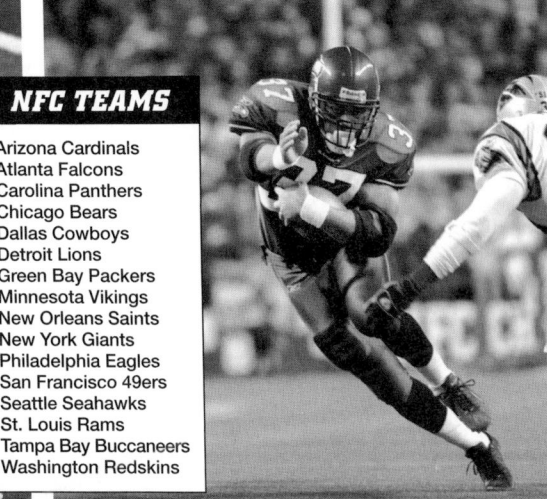

Running back Shaun Alexander of the Seattle Seahawks was named NFL MVP.

2005 NFL FINAL STANDINGS

AFC EAST

TEAM	W	L	T	PCT	PF	PA
y-Patriots	10	6	0	.625	379	338
Dolphins	9	7	0	.563	318	317
Bills	5	11	0	.313	271	367
Jets	4	12	0	.250	240	355

AFC NORTH

TEAM	W	L	T	PCT	PF	PA
y-Bengals	11	5	0	.688	421	350
x-Steelers	11	5	0	.688	389	258
Ravens	6	10	0	.375	265	299
Browns	6	10	0	.375	232	301

AFC SOUTH

TEAM	W	L	T	PCT	PF	PA
*z-Colts	14	2	0	.875	439	247
x-Jaguars	12	4	0	.750	361	269
Titans	4	12	0	.250	299	421
Texans	2	14	0	.125	260	431

AFC WEST

TEAM	W	L	T	PCT	PF	PA
y-Broncos	13	3	0	.813	395	258
Chiefs	10	6	0	.625	403	325
Chargers	9	7	0	.563	418	312
Raiders	4	12	0	.250	290	383

NFC EAST

TEAM	W	L	T	PCT	PF	PA
x-Giants	11	5	0	.688	422	314
x-Redskins	10	6	0	.625	359	293
Cowboys	9	7	0	.563	325	308
Eagles	6	10	0	.375	310	388

NFC NORTH

TEAM	W	L	T	PCT	PF	PA
y-Bears	11	5	0	.688	260	202
Vikings	9	7	0	.563	306	344
Lions	5	11	0	.313	254	345
Packers	4	12	0	.250	298	344

NFC SOUTH

TEAM	W	L	T	PCT	PF	PA
y-Buccaneers	11	5	0	.688	300	274
x-Panthers	11	5	0	.688	391	259
Falcons	8	8	0	.500	351	341
Saints	3	13	0	.188	235	398

NFC WEST

TEAM	W	L	T	PCT	PF	PA
*z-Seahawks	13	3	0	.813	452	271
Rams	6	10	0	.375	363	429
Cardinals	5	11	0	.313	311	387
49ers	4	12	0	.250	239	428

* clinched home-field advantage throughout the playoffs, x-clinched playoff berth, y-clinched division title, z-clinched first-round bye

KEY W=win; L=loss; T=tie; PCT=winning percentage; PF=points for; PA=points against

2005 NFL PLAYOFFS

| | | | AFC | | | | | NFC | | |

AFC bracket:
- New England Patriots 28
- Jacksonville Jaguars 3
- New England Patriots 13
- Denver Broncos 27
- Denver Broncos 17
- **PITTSBURGH STEELERS 21**
- Seattle Seahawks 10
- Indianapolis Colts 18
- Pittsburgh Steelers 34
- Pittsburgh Steelers 21
- Pittsburgh Steelers 31
- Cincinnati Bengals 17

NFC bracket:
- Washington Redskins 17
- Tampa Bay Buccaneers 10
- Washington Redskins 10
- Seattle Seahawks 34
- Seattle Seahawks 20
- Carolina Panthers 14
- Chicago Bears 21
- Carolina Panthers 29
- Carolina Panthers 23
- New York Giants 0

WILD CARD · DIV. PLAYOFF · CONF. CHAMPIONSHIP · CONF. CHAMPIONSHIP · DIV. PLAYOFF · WILD CARD

AFC WILD-CARD GAMES

NEW ENGLAND PATRIOTS 28
JACKSONVILLE JAGUARS 3

	1Q	2Q	3Q	4Q	T
JAGUARS	0	3	0	0	3
PATRIOTS	0	7	14	7	28

1ST QUARTER
None
2ND QUARTER
TD NE: Troy Brown, 11-yard pass from Tom Brady (Adam Vinatieri kick), 2:52. Drive: 6 plays, 37 yards in 2:05.
FG Jax: Josh Scobee, 36 yards, 13:55. Drive: 12 plays, 56 yards in 5:45.
3RD QUARTER
TD NE: David Givens, 3-yard pass from Tom Brady (Adam Vinatieri kick), 7:47. Drive: 12 plays, 81 yards in 6:42.
TD NE: Benjamin Watson, 63-yard pass from Tom Brady (Adam Vinatieri kick), 11:57. Drive: 5 plays, 71 yards in 2:53.
4TH QUARTER
TD NE: Asante Samuel, 73-yard interception return (Adam Vinatieri kick), 0:14.

PITTSBURGH STEELERS 31
CINCINNATI BENGALS 17

	1Q	2Q	3Q	4Q	T
STEELERS	0	14	14	3	31
BENGALS	10	7	0	0	17

1ST QUARTER
FG Cin: Shayne Graham, 23 yards. Drive: 9 plays, 84 yards in 4:25.
TD Cin: Rudi Johnson, 20-yard run (Shayne Graham kick), 13:51. Drive: 7 plays, 76 yards in 3:26.
2ND QUARTER
TD Pitt: Willie Parker, 19-yard pass from Ben Roethlisberger (Jeff Reed kick). Drive: 8 plays, 60 yards in 2:58.
TD Cin: T.J. Houshmandzadeh, 7-yard pass from Jon Kitna (Shayne Graham kick). Drive: 15 plays, 67 yards in 6:58.
TD Pitt: Hines Ward, 5-yard pass from Ben Roethlisberger (Jeff Reed kick). Drive: 6 plays, 76 yards in 2:25.
3RD QUARTER
TD Pitt: Jerome Bettis, 5-yard run (Jeff Reed kick). Drive: 8 plays, 66 yards in 4:39.
TD Pitt: Cedrick Wilson, 43-yard pass from Ben Roethlisberger (Jeff Reed kick). Drive: 3 plays, 50 yards in 1:25.
4TH QUARTER
FG Pitt: Jeff Reed, 21 yards, 4:31. Drive: 6 plays, 37 yards in 2:56.

FAST FACT

New Orleans has hosted the Super Bowl the most times (nine). Miami, the site of Super Bowl XLI, will tie that mark on February 4, 2007.

NFC WILD-CARD GAMES

WASHINGTON REDSKINS 17
TAMPA BAY BUCCANEERS 10

	1Q	2Q	3Q	4Q	T
REDSKINS	14	3	0	0	17
BUCCANEERS	0	3	7	0	10

1ST QUARTER
TD Wash: Clinton Portis 6-yard run (John Hall kick), 6:20. Drive: 1 play, 6 yards in :05.
TD Wash: Sean Taylor, 51-yard fumble return (John Hall kick), 10:45.
2ND QUARTER
FG Tam: Matt Bryant, 43 yards, 4:58. Drive: 11 plays, 38 yards in 5:28.
FG Wash: John Hall, 47 yards, 9:26. Drive: 10 plays, 40 yards in 4:28.
3RD QUARTER
TD Tam: Chris Simms, 2-yard run (Matt Bryant kick), 5:20. Drive: 7 plays, 51 yards in 3:23.
4TH QUARTER
None

CAROLINA PANTHERS 23
NEW YORK GIANTS 0

	1Q	2Q	3Q	4Q	T
PANTHERS	0	10	7	6	23
GIANTS	0	0	0	0	0

1ST QUARTER
None
2ND QUARTER
TD Car: Steve Smith, 22-yard pass from Jake Delhomme (John Kasay kick), 5:19. Drive: 12 plays, 77 yards in 7:46.
FG Car: John Kasay, 4 plays, 2 yards in :58.
3RD QUARTER
TD Car: Steve Smith, 12-yard run (John Kasay kick), 8:03. Drive: 1 play, 12 yards in :06.
4TH QUARTER
FG Car: John Kasay, 45 yards, 1:27. Drive: 10 plays, 55 yards in 6:07.
FG Car: John Kasay, 18 yards, 12:20. Drive: 14 plays, 55 yards in 8:55.

AFC DIVISIONAL GAMES

PITTSBURGH STEELERS 21
INDIANAPOLIS COLTS 18

	1Q	2Q	3Q	4Q	T
STEELERS	14	0	7	0	21
COLTS	0	3	0	15	18

1ST QUARTER
TD Pitt: Antwaan Randle El, 6-yard pass from Ben Roethlisberger (Jeff Reed kick), 5:35. Drive: 10 plays, 84 yards in 5:35.
TD Pitt: Heath Miller, 7-yard pass from Ben Roethlisberger (Jeff Reed kick), 11:48. Drive: 7 plays, 72 yards in 2:53.
2ND QUARTER
FG Ind: Mike Vanderjagt, 20 yards, 13:40. Drive: 15 plays, 96 yards in 9:39.
3RD QUARTER
TD Pitt: Jerome Bettis, 1-yard run (Jeff Reed kick), 13:34. Drive: 6 plays, 30 yards in 3:21.
4TH QUARTER
TD Ind: Dallas Clark, 50-yard pass from Peyton Manning (Mike Vanderjagt kick), 0:51. Drive: 6 plays, 72 yards in 2:17.
TD Ind: Edgerrin James, 3-yard run (Peyton Manning pass to Reggie Wayne for two-point conversion), 10:36. Drive: 6 plays, 80 yards in 1:39.

DENVER BRONCOS 27
NEW ENGLAND PATRIOTS 13

	1Q	2Q	3Q	4Q	T
PATRIOTS	0	3	3	7	13
BRONCOS	0	10	7	10	27

1ST QUARTER
None
2ND QUARTER
FG NE: Adam Vinatieri, 40 yards, 11:12. Drive: 7 plays, 67 yards in 2:22.
TD Den: Mike Anderson, 1-yard run (Jason Elam kick), 13:18. Drive: 1 play, 40 yards in :09.
FG Den: Jason Elam, 50 yards, 14:17. Drive: 4 plays, 7 yards in :50.
3RD QUARTER
FG NE: Adam Vinatieri, 32 yards, 7:11. Drive: 11 plays, 58 yards in 5:32.
TD Den: Mike Anderson, 1-yard run (Jason Elam kick), 14:17. Drive: 1 play, 1 yard in :04.
4TH QUARTER
TD Den: Rod Smith, 4-yard pass from Jake Plummer (Jason Elam kick), 6:22. Drive: 3 plays, 15 yards in 1:32.
TD NE: David Givens, 4-yard pass from Tom Brady (Adam Vinatieri kick), 6:55. Drive: 2 plays, 77 yards in :33.
FG Den: Jason Elam, 34 yards, 11:40. Drive: 8 plays, 61 yards in 4:41.

TRIVIA CHALLENGE

Only one team has ever beaten the Number 1, Number 2, and Number 3 seeds in its conference to reach the Super Bowl. Name that team.

Pittsburgh. In 2005, the Steelers beat Indianapolis, Denver, and Cincinnati.

NFC DIVISIONAL GAMES

SEATTLE SEAHAWKS 20
WASHINGTON REDSKINS 10

	1Q	2Q	3Q	4Q	T
REDSKINS	0	3	0	7	10
SEAHAWKS	0	7	7	6	20

1ST QUARTER
None
2ND QUARTER
FG Wash: John Hall, 26 yards, 6:01. Drive: 10 plays, 32 yards in 5:03.
TD Sea: Darrell Jackson, 29-yard pass from Matt Hasselbeck (Josh Brown kick), 11:38. Drive: 12 plays, 74 yards in 5:37.
3RD QUARTER
TD Sea: Matt Hasselbeck, 6-yard run (Josh Brown kick), 5:25. Drive: 10 plays, 81 yards in 4:20.
4TH QUARTER
FG Sea: Josh Brown, 33 yards, 0:44. Drive: 6 plays, 48 yards, 2:39.
TD Wash: Santana Moss, 20-yard pass from Mark Brunell (John Hall kick), 3:01. Drive: 4 plays, 76 yards in 2:17.
FG Sea: Josh Brown, 31 yards, 12:06. Drive: 9 plays, 60 yards in 5:07.

CAROLINA PANTHERS 29
CHICAGO BEARS 21

	1Q	2Q	3Q	4Q	T
PANTHERS	7	9	7	6	29
BEARS	0	7	7	7	21

1ST QUARTER
TD Car: Steve Smith, 58-yard pass from Jake Delhomme (John Kasay kick), 0:55. Drive: 2 plays, 60 yards in :55.
2ND QUARTER
FG Car: John Kasay, 20 yards, 0:03. Drive: 10 plays, 62 yards in 4:01.
FG Car: John Kasay, 38 yards, 8:34. Drive: 8 plays, 40 yards in 4:26.
TD Chi: Adrian Peterson, 1-yard run (Robbie Gould kick), 13:03. Drive: 9 plays, 67 yards in 4:29.
FG Car: John Kasay, 37 yards, 15:00. Drive: 8 plays, 51 yards in 1:57.
3RD QUARTER
TD Chi: Desmond Clark, 1-yard pass from Rex Grossman (Robbie Gould kick), 3:39. Drive: 8 plays, 68 yards in 3:39.
TD Car: Steve Smith, 39-yard pass from Jake Delhomme (John Kasay kick), 12:53. Drive: 5 plays, 56 yards in 3:24.
4TH QUARTER
TD Chi: Jason Mckie, 3-yard run (Robbie Gould kick), 2:37. Drive: 11 plays, 66 yards in 4:44.
TD Car: Kris Magnum, 1-yard pass from Jake Delhomme (Pat failed), 6:56. Drive: 7 plays, 62 yards in 4:19.

AFC CONFERENCE CHAMPIONSHIP

PITTSBURGH STEELERS 34
DENVER BRONCOS 17

	1Q	2Q	3Q	4Q	T
STEELERS	3	21	0	10	34
BRONCOS	0	3	7	7	17

1ST QUARTER
FG Pitt: Jeff Reed, 47 yards, 10:49. Drive: 12 plays, 62 yards in 6:29.
2ND QUARTER
TD Pitt: Cedrick Wilson, 12-yard pass from Ben Roethlisberger (Jeff Reed kick), 0:06. Drive: 5 plays, 39 yards in 2:53.
FG Den: Jason Elam, 23 yards, 5:37. Drive: 12 plays, 55 yards in 5:31.
TD Pitt: Jerome Bettis, 3-yard run, 13:05. Drive: 14 plays, 80 yards in 7:28.
TD Pitt: Hines Ward, 17-yard pass from Ben Roethlisberger (Jeff Reed kick), 14:53. Drive: 4 plays, 38 yards in 1:41.
3RD QUARTER
TD Den: Ashley Lelie, 30-yard pass from Jake Plummer (Jason Elam kick), 11:24. Drive: 5 plays, 80 yards in 2:24.
4TH QUARTER
FG Pitt: Jeff Reed, 42 yards, 1:22. Drive: 8 plays, 47 yards in 4:58.
TD Den: Mike Anderson, 3-yard run (Jason Elam kick), 7:08. Drive: 7 plays, 85 yards in 3:47.
TD Pitt: Ben Roethlisberger, 4-yard run (Jeff Reed kick), 12:01. Drive: 5 plays, 17 yards in 1:53.

NFC CONFERENCE CHAMPIONSHIP

SEATTLE SEAHAWKS 34
CAROLINA PANTHERS 14

	1Q	2Q	3Q	4Q	T
PANTHERS	0	7	0	7	14
SEAHAWKS	10	10	7	7	34

1ST QUARTER
TD Sea: Jerramy Stevens, 17-yard pass from Matt Hasselbeck (Josh Brown kick), 9:29. Drive: 5 plays, 57 yards in 2:16.
FG Sea: Josh Brown, 24 yards, 12:37. Drive: 6 plays, 14 yards in 2:44.
2ND QUARTER
TD Sea: Shaun Alexander, 1-yard run (Josh Brown kick), 0:07. Drive: 4 plays, 17 yards in :57.
TD Car: Steve Smith, 59-yard punt return (John Kasay kick), 5:55.
FG Sea: Josh Brown, 39 yards, 10:57. Drive: 10 plays, 57 yards in 5:02.
3RD QUARTER
TD Sea: Darrell Jackson, 20 yard pass from Matt Hasselbeck (Josh Brown kick), 3:51. Drive: 8 plays, 65 yards in 3:51.
4TH QUARTER
TD Sea: Shaun Alexander, 1-yard run (Josh Brown kick), 9:00. Drive: 8 plays, 53 yards in 4:48.
TD Car: Drew Carter, 47-yard pass from Jake Delhomme (John Kasay kick), 9:51. Drive: 4 plays, 80 yards in :51.

SUPER BOWL XL

PITTSBURGH STEELERS 21
SEATTLE SEAHAWKS 10

FEBRUARY 5, 2006
FORD FIELD, DETROIT, MICHIGAN

	1Q	2Q	3Q	4Q	T
STEELERS	0	7	7	7	21
SEAHAWKS	3	0	7	0	10

1ST QUARTER
FG Sea: Josh Brown, 47 yards, 14:38. Drive: 7 plays, 22 yards in 3:34.

2ND QUARTER
TD Pitt: Ben Roethlisberger, 1-yard run (Jeff Reed kick), 13:05. Drive: 11 plays, 59 yards in 6:20.

3RD QUARTER
TD Pitt: Willie Parker, 75-yard run (Jeff Reed kick), 0:22.
TD Sea: Jerramy Stevens, 16-yard pass from Matt Hasselbeck (Josh Brown kick), 8:15. Drive: 3 plays, 20 yards in :53.

4TH QUARTER
TD Pitt: Hines Ward, 43-yard pass from Antwaan Randle El (Jeff Reed kick), 6:04. Drive: 4 plays, 56 yards in 1:50.

LEGENDS

Joe Namath led one of the great upsets in NFL history.

MARVIN E. NEWMAN

■ **Joe Namath, quarterback,** b. May 31, 1943, Beaver Falls, Pennsylvania. "Broadway Joe" was one of the most exciting quarterbacks ever to play pro football. He earned respect for the old American Football League and helped bring about its merger with the NFL. After the AFL had been thrashed by the NFL in the first two championship games between the rival leagues, Namath brashly predicted his Jets would defeat the NFL's Baltimore Colts in Super Bowl III. He then went out and pulled off a 16-7 upset victory. With his powerful arm and lightning-quick release, Namath was the first quarterback to pass for more than 4,000 yards in a season. He was the AFL Rookie of the Year in 1965, and despite a career filled with knee injuries, completed 1,886 passes for 27,663 yards and 173 touchdowns in 12 seasons with the Jets and one with the Los Angeles Rams. He was inducted into the Pro Football Hall of Fame in 1985.

■ **Deacon Jones, defensive end,** b. December 9, 1938, Eatonville, Florida. David D. (Deacon) Jones is the grandfather of the "sack" — a term he is credited with inventing. Jones spent most of his 14-year career with the Los Angeles Rams, anchoring their famous defensive line, the Fearsome Foursome. At 6'4" and 272 pounds, he led the way for big, fast linemen like today's Richard Seymour (Patriots) and Dwight Freeney (Colts). Deacon played in eight Pro Bowls and was a unanimous all-league pick for six straight years (1965-70). He missed just five of a possible 196 regular-season games in his career, and was inducted into the Pro Football Hall of Fame in 1980.

■ **Mike Ditka, tight end,** b. October 18, 1939, Carnegie, Pennsylvania. Ditka is best known today for his successful run as the head coach of the Chicago Bears (1982-92, including a victory in Super Bowl XX) and later the New Orleans Saints (1997-99). But before that, he was a legendary player. Ditka is the first tight end ever elected to the Pro Football Hall of Fame (1988). He was the NFL Rookie of the Year in 1961, and was named to five Pro Bowls. Ditka played 12 seasons in the NFL, six with the Chicago Bears. He finished his career with 427 receptions for 5,812 yards and 43 touchdowns. He was known for his outstanding blocking, but was also a reliable receiver — a rarity for a tight end in his day.

SUPER BOWL XL (cont.)

TEAM STATS

	SEAHAWKS	STEELERS
First Downs	20	14
Rushing	5	6
Passing	15	8
Penalty	0	0
3rd-Down Conversions	5-17	8-15
4th-Down Conversions	1-2	0-0
Total Net Yards	396	339
Total Plays	77	56
Average Gain	5.1	6.1
Net Yards Rushing	137	181
Rushes	25	33
Avg. Per Rush	5.5	5.5

	SEAHAWKS	STEELERS
Net Yards Passing	259	158
Comp.-Att.	26-49	10-22
Yards Per Pass	5.0	6.9
Sacked-Yards Lost	3-14	1-8
Had Intercepted	1	2
Punts-Average	6-50.2	6-48.7
Return Yards	174	99
Punts-Returns	4-27	2-32
Kickoffs-Returns	4-71	2-43
Int.-Returns	2-76	1-24
Penalties-Yards	7-70	3-20
Fumbles-Lost	0-0	0-0
Time of Pos.	33:02	26:58

PLAYER STATISTICS: SEAHAWKS

OFFENSE

PASSING	COMP-ATT	YDS	TD	INT
Matt Hasselbeck	26-49	273	1	1

RUSHING	ATT	YDS	TD	LG
Shaun Alexander	20	95	0	21
Matt Hasselbeck	3	35	0	18
Mack Strong	2	7	0	7

RECEIVING	REC	YDS	TD	LG
Bobby Engram	6	70	0	21
Joe Jurevicius	5	93	0	35
Darrell Jackson	5	50	0	20
Jerramy Stevens	3	25	1	16
Mack Strong	2	15	0	13
Ryan Hannam	2	12	0	9
Shaun Alexander	2	2	0	4
Maurice Morris	1	6	0	6

DEFENSE	T-A	SCK	INT	FF
Lofa Tatupu	6-3	0	0	0
LeRoy Hill	7-1	0	0	0
Michael Boulware	2-3	0	1	0
Etric Pruitt	4-0	0	0	0
D.D. Lewis	2-2	0	0	0
Marcus Trufant	3-0	0	0	0
Jordan Babineaux	2-0	0	0	0
Grant Wistrom	2-0	1	0	8
Niko Koutouvides	2-0	0	0	0
Rocky Bernard	2-0	0	0	0
Marcus Tubbs	2-0	0	0	0
Marquand Manuel	1-0	0	0	0
Chartric Darby	1-0	0	0	0
Isaiah Kacyvenski	1-0	0	0	0
Matt Hasselbeck	1-0	0	0	0
Kelly Herndon	0-1	0	1	0

PLAYER STATISTICS: STEELERS

OFFENSE

PASSING	COMP-ATT	YDS	TD	INT
Ben Roethlisberger	9-21	123	0	2
Antwaan Randle El	1-1	43	1	0

RUSHING	ATT	YDS	TD	LG
Willie Parker	10	93	1	75
Jerome Bettis	14	43	0	12
Ben Roethlisberger	7	25	1	10
Hines Ward	1	18	0	18
Verron Haynes	1	2	0	2

RECEIVING	REC	YDS	TD	LG
Hines Ward	5	123	1	43
Antwaan Randle El	3	22	0	8
Cedrick Wilson	1	20	0	20
Willie Parker	1	1	0	1

DEFENSE	T-A	SCK	INT	FF
Ike Taylor	6-1	0	1	0
Deshea Townsend	5-1	1	0	0
James Farrior	4-2	0	0	0
Clark Haggans	5-0	1	0	0
Troy Polamalu	4-1	0	0	0
Larry Foote	4-1	0	0	0
Casey Hampton	4-0	1	0	0
Aaron Smith	3-1	0	0	0
Brett Keisel	2-0	0	0	0
Joey Porter	3-0	0	0	0
James Harrison	2-1	0	0	0
Tyrone Carter	2-1	0	0	0
Chris Hope	1-2	0	0	0
Bryant McFadden	2-0	0	0	0
Antwaan Randle El	2-0	0	0	0
Kimo von Oelhoffen	2-0	0	0	0
Clint Kriewaldt	1-1	0	0	0
Chidi Iwuoma	1-0	0	0	0
Ricardo Colclough	1-0	0	0	0
Chris Hoke	1-0	0	0	0

KEY COMP-ATT=completions-attempts; YDS=yards; TD=touchdowns; INT=interceptions; ATT=attempts; LG=long; REC=receptions; T-A=tackles-assists; SCK=sacks; FF=forced fumbles

THE ASSOCIATED PRESS 2005 ALL-PRO TEAM

OFFENSE

QUARTERBACK Peyton Manning, Indianapolis Colts

RUNNING BACKS Shaun Alexander, Seattle Seahawks; Tiki Barber, NY Giants

FULLBACK Mack Strong, Seattle Seahawks

TIGHT END Antonio Gates, San Diego Chargers

WIDE RECEIVERS Steve Smith, Carolina Panthers; Chad Johnson, Cincinnati Bengals

TACKLES Walter Jones, Seattle Seahawks; Willie Anderson, Cincinnati Bengals

GUARDS Steve Hutchinson, Seattle Seahawks; Alan Faneca, Pittsburgh Steelers; Brian Waters, Kansas City Chiefs

CENTER Jeff Saturday, Indianapolis Colts

KICKER Neil Rackers, Arizona Cardinals

KICK RETURNER Jerome Mathis, Houston Texans

Brian Urlacher
Chicago Bears

DEFENSE

ENDS Dwight Freeney, Indianapolis Colts; Osi Umenyiora, NY Giants

TACKLES Jamal Williams, San Diego Chargers; Richard Seymour, New England Patriots

OUTSIDE LINEBACKERS Lance Briggs, Chicago Bears; Derrick Brooks, Tampa Bay Buccaneers

INSIDE LINEBACKERS Brian Urlacher, Chicago Bears; Al Wilson, Denver Broncos

CORNERBACKS Ronde Barber, Tampa Bay Buccaneers; Champ Bailey, Denver Broncos

SAFETIES Troy Polamalu, Tampa Bay Buccaneers; Bob Sanders, Indianapolis Colts

PUNTER Brian Moorman, Buffalo Bills

2005 REGULAR-SEASON RESULTS — AFC

BALTIMORE RAVENS

WEEK	OPPONENT	SCORE	W/L/T
1	COLTS	7–24	L
2	at Titans	10–25	L
3	BYE WEEK	–	–
4	JETS	13–3	W
5	at Lions	17–35	L
6	BROWNS	16–3	W
7	at Bears	6–10	L
8	at Steelers	19–20	L
9	BENGALS	9–21	L
10	at Jaguars	3–30	L
11	STEELERS	16–13	W
12	at Bengals	29–42	L
13	TEXANS	16–15	W
14	at Broncos	10–12	L
15	PACKERS	48–3	W
16	VIKINGS	30–23	W
17	at Browns	16–20	L

BUFFALO BILLS

WEEK	OPPONENT	SCORE	W/L/T
1	TEXANS	22–7	W
2	at Buccaneers	19–3	L
3	FALCONS	24–16	L
4	at Saints	19–7	L
5	DOLPHINS	20–14	W
6	JETS	27–17	W
7	at Raiders	38–17	L
8	at Patriots	21–16	L
9	BYE WEEK	–	–
10	CHIEFS	14–3	W
11	at Chargers	48–10	L
12	PANTHERS	13–9	L
13	at Dolphins	24–23	L
14	PATRIOTS	35–7	L
15	BRONCOS	28–17	L
16	at Bengals	37–27	W
17	at Jets	30–26	L

CINCINNATI BENGALS

WEEK	OPPONENT	SCORE	W/L/T
1	at Browns	27–13	W
2	VIKINGS	37–8	W
3	at Bears	24–7	W
4	TEXANS	16–10	W
5	at Jaguars	20–23	L
6	at Titans	31–23	W
7	STEELERS	13–27	L
8	PACKERS	21–14	W
9	at Ravens	21–9	W
10	BYE WEEK	–	–
11	COLTS	37–45	L
12	RAVENS	42–29	W
13	at Steelers	38–31	W
14	BROWNS	23–20	W
15	at Lions	41–17	W
16	BILLS	27–37	L
17	at Chiefs	3–37	L

Note: Home games are capitalized.

CLEVELAND BROWNS

WEEK	OPPONENT	SCORE	W/L/T
1	BENGALS	13–27	L
2	at Packers	26–24	W
3	at Colts	6–13	L
4	BYE WEEK	–	–
5	BEARS	20–10	W
6	at Ravens	3–16	L
7	LIONS	10–13	L
8	at Texans	16–19	L
9	TITANS	20–14	W
10	at Steelers	21–34	L
11	DOLPHINS	22–0	W
12	at Vikings	12–24	L
13	JAGUARS	14–20	L
14	at Bengals	20–23	L
15	at Raiders	9–7	W
16	STEELERS	0–41	L
17	RAVENS	20–16	W

2005 REGULAR-SEASON RESULTS — AFC (cont.)

DENVER BRONCOS

WEEK	OPPONENT	SCORE	W/L/T
1	at Dolphins	10–34	L
2	CHARGERS	20–17	W
3	CHIEFS	30–10	W
4	at Jacksonville	20–7	W
5	REDSKINS	21–19	W
6	PATRIOTS	28–20	W
7	at Giants	23–24	L
8	EAGLES	49–21	W
9	BYE WEEK	—	—
10	at Raiders	31–17	W
11	JETS	27–0	W
12	at Cowboys	24–21	W
13	at Chiefs	27–31	L
14	RAVENS	12–10	W
15	at Bills	28–17	W
16	RAIDERS	22–3	W
17	at Chargers	23–7	W

HOUSTON TEXANS

WEEK	OPPONENT	SCORE	W/L/T
1	at Bills	7–22	L
2	STEELERS	7–27	L
3	BYE WEEK	—	—
4	at Bengals	10–16	L
5	TITANS	20–34	L
6	at Seahawks	10–42	L
7	COLTS	20–38	L
8	BROWNS	19–16	W
9	at Jaguars	14–21	L
10	at Colts	17–31	L
11	CHIEFS	17–45	L
12	RAMS	27–33	L
13	at Ravens	15–16	L
14	at Titans	10–13	L
15	CARDINALS	30–19	W
16	Jaguars	20–38	L
17	at 49ers	17–20	L

INDIANAPOLIS COLTS

WEEK	OPPONENT	SCORE	W/L/T
1	at Ravens	24–7	W
2	Jaguars	10–3	W
3	BROWNS	13–6	W
4	at Titans	31–10	W
5	at 49ers	28–3	W
6	RAMS	45–28	W
7	at Texans	38–20	W
8	BYE WEEK	—	—
9	at Patriots	40–21	W
10	TEXANS	31–17	W
11	at Bengals	45–37	W
12	STEELERS	26–7	W
13	TENNESSEE	35–3	W
14	at Jaguars	26–18	W
15	CHARGERS	17–26	L
16	at Seahawks	13–28	L
17	CARDINALS	17–13	W

JACKSONVILLE JAGUARS

WEEK	OPPONENT	SCORE	W/L/T
1	SEAHAWKS	26–14	W
2	at Colts	3–10	L
3	at Jets	26–20	W
4	BRONCOS	7–20	L
5	BENGALS	23–20	W
6	at Steelers	23–17	W
7	BYE WEEK	—	—
8	at Rams	21–24	L
9	TEXANS	21–14	W
10	RAVENS	30–3	W
11	at Titans	31–28	W
12	at Cardinals	24–17	W
13	at Browns	20–14	W
14	COLTS	18–26	L
15	49ERS	10–9	W
16	at Texans	38–20	W
17	TITANS	40–14	W

KANSAS CITY CHIEFS

WEEK	OPPONENT	SCORE	W/L/T
1	JETS	27–7	W
2	at Raiders	23–17	W
3	at Broncos	10–30	L
4	EAGLES	31–37	L
5	BYE WEEK	—	—
6	REDSKINS	28–21	W
7	at Dolphins	30–20	W
8	at Chargers	20–28	L
9	RAIDERS	27–23	W
10	at Bills	3–14	L
11	at Texans	45–17	W
12	PATRIOTS	26–16	W
13	BRONCOS	31–27	W
14	at Cowboys	28–31	L
15	at Giants	17–27	L
16	CHARGERS	20–7	W
17	BENGALS	37–3	W

MIAMI DOLPHINS

WEEK	OPPONENT	SCORE	W/L/T
1	BRONCOS	34–10	W
2	at Jets	7–17	L
3	PANTHERS	27–24	W
4	BYE WEEK	—	—
5	at Bills	14–20	L
6	at Buccaneers	13–27	L
7	CHIEFS	20–30	L
8	at Saints	21–6	W
9	FALCONS	10–17	L
10	PATRIOTS	16–23	L
11	at Browns	0–22	L
12	at Raiders	33–21	W
13	BILLS	24–23	W
14	at Chargers	23–21	W
15	JETS	24–20	W
16	TITANS	24–10	W
17	at Patriots	28–26	W

2005 REGULAR-SEASON RESULTS — AFC (cont.)

NEW ENGLAND PATRIOTS

WEEK	OPPONENT	SCORE	W/L/T
1	RAIDERS	30–20	W
2	at Panthers	27–17	L
3	at Steelers	23–20	W
4	CHARGERS	41–17	L
5	at Falcons	31–28	W
6	at Broncos	28–20	L
7	BYE WEEK	—	—
8	BILLS	21–16	W
9	COLTS	40–21	L
10	at Dolphins	23–16	W
11	SAINTS	24–17	W
12	at Chiefs	26–16	L
13	JETS	16–3	W
14	at Bills	35–7	W
15	BUCCANEERS	28–0	W
16	at Jets	31–21	W
17	DOLPHINS	28–26	L

NEW YORK JETS

WEEK	OPPONENT	SCORE	W/L/T
1	at Chiefs	7–27	L
2	DOLPHINS	17–7	W
3	JAGUARS	20–26	L
4	at Ravens	3–13	L
5	BUCCANEERS	14–12	W
6	at Bills	17–27	L
7	at Falcons	14–27	L
8	BYE WEEK	—	—
9	CHARGERS	26–31	L
10	at Panthers	3–30	L
11	at Broncos	0–27	L
12	SAINTS	19–21	L
13	at Patriots	3–16	L
14	Raiders	26–10	W
15	DOLPHINS	20–24	L
16	PATRIOTS	21–31	L
17	BILLS	30–26	W

OAKLAND RAIDERS

WEEK	OPPONENT	SCORE	W/L/T
*1	at Patriots	20–30	L
2	CHIEFS	17–23	L
3	at Eagles	20–23	L
4	COWBOYS	19–13	W
5	BYE WEEK	—	—
6	CHARGERS	14–27	L
7	BILLS	38–17	W
8	at Titans	34–25	W
9	at Chiefs	23–27	L
10	BRONCOS	17–31	L
11	at Redskins	16–13	W
12	DOLPHINS	21–33	L
13	at Chargers	10–34	L
14	at Jets	10–26	L
15	BROWNS	7–9	L
16	at Broncos	3–22	L
17	GIANTS	21–30	L

PITTSBURGH STEELERS

WEEK	OPPONENT	SCORE	W/L/T
1	TITANS	34–7	W
2	at Texans	27–7	W
3	PATRIOTS	20–23	L
4	BYE WEEK	—	—
5	at Chargers	24–22	W
6	JAGUARS	17–23	L
7	at Bengals	27–13	W
8	RAVENS	20–19	W
9	at Packers	20–10	W
10	BROWNS	34–21	W
11	at Ravens	13–16	L
12	at Colts	7–26	L
13	BENGALS	38–31	L
14	BEARS	21–9	W
15	at Vikings	18–3	W
16	at Browns	41–0	W
17	LIONS	35–21	W

SAN DIEGO CHARGERS

WEEK	OPPONENT	SCORE	W/L/T
1	COWBOYS	24–28	L
2	at Broncos	17–20	L
3	GIANTS	45–23	W
4	at Patriots	41–17	W
5	STEELERS	22–24	L
6	at Raiders	27–14	W
7	at Eagles	17–20	L
8	CHIEFS	28–20	W
9	at Jets	31–26	W
10	BYE WEEK	—	—
11	BILLS	48–10	W
12	at Redskins	23–17	W
13	RAIDERS	34–10	W
14	DOLPHINS	21–23	L
15	at Colts	26–17	W
16	at Chiefs	7–20	L
17	BRONCOS	7–23	L

TENNESSEE TITANS

WEEK	OPPONENT	SCORE	W/L/T
1	at Steelers	7–34	L
2	RAVENS	25–10	W
3	at Rams	27–31	L
4	COLTS	10–31	L
5	at Texans	43–20	W
6	BENGALS	23–31	L
7	at Cardinals	10–20	L
8	RAIDERS	25–34	L
9	at Browns	14–20	L
10	BYE WEEK	—	—
11	JAGUARS	28–31	L
12	49ERS	33–22	W
13	at Colts	3–35	L
14	TEXANS	13–10	W
15	SEAHAWKS	24–28	L
16	at Dolphins	10–24	L
17	at Jaguars	13–40	L

2005 REGULAR-SEASON RESULTS – NFC

ARIZONA CARDINALS

WEEK	OPPONENT	SCORE	W/L/T
1	at Giants	19–42	L
2	RAMS	12–17	L
3	at Seahawks	12–37	L
4	49ERS	31–14	W
5	PANTHERS	20–24	W
6	BYE WEEK	–	–
7	TITANS	20–10	W
8	at Cowboys	13–34	L
9	SEAHAWKS	19–33	L
10	at Lions	21–29	L
11	at Rams	38–28	W
12	JAGUARS	17–24	L
13	at 49ers	17–10	W
14	REDSKINS	13–17	L
15	at Texans	19–30	L
16	EAGLES	27–21	W
17	at Colts	13–17	L

DID YOU KNOW?

Three NFL tight ends who never played college football scored touchdowns for their teams in 2005: Wesley Duke of Denver, Antonio Gates of San Diego, and Marcus Pollard of Detroit.

FAST FACT

Members of the winning team in Super Bowl XL each received $73,000. The loser's share was $38,000 per player.

TODAY'S STARS

JOE MURPHY/WIREIMAGE.COM

Marvin Harrison is half of the top TD-pass combination in NFL history.

■ **Marvin Harrison, wide receiver,** b. August 25, 1972, Philadelphia, Pennsylvania. Peyton Manning's favorite receiver had another spectacular season in 2005, catching 82 passes for 1,146 yards and 12 touchdowns. Harrison and Manning now own the record for most touchdown passes thrown/caught by a duo (94, breaking the previous record of 85 held by Steve Young and Jerry Rice). Harrison was named to his seventh straight Pro Bowl.

■ **Shaun Alexander, running back,** b. August 30, 1977, Florence, Kentucky. Alexander was named the NFL's Most Valuable Player for the 2005 season for leading the Seattle Seahawks to the NFC championship. Starting all 16 regular-season games, Alexander rushed 370 times for 1,880 yards and a league-record 28 touchdowns (27 rushing and one receiving). He also became the only player in NFL history to score at least 15 touchdowns in five straight seasons.

■ **Carson Palmer, quarterback,** b. December 27, 1979, Mission Viejo, California. In his third year as a Bengal, Palmer led Cincinnati to an 11-5 record and its first winning season since 1990. Palmer paced the NFL in three major passing categories: TD passes (a team-record 32), completion percentage (67.8) and touchdown/interception differential (plus 20: 32 TDs/12 picks). The Bengals were beaten by Pittsburgh in the wild card round of the playoffs, after Palmer was knocked out of the game early with an injured knee.

ATLANTA FALCONS

WEEK	OPPONENT	SCORE	W/L/T
1	EAGLES	14–10	W
2	at Seahawks	18–21	L
3	at Bills	24–16	W
4	VIKINGS	30–10	W
5	PATRIOTS	28–31	L
6	at Saints	34–31	W
7	JETS	27–14	W
8	BYE WEEK	—	—
9	at Dolphins	17–10	W
10	PACKERS	25–33	L
11	BUCCANEERS	27–30	L
12	at Lions	27–7	W
13	at Panthers	6–24	L
14	SAINTS	36–17	W
15	at Bears	3–16	L
16	at Buccaneers	24–27	L
17	PANTHERS	11–44	L

CAROLINA PANTHERS

WEEK	OPPONENT	SCORE	W/L/T
1	SAINTS	20–23	L
2	PATRIOTS	27–17	W
3	at Dolphins	24–27	L
4	PACKERS	32–29	W
5	CARDINALS	24–20	W
6	at Lions	21–20	W
7	BYE WEEK	—	—
8	VIKINGS	38–13	W
9	at Buccaneers	34–14	W
10	JETS	30–3	W
11	at Bears	3–13	L
12	at Bills	13–9	W
13	FALCONS	24–6	W
14	BUCCANEERS	10–20	L
15	at Saints	27–10	W
16	COWBOYS	20–24	L
17	at Falcons	44–11	W

CHICAGO BEARS

WEEK	OPPONENT	SCORE	W/L/T
1	at Redskins	7–9	L
2	LIONS	38–6	W
3	BENGALS	7–24	L
4	BYE WEEK	—	—
5	at Browns	10–20	L
6	VIKINGS	28–3	W
7	RAVENS	10–6	W
8	at Lions	19–13	W
9	at Saints	20–17	W
10	49ERS	17–9	W
11	PANTHERS	13–3	W
12	at Buccaneers	13–10	W
13	PACKERS	19–7	W
14	at Steelers	9–21	L
15	FALCONS	16–3	W
16	at Packers	24–17	W
17	at Vikings	10–34	L

DALLAS COWBOYS

WEEK	OPPONENT	SCORE	W/L/T
1	at Chargers	28–24	W
2	REDSKINS	13–14	L
3	at 49ers	34–31	W
4	at Raiders	13–19	L
5	EAGLES	33–10	W
6	GIANTS	16–13	W
7	at Seahawks	10–13	L
8	CARDINALS	34–13	W
9	BYE WEEK	—	—
10	at Eagles	21–20	W
11	LIONS	20–7	W
12	BRONCOS	21–24	L
13	at Giants	10–17	L
14	CHIEFS	31–28	W
15	at Redskins	7–35	L
16	at Panthers	24–20	W
17	RAMS	10–20	L

DETROIT LIONS

WEEK	OPPONENT	SCORE	W/L/T
1	PACKERS	17–3	W
2	at Bears	6–38	L
3	BYE WEEK	—	—
4	at Buccaneers	13–17	L
5	RAVENS	35–17	W
6	PANTHERS	20–21	L
7	at Browns	13–10	W
8	BEARS	13–19	L
9	at Vikings	14–27	L
10	CARDINALS	29–21	W
11	at Cowboys	7–20	L
12	FALCONS	7–27	L
13	VIKINGS	16–21	L
14	at Packers	13–16	L
15	BENGALS	17–41	L
16	at Saints	13–12	W
17	at Steelers	21–35	L

GREEN BAY PACKERS

WEEK	OPPONENT	SCORE	W/L/T
1	at Lions	3–17	L
2	BROWNS	24–26	L
3	BUCCANEERS	16–17	L
4	at Panthers	29–32	L
5	SAINTS	52–3	W
6	BYE WEEK	—	—
7	at Vikings	20–23	L
8	at Bengals	14–21	L
9	STEELERS	10–20	L
10	at Falcons	33–25	W
11	VIKINGS	17–20	L
12	at Eagles	14–29	L
13	at Bears	7–19	L
14	LIONS	16–13	W
15	at Ravens	3–48	L
16	BEARS	17–24	L
17	SEAHAWKS	23–17	W

Note: Home games are capitalized.

2005 REGULAR-SEASON RESULTS – NFC (cont.)

MINNESOTA VIKINGS

WEEK	OPPONENT	SCORE	W/L/T
1	BUCCANEERS	13–24	L
2	at Bengals	8–37	L
3	SAINTS	33–16	W
4	at Falcons	10–30	L
5	BYE WEEK	—	—
6	at Bears	3–28	L
7	PACKERS	23–20	W
8	at Panthers	13–38	L
9	LIONS	27–14	W
10	at Giants	24–21	W
11	at Packers	20–17	W
12	BROWNS	24–12	W
13	at Lions	21–16	W
14	RAMS	27–13	W
15	STEELERS	3–18	L
16	at Ravens	23–30	L
17	BEARS	34–10	W

NEW ORLEANS SAINTS

WEEK	OPPONENT	SCORE	W/L/T
1	at Panthers	23–20	W
2	GIANTS	10–27	L
3	at Vikings	16–33	L
4	BILLS	19–7	W
5	at Packers	3–52	L
6	FALCONS	31–34	L
7	at Rams	17–28	L
8	DOLPHINS	6–21	L
9	BEARS	17–20	L
10	BYE WEEK	—	—
11	at Patriots	17–24	L
12	at Jets	21–19	W
13	BUCCANEERS	3–10	L
14	at Falcons	17–36	L
15	PANTHERS	10–27	L
16	LIONS	12–13	L
17	at Buccaneers	13–27	L

NEW YORK GIANTS

WEEK	OPPONENT	SCORE	W/L/T
1	CARDINALS	42–19	W
2	at Saints	27–10	W
3	at Chargers	23–45	L
4	RAMS	44–24	W
5	BYE WEEK	—	—
6	at Cowboys	13–16	L
7	BRONCOS	24–23	W
8	REDSKINS	36–0	W
9	at 49ers	24–6	W
10	VIKINGS	21–24	L
11	EAGLES	27–17	W
12	at Seahawks	21–24	L
13	COWBOYS	17–10	W
14	at Eagles	26–23	W
15	CHIEFS	27–17	W
16	at Redskins	20–35	L
17	at Raiders	30–21	W

PHILADELPHIA EAGLES

WEEK	OPPONENT	SCORE	W/L/T
1	at Falcons	10–14	L
2	49ERS	42–3	W
3	RAIDERS	23–20	W
4	at Chiefs	37–31	W
5	at Cowboys	10–33	L
6	BYE WEEK	—	—
7	CHARGERS	20–17	W
8	at Broncos	21–49	L
9	at Redskins	10–17	L
10	COWBOYS	20–21	L
11	at Giants	17–27	L
12	PACKERS	19–14	W
13	SEAHAWKS	0–42	L
14	GIANTS	23–26	L
15	at Rams	17–16	W
16	at Cardinals	21–27	L
17	REDSKINS	20–31	L

SAN FRANCISCO 49ERS

WEEK	OPPONENT	SCORE	W/L/T
1	RAMS	28–25	W
2	at Eagles	3–42	L
3	COWBOYS	34–31	L
4	at Cardinals	14–31	L
5	COLTS	28–3	L
6	BYE WEEK	—	—
7	at Redskins	17–52	L
8	BUCCANEERS	10–15	W
9	GIANTS	24–6	L
10	at Bears	9–17	L
11	SEAHAWKS	27–25	L
12	at Titans	22–33	L
13	CARDINALS	17–10	L
14	at Seahawks	3–41	L
15	at Jaguars	9–10	L
16	at Rams	24–20	W
17	TEXANS	20–17	W

SEATTLE SEAHAWKS

WEEK	OPPONENT	SCORE	W/L/T
1	at Jaguars	14–26	L
2	FALCONS	21–18	W
3	CARDINALS	37–12	W
4	at Redskins	17–20	L
5	at Rams	37–31	W
6	TEXANS	42–10	W
7	COWBOYS	13–10	W
8	BYE WEEK	—	—
9	at Cardinals	33–19	W
10	RAMS	31–16	W
11	at 49ers	27–25	W
12	GIANTS	24–21	W
13	at Eagles	42–0	W
14	49ERS	41–3	W
15	at Titans	28–24	W
16	COLTS	28–13	W
17	at Packers	17–23	L

ST. LOUIS RAMS

WEEK	OPPONENT	SCORE	W/L/T
1	at 49ers	25–28	L
2	at Cardinals	17–12	W
3	TITANS	31–27	W
4	at Giants	24–44	L
5	SEAHAWKS	31–37	L
6	at Colts	28–45	L
7	SAINTS	28–17	W
8	JAGUARS	24–21	W
9	BYE WEEK	—	—
10	at Seahawks	16–31	L
11	CARDINALS	28–38	L
12	at Texans	33–27	W
13	REDSKINS	9–24	L
14	at Vikings	13–27	L
15	EAGLES	16–17	L
16	49ERS	20–24	L
17	at Cowboys	20–10	W

TAMPA BAY BUCCANEERS

WEEK	OPPONENT	SCORE	W/L/T
1	at Vikings	24–13	W
2	BILLS	19–3	W
3	at Packers	17–16	W
4	LIONS	17–13	W
5	at Jets	12–14	L
6	DOLPHINS	27–13	W
7	BYE WEEK	—	—
8	at 49ers	10–15	L
9	PANTHERS	14–34	L
10	REDSKINS	36–35	W
11	at Falcons	30–27	W
12	BEARS	10–13	L
13	at Saints	10–3	W
14	at Panthers	20–10	W
15	at Patriots	0–28	L
16	FALCONS	27–24	W
17	SAINTS	27–13	W

WASHINGTON REDSKINS

WEEK	OPPONENT	SCORE	W/L/T
1	BEARS	9–7	W
2	at Cowboys	14–13	W
3	BYE WEEK	—	—
4	SEAHAWKS	20–17	W
5	at Broncos	19–21	L
6	at Chiefs	21–28	L
7	49ERS	52–17	W
8	at Giants	0–36	L
9	EAGLES	17–10	W
10	at Buccaneers	35–36	L
11	RAIDERS	13–16	L
12	CHARGERS	17–23	L
13	at Rams	24–9	W
14	at Cardinals	17–13	W
15	COWBOYS	35–7	W
16	GIANTS	35–20	W
17	at Eagles	31–20	W

DID YOU KNOW?

Shaun Alexander of the Seattle Seahawks registered the ninth highest rushing total in league history in 2005 with 1,880 yards. The record for most yards rushed for in a season is 2,105 by Eric Dickerson of the Los Angeles Rams in 1983.

2005 INDIVIDUAL LEADERS — AFC

TOUCHDOWNS	TEAM	TD	RSH	REC	RET	PTS
Larry Johnson	KC	21	20	1	0	126
LaDainian Tomlinson	SD	20	18	2	0	120
Edgerrin James	IND	14	13	1	0	84
Mike Anderson	DEN	13	12	1	0	78
Corey Dillon	NE	13	12	1	0	78
Marvin Harrison	IND	12	0	12	0	72
Rudi Johnson	CIN	12	12	0	0	72
Chris Chambers	MIA	11	0	11	0	66
LaMont Jordan	OAK	11	9	2	0	68
Hines Ward	PIT	11	0	11	0	66
Antonio Gates	SD	10	0	10	0	60
Jerome Bettis	PIT	9	9	0	0	54
Chad Johnson	CIN	9	0	9	0	54

KEY TD=touchdowns; RSH=rushing touchdowns; REC=receiving touchdowns; RET=returns; PTS=points

2005 INDIVIDUAL LEADERS — AFC (cont.)

KICKING	TEAM	FGM	FGA	LONG	XPM	XPA	PTS
Matt Stover	BAL	30	34	49	23	23	113
Rian Lindell	BUF	29	35	53	26	26	113
Shayne Graham	CIN	28	32	49	47	47	131
Phil Dawson	CLE	27	29	44	19	21	100
Lawrence Tynes	KC	27	33	52	44	45	125
Kris Brown	HOU	26	34	53	24	24	102
Olindo Mare	MIA	25	30	53	33	33	108
Jason Elam	DEN	24	32	51	43	44	115
Jeff Reed	PIT	24	29	44	45	45	117
Rob Bironas	TEN	23	29	53	30	32	99

PASSER RATING	TEAM	YDS	ATT	COMP	TD	INT	LONG	RATING
Peyton Manning	IND	3,747	453	305	28	10	80	104.1
Carson Palmer	CIN	3,836	509	345	32	12	70	101.1
Ben Roethlisberger	PIT	2,385	268	168	17	9	85	98.6
Tom Brady	NE	4,110	530	334	26	14	71	92.3
Jake Plummer	DEN	3,366	456	277	18	7	72	90.2
Trent Green	KC	4,014	507	317	17	10	60	90.1
Byron Leftwich	JAC	2,123	302	175	15	5	45	89.3
Drew Bees	SD	3,576	500	323	24	15	54	89.2
Kelly Holcomb	BUF	1,509	230	155	10	8	65	85.6
Steve McNair	TEN	3,161	476	292	16	11	57	82.4

RECEPTIONS	TEAM	REC	YDS	AVG	TD	LONG
Chad Johnson	CIN	97	1,432	14.8	9	70
Antonio Gates	SD	89	1,101	12.4	10	38
Derrick Mason	BAL	86	1,073	12.5	3	39
Rod Smith	DEN	85	1,105	13.0	6	72
Reggie Wayne	IND	83	1,055	12.7	5	66
Chris Chambers	MIA	82	1,118	13.6	11	77
Marvin Harrison	IND	82	1,146	14.0	12	80
Eric Moulds	BUF	81	816	10.1	4	55
Deion Branch	NE	78	998	12.8	5	51
Tony Gonzalez	KC	78	905	11.6	2	39

RUSHING	TEAM	YDS	ATT	AVG	TD	LONG
Larry Johnson	KC	1,750	336	5.2	20	49
Edgerrin James	IND	1,506	360	4.2	13	33
LaDainian Tomlinson	SD	1,462	339	4.3	18	62
Rudi Johnson	CIN	1,458	337	4.3	12	33
Willis McGahee	BUF	1,247	325	3.8	5	27
Reuben Droughns	CLE	1,232	309	4.0	2	75
Willie Parker	PIT	1,202	255	4.7	4	80
LaMont Jordan	OAK	1,025	272	3.8	9	26
Mike Anderson	DEN	1,014	239	4.2	12	44
Domanick Davis	HOU	976	230	4.2	2	44
Tatum Bell	DEN	921	173	5.3	8	68

Larry Johnson,
Kansas City Chiefs

DAVID E. KLUTHO

KEY FGM=field goals made; FGA=field goals attempted; XPM=extra points made; XPA=extra points attempted; PTS=points; YDS=yards; ATT=attempts; COMP=completions; TD=touchdowns; INT=interceptions; REC=receptions; AVG=average

2005 INDIVIDUAL LEADERS — AFC (cont.)

RECEIVING YARDS	TEAM	REC	YDS	AVG	TD	LONG
Chad Johnson	CIN	97	1,432	14.8	9	70
Marvin Harrison	IND	82	1,146	14.0	12	80
Chris Chambers	MIA	82	1,118	13.6	11	77
Rod Smith	DEN	85	1,105	13.0	6	72
Eddie Kennison	KC	68	1,102	16.2	5	55
Antonio Gates	SD	89	1,101	12.4	10	38
Derrick Mason	BAL	16	1,073	12.5	3	39
Reggie Wayne	IND	83	1,055	12.7	5	66
Jimmy Smith	JAC	70	1,023	14.6	6	45
Antonio Bryant	CLE	69	1,009	14.6	4	54

Derrick Burgess, Oakland Raiders

INTERCEPTIONS	TEAM	INT	YDS	TD	LONG
Ty Law	NYJ	10	195	1	74
Deltha O'Neal	CIN	10	103	0	37
Champ Bailey	DEN	8	139	2	65
Greg Wesley	KC	6	106	0	51
David Barrett	NYJ	5	28	0	13
Nick Ferguson	DEN	5	59	0	30
Tory James	CIN	5	5	0	5
Cato June	IND	5	115	2	36
Rashean Mathis	JAC	5	79	1	41
Odell Thurman	CIN	5	59	1	30
Terry Cousin	JAC	4	18	0	14

SACKS	TEAM	SACKS	TACKLES*
Derrick Burgess	OAK	16	50
Kyle Vanden Bosch	TEN	12.5	40
Aaron Schobel	BUF	12	54
Jason Taylor	MIA	12	52
Robert Mathis	IND	11.5	29
Jared Allen	KC	11	51
Dwight Freeney	IND	11	30
John Abraham	NYJ	10.5	44
Joey Porter	PIT	10.5	39
Shawne Merriman	SD	10	41

PUNTING	TEAM	NO.	YDS	AVG	NAVG	LG	TB	BLK	IN 20	RET	RET AVG	RET TD
Brian Moorman	BUF	71	3,242	45.7	39.1	68	9	0	22	42	6.8	0
Shane Lechler	OAK	82	3,744	45.7	37.9	64	9	0	26	39	11.8	0
Josh Miller	NE	76	3,431	45.1	38.3	59	4	1	22	42	9.6	0
Hunter Smith	IND	52	2,301	44.3	37.1	58	5	0	23	25	10.9	0
Todd Sauerbrun	DEN	72	3,157	43.8	38.0	66	6	1	24	36	7.4	0
Mike Scifres	SD	71	3,104	43.7	38.0	71	8	0	25	26	9.4	0
Ben Graham	NYJ	74	3,233	43.7	37.9	59	6	0	18	36	8.5	0
Donnie Jones	MIA	88	3,827	43.5	39.3	63	7	0	31	46	4.9	0
Dave Zastudil	BAL	84	3,653	43.5	35.7	60	7	1	11	55	8.7	0
Craig Hentrich	TEN	78	3,371	43.2	37.8	59	14	0	21	32	4.5	0

2005 INDIVIDUAL LEADERS — NFC

TOUCHDOWNS	TEAM	TD	RSH	REC	RET	PTS
Shaun Alexander	SEA	28	27	1	0	168
Steve Smith	CAR	13	1	12	0	78
Stephen Davis	CAR	12	12	0	0	72
Tiki Barber	NYG	11	9	2	0	68
Clinton Portis	WAS	11	11	0	0	68
Larry Fitzgerald	ARI	10	0	10	0	60
Joey Galloway	TB	10	0	10	0	60
Steven Jackson	STL	10	8	2	0	60
Joe Jurevicius	SEA	10	0	10	0	60
Torry Holt	STL	9	0	9	0	54

KEY NO.=number; NAVG=net average; LG=long; TB=touchback; BLK=blocked; IN 20=inside 20-yard line; RET=returned; RET AVG=return average; RET TD=returned for a touchdown

*Unassisted tackles

2005 INDIVIDUAL LEADERS — NFC (cont.)

KICKING	TEAM	FGM	FGA	LONG	XPM	XPA	PTS
Neil Rackers	ARI	40	42	54	20	20	140
Jay Feely	NYG	35	42	52	43	43	148
Jeff Wilkins	STL	27	31	53	36	36	117
John Kasay	CAR	26	34	52	43	44	121
Joe Nedney	SF	26	28	56	19	19	97
John Carney	NO	25	32	49	22	22	97
Paul Edinger	MIN	25	34	56	31	31	106
Todd Peterson	ATL	23	25	43	35	35	104
Matt Bryant	TB	21	25	50	31	31	94
Robbie Gould	CHI	21	27	45	19	20	82

PASSER RATING	TEAM	YDS	ATT	COMP	TD	INT	LONG	RATING
Matt Hasselbeck	SEA	3,459	449	294	24	9	56	98.2
Marc Bulger	STL	2,297	287	192	14	9	57	94.4
Brad Johnson	MIN	1,885	294	184	12	4	80	88.9
Jake Delhomme	CAR	3,421	435	262	24	16	80	88.1
Mark Brunell	WAS	3,050	454	262	23	10	78	85.9
Kurt Warner	ARI	2,713	375	242	11	9	63	85.8
Donovan McNabb	PHI	2,507	357	211	16	9	91	85.0
Drew Bledsoe	DAL	3,639	499	300	23	17	71	83.7
Chris Simms	TB	2,035	313	191	10	7	78	81.4
Eli Manning	NYG	3,762	557	294	24	17	78	75.9
Josh McCown	ARI	1,836	270	163	9	11	49	74.9

RECEPTIONS	TEAM	REC	YDS	AVG	TD	LONG
Larry Fitzgerald	ARI	103	1,409	13.7	10	47
Steve Smith	CAR	103	1,563	15.2	12	80
Anquan Boldin	ARI	102	1,402	13.7	7	54
Torry Holt	STL	102	1,331	13.0	9	44
Donald Driver	GB	86	1,221	14.2	5	59
Santana Moss	WAS	84	1,483	17.7	9	78
Joey Galloway	TB	83	1,287	15.5	10	80
Plaxico Burress	NYG	76	1,214	16.0	7	78
Chris Cooley	WAS	71	774	10.9	7	32
Keyshawn Johnson	DAL	71	839	11.8	6	34

RECEIVING YARDS	TEAM	REC	YDS	AVG	TD	LONG
Steve Smith	CAR	103	1,563	15.2	12	80
Santana Moss	WAS	84	1,483	17.7	9	78
Larry Fitzgerald	ARI	103	1,409	13.7	10	47
Anquan Boldin	ARI	102	1,402	13.7	7	54
Torry Holt	STL	102	1,331	13.0	9	44
Joey Galloway	TB	83	1,287	15.5	10	80
Donald Driver	GB	86	1,221	14.2	5	59
Plaxico Burress	NYG	76	1,214	16.0	7	78
Terry Glenn	DAL	62	1,136	18.3	7	71
Donté Stallworth	NO	70	945	13.5	7	43

Steve Smith,
Carolina Panthers

2005 INDIVIDUAL LEADERS — NFC (cont.)

RUSHING	TEAM	YDS	ATT	AVG	TD	LONG
Shaun Alexander	SEA	1,880	370	5.1	27	88
Tiki Barber	NYG	1,860	357	5.2	9	95
Clinton Portis	WAS	1,516	352	4.3	11	47
Warrick Dunn	ATL	1,416	280	5.1	3	65
Thomas Jones	CHI	1,335	314	4.3	9	42
Carnell Williams	TB	1,178	290	4.1	6	71
Steven Jackson	STL	1,046	254	4.1	8	51
Julius Jones	DAL	993	257	3.9	5	51
DeShaun Foster	CAR	879	205	4.3	2	70
Kevin Jones	DET	664	186	3.6	5	40

*Darren Sharper,
Minnesota Vikings*

INTERCEPTIONS	TEAM	INT	YDS	TD	LONG
Darren Sharper	MIN	9	276	2	92
Nathan Vasher	CHI	8	145	1	46
Chris Gamble	CAR	7	157	1	61
Dre' Bly	DET	6	54	0	28
DeAngelo Hall	ATL	6	177	0	65
Ken Lucas	CAR	6	70	0	32
Ronde Barber	TB	5	105	0	42
Charles Tillman	CHI	5	172	1	95
Mike Adams	SF	4	36	1	40

SACKS	TEAM	SACKS	TACKLES*
Osi Umenyiora	NYG	14.5	49
Simeon Rice	TB	14.0	33
Michael Strahan	NYG	11.5	61
Rod Coleman	ATL	10.5	35
Julius Peppers	CAR	10.5	38
Adewale Ogunleye	CHI	10.0	36
Leonard Little	STL	9.5	45
Bryce Fisher	SEA	9.0	34
Rocky Bernard	SEA	8.5	43
Will Smith	NO	8.5	48

TRIVIA CHALLENGE

What former linebacker is the only player in NFL history to win Super Bowl rings with three different teams?

Matt Millen won rings with the Raiders (Super Bowls XV and XVIII), the 49ers (XXIV), and the Redskins (XXVI).

PUNTING	TEAM	NO.	YDS	AVG	NAVG	LG	TB	BLK	IN 20	RET	RET AVG	RET TD
Josh Bidwell	TB	90	4,101	45.6	37.5	61	13	0	24	49	9.5	0
Chris Kluwe	MIN	71	3,130	44.1	35.8	62	6	0	17	41	11.5	0
Scott Player	ARI	73	3,206	43.9	37.0	60	7	1	18	39	8.4	1
Nick Harris	DET	84	3,656	43.5	36.9	60	2	0	34	50	10.4	2
Jason Baker	CAR	72	3,118	43.3	38.9	59	4	0	23	36	6.5	0
Mitch Berger	NO	71	3,066	43.2	38.7	69	3	0	28	33	7.9	0
Bryan Barker	STL	50	2,137	42.7	35.6	63	4	0	13	31	8.9	0
Mat McBriar	DAL	81	3,439	42.5	37.1	63	9	0	28	33	7.6	0
Michael Koenen	ATL	78	3,300	42.3	36.9	67	9	0	23	35	6.8	0
Jeff Feagles	NYG	73	3,070	42.1	37.0	56	3	0	26	36	8.6	1

*Unassisted tackles

TEAM-BY-TEAM STATS — AFC

BALTIMORE RAVENS

PASSING

PLAYER	ATT	COMP	YDS	PCT COMP	YDS/ATT	TD	INT	RATING
Kyle Boller	293	171	1,799	58.4	6.14	12	3.8	71.8

RUSHING

PLAYER	NO.	YDS	AVG	LG	TD
Jamal Lewis	269	906	3.4	25	3
Chester Taylor	117	487	4.2	52	0
Anthony Wright	18	68	3.8	22	0
Kyle Boller	23	66	2.9	9	1
Mark Clayton	8	33	4.1	11	1
Kordell Stewart	4	24	6.0	13	0
Jamel White	6	17	2.8	5	0

RECEIVING

PLAYER	NO.	YDS	AVG	LG	TD
Derrick Mason	86	1,073	12.5	39	3
Todd Heap	75	855	11.4	48	7
Mark Clayton	44	471	10.7	47	2
Chester Taylor	41	292	7.1	20	1
Jamal Lewis	32	191	6.0	15	1
Daniel Wilcox	20	154	7.7	17	1
Randy Hymes	11	132	12.0	21	2
Justin Green	7	32	4.6	8	0

KICKING

PLAYER	FGM	FGA	PCT	XPM	XPA
Matt Stover	30	34	88.2	23	23

PUNTING

PLAYER	NO.	AVG	NET AVG	TB	IN 20	LG	BLK
Dave Zastudil	84	43.5	35.7	7	11	60	1
Aaron Elling	1	32.0	32.0	0	1	32	0

INTERCEPTIONS Deion Sanders, 2　　　SACKS Adalius Thomas, 9

BUFFALO BILLS

PASSING

PLAYER	ATT	COMP	YDS	PCT COMP	YDS/ATT	TD	INT	RATING
Kelly Holcomb	230	155	1,509	67.4	6.56	10	8	85.6
J.P. Losman	228	113	1,340	49.6	5.88	8	8	64.9

RUSHING

PLAYER	NO.	YDS	AVG	LG	TD
Willis McGahee	325	1,247	3.8	27	5
Shaud Williams	45	161	3.6	28	0
J.P. Losman	31	154	5.0	30	0
Lee Evans	4	38	9.5	39	0
Kelly Holcomb	18	11	0.6	8	1

RECEIVING

PLAYER	NO.	YDS	AVG	LG	TD
Eric Moulds	81	816	10.1	55	4
Lee Evans	48	743	15.5	65	7
Josh Reed	32	449	14.0	51	2
Willis McGahee	28	178	6.4	19	0
Mark Campbell	19	139	7.3	27	0
Shaud Williams	17	118	6.9	23	0
Roscoe Parrish	15	148	9.9	28	1
Daimon Shelton	13	98	7.5	21	1

KICKING

PLAYER	FGM	FGA	PCT	XPM	XPA
Rian Lindell	29	35	82.9	26	26

PUNTING

PLAYER	NO.	AVG	NET AVG	TB	IN 20	LG	BLK
Brian Moorman	71	45.7	39.1	9	22	68	0

INTERCEPTIONS Terrence McGee, 4　　　SACKS Aaron Schobel, 12

KEY ATT=attempts; COMP=completions; YDS=yards; PCT COMP=completion percentage; YDS/ATT=yards per attempt; TD=touchdowns; INT=interceptions; NO.=number; AVG=average; LG=long; FGM=field goals made; FGA=field goals attempted; PCT=percentage; XPM=extra points made; XPA=extra points attempted; NET AVG=net average; TB=touchbacks; IN 20=inside 20-yard line; BLK=blocked

CINCINNATI BENGALS

PASSING

PLAYER	ATT	COMP	YDS	PCT COMP	YDS/ATT	TD	INT	RATING
Carson Palmer	509	345	3,836	67.8	7.54	32	12	101.1
Jon Kitna	29	17	99	58.6	3.41	0	2	36.4

RUSHING

PLAYER	NO.	YDS	AVG	LG	TD
Rudi Johnson	337	1,458	4.3	33	12
Chris Perry	61	279	4.6	30	0
T.J. Houshmandzadeh	8	62	7.8	17	1
Carson Palmer	34	41	1.2	14	1
Chad Johnson	5	33	6.6	11	0
Jeremi Johnson	8	14	1.8	5	0

RECEIVING

PLAYER	NO.	YDS	AVG	LG	TD
Chad Johnson	97	1,432	14.8	70	9
T.J. Houshmandzadeh	78	956	12.3	43	7
Chris Perry	51	328	6.4	28	2
Chris Henry	31	422	13.6	47	6
Rudi Johnson	23	90	3.9	15	0
Kevin Walter	19	211	11.1	33	1
Matt Schobel	18	193	10.7	28	1

KICKING

PLAYER	FGM	FGA	PCT	XPM	XPA
Shayne Graham	28	32	87.5	47	47

PUNTING

PLAYER	NO.	AVG	NET AVG	TB	IN 20	LG	BLK
Kyle Larson	60	43.2	35.6	8	13	75	1

INTERCEPTIONS Deltha O'Neal, 10 **SACKS** Justin Smith, 6

CLEVELAND BROWNS

PASSING

PLAYER	ATT	COMP	YDS	PCT COMP	YDS/ATT	TD	INT	RATING
Trent Dilfer	333	199	2,321	59.8	6.97	11	12	76.9
Charlie Frye	164	98	1,002	59.8	6.11	4	5	72.8
Frisman Jackson	0	0	0	—	—	0	0	—

RUSHING

PLAYER	NO.	YDS	AVG	LG	TD
Reuben Droughns	309	1,232	4.0	75	2
William Green	20	78	3.9	17	0
Charlie Frye	18	60	3.3	16	1
Trent Dilfer	20	46	2.3	12	0
Dennis Northcutt	2	33	16.5	31	0
Jason Wright	11	27	2.5	6	1

RECEIVING

PLAYER	NO.	YDS	AVG	LG	TD
Antonio Bryant	69	1,009	14.6	54	4
Steve Heiden	43	401	9.3	62	3
Dennis Northcutt	42	441	10.5	58	2
Reuben Droughns	39	369	9.5	51	0
Braylon Edwards	32	512	16.0	80	3
Frisman Jackson	24	287	12.0	68	1
Aaron Shea	18	153	8.5	27	1
Terrelle Smith	12	58	4.8	9	1

KICKING

PLAYER	FGM	FGA	PCT	XPM	XPA
Phil Dawson	27	29	93.1	19	21

PUNTING

PLAYER	NO.	AVG	NET AVG	TB	IN 20	LG	BLK
Kyle Richardson	78	40.8	34.0	9	22	61	0

INTERCEPTIONS Brian Russell, 3 **SACKS** Chaun Thompson, Alvin McKinley, 5

FOOTBALL PRO

DENVER BRONCOS

PASSING

PLAYER	ATT	COMP	YDS	PCT COMP	YDS/ATT	TD	INT	RATING
Jake Plummer	456	277	3,366	60.7	7.38	18	7	90.2

RUSHING

PLAYER	NO.	YDS	AVG	LG	TD
Mike Anderson	239	1,014	4.2	44	12
Tatum Bell	173	921	5.3	68	8
Ron Dayne	53	270	5.1	55	1
Jake Plummer	46	151	3.3	22	2
Ashley Lelie	5	84	16.8	39	0

RECEIVING

PLAYER	NO.	YDS	AVG	LG	TD
Rod Smith	85	1,105	13.0	72	6
Ashley Lelie	42	770	18.3	56	1
Jeb Putzier	37	481	13.0	32	0
Charlie Adams	21	203	9.7	21	0
Stephen Alexander	21	170	8.1	15	1
Mike Anderson	18	212	11.8	66	1
Tatum Bell	18	104	5.8	14	0
Kyle Johnson	17	160	9.4	33	5
Todd Devoe	9	87	9.7	44	1

KICKING

PLAYER	FGM	FGA	PCT	XPM	XPA
Jason Elam	24	32	75.0	43	44

PUNTING

PLAYER	NO.	AVG	NET AVG	TB	IN 20	LG	BLK
Todd Sauerbrun	72	43.8	38.0	6	24	66	1

INTERCEPTIONS Champ Bailey, 8

SACKS John Lynch, Trevor Pryce, Ebenezer Ekuban, 4

HOUSTON TEXANS

PASSING

PLAYER	ATT	COMP	YDS	PCT COMP	YDS/ATT	TD	INT	RATING
David Carr	423	256	2,488	60.5	5.88	14	11	77.2

RUSHING

PLAYER	NO.	YDS	AVG	LG	TD
Domanick Davis	230	976	4.2	44	2
Jonathan Wells	90	325	3.6	14	4
David Carr	56	308	5.5	20	1
Vernand Morency	46	184	4.0	25	2

RECEIVING

PLAYER	NO.	YDS	AVG	LG	TD
Andre Johnson	63	688	10.9	53	2
Jabar Gaffney	55	492	8.9	29	2
Domanick Davis	39	337	8.6	33	4
Corey Bradford	34	436	12.8	50	5
Marcellus Rivers	24	168	7.0	20	0
Jonathan Wells	22	179	8.1	20	0
Vernand Morency	10	87	8.7	16	0

KICKING

PLAYER	FGM	FGA	PCT	XPM	XPA
Kris Brown	26	34	76.5	24	24

PUNTING

PLAYER	NO.	AVG	NET AVG	TB	IN 20	LG	BLK
Chad Stanley	77	38.8	35.7	1	29	61	0

INTERCEPTIONS Glenn Earl, 2

SACKS Shantee Orr, 7

INDIANAPOLIS COLTS

PASSING

PLAYER	ATT	COMP	YDS	PCT COMP	YDS/ATT	TD	INT	RATING
Peyton Manning	453	305	3,747	67.3	8.27	28	10	104.1

RUSHING

PLAYER	NO.	YDS	AVG	LG	TD
Edgerrin James	360	1,506	4.2	33	13
Dominic Rhodes	40	118	3.0	24	4
Peyton Manning	33	45	1.4	12	0
Ran Carthon	13	18	1.4	7	1

RECEIVING

PLAYER	NO.	YDS	AVG	LG	TD
Reggie Wayne	83	1,055	12.7	66	5
Marvin Harrison	82	1,146	14.0	80	12
Edgerrin James	44	337	7.7	20	1
Brandon Stokley	41	543	13.2	45	1
Dallas Clark	37	488	13.2	56	4
Bryan Fletcher	18	202	11.2	23	3
Troy Walters	14	152	10.9	39	3
Dominic Rhodes	12	88	7.3	15	0

KICKING

PLAYER	FGM	FGA	PCT	XPM	XPA
Mike Vanderjagt	23	25	92.0	52	52

PUNTING

PLAYER	NO.	AVG	NET AVG	TB	IN 20	LG	BLK
Hunter Smith	52	44.3	37.1	5	23	58	0

INTERCEPTIONS Cato June, 5   **SACKS** Robert Mathis, 11.5

JACKSONVILLE JAGUARS

PASSING

PLAYER	ATT	COMP	YDS	PCT COMP	YDS/ATT	TD	INT	RATING
Byron Leftwich	302	175	2,123	57.9	7.03	15	5	89.3
David Garrard	168	98	1,117	58.3	6.65	4	1	83.9

RUSHING

PLAYER	NO.	YDS	AVG	LG	TD
Fred Taylor	194	787	4.1	71	3
Greg Jones	151	575	3.8	27	4
David Garrard	31	172	5.5	28	3
Alvin Pearman	39	149	3.8	45	1
LaBrandon Toefield	36	142	3.9	32	4
Byron Leftwich	31	67	2.2	9	2

RECEIVING

PLAYER	NO.	YDS	AVG	LG	TD
Jimmy Smith	70	1,023	14.6	45	6
Ernest Wilford	41	681	16.6	39	7
Matt Jones	36	432	12.0	42	5
Reggie Williams	35	445	12.7	41	0
Alvin Pearman	32	240	7.5	19	0
Kyle Brady	18	157	8.7	33	1
George Wrighster	13	120	9.2	27	2
Fred Taylor	13	83	6.4	13	0
Greg Jones	10	65	6.5	10	0

KICKING

PLAYER	FGM	FGA	PCT	XPM	XPA
Josh Scobee	23	30	76.7	38	39

PUNTING

PLAYER	NO.	AVG	NET AVG	TB	IN 20	LG	BLK
Chris Hanson	82	42.9	36.9	11	33	74	1

INTERCEPTIONS Rashean Mathis, 5   **SACKS** Reggie Hayward, 8.5

KANSAS CITY CHIEFS

PASSING

PLAYER	ATT	COMP	YDS	PCT COMP	YDS/ATT	TD	INT	RATING
Trent Green	507	317	4,014	62.5	7.92	17	10	90.1

RUSHING

PLAYER	NO.	YDS	AVG	LG	TD
Larry Johnson	336	1,750	5.2	49	20
Priest Holmes	119	451	3.8	35	6
Trent Green	35	82	2.3	13	0
Eddie Kennison	7	43	6.1	23	0
Dee Brown	7	21	3.0	7	0
Tony Richardson	6	20	3.3	8	0

RECEIVING

PLAYER	NO.	YDS	AVG	LG	TD
Tony Gonzalez	78	905	11.6	39	2
Eddie Kennison	68	1,102	16.2	55	5
Samie Parker	36	533	14.8	49	3
Dante Hall	34	436	12.8	52	3
Larry Johnson	33	343	10.4	36	1
Priest Holmes	21	197	9.4	60	1
Chris Horn	18	187	10.4	50	0
Tony Richardson	9	68	7.6	22	1

KICKING

PLAYER	FGM	FGA	PCT	XPM	XPA
Lawrence Tynes	27	33	81.8	44	45

PUNTING

PLAYER	NO.	AVG	NET AVG	TB	IN 20	LG	BLK
Dustin Colquitt	65	39.4	35.2	5	27	62	0

INTERCEPTIONS Greg Wesley, 6   SACKS Jared Allen, 11

MIAMI DOLPHINS

PASSING

PLAYER	ATT	COMP	YDS	PCT COMP	YDS/ATT	TD	INT	RATING
Gus Frerotte	494	257	2,996	52.0	6.06	18	13	71.9
Sage Rosenfels	61	34	462	55.7	7.57	4	3	81.5

RUSHING

PLAYER	NO.	YDS	AVG	LG	TD
Ronnie Brown	207	907	4.4	65	4
Ricky Williams	168	743	4.4	35	6
Chris Chambers	12	92	7.7	61	0
Gus Frerotte	27	61	2.3	14	0

RECEIVING

PLAYER	NO.	YDS	AVG	LG	TD
Chris Chambers	82	1,118	69.9	77	11
Randy McMichael	60	582	36.4	30	5
Marty Booker	39	686	45.7	60	3
Ronnie Brown	32	232	15.5	38	1
Wes Welker	29	434	27.1	47	0
Ricky Williams	17	93	7.8	19	0
Lorenzo Diamond	8	54	3.4	18	0

KICKING

PLAYER	FGM	FGA	PCT	XPM	XPA
Olindo Mare	25	30	83.3	33	33

PUNTING

PLAYER	NO.	AVG	NET AVG	TB	IN 20	LG	BLK
Donnie Jones	88	43.5	39.3	7	31	63	0

INTERCEPTIONS Lance Schulters, 4   SACKS Jason Taylor, 12

NEW ENGLAND PATRIOTS

PASSING

PLAYER	ATT	COMP	YDS	PCT COMP	YDS/ATT	TD	INT	RATING
Tom Brady	530	334	4,110	63.0	7.75	26	14	92.3

RUSHING

PLAYER	NO.	YDS	AVG	LG	TD
Corey Dillon	209	733	3.5	29	12
Patrick Pass	54	245	4.5	31	3
Heath Evans	51	192	3.8	21	0
Kevin Faulk	51	145	2.8	13	0
Tom Brady	27	89	3.3	15	1
Michael Cloud	23	59	2.6	15	0

RECEIVING

PLAYER	NO.	YDS	AVG	LG	TD
Deion Branch	78	998	12.8	51	5
David Givens	59	738	12.5	40	2
Troy Brown	39	466	11.9	71	2
Ben Watson	29	441	15.2	35	4
Kevin Faulk	29	260	9.0	23	0
Patrick Pass	22	227	10.3	39	0
Corey Dillon	22	181	8.2	25	1
Tim Dwight	19	332	17.5	59	3
Daniel Graham	16	235	14.7	45	3
Heath Evans	10	88	8.8	19	0

KICKING

PLAYER	FGM	FGA	PCT	XPM	XPA
Adam Vinatieri	20	25	80.0	40	41

PUNTING

PLAYER	NO.	AVG	NET AVG	TB	IN 20	LG	BLK
Josh Miller	76	45.1	38.3	4	22	59	1

INTERCEPTIONS Asante Samuel, 3   **SACKS** Rosevelt Colvin, 7

NEW YORK JETS

PASSING

PLAYER	ATT	COMP	YDS	PCT COMP	YDS/ATT	TD	INT	RATING
Brooks Bollinger	266	150	1,558	56.4	5.86	7	6	72.9
Vinny Testaverde	106	60	777	56.6	7.33	1	6	59.4

RUSHING

PLAYER	NO.	YDS	AVG	LG	TD
Curtis Martin	220	735	3.3	49	5
Cedric Houston	81	302	3.7	17	2
Brooks Bollinger	35	135	3.9	15	0
B.J. Askew	13	59	4.5	14	0

RECEIVING

PLAYER	NO.	YDS	AVG	LG	TD
Laveranues Coles	73	845	11.6	43	5
Justin McCareins	43	713	16.6	45	2
Doug Jolley	29	324	11.2	60	1
Jerald Sowell	28	155	5.5	28	2
Curtis Martin	24	118	4.9	14	0
Jerricho Cotchery	19	251	13.2	45	0
Chris Baker	18	269	14.9	47	1

KICKING

PLAYER	FGM	FGA	PCT	XPM	XPA
Mike Nugent	22	28	78.6	24	24

PUNTING

PLAYER	NO.	AVG	NET AVG	TB	IN 20	LG	BLK
Ben Graham	74	43.7	37.9	6	18	59	0

INTERCEPTIONS Ty Law, 10   **SACKS** John Abraham, 10.5

FOOTBALL PRO

OAKLAND RAIDERS

PASSING

PLAYER	ATT	COMP	YDS	PCT COMP	YDS/ATT	TD	INT	RATING
Kerry Collins	565	302	3,759	53.5	6.65	20	12	77.3
Marques Tuiasosopo	26	14	124	53.8	4.77	1	2	47.6

RUSHING

PLAYER	NO.	YDS	AVG	LG	TD
LaMont Jordan	272	1,025	3.8	26	9
Zack Crockett	60	208	3.5	24	1
Alvis Whitted	2	51	25.5	27	0
Kerry Collins	17	39	2.3	18	1

RECEIVING

PLAYER	NO.	YDS	AVG	LG	TD
Jerry Porter	76	942	12.4	49	5
LaMont Jordan	70	563	8.0	28	2
Randy Moss	60	1,005	16.8	79	8
Doug Gabriel	37	554	15.0	38	3
Courtney Anderson	24	303	12.6	36	3
Alvis Whitted	14	183	13.1	26	0
Randal Williams	13	164	12.6	34	0
Zack Crockett	13	111	8.5	23	0
John Paul Foschi	6	37	6.2	11	0

KICKING

PLAYER	FGM	FGA	PCT	XPM	XPA
Sebastian Janikowski	20	30	66.7	30	30

PUNTING

PLAYER	NO.	AVG	NET AVG	TB	IN 20	LG	BLK
Shane Lechler	82	45.7	37.9	9	26	64	0

INTERCEPTIONS Stuart Schweigert, 2　　**SACKS** Derrick Burgess, 16

PITTSBURGH STEELERS

PASSING

PLAYER	ATT	COMP	YDS	PCT COMP	YDS/ATT	TD	INT	RATING
Ben Roethlisberger	268	168	2,385	62.7	8.90	17	9	98.6
Tommy Maddox	71	34	406	47.9	5.72	2	4	51.7

RUSHING

PLAYER	NO.	YDS	AVG	LG	TD
Willie Parker	255	1,202	4.7	80	4
Jerome Bettis	110	368	3.3	39	9
Verron Haynes	74	274	3.7	20	3
Duce Staley	38	148	3.9	17	1
Antwaan Randle El	12	73	6.1	43	0
Ben Roethlisberger	31	69	2.2	15	3
Charlie Batch	11	30	2.7	15	1

RECEIVING

PLAYER	NO.	YDS	AVG	LG	TD
Hines Ward	69	975	14.1	85	11
Heath Miller	39	459	11.8	50	6
Antwaan Randle El	35	558	15.9	63	1
Cedrick Wilson	26	451	17.3	46	0
Willie Parker	18	218	12.1	48	1
Verron Haynes	11	113	10.3	18	0
Quincy Morgan	9	150	16.7	31	2
Dan Kreider	7	43	6.1	9	0

KICKING

PLAYER	FGM	FGA	PCT	XPM	XPA
Jeff Reed	24	29	82.8	45	45

PUNTING

PLAYER	NO.	AVG	NET AVG	TB	IN 20	LG	BLK
Chris Gardocki	67	41.8	34.7	7	22	65	0

INTERCEPTIONS Chris Hope, 3　　**SACKS** Joey Porter, 10.5

SAN DIEGO CHARGERS

PASSING

PLAYER	ATT	COMP	YDS	PCT COMP	YDS/ATT	TD	INT	RATING
Drew Brees	500	323	3,576	64.6	7.15	24	15	89.2
Philip Rivers	22	12	115	54.5	5.23	0	1	50.4

RUSHING

PLAYER	NO.	YDS	AVG	LG	TD
LaDainian Tomlinson	339	1462	4.3	62	18
Michael Turner	57	335	5.9	83	3
Lorenzo Neal	29	98	3.4	9	0
Eric Parker	4	55	13.8	30	0
Darren Sproles	8	50	6.3	21	0

RECEIVING

PLAYER	NO.	YDS	AVG	LG	TD
Antonio Gates	89	1,101	12.4	38	10
Keenan McCardell	70	917	13.1	54	9
Eric Parker	57	725	12.7	49	3
LaDainian Tomlinson	51	370	7.3	41	2
Reche Caldwell	28	352	12.6	43	1
Lorenzo Neal	24	145	6.0	21	1
Justin Peelle	11	38	3.5	11	1
Vincent Jackson	3	59	19.7	21	0

KICKING

PLAYER	FGM	FGA	PCT	XPM	XPA
Nate Kaeding	21	24	87.5	49	49

PUNTING

PLAYER	NO.	AVG	NET AVG	TB	IN 20	LG	BLK
Mike Scifres	71	43.7	38.0	8	25	71	0

INTERCEPTIONS Bhawoh Jue, 3   SACKS Shawne Merriman, 10

TENNESSEE TITANS

PASSING

PLAYER	ATT	COMP	YDS	PCT COMP	YDS/ATT	TD	INT	RATING
Steve McNair	476	292	3,161	61.3	6.64	16	11	82.4
Billy Volek	88	50	474	56.8	5.39	4	2	77.6

RUSHING

PLAYER	NO.	YDS	AVG	LG	TD
Chris Brown	224	851	3.8	38	5
Travis Henry	88	335	3.8	29	0
Steve McNair	32	139	4.3	19	1
Jarrett Payton	33	105	3.2	15	2
Matt Mauck	7	39	5.6	12	0

RECEIVING

PLAYER	NO.	YDS	AVG	LG	TD
Drew Bennett	58	738	12.7	55	4
Erron Kinney	55	543	9.9	27	2
Ben Troupe	55	530	9.6	35	4
Bo Scaife	37	273	7.4	19	2
Chris Brown	25	327	13.1	57	2
Brandon Jones	23	299	13.0	38	2
Tyrone Calico	22	191	8.7	18	0
Roydell Williams	21	299	14.2	50	2
Courtney Roby	21	289	13.8	32	1

KICKING

PLAYER	FGM	FGA	PCT	XPM	XPA
Rob Bironas	23	29	79.3	30	32

PUNTING

PLAYER	NO.	AVG	NET AVG	TB	IN 20	LG	BLK
Craig Hentrich	78	43.2	37.8	14	21	59	0

INTERCEPTIONS Reynaldo Hill, 3   SACKS Kyle Vanden Bosch, 12.5

TEAM-BY-TEAM STATS — NFC

ARIZONA CARDINALS

PASSING

PLAYER	ATT	COMP	YDS	PCT COMP	YDS/ATT	TD	INT	RATING
Kurt Warner	375	242	2,713	64.5	7.23	11	9	85.8
Josh McCown	270	163	1,836	60.4	6.80	9	11	74.9

RUSHING

PLAYER	NO.	YDS	AVG	LG	TD
Marcel Shipp	157	451	2.9	19	0
J.J. Arrington	112	370	3.3	32	2
Josh McCown	29	139	4.8	12	0
Obafemi Ayanbadejo	22	46	2.1	11	0
Anquan Boldin	12	45	3.8	11	0

RECEIVING

PLAYER	NO.	YDS	AVG	LG	TD
Larry Fitzgerald	103	1409	13.7	47	10
Anquan Boldin	102	1402	13.7	54	7
Bryant Johnson	40	432	10.8	41	1
Marcel Shipp	35	255	7.3	28	0
Obafemi Ayanbadejo	34	231	6.8	18	0
Adam Bergen	28	270	9.6	32	1
J.J. Arrington	25	139	5.6	15	0
LeRon McCoy	18	191	10.6	24	1

KICKING

PLAYER	FGM	FGA	PCT	XPM	XPA
Neil Rackers	40	42	95.2	20	20

PUNTING

PLAYER	NO.	AVG	NET AVG	TB	IN 20	LG	BLK
Scott Player	73	43.9	37.0	7	18	60	1

INTERCEPTIONS Karlos Dansby, 3   **SACKS** Adrian Wilson, 8

ATLANTA FALCONS

PASSING

PLAYER	ATT	COMP	YDS	PCT COMP	YDS/ATT	TD	INT	RATING
Michael Vick	387	214	2,412	55.3	6.23	15	13	73.1
Matt Schaub	64	33	495	51.6	7.73	4	0	98.1

RUSHING

PLAYER	NO.	YDS	AVG	LG	TD
Warrick Dunn	280	1,416	5.1	65	3
Michael Vick	102	597	5.9	32	6
T.J. Duckett	121	380	3.1	25	8

RECEIVING

PLAYER	NO.	YDS	AVG	LG	TD
Alge Crumpler	65	877	13.5	48	5
Brian Finneran	50	611	12.2	53	2
Michael Jenkins	36	508	14.1	58	3
Roddy White	29	446	15.4	54	3
Warrick Dunn	29	220	7.6	24	1
Justin Griffith	21	111	5.3	17	3
T.J. Duckett	6	63	10.5	19	0

KICKING

PLAYER	FGM	FGA	PCT	XPM	XPA
Todd Peterson	23	25	92.0	35	35

PUNTING

PLAYER	NO.	AVG	NET AVG	TB	IN 20	LG	BLK
Michael Koenen	78	42.3	36.9	9	23	67	0

INTERCEPTIONS DeAngelo Hall, 6   **SACKS** Rod Coleman, 10.5

KEY ATT=attempts; COMP=completions; YDS=yards; PCT COMP=completion percentage; YDS/ATT=yards per attempt; TD=touchdowns; INT=interceptions; NO.=number; AVG=average; LG=long; FGM=field goals made; FGA=field goals attempted; PCT=percentage; XPM=extra points made; XPA=extra points attempted; NET AVG=net average; TB=touchbacks; IN 20=inside 20-yard line; BLK=blocked

CAROLINA PANTHERS

PASSING

PLAYER	ATT	COMP	YDS	PCT COMP	YDS/ATT	TD	INT	RATING
Jake Delhomme	435	262	3,421	60.2	7.86	24	16	88.1

RUSHING

PLAYER	NO.	YDS	AVG	LG	TD
DeShaun Foster	205	879	4.3	70	2
Stephen Davis	180	549	3.1	39	12
Nick Goings	37	133	3.6	17	0
Jamal Robertson	14	41	2.9	11	1
Jake Delhomme	24	31	1.3	12	1

RECEIVING

PLAYER	NO.	YDS	AVG	LG	TD
Steve Smith	103	1,563	15.2	80	12
DeShaun Foster	34	372	10.9	47	1
Ricky Proehl	25	441	17.6	69	4
Keary Colbert	25	282	11.3	42	2
Kris Mangum	23	202	8.8	24	2
Nick Goings	14	151	10.8	30	0
Brad Hoover	14	87	6.2	12	0

KICKING

PLAYER	FGM	FGA	PCT	XPM	XPA
John Kasay	26	34	76.5	43	44

PUNTING

PLAYER	NO.	AVG	NET AVG	TB	IN 20	LG	BLK
Jason Baker	72	43.3	38.9	4	23	59	0

INTERCEPTIONS Chris Gamble, 7   SACKS Julius Peppers, 10.5

CHICAGO BEARS

PASSING

PLAYER	ATT	COMP	YDS	PCT COMP	YDS/ATT	TD	INT	RATING
Kyle Orton	368	190	1,869	51.6	5.08	9	13	59.7
Rex Grossman	39	20	259	51.3	6.64	1	2	59.7
Jeff Blake	9	8	55	88.9	6.11	1	0	129.2
Brad Maynard	2	1	18	50.0	9.00	0	0	81.3

RUSHING

PLAYER	NO.	YDS	AVG	LG	TD
Thomas Jones	314	1,335	4.3	42	9
Adrian Peterson	76	391	5.1	36	2
Cedric Benson	67	272	4.1	36	0
Kyle Orton	24	44	1.8	15	0
Bernard Berrian	2	31	15.5	37	0

RECEIVING

PLAYER	NO.	YDS	AVG	LG	TD
Muhsin Muhammad	64	750	11.7	33	4
Justin Gage	31	346	11.2	25	2
Thomas Jones	26	143	5.5	41	0
Desmond Clark	24	229	9.5	31	2
Mark Bradley	18	230	12.8	54	0
Bernard Berrian	13	246	18.9	54	0

KICKING

PLAYER	FGM	FGA	PCT	XPM	XPA
Robbie Gould	21	27	77.8	19	20

PUNTING

PLAYER	NO.	AVG	NET AVG	TB	IN 20	LG	BLK
Brad Maynard	96	41.0	35.3	11	24	63	1

INTERCEPTIONS Nathan Vasher, 8   SACKS Adewale Ogunleye, 10

DALLAS COWBOYS

PASSING

PLAYER	ATT	COMP	YDS	PCT COMP	YDS/ATT	TD	INT	RATING
Drew Bledsoe	499	300	3,639	60.1	7.29	23	17	83.7

RUSHING

PLAYER	NO.	YDS	AVG	LG	TD
Julius Jones	257	993	3.9	51	5
Marion Barber	138	538	3.9	28	5
Tyson Thompson	46	182	4.0	16	0
Anthony Thomas	36	80	2.2	12	0
Drew Bledsoe	34	50	1.5	9	2

RECEIVING

PLAYER	NO.	YDS	AVG	LG	TD
Keyshawn Johnson	71	839	11.8	34	6
Jason Witten	66	757	11.5	34	6
Terry Glenn	62	1,136	18.3	71	7
Julius Jones	35	218	6.2	26	0
Patrick Crayton	22	341	15.5	63	2
Marion Barber	18	115	6.4	21	0
Lousaka Polite	9	72	8.0	15	1

KICKING

PLAYER	FGM	FGA	PCT	XPM	XPA
Jose Cortez	12	16	75.0	13	14

PUNTING

PLAYER	NO.	AVG	NET AVG	TB	IN 20	LG	BLK
Mat McBriar	81	42.5	37.1	9	28	63	0

INTERCEPTIONS Aaron Glenn, 4   SACKS DeMarcus Ware, Greg Ellis, 8

DETROIT LIONS

PASSING

PLAYER	ATT	COMP	YDS	PCT COMP	YDS/ATT	TD	INT	RATING
Joey Harrington	330	188	2,021	57.0	6.12	12	12	72.0
Jeff Garcia	173	102	937	59.0	5.42	3	6	65.1

RUSHING

PLAYER	NO.	YDS	AVG	LG	TD
Kevin Jones	186	664	3.6	40	5
Artose Pinner	106	349	3.3	19	3
Shawn Bryson	64	306	4.8	77	1
Joey Harrington	24	80	3.3	15	0

RECEIVING

PLAYER	NO.	YDS	AVG	LG	TD
Marcus Pollard	46	516	11.2	86	3
Roy Williams	45	687	15.3	51	8
Scottie Vines	40	417	10.4	40	0
Shawn Bryson	37	284	7.7	63	0
Mike Williams	29	350	12.1	49	1
Artose Pinner	21	181	8.6	24	0
Kevin Jones	20	109	5.5	28	0
Kevin Johnson	17	133	7.8	25	0
Charles Rogers	14	197	14.1	35	1

KICKING

PLAYER	FGM	FGA	PCT	XPM	XPA
Jason Hanson	19	24	79.2	27	27

PUNTING

PLAYER	NO.	AVG	NET AVG	TB	IN 20	LG	BLK
Nick Harris	84	43.5	36.9	2	34	60	0

INTERCEPTIONS Dre' Bly, 6   SACKS Kalimba Edwards, 7

GREEN BAY PACKERS

PASSING

PLAYER	ATT	COMP	YDS	PCT COMP	YDS/ATT	TD	INT	RATING
Brett Favre	607	372	3,881	61.3	6.39	20	29	70.9
Aaron Rodgers	16	9	65	56.3	4.06	0	1	39.8

RUSHING

PLAYER	NO.	YDS	AVG	LG	TD
Samkon Gado	143	582	4.1	64	6
Ahman Green	77	255	3.3	13	0
Tony Fisher	60	173	2.9	17	1

RECEIVING

PLAYER	NO.	YDS	AVG	LG	TD
Donald Driver	86	1,221	14.2	59	5
Antonio Chatman	49	549	11.2	25	4
Tony Fisher	48	347	7.2	15	1
Donald Lee	33	294	8.9	27	2
William Henderson	30	264	8.8	32	0
Robert Ferguson	27	366	13.6	51	3
David Martin	27	224	8.3	21	3
Bubba Franks	25	207	8.3	24	1

KICKING

PLAYER	FGM	FGA	PCT	XPM	XPA
Ryan Longwell	20	27	74.1	30	31

PUNTING

PLAYER	NO.	AVG	NET AVG	TB	IN 20	LG	BLK
B.J. Sander	64	39.2	33.9	2	11	53	0

INTERCEPTIONS Al Harris, 3   **SACKS** Kabeer Gbaja-Biamila, 8

MINNESOTA VIKINGS

PASSING

PLAYER	ATT	COMP	YDS	PCT COMP	YDS/ATT	TD	INT	RATING
Brad Johnson	294	184	1,885	62.6	6.41	12	4	88.9
Daunte Culpepper	216	139	1,564	64.4	7.24	6	12	72.0

RUSHING

PLAYER	NO.	YDS	AVG	LG	TD
Mewelde Moore	155	662	4.3	33	1
Michael Bennett	126	473	3.8	61	3
Daunte Culpepper	24	147	6.1	18	1
Ciatrick Fason	32	62	1.9	15	4
Brad Johnson	18	53	2.9	16	0

RECEIVING

PLAYER	NO.	YDS	AVG	LG	TD
Jermaine Wiggins	69	568	8.2	24	1
Travis Taylor	50	604	12.1	31	4
Mewelde Moore	37	339	9.2	29	2
Marcus Robinson	31	515	16.6	68	5
Nate Burleson	30	328	10.9	20	1
Michael Bennett	27	124	4.6	20	2
Troy Williamson	24	372	15.5	56	2
Koren Robinson	22	347	15.8	80	1

KICKING

PLAYER	FGM	FGA	PCT	XPM	XPA
Paul Edinger	25	34	73.5	31	31

PUNTING

PLAYER	NO.	AVG	NET AVG	TB	IN 20	LG	BLK
Chris Kluwe	71	44.1	35.8	6	17	62	0

INTERCEPTIONS Darren Sharper, 9   **SACKS** Lance Johnstone, 7.5

NEW ORLEANS SAINTS

PASSING

PLAYER	ATT	COMP	YDS	PCT COMP	YDS/ATT	TD	INT	RATING
Aaron Brooks	431	240	2,882	55.7	6.69	13	17	70.0

RUSHING

PLAYER	NO.	YDS	AVG	LG	TD
Antowain Smith	166	659	4.0	42	3
Aaron Stecker	95	363	3.8	32	0
Deuce McAllister	93	335	3.6	26	3

RECEIVING

PLAYER	NO.	YDS	AVG	LG	TD
Donté Stallworth	70	945	13.5	43	7
Joe Horn	49	654	13.3	30	1
Zachary Hilton	35	396	11.3	29	1
Aaron Stecker	35	281	8.0	41	0
Az-Zahir Hakim	34	489	14.4	42	2
Devery Henderson	22	343	15.6	66	3
Deuce McAllister	17	117	6.9	22	0
Ernie Conwell	13	165	12.7	31	1

KICKING

PLAYER	FGM	FGA	PCT	XPM	XPA
John Carney	25	32	78.1	22	22

PUNTING

PLAYER	NO.	AVG	NET AVG	TB	IN 20	LG	BLK
Mitch Berger	71	43.2	38.7	3	28	69	0

INTERCEPTIONS Jason Craft, 3   **SACKS** Will Smith, 8.5

NEW YORK GIANTS

PASSING

PLAYER	ATT	COMP	YDS	PCT COMP	YDS/ATT	TD	INT	RATING
Eli Manning	557	294	3,762	52.8	6.75	24	17	75.9
Tiki Barber	1	0	0	0.0	0.00	0	0	39.6

RUSHING

PLAYER	NO.	YDS	AVG	LG	TD
Tiki Barber	357	1860	5.2	95	9
Derrick Ward	35	123	3.5	12	0
Brandon Jacobs	38	99	2.6	21	7

RECEIVING

PLAYER	NO.	YDS	AVG	LG	TD
Plaxico Burress	76	1,214	16.0	78	7
Jeremy Shockey	65	891	13.7	59	7
Amani Toomer	60	684	11.4	37	7
Tiki Barber	54	530	9.8	48	2
Jim Finn	13	98	7.5	15	0
Tim Carter	10	186	18.6	44	0
Visanthe Shiancoe	8	91	11.4	17	0

KICKING

PLAYER	FGM	FGA	PCT	XPM	XPA
Jay Feely	35	42	83.3	43	43

PUNTING

PLAYER	NO.	AVG	NET AVG	TB	IN 20	LG	BLK
Jeff Feagles	73	42.1	37.0	3	26	56	0

INTERCEPTIONS Brent Alexander, 4   **SACKS** Osi Umenyiora, 14.5

PHILADELPHIA EAGLES

PASSING

PLAYER	ATT	COMP	YDS	PCT COMP	YDS/ATT	TD	INT	RATING
Donovan McNabb	357	211	2,507	59.1	7.02	16	9	85.0

RUSHING

PLAYER	NO.	YDS	AVG	LG	TD
Brian Westbrook	156	617	4.0	31	3
Ryan Moats	55	278	5.1	59	3
Lamar Gordon	54	182	3.4	11	1
Mike McMahon	34	118	3.5	19	3
Reno Mahe	20	87	4.4	13	0

RECEIVING

PLAYER	NO.	YDS	AVG	LG	TD
L.J. Smith	61	682	11.2	48	3
Brian Westbrook	61	616	10.1	62	4
Greg Lewis	48	561	11.7	34	1
Terrell Owens	47	763	16.2	91	6
Reggie Brown	43	571	13.3	56	4
Billy McMullen	18	268	14.9	38	1
Josh Parry	13	89	6.8	13	0
Reno Mahe	12	68	5.7	12	0

KICKING

PLAYER	FGM	FGA	PCT	XPM	XPA
David Akers	16	22	72.7	23	23

PUNTING

PLAYER	NO.	AVG	NET AVG	TB	IN 20	LG	BLK
Dirk Johnson	39	41.4	38.4	0	11	59	0

INTERCEPTIONS Sheldon Brown, 4   **SACKS** Jevon Kearse, 7.5

SAN FRANCISCO 49ERS

PASSING

PLAYER	ATT	COMP	YDS	PCT COMP	YDS/ATT	TD	INT	RATING
Alex Smith	165	84	875	50.9	5.30	1	11	40.8
Tim Rattay	97	56	667	57.7	6.88	5	6	70.3

RUSHING

PLAYER	NO.	YDS	AVG	LG	TD
Frank Gore	127	608	4.8	72	3
Kevan Barlow	176	581	3.3	29	3
Maurice Hicks	59	308	5.2	73	3
Alex Smith	30	103	3.4	19	0

RECEIVING

PLAYER	NO.	YDS	AVG	LG	TD
Brandon Lloyd	48	733	15.3	89	5
Arnaz Battle	32	363	11.3	39	3
Kevan Barlow	31	241	7.8	24	0
Johnnie Morton	21	288	13.7	30	0
Frank Gore	15	131	8.7	47	0
Maurice Hicks	12	47	3.9	11	0
Terry Jackson	10	67	6.7	12	0
Terry Jones	9	76	8.4	21	0
Jason McAddley	7	125	17.9	38	0

KICKING

PLAYER	FGM	FGA	PCT	XPM	XPA
Joe Nedney	26	28	92.9	19	19

PUNTING

PLAYER	NO.	AVG	NET AVG	TB	IN 20	LG	BLK
Andy Lee	107	41.6	36.3	3	15	58	1

INTERCEPTIONS Shawntae Spencer, 4   **SACKS** Bryant Young, 8

SEATTLE SEAHAWKS

PASSING

PLAYER	ATT	COMP	YDS	PCT COMP	YDS/ATT	TD	INT	RATING
Matt Hasselbeck	449	294	3,459	65.5	7.70	24	9	98.2
Seneca Wallace	25	13	173	52.0	6.92	1	1	70.9

RUSHING

PLAYER	NO.	YDS	AVG	LG	TD
Shaun Alexander	370	1,880	5.1	88	27
Maurice Morris	71	288	4.1	49	1
Matt Hasselbeck	36	124	3.4	23	1
Leonard Weaver	17	80	4.7	24	0

RECEIVING

PLAYER	NO.	YDS	AVG	LG	TD
Bobby Engram	67	778	11.6	56	3
Joe Jurevicius	55	694	12.6	52	10
Jerramy Stevens	45	554	12.3	35	5
Darrell Jackson	38	482	12.7	48	3
D.J. Hackett	28	400	14.3	47	2
Mack Strong	22	166	7.5	27	0
Shaun Alexander	15	78	5.2	9	1
Ryan Hannam	13	89	6.8	20	1

KICKING

PLAYER	FGM	FGA	PCT	XPM	XPA
Josh Brown	18	25	72.0	56	57

PUNTING

PLAYER	NO.	AVG	NET AVG	TB	IN 20	LG	BLK
Tom Rouen	61	41.6	35.0	7	20	62	0
Leo Araguz	18	40.2	34.7	1	4	53	0
Josh Brown	1	20.0	20.0	0	1	20	0

INTERCEPTIONS Michael Boulware, 4   **SACKS** Bryce Fisher, 9

ST. LOUIS RAMS

PASSING

PLAYER	ATT	COMP	YDS	PCT COMP	YDS/ATT	TD	INT	RATING
Marc Bulger	287	192	2,297	66.9	8.00	14	9	94.4
Jamie Martin	177	124	1,277	70.1	7.21	5	7	83.5

RUSHING

PLAYER	NO.	YDS	AVG	LG	TD
Steven Jackson	254	1,046	4.1	51	8
Marshall Faulk	65	292	4.5	20	0
Aveion Cason	10	65	6.5	14	1
Ryan Fitzpatrick	14	64	4.6	14	2

RECEIVING

PLAYER	NO.	YDS	AVG	LG	TD
Torry Holt	102	1331	13.0	44	9
Kevin Curtis	60	801	13.4	83	6
Shaun McDonald	46	523	11.4	31	0
Marshall Faulk	44	291	6.6	18	1
Steven Jackson	43	320	7.4	27	2
Isaac Bruce	36	525	14.6	46	3
Dane Looker	23	237	10.3	23	0
Brandon Manumaleuna	13	129	9.9	33	1

KICKING

PLAYER	FGM	FGA	PCT	XPM	XPA
Jeff Wilkins	27	31	87.1	36	36

PUNTING

PLAYER	NO.	AVG	NET AVG	TB	IN 20	LG	BLK
Bryan Barker	50	42.7	35.6	4	13	63	0
Reggie Hodges	22	38.0	31.0	1	3	55	0

INTERCEPTIONS Mike Furrey, 4   **SACKS** Leonard Little, 9.5

TAMPA BAY BUCCANEERS

PASSING

PLAYER	ATT	COMP	YDS	PCT COMP	YDS/ATT	TD	INT	RATING
Chris Simms	313	191	2,035	61.0	6.50	10	7	81.4
Brian Griese	174	112	1,136	64.4	6.53	7	7	79.6

RUSHING

PLAYER	NO.	YDS	AVG	LG	TD
Carnell Williams	290	1,178	4.1	71	6
Michael Pittman	70	436	6.2	64	1
Earnest Graham	28	83	3.0	16	0
Mike Alstott	34	80	2.4	9	6
Chris Simms	19	31	1.6	10	0

RECEIVING

PLAYER	NO.	YDS	AVG	LG	TD
Joey Galloway	83	1,287	15.5	80	10
Alex Smith	41	367	9.0	24	2
Michael Pittman	36	300	8.3	41	1
Ike Hilliard	35	282	8.1	22	1
Michael Clayton	32	372	11.6	41	0
Mike Alstott	25	222	8.9	24	1
Carnell Williams	20	81	4.1	15	0
Anthony Becht	16	112	7.0	17	0
Jameel Cook	7	43	6.1	11	1
Edell Shepherd	6	103	17.2	46	1

KICKING

PLAYER	FGM	FGA	PCT	XPM	XPA
Matt Bryant	21	25	84.0	31	31
Todd France	1	2	50.0	1	1

PUNTING

PLAYER	NO.	AVG	NET AVG	TB	IN 20	LG	BLK
Josh Bidwell	90	45.6	37.5	13	24	61	0

INTERCEPTIONS Ronde Barber, 5   SACKS Simeon Rice, 14

WASHINGTON REDSKINS

PASSING

PLAYER	ATT	COMP	YDS	PCT COMP	YDS/ATT	TD	INT	RATING
Mark Brunell	454	262	3,050	57.7	6.72	23	10	85.9
Patrick Ramsey	25	15	279	60.0	11.16	1	1	95.3

RUSHING

PLAYER	NO.	YDS	AVG	LG	TD
Clinton Portis	352	1,516	4.3	47	11
Ladell Betts	89	338	3.8	22	1
Rock Cartwright	27	199	7.4	52	2
Mark Brunell	42	111	2.6	25	0
James Thrash	1	8	8.0	8	0

RECEIVING

PLAYER	NO.	YDS	AVG	LG	TD
Santana Moss	84	1,483	17.7	78	9
Chris Cooley	71	774	10.9	32	7
Clinton Portis	30	216	7.2	23	0
David Patten	22	217	9.9	32	0
Robert Royal	18	131	7.3	29	1
James Thrash	14	194	13.9	41	0
Mike Sellers	12	72	6.0	19	7

KICKING

PLAYER	FGM	FGA	PCT	XPM	XPA
John Hall	12	14	85.7	27	27
Nick Novak	5	7	71.4	15	15

PUNTING

PLAYER	NO.	AVG	NET AVG	TB	IN 20	LG	BLK
Derrick Frost	76	40.4	36.7	6	23	55	0

INTERCEPTIONS Lemar Marshall, 4   SACKS Phillip Daniels, 8

SUPER BOWL RESULTS

SUPER BOWL	DATE	WINNER	LOSER	SCORE	SITE	ATTENDANCE
XL	2-5-06	Steelers	Seahawks	21–10	Detroit, MI	68,206
XXXIX	2-6-05	Patriots	Eagles	24–21	Jacksonville, FL	78,125
XXXVIII	2-1-04	Patriots	Panthers	32–29	Houston, TX	71,525
XXXVII	1-26-03	Buccaneers	Raiders	48–21	San Diego, CA	67,603
XXXVI	2-3-02	Patriots	Rams	20–17	New Orleans, LA	72,922
XXXV	1-28-01	Ravens	Giants	34–7	Tampa, FL	71,921
XXXIV	1-30-00	Rams	Titans	23–16	Atlanta, GA	72,625
XXXIII	1-31-99	Broncos	Falcons	34–19	Miami, FL	74,803
XXXII	1-25-98	Broncos	Packers	31–24	San Diego, CA	68,912
XXXI	1-26-97	Packers	Patriots	35–21	New Orleans, LA	72,301
XXX	1-28-96	Cowboys	Steelers	27–17	Tempe, AZ	76,347
XXIX	1-29-95	49ers	Chargers	49–26	Miami, FL	74,107
XXVIII	1-30-94	Cowboys	Bills	30–13	Atlanta, GA	72,817
XXVII	1-31-93	Cowboys	Bills	52–17	Pasadena, CA	98,374
XXVI	1-26-92	Redskins	Bills	37–24	Minneapolis, MN	63,130
XXV	1-27-91	Giants	Bills	20–19	Tampa, FL	73,813
XXIV	1-28-90	49ers	Broncos	55–10	New Orleans, LA	72,919
XXIII	1-22-89	49ers	Bengals	20–16	Miami, FL	75,129
XXII	1-31-88	Redskins	Broncos	42–10	San Diego, CA	73,302
XXI	1-25-87	Giants	Broncos	39–20	Pasadena, CA	101,063
XX	1-26-86	Bears	Patriots	46–10	New Orleans, LA	73,818
XIX	1-20-85	49ers	Dolphins	38–16	Stanford, CA	84,059
XVIII	1-22-84	Raiders	Redskins	38–9	Tampa, FL	72,920
XVII	1-30-83	Redskins	Dolphins	27–17	Pasadena, CA	103,667
XVI	1-24-82	49ers	Bengals	26–21	Pontiac, MI	81,270
XV	1-25-81	Raiders	Eagles	27–10	New Orleans, LA	76,135
XIV	1-20-80	Steelers	Rams	31–19	Pasadena, CA	103,985
XIII	1-21-79	Steelers	Cowboys	35–31	Miami, FL	79,484
XII	1-15-78	Cowboys	Broncos	27–10	New Orleans, LA	76,400
XI	1-9-77	Raiders	Vikings	32–14	Pasadena, CA	103,438
X	1-18-76	Steelers	Cowboys	21–17	Miami, FL	80,187
IX	1-12-75	Steelers	Vikings	16–6	New Orleans, LA	80,997
VIII	1-13-74	Dolphins	Vikings	24–7	Houston, TX	71,882
VII	1-14-73	Dolphins	Redskins	14–7	Los Angeles, CA	90,182
VI	1-16-72	Cowboys	Dolphins	24–3	New Orleans, LA	81,023
V	1-17-71	Colts	Cowboys	16–13	Miami, FL	79,204
IV	1-11-70	Chiefs	Vikings	23–7	New Orleans, LA	80,562
III	1-12-69	Jets	Colts	16–7	Miami, FL	75,389
II	1-14-68	Packers	Raiders	33–14	Miami, FL	75,546
I	1-15-67	Packers	Chiefs	35–10	Los Angeles, CA	61,946

SUPER BOWL MVPS

SUPER BOWL	PLAYER/TEAM	POSITION	SUPER BOWL	PLAYER/TEAM	POSITION
XL	Hines Ward, Steelers	WR	XIX	Joe Montana, 49ers	QB
XXXIX	Deion Branch, Patriots	WR	XVIII	Marcus Allen, Raiders	RB
XXXVIII	Tom Brady, Patriots	QB	XVII	John Riggins, Redskins	RB
XXXVII	Dexter Jackson, Buccaneers	S	XVI	Joe Montana, 49ers	QB
XXXVI	Tom Brady, Patriots	QB	XV	Jim Plunkett, Raiders	QB
XXXV	Ray Lewis, Ravens	LB	XIV	Terry Bradshaw, Steelers	QB
XXXIV	Kurt Warner, Rams	QB	XIII	Terry Bradshaw, Steelers	QB
XXXIII	John Elway, Broncos	QB	XII (tie)	Randy White, Cowboys	DT
XXXII	Terrell Davis, Broncos	RB		Harvey Martin, Cowboys	DE
XXXI	Desmond Howard, Packers	KR	XI	Fred Biletnikoff, Raiders	WR
XXX	Larry Brown, Cowboys	DB	X	Lynn Swann, Steelers	WR
XXIX	Steve Young, 49ers	QB	IX	Franco Harris, Steelers	RB
XXVIII	Emmitt Smith, Cowboys	RB	VIII	Larry Csonka, Dolphins	RB
XXVII	Troy Aikman, Cowboys	QB	VII	Jake Scott, Dolphins	S
XXVI	Mark Rypien, Redskins	QB	VI	Roger Staubach, Cowboys	QB
XXV	Ottis Anderson, Giants	RB	V	Chuck Howley, Cowboys	LB
XXIV	Joe Montana, 49ers	QB	IV	Len Dawson, Chiefs	QB
XXIII	Jerry Rice, 49ers	WR	III	Joe Namath, Jets	QB
XXII	Doug Williams, Redskins	QB	II	Bart Starr, Packers	QB
XXI	Phil Simms, Giants	QB	I	Bart Starr, Packers	QB
XX	Richard Dent, Bears	DE			

KEY QB=quarterback; S=safety; LB=linebacker; RB=running back; KR=kick returner; DB=defensive back; WR=wide receiver; DE=defensive end; DT=defensive tackle

2005-06 TIME LINE

April 23, 2005: Quarterback Alex Smith of Utah is drafted by the San Francisco 49ers with the first overall pick in the 2005 NFL Draft. Auburn University makes draft history by becoming the first college team to have its entire offensive backfield — two running backs and a quarterback — selected in the first round.

August 31, 2005: The Green Bay Packers, led by Mississippi native Brett Favre, pack a planeful of emergency supplies to help victims of Hurricane Katrina. The team brings the supplies to Nashville, Tennessee, where they are trucked to hard-hit Hattiesburg, Mississippi.

September 18, 2005: Running back LaDainian Tomlinson of the San Diego Chargers sets the NFL record for consecutive games with a rushing touchdown when he scores for the 14th straight game, against Denver.

October 30, 2005: Terrell Owens plays his final football game of the season after a dispute with his team, the Philadelphia Eagles. Owens catches three balls for 154 yards and a touchdown against Denver. He finishes '05 having played in just seven games, amassing 763 yards, and scoring six touchdowns.

October 31, 2005: Pittsburgh Steelers quarterback Ben Roethlisberger injures his right knee in a game against Baltimore. Big Ben misses the team's next three games. He goes on to lead the Steelers to wins in their last eight games, including the Super Bowl win over Seattle.

December 18, 2005: After winning their first 13 games, the Indianapolis Colts are beaten for the first time in the season. The Colts are stunned at home by the San Diego Chargers, 26-17.

January 1, 2006: Doug Flutie of the New England Patriots becomes the first NFL player to successfully dropkick the ball since 1948. Flutie's kick is a late-game extra point attempt for the Pats, who lose to Miami, 28-26.

January 7, 2006: Coach Joe Gibbs of the Washington Redskins, who had come out of retirement at the start of the previous season, returns to the playoffs for the first time in 13 years. His Redskins win 17-10 at Tampa Bay. Gibbs gets his 17th playoff win, third-best all time.

January 8, 2006: On his first pass of the playoffs, Cincinnati Bengals quarterback Carson Palmer tears the anterior cruciate ligament in his left knee. Palmer's lone pass results in a 66-yard reception, making it the longest completion in Bengals' playoff history. The Pittsburgh Steelers win the game, 31-17.

January 14, 2006: The New England Patriots, two-time defending Super Bowl champions, are eliminated from the playoffs by the Denver Broncos, 27-13. The defeat ends New England's record 10-game playoff winning streak, dating back to the 1998 season.

January 22, 2006: Seattle and Pittsburgh advance to the Super Bowl. The Seahawks defeat the Carolina Panthers, 34-14, to win the NFC Championship. The Steelers roll over Denver, 34-17, for the AFC crown.

February 5, 2006: The Steelers use a trick play and running back Willie Parker's Super Bowl-record 75-yard touchdown run to win the Super Bowl, 21-10. Hines Ward is named the game's MVP. It is Pittsburgh's record-tying fifth Super Bowl title and the AFC's fifth Super Bowl victory in the past six seasons.

**Dan Marino,
Miami Dolphins**

JOHN BIEVER

ALL-TIME NFL INDIVIDUAL
STATISTICAL LEADERS — CAREER LEADERS

SCORING

PLAYER	YRS	TD	FG	PAT	PTS
Gary Anderson	23	0	538	820	2,434
Morten Andersen	23	0	520	798	2,358
George Blanda	26	9	335	942	2,002
Norm Johnson	18	0	366	638	1,736
Nick Lowery	18	0	383	562	1,711
Jan Stenerud	19	0	373	580	1,699
†John Carney	18	0	390	464	1,634
Eddie Murray	19	0	352	538	1,594
†Matt Stover	15	0	380	454	1,594
Al Del Greco	17	0	347	543	1,584
†Jason Elam	13	0	341	534	1,557
Steve Christie	15	6	336	468	1,476
Pat Leahy	18	0	304	558	1,470
Jim Turner	16	1	304	521	1,439
Matt Bahr	17	0	300	522	1,422
†Jason Hanson	14	0	327	439	1,420
Mark Moseley	16	0	300	482	1,382
Jim Bakken	17	0	282	534	1,380
Fred Cox	15	0	282	519	1,365
Lou Groza	17	1	234	641	1,349

RUSHING

PLAYER	YRS	ATT	YDS	AVG	LG	TD
†Emmitt Smith	15	4,409	18,355	4.2	75	164
Walter Payton	13	3,838	16,726	4.4	76	110
Barry Sanders	10	3,062	15,269	5.0	85	99
†Curtis Martin	11	3,518	14,101	4.0	70	90
†Jerome Bettis	13	3,479	13,662	3.9	71	91
Eric Dickerson	11	2,996	13,259	4.4	85	90
Tony Dorsett	12	2,936	12,739	4.3	99	77
Jim Brown	9	2,359	12,312	5.2	80	106
†Marshall Faulk	12	2,836	12,279	4.3	71	100
Marcus Allen	16	3,022	12,243	4.1	61	123
Franco Harris	13	2,949	12,120	4.1	75	91
Thurman Thomas	13	2,877	12,074	4.2	80	65
John Riggins	14	2,916	11,352	3.9	66	104
O.J. Simpson	11	2,404	11,236	4.7	94	61
Ricky Watters	10	2,622	10,643	4.1	57	78
†Eddie George	9	2,865	10,441	3.6	76	68
†Corey Dillon	9	2,419	10,429	4.3	96	69
Ottis Anderson	14	2,562	10,273	4.0	76	81
Earl Campbell	8	2,187	9,407	4.3	81	74
†Edgerrin James	7	2,188	9,226	4.2	72	64

TOUCHDOWNS

PLAYER	YRS	RUSH	REC	RET	TD
Jerry Rice	20	10	197	0	208
Emmitt Smith	15	164	11	0	175
Marcus Allen	16	123	21	1	145
†Marshall Faulk	12	100	36	0	136
Cris Carter	16	0	130	1	131
Jim Brown	9	106	20	0	126
Walter Payton	13	110	15	0	125
John Riggins	14	104	12	0	116
Lenny Moore	12	63	48	2	113
†Marvin Harrison	10	0	110	0	110

PLAYER	YRS	RUSH	REC	RET	TD
Barry Sanders	10	99	10	0	109
†Tim Brown	17	1	100	4	105
Don Hutson	11	3	99	3	105
†Terrell Owens	10	2	101	0	103
Steve Largent	14	1	100	0	101
†Shaun Alexander	6	89	11	0	100
Franco Harris	13	91	9	0	100
†Curtis Martin	11	90	10	0	100
†Randy Moss	8	0	98	1	99
Eric Dickerson	11	90	6	0	96

PASSING — EFFICIENCY*

PLAYER	YRS	ATT	COMP	PCT COMP	YDS	YDS/ATT	TD	INT	RATING
Steve Young	15	4,149	2,667	64.3	33,124	7.98	232	107	96.8
†Kurt Warner	8	2,340	1,537	65.7	19,214	8.21	119	78	94.1
†Peyton Manning	8	4,333	2,769	63.9	33,189	7.66	244	130	93.5
Joe Montana	15	5,391	3,409	63.2	40,551	7.52	273	139	92.3
†Daunte Culpepper	7	2,607	1,678	64.4	20,162	7.73	135	86	91.5
†Marc Bulger	4	1,518	987	65.0	11,932	7.86	71	51	90.6
†Tom Brady	6	2,548	1,577	61.9	18,035	7.08	123	66	88.5
†Trent Green	8	3,329	2,022	60.7	25,621	7.70	150	92	88.3
†Matt Hasselbeck	7	2,205	1,342	60.9	15,925	7.22	96	57	86.6
Dan Marino	17	8,358	4,967	59.4	61,361	7.34	420	252	86.4

PASSING — YARDS

PLAYER	YRS	ATT	COMP	PCT COMP	YDS
Dan Marino	17	8,358	4,967	59.4	61,361
†Brett Favre	15	7,611	4,678	61.5	53,615
John Elway	16	7,250	4,123	56.9	51,475
Warren Moon	17	6,823	3,988	58.4	49,325
Fran Tarkenton	18	6,467	3,686	57.0	47,003
†Vinny Testaverde	19	6,526	3,691	56.6	45,252

PLAYER	YRS	ATT	COMP	PCT COMP	YDS
†Drew Bledsoe	13	6,548	3,749	57.3	43,447
Dan Fouts	15	5,604	3,297	58.8	43,040
Joe Montana	15	5,391	3,409	63.2	40,551
Johnny Unitas	18	5,186	2,830	54.6	40,239
Dave Krieg	19	5,311	3,105	58.5	38,147
Boomer Esiason	14	5,205	2,969	57.0	37,920

*1,500 or more attempts. The passer ratings are based on performance standards established for completion percentage, interception percentage, touchdown percentage, and average gain. Passers are allocated points according to how their marks compare with those standards.
†Active in 2005

KEY YRS=years; TD=touchdowns; FG=field goals; PAT=extra points; PTS=points; ATT=attempts; AVG=average; LG=long; RUSH=rushing; REC=receiving; RET=returns; COMP=completions; PCT COMP=completion percentage; YDS/ATT=yards per attempt; INT=interceptions; COMP YDS=completion yards

PASSING — TOUCHDOWNS

PLAYER	TD
Dan Marino	420
†Brett Favre	396
Fran Tarkenton	342
John Elway	300
Warren Moon	291
Johnny Unitas	290
Joe Montana	273
†Vinny Testaverde	269
Dave Krieg	261
Sonny Jurgensen	255
Dan Fouts	254
Boomer Esiason	247
†Drew Bledsoe	244
John Hadl	244
†Peyton Manning	244
Len Dawson	239
Jim Kelly	237

SACKS

PLAYER	SACKS
Bruce Smith	200.0
Reggie White	198.0
Kevin Greene	160.0
Chris Doleman	150.5
Richard Dent	137.5

Note: Officially compiled since 1982

Bruce Smith,
Buffalo Bills

JOHN IACONO

INTERCEPTIONS

PLAYER	YRS	NO.	YDS	AVG	LG	TD
Paul Krause	16	81	1,185	14.6	81	3
Emlen Tunnell	14	79	1,282	16.2	55	4
Rod Woodson	17	71	1,483	20.9	98	12
Dick "Night Train" Lane	14	68	1,207	17.8	80	5
Ken Riley	15	65	596	9.2	66	5

RECEIVING — RECEPTIONS

PLAYER	YRS	NO.	YDS	AVG	LG	TD
Jerry Rice	20	1,549	22,895	14.8	96	197
Cris Carter	16	1,101	13,899	12.6	80	130
Tim Brown	17	1,094	14,934	13.7	80	100
Andre Reed	16	951	13,198	13.9	83	87
Art Monk	16	940	12,721	13.5	79	68
†Marvin Harrison	10	927	12,331	13.3	80	110
†Jimmy Smith	12	862	12,287	14.3	75	67
Irving Fryar	17	851	12,785	15.0	80	84
Larry Centers	14	827	6,797	8.2	54	28
†Keenan McCardell	14	825	10,680	12.9	76	62
Steve Largent	14	819	13,089	16.0	74	100
Shannon Sharpe	14	815	10,060	12.3	82	62

RECEIVING — YARDS

PLAYER	YDS
Jerry Rice	22,895
Tim Brown	14,934
James Lofton	14,004
Cris Carter	13,899
Henry Ellard	13,777
Andre Reed	13,198
Steve Largent	13,089
Irving Fryar	12,785
Art Monk	12,721
†Marvin Harrison	12,331

† Active in 2005

SINGLE-SEASON LEADERS

SCORING — POINTS

PLAYER	YEAR	TD	PAT	FG	PTS
Paul Hornung, Packers	1960	15	41	15	176
Shaun Alexander, Seahawks	2005	28	0	0	168
Gary Anderson, Vikings	1998	0	59	35	164
Jeff Wilkins, Rams	2003	0	46	39	163
Priest Holmes, Chiefs	2003	27	0	0	162
Mark Moseley, Redskins	1983	0	62	33	161
Marshall Faulk, Rams	2000	26	0	0	160
Gino Cappelletti, Patriots	1964	7	36	25	155
Emmitt Smith, Cowboys	1995	25	0	0	150
Chip Lohmiller, Redskins	1991	0	56	31	149

Note: Cappelletti's 1964 total includes a 2-point conversion.

FIELD GOALS

PLAYER	YEAR	ATT	NO.
Neil Rackers, Cardinals	2005	42	40
Jeff Wilkins, Rams	2003	42	39
Olindo Mare, Dolphins	1999	46	39
John Kasay, Panthers	1996	45	37
Mike Vanderjagt, Colts	2003	37	37
Cary Blanchard, Colts	1996	40	36

Five tied with 35 (Jay Feely, 2005).

TOUCHDOWNS

PLAYER	YEAR	RUSH	REC	RET	TOTAL
Priest Holmes, Chiefs	2003	27	0	0	27
Shaun Alexander, Seahawks	2005	27	1	0	28
Marshall Faulk, Rams	2000	18	8	0	26
Emmitt Smith, Cowboys	1995	25	0	0	25
John Riggins, Redskins	1983	24	0	0	24
Priest Holmes, Chiefs	2002	21	3	0	24
O.J. Simpson, Bills	1975	16	7	0	23
Jerry Rice, 49ers	1987	1	22	0	23

Three tied with 22.

RUSHING — YARDS GAINED

PLAYER	YEAR	ATT	YDS	AVG
Eric Dickerson, Rams	1984	379	2,105	5.6
Jamal Lewis, Ravens	2003	387	2,066	5.3
Barry Sanders, Lions	1997	335	2,053	6.1
Terrell Davis, Broncos	1998	392	2,008	5.1
O.J. Simpson, Bills	1973	332	2,003	6.0
Earl Campbell, Oilers	1980	373	1,934	5.2
Barry Sanders, Lions	1994	331	1,883	5.7
Ahman Green, Packers	2003	355	1,883	5.3
Shaun Alexander, Seahawks	2005	370	1,880	5.1
Jim Brown, Browns	1963	291	1,863	6.4
Tiki Barber, Giants	2005	357	1,860	5.1

SINGLE-SEASON LEADERS (cont.)

RUSHING — AVERAGE GAIN

PLAYER	YEAR	AVG
Beattie Feathers, Bears	1934	8.44
Randall Cunningham, Eagles	1990	7.98
Michael Vick, Falcons	2004	7.50
Michael Vick, Falcons	2002	6.88
Bobby Douglass, Bears	1972	6.87

Minimum 100 attempts.

RUSHING — TOUCHDOWNS

PLAYER	YEAR	NO.
Shaun Alexander, Seahawks	2005	27
Priest Holmes, Chiefs	2003	27
Emmitt Smith, Cowboys	1995	25
John Riggins, Redskins	1983	24

Five tied with 21.

PASSING — YARDS GAINED

PLAYER	YEAR	ATT	COMP	PCT	YDS
Dan Marino, Dolphins	1984	564	362	64.2	5,084
Kurt Warner, Rams	2001	546	375	68.7	4,830
Dan Fouts, Chargers	1981	609	360	59.1	4,802
Dan Marino, Dolphins	1986	623	378	60.7	4,746
Daunte Culpepper, Vikings	2004	548	379	69.2	4,717
Dan Fouts, Chargers	1980	589	348	59.1	4,715
Warren Moon, Oilers	1991	655	404	61.7	4,690
Warren Moon, Oilers	1990	584	362	62.0	4,689
Rich Gannon, Raiders	2002	618	418	67.6	4,689
Neil Lomax, Cardinals	1984	560	345	61.6	4,614
Peyton Manning, Colts	2004	497	336	67.6	4,557

PASSER RATING

PLAYER	YEAR	RATING
Peyton Manning, Colts	2004	121.1
Steve Young, 49ers	1994	112.8
Joe Montana, 49ers	1989	112.4
Daunte Culpepper, Vikings	2004	110.9
Milt Plum, Browns	1960	110.4
Sammy Baugh, Redskins	1945	109.9
Kurt Warner, Rams	1999	109.2

PASSING — TOUCHDOWNS

PLAYER	YEAR	NO.
Peyton Manning, Colts	2004	49
Dan Marino, Dolphins	1984	48
Dan Marino, Dolphins	1986	44
Kurt Warner, Rams	1999	41
Brett Favre, Packers	1996	39
Daunte Culpepper, Vikings	2004	39

Four tied with 36.

RECEIVING — RECEPTIONS

PLAYER	YEAR	NO.	YDS
Marvin Harrison, Colts	2002	143	1,722
Herman Moore, Lions	1995	123	1,686
Cris Carter, Vikings	1994	122	1,256
Jerry Rice, 49ers	1995	122	1,848
Cris Carter, Vikings	1995	122	1,371
Isaac Bruce, Rams	1995	119	1,781
Torry Holt, Rams	2003	117	1,696
Jimmy Smith, Jaguars	1999	116	1,636
Marvin Harrison, Colts	1999	115	1,663
Rod Smith, Broncos	2001	113	1,343

Four tied with 112.

RECEIVING — YARDS GAINED

PLAYER	YEAR	YDS
Jerry Rice, 49ers	1995	1,848
Isaac Bruce, Rams	1995	1,781
Charley Hennigan, Oilers	1961	1,746
Marvin Harrison, Colts	2002	1,722
Torry Holt, Rams	2003	1,696
Herman Moore, Lions	1995	1,686

RECEIVING — TOUCHDOWNS

PLAYER	YEAR	NO.
Jerry Rice, 49ers	1987	22
Mark Clayton, Dolphins	1984	18
Sterling Sharpe, Packers	1994	18

Eight tied with 17.

INTERCEPTIONS

PLAYER	YEAR	NO.
Dick "Night Train" Lane, Rams	1952	14
Dan Sandifer, Redskins	1948	13
Spec Sanders, N.Y. Yankees	1950	13
Lester Hayes, Raiders	1980	13

Nine tied with 12.

SACKS

PLAYER	YEAR	NO.
Michael Strahan, N.Y. Giants	2001	22.5
Mark Gastineau, Jets	1984	22.0
Reggie White, Eagles	1987	21.0
Chris Doleman, Vikings	1989	21.0
Lawrence Taylor, N.Y. Giants	1986	20.5

PRO BOWL RESULTS

DATE	RESULT	DATE	RESULT	DATE	RESULT
2-12-06	NFC 23, AFC 17	2-1-98	AFC 29, NFC 24	2-4-90	NFC 27, AFC 21
2-13-05	AFC 38, NFC 27	2-2-97	AFC 26, NFC 23	1-29-89	NFC 34, AFC 3
2-8-04	NFC 55, AFC 52	2-4-96	NFC 20, AFC 13	2-7-88	AFC 15, NFC 6
2-2-03	AFC 45, NFC 20	2-5-95	AFC 41, NFC 13	2-1-87	AFC 10, NFC 6
2-9-02	AFC 38, NFC 30	2-6-94	NFC 17, AFC 3	2-2-86	NFC 28, AFC 24
2-4-01	AFC 38, NFC 17	2-7-93	AFC 23, NFC 20	1-27-85	AFC 22, NFC 14
2-6-00	NFC 51, AFC 31	2-2-92	NFC 21, AFC 15	1-29-84	NFC 45, AFC 3
2-7-99	AFC 23, NFC 10	2-3-91	AFC 23, NFC 21	2-6-83	NFC 20, AFC 19

PRO BOWL RESULTS (cont.)

DATE	RESULT	DATE	RESULT	DATE	RESULT
1-31-82	AFC 16, NFC 13	1-21-68	AFL East 25, West 24	1-13-57	West 19, East 10
2-1-81	NFC 21, AFC 7	1-22-67	NFL East 20, West 10	1-15-56	East 31, West 30
1-27-80	NFC 37, AFC 27	1-21-67	AFL East 30, West 23	1-16-55	West 26, East 19
1-29-79	NFC 13, AFC 7	1-15-66	NFL East 36, West 7	1-17-54	East 20, West 9
1-23-78	NFC 14, AFC 13	1-15-66	AFL All-Stars 30, Buffalo 19	1-10-53	N. Conf. 27, A. Conf. 7
1-17-77	AFC 24, NFC 14	1-16-65	AFL West 38, East 14	1-12-52	N. Conf. 30, A. Conf. 13
1-26-76	NFC 23, AFC 20	1-10-65	NFL West 34, East 14	1-14-51	A. Conf. 28, N. Conf. 27
1-20-75	NFC 17, AFC 10	1-19-64	AFL West 27, East 24	12-27-42	NFL All-Stars 17,
1-20-74	AFC 15, NFC 13	1-12-64	NFL West 31, East 17		Washington 14
1-21-73	AFC 33, NFC 28	1-13-63	NFL East 30, West 20	1-4-42	Chi. Bears 35,
1-23-72	AFC 26, NFC 13	1-13-63	AFL West 21, East 14		NFL All-Stars 24
1-24-71	NFC 27, AFC 6	1-14-62	NFL West 31, East 30	12-29-40	Chi. Bears 28,
1-18-70	NFL West 16, East 13	1-7-62	AFL West 47, East 27		NFL All-Stars 14
1-17-70	AFL West 26, East 3	1-15-61	West 35, East 31	1-14-40	Green Bay 16,
1-19-69	NFL West 10, East 7	1-17-60	West 38, East 21		NFL All-Stars 7
1-19-69	AFL West 38, East 25	1-11-59	East 28, West 21	1-15-39	N.Y. Giants 13,
1-21-68	NFL West 38, East 20	1-12-58	West 26, East 7		Pro All-Stars 10

2006 NFL DRAFT — FIRST ROUND   April 29-30, 2006, New York, NY

PICK	TEAM	PLAYER	POS.	HT.	WT.	SCHOOL
1	Houston	Mario Williams	DE	6-7	290	N.C. State
2	New Orleans	Reggie Bush	RB	5-11	201	USC
3	Tennessee	Vince Young	QB	6-4	229	Texas
4	N.Y. Jets	D. Ferguson	OT	6-6	312	Virginia
5	Green Bay	A.J. Hawk	LB	6-1	248	Auburn
6	San Francisco	Vernon Davis	TE	6-3^{1}/$_{2}$	254	Maryland
7	Oakland	Michael Huff	S	6-0	204	Texas
8	Buffalo	Donte Whitner	S	5-10	204	Ohio State
9	Detroit	Ernie Sims	LB	5-11	231	Florida State
10	Arizona	Matt Leinart	QB	6-5	223	USC
11	Denver	Jay Cutler	QB	6-3^{1}/$_{2}$	226	Vanderbilt
12	Baltimore	Haloti Ngata	DT	6-4	248	Oregon
13	Cleveland	Kamerion Wimbley	DE	6-4	313	Florida State
14	Philadelphia	Brodrick Bunkley	DT	6-2^{1}/$_{2}$	306	Florida State
15	St. Louis	Tye Hill	CB	5-9^{1}/$_{2}$	185	Clemson
16	Miami	Jason Allen	S	6-1	209	Tennessee
17	Minnesota	Chad Greenway	LB	6-2^{1}/$_{2}$	242	Iowa
18	Dallas	Bobby Carpenter	LB	6-2^{1}/$_{2}$	256	Ohio State
19	San Diego	Antonio Cromartie	CB	6-2	208	Florida State
20	Kansas City	Tamba Hali	DE	6-3	275	Penn State
21	New England	Laurence Maroney	RB	6-0	217	Minnesota
22	San Francisco	Manny Lawson	DE	6-5^{1}/$_{2}$	241	N.C. State
23	Tampa Bay	Davin Joseph	OG	6-2^{1}/$_{2}$	311	Oklahoma
24	Cincinnati	Johnathan Joseph	CB	5-11	193	South Carolina
25	Pittsburgh	Santonio Holmes	WR	5-10^{1}/$_{2}$	188	Ohio State
26	Buffalo	John McCargo	DT	6-1^{1}/$_{2}$	302	N.C. State
27	Carolina	DeAngelo Williams	RB	5-9	214	Memphis
28	Jacksonville	Marcedes Lewis	TE	6-6^{1}/$_{2}$	261	UCLA
29	N.Y. Jets	Nick Mangold	C	6-3^{1}/$_{2}$	300	Ohio State
30	Indianapolis	Joseph Addai	RB	5-11^{1}/$_{2}$	214	LSU
31	Seattle	Kelly Jennings	CB	5-11	180	Miami (Florida)
32	N.Y. Giants	Mathias Kiwanuka	DE	6-5^{1}/$_{2}$	266	Boston College

KEY QB=quarterback; RB=running back; WR=wide receiver; CB=cornerback; DE=defensive end; OLB=outside linebacker; OT=offensive tackle; FS=free safety; DT=defensive tackle; C=center; TE=tight end; G=guard

FOOTBALL COLLEGE

The 2005 college football season was a fitting lead-up to the remarkable national championship game played on January 4, 2006, at the Rose Bowl.

The teams that competed in that game — USC and Texas — had begun the season ranked Number 1 and Number 2 in most preseason polls. The two teams remained that way during the regular season. Each racked up impressive wins week after week. As the season unfolded, it became clear that the only thing standing between coach Pete Carroll's USC team and a record third-straight national title would be coach Mack Brown's Texas squad.

Despite a strong — and surprising — season from Penn State (which finished the regular season at 10–1) and impressive performances from Ohio State (9–2), Notre Dame (9–2), and Oregon (10–1), the only undefeated teams at bowl time were USC and Texas.

By the time the Rose Bowl kicked off on the evening of January 4, USC was riding the nation's longest winning streak (34) and Texas was being regarded as an underdog. ESPN even had a series of *SportsCenter* segments attempting to answer the question of whether USC was the best team of all time.

But ESPN and a few other folks were in for a surprise: Vince Young, the enormously gifted quarterback for the Longhorns showed that he not only had the size and speed to be a great player, but a gift for performing at his best on the game's biggest stage.

Young led the Longhorns to a 41–38 come-from-behind win. He rushed for 200 yards and three touchdowns (including the game-winner), and passed for 267 yards (completing 30 of his 40 attempts). He was named the game's Most Valuable Player. Four days after the game, Young, a junior, announced he would be entering the 2006 NFL Draft. He was immediately regarded as one of the draft's top prospects.

Young, however, wasn't recognized as the nation's best player in 2005. That honor went to USC running back Reggie Bush, who became the second-straight Trojan and the third in four seasons to win the Heisman Trophy (following quarterbacks Carson Palmer, who won in 2002, and Matt Leinart, who won in 2004).

Young did win the Maxwell Award, as the nation's best all-around player. Mike Hass of Oregon State was presented with the Fred Biletnikoff award as the nation's top receiver. He is the only player in Pac-10 history (and just the 10th in NCAA history) to have three 1,000-yard receiving seasons. Linebacker Paul Posluszny of Penn State was named the winner of the Chuck Bednarik Trophy, as the nation's best defensive player. He was just the fourth player in school history to record more than 100 tackles in consecutive seasons.

Quarterback Vince Young (10) dives for the first of three touchdowns he scored to lead Texas over USC in the national championship game.

ROBERT BECK

FINAL 2005 COLLEGE FOOTBALL POLLS

THE ASSOCIATED PRESS

	TEAM	RECORD	POINTS
1.	Texas	13–0	1,625
2.	USC	12–1	1,560
3.	Penn State	11–1	1,484
4.	Ohio State	10–2	1,428
5.	West Virginia	11–1	1,325
6.	LSU	11–2	1,314
7.	Virginia Tech	11–2	1,197
8.	Alabama	10–2	1,081
9.	Notre Dame	9–3	1,019
10.	Georgia	10–3	994
11.	TCU	11–1	937
12.	Florida	9–3	817
13.	Oregon	10–2	817
14.	Auburn	9–3	799
15.	Wisconsin	10–3	786
16.	UCLA	10–2	778
17.	Miami (Florida)	9–3	589
18.	Boston	9–3	545
19.	Louisville	9–3	410
20.	Texas Tech	9–3	359
21.	Clemson	8–4	339
22.	Oklahoma	8–4	329
23.	Florida State	8–5	232
24.	Nebraska	8–4	128
25.	California	8–4	45

USA TODAY COACHES

	TEAM	RECORD	POINTS
1.	Texas	13–0	1,550
2.	USC	12–1	1,483
3.	Penn State	11–1	1,421
4.	Ohio State	10–2	1,357
5.	LSU	11–2	1,281
6.	West Virginia	11–1	1,235
7.	Virginia Tech	11–2	1,176
8.	Alabama	10–2	1,066
9.	TCU	11–1	914
10.	Georgia	10–3	900
11.	Notre Dame	9–3	866
12.	Oregon	10–2	837
13.	UCLA	10–2	774
14.	Auburn	9–3	760
15.	Wisconsin	10–3	739
16.	Florida	9–3	718
17.	Boston	9–3	584
18.	Miami (Florida)	9–3	558
19.	Texas Tech	9–3	422
20.	Louisville	9–3	342
21.	Clemson	8–4	310
22.	Oklahoma	8–4	274
23.	Florida State	8–5	209
24.	Nebraska	8–4	109
25.	California	8–4	68

2005–06 COLLEGE BOWL AND PLAYOFF RESULTS

BOWL GAME	DATE	SITE	RESULT
ROSE	Jan. 4	Pasadena, California	Texas 41, USC 38
ORANGE	Jan. 3	Miami, Florida	Penn State 26, Florida State 23
SUGAR	Jan. 2	Atlanta, Georgia	West Virginia 38, Georgia 35
FIESTA	Jan. 2	Tempe, Arizona	Ohio State 34, Notre Dame 20
CAPITAL ONE	Jan. 2	Orlando, Florida	Wisconsin 24, Auburn 10
GATOR	Jan. 2	Jacksonville, Florida	Virginia Tech 35, Louisville 24
OUTBACK	Jan. 2	Tampa, Florida	Florida 31, Iowa 24
COTTON	Jan. 2	Dallas, Texas	Alabama 13, Texas Tech 10
HOUSTON	Dec. 31	Houston, Texas	TCU 27, Iowa State 24
LIBERTY	Dec. 31	Memphis, Tennessee	Tulsa 31, Fresno State 24
MEINEKE CAR CARE	Dec. 31	Charlotte, North Carolina	NC State 14, South Florida 0
PEACH	Dec. 30	Atlanta, Georgia	LSU 40, Miami-Florida 3
INDEPENDENCE	Dec. 30	Shreveport, Louisiana	Missouri 38, South Carolina 31
SUN	Dec. 30	El Paso, Texas	UCLA 50, Northwestern 38
MUSIC CITY	Dec. 30	Nashville, Tennessee	Virginia 34, Minnesota 31
HOLIDAY	Dec. 29	San Diego, California	Oklahoma 17, Oregon 14
EMERALD	Dec. 29	San Francisco, California	Utah 38, Georgia Tech 10
ALAMO	Dec. 28	San Antonio, Texas	Nebraska 32, Michigan 28
MPC COMPUTERS	Dec. 28	Boise, Idaho	Boston College 27, Boise State 21
INSIGHT	Dec. 27	Phoenix, Arizona	Arizona State 45, Rutgers 40
CHAMPS SPORTS	Dec. 27	Orlando, Florida	Clemson 19, Colorado 10
MOTOR CITY	Dec. 26	Detroit, Michigan	Memphis 38, Akron 31
HAWAII	Dec. 24	Honolulu, Hawaii	Nevada 49, UCF 48
FORT WORTH	Dec. 23	Fort Worth, Texas	Kansas 42, Houston 13
POINSETTIA	Dec. 22	San Diego, California	Navy 51, Colorado State 30
LAS VEGAS	Dec. 22	Las Vegas, Nevada	California 35, BYU 28
GMAC	Dec. 21	Mobile, Alabama	Toledo 45, Texas-El Paso 13
NEW ORLEANS	Dec. 20	Lafayette, Louisiana	Southern Miss 31, Arkansas State 19

PETER READ MILLER

Reggie Bush averaged 8.7 yards per carry.

2005 HEISMAN VOTING

PLAYER, SCHOOL	POSITION	1ST	2ND	3RD	TOTAL
Reggie Bush, USC	RB	784	89	11	2451
Vince Young, Texas	QB	79	613	145	1,608
Matt Leinart, USC	QB	18	147	449	797
Brady Quinn, Notre Dame	QB	7	21	128	191
Michael Robinson, Penn State	QB	2	7	29	49
A.J. Hawk, Ohio State	LB	0	3	23	29
DeAngelo Williams, Memphis	RB	1	2	19	26
Drew Olson, UCLA	QB	1	2	14	21
Jerome Harrison, Wash. State	RB	0	4	12	20
Elvis Dumervil, Louisville	DL	0	0	9	9

2005 AP ALL-AMERICA TEAM

OFFENSE

QB Vince Young, Texas, junior
RB Reggie Bush, USC, junior
　　 Jerome Harrison, Wash. State, senior
WR Dwayne Jarrett, USC, sophomore
　　 Mike Hass, Oregon State, senior
TE Vernon Davis, Maryland, junior
C Greg Eslinger, Minnesota, senior
OL Jonathan Scott, Texas, senior
　　 Marcus McNeill, Auburn, senior
　　 Max Jean-Gilles, Georgia, senior
　　 D'Brickashaw Ferguson, Virginia, senior
K Mason Crosby, Colorado, junior
AP Maurice Drew, UCLA, junior

DEFENSE

DL Tamba Hali, Penn State, senior
　　 Haloti Ngata, Oregon, junior
　　 Elvis Dumervil, Louisville, senior
　　 Rodrique Wright, Texas, senior
LB A.J. Hawk, Ohio State, senior
　　 Paul Posluszny, Penn State, junior
　　 DeMeco Ryans, Alabama, senior
DB Jimmy Williams, Virginia Tech, senior
　　 Darnell Bing, USC, junior
　　 Michael Huff, Texas, senior
　　 Greg Blue, Georgia, senior
P Ryan Plackemeier, Wake Forest, senior

KEY
QB=quarterback;
RB=running back;
WR=wide receiver;
TE=tight end; C=center;
OL=offensive lineman;
K= kicker; DL=defensive
lineman; LB=linebacker;
DB=defensive back;
P=punter; AP=all purpose

2005 NCAA DIVISION I-A CONFERENCE STANDINGS

Atlantic Coast Conference

TEAM	CONFERENCE				OVERALL			
	W	L	PF	PA	W	L	PF	PA
Atlantic Division								
Boston College	5	3	181	160	9	3	310	191
Florida State	5	3	219	180	8	5	376	286
Clemson	4	4	222	161	8	4	316	211
North Carolina State	3	5	136	182	7	5	249	212
Maryland	3	5	190	217	5	6	270	275
Wake Forest	3	5	202	227	4	7	269	316
Coastal Division								
Virginia Tech	7	1	263	86	11	2	440	168
Miami (Florida)	6	2	238	118	9	3	325	171
Georgia Tech	5	3	154	162	7	5	222	241
North Carolina	4	4	148	188	5	6	198	288
Virginia	3	5	177	202	7	5	320	279
Duke	0	8	95	342	1	10	177	408

Big East Conference

TEAM	CONFERENCE				OVERALL			
	W	L	PF	PA	W	L	PF	PA
West Virginia	7	0	244	104	11	1	385	214
Louisville	5	2	273	175	9	3	521	285
Rutgers	4	3	188	199	7	5	344	307
South Florida	4	3	188	135	6	6	276	216
Pittsburgh	4	3	189	178	5	6	267	243
Connecticut	2	5	115	170	5	6	272	211
Cincinatti	2	5	117	230	4	7	192	345
Syracuse	0	7	73	196	1	10	152	295

KEY W=win; L=loss; PF=points for; PA=points against

Big Ten Conference

TEAM	CONFERENCE				OVERALL			
	W	L	PF	PA	W	L	PF	PA
Penn State	7	1	282	141	11	1	413	204
Ohio State	7	1	275	118	10	2	392	183
Wisconsin	5	3	246	228	10	3	446	309
Iowa	5	3	232	165	7	5	360	240
Michigan	5	3	219	178	7	5	345	244
Northwestern	5	3	253	254	7	5	388	407
Minnesota	4	4	255	273	7	5	429	348
Purdue	3	5	222	212	5	6	330	309
Michigan State	2	6	237	247	5	6	372	316
Indiana	1	7	155	303	4	7	248	361
Illinois	0	8	94	351	2	9	187	435

Big 12 Conference (North)

TEAM	CONFERENCE				OVERALL			
	W	L	PF	PA	W	L	PF	PA
Colorado	5	3	219	167	7	6	305	307
Nebraska	4	4	201	208	8	4	296	252
Iowa State	4	4	232	158	7	5	339	230
Missouri	4	4	200	236	7	5	369	350
Kansas	3	5	127	210	7	5	269	264
Kansas State	2	6	179	258	5	6	289	305

Big 12 Conference (South)

TEAM	CONFERENCE				OVERALL			
	W	L	PF	PA	W	L	PF	PA
Texas	8	0	405	137	13	0	652	213
Texas Tech	6	2	264	182	9	3	473	226
Oklahoma	6	2	241	190	8	4	323	277
Texas A&M	3	5	218	279	5	6	352	343
Baylor	2	6	140	244	5	6	236	291
Oklahoma State	1	7	164	321	4	7	222	344

Conference USA (East)

TEAM	CONFERENCE				OVERALL			
	W	L	PF	PA	W	L	PF	PA
University of Central Florida (UCF)	7	1	245	204	8	5	373	373
Memphis	5	3	207	201	7	5	326	276
Southern Mississippi	5	3	238	182	7	5	355	272
East Carolina	4	4	194	232	5	6	267	371
Alabama-Birmingham	3	5	235	212	5	6	307	264
Marshall	3	5	135	199	4	7	204	285

Conference USA (West)

TEAM	CONFERENCE				OVERALL			
	W	L	PF	PA	W	L	PF	PA
Tulsa	6	2	276	180	9	4	430	305
Texas-El Paso	5	3	269	236	8	4	382	311
Houston	4	4	241	218	6	6	337	324
Southern Methodist (SMU)	4	4	177	176	5	6	229	280
Tulane	1	7	171	257	2	9	234	348
Rice	1	7	201	292	1	10	241	447

Mid-American Conference (East)

TEAM	CONFERENCE				OVERALL			
	W	L	PF	PA	W	L	PF	PA
Miami (Ohio)	5	3	272	194	7	4	371	258
Akron	5	3	204	174	7	6	307	318
Bowling Green	5	3	240	193	6	5	372	304
Ohio	3	5	162	243	4	7	192	336
Buffalo	1	7	107	241	1	10	110	327
Kent State	0	8	102	236	1	10	180	331

FAST FACT

Boston College has the longest current streak of bowl game wins in the nation, having brought home a bowl trophy in six straight seasons. BC's last loss in post-season play was to Colorado in the 1999 Insight Bowl.

2005 NCAA DIVISION I-A CONFERENCE STANDINGS (cont.)

Mid-American Conference (West)

TEAM	CONFERENCE				OVERALL			
	W	L	PF	PA	W	L	PF	PA
Toledo	6	2	266	173	9	3	429	261
Northern Illinois	6	2	263	169	7	5	389	274
Western Michigan	5	3	282	267	7	4	354	342
Central Michigan	5	3	230	190	6	5	260	260
Ball State	4	4	230	259	4	7	233	416
Eastern Michigan	3	5	183	202	4	7	240	295

Mountain West Conference

TEAM	CONFERENCE				OVERALL			
	W	L	PF	PA	W	L	PF	PA
Texas Christian (TCU)	8	0	306	151	11	1	398	223
Brigham Young	5	3	297	237	6	6	396	351
Colorado State	5	3	197	210	6	6	321	369
Utah	4	4	247	217	7	5	360	289
New Mexico	4	4	230	250	6	5	326	327
San Diego State	4	4	206	184	5	7	323	325
Air Force	3	5	262	278	4	7	330	349
Wyoming	2	6	195	251	4	7	271	297
University of Nevada-Las Vegas (UNLV)	1	7	135	297	2	9	207	381

Pacific-Ten Conference

TEAM	CONFERENCE				OVERALL			
	W	L	PF	PA	W	L	PF	PA
Southern California (USC)	8	0	383	149	12	1	638	297
Oregon	7	1	278	189	10	2	414	278
California-Los Angeles (UCLA)	6	2	271	306	10	2	469	410
California	4	4	243	190	8	4	395	254
Arizona State	4	4	251	247	7	5	442	359
Stanford	4	4	180	241	5	6	269	337
Oregon State	3	5	195	261	5	6	293	365
Arizona	2	6	173	220	3	8	252	290
Washington State	1	7	227	292	4	7	368	346
Washington	1	7	169	275	2	9	237	337

Southeastern Conference (East)

TEAM	CONFERENCE				OVERALL			
	W	L	PF	PA	W	L	PF	PA
Georgia	6	2	209	134	10	3	384	213
Florida	5	3	205	178	9	3	343	226
South Carolina	5	3	175	193	7	5	284	279
Tennessee	3	5	147	138	5	6	205	205
Vanderbilt	3	5	223	271	5	6	299	321
Kentucky	2	6	160	277	3	8	239	375

Southeastern Conference (West)

TEAM	CONFERENCE				OVERALL			
	W	L	PF	PA	W	L	PF	PA
Louisiana State University (LSU)	7	1	214	114	11	2	383	185
Auburn	7	1	262	122	9	3	386	186
Alabama	6	2	159	87	10	2	263	128
Arkansas	2	6	173	169	4	7	283	271
Mississippi State	1	7	78	211	3	8	153	259
Mississippi (Ole Miss)	1	7	97	208	3	8	148	245

Sun Belt Conference

TEAM	CONFERENCE				OVERALL			
	W	L	PF	PA	W	L	PF	PA
Louisiana-Lafayette	5	2	203	161	6	5	286	304
Arkansas State	5	2	182	163	6	6	294	303
Louisiana-Monroe	5	2	194	186	5	6	239	339
Florida International	3	4	172	191	5	6	257	323
Middle Tennessee	3	4	176	124	4	7	210	206
Troy	3	4	100	121	4	7	175	255
Florida Atlantic	2	5	109	179	2	9	148	339
North Texas	2	5	131	142	2	9	157	346

Western Athletic Conference

TEAM	CONFERENCE				OVERALL			
	W	L	PF	PA	W	L	PF	PA
Nevada	7	1	297	224	9	3	410	383
Boise State	7	1	339	178	9	4	469	317
Fresno State	6	2	292	143	8	5	491	292
Louisiana Tech	6	2	259	192	7	4	316	281
Hawaii	4	4	264	244	5	7	368	428
San Jose State	2	6	173	241	3	8	248	357
Utah State	2	6	167	270	3	8	208	360
Idaho	2	6	180	313	2	9	243	419
New Mexico State	0	8	147	313	0	12	198	465

Independents

TEAM	OVERALL			
	W	L	PF	PA
Temple	0	11	107	498
Army	4	7	220	294
Navy	8	4	410	313
Notre Dame	9	3	440	294

2005 NCAA DIVISION I-AA CONFERENCE STANDINGS

Atlantic 10 Conference (North)

TEAM	CONFERENCE				OVERALL			
	W	L	PF	PA	W	L	PF	PA
New Hampshire	7	1	344	211	11	2	542	289
Massachusetts	6	2	178	95	7	4	259	146
Hofstra	5	3	206	171	7	4	338	222
Maine	3	5	150	251	5	6	216	283
Rhode Island	2	6	187	231	4	7	312	306
Northeastern	2	6	182	250	2	9	248	340

Atlantic 10 Conference (South)

TEAM	CONFERENCE				OVERALL			
	W	L	PF	PA	W	L	PF	PA
Richmond	7	1	240	150	9	4	349	231
James Madison	5	3	243	130	7	4	391	168
Delaware	3	5	163	187	6	5	274	264
Towson	3	5	208	329	6	5	345	372
William & Mary	3	5	237	240	5	6	358	283
Villanova	2	6	185	278	4	7	257	350

Big Sky Conference

TEAM	CONFERENCE				OVERALL			
	W	L	PF	PA	W	L	PF	PA
Montana	5	2	173	109	8	4	306	218
Montana State	5	2	194	175	7	4	276	251
Eastern Washington	5	2	251	151	7	5	420	281
Portland State	4	3	230	182	6	5	313	273
Weber State	4	3	172	171	6	5	277	277
Idaho State	3	4	184	215	5	6	298	304
Northern Arizona	1	6	125	236	3	8	233	328
Sacramento State	1	6	128	218	2	9	192	352

Big South Conference

TEAM	CONFERENCE				OVERALL			
	W	L	PF	PA	W	L	PF	PA
Coastal Carolina	3	1	126	100	9	2	338	220
Charleston Southern	3	1	115	98	7	4	313	303
Gardner-Webb	2	2	114	140	5	6	386	367
Virginia Military Institute	2	2	110	112	3	8	230	319
Liberty	0	4	74	89	1	10	146	348

FOOTBALL COLLEGE

2005 NCAA DIVISION I-AA CONFERENCE STANDINGS (cont.)

Gateway Conference

TEAM	CONFERENCE				OVERALL			
	W	L	PF	PA	W	L	PF	PA
Northern Iowa	5	2	165	147	11	4	449	357
Southern Illinois	5	2	227	190	9	4	449	298
Youngstown State	5	2	185	107	8	3	306	178
Illinois State	4	3	285	177	7	4	431	234
Western Kentucky	4	3	204	193	6	5	339	292
Western Illinois	3	4	204	216	5	6	352	371
Missouri State	2	5	160	228	4	6	273	312
Indiana State	0	7	148	320	0	11	193	476

Great West Conference

TEAM	CONFERENCE				OVERALL			
	W	L	PF	PA	W	L	PF	PA
California Polytechnic	4	1	125	66	9	4	354	232
University of California-Davis	4	1	111	78	6	5	217	184
North Dakota State	3	2	142	95	7	4	320	151
South Dakota State	3	2	134	100	6	5	363	251
Southern Utah	1	4	79	162	1	9	126	328
Northern Colorado	0	5	59	149	4	7	255	285

Ivy League

TEAM	CONFERENCE				OVERALL			
	W	L	PF	PA	W	L	PF	PA
Brown	6	1	252	166	9	1	368	218
Harvard	5	2	231	137	7	3	310	224
Princeton	5	2	192	109	7	3	245	163
Cornell	4	3	167	132	6	4	268	180
Yale	4	3	174	140	4	6	228	207
Penn	3	4	151	155	5	5	269	204
Dartmouth	1	6	64	162	2	8	126	260
Columbia	0	7	63	293	2	8	116	337

Metro Atlantic Athletic Conference

TEAM	CONFERENCE				OVERALL			
	W	L	PF	PA	W	L	PF	PA
Duquesne	4	0	133	45	7	3	264	161
Marist	3	1	121	83	7	4	305	283
La Salle	2	2	83	129	4	7	266	373
Iona	1	3	103	124	3	7	171	280
St Peter's	0	4	74	133	1	9	200	379

Mid-Eastern Athletic Conference

TEAM	CONFERENCE				OVERALL			
	W	L	PF	PA	W	L	PF	PA
Hampton	8	0	250	96	11	1	376	168
South Carolina State	7	1	276	116	9	2	378	166
Delaware State	6	2	174	118	7	4	225	213
Florida A&M	6	3	187	201	6	5	196	261
Bethune-Cookman	4	4	263	214	7	4	384	251
Norfolk State	2	6	194	266	4	7	292	346
North Carolina A&T	2	6	141	238	3	8	188	276
Howard	1	7	87	179	4	7	173	228
Morgan State	1	7	146	285	2	9	248	375

Northeast Conference

TEAM	CONFERENCE				OVERALL			
	W	L	PF	PA	W	L	PF	PA
Central Connecticut State	5	2	161	145	7	4	273	274
Stony Brook	5	2	164	157	6	5	220	270
Monmouth (New Jersey)	4	3	159	94	6	4	266	190
Albany (New York)	4	3	133	87	5	6	188	194
Wagner	3	4	159	204	6	5	287	294
Sacred Heart	3	4	160	195	4	6	239	287
St. Francis (Pennsylvania)	3	4	196	219	3	8	287	343
Robert Morris	1	6	154	185	2	8	243	256

Ohio Valley Conference

TEAM	CONFERENCE				OVERALL			
	W	L	PF	PA	W	L	PF	PA
Eastern Illinois	8	0	273	124	9	3	319	230
Eastern Kentucky	7	1	299	132	7	4	346	233
Jacksonville State	6	2	211	131	6	5	292	224
Tennessee-Martin	4	4	224	201	6	5	297	319
Samford	4	4	182	222	5	6	279	322
Tennessee Tech	3	5	191	269	4	7	269	351
Southeast Missouri State	2	6	212	238	2	9	268	374
Tennessee State	1	7	99	246	2	9	136	303
Murray State	0	7	143	276	2	9	218	377

Patriot League

TEAM	CONFERENCE				OVERALL			
	W	L	PF	PA	W	L	PF	PA
Colgate	5	1	152	96	8	4	283	245
Lafayette	5	1	151	95	8	4	273	204
Lehigh	4	2	207	97	8	3	399	228
Holy Cross	3	3	167	141	6	5	317	263
Georgetown	2	4	77	177	4	7	110	292
Fordham	2	4	86	155	2	9	150	320
Bucknell	0	6	110	189	1	10	179	332

Pioneer Football League (North)

TEAM	CONFERENCE				OVERALL			
	W	L	PF	PA	W	L	PF	PA
San Diego	4	0	191	78	11	1	511	205
Dayton	3	1	142	79	9	1	403	141
Drake	2	2	148	90	6	4	376	229
Valparaiso	1	3	86	185	3	8	187	424
Butler	0	4	45	180	0	11	154	468

Pioneer Football League (South)

TEAM	CONFERENCE				OVERALL			
	W	L	PF	PA	W	L	PF	PA
Morehead State	3	0	106	37	8	4	407	336
Jacksonville (Florida)	2	1	66	70	4	4	236	211
Davidson	1	2	70	58	4	6	201	237
Austin Peay	0	3	44	121	2	9	140	412

Southern Conference

TEAM	CONFERENCE				OVERALL			
	W	L	PF	PA	W	L	PF	PA
Appalachian State	6	1	271	117	12	3	455	282
Georgia Southern	5	2	242	107	8	4	456	277
Furman	4	2	219	171	11	3	488	383
Western Carolina	4	3	155	164	5	4	179	178
Wofford	3	3	93	134	6	5	249	292
Chattanooga-Tennessee	3	4	156	218	6	5	245	339
Citadel	2	5	127	199	4	7	194	316
Elon	0	7	69	222	3	8	173	281

Southland Conference

TEAM	CONFERENCE				OVERALL			
	W	L	PF	PA	W	L	PF	PA
Texas State	5	1	203	114	11	3	518	284
Nicholls State	5	1	198	151	6	4	308	226
McNeese State	3	3	132	191	5	4	221	287
Northwestern State	3	3	139	121	5	5	215	240
Southeast Louisiana	2	4	153	170	4	6	279	275
Sam Houston State	2	4	159	146	3	7	270	288
Stephen F. Austin	1	5	139	230	5	6	324	380

DID YOU KNOW?

Minnesota became the first school in NCAA history to have two running backs each rush for 1,000 yards in a season for three consecutive seasons. Laurence Maroney reached the 1,000-yard mark in 2003, 2004, and 2005. Marion Barber III joined Maroney in 2003 and 2004. In 2005, Gary Russell became the other Minnesota running back to rush for at least 1,000 yards.

2005 NCAA DIVISION I-AA CONFERENCE STANDINGS (cont.)

Southwestern Athletic Conference (East)

TEAM	CONFERENCE				OVERALL			
	W	L	PF	PA	W	L	PF	PA
Alabama A&M	7	2	224	165	9	3	299	224
Alabama State	6	3	317	200	6	5	358	255
Alcorn State	5	4	208	227	6	5	253	282
Mississippi Valley State (MVSU)	5	4	277	254	6	5	360	292
Jackson State	2	7	180	325	2	9	201	365

Southwestern Athletic Conference (West)

TEAM	CONFERENCE				OVERALL			
	W	L	PF	PA	W	L	PF	PA
Grambling State	9	0	395	175	11	1	529	236
Southern	4	5	250	239	4	5	250	239
Prairie View	3	6	150	276	5	6	229	296
Arkansas-Pine Bluff	3	6	212	252	3	8	238	296
Texas Southern	1	8	194	294	1	10	222	385

Independents

TEAM	OVERALL			
	W	L	PF	PA
Winston-Salem	6	4	231	215
Savannah State	0	11	215	480

2005 NCAA INDIVIDUAL LEADERS: DIVISION I-A

SCORING

	TD	PTS
Lendale White, USC	26	156
Brian Calhoun, Wisconsin	24	144
Michael Bush, Louisville	24	144
Taurean Henderson, Texas Tech	22	132
Maurice Drew, UCLA	20	120
Mario Danelo, USC	0	116
DeAngelo Williams, Memphis	19	114
Reggie Bush, USC	19	114
Brandon Coutu, Georgia	0	114
Gary Russell, Minnesota	19	114

TRIVIA CHALLENGE

What wide receiver holds the NCAA record for most consecutive games with a pass reception, and how long was his streak?

Miami (Ohio) wide receiver Michael Larkin caught a pass in 50 consecutive games during his career (2001-2004). His only game without a reception was his first as a collegian.

FIELD GOALS

	FGM	FGA	PCT
Jad Dean, Clemson	24	31	77.4
Darren McCaleb, Southern Mississippi	23	26	88.5
Brandon Coutu, Georgia	23	29	79.3
Alexis Serna, Oregon State	23	28	82.1
Josh Huston, Ohio State	22	28	78.6
Stephen Gostowski, Memphis	22	25	88.0
Mason Crosby, Colorado	22	29	75.9

RUSHING

	G	CARRIES	YDS	AVG	TD
DeAngelo Williams, Memphis	11	309	1,959	6.3	18
Jerome Harrison, Washington State	9	308	1,900	6.2	16
Reggie Bush, USC	13	200	1,740	8.7	16
Brian Calhoun, Wisconsin	13	348	1,636	4.7	22
Garrett Wolfe, Northern Illinois	9	243	1,588	6.5	16
Tyrell Sutton, Northwestern	12	250	1,474	5.9	16
Laurence Maroney, Minnesota	11	281	1,464	5.2	10
B.J. Mitchell, Nevada	12	261	1,399	5.4	12
Andre Hall, Southern Florida	12	270	1,374	5.1	13
Albert Young, Iowa	12	249	1,334	5.4	8

KEY TD=touchdowns; PTS=points; FGM=field goals made; FGA=field goals attempted; PCT=percentage; G=games; YDS=yards; AVG=average; TD=touchdowns

TODAY'S STARS

Brady Quinn is a leading Heisman Trophy candidate.

AL TIELEMANS

■ **Brady Quinn, quarterback,** b. October 27, 1984, Dublin, Ohio. Just a junior, Quinn already owns every major Notre Dame passing record, including: single-season/career yardage (3,919/8,336), single-season/career attempts (450/1,135), single-season/career completions (292/640), and single-season/career touchdown passes (32/58). Quinn is the first Fighting Irish quarterback to throw for more than 3,000 yards in one season. Against BYU on October 22, 2005, Quinn became the first Irish passer to throw for six touchdowns in a game. Quinn helped lead Notre Dame to a 9-3 record. He finished fourth in the Heisman voting, behind winner Reggie Bush (USC), Vince Young (Texas), and Matt Leinart (USC).

■ **Ted Ginn, Jr., wide receiver/kick returner,** b. April 12, 1985, Cleveland, Ohio. Entering his junior season at Ohio State, Ginn is already one of the college game's most electrifying players. After just two seasons, he already shares the Big Ten Conference record for punts returned for touchdowns in a career (five). In the Buckeyes' 34–20 win over Notre Dame in the 2006 Fiesta Bowl, Ginn had a career-high 167 receiving yards and two touchdowns (one receiving and one rushing). He enters the 2006 regular season with 14 touchdowns in his college career.

■ **Brian Brohm, quarterback,** b. Sept. 23, 1985, Louisville, Kentucky. The Louisville Cardinals went 8–2 in games Brohm started in 2005 (and were 9–3 overall). For the season, his first year as a starter, he passed for 2,833 yards and 19 touchdowns in 10 games. He led the Big East conference in passing yards and total offense. Brohm was also a promising baseball prospect in high school, and was drafted as an outfielder by the Colorado Rockies.

2005 NCAA INDIVIDUAL LEADERS: DIVISION I-A (cont.)

PASSING EFFICIENCY	ATTS	COMP PCT	YDS	INT	TD	RATING
Rudy Carpenter, Arizona State	228	68.4	2,273	2	17	175.01
Brian Brohm, Louisville	301	68.8	2,883	5	19	166.73
Vince Young, Texas	325	65.2	3,036	10	26	163.95
Troy Smith, Ohio State	237	62.9	2,282	4	16	162.66
Drew Olson, UCLA	378	64.0	3,198	6	34	161.59
Phil Horvath, Northern Illinois	238	70.6	1,995	8	18	159.23
Brady Quinn, Notre Dame	450	64.9	3,919	7	32	158.40
Matt Leinart, USC	431	65.7	3,815	8	28	157.74
Colt Brennan, Hawaii	515	68.0	4,301	13	35	155.49
Drew Stanton, Michigan State	355	66.5	3,077	12	22	152.98

KEY ATTS=attempts; COMP PCT=completion percentage; YDS=yards; INT=interceptions; TD=touchdowns

FAST FACT

Texas collected its 800th all-time win when it defeated USC in the national championship game at the Rose Bowl on January 4, 2006. Only two Division I schools have more overall wins – Michigan (849) and Notre Dame (811).

2005 NCAA INDIVIDUAL LEADERS: DIVISION I-A (cont.)

RECEIVING	G	REC	YDS	YDS/G	TD
Mike Hass, Oregon State	11	90	1,532	139.27	6
Jeff Samardzija, Notre Dame	12	78	1,274	104.80	15
Dwayne Jarrett, USC	13	91	1,274	98.00	16
Greg Jennings, Western Michigan	11	98	1,259	114.45	14
Garrett Mills, Tulsa	13	87	1,235	95.00	9
Ryan Grice-Mullen, Hawaii	12	85	1,228	102.33	12
David Anderson, Colorado State	12	86	1,221	101.75	8
Derek Hagan, Arizona State	12	77	1,210	100.83	8
Domenik Hixon, Akron	13	75	1,210	93.08	8
Brandon Marshall, Central Florida	13	74	1,195	91.92	11

INTERCEPTIONS	INT	YDS	TD
Aaron Gipson, Oregon	7	117	1
Alan Zemaitis, Penn State	6	35	0
Dion Byrum, Ohio	6	150	2
Jelani Jordan, Bowling Green	6	66	0
Anthony Smith, Syracuse	6	73	0
Marcus Hamilton, Virginia	6	28	0
Nick Graham, Tulsa	6	66	0
Clint Ingram, Oklahoma	5	63	1
Gabriel Fulbright, New Mexico	5	77	0
Quincy Butler, TCU	5	76	0

**Mike Hass,
Oregon State**

HARRY HOW/GETTY IMAGES

2005 NCAA INDIVIDUAL LEADERS: DIVISION I-AA

SCORING	TD	PTS
David Ball, New Hampshire	24	146
Nick Hartigan, Brown	21	126
Jayson Foster, Georgia Southern	21	126
Kevin Richardson, Appalachian State	21	126
Jerome Felton, Furman	20	124
Henry Tolbert, Gram State	20	120
David Horn, Northern Iowa	19	114
Alonzo Coleman, Hampton	19	114
Eric Rath, Lehigh	18	108
Omar Cuff, Delaware	18	108

FIELD GOALS	FGM	FGA	PCT
Andrew Paterini, Hampton	20	30	66.7
Parker Douglass, South Dakota State	19	25	76.0
Steve Morgan, Brown	18	23	78.3
Jaret Johnson, Idaho State	17	18	94.4
Rob Zarrilli, Hofstra	17	19	89.5
Derek Javarone, Princeton	16	18	88.9
Joseph Fore, Richmond	16	20	80.0

RUSHING	G	CARRIES	YDS	AVG	TD
Nick Hartigan, Brown	10	314	1,727	5.5	20
Joe Rubin, Portland State	11	345	1,702	4.9	17
James Noble, California Polytechnic	11	223	1,578	7.1	16
Scott Phaydayong, Drake	10	204	1,552	7.6	8
Jermaine Austin, Georgia Southern	12	233	1,546	6.6	14
Jayson Foster, Georgia Southern	12	239	1,481	6.2	21
Arkee Whitlock, Southern Illinois	12	270	1,458	5.4	14
Kevin Richardson, Appalachian State	15	266	1,433	5.4	19
Donald Chapman, Tennessee-Martin	11	302	1,396	4.6	16
Jordan Scott, Colgate	10	320	1,364	4.3	10

TRIVIA CHALLENGE

There have been two NCAA games that have gone to seven overtimes, but only three teams have participated in those games (meaning one team played in both games). Name all three teams.

Arkansas, Mississippi, and Kentucky. Arkansas won both games, 58-56 over Ole Miss in 2001 and 71-63 over Kentucky in 2003.

KEY G=games; REC=receptions; YDS=yards; YDS/G=yards per game; TD=touchdowns; INT=interceptions; PTS=points; FGM=field goals made; FGA=field goals attempted; PCT=percentage; AVG=average

PASSING EFFICIENCY	ATTS	COMP PCT	YDS	INT	TD	RATING
Bruce Eugene, Grambling State	456	56.1	4,408	6	56	175.24
Joshua Johnson, San Diego	371	70.1	3,256	8	36	171.51
Ricky Santos, New Hampshire	429	70.2	3,797	9	39	170.32
Erik Meyer, East Washington	411	65.5	4,003	5	30	168.92
Eric Sanders, North Iowa	312	68.3	2,929	5	23	168.25
Tarvaris Jackson, Alabama State	320	60.9	2,941	5	29	164.92
Kevin Hoyng, Dayton	193	59.1	1,989	5	14	164.39
Justin Rascati, James Madison	214	69.6	1,822	5	17	162.69
Connor Jostes, Drake	186	59.7	1,580	5	19	159.37
Steve LaFalce, Western Illinois	298	67.5	2,586	8	19	156.02

RECEIVING	G	REC	YDS	YDS/G	TD
David Ball, New Hampshire	13	87	1,551	119.31	24
Laurent Robinson, Illinois State	11	86	1,465	133.18	12
Michael Caputo, St. Francis (PA)	11	92	1,433	130.27	12
Eric Kimble, East Washington	12	87	1,419	118.25	12
Henry Tolbert, Grambling State	12	74	1,391	115.92	19
Tony Kays, California-Davis	11	93	1,213	110.27	3
Andre Ralston, Eastern Kentucky	11	62	1,150	104.55	8
Raul Vijl, Eastern Washington	12	72	1,080	90.00	8
Tyrone Timmons, MVSU	11	62	1,059	96.27	8
Alvance Robinson, Alabama State	11	63	1,046	95.09	12

INTERCEPTIONS	INT	YDS	TD
Jay McCareins, Princeton	9	236	2
James Gasparella, Brown	7	42	0
Bobbie Williams, Bethune-Cookman	6	80	0
Casey Klaus, Dayton	6	146	1
Brian Ford, Wofford	6	5	0
Kedrick Coleman, Stephen F. Austin	6	112	0
Codera Jackson, Youngstown State	6	103	1
Courtney Brown, California Polytechnic	7	54	1
Michael Ford, Duquesne	5	164	2
Duriel Adams, Southeastern Louisiana	5	110	0
Pat FitzGerald, Davidson	5	22	0

Bruce Eugene, Grambling State

DID YOU KNOW?

Vince Young became the first Division I-A player in history to finish a season with 3,000 yards passing (3,036) and 1,000 yards rushing (1,050).

KEY ATTS=attempts; COMP PCT=completion percentage; YDS=yards; INT=interceptions; TD=touchdowns; G=games; REC=receptions; YDS/G=yards per game

NATIONAL CHAMPIONSHIPS

YEAR	CHAMPION	RECORD	HEAD COACH
2005	Texas	13–0	Mack Brown
2004	USC	13–0	Pete Carroll
2003	USC	12–1	Pete Carroll
(split)	LSU	13–1	Nick Saban
2002	Ohio State	14–0	Jim Tressel
2001	Miami (Florida)	12–0	Larry Coker
2000	Oklahoma	13–0	Bob Stoops
1999	Florida State	12–0	Bobby Bowden
1998	Tennessee	13–0	Phillip Fulmer
1997	Michigan	12–0	Lloyd Carr
(split)	Nebraska (ESPN)	13–0	Tom Osborne
1996	Florida	12–1	Steve Spurrier
1995	Nebraska	12–0–0	Tom Osborne
1994	Nebraska	13–0–0	Tom Osborne
1993	Florida State	12–1–0	Bobby Bowden
1992	Alabama	13–0–0	Gene Stallings
1991	Miami (Florida)	12–0–0	Dennis Erickson
(split)	Washington (CNN)	12–0–0	Don James
1990	Colorado	11–1–1	Bill McCartney
(split)	Georgia Tech (UPI)	11–0–1	Bobby Ross
1989	Miami (Florida)	11–1–0	Dennis Erickson
1988	Notre Dame	12–0–0	Lou Holtz
1987	Miami (Florida)	12–0–0	Jimmy Johnson
1986	Penn State	12–0–0	Joe Paterno
1985	Oklahoma	11–1–0	Barry Switzer
1984	Brigham Young	13–0–0	LaVell Edwards

YEAR	CHAMPION	RECORD	HEAD COACH
1983	Miami (Florida)	11–1–0	Howard Schnellenberger
1982	Penn State	11–1–0	Joe Paterno
1981	Clemson	12–0–0	Danny Ford
1980	Georgia	12–0–0	Vince Dooley
1979	Alabama	12–0–0	Bear Bryant
1978	Alabama	11–1–0	Bear Bryant
(split)	USC (UPI)	12–1–0	John Robinson
1977	Notre Dame	11–1–0	Dan Devine
1976	Pittsburgh	12–0–0	Johnny Majors
1975	Oklahoma	11–1–0	Barry Switzer
1974	Oklahoma (AP)	11–0–0	Barry Switzer
(split)	USC (UPI)	10–1–1	John McKay
1973	Notre Dame	11–0–0	Ara Parseghian
(split)	Alabama (UPI)	11–1–0	Bear Bryant
1972	USC	12–0–0	John McKay
1971	Nebraska	13–0–0	Bob Devaney
1970	Nebraska	11–0–1	Bob Devaney
(split)	Texas (UPI)	10–1–0	Darrell Royal
1969	Texas	11–0–0	Darrell Royal
1968	Ohio State	10–0–0	Woody Hayes
1967	USC	10–1–0	John McKay
1966	Notre Dame	9–0–1	Ara Parseghian
1965	Alabama	9–1–1	Bear Bryant
(split)	Michigan State (UPI)	10–1–0	Duffy Daugherty
1964	Alabama	10–1–0	Bear Bryant
1963	Texas	11–0–0	Darrell Royal

Note: National Champion selectors: Helms Athletic Foundation (H), 1883–1935; The Dickinson System (D), 1924–40; The Associated Press (AP), 1936–present; United Press International (UPI), 1958–90; USA Today/CNN (CNN), 1991–96; USA Today/ESPN (ESPN), 1997–present. In 1996, the NCAA introduced overtime to break ties.

NATIONAL CHAMPIONSHIPS (cont.)

YEAR	CHAMPION	RECORD	HEAD COACH	YEAR	CHAMPION	RECORD	HEAD COACH
1962	USC	11-0-0	John McKay	(split)	Stanford (D)(H)	10-0-1	Pop Warner
1961	Alabama	11-0-0	Bear Bryant	1925	Alabama (H)	10-0-0	Wallace Wade
1960	Minnesota	8-2-0	Murray Warmath	(split)	Dartmouth (D)	8-0-0	Jesse Hawley
1959	Syracuse	11-0-0	Ben Schwartzwalder	1924	Notre Dame	10-0-0	Knute Rockne
1958	Louisiana State	11-0-0	Paul Dietzel	1923	Illinois	8-0-0	Bob Zuppke
1957	Auburn	10-0-0	Shug Jordan	1922	Cornell	8-0-0	Gil Dobie
(split)	Ohio State (UPI)	9-1-0	Woody Hayes	1921	Cornell	8-0-0	Gil Dobie
1956	Oklahoma	10-0-0	Bud Wilkinson	1920	California	9-0-0	Andy Smith
1955	Oklahoma	11-0-0	Bud Wilkinson	1919	Harvard	9-0-1	Bob Fisher
1954	Ohio State	10-0-0	Woody Hayes	1918	Pittsburgh	4-1-0	Pop Warner
(split)	UCLA (UPI)	9-0-0	Red Sanders	1917	Georgia Tech	9-0-0	John Heisman
1953	Maryland	10-1-0	Jim Tatum	1916	Pittsburgh	8-0-0	Pop Warner
1952	Michigan State	9-0-0	Biggie Munn	1915	Cornell	9-0-0	Al Sharpe
1951	Tennessee	10-1-0	Robert Neyland	1914	Army	9-0-0	Charley Daly
1950	Oklahoma	10-1-0	Bud Wilkinson	1913	Harvard	9-0-0	Percy Haughton
1949	Notre Dame	10-0-0	Frank Leahy	1912	Harvard	9-0-0	Percy Haughton
1948	Michigan	9-0-0	Bennie Oosterbaan	1911	Princeton	8-0-2	Bill Roper
1947	Notre Dame	9-0-0	Frank Leahy	1910	Harvard	8-0-1	Percy Haughton
(split)	Michigan	10-0-0	Fritz Crisler	1909	Yale	10-0-0	Howard Jones
1946	Notre Dame	8-0-1	Frank Leahy	1908	Pennsylvania	11-0-1	Sol Metzger
1945	Army	9-0-0	Red Blaik	1907	Yale	9-0-1	Bill Knox
1944	Army	9-0-0	Red Blaik	1906	Princeton	9-0-1	Bill Roper
1943	Notre Dame	9-1-0	Frank Leahy	1905	Chicago	10-0-0	Amos Alonzo Stagg
1942	Ohio State	9-1-0	Paul Brown	1904	Pennsylvania	12-0-0	Carl Williams
1941	Minnesota	8-0-0	Bernie Bierman	1903	Princeton	11-0-0	Art Hillebrand
1940	Minnesota	8-0-0	Bernie Bierman	1902	Michigan	11-0-0	Fielding Yost
1939	Texas A&M (AP)	11-0-0	Homer Norton	1901	Michigan	11-0-0	Fielding Yost
(split)	USC (D)	8-0-2	Howard Jones	1900	Yale	12-0-0	Malcolm McBride
1938	TCU (AP)	11-0-0	Dutch Meyer	1899	Harvard	10-0-1	Benjamin H. Dibblee
(split)	Notre Dame (D)	8-1-0	Elmer Layden	1898	Harvard	11-0-0	W. Cameron Forbes
1937	Pittsburgh	9-0-1	Jock Sutherland	1897	Pennsylvania	15-0-0	George W. Woodruff
1936	Minnesota	7-1-0	Bernie Bierman	1896	Princeton	10-0-1	Garrett Cochran
1935	Minnesota (H)	8-0-0	Bernie Bierman	1895	Pennsylvania	14-0-0	George W. Woodruff
(split)	SMU (D)	12-1-0	Matty Bell	1894	Yale	16-0-0	William C. Rhodes
1934	Minnesota	8-0-0	Bernie Bierman	1893	Princeton	11-0-0	Tom Trenchard
1933	Michigan	8-0-0	Harry Kipke	1892	Yale	13-0-0	Walter Camp
1932	USC (H)	10-0-0	Howard Jones	1891	Yale	13-0-0	Walter Camp
(split)	Michigan (D)	8-0-0	Harry Kipke	1890	Harvard	11-0-0	G. Stewart/G.Adams
1931	USC	10-1-0	Howard Jones	1889	Princeton	10-0-0	Edgar Poe
1930	Notre Dame	10-0-0	Knute Rockne	1888	Yale	13-0-0	Walter Camp
1929	Notre Dame	9-0-0	Knute Rockne	1887	Yale	9-0-0	Harry W. Beecher
1928	Georgia Tech (H)	10-0-0	Bill Alexander	1886	Yale	9-0-1	Robert N. Corwin
(split)	USC (D)	9-0-1	Howard Jones	1885	Princeton	9-0-0	Charles DeCamp
1927	Illinois	7-0-1	Bob Zuppke	1884	Yale	8-0-1	Eugene L. Richards
1926	Alabama (H)	9-0-1	Wallace Wade	1883	Yale	8-0-0	Ray Tompkins

MAJOR BOWL GAME RESULTS

ROSE BOWL

DATE	RESULT	DATE	RESULT
2006	Texas 41, USC 38	1989	Michigan 22, USC 14
2005	Texas 38, Michigan 37	1988	Michigan State 20, USC 17
2004	USC 28, Michigan 14	1987	Arizona State 22, Michigan 15
2003	Oklahoma 34, Washington State 14	1986	UCLA 45, Iowa 28
2002	Miami 37, Nebraska 14	1985	USC 20, Ohio State 17
2001	Washington 34, Purdue 24	1984	UCLA 45, Illinois 9
2000	Wisconsin 17, Stanford 9	1983	UCLA 24, Michigan 14
1999	Wisconsin 38, UCLA 31	1982	Washington 28, Iowa 0
1998	Michigan 21, Washington State 16	1981	Michigan 23, Washington 6
1997	Ohio State 20, Arizona State 17	1980	USC 17, Ohio State 16
1996	USC 41, Northwestern 32	1979	USC 17, Michigan 10
1995	Penn State 38, Oregon 20	1978	Washington 27, Michigan 20
1994	Wisconsin 21, UCLA 16	1977	USC 14, Michigan 6
1993	Michigan 38, Washington 31	1976	UCLA 23, Ohio State 10
1992	Washington 34, Michigan 14	1975	USC 18, Ohio State 17
1991	Washington 46, Iowa 34	1974	Ohio State 42, USC 21
1990	USC 17, Michigan 10	1973	USC 42, Ohio State 17

ROSE BOWL (cont.)

DATE	RESULT	DATE	RESULT
1972	Stanford 13, Michigan 12	1943	Georgia 9, UCLA 0
1971	Stanford 27, Ohio State 17	1942	Oregon State 20, Duke 16
1970	USC 10, Michigan 3	1941	Stanford 21, Nebraska 13
1969	Ohio State 27, USC 16	1940	USC 14, Tennessee 0
1968	USC 14, Indiana 3	1939	USC 7, Duke 3
1967	Purdue 14, USC 13	1938	California 13, Alabama 0
1966	UCLA 14, Michigan State 12	1937	Pittsburgh 21, Washington 0
1965	Michigan 34, Oregon State 7	1936	Stanford 7, SMU 0
1964	Illinois 17, Washington 7	1935	Alabama 29, Stanford 13
1963	USC 42, Wisconsin 37	1934	Columbia 7, Stanford 0
1962	Minnesota 21, UCLA 3	1933	USC 35, Pittsburgh 0
1961	Washington 17, Minnesota 7	1932	USC 21, Tulane 12
1960	Washington 44, Wisconsin 8	1931	Alabama 24, Washington State 0
1959	Iowa 38, California 12	1930	USC 47, Pittsburgh 14
1958	Ohio State 10, Oregon 7	1929	Georgia Tech 8, California 7
1957	Iowa 35, Oregon State 19	1928	Stanford 7, Pittsburgh 6
1956	Michigan State 17, UCLA 14	1927	Stanford 7, Alabama 7
1955	Ohio State 20, USC 7	1926	Alabama 20, Washington 19
1954	Michigan State 28, UCLA 20	1925	Notre Dame 27, Stanford 10
1953	USC 7, Wisconsin 0	1924	Washington 14, Navy 14
1952	Illinois 40, Stanford 7	1923	USC 14, Penn State 3
1951	Michigan 14, California 6	1922	California 0, Washington & Jefferson 0
1950	Ohio State 17, California 14	1921	California 28, Ohio State 0
1949	Northwestern 20, California 14	1920	Harvard 7, Oregon 6
1948	Michigan 49, USC 0	1919	Great Lakes 17, Mare Island 0
1947	Illinois 45, UCLA 14	1918	Mare Island 19, Camp Lewis 7
1946	Alabama 34, USC 14	1917	Oregon 14, Pennsylvania 0
1945	USC 25, Tennessee 0	1916	Washington State 14, Brown 0
1944	USC 29, Washington 0	1902	Michigan 49, Stanford 0

Note: From 1903–15, no Rose Bowl football game was held. In 1903, polo replaced football. From 1904–1915, chariot races were held. Football returned in 1916.

ORANGE BOWL

DATE	RESULT	DATE	RESULT
January 3, 2006	Penn State 26, Florida State 23	January 1, 1976	Oklahoma 14, Michigan 6
January 4, 2005	USC 55, Oklahoma 19	January 1, 1975	Notre Dame 13, Alabama 11
January 1, 2004	Miami (Florida) 16, Florida State 14	January 1, 1974	Penn State 16, LSU 9
January 2, 2003	USC 38, Iowa 17	January 1, 1973	Nebraska 40, Notre Dame 6
January 2, 2002	Florida 56, Maryland 23	January 1, 1972	Nebraska 38, Alabama 6
January 3, 2001	Oklahoma 13, Florida State 2	January 1, 1971	Nebraska 17, LSU 12
January 1, 2000	Michigan 35, Alabama 34 (OT)	January 1, 1970	Penn State 10, Missouri 3
January 2, 1999	Florida 31, Syracuse 10	January 1, 1969	Penn State 15, Kansas 14
January 2, 1998	Nebraska 42, Tennessee 17	January 1, 1968	Oklahoma 26, Tennessee 24
December 31, 1996	Nebraska 41, Virginia Tech 21	January 2, 1967	Florida 27, Georgia Tech 12
January 1, 1996	Florida State 31, Notre Dame 26	January 1, 1966	Alabama 39, Nebraska 28
January 1, 1995	Nebraska 24, Miami (Florida) 17	January 1, 1965	Texas 21, Alabama 17
January 1, 1994	Florida State 18, Nebraska 16	January 1, 1964	Nebraska 13, Auburn 7
January 1, 1993	Florida State 27, Nebraska 14	January 1, 1963	Alabama 17, Oklahoma 0
January 1, 1992	Miami (Florida) 22, Nebraska 0	January 1, 1962	LSU 25, Colorado 7
January 1, 1991	Colorado 10, Notre Dame 9	January 2, 1961	Missouri 21, Navy 14
January 1, 1990	Notre Dame 21, Colorado 6	January 1, 1960	Georgia 14, Missouri 0
January 2, 1989	Miami (Florida) 23, Nebraska 3	January 1, 1959	Oklahoma 21, Syracuse 6
January 1, 1988	Miami (Florida) 20, Oklahoma 14	January 1, 1958	Oklahoma 48, Duke 21
January 1, 1987	Oklahoma 42, Arkansas 8	January 1, 1957	Colorado 27, Clemson 21
January 1, 1986	Oklahoma 25, Penn State 10	January 2, 1956	Oklahoma 20, Maryland 6
January 1, 1985	Washington 28, Oklahoma 17	January 1, 1955	Duke 34, Nebraska 7
January 2, 1984	Miami (Florida) 31, Nebraska 30	January 1, 1954	Oklahoma 7, Maryland 0
January 1, 1983	Nebraska 21, LSU 20	January 1, 1953	Alabama 61, Syracuse 6
January 1, 1982	Clemson 22, Nebraska 15	January 1, 1952	Georgia Tech 17, Baylor 14
January 1, 1981	Oklahoma 18, Florida State 17	January 1, 1951	Clemson 15, Miami (Florida) 14
January 1, 1980	Oklahoma 24, Florida State 7	January 2, 1950	Santa Clara 21, Kentucky 13
January 1, 1979	Oklahoma 31, Nebraska 24	January 1, 1949	Texas 41, Georgia 28
January 2, 1978	Arkansas 31, Oklahoma 6	January 1, 1948	Georgia Tech 20, Kansas 14
January 1, 1977	Ohio State 27, Colorado 10	January 1, 1947	Rice 8, Tennessee 0

MAJOR BOWL GAME RESULTS (cont.)

ORANGE BOWL (cont.)

DATE	RESULT	DATE	RESULT
January 1, 1946	Miami (Florida) 13, Holy Cross 6	January 1, 1940	Georgia Tech 21, Missouri 7
January 1, 1945	Tulsa 26, Georgia Tech 12	January 2, 1939	Tennessee 17, Oklahoma 0
January 1, 1944	LSU 19, Texas A&M 14	January 1, 1938	Auburn 6, Michigan State 0
January 1, 1943	Alabama 37, Boston College 21	January 1, 1937	Duquesne 13, Mississippi State 12
January 1, 1942	Georgia 40, TCU 26	January 1, 1936	Catholic 20, Mississippi 19
January 1, 1941	Mississippi State 14, Georgetown 7	January 1, 1935	Bucknell 26, Miami (Florida) 0

SUGAR BOWL

DATE	RESULT	DATE	RESULT
January 2, 2006	West Virginia 38, Georgia 35	January 1, 1970	Mississippi 27, Arkansas 22
January 3, 2005	Auburn 16, Virginia Tech 13	January 1, 1969	Arkansas 16, Georgia 2
January 4, 2004	LSU 21, Oklahoma 14	January 1, 1968	LSU 20, Wyoming 13
January 1, 2003	Georgia 26, Florida State 13	January 1, 1967	Alabama 34, Nebraska 7
January 1, 2002	LSU 47, Illinois 34	January 1, 1966	Missouri 20, Florida 18
January 2, 2001	Miami (Florida) 37, Florida 20	January 1, 1965	LSU 13, Syracuse 10
January 4, 2000	Florida State 46, Virginia Tech 29	January 1, 1964	Alabama 12, Mississippi 7
January 1, 1999	Ohio State 24, Texas A&M 14	January 1, 1963	Mississippi 17, Arkansas 13
January 1, 1998	Florida State 31, Ohio State 14	January 1, 1962	Alabama 10, Arkansas 3
January 2, 1997	Florida 52, Florida State 20	January 2, 1961	Mississippi 14, Rice 6
December 31, 1995	Virginia Tech 28, Texas 10	January 1, 1960	Mississippi 21, LSU 0
January 2, 1995	Florida State 23, Florida 17	January 1, 1959	LSU 7, Clemson 0
January 1, 1994	Florida 41, West Virginia 7	January 1, 1958	Mississippi 39, Texas 7
January 1, 1993	Alabama 34, Miami (Florida) 13	January 1, 1957	Baylor 13, Tennessee 7
January 1, 1992	Notre Dame 39, Florida 28	January 2, 1956	Georgia Tech 7, Pittsburgh 0
January 1, 1991	Tennessee 23, Virginia 22	January 2, 1955	Navy 21, Mississippi 0
January 1, 1990	Miami (Florida) 33, Alabama 25	January 1, 1954	Georgia Tech 42, West Virginia 19
January 2, 1989	Florida State 13, Auburn 7	January 1, 1953	Georgia Tech 24, Mississippi 7
January 1, 1988	Auburn 16, Syracuse 16	January 1, 1952	Maryland 28, Tennessee 13
January 1, 1987	Nebraska 30, LSU 15	January 1, 1951	Kentucky 13, Oklahoma 7
January 1, 1986	Tennessee 35, Miami (Florida) 7	January 2, 1950	Oklahoma 35, LSU 0
January 1, 1985	Nebraska 28, LSU 10	January 1, 1949	Oklahoma 14, North Carolina 6
January 2, 1984	Auburn 9, Michigan 7	January 1, 1948	Texas 27, Alabama 7
January 1, 1983	Penn State 27, Georgia 23	January 1, 1947	Georgia 20, North Carolina 10
January 1, 1982	Pittsburgh 24, Georgia 20	January 1, 1946	Oklahoma State 33, Saint Mary's 13
January 1, 1981	Georgia 17, Notre Dame 10	January 1, 1945	Duke 29, Alabama 26
January 1, 1980	Alabama 24, Arkansas 9	January 1, 1944	Georgia Tech 20, Tulsa 18
January 1, 1979	Alabama 14, Penn State 7	January 1, 1943	Tennessee 14, Tulsa 7
January 2, 1978	Alabama 35, Ohio State 6	January 1, 1942	Fordham 2, Missouri 0
January 1, 1977	Pittsburgh 27, Georgia 3	January 1, 1941	Boston College 19, Tennessee 13
December 31, 1975	Alabama 13, Penn State 6	January 1, 1940	Texas A&M 14, Tulane 13
December 31, 1974	Nebraska 13, Florida 10	January 2, 1939	TCU 15, Carnegie Mellon 7
December 31, 1973	Notre Dame 24, Alabama 23	January 1, 1938	Santa Clara 6, LSU 0
December 31, 1972	Oklahoma 14, Penn State 0	January 1, 1937	Santa Clara 21, LSU 14
January 1, 1972	Oklahoma 40, Auburn 22	January 1, 1936	TCU 3, LSU 2
January 1, 1971	Tennessee 34, Air Force 13	January 1, 1935	Tulane 20, Temple 14

COTTON BOWL

DATE	RESULT	DATE	RESULT
January 2, 2006	Alabama 13, Texas Tech 10	January 1, 1991	Miami (Florida) 46, Texas 3
January 1, 2005	Tennessee 38, Texas A&M 7	January 1, 1990	Tennessee 31, Arkansas 27
January 2, 2004	Mississippi 31, Oklahoma State 28	January 2, 1989	UCLA 17, Arkansas 3
January 1, 2003	Texas 35, LSU 20	January 1, 1988	Texas A&M 35, Notre Dame 10
January 1, 2002	Oklahoma 10, Arkansas 3	January 1, 1987	Ohio State 28, Texas A&M 12
January 1, 2001	Kansas State 35, Tennessee 21	January 1, 1986	Texas A&M 36, Auburn 16
January 1, 2000	Arkansas 27, Texas 6	January 1, 1985	Boston College 45, Houston 28
January 1, 1999	Texas 38, Mississippi State 11	January 2, 1984	Georgia 10, Texas 9
January 1, 1998	UCLA 29, Texas A&M 23	January 1, 1983	SMU 7, Pittsburgh 3
January 1, 1997	BYU 19, Kansas State 15	January 1, 1982	Texas 14, Alabama 12
January 1, 1996	Colorado 38, Oregon 6	January 1, 1981	Alabama 30, Baylor 2
January 2, 1995	USC 55, Texas Tech 14	January 1, 1980	Houston 17, Nebraska 14
January 1, 1994	Notre Dame 24, Texas A&M 21	January 1, 1979	Notre Dame 35, Houston 34
January 1, 1993	Notre Dame 28, Texas A&M 3	January 2, 1978	Notre Dame 38, Texas 10
January 1, 1992	Florida State 10, Texas A&M 2	January 1, 1977	Houston 30, Maryland 21

LEGENDS

Ernie Davis was the first African American to win the Heisman Trophy.

■ **Ernie Davis, running back,** b. December 14, 1939, New Salem, Pennsylvania; d. May 18, 1963. In 1961, while a senior at Syracuse, Davis became the first African American to win the Heisman Trophy. The powerful 6' 2", 212-pound running back rushed for 2,386 yards, gained 3,414 all-purpose yards, and scored 35 touchdowns in three seasons. As a sophomore, he helped lead the Orange to its only national championship. Sadly, Davis never played in the NFL. He was stricken with leukemia and died at the age of 23.

■ **Ty Detmer, quarterback,** b. October 30, 1967. A member of the NCAA's All-Decade team for the 1990's, Detmer played for Brigham Young University, where he set 59 NCAA records during his career, including most touchdown passes (121), yards passing (15,031), completions (958), attempts (1,530), and total offense (14,653 yards). In 1990, Detmer won the Heisman Trophy, and two years later was drafted by the Green Bay Packers in the ninth round of the NFL Draft. He had his best pro season with the Philadelphia Eagles in 1996, leading the team to a 10–6 mark and a playoff berth. Detmer completed his 14th NFL season in 2005, with the Atlanta Falcons.

■ **Anthony Carter, wide receiver,** b. Sept. 17, 1960, Riviera Beach, Florida. The speedy, sure-handed wide receiver was a three-time All-America at Michigan. He set the mark for most all-purpose yards per play in NCAA history (17.4). Carter had 14 touchdown catches in his senior season, and wound up with 37 for his career — the previous Michigan record was 16 career touchdowns. Michigan went 35–13 with Carter on the roster and appeared in four straight bowl games. He was inducted into the College Football Hall of Fame in 2001 after a 12-year professional career.

MAJOR BOWL GAME RESULTS (cont.)

COTTON BOWL (cont.)

DATE	RESULT	DATE	RESULT
January 1, 1976	Arkansas 31, Georgia 10	January 2, 1961	Duke 7, Arkansas 6
January 1, 1975	Penn State 41, Baylor 20	January 1, 1960	Syracuse 23, Texas 14
January 1, 1974	Nebraska 19, Texas 3	January 1, 1959	TCU 0, Air Force 0
January 1, 1973	Texas 17, Alabama 13	January 1, 1958	Navy 20, Rice 7
January 1, 1972	Penn State 30, Texas 6	January 1, 1957	TCU 28, Syracuse 27
January 1, 1971	Notre Dame 24, Texas 11	January 2, 1956	Mississippi 14, TCU 13
January 1, 1970	Texas 21, Notre Dame 17	January 1, 1955	Georgia Tech 14, Arkansas 6
January 1, 1969	Texas 36, Tennessee 13	January 1, 1954	Rice 28, Alabama 6
January 1, 1968	Texas A&M 20, Alabama 16	January 1, 1953	Texas 16, Tennessee 0
December 31, 1966	Georgia 24, SMU 9	January 1, 1952	Kentucky 20, TCU 7
January 1, 1966	LSU 14, Arkansas 7	January 1, 1951	Tennessee 20, Texas 14
January 1, 1965	Arkansas 10, Nebraska 7	January 2, 1950	Rice 27, North Carolina 13
January 1, 1964	Texas 28, Navy 6	January 1, 1949	SMU 21, Oregon 13
January 1, 1963	LSU 13, Texas 0	January 1, 1948	SMU 13, Penn State 13
January 1, 1962	Texas 12, Mississippi 7	January 1, 1947	Arkansas 0, LSU 0

MAJOR BOWL GAME RESULTS (cont.)

COTTON BOWL (cont.)

DATE	RESULT	DATE	RESULT
January 1, 1946	Texas 40, Missouri 27	January 1, 1941	Texas A&M 13, Fordham 12
January 1, 1945	Oklahoma State 34, TCU 0	January 1, 1940	Clemson 6, Boston College 3
January 1, 1944	Texas 7, Randolph Field 7	January 2, 1939	St. Mary's (CA) 20, Texas Tech 13
January 1, 1943	Texas 14, Georgia Tech 7	January 1, 1938	Rice 28, Colorado 14
January 1, 1942	Alabama 29, Texas A&M 21	January 1, 1937	TCU 16, Marquette 6

FIESTA BOWL

DATE	RESULT	DATE	RESULT
January 2, 2006	Ohio State 34, Notre Dame 20	January 1, 1988	Florida State 31, Nebraska 28
January 1, 2005	Utah 35, Pittsburgh 7	January 2, 1987	Penn State 14, Miami (Florida) 10
January 2, 2004	Ohio State 35, Kansas St. 28	January 1, 1986	Michigan 27, Nebraska 23
January 3, 2003	Ohio State 31, Miami (Florida) 24	January 1, 1985	UCLA 39, Miami (Florida) 37
January 1, 2002	Oregon 38, Colorado 16	January 1, 1984	Ohio State 28, Pittsburgh 23
January 1, 2001	Oregon State 41, Notre Dame 9	January 1, 1983	Arizona State 32, Oklahoma 21
January 2, 2000	Nebraska 31, Tennessee 21	January 1, 1982	Penn State 26, USC 10
January 4, 1999	Tennessee 23, Florida State 16	December 26, 1980	Penn State 31, Ohio State 19
December 31, 1997	Kansas State 35, Syracuse 18	December 25, 1979	Pittsburgh 16, Arizona 10
January 1, 1997	Penn State 38, Texas 15	December 25, 1978	Arkansas 10, UCLA 10
January 2, 1996	Nebraska 62, Florida 24	December 25, 1977	Penn State 42, Arizona State 30
January 1, 1995	Colorado 41, Notre Dame 24	December 25, 1976	Oklahoma 41, Wyoming 7
January 1, 1994	Arizona 29, Miami (Florida) 0	December 26, 1975	Arizona State 17, Nebraska 14
January 1, 1993	Syracuse 26, Colorado 22	December 28, 1974	Oklahoma State 16, BYU 6
January 1, 1992	Penn State 42, Tennessee 17	December 21, 1973	Arizona State 28, Pittsburgh 7
January 1, 1991	Louisville 34, Alabama 7	December 23, 1972	Arizona State 49, Missouri 35
January 1, 1990	Florida State 41, Nebraska 17	December 27, 1971	Arizona State 45, Florida State 38
January 2, 1989	Notre Dame 34, West Virginia 21		

NCAA DIVISION I-AA CHAMPIONSHIPS

YEAR	WINNER	RUNNER-UP	SCORE	YEAR	WINNER	RUNNER-UP	SCORE
2005	Appalachian State	Northern Iowa	21–16	1991	Youngstown State	Marshall	25–17
2004	James Madison	Montana	31–21	1990	Georgia Southern	Nevada-Reno	36–13
2003	Delaware	Colgate	40–0	1989	Georgia Southern	Stephen F. Austin	37–34
2002	Western Kentucky	McNeese State	34–14	1988	Furman	Georgia Southern	17–12
2001	Montana	Furman	13–6	1987	Louisiana Monroe	Marshall	43–42
2000	Georgia Southern	Montana	27–25	1986	Georgia Southern	Arkansas State	48–21
1999	Georgia Southern	Youngstown State	59–24	1985	Georgia Southern	Furman	44–42
1998	Massachusetts	Georgia Southern	55–43	1984	Montana State	Louisiana Tech	19–6
1997	Youngstown State	McNeese State	10–9	1983	Southern Illinois	Western Carolina	43–7
1996	Marshall	Montana	49–29	1982	Eastern Kentucky	Delaware	17–14
1995	Montana	Marshall	22–20	1981	Idaho State	Eastern Kentucky	34–23
1994	Youngstown State	Boise State	28–14	1980	Boise State	Eastern Kentucky	31–29
1993	Youngstown State	Marshall	17–5	1979	Eastern Kentucky	Lehigh	30–7
1992	Marshall	Youngstown State	31–28	1978	Florida A&M	Massachusetts	35–28

HEISMAN MEMORIAL TROPHY

Awarded to the nation's best college player by the Downtown Athletic Club (DAC) of New York City. The trophy is named after John W. Heisman, who coached Georgia Tech to the national championship in 1917 and later served as DAC athletic director.

YEAR	WINNER, COLLEGE	RUNNER-UP, COLLEGE
2005	Reggie Bush, USC	Vince Young, Texas
2004	*† Matt Leinart, USC	Adrian Peterson, Oklahoma
2003	* Jason White, Oklahoma	Larry Fitzgerald, Pittsburgh
2002	Carson Palmer, USC	Brad Banks, Iowa
2001	Eric Crouch, Nebraska	Rex Grossman, Florida
2000	Chris Weinke, Florida State	Josh Heupel, Oklahoma
1999	Ron Dayne, Wisconsin	Joe Hamilton, Georgia Tech
1998	Ricky Williams, Texas	Michael Bishop, Kansas State

*Juniors (all others were seniors)
†Winners who played for national championship teams the same year

HEISMAN MEMORIAL TROPHY (cont.)

YEAR	WINNER, COLLEGE	RUNNER-UP, COLLEGE
1997	†Charles Woodson, Michigan	Peyton Manning, Tennessee
1996	†Danny Wuerffel, Florida	Troy Davis, Iowa State
1995	Eddie George, Ohio State	Tommie Frazier, Nebraska
1994	Rashaan Salaam, Colorado	Ki-Jana Carter, Penn State
1993	†Charlie Ward, Florida State	Heath Shuler, Tennessee
1992	Gino Torretta, Miami (Florida)	Marshall Faulk, San Diego State
1991	* Desmond Howard, Michigan	Casey Weldon, Florida State
1990	* Ty Detmer, BYU	Raghib Ismail, Notre Dame
1989	* Andre Ware, Houston	Anthony Thompson, Indiana
1988	* Barry Sanders, Oklahoma State	Rodney Peete, USC
1987	Tim Brown, Notre Dame	Don McPherson, Syracuse
1986	Vinny Testaverde, Miami (Florida)	Paul Palmer, Temple
1985	Bo Jackson, Auburn	Chuck Long, Iowa
1984	Doug Flutie, Boston College	Keith Byars, Ohio State
1983	Mike Rozier, Nebraska	Steve Young, BYU
1982	* Herschel Walker, Georgia	John Elway, Stanford
1981	Marcus Allen, USC	Herschel Walker, Georgia
1980	George Rogers, South Carolina	Hugh Green, Pittsburgh
1979	Charles White, USC	Billy Sims, Oklahoma
1978	* Billy Sims, Oklahoma	Chuck Fusina, Penn State
1977	Earl Campbell, Texas	Terry Miller, Oklahoma State
1976	†Tony Dorsett, Pittsburgh	Ricky Bell, USC
1975	Archie Griffin, Ohio State	Chuck Muncie, California
1974	* Archie Griffin, Ohio State	Anthony Davis, USC
1973	John Cappelletti, Penn State	John Hicks, Ohio State
1972	Johnny Rodgers, Nebraska	Greg Pruitt, Oklahoma
1971	Pat Sullivan, Auburn	Ed Marinaro, Cornell
1970	Jim Plunkett, Stanford	Joe Theismann, Notre Dame
1969	Steve Owens, Oklahoma	Mike Phipps, Purdue
1968	O.J. Simpson, USC	Leroy Keyes, Purdue
1967	Gary Beban, UCLA	O.J. Simpson, USC
1966	Steve Spurrier, Florida	Bob Griese, Purdue
1965	Mike Garrett, USC	Howard Twilley, Tulsa
1964	John Huarte, Notre Dame	Jerry Rhome, Tulsa
1963	* Roger Staubach, Navy	Billy Lothridge, Georgia Tech
1962	Terry Baker, Oregon State	Jerry Stovall, LSU
1961	Ernie Davis, Syracuse	Bob Ferguson, Ohio State
1960	Joe Bellino, Navy	Tom Brown, Minnesota
1959	Billy Cannon, LSU	Rich Lucas, Penn State
1958	Pete Dawkins, Army	Randy Duncan, Iowa
1957	John David Crow, Texas A&M	Alex Karras, Iowa
1956	Paul Hornung, Notre Dame	Johnny Majors, Tennessee
1955	Howard Cassady, Ohio State	Jim Swink, TCU
1954	Alan Ameche, Wisconsin	Kurt Burris, Oklahoma
1953	John Lattner, Notre Dame	Paul Giel, Minnesota
1952	Billy Vessels, Oklahoma	Jack Scarbath, Maryland
1951	Dick Kazmaier, Princeton	Hank Lauricella, Tennessee
1950	* Vic Janowicz, Ohio State	Kyle Rote, SMU
1949	†Leon Hart, Notre Dame	Charlie Justice, North Carolina
1948	* Doak Walker, SMU	Charlie Justice, North Carolina
1947	†John Lujack, Notre Dame	Bob Chappius, Michigan
1946	Glenn Davis, Army	Charley Trippi, Georgia
1945	*†Doc Blanchard, Army	Glenn Davis, Army
1944	Les Horvath, Ohio State	Glenn Davis, Army
1943	Angelo Bertelli, Notre Dame	Bob Odell, Pennsylvania
1942	Frank Sinkwich, Georgia	Paul Governali, Columbia
1941	†Bruce Smith, Minnesota	Angelo Bertelli, Notre Dame
1940	Tom Harmon, Michigan	John Kimbrough, Texas A&M
1939	Nile Kinnick, Iowa	Tom Harmon, Michigan
1938	†Davey O'Brien, TCU	Marshall Goldberg, Pittsburgh
1937	Clint Frank, Yale	Byron White, Colorado
1936	Larry Kelley, Yale	Sam Francis, Nebraska
1935	Jay Berwanger, Chicago	Monk Meyer, Army

*Juniors (all others were seniors)
†Winners who played for national championship teams the same year
 Note: Former Heisman winners and members of the national media cast votes with ballots allowing for three names (3 points for first, 2 points for second, and 1 point for third).

MAXWELL AWARD

Given to the nation's most outstanding college football player by the Maxwell Football Club of Philadelphia.

YEAR	PLAYER, COLLEGE	YEAR	PLAYER, COLLEGE
2005	Vince Young, Texas	1970	Jim Plunkett, Stanford
2004	Jason White, Oklahoma	1969	Mike Reid, Penn State
2003	Eli Manning, Mississippi	1968	O.J. Simpson, USC
2002	Larry Johnson, Penn State	1967	Gary Beban, UCLA
2001	Ken Dorsey, Miami (Florida)	1966	Jim Lynch, Notre Dame
2000	Drew Brees, Purdue	1965	Tommy Nobis, Texas
1999	Ron Dayne, Wisconsin	1964	Glenn Ressler, Penn State
1998	Ricky Williams, Texas	1963	Roger Staubach, Navy
1997	Peyton Manning, Tennessee	1962	Terry Baker, Oregon State
1996	Danny Wuerffel, Florida	1961	Bob Ferguson, Ohio State
1995	Eddie George, Ohio State	1960	Joe Bellino, Navy
1994	Kerry Collins, Penn State	1959	Rich Lucas, Penn State
1993	Charlie Ward, Florida State	1958	Pete Dawkins, Army
1992	Gino Torretta, Miami (Florida)	1957	Bob Reifsnyder, Navy
1991	Desmond Howard, Michigan	1956	Tommy McDonald, Oklahoma
1990	Ty Detmer, BYU	1955	Howard Cassidy, Ohio State
1989	Anthony Thompson, Indiana	1954	Ron Beagle, Navy
1988	Barry Sanders, Oklahoma State	1953	John Lattner, Notre Dame
1987	Don McPherson, Syracuse	1952	John Lattner, Notre Dame
1986	Vinny Testaverde, Miami (Florida)	1951	Dick Kazmaier, Princeton
1985	Chuck Long, Iowa	1950	Reds Bagnell, Pennsylvania
1984	Doug Flutie, Boston College	1949	Leon Hart, Notre Dame
1983	Mike Rozier, Nebraska	1948	Chuck Bednarik, Pennsylvania
1982	Herschel Walker, Georgia	1947	Doak Walker, SMU
1981	Marcus Allen, USC	1946	Charley Trippi, Georgia
1980	Hugh Green, Pittsburgh	1945	Doc Blanchard, Army
1979	Charles White, USC	1944	Glenn Davis, Army
1978	Chuck Fusina, Penn State	1943	Bob Odell, Pennsylvania
1977	Ross Browner, Notre Dame	1942	Paul Governali, Columbia
1976	Tony Dorsett, Pittsburgh	1941	Bill Dudley, Virginia
1975	Archie Griffin, Ohio State	1940	Tom Harmon, Michigan
1974	Steve Joachim, Temple	1939	Nile Kinnick, Iowa
1973	John Cappelletti, Penn State	1938	Davey O'Brien, TCU
1972	Brad Van Pelt, Michigan State	1937	Clint Frank, Yale
1971	Ed Marinaro, Cornell		

VINCE LOMBARDI/ROTARY AWARD

Given to the most outstanding college lineman of the year. The award is sponsored by the Rotary Club of Houston, Texas.

YEAR	PLAYER, COLLEGE	YEAR	PLAYER, COLLEGE
2005	A.J. Hawk, Ohio State	1984	Tony Degrate, Texas
2004	David Pollack, Georgia	1983	Dean Steinkuhler, Nebraska
2003	Tommie Harris, Oklahoma	1982	Dave Rimington, Nebraska
2002	Terrell Suggs, Arizona State	1981	Kenneth Sims, Texas
2001	Julius Peppers, North Carolina	1980	Hugh Green, Pittsburgh
		1979	Brad Budde, USC
2000	Jamal Reynolds, Florida State	1978	Bruce Clark, Penn State
1999	Corey Moore, Virginia Tech	1977	Ross Browner, Notre Dame
1998	Dat Nguyen, Texas A&M	1976	Wilson Whitley, Houston
1997	Grant Wistrom, Nebraska	1975	Lee Roy Selmon, Oklahoma
1996	Orlando Pace, Ohio State	1974	Randy White, Maryland
1995	Orlando Pace, Ohio State	1973	John Hicks, Ohio State
1994	Warren Sapp, Miami (Florida)	1972	Rich Glover, Nebraska
1993	Aaron Taylor, Notre Dame	1971	Walt Patulski, Notre Dame
1992	Marvin Jones, Florida State	1970	Jim Stillwagon, Ohio State
1991	Steve Emtman, Washington		
1990	Chris Zorich, Notre Dame		
1989	Percy Snow, Michigan State		
1988	Tracy Rocker, Auburn		
1987	Chris Spielman, Ohio State		
1986	Cornelius Bennett, Alabama		
1985	Tony Casillas, Oklahoma		

A.J. Hawk, Ohio State

DAMIAN STROHMEYER

DID YOU KNOW?

Four schools made the first bowl appearances in their program's history following the 2005 regular season. However none of them — Central Florida, South Florida, Akron, or Arkansas State — managed to get a bowl win.

DAVEY O'BRIEN NATIONAL QUARTERBACK AWARD

Given to the nation's top quarterback by the Davey O'Brien Educational and Charitable Trust of Fort Worth. Named for TCU Hall of Fame quarterback Davey O'Brien (1936-38).

YEAR	PLAYER, COLLEGE	YEAR	PLAYER, COLLEGE
2005	Vince Young, Texas	1992	Gino Torretta, Miami (Florida)
2004	Jason White, Oklahoma	1991	Ty Detmer, BYU
2003	Jason White, Oklahoma	1990	Ty Detmer, BYU
2002	Brad Banks, Iowa	1989	Andre Ware, Houston
2001	Eric Crouch, Nebraska	1988	Troy Aikman, UCLA
2000	Chris Weinke, Florida State	1987	Don McPherson, Syracuse
1999	Joe Hamilton, Georgia Tech	1986	Vinny Testaverde, Miami (Florida)
1998	Michael Bishop, Kansas State	1985	Chuck Long, Iowa
1997	Peyton Manning, Tennessee	1984	Doug Flutie, Boston College
1996	Danny Wuerffel, Florida	1983	Steve Young, BYU
1995	Danny Wuerffel, Florida	1982	Todd Blackledge, Penn State
1994	Kerry Collins, Penn State	1981	Jim McMahon, BYU
1993	Charlie Ward, Florida State		

2005-06 TIME LINE

■ **September 10, 2005:** Number 20 Notre Dame defeats Number 3 Michigan, 17–10, at Ann Arbor, Michigan. Charlie Weis becomes the first ND coach to win his first two games on the road since the legendary Knute Rockne did it in 1918.

■ **October 15, 2005:** A wild Saturday: West Virginia rallies from 17 down to beat Louisville in triple overtime; Michigan beats Penn State on the last play of the game; Wisconsin comes back from 10 down to win at Minnesota; and, in the Game of the Year, USC beats Notre Dame, 34–31, on the game's final play.

■ **October 22, 2005:** Number 5 Alabama runs its record to 7-0 with a 6–3 win over Number 17 Tennessee. The game is decided by a field goal by Jamie Christensen with 13 seconds to play. It is the second straight game in which Christensen has kicked the game-winner in the final seconds.

■ **October 29, 2005:** One of the nation's undefeated stumbles, as Number 4 Georgia falls to Number 16 Florida, 14–10. Georgia (whose regular quarterback, D.J. Shockley, was injured) is eliminated from national title contention.

■ **November 5, 2005:** Number 3 Virginia Tech's bid for an undefeated season is halt-ed at home by Number 5 Miami, 27–7.

■ **November 12, 2005:** The national title race is whittled to two (USC and Texas), as the nation's other unbeaten team, Number 4 Alabama, loses in over-time to Number 5 LSU.

■ **December 10, 2005:** Reggie Bush of USC wins the Heisman Trophy.

■ **December 28, 2005:** In one of the most frantic finishes in college football history, Nebraska outlasts Michigan, 32–28 in the Alamo Bowl. On the game's final play, Michigan returned a kickoff to the Nebraska 13-yard-line on eight laterals.

■ **January 3, 2006:** The next-to-last bowl game of the 2005 season matches up the game's all-time winningest coaches. Joe Paterno's Penn State team defeats Bobby Bowden's Florida State squad in the Orange Bowl, giving Paterno 354 career victories versus Bowden's 359.

■ **January 4, 2006:** In one of college football's greatest games ever, Texas ruins USC's bid for a third straight national championship with a thrilling 41–38 victory. The Longhorns win their school's first national championship in 36 years.

BASEBALL

Outfielder Jermaine Dye of the Chicago White Sox was named World Series MVP.

JOHN BIEVER

I n the mid-19th century, men gathered on the Elysian Fields of New Jersey for games of what was then called "base ball." The sport grew to become America's national pastime. But in 2005 (and 2006), baseball took on an international flavor like never before.

At July's All-Star Game, the Home Run Derby pitted players as representatives of their countries, and Venezuela's Bobby Abreu conquered a field that included players from the United States, Canada, the Dominican Republic, Panama, Puerto Rico, South Korea, and the Netherlands. In October, the Chicago White Sox became the first team with a foreign-born manager (Ozzie Guillen of Venezuela) to win the World Series. Finally, in March 2006, the first World Baseball Classic was held. Sixteen nations participated. On March 20, Japan defeated Cuba, 10–6, to win the Classic.

Baseball's steroids problem soon returned to center stage. A new book called *Game of Shadows* by Mark Fainaru-Wada and Lance Williams detailed Barry Bonds' alleged steroid use. Major League Baseball announced it would investigate the charges. Bonds entered 2006 six home runs shy of Babe Ruth's career total of 714, and 47 away from Hank Aaron's all-time record of 755.

In 2005, baseball introduced new penalties for steroid use. In the first year of the new program, 13 players were suspended. After the season, the MLB stiffened the penalties to a 50-game suspension for a first offense, 100 games for a second offense and a lifetime ban for a third positive test.

Fans continued to be enthusiastic about the game, setting many attendance records. The New York Yankees became just the third franchise to reach the four million mark in attendance. The Yankees were led by American League Most Valuable Player Alex Rodriguez. The Bronx Bombers rallied from an 11–19 start to catch the Boston Red Sox and win their eighth straight division title.

The Atlanta Braves won their 14th straight division crown, riding the hot bat of Andruw Jones (a club-record 51 home runs). The Braves had to outlast four other teams that each finished with at least a .500 winning percentage. (The San Diego Padres won the N.L. West with the worst record ever for a division champion, 82–80.)

The Houston Astros rode their trio of pitching aces (Roger Clemens, Andy Pettitte, and Roy Oswalt) to a wild-card victory. Houston followed with a thrilling Division Series win over the Braves and an upset of the St. Louis Cardinals, to reach its first-ever World Series.

Once in the Series, however, the Astros ran into the hottest team in baseball. The White Sox let their brilliant starting pitching carry them to their first pennant since 1959, going a combined 7–1 in the first two rounds of the playoffs. The Series itself was thrilling, if brief. Centerfielder Scott Podsednik, who hadn't hit a home run all year, smoked a game-winning homer in Game 2, and reserve Geoff Blum won the longest game in Series history with a 15th inning home run in Game 3. One night later, the Sox won their first World Series title since 1917 with a 1–0 victory.

On that night, baseball's problems seemed far away. All the game's virtues were on display, personified by the new champions. As Guillen hoisted the trophy, the sport seemed to be moving past its Steroid Era and entering its International Era. For baseball, it's a whole new world.

2005 MAJOR LEAGUE BASEBALL FINAL STANDINGS

NATIONAL LEAGUE

EASTERN DIVISION

TEAM	W	L	PCT	GB	HOME	AWAY
Atlanta	90	72	.556	-	53-28	37-44
Philadelphia	88	74	.543	2	46-35	42-39
NY Mets	83	79	.512	7	48-33	35-46
Florida	83	79	.512	7	45-36	38-43
Washington	81	81	.500	9	41-40	40-41

CENTRAL DIVISION

TEAM	W	L	PCT	GB	HOME	AWAY
St. Louis	100	62	.617	-	50-31	50-31
†Houston	89	73	.549	11	53-28	36-45
Milwaukee	81	81	.500	19	46-35	35-46
Chicago Cubs	79	83	.488	21	38-43	41-40
Cincinnati	73	89	.451	27	42-39	31-50
Pittsburgh	67	95	.414	33	34-47	33-48

WESTERN DIVISION

TEAM	W	L	PCT	GB	HOME	AWAY
San Diego	82	80	.506	-	46-35	36-45
Arizona	77	85	.475	5	36-45	41-40
San Francisco	75	87	.463	7	37-44	38-43
LA Dodgers	71	91	.438	11	40-41	31-50
Colorado	67	95	.414	15	40-41	27-54

†Wild-card team

AMERICAN LEAGUE

EASTERN DIVISION

TEAM	W	L	PCT	GB	HOME	AWAY
NY Yankees	95	67	.586	-	53-28	42-39
†Boston	95	67	.586	-	54-27	41-40
Toronto	80	82	.494	15	43-38	37-44
Baltimore	74	88	.457	21	36-45	38-43
Tampa Bay	67	95	.414	28	40-41	27-54

CENTRAL DIVISION

TEAM	W	L	PCT	GB	HOME	AWAY
Chicago Sox	99	63	.611	-	47-34	52-29
Cleveland	93	69	.574	6	43-38	50-31
Minnesota	83	79	.512	16	45-36	38-43
Detroit	71	91	.438	28	39-42	32-49
Kansas City	56	106	.346	43	34-47	22-59

WESTERN DIVISION

TEAM	W	L	PCT	GB	HOME	AWAY
LA Angels	95	67	.586	-	49-32	46-35
Oakland	88	74	.543	7	45-36	43-38
Texas	79	83	.488	16	44-37	35-46
Seattle	69	93	.426	26	39-42	30-51

†Wild-card team

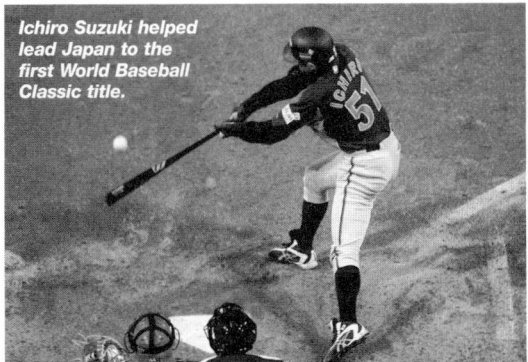

Ichiro Suzuki helped lead Japan to the first World Baseball Classic title.

Pitcher Roy Oswalt's 20 victories were a huge part of the Houston Astros' wild-card success.

MAJOR LEAGUE TEAMS

NATIONAL LEAGUE
Arizona Diamondbacks
Atlanta Braves
Chicago Cubs
Cincinnati Reds
Colorado Rockies
Florida Marlins
Houston Astros
Los Angeles Dodgers
Milwaukee Brewers
New York Mets
Philadelphia Phillies
Pittsburgh Pirates
San Diego Padres
San Francisco Giants
St. Louis Cardinals
Washington Nationals

AMERICAN LEAGUE
Baltimore Orioles
Boston Red Sox
Chicago White Sox
Cleveland Indians
Detroit Tigers
Kansas City Royals
Los Angeles Angels
Minnesota Twins
New York Yankees
Oakland Athletics
Seattle Mariners
Tampa Bay Devil Rays
Texas Rangers
Toronto Blue Jays

MLB 2005 PLAYOFFS – NATIONAL LEAGUE

NATIONAL LEAGUE DIVISION SERIES

October 4	Cardinals 8, Padres 5	October 8	Cardinals 7, Padres 4
October 6	Cardinals 6, Padres 2		

(ST. LOUIS CARDINALS WON SERIES, 3–0)

October 5	Astros 10, Braves 5	October 8	Astros 7, Braves 3
October 6	Braves 7, Astros 1	October 9	Astros 7, Braves 6

(HOUSTON ASTROS WON SERIES, 3–1)

NATIONAL LEAGUE CHAMPIONSHIP SERIES

October 12	Cardinals 5, Astros 3	October 16	Astros 2, Cardinals 1
October 13	Astros 4, Cardinals 1	October 17	Cardinals 5, Astros 4
October 15	Astros 4, Cardinals 3	October 19	Astros 5, Cardinals 1

(HOUSTON ASTROS WON SERIES, 4–2)

GAME 1

Astros	0	0	0	0	0	0	2	0	1	**3**
Cardinals	2	1	0	0	2	0	0	0	x	**5**

W—Carpenter. **L**—Pettitte. **SV**—Isringhausen. **E**—StL: Eckstein. **LOB**—Hou: 6; StL: 4. **2B**—Hou: Berkman, Ensberg. **HR**—Hou: Burke; StL: Sanders. **S**—Hou: Pettitte; StL: Carpenter. **SF**—Hou: Ausmus. **GIDP**—Hou: Berkman; StL: Sanders, Molina. **T**—2:29. **A**—52,332.

Recap: Chris Carpenter scattered five hits over eight innings, and Reggie Sanders continued his strong post-season with a two-run homer in the first. Chris Burke, pinch-hitting for Houston starter Andy Pettitte, provided the only punch for the Astros with a two-run homer in the seventh.

GAME 2

Astros	0	1	0	0	1	0	0	2	0	**4**
Cardinals	0	0	0	0	0	1	0	0	0	**1**

W—Oswalt. **L**—Mulder. **SV**—Lidge. **E**—Hou: Ensberg. **LOB**—Hou: 7; StL: 8. **S**—Hou: Oswalt. **2B**—Hou: Ausmus, Berkman; StL: Molina 2. **3B**—Hou: Burke, Everett. **HR**—StL: Pujols. **SB**—Hou: Ausmus. **CS**—Hou: Taveras. **GIDP**—Hou: Ensberg. **WP**—StL: Tavarez. **PB**—StL: Molina **T**—3:03. **A**—52,358.

Recap: Roy Oswalt handcuffed St. Louis for seven innings, giving up five hits. Chris Burke, getting his first post-season start for the Astros, came through with two runs and an RBI single in the eighth that gave Houston life and evened the series on the road. Albert Pujols homered for St. Louis.

GAME 3

Cardinals	0	0	0	0	1	1	0	0	1	**3**
Astros	0	0	0	2	0	2	0	0	x	**4**

W—Clemens. **L**—Morris. **SV**—Lidge. **E**—StL: Luna. **LOB**—StL: 7; Hou: 8. **S**—StL: Morris. **SF**—StL: Eckstein; Walker. **2B**—StL: Mabry; Hou: Lamb, Everett. **HR**—Hou: Lamb. **SB**—StL: Edmonds. **T**—3:00. **A**—42,823.

Recap: Roger Clemens got some vindication for last season's Game 7 loss to the Cardinals. In both games, Clemens had a 2–0 lead and lost it. This year, he and the Astros found a way to win. Despite not having his best stuff, Clemens kept the Astros in the game for six tough innings. Mike Lamb homered, and Chad Qualls and Brad Lidge closed out the game for Houston.

GAME 4

Cardinals	0	0	0	1	0	0	0	0	0	**1**
Astros	0	0	0	1	0	0	1	0	x	**2**

W—Qualls. **L**—Marquis. **SV**—Lidge. **E**—StL: Marquis. **LOB**—StL: 5.; Hou: 11. **S**—Hou: Biggio. **SF**—StL: Pujols; Hou: Ensberg. **2B**—StL: Edmonds. **HR**—Hou: Lane. **GIDP**—StL: Edmonds, Mabry. **T**—3:11. **A**—43,010.

Recap: In a dogfight of the teams' Number 4 starters, the Astros' Brandon Backe gave up only one run on two hits over five innings and was nearly matched by the Cardinals' Jeff Suppan, who gave up one run on *three* hits over five innings. Houston manufactured the winning run in the seventh with a sacrifice fly from Morgan Ensberg, and its bullpen closed the deal. Chad Qualls threw his third straight perfect inning of relief to get the victory, and Brad Lidge got out of a jam in the ninth to pick up his third save of the series.

GAME 5

Cardinals	0	0	2	0	0	0	0	0	3	**5**
Astros	0	1	0	0	0	0	3	0	0	**4**

W—Isringhausen. **L**—Lidge. **E**—StL: Luna; Hou: Everett. **LOB**—StL: 8; Hou: 7. **S**—Hou: Burke, Pettitte. **2B**—StL: Molina; Hou: Ausmus. **HR**—StL: Pujols; Hou: Berkman. **SB**—StL: Sanders, Eckstein. **CS**—StL: Eckstein. **HBP**—StL: Eckstein; Hou: Lane. **T**—3:19. **A**—43,470.

Recap: St. Louis, facing a mountain named Pettitte-Oswalt-Clemens blocking its path back to the World Series, took the first improbable step around the obstacle. They didn't conquer Pettitte, who was much sharper than in Game 1, giving up two runs on just two hits over seven innings and leaving with a 4–2 lead. They didn't solve Houston's middle relief, which was locking things down, as they had been doing all series. Dependable Brad Lidge came in to close out the Cardinals and take Houston to its first World Series. But somebody forgot to tell Albert Pujols to step aside. Pujols stunned Lidge and the Houston fans with a three-run homer in the ninth to pull St. Louis within a game of Houston in the series.

KEY W=winning pitcher; L=losing pitcher; SV=save; E=errors; LOB=left on base; S=sacrifice; SF=sacrifice fly; 2B=double; 3B=triple; HR=home run; SB=stolen bases; CS=caught stealing; HBP=hit by pitch; GIDP=grounded into double plays; WP=wild pitch; PB=passed ball; T=time; A=attendance

NATIONAL LEAGUE CHAMPIONSHIP SERIES (cont.)

GAME 6										
Astros	0	0	2	1	0	1	1	0	0	**5**
Cardinals	0	0	0	0	1	0	0	0	0	**1**

W—Oswalt. **L**—Mulder. **LOB**—Hou: 7; StL: 6. **S**—Hou: Oswalt, Everett, Taveras. **SF**—StL: Rodriguez. **2B**—StL: Walker. **HR**—Hou: Lane. **HBP**—StL: Eckstein, Grudzielanek. **WP**—Hou: Tavarez; StL: Mulder 2. **T**—2:53. **A**—52,438.

Recap: Roy Oswalt took the Houston Astros' 44-year-old quest for a World Series berth on his shoulders and denied St. Louis its second straight Series appearance. Oswalt, now 4–0 in his postseason career, struck out six and gave up three hits in seven innings. Houston got the lead in the third in typical fashion: a wild pitch and Craig Biggio's RBI single made it 2–0. That gave Oswalt all he needed to "go right at 'em." Jason Lane added a solo homer in the fourth.

DID YOU KNOW?

Bobby Abreu of the Philadelphia Phillies set a Home Run Derby record for both a single round (24, in Round 1) and overall (41) in winning the contest at the 2005 All-Star Game.

MLB 2005 PLAYOFFS – AMERICAN LEAGUE

AMERICAN LEAGUE DIVISION SERIES

October 4	Yankees 4, Angels 2	October 9	Yankees 3, Angels 2
October 6	Angels 5, Yankees 3	October 10	Angels 5, Yankees 3
October 7	Angels 11, Yankees 7		

(LOS ANGELES ANGELS WON SERIES, 3–2)

October 4	White Sox 14, Red Sox 2	October 7	White Sox 5, Red Sox 3
October 5	White Sox 5, Red Sox 4		

(CHICAGO WHITE SOX WON SERIES, 3–0)

AMERICAN LEAGUE CHAMPIONSHIP SERIES

October 11	Angels 3, White Sox 2	October 15	White Sox 8, Angels 2
October 12	White Sox 2, Angels 1	October 18	White Sox 6, Angels 3
October 14	White Sox 5, Angels 2		

(CHICAGO WHITE SOX WON SERIES, 4–1)

GAME 1										
Angels	0	1	2	0	0	0	0	0	0	**3**
White Sox	0	0	1	1	0	0	0	0	0	**2**

W—Byrd. **L**—Contreras. **SV**—Rodriguez. **E**—LA: Figgins. **LOB**—LA: 4; Chi: 6. **S**—LA: Figgins. **HR**—LA: Anderson; Chi: Crede. **SB**—LA: Figgins, Erstad. **CS**—Chi: Podsednik, Pierzynski. **HBP**—Chi: Rowand. **T**—2:47. **A**—40,659.

Recap: Working on three days rest, Paul Byrd and the jet-lagged Angels gave up five hits in six-plus innings to the well-rested White Sox. Garret Anderson led off the second inning with his third homer of the postseason. In the third, Los Angeles scrambled for a 3–0 lead with a hit-and-run single, a sacrifice bunt, an infield hit, and a bouncer back to the mound. A Joe Crede homer and A.J. Pierzynski's tough two-out RBI single in the fourth closed it to 3–2, but Byrd and the Angels bullpen held on to take the opener.

GAME 2										
Angels	0	0	0	0	1	0	0	0	0	**1**
White Sox	1	0	0	0	0	0	0	0	1	**2**

W—Buehrle. **L**—Escobar. **E**—LA: Washburn, Guerrero, Paul; Chi: Uribe. **LOB**—LA: 4; Chi: 7. **2B**—LA: Cabrera; Chi: Rowand, Crede, 2. **HR**—LA: Quinlan. **SB**—Chi: Ozuna. **HBP**—LA: B. Molina; Chi: Iguchi. **GIDP**—LA: Kennedy, Guerrero. **PB**—Chi: Pierzynski. **T**—2:34. **A**—41,013.

Recap: A.J. Pierzynski struck out swinging to end the ninth inning and send the game into extra innings — or so the Angels thought. Pierzynski and home plate umpire Doug Eddings saw things differently. Pierzynski saw a third strike that hit the dirt and ran to first base. Eddings called him safe when Angels catcher Josh Paul rolled the ball back to the

mound, believing the inning over. Joe Crede followed with a two-out double, and Mark Buehrle pitched a complete-game five-hitter to decide this controversial game and even the series at a game apiece.

GAME 3										
White Sox	3	0	1	0	1	0	0	0	0	**5**
Angels	0	0	0	0	0	2	0	0	0	**2**

W—Garland. **L**—Lackey. **LOB**—Chi: 6; LA: 1. **2B**—Chi: Dye, Iguchi; LA: Erstad. **HR**—Chi: Konerko; LA: Cabrera. **GIDP**—Chi: Rowand; LA: Guerrero. **T**—2:42. **A**—44,725.

Recap: No controversy in this one. Jon Garland pitched Chicago's second straight complete game, a four-hitter, and Paul Konerko hit a two-run homer to help the White Sox dominate John Lackey and the quiet Angels bats and take the series lead, two games to one.

GAME 4										
White Sox	3	0	1	1	1	0	0	2	0	**8**
Angels	0	1	0	1	0	0	0	0	0	**2**

W—Garcia. **L**—Santana. **E**—Chi: Garcia; LA: Cabrera. **LOB**—Chi: 5; LA: 4. **2B**—Chi: Rowand; LA: Kotchman. **3B**—Chi: Podsednik. **HR**—Chi: Konerko, Pierzynski. **SB**—Chi: Podsednik 2, Dye. **CS**—Chi: Crede. **HBP**—Chi: Iguchi. **GIDP**—Chi: Uribe; LA: Finley. **T**—2:46. **A**—44,857.

Recap: Chicago put itself on the verge of its first World Series appearance since 1959 with Freddy Garcia's complete-game victory — the third-straight for the White Sox. Paul Konerko homered in the first inning again, daring the Angels to play catch-up against his determined White Sox.

AMERICAN LEAGUE CHAMPIONSHIP SERIES (cont.)

GAME 5

White Sox	0	1	0	0	1	0	1	1	2	**6**
Angels	0	0	1	0	2	0	0	0	0	**3**

W—Contreras. **L**—Byrd. **SV**— . **E**—Chi: Contreras; LA: Escobar, Kennedy. **PB**—Chi: Pierzynski. **LOB**—Chi: 9; LA: 4. **2B**—Chi: Rowand, Uribe, Dye, Konerko; LA: Rivera, Figgins. **HR**—Chi: Crede. **S**—Chi: Pierzynski; LA: Figgins. **SF**—Chi: Crede; Rowand; LA: Anderson. **HBP**—Chi: Iguchi. **T**—3:11. **A**—44,712.

Recap: Chicago made it an even four in a row — victories, complete games, and emphatic statements that they are the team to beat in the World Series. Jose Contreras retired the last 15 batters in the game. The victory gave the White Sox the most consecutive complete games in a postseason since the 1956 New York Yankees. Joe Crede tied the game in the seventh with a leadoff homer. Pierzynski, who seemed to be in the middle of every contested call in this series, was called out — then called safe — on a tag play at first. Crede followed with a single to put Chicago up for good.

2005 WORLD SERIES

October 23	White Sox 5, Astros 3	October 26	White Sox 7, Astros 5
October 24	White Sox 7, Astros 6	October 27	White Sox 1, Astros 0

(CHICAGO WHITE SOX WON SERIES, 4–0)

GAME 1

Astros	0	1	2	0	0	0	0	0	0	**3**
White Sox	1	2	0	1	0	0	0	1	x	**5**

W—Contreras. **L**—Rodriguez. **SV**—Jenks. **E**—Hou: Everett. **LOB**—Hou: 6; Chi: 9. **S**—Hou: Taveras; Chi: Everett. **2B**—Hou: Berkman, Taveras 2; Chi: Uribe. **3B**—Chi: Podsednik. **HR**—Hou: Lamb; Chi: Dye, Crede. **SB**—Hou: Burke; Chi: Podsednik, Pierzynski. **HBP**—Hou: Bagwell 2, Ausmus. **GIDP**—Hou: Lane; Chi: Iguchi, Pierzynski. **T**—3:13. **A**—41,206.

Recap: Chicago was trying to win its first World Series game since 1959. Houston was trying to win its first World Series game ever. Roger Clemens, trying to become the oldest pitcher to win a World Series game, was not sharp, and came out after two innings with a hamstring injury. Joe Crede broke a 3–3 tie in the fourth with a solo homer. That was enough for Jose Contreras and the rarely-seen White Sox bullpen, which shut down and shut out the Astros after the third.

GAME 2

Astros	0	1	1	0	2	0	0	0	2	**6**
White Sox	0	2	0	0	0	0	4	0	1	**7**

W—Cotts. **L**—Lidge. **LOB**—Hou: 4; Chi: 5. **SF**—Hou: Berkman. **2B**—Hou: Ausmus, Berkman; Chi: Uribe 2, Rowand. **3B**—Hou: Taveras. **HR**—Hou: Ensberg; Chi: Konerko, Podsednik. **SB**—Hou: Lane; Chi: Uribe. **CS**—Chi: Everett. **HBP**—Chi: Dye. **T**—3:11. **A**—41,432.

Recap: Andy Pettitte delivered another strong performance. He had left Game 5 of the championship series with a 4–2 lead after seven innings, only to see Albert Pujols defeat Brad Lidge and the Astros with a three-run homer. He left this game after six innings, again leading 4–2. Paul Konerko's two-out grand slam in the seventh put Chicago ahead after a controversial call. The umpire awarded first base to Jermaine Dye on a swinging strike, when it appeared the ball hit him. Replays show that the ball hit his bat. Houston scored twice in the ninth to tie the game, setting the stage for another dramatic finish. Lidge came after Scott Podsednik, who had not homered in 507 at-bats this season, with a 2-and-1 fastball. Podsednik saw the pitch over the middle of the plate and knocked it over the right-center field fence for a walk-off homer.

GAME 3

White Sox	0	0	0	0	5	0	0	0	0	0	0	0	0	2	**7**
Astros	1	0	2	1	0	0	0	1	0	0	0	0	0	0	**5**

W— Marte. **L**—Astacio. **SV**— Buehrle. **E**—Chi: Uribe 2, Hernandez; Hou: Ensberg. **LOB**—Chi: 15; Hou: 15. **S**—Hou: Oswalt, Everett. **2B**—Chi: Konerko, Pierzynski; Hou: Biggio, Lane. **HR**—Chi: Crede, Blum; Hou: Lane. **SB**—Chi: Podsednik, Harris; Hou: Burke. **CS**—Hou: Everett. **HBP**—Chi: Crede, Konerko; Hou: Taveras. **GIDP**—Chi: Dye, Podsednik, Konerko; Hou: Ensberg, Ausmus. **T**—5:41. **A**—42,848.

Recap: In the longest game in World Series history, in which the two teams used 17 pitchers — the most in history — again it came down to a single deciding pitch and swing. With two outs in the 14th inning, former Astro Geoff Blum, batting for the first time in a World Series, slugged a two-out solo homer to break a 5–5 tie. Chicago, which had earlier — much earlier — come back from a 4–0 deficit to score five runs in the fifth inning against Roy Oswalt, added an insurance run with a bases-loaded walk. Starter Mark Buehrle — who pitched seven innings in Game 2 two nights earlier — got Chicago out of a jam in the bottom of the inning to get the last out.

GAME 4

White Sox	0	0	0	0	0	0	0	1	0	**1**
Astros	0	0	0	0	0	0	0	0	0	**0**

W—Garcia. **L**—Lidge. **SV**—Jenks. **LOB**—Chi: 7; Hou: 9. **S**—Chi: Podsednik; Hou: Taveras, Ausmus. **2B**—Chi: Dye, Crede, Pierzynski; Hou: Lamb. **3B**—Chi: Podsednik. **SB**—Hou: Berkman, Taveras. **HBP**—Hou: Taveras. **GIDP**—Hou: Everett. **WP**—Chi: Politte. **T**—3:20. **A**—42,936.

Recap: Chicago shut down Houston for the sweep — its eighth consecutive postseason win and first World Series title since 1917. White Sox starter Freddy Garcia and Houston's Brandon Backe pitched shutout ball for seven innings. Chicago broke through in the eighth off Brad Lidge, who would probably like to forget his recent postseason experience. Willie Harris, pinch-hitting for Garcia, singled, was sacrificed to second, and scored on Jermaine Dye's single up the middle. Reliever Neal Cotts got Chicago out of a first-and-second, one-out jam in the bottom of the inning, and Bobby Jenks preserved the victory in the ninth. Dye was named the series MVP.

TODAY'S STARS

■ **Andruw Jones, outfielder,** b. April 23, 1977, Willemstad, Curacao. Jones announced himself to the baseball world with his bat in 1996, then used his glove to become a star as the best defensive outfielder in baseball. In 2005, he put it all together for the best season of his career. As a 19-year-old rookie in 1996, Jones blasted two home runs in Game 1 of the World Series, the youngest player ever to do so. Two seasons later, he began a string of eight consecutive Gold Gloves in centerfield. In 2005, he hit 51 home runs, setting a new single-season record for a Braves player. He added 128 RBIs, the fourth time he's topped 100 RBIs, and made his fourth All-Star team, helping the Braves to their 14th straight division title.

■ **Manny Ramirez, outfielder,** b. May 30, 1972, Santo Domingo, Dominican Republic. He may sometimes look indifferent in the outfield or confused on the basepaths, but Ramirez is one of the best hitters in baseball. The 2005 season was the eighth straight in which he has smacked at least 30 home runs (he finished with 45) and driven in more than 100 runs (144). Since becoming a regular in 1994, Ramirez has more RBIs (1,409) than any other player in baseball. A nine-time All-Star, he's batted .300 or better nine times. He also comes through in the clutch. He is second all-time with 21 grand slams and was named MVP of the 2004 World Series, when the Red Sox won their first championship since 1918.

■ **Mariano Rivera, pitcher,** b. November 29, 1969, Panama City, Panama. Rivera is already known as the best closer in post-season history. Now, he is marching toward the title of best closer of all time. In 2005, he posted another dominant season: 7–4 with 43 saves in 47 chances, a 1.38 ERA, and 80 strikeouts in 78.1 innings. He made his seventh All-Star team and finished second in the Cy Young voting. His 379 saves (99 short of record-holder Lee Smith's 478) rank fifth all-time and first in American League history. His 34 saves and 0.81 ERA are post-season records.

Andruw Jones added a home-run title to his Gold Glove collection.

TOM DiPACE

TRIVIA CHALLENGE

The Chicago White Sox tied a major league record by going 11–1 in the 2005 postseason. Which World Series champion also went 11–1 on its way to a title?

The 1999 New York Yankees

MLB 2005 PLAYOFFS COMPOSITE BOX SCORES

NATIONAL LEAGUE CHAMPIONSHIP SERIES

HOUSTON ASTROS

BATTING	AB	R	H	HR	RBI	BA
Biggio	24	2	8	0	3	.333
Everett	23	2	7	0	2	.304
Ausmus	22	3	7	0	1	.318
Lane	21	3	5	2	3	.238
Ensberg	21	1	5	0	2	.238
Berkman	21	2	6	1	3	.286
Burke	20	5	6	1	3	.300
Lamb	16	3	3	1	2	.188
Taveras	14	1	5	0	0	.357
Palmeiro	3	0	1	0	0	.333
Clemens	2	0	1	0	0	.500
Backe	2	0	0	0	0	.000
Pettitte	2	0	0	0	0	.000
Vizcaino	2	0	0	0	0	.000
Bagwell	1	0	0	0	0	.000
Bruntlett	1	0	0	0	0	.000

PITCHING	G	IP	H	BB	SO	ERA
Oswalt	2	14.0	8	4	12	1.29
Pettitte	2	12.1	15	4	6	5.11
Clemens	1	6.0	6	2	1	3.00
Backe	1	5.2	2	3	7	1.59
Lidge	4	5.0	6	2	7	7.20
Qualls	4	4.2	0	0	4	0.00
Wheeler	3	2.2	2	0	2	0.00
Springer	1	1.0	0	1	1	0.00
Astacio	1	1.0	0	0	2	0.00
Gallo	2	0.2	0	0	0	0.00

ST. LOUIS CARDINALS

BATTING	AB	R	H	HR	RBI	BA
Grudzielanek	22	2	5	0	2	.227
Molina	22	1	7	0	0	.318
Eckstein	20	5	4	0	2	.200
Edmonds	19	2	4	0	0	.211
Walker	19	0	3	0	1	.158
Sanders	18	1	3	1	2	.167
Nunez	13	1	5	0	0	.385
Mabry	8	0	1	0	1	.125
Taguchi	6	0	0	0	0	.000
Carpenter	4	0	0	0	1	.000
Luna	4	0	0	0	0	.000
Mulder	3	0	0	0	0	.000
Rodriguez	2	1	0	0	1	.000
Suppan	2	0	0	0	0	.000
Marquis	1	0	0	0	0	.000
Morris	1	0	0	0	0	.000

PITCHING	G	IP	H	BB	SO	ERA
Carpenter	2	15.0	14	4	9	3.00
Mulder	2	11.2	14	3	8	3.09
Morris	1	5.1	8	1	3	5.06
Marquis	3	5.1	6	3	4	3.38
Suppan	1	5.0	3	3	5	1.80
Isringhausen	3	4.0	3	0	2	0.00
Tavarez	3	3.1	5	0	2	5.40
Flores	2	1.1	0	1	0	0.00
Thompson	2	1.0	2	0	0	0.00

AMERICAN LEAGUE CHAMPIONSHIP SERIES

CHICAGO WHITE SOX

BATTING	AB	R	H	HR	RBI	BA
Konerko	21	2	6	2	7	.286
Everett	20	2	5	0	3	.250
Crede	19	2	7	2	7	.368
Dye	19	3	5	0	3	.263
Pierzynski	18	1	3	1	2	.167
Rowand	18	3	3	0	1	.167
Iguchi	17	4	3	0	0	.176
Podsednik	17	4	5	0	0	.294
Uribe	16	1	4	0	0	.250
Ozuna	0	1	0	0	0	.000

PITCHING	G	IP	H	BB	SO	ERA
Contreras	2	17.1	12	2	6	3.12
Garcia	1	9.0	6	1	5	2.00
Garland	1	9.0	4	1	7	2.00
Buehrle	1	9.0	5	0	4	1.00
Cotts	1	0.2	0	0	0	0.00

LOS ANGELES ANGELS

BATTING	AB	R	H	HR	RBI	BA
Cabrera	20	1	4	1	3	.200
Guerrero	20	0	1	0	1	.050
Anderson	17	2	3	1	2	.176
Figgins	17	1	2	0	1	.118
B. Molina	17	0	2	0	1	.118
Erstad	17	1	4	0	0	.235
Kennedy	14	3	4	0	1	.286
Finley	9	1	2	0	0	.222
Rivera	9	1	1	0	0	.111
Kotchman	7	0	2	0	1	.286
Quinlan	3	1	1	1	1	.333
J. Molina	3	0	1	0	1	.333
DaVanon	1	0	0	0	0	.000
Izturis	0	0	0	0	0	.000
Paul	0	0	0	0	0	.000

PITCHING	G	IP	H	BB	SO	ERA
Byrd	2	10.2	10	2	2	3.38
Shields	4	6.0	4	1	5	0.00
Lackey	1	5.0	8	1	3	9.00
Washburn	1	4.2	4	1	1	0.00
Escobar	2	4.1	4	2	10	2.08
Santana	1	4.1	3	3	2	10.38
Donnelly	3	3.1	2	1	5	0.00
Rodriguez	2	2.1	2	3	3	0.00
Yan	1	2.0	3	1	2	9.00
Gregg	1	2.0	1	1	3	0.00

KEY AB=at-bats; R=runs; H=hits; HR=home runs; RBI=runs batted in; BA=batting average; G=games; IP=innings pitched; BB=bases on balls; SO=strikeouts; ERA=earned run average

2005 WORLD SERIES COMPOSITE BOX SCORES

CHICAGO WHITE SOX

BATTING	AB	R	H	HR	RBI	BA
Podsednik	21	2	6	1	2	.286
Iguchi	18	2	3	0	1	.167
Crede	17	2	5	2	3	.294
Rowand	17	2	5	0	0	.294
Uribe	16	2	4	0	2	.250
Konerko	16	1	4	1	4	.250
Dye	16	3	7	1	3	.438
Pierzynski	15	3	4	0	3	.267
Everett	9	1	4	0	0	.444
Garland	3	0	0	0	0	.000
Garcia	2	0	0	0	0	.000
Blum	1	1	1	1	1	1.000
Harris	1	1	1	0	0	1.000
Perez	1	0	0	0	0	.000
Widger	1	0	0	0	1	.000
Buehrle	0	0	0	0	0	.000
Cotts	0	0	0	0	0	.000
Hermanson	0	0	0	0	0	.000
Hernandez	0	0	0	0	0	.000
Jenks	0	0	0	0	0	.000
Marte	0	0	0	0	0	.000
Politte	0	0	0	0	0	.000
Vizcaino	0	0	0	0	0	.000

PITCHING	G	IP	H	BB	SO	ERA
Buehrle	2	7.1	7	0	6	4.91
Contreras	1	7.0	6	0	2	3.86
Garcia	1	7.0	4	3	7	0.00
Garland	1	7.0	7	2	4	2.57
Jenks	4	5.0	3	2	7	3.60
Politte	3	2.1	0	2	2	3.86
Marte	1	1.2	0	2	3	0.00
Cotts	4	1.1	1	1	2	0.00
Hernandez	1	1.0	0	4	2	0.00
Vizcaino	1	1.0	0	1	0	0.00

HOUSTON ASTROS

BATTING	AB	R	H	HR	RBI	BA
Biggio	18	3	4	0	1	.222
Ensberg	18	2	2	1	2	.111
Lane	18	1	4	1	2	.222
Ausmus	16	1	4	0	0	.250
Taveras	15	2	5	0	0	.333
Everett	15	2	1	0	0	.067
Berkman	13	0	5	0	6	.385
Lamb	10	1	2	1	1	.200
Bagwell	8	1	1	0	0	.125
Burke	5	1	0	0	0	.000
Vizcaino	2	0	1	0	2	.500
Backe	2	0	0	0	0	.000
Palmeiro	2	0	0	0	0	.000
Oswalt	1	0	0	0	0	.000
Estacio	0	0	0	0	0	.000
Bruntlett	0	0	0	0	0	.000
Gallo	0	0	0	0	0	.000
Lidge	0	0	0	0	0	.000
Qualls	0	0	0	0	0	.000
Rodriguez	0	0	0	0	0	.000
Springer	0	0	0	0	0	.000
Wheeler	0	0	0	0	0	.000

PITCHING	G	IP	H	BB	SO	ERA
Backe	1	7.0	5	0	7	0.00
Pettitte	1	6.0	8	0	4	3.00
Oswalt	1	6.0	8	5	3	7.50
Qualls	3	5.1	3	2	5	1.69
Lidge	3	3.2	4	0	6	4.91
Rodriguez	2	3.2	4	5	2	2.45
Clemens	1	2.0	4	0	1	13.50
Springer	2	2.0	2	0	1	4.50
Wheeler	2	2.0	2	1	1	13.50
Gallo	2	1.0	0	0	0	0.00
Estacio	1	0.2	4	2	0	27.00

DID YOU KNOW?

Game 4 of the National League Division Series between the Houston Astros and Atlanta Braves was the longest post-season game in innings played (18) in baseball history. (Houston won, 7–6.) Sixteen days later, the Astros played the longest game in time (5 hours 41 minutes) in World Series history. (They lost to the Chicago White Sox, 7–5.)

2005 MLB INDIVIDUAL LEADERS

NATIONAL LEAGUE BATTING

BATTING AVERAGE

Derrek Lee, Chi	.335
Albert Pujols, StL	.330
Miguel Cabrera, Fla	.323
Todd Helton, Col	.320
Sean Casey, Cin	.312
Chad Tracy, Ari	.308
Matt Holliday, Col	.307
Brady Clark, Mil	.306
David Wright, NY	.306
Jason Bay, Pit	.306
Randy Winn, SF	.306
Aramis Ramirez, Chi	.302

HITS

Derrek Lee, Chi	199
Miguel Cabrera, Fla	198
Jimmy Rollins, Phi	196
Albert Pujols, StL	195
Jose Reyes, NY	190
David Eckstein, StL	185
Brady Clark, Mil	183
Jason Bay, Pit	183
Juan Pierre, Fla	181
David Wright, NY	176

DOUBLES

Derrek Lee, Chi	50
Randy Winn, SF	47
Marcus Giles, Atl	45
Todd Helton, Col	45
Jason Bay, Pit	44
Two tied with 43.	

TRIPLES

Jose Reyes, NY	17
Juan Pierre, Fla	13
Rafael Furcal, Atl	11
Jimmy Rollins, Phi	11
Dave Roberts, SD	10
Brian Giles, SD	8

HOME RUNS

Andruw Jones, Atl	51
Derrek Lee, Chi	46
Albert Pujols, StL	41
Adam Dunn, Cin	40
Troy Glaus, Ari	37
Morgan Ensberg, Hou	36
Ken Griffey, Jr., Cin	35
Cliff Floyd, NY	34
Miguel Cabrera, Fla	33
Carlos Delgado, Fla	33

RUNS SCORED

Albert Pujols, StL	129
Derrek Lee, Chi	120
Jimmy Rollins, Phi	115
Jason Bay, Pit	110
Adam Dunn, Cin	107
Miguel Cabrera, Fla	106
Marcus Giles, Atl	104
Bobby Abreu, Phi	104
Rafael Furcal, Atl	100
Jeff Kent, LA	100

TOTAL BASES

Derrek Lee, Chi	393
Albert Pujols, StL	360
Miguel Cabrera, Fla	344
Andruw Jones, Atl	337
Jason Bay, Pit	335

STOLEN BASES

Jose Reyes, NY	60
Juan Pierre, Fla	57
Rafael Furcal, Atl	46
Jimmy Rollins, Phi	41
Ryan Freel, Cin	36
Willy Taveras, Hou	34

RUNS BATTED IN

Andruw Jones, Atl	128
Pat Burrell, Phi	117
Albert Pujols, StL	117
Miguel M. Cabrera, Fla	116
Carlos Delgado, Fla	115
Carlos Lee, Mil	114
Derrek Lee, Chi	107
Jeff Kent, LA	105
Chase Utley, Phi	105
Two tied with 102.	

SLUGGING PERCENTAGE

Derrek Lee, Chi	.662
Albert Pujols, StL	.609
Carlos Delgado, Fla	.582
Ken Griffey, Jr., Cin	.576
Andruw Jones, Atl	.575

ON-BASE PERCENTAGE

Todd Helton, Col	.445
Albert Pujols, StL	.430
Brian Giles, SD	.423
Derrek Lee, Chi	.418
Lance Berkman, Hou	.411

BASES ON BALLS

Brian Giles, SD	119
Bobby Abreu, Phi	117
Adam Dunn, Cin	114
Todd Helton, Col	106
Pat Burrell, Phi	99

Dontrelle Willis, Marlins

DAVID J. PHILLIP/AP

NATIONAL LEAGUE PITCHING

EARNED RUN AVERAGE

Roger Clemens, Hou	1.87
Andy Pettitte, Hou	2.39
Dontrelle Willis, Fla	2.63
Pedro Martinez, NY	2.82
Chris Carpenter, StL	2.83
Jake Peavy, SD	2.88
Roy Oswalt, Hou	2.94
John Smoltz, Atl	3.06
John Patterson, Was	3.13
Carlos Zambrano, Chi	3.26

SAVES

Chad Cordero, Was	47
Trevor Hoffman, SD	43
Brad Lidge, Hou	42
Todd Jones, Fla	40
Derrick Turnbow, Mil	39
Jason Isringhausen, StL	39
Billy Wagner, Phi	38
Ryan Dempster, Chi	33
Brian Fuentes, Col	31
Braden Looper, NY	28

WINS

Dontrelle Willis, Fla	22
Chris Carpenter, StL	21
Roy Oswalt, Hou	20
Chris Capuano, Mil	18
Andy Pettitte, Hou	17
Jon Lieber, Phi	17
Mark Mulder, StL	16
Jeff Suppan, StL	16
Josh Beckett, Fla	15
Pedro Martinez, NY	15
Livan Hernandez, Was	15

GAMES PITCHED

Scott Eyre, SF	86
Gary Majewski, Was	79
Duaner Sanchez, LA	79
Four tied with 78.	

INNINGS PITCHED

Livan Hernandez, Was	246.1
Roy Oswalt, Hou	241.2
Chris Carpenter, StL	241.2
Dontrelle Willis, Fla	236.1
John Smoltz, Atl	229.2
Brandon Webb, Ari	229.0
Greg Maddux, Chi	225.0

STRIKEOUTS

Jake Peavy, SD	216
Chris Carpenter, StL	213
Doug Davis, Mil	208
Pedro Martinez, NY	208
Brett Myers, Phi	208
Carlos Zambrano, Chi	202
A.J. Burnett, Fla	198
Javier Vazquez, Ari	192
Mark Prior, Chi	188
Two tied with 185.	

COMPLETE GAMES

Dontrelle Willis, Fla	7
Chris Carpenter, StL	7
A.J. Burnett, Fla	4
Roy Oswalt, Hou	4
Pedro Martinez, NY	4

SHUTOUTS

Dontrelle Willis, Fla	5
Chris Carpenter, StL	4
Jake Peavy, SD	3
Four tied with 2.	

Note: Players listed under batting average must have had at least 3.1 plate appearances per game.

AMERICAN LEAGUE BATTING

BATTING AVERAGE

Michael Young, Tex	.331
Alex Rodriguez, NY	.321
Vladimir Guerrero, LA	.317
Johnny Damon, Bos	.316
Brian Roberts, Bal	.314
Derek Jeter, NY	.309
Travis Hafner, Cle	.305
Victor Martinez, Cle	.305
Hideki Matsui, NY	.305
Miguel Tejada, Bal	.304
Ichiro Suzuki, Sea	.303

HITS

Michael Young, Tex	221
Ichiro Suzuki, Sea	206
Derek Jeter, NY	202
Miguel Tejada, Bal	199
Johnny Damon, Bos	197
Alex Rodriguez, NY	194
Carl Crawford, TB	194
Mark Teixeira, Tex	194
Hideki Matsui, NY	192
Chone Figgins, LA	186

DOUBLES

Miguel Tejada, Bal	50
Brian Roberts, Bal	45
Hideki Matsui, NY	45
Alfonso Soriano, Tex	43
Two tied with 42.	

Michael Young, Rangers

JOSH MERWIN

TRIPLES

Carl Crawford, TB	15
Ichiro Suzuki, Sea	12
Grady Sizemore, Cle	11
Chone Figgins, LA	10
Brandon Inge, Det	9
Brian Roberts, Bal	7

HOME RUNS

Alex Rodriguez, NY	48
David Ortiz, Bos	47
Manny Ramirez, Bos	45
Mark Teixeira, Tex	43
Paul Konerko, Chi	40
Richie Sexson, Sea	39
Alfonso Soriano, Tex	36
Gary Sheffield, NY	34
Travis Hafner, Cle	33
Vladimir Guerrero, LA	32
Jason Giambi, NY	32

RUNS SCORED

Alex Rodriguez, NY	124
Derek Jeter, NY	122
David Ortiz, Bos	119
Johnny Damon, Bos	117
Michael Young, Tex	114
Chone Figgins, LA	113
Manny Ramirez, Bos	112
Mark Teixeira, Tex	112
Grady Sizemore, Cle	111
Ichiro Suzuki, Sea	111

TOTAL BASES

Mark Teixeira, Tex	370
Alex Rodriguez, NY	369
David Ortiz, Bos	363
Michael Young, Tex	343
Miguel Tejada, Bal	337

STOLEN BASES

Chone Figgins, LA	62
Scott Podsednik, Chi	59
Carl Crawford, TB	46
Julio Lugo, TB	39
Ichiro Suzuki, Sea	33
Alfonso Soriano, Tex	30

RUNS BATTED IN

David Ortiz, Bos	148
Manny Ramirez, Bos	144
Mark Teixeira, Tex	144
Alex Rodriguez, NY	130
Gary Sheffield, NY	123
Richie Sexson, Sea	121
Jorge L. Cantu, TB	117
Hideki Matsui, NY	116
Travis Hafner, Cle	108
Vladimir Guerrero, LA	108

SLUGGING PERCENTAGE

Alex Rodriguez, NY	.610
David Ortiz, Bos	.604
Travis Hafner, Cle	.595
Manny Ramirez, Bos	.594
Mark Teixeira, Tex	.575

ON-BASE PERCENTAGE

Jason Giambi, NY	.440
Alex Rodriguez, NY	.421
Travis Hafner, Cle	.408
David Ortiz, Bos	.397
Vladimir Guerrero, LA	.394

BASES ON BALLS

Jason Giambi, NY	108
David Ortiz, Bos	102
Alex Rodriguez, NY	91
Richie Sexson, Sea	89
Paul Konerko, Chi	81

AMERICAN LEAGUE PITCHING

EARNED RUN AVERAGE

Kevin Millwood, Cle	2.86
Johan Santana, Min	2.87
Mark Buehrle, Chi	3.12
Jarrod Washburn, LA	3.20
John Lackey, LA	3.44
Carlos Silva, Min	3.44
Kenny Rogers, Tex	3.46
Bartolo Colon, LA	3.48
Jon Garland, Chi	3.50
Joe Blanton, Oak	3.53

SAVES

Bob Wickman, Cle	45
Francisco Rodriguez, LA	45
Joe Nathan, Min	43
Mariano Rivera, NY	43
Danys Baez, TB	41
Francisco Cordero, Tex	37
B.J. Ryan, Bal	36
Eddie Guardado, Sea	36
Dustin Hermanson, Chi	34
Miguel Batista, Tor	31

WINS

Bartolo Colon, LA	21
Jon Garland, Chi	18
Cliff Lee, Cle	18
Randy Johnson, NY	17
Tim Wakefield, Bos	16
Mark Buehrle, Chi	16
Johan Santana, Min	16
Five tied with 15.	

GAMES PITCHED

Mike Timlin, Bos	81
Scott Schoeneweis, Tor	80
Tom Gordon, NY	79
Bob Howry, Cle	79
Scot Shields, LA	78

INNINGS PITCHED

Mark Buehrle, Chi	236.2
Johan Santana, Min	231.2
Barry Zito, Oak	228.1
Freddy Garcia, Chi	228.0
Randy Johnson, NY	225.2
Tim Wakefield, Bos	225.1
Bartolo Colon, LA	222.2

STRIKEOUTS

Johan Santana, Min	238
Randy Johnson, NY	211
John Lackey, LA	199
Scott Kazmir, TB	174
Barry Zito, Oak	171
Dan Haren, Oak	163
C.C. Sabathia, Cle	161
Daniel Cabrera, Bal	157
Bartolo Colon, LA	157
Jose Contreras, Chi	154
Tim Wakefield, Bos	151
Mark Buehrle, Chi	149

COMPLETE GAMES

Roy Halladay, Tor	5
Jeremy Bonderman, Det	4
Randy Johnson, NY	4
Six tied with 3.	

SHUTOUTS

Jon Garland, Chi	3
Johan Santana, Min	2
Mike Mussina, NY	2
Roy Halladay, Tor	2

2005 REGULAR SEASON TEAM STATS

NATIONAL LEAGUE

TEAM BATTING

TEAM BATTING	G	AB	R	H	2B	3B	HR	RBI	TB	BB	SO	SB	OBP	SLG	BA
Florida	162	5,502	717	1,499	306	32	128	678	2,253	512	918	96	.339	.409	.272
Chicago	162	5,584	703	1,506	323	23	194	674	2,457	419	920	65	.324	.440	.270
Philadelphia	162	5,542	807	1,494	282	35	167	760	2,348	639	1,083	116	.348	.424	.270
St. Louis	162	5,538	805	1,494	287	26	170	757	2,343	534	947	83	.339	.423	.270
Colorado	162	5,542	740	1,477	280	34	150	704	2,275	509	1,103	65	.333	.411	.267
Atlanta	162	5,486	769	1,453	308	37	184	733	2,387	534	1,084	92	.333	.435	.265
Cincinnati	163	5,565	820	1,453	335	15	222	784	2,484	611	1,303	72	.339	.446	.261
San Francisco	162	5,462	649	1,427	299	26	128	617	2,162	431	901	71	.319	.396	.261
Milwaukee	162	5,448	726	1,413	327	19	175	689	2,303	531	1,162	79	.331	.423	.259
Pittsburgh	162	5,573	680	1,445	292	38	139	656	2,230	471	1,092	73	.322	.400	.259
New York	162	5,505	722	1,421	279	32	175	683	2,289	486	1,075	153	.322	.416	.258
San Diego	162	5,502	684	1,416	269	39	130	655	2,153	600	977	99	.333	.391	.257
Arizona	162	5,550	696	1,419	291	27	191	670	2,337	606	1,094	67	.332	.421	.256
Houston	163	5,462	693	1,400	281	32	161	654	2,228	481	1,037	115	.322	.408	.256
Los Angeles	162	5,433	685	1,374	284	21	149	653	2,147	541	1,094	58	.326	.395	.253
Washington	162	5,426	639	1,367	311	32	117	615	2,093	491	1,090	45	.322	.386	.252

TEAM PITCHING

TEAM PITCHING	W	L	ERA	CG	SHO	SV	INN	H	R	ER	BB	SO
St. Louis	100	62	3.49	15	14	48	1,445.2	1,399	634	560	443	974
Houston	89	73	3.51	6	11	45	1,443.0	1,336	609	563	440	1,164
New York	83	79	3.76	8	11	38	1,435.2	1,390	648	599	491	1,012
Washington	81	81	3.87	4	9	51	1,458.0	1,456	673	627	539	997
Atlanta	90	72	3.97	8	12	38	1,443.2	1,487	674	635	520	929
Milwaukee	81	81	3.98	7	6	46	1,438.0	1,382	697	636	569	1,173
San Diego	82	80	4.13	4	8	45	1,455.1	1,452	726	668	503	1,133
Florida	83	79	4.16	14	10	42	1,442.1	1,459	732	666	563	1,125
Chicago	79	83	4.19	8	15	39	1,440.0	1,357	714	671	576	1,256
Philadelphia	88	74	4.21	4	6	40	1,435.0	1,379	726	672	487	1,159
San Francisco	75	87	4.33	4	8	46	1,444.1	1,456	745	695	592	972
Los Angeles	71	91	4.38	6	9	40	1,427.1	1,434	755	695	471	1,004
Pittsburgh	67	95	4.42	4	14	35	1,436.0	1,456	769	706	612	958
Arizona	77	85	4.84	6	10	45	1,456.1	1,580	856	788	537	1,038
Colorado	67	95	5.13	4	4	37	1,418.2	1,600	862	808	604	981
Cincinnati	73	89	5.15	2	1	31	1,433.0	1,657	889	820	492	955

AMERICAN LEAGUE

TEAM BATTING

TEAM BATTING	G	AB	R	H	2B	3B	HR	RBI	TB	BB	SO	SB	OBP	SLG	BA
Boston	162	5,626	910	1,579	339	21	199	863	2,557	653	1,044	45	.357	.454	.281
New York	162	5,624	886	1,552	259	16	229	847	2,530	637	989	84	.355	.450	.276
Tampa Bay	162	5,552	750	1,519	289	40	157	717	2,359	412	990	151	.329	.425	.274
Detroit	162	5,602	723	1,521	283	45	168	678	2,398	384	1,038	66	.321	.428	.272
Cleveland	162	5,609	790	1,522	337	30	207	760	2,540	503	1,093	62	.334	.453	.271
Los Angeles	162	5,624	761	1,520	278	30	147	726	2,299	447	848	161	.325	.409	.270
Baltimore	162	5,551	729	1,492	296	27	189	700	2,409	447	902	83	.327	.434	.269
Texas	162	5,716	865	1,528	311	29	260	834	2,677	495	1,112	67	.329	.468	.267
Toronto	162	5,581	775	1,480	307	39	136	735	2,273	486	955	72	.331	.407	.265
Kansas City	162	5,503	701	1,445	289	34	126	653	2,180	424	1,008	53	.320	.396	.263
Chicago	162	5,529	741	1,450	253	23	200	713	2,349	435	1,002	137	.322	.425	.262
Oakland	162	5,627	772	1,476	310	20	155	739	2,291	537	819	31	.330	.407	.262
Minnesota	162	5,564	688	1,441	269	32	134	644	2,176	485	978	102	.323	.391	.259
Seattle	162	5,507	699	1,408	289	34	130	657	2,155	466	986	102	.317	.391	.256

TEAM PITCHING

TEAM PITCHING	W	L	ERA	CG	SHO	SV	INN	H	R	ER	BB	SO
Cleveland	93	69	3.61	6	10	51	1,452.2	1,363	642	582	413	1,050
Chicago	99	63	3.61	9	10	54	1,475.2	1,392	645	592	459	1,040
Los Angeles	95	67	3.68	7	11	54	1,464.1	1,419	643	598	443	1,126
Oakland	88	74	3.69	9	12	38	1,450.1	1,315	658	594	504	1,075
Minnesota	83	79	3.71	9	8	44	1,464.1	1,458	662	606	348	965
Toronto	80	82	4.06	9	8	35	1,447.0	1,475	705	653	444	958
Seattle	69	93	4.49	6	7	39	1,427.1	1,483	751	712	496	892
Detroit	71	91	4.51	7	2	37	1,435.2	1,504	787	719	461	907
New York	95	67	4.52	8	14	46	1,430.2	1,495	789	718	463	985
Baltimore	74	88	4.56	2	9	38	1,427.2	1,458	800	724	580	1,052
Boston	95	67	4.74	6	8	38	1,429.0	1,550	805	753	440	959
Texas	79	83	4.96	2	6	46	1,440.0	1,589	858	794	522	932
Tampa Bay	67	95	5.39	1	4	43	1,421.2	1,570	936	851	615	949
Kansas City	56	106	5.49	4	4	25	1,413.1	1,640	935	862	580	924

KEY G=games; GS=games started; AB=at bat; R=run; H=hit; 2B=double; 3B=triple; HR=home run; RBI=run batted in; TB=total bases; BB=walk; SO=strikeout; SB=stolen base; OBP=on-base percentage; SLG=slugging percentage; BA=batting average; W=win; L=loss; ERA=earned run average; CG=complete games; SHO=shutouts; SV=saves; INN=innings; ER=earned runs

NATIONAL LEAGUE TEAM-BY-TEAM STATS

ARIZONA DIAMONDBACKS

BATTING

BATTING	G	AB	R	H	2B	3B	HR	RBI	TB	BB	SO	SB	OBP	SLG	BA
Chad Tracy	145	503	73	155	34	4	27	72	278	35	78	3	.359	.553	.308
Tony Clark	130	349	47	106	22	2	30	87	222	37	88	0	.366	.636	.304
Shawn Green	158	581	87	166	37	4	22	73	277	62	95	8	.355	.477	.286
Alex Cintron	122	330	36	90	19	2	8	48	137	12	33	1	.298	.415	.273
Luis Gonzalez	155	579	90	157	37	0	24	79	266	78	90	4	.366	.459	.271
Royce Clayton	143	522	59	141	28	4	2	44	183	38	105	13	.320	.351	.270
Troy Glaus	149	538	78	139	29	1	37	97	281	84	145	4	.363	.522	.258
Craig Counsell	150	578	85	148	34	4	9	42	217	78	69	26	.350	.375	.256
Kelly Stinnett	59	129	15	32	4	0	6	12	54	12	32	0	.317	.419	.248
Quinton McCracken	134	215	23	51	4	3	1	13	64	23	35	4	.313	.298	.237
Luis Terrero	88	161	23	37	6	1	4	20	57	14	40	3	.313	.354	.230
Koyie Hill	34	78	6	17	5	0	0	6	22	11	27	0	.308	.282	.218
Jose Cruz, Jr.	64	202	23	43	9	0	12	28	88	42	54	0	.347	.436	.213
Chris Snyder	115	326	24	66	14	0	6	28	98	40	87	0	.297	.301	.202
Conor Jackson	40	85	8	17	3	0	2	8	26	12	11	0	.303	.306	.200

PITCHING

PITCHING	W–L	ERA	G	GS	CG	SV	INN	H	R	ER	BB	SO
Brandon Medders	4–1	1.78	27	0	0	0	30.1	21	6	6	11	31
Tim Worrell	1–1	2.27	32	0	0	0	31.2	30	13	8	9	22
Jose Valverde	3–4	2.44	61	0	0	15	66.1	51	19	18	20	75
Brandon Webb	14–12	3.54	33	33	1	0	229.0	229	98	90	59	172
Javier Vazquez	11–15	4.42	33	33	3	0	215.2	223	112	106	46	192
Mike Gosling	0–3	4.45	13	5	0	0	32.1	40	20	16	19	14
Brad Halsey	8–12	4.61	28	26	0	0	160.0	191	101	82	39	82
Shawn Estes	7–8	4.80	21	21	2	0	123.2	132	70	66	45	63
Claudio Vargas	9–6	4.81	21	19	0	0	119.2	124	66	64	40	90
Mike Koplove	2–1	5.07	44	0	0	0	49.2	48	31	28	20	28
Lance Cormier	7–3	5.11	67	0	0	0	79.1	86	50	45	43	63
Russ Ortiz	5–11	6.89	22	22	0	0	115.0	147	92	88	65	46
Brian Bruney	1–3	7.43	47	0	0	12	46.0	56	39	38	35	51
Greg Aquino	0–1	7.76	35	0	0	1	31.1	42	29	27	17	34

ATLANTA BRAVES

BATTING

BATTING	G	AB	R	H	2B	3B	HR	RBI	TB	BB	SO	SB	OBP	SLG	BA
Wilson Betemit	115	246	36	75	12	4	4	20	107	22	55	1	.359	.435	.305
Jeff Francoeur	70	257	41	77	20	1	14	45	141	11	58	3	.336	.549	.300
Pete Orr	112	150	32	45	8	1	1	8	58	6	23	7	.331	.387	.300
Chipper Jones	109	358	66	106	30	0	21	72	199	72	56	5	.412	.556	.296
Marcus Giles	152	577	104	168	45	4	15	63	266	64	108	16	.365	.461	.291
Rafael Furcal	154	616	100	175	31	11	12	58	264	62	78	46	.348	.429	.284
Brian McCann	59	180	20	50	7	0	5	23	72	18	26	1	.345	.400	.278
Julio Franco	108	233	30	64	12	1	9	42	105	27	57	4	.348	.451	.275
Ryan Langerhans	128	326	48	87	22	3	8	42	139	37	75	0	.348	.426	.267
Andruw Jones	160	586	95	154	24	3	51	128	337	64	112	5	.347	.575	.263
Johnny Estrada	105	357	31	93	26	0	4	39	131	20	38	0	.303	.367	.261
Adam LaRoche	141	451	53	117	28	0	20	78	205	39	87	0	.320	.455	.259
Brian Jordan	76	231	25	57	8	2	3	24	78	14	46	2	.295	.338	.247
Kelly Johnson	87	290	46	70	12	3	9	40	115	40	75	2	.334	.397	.241
Raul Mondesi	41	142	17	30	7	1	4	17	51	12	35	0	.271	.359	.211
Todd Hollandsworth	24	35	3	6	0	0	1	1	9	5	13	0	.275	.257	.171

PITCHING

PITCHING	W–L	ERA	G	GS	CG	SV	INN	H	R	ER	BB	SO
Jorge Sosa	13–3	2.55	44	20	0	0	134.0	122	42	38	64	85
John Smoltz	14–7	3.06	33	33	3	0	229.2	210	83	78	53	169
Blaine Boyer	4–2	3.11	43	0	0	0	37.2	32	13	13	17	33
Mike Hampton	5–3	3.50	12	12	1	0	69.1	74	28	27	18	27
Tim Hudson	14–9	3.52	29	29	2	0	192.0	194	79	75	65	115
Chris Reitsma	3–6	3.93	76	0	0	15	73.1	79	32	32	14	42
John Foster	4–2	4.15	62	0	0	1	34.2	27	17	16	19	32
Jim Brower	1–2	4.20	37	0	0	0	30.0	33	14	14	17	28
John Thomson	4–6	4.47	17	17	1	0	98.2	111	52	49	28	61
Horacio Ramirez	11–9	4.63	33	32	1	0	202.1	214	108	104	67	80
Kyle Davies	7–6	4.93	21	14	0	0	87.2	98	51	48	49	62
Roman Colon	1–5	5.28	23	4	0	0	44.1	47	28	26	14	30
Dan Kolb	3–8	5.93	65	0	0	11	57.2	78	39	38	29	39
Adam Bernero	4–3	6.51	36	0	0	0	47.0	61	35	34	12	37

BASEBALL

CHICAGO CUBS

BATTING	G	AB	R	H	2B	3B	HR	RBI	TB	BB	SO	SB	OBP	SLG	BA
Derrek Lee	158	594	120	199	50	3	46	107	393	85	109	15	.418	.662	.335
Matt Murton	51	140	19	45	3	2	7	14	73	16	22	2	.386	.521	.321
Todd Walker	110	397	50	121	25	3	12	40	188	31	40	1	.355	.474	.305
Aramis Ramirez	123	463	72	140	30	0	31	92	263	35	60	0	.358	.568	.302
Ronny Cedeno	41	80	13	24	3	0	1	6	30	5	11	1	.356	.375	.300
Nomar Garciaparra	62	230	28	65	12	0	9	30	104	12	24	0	.320	.452	.283
Michael Barrett	133	424	48	117	32	3	16	61	203	40	61	0	.345	.479	.276
Neifi Perez	154	572	59	157	33	1	9	54	219	18	47	8	.298	.383	.274
Jerry Hairston, Jr.	114	380	51	99	25	2	4	30	140	31	46	8	.336	.368	.261
Jeromy Burnitz	160	605	84	156	31	2	24	87	263	57	109	5	.322	.435	.258
Todd Hollandsworth	107	268	23	68	17	2	5	35	104	18	53	4	.301	.388	.254
Jose Macias	112	177	15	45	8	0	1	13	56	6	24	4	.274	.316	.254
Matt Lawton	19	78	8	19	2	0	1	5	24	4	8	1	.289	.308	.244
Henry Blanco	54	161	16	39	6	0	6	25	63	11	24	0	.287	.391	.242
Jason Dubois	52	142	15	34	12	0	7	22	67	7	49	0	.289	.472	.239
Corey Patterson	126	451	47	97	15	3	13	34	157	23	118	15	.254	.348	.215

PITCHING	W–L	ERA	G	GS	CG	SV	INN	H	R	ER	BB	SO
Will Ohman	2–2	2.91	69	0	0	0	43.1	32	14	14	24	45
Ryan Dempster	5–3	3.13	63	6	0	33	92.0	83	35	32	49	89
Carlos Zambrano	14–6	3.26	33	33	2	0	223.1	170	88	81	86	202
Mark Prior	11–7	3.67	27	27	1	0	166.2	143	73	68	59	188
Michael Wuertz	6–2	3.81	75	0	0	0	75.2	60	36	32	40	89
Jerome Williams	6–8	3.91	18	17	0	0	106.0	98	50	46	45	59
Kerry Wood	3–4	4.23	21	10	0	0	66.0	52	32	31	26	77
Greg Maddux	13–15	4.24	35	35	3	0	225.0	239	112	106	36	136
Roberto Novoa	4–5	4.43	49	0	0	0	44.2	47	22	22	25	47
Glendon Rusch	9–8	4.52	46	19	1	0	145.1	175	79	73	53	111
Mike Remlinger	0–3	4.91	35	0	0	0	33.0	31	19	18	12	30
Sergio Mitre	2–5	5.37	21	7	1	0	60.1	62	37	36	23	37
Todd Wellemeyer	2–1	6.12	22	0	0	1	32.1	32	23	22	22	32

CINCINNATI REDS

BATTING	G	AB	R	H	2B	3B	HR	RBI	TB	BB	SO	SB	OBP	SLG	BA
Sean Casey	137	529	75	165	32	0	9	58	224	48	48	2	.371	.423	.312
Ken Griffey, Jr.	128	491	85	148	30	0	35	92	283	54	93	0	.369	.576	.301
Felipe Lopez	148	580	97	169	34	5	23	85	282	57	111	15	.352	.486	.291
Joe Randa	92	332	44	96	26	1	13	48	163	33	52	0	.356	.491	.289
Rich Aurilia	114	426	61	120	23	2	14	68	189	37	67	2	.338	.444	.282
Javier Valentin	76	221	36	62	11	0	14	50	115	30	37	0	.362	.520	.281
Ryan Freel	103	369	69	100	19	3	4	21	137	51	59	36	.371	.371	.271
Jason LaRue	110	361	38	94	27	0	14	60	163	41	101	0	.355	.452	.260
Wily Mo Pena	99	311	42	79	17	0	19	51	153	20	116	2	.304	.492	.254
Adam Dunn	160	543	107	134	35	2	40	101	293	114	168	4	.387	.540	.247
Austin Kearns	112	387	62	93	26	1	18	67	175	48	107	0	.333	.452	.240
Jacob Cruz	110	127	12	30	10	0	4	18	52	16	46	0	.324	.409	.236
Edwin Encarnacion	69	211	25	49	16	0	9	31	92	20	60	3	.308	.436	.232
D'Angelo Jimenez	35	105	14	24	7	0	0	5	31	14	23	2	.319	.295	.229
Ray Olmedo	54	77	10	17	4	1	1	4	26	6	22	4	.282	.338	.221

PITCHING	W–L	ERA	G	GS	CG	SV	INN	H	R	ER	BB	SO
Brian Shackelford	1–0	2.43	37	0	0	0	29.2	21	9	8	9	17
Kent Mercker	3–1	3.65	78	0	0	4	61.2	64	27	25	19	45
Aaron Harang	11–13	3.83	32	32	1	0	211.2	217	93	90	51	163
David Weathers	7–4	3.94	73	0	0	15	77.2	71	36	34	29	61
Jason Standridge	2–2	4.06	32	0	0	0	31.0	38	14	14	16	17
Brandon Claussen	10–11	4.21	29	29	0	0	166.2	178	89	78	57	121
Matt Belisle	4–8	4.41	60	5	0	1	85.2	101	49	42	26	59
Todd Coffey	4–1	4.50	57	0	0	1	58.0	84	33	29	11	26
Ramon Ortiz	9–11	5.36	30	30	1	0	171.1	206	110	102	51	96
Ryan Wagner	3–2	6.11	42	0	0	0	45.2	56	33	31	17	39
Randy Keisler	2–1	6.27	24	4	0	0	56.0	64	45	39	28	43
Luke Hudson	6–9	6.38	19	16	0	0	84.2	83	62	60	50	53
Eric Milton	8–15	6.47	34	34	0	0	186.1	237	141	134	52	123
Ricky Stone	0–0	6.75	23	0	0	0	30.2	48	24	23	7	15
Paul Wilson	1–5	7.77	9	9	0	0	46.1	68	41	40	17	30

COLORADO ROCKIES

BATTING	G	AB	R	H	2B	3B	HR	RBI	TB	BB	SO	SB	OBP	SLG	BA
Ryan Shealy	36	91	14	30	7	0	2	16	43	13	22	1	.413	.473	.330
Todd Helton	144	509	92	163	45	2	20	79	272	106	80	3	.445	.534	.320
Jorge Piedra	61	112	19	35	8	1	6	16	63	10	15	2	.371	.563	.313
Eddy Garabito	42	88	15	27	5	0	1	8	35	8	12	3	.384	.398	.307
Matt Holliday	125	479	68	147	24	7	19	87	242	36	79	14	.361	.505	.307
Cory Sullivan	139	378	64	111	15	4	4	30	146	28	83	12	.343	.386	.294
Luis Gonzalez	128	404	51	118	25	0	9	44	170	20	63	3	.333	.421	.292
Clint Barmes	81	350	55	101	19	1	10	46	152	16	36	6	.330	.434	.289
Garrett Atkins	138	519	62	149	31	1	13	89	221	45	72	0	.347	.426	.287
Aaron Miles	99	324	37	91	12	3	2	28	115	8	38	4	.306	.355	.281
Brad Hawpe	101	305	38	80	10	3	9	47	123	43	70	2	.350	.403	.262
Preston Wilson	71	267	39	69	15	1	15	47	131	25	77	3	.322	.491	.258
Todd Greene	38	126	10	32	4	0	7	23	57	7	21	0	.299	.452	.254
Danny Ardoin	80	210	28	48	10	0	6	22	76	20	69	1	.320	.362	.229
Desi Relaford	73	210	24	47	13	2	1	16	67	22	42	3	.308	.319	.224
J.D. Closser	92	237	31	52	12	2	7	27	89	32	48	1	.314	.376	.219
Omar Quintanilla	39	128	16	28	1	1	0	7	31	9	15	2	.270	.242	.219
Dustan Mohr	98	266	34	57	10	3	17	38	124	23	94	1	.280	.466	.214

PITCHING	W–L	ERA	G	GS	CG	SV	INN	H	R	ER	BB	SO
Jay Witasick	0–4	2.52	32	0	0	0	35.2	27	11	10	12	40
Brian Fuentes	2–5	2.91	78	0	0	31	74.1	59	25	24	34	91
Mike DeJean	2–3	3.19	38	0	0	0	36.2	26	14	13	12	35
Aaron Cook	7–2	3.67	13	13	2	0	83.1	101	38	34	16	24
Shawn Chacon	1–7	4.09	13	12	0	0	72.2	69	33	33	36	39
David Cortes	2–0	4.10	50	0	0	2	52.2	50	24	24	10	36
Sunny Kim	5–1	4.22	12	8	1	0	53.1	56	26	25	13	38
Byung-Hyun Kim	5–12	4.86	40	22	0	0	148.0	156	82	80	71	115
Jason Jennings	6–9	5.02	20	20	1	0	122.0	130	73	68	62	75
Marcos Carvajal	0–2	5.09	39	0	0	0	53.0	52	30	30	21	47
Jamey Wright	8–16	5.46	34	27	0	0	171.1	201	119	104	81	101
Jeff Francis	14–12	5.68	33	33	0	0	183.2	228	119	116	70	128
Scott Dohmann	2–1	6.10	32	0	0	0	31.0	33	21	21	19	35
Jose Acevedo	2–4	6.47	36	5	0	1	64.0	86	48	46	16	31
Joe Kennedy	4–8	7.04	16	16	0	0	92.0	128	81	72	44	52

FLORIDA MARLINS

BATTING	G	AB	R	H	2B	3B	HR	RBI	TB	BB	SO	SB	OBP	SLG	BA
Miguel Cabrera	158	613	106	198	43	2	33	116	344	64	125	1	.385	.561	.323
Lenny Harris	83	70	5	22	4	0	1	13	29	7	11	0	.385	.414	.314
Jeff Conine	131	335	42	102	20	2	3	33	135	38	58	2	.374	.403	.304
Luis Castillo	122	439	72	132	12	4	4	30	164	65	32	10	.391	.374	.301
Carlos Delgado	144	521	81	157	41	3	33	115	303	72	121	0	.399	.582	.301
Juan Encarnacion	141	506	59	145	27	3	16	76	226	41	104	6	.349	.447	.287
Paul Lo Duca	132	445	45	126	23	1	6	57	169	34	31	4	.334	.380	.283
Juan Pierre	162	656	96	181	19	13	2	47	232	41	45	57	.326	.354	.276
Alex Gonzalez	130	435	45	115	30	0	5	45	160	31	81	5	.319	.368	.264
Chris Aguila	65	78	11	19	3	0	0	4	22	3	19	0	.272	.282	.244
Damion Easley	102	267	37	64	19	1	9	30	112	26	47	4	.312	.419	.240
Mike Lowell	150	500	56	118	36	1	8	58	180	46	58	4	.298	.360	.236
Matt Treanor	58	134	10	27	8	0	0	13	35	16	28	0	.301	.261	.201

PITCHING	W–L	ERA	G	GS	CG	SV	INN	H	R	ER	BB	SO
Todd Jones	1–5	2.10	68	0	0	40	73.0	61	19	17	14	62
Dontrelle Willis	22–10	2.63	34	34	7	0	236.1	213	79	69	55	170
Jim Mecir	1–4	3.12	52	0	0	0	43.1	39	17	15	17	34
Josh Beckett	15–8	3.38	29	29	2	0	178.2	153	75	67	58	166
A.J. Burnett	12–12	3.44	32	32	4	0	209.0	184	97	80	79	198
Nate Bump	0–3	4.03	31	0	0	0	38.0	43	18	17	12	18
Jason Vargas	5–5	4.03	17	13	1	0	73.2	71	34	33	31	59
Brian Moehler	6–12	4.55	37	25	0	0	158.1	198	82	80	42	95
Guillermo Mota	2–2	4.70	56	0	0	2	67.0	65	38	35	32	60
Antonio Alfonseca	1–1	4.94	33	0	0	0	27.1	29	15	15	14	16
Ismael Valdez	2–2	5.33	14	7	0	0	50.2	64	32	30	22	27
Randy Messenger	0–0	5.35	29	0	0	0	37.0	39	22	22	30	29
Al Leiter	3–7	6.64	17	16	0	0	80.0	88	61	59	60	52
Travis Smith	0–0	6.75	12	0	0	0	10.2	17	8	8	5	9
John Riedling	4–1	7.16	29	0	0	0	27.2	34	23	22	13	16

BASEBALL

HOUSTON ASTROS

BATTING	G	AB	R	H	2B	3B	HR	RBI	TB	BB	SO	SB	OBP	SLG	BA
Lance Berkman	132	468	76	137	34	1	24	82	245	91	72	4	.411	.524	.293
Willy Taveras	152	592	82	172	13	4	3	29	202	25	103	34	.325	.341	.291
Orlando Palmeiro	114	204	22	58	17	2	3	20	88	15	23	3	.341	.431	.284
Morgan Ensberg	150	526	86	149	30	3	36	101	293	85	119	6	.388	.557	.283
Jason Lane	145	517	65	138	34	4	26	78	258	32	105	6	.316	.499	.267
Craig Biggio	155	590	94	156	40	1	26	69	276	37	90	11	.325	.468	.264
Brad Ausmus	134	387	35	100	19	0	3	47	128	51	48	5	.351	.331	.258
Jeff Bagwell	39	100	11	25	4	0	3	19	38	18	21	0	.358	.380	.250
Chris Burke	108	318	49	79	19	2	5	26	117	23	62	11	.309	.368	.248
Adam Everett	152	549	58	136	27	2	11	54	200	26	103	21	.290	.364	.248
Jose Vizcaino	98	187	15	46	10	2	1	23	63	15	40	2	.299	.337	.246
Mike Lamb	125	322	41	76	13	5	12	53	135	22	65	1	.284	.419	.236
Eric Bruntlett	91	109	19	24	5	2	4	14	45	10	25	7	.292	.413	.220
Luke Scott	34	80	6	15	4	2	0	4	23	9	23	1	.270	.288	.188
Raul Chavez	37	99	6	17	3	0	2	6	26	4	18	1	.210	.263	.172

PITCHING	W–L	ERA	G	GS	CG	SV	INN	H	R	ER	BB	SO
Roger Clemens	13–8	1.87	32	32	1	0	211.1	151	51	44	62	185
Dan Wheeler	2–3	2.21	71	0	0	3	73.1	53	18	18	19	69
Brad Lidge	4–4	2.29	70	0	0	42	70.2	58	21	18	23	103
Andy Pettitte	17–9	2.39	33	33	0	0	222.1	188	66	59	41	171
Roy Oswalt	20–12	2.94	35	35	4	0	241.2	243	85	79	48	184
Chad Qualls	6–4	3.28	77	0	0	0	79.2	73	33	29	23	60
Chad Harville	0–2	4.46	37	0	0	0	38.1	36	21	19	24	33
Russ Springer	4–4	4.73	62	0	0	0	59.0	49	34	31	21	54
Brandon Backe	10–8	4.76	26	25	1	0	149.1	151	82	79	67	97
Mike Burns	0–0	4.94	27	0	0	0	31.0	29	18	17	8	20
Wandy Rodriguez	10–10	5.53	25	22	0	0	128.2	135	82	79	53	80
Ezequiel Astacio	3–6	5.67	22	14	0	0	81.0	100	56	51	25	66

LOS ANGELES DODGERS

BATTING	G	AB	R	H	2B	3B	HR	RBI	TB	BB	SO	SB	OBP	SLG	BA
Willy Aybar	26	86	12	28	8	0	1	10	39	18	11	3	.448	.453	.326
Jose Cruz, Jr.	47	156	23	47	14	2	6	22	175	23	43	0	.391	.532	.301
Antonio Perez	98	259	28	77	13	2	3	23	103	21	61	11	.360	.398	.297
Milton Bradley	75	283	49	82	14	1	13	38	137	25	47	6	.350	.484	.290
Jeff Kent	149	553	100	160	36	0	29	105	283	72	85	6	.377	.512	.289
J.D. Drew	72	252	48	72	12	1	15	36	131	51	50	1	.412	.520	.286
Ricky Ledee	102	237	31	66	16	1	7	39	105	20	55	0	.335	.443	.278
Dioner Navarro	50	176	21	48	9	0	3	14	66	20	21	0	.354	.375	.273
Oscar Robles	110	364	44	99	18	1	5	34	134	31	33	0	.332	.368	.272
Olmedo Saenz	109	319	39	84	24	0	15	63	153	27	63	0	.325	.480	.263
Cesar Izturis	106	444	48	114	19	2	2	31	143	25	51	8	.302	.322	.257
Hee-Seop Choi	133	320	40	81	15	2	15	42	145	34	80	1	.336	.453	.253
Mike Edwards	88	239	23	59	9	2	3	15	81	16	34	1	.300	.339	.247
Jason Phillips	121	399	38	95	20	0	10	55	145	25	50	0	.287	.363	.238
Jayson Werth	102	337	46	79	22	2	7	43	126	48	114	11	.338	.374	.234
Jason Repko	129	276	43	61	15	3	8	30	106	16	80	5	.281	.384	.221

PITCHING	W–L	ERA	G	GS	CG	SV	INN	H	R	ER	BB	SO
Elmer Dessens	1–2	3.56	28	7	0	0	65.2	63	30	26	19	37
Derek Lowe	12–15	3.61	35	35	2	0	222.0	223	113	89	55	146
Duaner Sanchez	4–7	3.73	79	0	0	8	82.0	75	36	34	36	71
Brad Penny	7–9	3.90	29	29	1	0	175.1	185	78	76	41	122
Giovanni Carrara	7–4	3.93	72	0	0	0	75.2	65	35	33	38	56
Franquelis Osoria	0–2	3.94	24	0	0	0	29.2	28	14	13	8	15
Jeff Weaver	14–11	4.22	34	34	3	0	224.0	220	111	105	43	157
Odalis Perez	7–8	4.56	19	19	0	0	108.2	109	59	55	28	74
Steve Schmoll	2–2	5.01	48	0	0	3	46.2	47	29	26	22	29
D.J. Houlton	6–9	5.16	35	19	0	0	129.0	145	79	74	52	90
Yhency Brazoban	4–10	5.33	74	0	0	21	72.2	70	46	43	32	61
Scott Erickson	1–4	6.02	19	8	0	0	55.1	62	37	37	25	15
Edwin Jackson	2–2	6.28	7	6	0	0	28.2	31	22	20	17	13

MILWAUKEE BREWERS

BATTING	G	AB	R	H	2B	3B	HR	RBI	TB	BB	SO	SB	OBP	SLG	BA
Brady Clark	145	599	94	183	31	1	13	53	255	47	55	10	.372	.426	.306
Wes Helms	95	168	18	50	13	1	4	24	77	14	30	0	.356	.458	.298
Geoff Jenkins	148	538	87	157	42	1	25	86	276	56	138	0	.375	.513	.292
Bill Hall	146	501	69	146	39	6	17	62	248	39	103	18	.342	.495	.291
Jeff Cirillo	77	185	29	52	15	0	4	23	79	23	22	4	.373	.427	.281
Lyle Overbay	158	537	80	148	34	1	19	72	241	78	98	1	.367	.449	.276
Damian Miller	114	385	50	105	25	1	9	43	159	37	94	0	.340	.413	.273
Carlos Lee	162	618	85	164	41	0	32	114	301	57	87	13	.324	.487	.265
Russell Branyan	85	202	23	52	11	0	12	31	99	39	80	1	.378	.490	.257
J.J. Hardy	124	372	46	92	22	1	9	50	143	44	48	0	.327	.384	.247
Rickie Weeks	96	360	56	86	13	2	13	42	142	40	96	15	.333	.394	.239
Junior Spivey	49	182	22	43	8	1	5	17	68	18	57	7	.308	.374	.236
Chad Moeller	66	199	23	41	9	1	7	23	73	13	48	0	.257	.367	.206
Chris Magruder	101	138	16	28	9	0	2	13	43	7	33	3	.265	.312	.203

PITCHING	W–L	ERA	G	GS	CG	SV	INN	H	R	ER	BB	SO
Derrick Turnbow	7–1	1.74	69	0	0	39	67.1	49	15	13	24	64
Rick Helling	3–1	2.39	15	7	0	0	49.0	39	13	13	18	42
Ben Sheets	10–9	3.33	22	22	3	0	156.2	142	66	58	25	141
Matt Wise	4–4	3.36	49	0	0	1	64.1	37	25	24	25	62
Doug Davis	11–11	3.84	35	35	2	0	222.2	196	103	95	93	208
Justin Lehr	1–1	3.89	23	0	0	0	34.2	32	19	15	18	23
Chris Capuano	18–12	3.99	35	35	0	0	219.0	212	105	97	91	176
Tomo Ohka	7–6	4.35	22	20	1	0	126.1	145	65	61	28	81
Jorge de la Rosa	2–2	4.46	38	0	0	0	42.1	48	23	21	38	42
Julio Santana	3–5	4.50	41	0	0	1	42.0	34	21	21	19	49
Ricky Bottalico	2–2	4.54	40	0	0	2	41.2	43	24	21	19	29
Victor Santos	4–13	4.57	29	24	1	0	141.2	153	87	72	60	89
Wes Obermueller	1–4	5.26	23	8	0	0	65.0	74	41	38	36	33
Gary Glover	5–4	5.57	15	11	0	0	64.2	74	41	40	20	58
Dana Eveland	1–1	5.97	27	0	0	1	31.2	40	21	21	18	23

NEW YORK METS

BATTING	G	AB	R	H	2B	3B	HR	RBI	TB	BB	SO	SB	OBP	SLG	BA
David Wright	160	575	99	176	42	1	27	102	301	72	113	17	.388	.523	.306
Chris Woodward	81	173	16	49	10	0	3	18	68	13	46	0	.337	.393	.283
Mike Cameron	76	308	47	84	23	2	12	39	147	29	85	13	.342	.477	.273
Cliff Floyd	150	550	85	150	22	2	34	98	278	63	98	12	.358	.505	.273
Jose Reyes	161	696	99	190	24	17	7	58	269	27	78	60	.300	.386	.273
Carlos Beltran	151	582	83	155	34	2	16	78	241	56	96	17	.330	.414	.266
Marlon Anderson	123	235	31	62	9	0	7	19	92	18	45	6	.316	.391	.264
Victor Diaz	89	280	41	72	17	3	12	38	131	30	82	6	.329	.468	.257
Kazuo Matsui	87	267	31	68	9	4	3	24	94	14	43	6	.300	.352	.255
Miguel Cairo	100	327	31	82	18	0	2	19	106	19	31	13	.296	.324	.251
Mike Piazza	113	398	41	100	23	0	19	62	180	41	67	0	.326	.452	.251
Ramon Castro	99	209	26	51	16	0	8	41	91	25	58	1	.321	.435	.244
Doug Mientkiewicz	87	275	36	66	13	0	11	29	112	32	39	0	.322	.407	.240

PITCHING	W–L	ERA	G	GS	CG	SV	INN	H	R	ER	BB	SO
Juan Padilla	3–1	1.49	24	0	0	1	36.1	24	7	6	13	17
Roberto Hernandez	8–6	2.58	67	0	0	4	69.2	57	20	20	28	61
Jae Seo	8–2	2.59	14	14	1	0	90.1	84	26	26	16	59
Pedro Martinez	15–8	2.82	31	31	4	0	217.0	159	69	68	47	208
Aaron Heilman	5–3	3.17	53	7	1	5	108.0	87	40	38	37	106
Tom Glavine	13–13	3.53	33	33	2	0	211.1	227	88	83	61	105
Braden Looper	4–7	3.94	60	0	0	28	59.1	65	31	26	22	27
Kris Benson	10–8	4.13	28	28	0	0	174.1	171	86	80	49	95
Steve Trachsel	1–4	4.14	6	6	0	0	37.0	37	20	17	12	24
Victor Zambrano	7–12	4.17	31	27	0	0	166.1	170	85	77	77	112
Kazuhisa Ishii	3–9	5.14	19	16	0	0	91.0	87	59	52	49	53
Heath Bell	1–3	5.59	42	0	0	0	46.2	56	30	29	13	43

PHILADELPHIA PHILLIES

BATTING	G	AB	R	H	2B	3B	HR	RBI	TB	BB	SO	SB	OBP	SLG	BA
Kenny Lofton	110	367	67	123	15	5	2	36	154	32	41	22	.392	.420	.335
Placido Polanco	43	158	26	50	7	0	3	20	66	12	9	0	.376	.418	.316
Jason Michaels	105	289	54	88	16	2	4	31	120	44	45	3	.399	.415	.304
Chase Utley	147	543	93	158	39	6	28	105	293	69	109	16	.376	.540	.291
Jimmy Rollins	158	677	115	196	38	11	12	54	292	47	71	41	.338	.431	.290
Ryan Howard	88	312	52	90	17	2	22	63	177	33	100	0	.356	.567	.288
Bobby Abreu	162	588	104	168	37	1	24	102	279	117	134	31	.405	.474	.286
Pat Burrell	154	562	78	158	27	1	32	117	283	99	160	0	.389	.504	.281
Mike Lieberthal	118	392	48	103	25	0	12	47	164	35	35	0	.336	.418	.263
Todd Pratt	60	175	17	44	4	0	7	23	69	19	50	0	.332	.394	.251
David Bell	150	557	53	138	31	1	10	61	201	47	69	0	.310	.361	.248
Tomas Perez	94	159	17	37	7	0	0	22	44	11	27	1	.289	.277	.233
Endy Chavez	91	107	17	23	3	3	0	10	35	4	13	2	.243	.299	.215
Jim Thome	59	193	26	40	7	0	7	30	68	45	59	0	.360	.352	.207

PITCHING	W–L	ERA	G	GS	CG	SV	INN	H	R	ER	BB	SO
Billy Wagner	4–3	1.51	75	0	0	38	77.2	45	17	13	20	87
Aaron Fultz	4–0	2.24	62	0	0	0	72.1	47	21	18	23	54
Robinson Tejeda	4–3	3.57	26	13	0	0	85.2	67	36	34	51	72
Geoff Geary	2–1	3.72	40	0	0	0	58.0	54	29	24	21	42
Brett Myers	13–8	3.72	34	34	2	0	215.1	193	94	89	68	208
Ugueth Urbina	4–3	4.13	56	0	0	1	52.1	35	25	24	25	66
Ryan Madson	6–5	4.14	78	0	0	0	87.0	84	44	40	25	79
Jon Lieber	17–13	4.20	35	35	1	0	218.1	223	107	102	41	149
Randy Wolf	6–4	4.39	13	13	0	0	80.0	87	40	39	26	61
Cory Lidle	13–11	4.53	31	31	1	0	184.2	210	105	93	40	121
Vicente Padilla	9–12	4.71	27	27	0	0	147.0	146	79	77	74	103
Rheal Cormier	4–2	5.89	57	0	0	0	47.1	56	33	31	16	34
Gavin Floyd	1–2	10.04	7	4	0	0	26.0	30	31	29	16	17

PITTSBURGH PIRATES

BATTING	G	AB	R	H	2B	3B	HR	RBI	TB	BB	SO	SB	OBP	SLG	BA
Chris Duffy	39	126	22	43	4	2	1	9	54	7	22	2	.385	.429	.341
Jason Bay	162	599	110	183	44	6	32	101	335	95	142	21	.402	.559	.306
Freddy Sanchez	132	453	54	132	26	4	5	35	181	27	36	2	.336	.400	.291
Matt Lawton	101	374	53	102	28	1	10	44	162	58	61	16	.380	.433	.273
Rob Mackowiak	142	463	57	126	21	3	9	58	180	43	100	8	.337	.389	.272
Bobby Hill	58	93	12	25	6	0	0	11	31	9	17	0	.343	.333	.269
Jose Castillo	101	370	49	99	16	3	11	53	154	23	59	2	.307	.416	.268
Craig Wilson	59	197	23	52	14	1	5	22	83	30	69	3	.387	.421	.264
Daryle Ward	133	407	46	106	21	1	12	63	165	37	60	0	.318	.405	.260
Ty Wigginton	57	155	20	40	9	1	7	25	72	14	30	0	.324	.465	.258
Nate McLouth	41	109	20	28	6	0	5	12	49	3	20	2	.305	.450	.257
Jack Wilson	158	587	60	151	24	7	8	52	213	31	58	7	.299	.363	.257
Ryan Doumit	75	231	25	59	13	1	6	35	92	11	48	2	.324	.398	.255
Tike Redman	135	319	33	80	12	4	2	26	106	19	27	4	.292	.332	.251
Humberto Cota	93	297	29	72	20	1	7	43	115	17	80	0	.285	.387	.242
David Ross	40	108	9	24	8	0	3	15	41	6	24	0	.263	.380	.222
Brad Eldred	55	190	23	42	9	0	12	27	87	13	77	1	.279	.458	.221
Michael Restovich	52	84	10	18	3	1	2	5	43	8	24	0	.283	.345	.214

PITCHING	W–L	ERA	G	GS	CG	SV	INN	H	R	ER	BB	SO
Zach Duke	8–2	1.81	14	14	0	0	84.2	79	20	17	23	58
Paul Maholm	3–1	2.18	6	6	0	0	41.1	31	10	10	17	26
Mike Gonzalez	1–3	2.70	51	0	0	3	50.0	35	15	15	31	58
Salomon Torres	5–5	2.76	78	0	0	3	94.2	76	34	29	36	55
Rick White	4–7	3.72	71	0	0	2	75.0	90	39	31	29	40
Dave Williams	10–11	4.41	25	25	1	0	138.2	137	74	68	58	88
Ryan Vogelsong	2–2	4.43	44	0	0	0	81.1	82	43	40	40	52
Brian Meadows	3–1	4.58	65	0	0	0	74.2	84	42	38	21	44
Jose Mesa	2–8	4.76	55	0	0	27	56.2	61	30	30	26	37
John Grabow	2–3	4.85	63	0	0	0	52.0	46	31	28	25	42
Mark Redman	5–15	4.90	30	30	2	0	178.1	188	100	97	56	101
Josh Fogg	6–11	5.05	34	28	0	0	169.1	196	106	95	53	85
Kip Wells	8–18	5.09	33	33	1	0	182.0	186	116	103	99	132
Ian Snell	1–2	5.14	15	5	0	0	42.0	43	25	24	24	34
Oliver Perez	7–5	5.85	20	20	0	0	103.0	102	68	67	70	97

ST. LOUIS CARDINALS

BATTING	G	AB	R	H	2B	3B	HR	RBI	TB	BB	SO	SB	OBP	SLG	BA
Albert Pujols	161	591	129	195	38	2	41	117	360	97	65	16	.430	.609	.330
Jason Marquis	43	87	10	27	8	1	1	10	40	2	11	0	.326	.460	.310
John Rodriguez	56	149	15	44	6	0	5	24	65	19	45	2	.382	.436	.295
David Eckstein	158	630	90	185	26	7	8	61	249	58	44	11	.363	.395	.294
Mark Grudzielanek	137	528	64	155	30	3	8	59	215	26	81	8	.334	.407	.294
Larry Walker	100	315	66	91	20	1	15	52	158	41	64	2	.384	.502	.289
So Taguchi	143	396	45	114	21	2	8	53	163	20	62	11	.322	.412	.288
Hector Luna	64	137	26	39	10	2	1	18	56	9	25	10	.344	.409	.285
Abraham Nunez	139	421	64	120	13	2	5	44	152	37	63	0	.343	.361	.285
Reggie Sanders	93	295	49	80	14	2	21	54	161	28	75	14	.340	.546	.271
Jim Edmonds	142	467	88	123	37	1	29	89	249	91	139	5	.385	.533	.263
Yadier Molina	114	385	36	97	15	1	8	49	138	23	30	2	.295	.358	.252
John Mabry	112	246	26	59	15	1	8	32	100	20	63	0	.295	.407	.240
Scott Rolen	56	196	28	46	12	1	5	28	75	25	28	1	.323	.383	.235
Scott Seabol	59	105	11	23	5	0	1	10	31	8	23	0	.272	.295	.219
Einar Diaz	58	130	14	27	6	0	1	17	36	5	12	0	.248	.277	.208

PITCHING	W–L	ERA	G	GS	CG	SV	INN	H	R	ER	BB	SO
Jason Isringhausen	1–2	2.14	63	0	0	39	59.0	43	14	14	27	51
Al Reyes	4–2	2.15	65	0	0	3	62.2	38	15	15	20	67
Cal Eldred	1–0	2.19	31	1	0	0	37.0	35	9	9	18	29
Chris Carpenter	21–5	2.83	33	33	7	0	241.2	204	82	76	51	213
Brad Thompson	4–0	2.95	40	0	0	1	55.0	46	22	18	15	29
Ray King	4–4	3.38	77	0	0	0	40.0	46	17	15	16	23
Julian Tavarez	2–3	3.43	74	0	0	4	65.2	68	28	25	19	47
Randy Flores	3–1	3.46	50	0	0	1	41.2	37	22	16	13	43
Jeff Suppan	16–10	3.57	32	32	0	0	194.1	206	93	77	63	114
Mark Mulder	16–8	3.64	32	32	3	0	205.0	212	90	83	70	111
Matt Morris	14–10	4.11	31	31	2	0	192.2	209	101	88	37	117
Jason Marquis	13–14	4.13	33	32	3	0	207.0	206	110	95	69	100

SAN DIEGO PADRES

BATTING	G	AB	R	H	2B	3B	HR	RBI	TB	BB	SO	SB	OBP	SLG	BA
Miguel Olivo	37	115	16	35	7	1	4	16	98	4	31	6	.341	.487	.304
Brian Giles	158	545	92	164	38	8	15	83	263	119	64	13	.423	.483	.301
Mark Sweeney	135	221	31	65	12	1	8	40	103	40	58	4	.395	.466	.294
Ramon Hernandez	99	369	36	107	19	2	12	58	166	18	40	1	.322	.450	.290
Mark Loretta	105	404	54	113	16	1	3	38	140	45	34	8	.360	.347	.280
Dave Roberts	115	411	65	113	19	10	8	38	176	53	59	23	.356	.428	.275
Eric Young	56	142	22	39	9	0	2	12	54	18	12	7	.356	.380	.275
Robert Fick	93	230	25	61	10	2	3	30	84	26	33	0	.340	.365	.265
Xavier Nady	124	326	40	85	15	2	13	43	143	22	67	2	.321	.439	.261
Phil Nevin	73	281	31	72	11	1	9	47	112	19	67	1	.301	.399	.256
Joe Randa	58	223	27	57	17	1	4	20	94	14	29	0	.303	.395	.256
Damian Jackson	118	275	44	70	9	0	5	23	94	30	45	15	.335	.342	.255
Sean Burroughs	93	284	20	71	7	2	1	17	85	24	41	4	.318	.299	.250
Khalil Greene	121	436	51	109	30	2	15	70	188	25	93	5	.296	.431	.250
Ryan Klesko	137	443	61	110	19	1	18	58	185	75	80	3	.358	.418	.248
Geoff Blum	78	224	26	54	13	1	5	22	84	24	28	3	.321	.375	.241
Ben Johnson	31	75	10	16	8	1	3	13	35	11	23	0	.310	.467	.213

PITCHING	W–L	ERA	G	GS	CG	SV	INN	H	R	ER	BB	SO
Clay Hensley	1–1	1.70	24	1	0	0	47.2	33	12	9	17	28
Scott Linebrink	8–1	1.83	73	0	0	1	73.2	55	17	15	23	70
Rudy Seanez	7–1	2.69	57	0	0	0	60.1	49	19	18	22	84
Jake Peavy	13–7	2.88	30	30	3	0	203.0	162	70	65	50	216
Trevor Hoffman	1–6	2.97	60	0	0	43	57.2	52	23	19	12	54
Pedro Astacio	4–2	3.17	12	10	0	0	59.2	54	21	21	26	33
Paul Quantrill	1–1	3.41	22	0	0	0	31.2	37	13	12	2	24
Akinori Otsuka	2–8	3.59	66	0	0	1	62.2	55	28	25	34	60
Chris Hammond	5–1	3.84	55	0	0	0	58.2	51	25	25	14	34
Adam Eaton	11–5	4.27	24	22	0	0	128.2	140	70	61	44	100
Brian Lawrence	7–15	4.83	33	33	1	0	195.2	211	106	105	57	109
Woody Williams	9–12	4.85	28	28	0	0	159.2	174	92	86	51	106
Dennys Reyes	3–2	5.15	36	1	0	0	43.2	57	30	25	32	35
Tim Stauffer	3–6	5.33	15	14	0	0	81.0	92	50	48	29	49
Darrell May	1–3	5.61	22	8	0	0	59.1	73	38	37	20	32
Chan Ho Park	4–3	5.91	10	9	0	0	45.2	50	33	30	26	33

SAN FRANCISCO GIANTS

BATTING	G	AB	R	H	2B	3B	HR	RBI	TB	BB	SO	SB	OBP	SLG	BA
Randy Winn	58	231	39	83	22	5	14	26	308	11	38	7	.391	.680	.359
Moises Alou	123	427	67	137	21	3	19	63	221	56	43	5	.400	.518	.321
Ray Durham	142	497	67	144	33	0	12	62	213	48	59	6	.356	.429	.290
Barry Bonds	14	42	8	12	1	0	5	10	28	9	6	0	.404	.667	.286
Edgardo Alfonzo	109	368	36	102	17	1	2	43	127	27	34	2	.327	.345	.277
J.T. Snow	117	367	40	101	17	2	4	40	134	32	61	1	.343	.365	.275
Omar Vizquel	152	568	66	154	28	4	3	45	199	56	58	24	.341	.350	.271
Deivi Cruz	81	209	26	56	10	1	5	19	83	10	31	0	.301	.397	.268
Jason Ellison	131	352	49	93	18	2	4	24	127	24	44	14	.316	.361	.264
Lance Niekro	113	278	32	70	16	3	12	46	128	17	53	0	.295	.460	.252
Pedro Feliz	156	569	69	142	30	4	20	81	240	38	102	0	.295	.422	.250
Mike Matheny	134	443	42	107	34	0	13	59	180	29	91	0	.295	.406	.242
Michael Tucker	104	250	32	60	16	1	5	33	93	28	48	4	.317	.372	.240
Yorvit Torrealba	34	93	18	21	8	0	1	7	32	9	25	1	.301	.344	.226
Todd Linden	60	171	20	37	8	0	4	13	57	10	54	3	.280	.333	.216
Marquis Grissom	44	137	8	29	4	0	2	15	39	7	18	1	.248	.285	.212

PITCHING	W–L	ERA	G	GS	CG	SV	INN	H	R	ER	BB	SO
Matt Cain	2–1	2.33	7	7	1	0	46.1	24	12	12	19	30
Scott Munter	2–0	2.56	45	0	0	0	38.2	40	15	11	12	11
Scott Eyre	2–2	2.63	86	0	0	0	68.1	48	21	20	26	65
Noah Lowry	13–13	3.78	33	33	0	0	204.2	193	92	86	76	172
Jeremy Accardo	1–5	3.94	28	0	0	0	29.2	26	13	13	9	16
Jeff Fassero	4–7	4.05	48	6	0	0	91.0	92	48	41	31	60
LaTroy Hawkins	1–4	4.10	45	0	0	2	37.1	40	18	17	17	30
Tyler Walker	6–4	4.23	67	0	0	23	61.2	68	31	29	27	54
Jason Schmidt	12–7	4.40	29	29	0	0	172.0	160	90	84	85	165
Brett Tomko	8–15	4.48	33	30	3	1	190.2	205	99	95	57	114
Armando Benitez	2–3	4.50	30	0	0	19	30.0	25	17	15	16	23
Kevin Correia	2–5	4.63	16	11	0	0	58.1	61	31	30	31	44
Brad Hennessey	5–8	4.64	21	21	0	0	118.1	127	63	61	52	64
Jason Christiansen	6–1	5.36	56	0	0	0	42.0	48	27	25	15	17
Kirk Rueter	2–7	5.95	20	18	0	0	107.1	131	78	71	47	25
Jim Brower	2–1	6.53	32	0	0	1	30.1	40	22	22	15	25

WASHINGTON NATIONALS

BATTING	G	AB	R	H	2B	3B	HR	RBI	TB	BB	SO	SB	OBP	SLG	BA
Nick Johnson	131	453	66	131	35	3	15	74	217	80	87	3	.408	.479	.289
Ryan Church	102	268	41	77	15	3	9	42	125	24	70	3	.353	.466	.287
Jose Guillen	148	551	81	156	32	2	24	76	264	31	102	1	.338	.479	.283
Jose Vidro	87	309	38	85	21	2	7	32	131	31	30	0	.339	.424	.275
Brian Schneider	116	369	38	99	20	1	10	44	151	29	48	1	.330	.409	.268
Marlon Byrd	74	216	20	57	15	2	2	26	86	18	47	5	.318	.380	.264
Preston Wilson	68	253	34	66	14	1	10	43	112	20	71	3	.329	.443	.261
Carlos Baerga	93	158	18	40	7	0	2	19	53	7	17	0	.318	.335	.253
Vinny Castilla	142	494	53	125	36	1	12	66	199	43	82	4	.319	.403	.253
Jamey Carroll	113	303	44	76	8	1	0	22	86	34	55	3	.333	.284	.251
Brad Wilkerson	148	565	76	140	42	7	11	57	229	84	147	8	.351	.405	.248
Gary Bennett	68	199	11	44	7	0	1	21	54	21	37	0	.298	.271	.221
Junior Spivey	28	77	15	17	7	0	2	7	30	11	26	2	.330	.390	.221
Cristian Guzman	142	456	39	100	19	6	4	31	143	25	76	7	.260	.314	.219

PITCHING	W–L	ERA	G	GS	CG	SV	INN	H	R	ER	BB	SO
Chad Cordero	2–4	1.82	74	0	0	47	74.1	55	24	15	17	61
Hector Carrasco	5–4	2.04	64	5	0	2	88.1	59	23	20	38	75
Luis Ayala	8–7	2.66	68	0	0	1	71.0	75	23	21	14	40
Gary Majewski	4–4	2.93	79	0	0	1	86.0	80	32	28	37	50
John Patterson	9–7	3.13	31	31	2	0	198.1	172	71	69	65	185
Joey Eischen	2–1	3.22	57	0	0	0	36.1	34	14	13	19	30
Tomo Ohka	4–3	3.33	10	9	0	0	54.0	44	23	20	27	17
Mike Stanton	2–1	3.58	30	0	0	0	27.2	31	13	11	9	14
Jon Rauch	2–4	3.60	15	1	0	0	30.0	24	12	12	11	23
Esteban Loaiza	12–10	3.77	34	34	0	0	217.0	227	93	91	55	173
Livan Hernandez	15–10	3.98	35	35	2	0	246.1	268	116	109	84	147
Tony Armas	7–7	4.97	19	19	0	0	101.1	100	57	56	54	59
Ryan Drese	3–6	4.98	11	11	0	0	59.2	66	38	33	22	26
Sunny Kim	1–2	6.14	12	2	0	0	29.1	41	20	20	8	17
Zach Day	1–2	6.75	12	5	0	0	36.0	41	29	27	25	16

AMERICAN LEAGUE TEAM-BY-TEAM STATS

BALTIMORE ORIOLES

BATTING

	G	AB	R	H	2B	3B	HR	RBI	TB	BB	SO	SB	OBP	SLG	BA
Brian Roberts	143	561	92	176	45	7	18	73	289	67	83	27	.387	.515	.314
Miguel Tejada	162	654	89	199	50	5	26	98	337	40	83	5	.349	.515	.304
Bernie Castro	24	80	14	23	3	1	0	7	28	9	10	6	.360	.350	.288
Melvin Mora	149	593	86	168	30	1	27	88	281	50	112	7	.348	.474	.283
Luis Matos	121	389	53	109	20	2	4	32	145	27	58	17	.340	.373	.280
Chris Gomez	89	219	27	61	11	0	1	18	75	27	17	2	.359	.342	.279
Javy Lopez	103	395	47	110	24	1	15	49	181	19	68	0	.322	.458	.278
Jay Gibbons	139	488	72	135	33	3	26	79	252	28	56	0	.317	.516	.277
Rafael Palmeiro	110	369	47	98	13	0	18	60	165	43	43	2	.339	.447	.266
B.J. Surhoff	91	303	30	78	11	2	5	34	108	11	32	0	.282	.356	.257
Sal Fasano	64	160	25	40	3	0	11	20	76	9	41	0	.310	.475	.250
Larry Bigbie	67	206	22	51	9	1	5	21	77	21	49	3	.314	.374	.248
Sammy Sosa	102	380	39	84	15	1	14	45	143	39	84	1	.295	.376	.221
David Newhan	96	218	31	44	9	0	5	21	68	22	45	9	.279	.312	.202
Eric Byrnes	52	167	17	32	7	1	3	11	50	11	33	3	.246	.299	.192
Geronimo Gil	64	125	7	24	3	0	4	17	39	5	23	0	.220	.312	.192

PITCHING

	W–L	ERA	G	GS	CG	SV	INN	H	R	ER	BB	SO
B.J. Ryan	1–4	2.43	69	0	0	36	70.1	54	20	19	26	100
Chris Ray	1–3	2.66	41	0	0	0	40.2	34	15	12	18	43
James Baldwin	0–0	3.20	20	0	0	0	39.1	36	18	14	9	20
Todd Williams	5–5	3.30	72	0	0	1	76.1	72	34	28	26	38
Bruce Chen	13–10	3.83	34	32	1	0	197.1	187	94	84	63	133
Erik Bedard	6–8	4.00	24	24	0	0	141.2	139	66	63	57	125
Steve Kline	2–4	4.28	67	0	0	0	61.0	59	34	29	30	36
Daniel Cabrera	10–13	4.52	29	29	0	0	161.1	144	92	81	87	157
Rodrigo Lopez	15–12	4.90	35	35	0	0	209.1	232	126	114	63	118
Eric DuBose	2–3	5.52	15	3	0	0	29.1	28	21	18	19	17
Jorge Julio	3–5	5.90	67	0	0	0	71.2	76	50	47	24	58
Sidney Ponson	7–11	6.21	23	23	1	0	130.1	177	97	90	48	68
John Maine	2–3	6.30	10	8	0	0	40.0	39	30	28	24	24
Hayden Penn	3–2	6.34	8	8	0	0	38.1	46	30	27	21	18
Steve Reed	1–2	6.61	30	0	0	0	32.2	41	24	24	11	15

BOSTON RED SOX

BATTING

	G	AB	R	H	2B	3B	HR	RBI	TB	BB	SO	SB	OBP	SLG	BA
Tony Graffanino	51	188	39	60	12	1	4	20	86	9	23	4	.355	.457	.319
Johnny Damon	148	624	117	197	35	6	10	75	274	53	69	18	.366	.439	.316
David Ortiz	159	601	119	180	40	1	47	148	363	102	124	1	.397	.604	.300
Bill Mueller	150	519	69	153	34	3	10	62	223	59	74	0	.369	.430	.295
Manny Ramirez	152	554	112	162	30	1	45	144	329	80	119	1	.388	.594	.292
John Olerud	87	173	18	50	7	0	7	37	78	16	20	0	.344	.451	.289
Roberto Petagine	18	32	4	9	2	0	1	9	14	4	5	0	.361	.438	.281
Jason Varitek	133	470	70	132	30	1	22	70	230	62	117	2	.366	.489	.281
Kevin Youkilis	44	79	11	22	7	0	1	9	32	14	19	0	.400	.405	.278
Edgar Renteria	153	623	100	172	36	4	8	70	240	55	100	9	.335	.385	.276
Trot Nixon	124	408	64	112	29	1	13	67	182	53	59	2	.357	.446	.275
Kevin Millar	134	449	57	122	28	1	9	50	179	54	74	0	.355	.399	.272
Alex Cora	47	104	14	28	3	2	2	16	41	6	12	1	.310	.394	.269
Adam Hyzdu	12	16	1	4	1	0	0	0	5	2	3	0	.333	.313	.250
Gabe Kapler	36	97	15	24	7	0	1	9	34	3	15	1	.282	.351	.247
Doug Mirabelli	50	136	16	31	7	0	6	18	56	14	48	2	.309	.412	.228
Adam Stern	36	15	4	2	0	0	1	2	5	0	4	1	.188	.333	.133

PITCHING

	W–L	ERA	G	GS	CG	SV	INN	H	R	ER	BB	SO
Lenny DiNardo	0–1	1.84	8	1	0	0	14.2	13	6	3	5	15
Mike Timlin	7–3	2.24	81	0	0	13	80.1	86	23	20	20	59
Jonathan Papelbon	3–1	2.65	17	3	0	0	34.0	33	11	10	17	34
Mike Myers	3–1	3.13	65	0	0	0	37.1	30	14	13	13	21
Chad Bradford	2–1	3.86	31	0	0	0	23.1	29	10	10	4	10
Tim Wakefield	16–12	4.15	33	33	3	0	225.1	210	113	104	68	151
David Wells	15–7	4.45	30	30	2	0	184.0	220	95	91	21	107
Bronson Arroyo	14–10	4.51	35	32	0	0	205.1	213	116	103	54	100
Matt Clement	13–6	4.57	32	32	1	0	191.0	192	102	97	68	146
Curt Schilling	8–8	5.69	32	11	0	9	93.1	121	59	59	22	87
Keith Foulke	5–5	5.91	43	0	0	15	45.2	53	30	30	18	34
Jeremi Gonzalez	2–1	6.11	28	3	0	0	56.0	64	39	38	16	28

BASEBALL

CHICAGO WHITE SOX

BATTING

BATTING	G	AB	R	H	2B	3B	HR	RBI	TB	BB	SO	SB	OBP	SLG	BA
Joe Borchard	7	12	0	5	2	0	0	0	7	0	4	0	.417	.583	.417
Scott Podsednik	129	507	80	147	28	1	0	25	177	47	75	59	.351	.349	.290
Paul Konerko	158	575	98	163	24	0	40	100	307	81	109	0	.375	.534	.283
Tadahito Iguchi	135	511	74	142	25	6	15	71	224	47	114	15	.342	.438	.278
Pablo Ozuna	70	203	27	56	7	2	0	11	67	7	26	14	.313	.330	.276
Jermain Dye	145	529	74	145	29	2	31	86	271	39	99	11	.333	.512	.274
Aaron Rowand	157	578	77	156	30	5	13	69	235	32	116	16	.329	.407	.270
A.J. Pierzynski	128	460	61	118	21	0	18	56	193	23	68	0	.308	.420	.257
Willie Harris	56	121	17	31	2	1	1	8	38	13	25	10	.333	.314	.256
Joe Crede	132	432	54	109	21	0	22	62	196	25	66	1	.303	.454	.252
Juan Uribe	146	481	58	121	23	3	16	71	198	34	77	4	.301	.412	.252
Carl Everett	135	490	58	123	17	2	23	87	213	42	99	4	.311	.435	.251
Chris Widger	45	141	18	34	8	0	4	11	54	10	22	0	.296	.383	.241
Timo Perez	76	179	13	39	8	0	2	15	53	12	25	2	.266	.296	.218
Geoff Blum	31	95	6	19	2	1	1	3	26	4	15	0	.232	.274	.200
Brian N. Anderson	13	34	3	6	1	0	2	3	13	0	12	1	.176	.382	.176
Ross Gload	28	42	2	7	2	0	0	5	9	2	9	0	.205	.214	.167

PITCHING

PITCHING	W–L	ERA	G	GS	CG	SV	INN	H	R	ER	BB	SO
Neal Cotts	4–0	1.94	69	0	0	19	60.1	38	15	13	29	58
Cliff Politte	7–1	2.00	68	0	0	1	67.1	42	15	15	21	57
Dustin Hermanson	2–4	2.04	57	0	0	34	57.1	46	17	13	17	33
Bobby Jenks	1–1	2.75	32	0	0	6	39.1	34	15	12	15	50
Mark Buehrle	16–8	3.12	33	33	3	0	236.2	240	99	82	40	149
Jon Garland	18–10	3.50	32	32	3	0	221.0	212	93	86	47	115
Jose Contreras	15–7	3.61	32	32	1	0	204.2	177	91	82	75	154
Luis Vizcaino	6–5	3.73	65	0	0	0	70.0	74	30	29	29	43
Damaso Marte	3–4	3.77	66	0	0	4	45.1	45	21	19	33	54
Freddy Garcia	14–8	3.87	33	33	2	0	228.0	225	102	98	60	146
Brandon McCarthy	3–2	4.03	12	10	0	0	67.0	62	30	30	17	48
Orlando Hernandez	9–9	5.12	24	22	0	1	128.1	137	77	73	50	91

CLEVELAND INDIANS

BATTING

BATTING	G	AB	R	H	2B	3B	HR	RBI	TB	BB	SO	SB	OBP	SLG	BA
Victor Martinez	147	547	73	167	33	0	20	80	260	63	78	0	.378	.475	.305
Travis Hafner	137	486	94	148	42	0	33	108	289	79	123	0	.408	.595	.305
Coco Crisp	145	594	86	178	42	4	16	69	276	44	81	15	.345	.465	.300
Jhonny Peralta	141	504	82	147	35	4	24	78	262	58	128	0	.366	.520	.292
Grady Sizemore	158	640	111	185	37	11	22	81	310	52	132	22	.348	.484	.289
Ronnie Belliard	145	536	71	152	36	1	17	78	241	35	72	2	.325	.450	.284
Ben Broussard	142	466	59	119	30	5	19	68	216	32	98	2	.307	.464	.255
Ramon Vasquez	12	24	1	6	3	0	0	1	9	2	3	0	.308	.375	.250
Aaron Boone	143	511	61	124	19	1	16	60	193	35	92	9	.299	.378	.243
Casey Blake	147	523	72	126	32	1	23	58	229	43	116	4	.308	.438	.241
Jose Hernandez	84	234	28	54	7	0	6	31	79	14	60	1	.277	.338	.231
Jason Dubois	14	45	6	10	0	0	2	2	16	5	25	0	.300	.356	.222
Jim Liefer	19	56	5	11	2	0	1	8	16	1	15	0	.211	.286	.196
Josh Bard	34	83	6	16	4	0	1	9	23	9	11	0	.266	.277	.193
Jason Davis	11	2	0	0	0	0	0	0	0	0	2	0	.000	.000	.000
Ryan Garko	1	1	0	0	0	0	0	0	0	0	1	0	.000	.000	.000
Franklin Gutierrez	7	1	2	0	0	0	0	0	0	0	1	0	.500	.000	.000

PITCHING

PITCHING	W–L	ERA	G	GS	CG	SV	INN	H	R	ER	BB	SO
Fernando Cabrera	2–1	1.47	15	0	0	0	30.2	24	7	5	11	29
Arthur Rhodes	3–1	2.08	47	0	0	0	43.1	33	13	10	12	43
Bob Howry	7–4	2.47	79	0	0	3	73.0	49	23	20	16	48
Bob Wickman	0–4	2.47	64	0	0	45	62.0	57	17	17	21	41
Rafael Betancourt	4–3	2.79	54	0	0	1	67.2	57	23	21	17	73
Kevin Millwood	9–11	2.86	30	30	1	0	192.0	182	72	61	52	146
David Riske	3–4	3.10	58	0	0	1	72.2	55	28	25	15	48
Cliff Lee	18–5	3.79	32	32	1	0	202.0	194	91	85	52	143
C.C. Sabathia	15–10	4.03	31	31	1	0	196.2	185	92	88	62	161
Jake Westbrook	15–15	4.49	34	34	2	0	210.2	218	121	105	56	119
Scott Elarton	11–9	4.61	31	31	1	0	181.2	189	100	93	48	103
Jason Davis	4–2	4.69	11	4	0	0	40.1	44	22	21	20	32

DETROIT TIGERS

BATTING	G	AB	R	H	2B	3B	HR	RBI	TB	BB	SO	SB	OBP	SLG	BA
Placido Polanco	86	343	58	116	20	2	6	36	158	21	16	4	.386	.461	.338
Carlos Guillen	87	334	48	107	15	4	5	23	145	24	45	2	.368	.434	.320
Magglio Ordonez	82	305	38	92	17	0	8	46	133	30	35	0	.359	.436	.302
Chris Shelton	107	388	61	116	22	3	18	59	198	34	87	0	.360	.510	.299
Craig Monroe	157	567	69	157	30	3	20	89	253	40	95	8	.322	.446	.277
Ivan Rodriguez	129	504	71	139	33	5	14	50	224	11	93	7	.290	.444	.276
Curtis Granderson	47	162	18	44	6	3	8	20	80	10	43	1	.314	.494	.272
Dmitri Young	126	469	61	127	25	3	21	72	221	29	100	1	.325	.471	.271
Brandon Inge	160	616	75	161	31	9	16	72	258	63	140	7	.330	.419	.261
John McDonald	31	73	10	19	3	1	0	4	24	5	12	1	.308	.329	.260
Nook Logan	129	322	47	83	12	5	1	17	108	21	52	23	.305	.335	.258
Carlos Pena	79	260	37	61	9	0	18	44	124	31	95	0	.325	.477	.235
Omar Infante	121	406	36	90	28	2	9	43	149	16	73	8	.254	.367	.222
Vance Wilson	61	152	18	30	4	0	3	19	43	11	26	0	.275	.283	.197
Marcus Thames	38	107	11	21	2	0	7	16	44	9	38	0	.263	.411	.196

PITCHING	W–L	ERA	G	GS	CG	SV	INN	H	R	ER	BB	SO
Vic Darensbourg	1–1	2.82	22	0	0	0	22.1	24	7	7	7	9
Fernando Rodney	2–3	2.86	39	0	0	9	44.0	39	14	14	17	42
Jason Grilli	1–1	3.38	3	2	0	0	16.0	14	6	6	6	5
Chris Spurling	3–4	3.44	56	0	0	0	70.2	58	30	27	22	26
Craig Dingman	2–3	3.66	34	0	0	4	32.0	30	14	13	9	24
Franklyn German	4–0	3.66	58	0	0	1	59.0	63	26	24	34	38
Jamie Walker	4–3	3.70	66	0	0	0	48.2	49	22	20	13	30
Nate Robertson	7–16	4.48	32	32	2	0	196.2	202	113	98	65	122
Jason Johnson	8–13	4.54	33	33	1	0	210.0	233	117	106	49	93
Jeremy Bonderman	14–13	4.57	29	29	4	0	189.0	199	101	96	57	145
Mike Maroth	14–14	4.74	34	34	0	0	209.0	235	123	110	51	115
Sean Douglass	5–5	5.56	18	16	0	0	87.1	92	57	54	33	55
Roman Colon	1–1	6.12	12	3	0	0	25.0	35	17	17	7	17

KANSAS CITY ROYALS

BATTING	G	AB	R	H	2B	3B	HR	RBI	TB	BB	SO	SB	OBP	SLG	BA
Mike Sweeney	122	470	63	141	39	0	21	83	243	33	61	3	.347	.517	.300
Aaron Guiel	33	109	18	32	5	0	4	7	49	6	21	1	.355	.450	.294
David DeJesus	122	461	69	135	31	6	9	56	205	42	76	5	.359	.445	.293
Emil Brown	150	545	75	156	31	5	17	86	248	48	108	10	.349	.455	.286
Matt Diaz	34	89	7	25	4	2	1	9	36	4	15	0	.323	.404	.281
Terence Long	137	455	62	127	21	3	6	53	172	30	56	3	.321	.378	.279
Matt Stairs	127	396	55	109	26	1	13	66	176	60	69	1	.373	.444	.275
Angel Berroa	159	608	68	164	21	5	11	55	228	18	108	7	.305	.375	.270
Paul Phillips	23	67	6	18	4	1	1	9	27	0	5	0	.269	.403	.269
Denny Hocking	23	60	14	16	1	0	0	7	17	10	10	0	.371	.283	.267
Mark Teahen	130	447	60	110	29	4	7	55	168	40	107	7	.309	.376	.246
John Buck	118	401	40	97	21	1	12	47	156	23	94	2	.287	.389	.242
Chip Ambres	53	145	25	35	8	0	4	9	55	16	32	3	.323	.379	.241
Joe McEwing	83	180	16	43	7	0	1	6	53	6	35	4	.263	.294	.239
Justin Huber	25	78	6	17	3	0	0	6	20	5	20	0	.271	.256	.218
Andres Blanco	26	79	6	17	0	1	0	5	19	0	5	0	.220	.241	.215
Donnie Murphy	32	77	4	12	5	0	1	8	20	9	23	0	.241	.260	.156

PITCHING	W–L	ERA	G	GS	CG	SV	INN	H	R	ER	BB	SO
Andrew Sisco	2–5	3.11	67	0	0	0	75.1	68	27	26	42	76
Mike MacDougal	5–6	3.33	68	0	0	21	70.1	69	32	26	24	72
Ambiorix Burgos	3–5	3.98	59	0	0	2	63.1	60	29	28	31	65
Mike Wood	5–8	4.46	47	10	0	2	115.0	129	66	57	52	60
D.J. Carrasco	6–8	4.79	21	20	1	0	114.2	129	67	61	51	49
Jeremy Affeldt	0–2	5.26	49	0	0	0	49.2	56	35	29	29	39
Runelvys Hernandez	8–14	5.52	29	29	0	0	159.2	172	101	98	70	88
Zack Greinke	5–17	5.80	33	33	2	0	183.0	233	125	118	53	114
J.P. Howell	3–5	6.19	15	15	0	0	72.2	73	55	50	39	54
Shawn Camp	1–4	6.43	29	0	0	0	49.0	69	40	35	13	28
Jose Lima	5–16	6.99	32	32	1	0	168.2	219	140	131	61	80
Leo Nunez	3–2	7.55	41	0	0	0	53.2	73	45	45	18	32

LOS ANGELES ANGELS

BATTING	G	AB	R	H	2B	3B	HR	RBI	TB	BB	SO	SB	OBP	SLG	BA
Vladimir Guerrero	141	520	95	165	29	2	32	108	294	61	48	13	.333	.333	.333
Adam Kennedy	129	416	49	125	23	0	2	37	154	29	64	19	.354	.370	.300
Bengie Molina	119	410	45	121	17	0	15	69	183	27	41	0	.336	.446	.295
Chone Figgins	158	642	113	186	25	10	8	57	255	64	101	62	.352	.397	.290
Garrett Anderson	142	575	68	163	34	1	17	96	250	23	84	1	.308	.435	.283
Casey Kotchman	47	126	16	35	5	0	7	22	61	15	18	1	.352	.484	.278
Darin Erstad	153	609	86	166	33	3	7	66	226	47	109	10	.325	.371	.273
Juan Rivera	106	350	46	95	17	1	15	59	159	23	44	1	.316	.454	.271
Orlando Cabrera	141	540	70	139	28	3	8	57	197	38	50	21	.309	.365	.257
Maicer Izturis	77	191	18	47	8	4	1	15	66	17	21	9	.306	.346	.246
Robb Quinlan	54	134	17	31	8	0	5	14	54	7	26	0	.273	.403	.231
Jeff DaVanon	108	225	42	52	10	1	2	15	70	39	44	11	.347	.311	.231
Jose Molina	75	184	14	42	4	0	6	25	64	13	41	2	.286	.348	.228
Steve Finley	112	406	41	90	20	3	12	54	152	26	71	8	.271	.374	.222
Josh Paul	34	37	4	7	1	0	2	4	14	2	9	0	.231	.378	.189
Zach Sorensen	12	12	3	2	1	0	0	0	3	0	2	0	.167	.250	.167
Curtis Pride	11	11	2	1	1	0	0	0	2	0	4	0	.091	.182	.091

PITCHING	W–L	ERA	G	GS	CG	SV	INN	H	R	ER	BB	SO
Francisco Rodriguez	2–5	2.67	66	0	0	45	67.1	45	20	20	32	91
Scot Shields	10–11	2.75	78	0	0	7	91.2	66	33	28	37	98
Kelvim Escobar	3–2	3.02	16	7	0	1	59.2	45	21	20	21	63
Jarrod Washburn	8–8	3.20	29	29	1	0	177.1	184	66	63	51	94
John Lackey	14–5	3.44	33	33	1	0	209.0	208	85	85	71	199
Bartolo Colon	21–8	3.48	33	33	2	0	222.2	215	93	86	43	157
Brendan Donnelly	9–3	3.72	65	0	0	0	65.1	60	30	27	19	53
Paul Byrd	12–11	3.74	31	31	2	0	204.1	216	95	85	28	102
Joel Peralta	1–0	3.89	28	0	0	0	34.2	28	15	15	14	30
Esteban Yan	1–1	4.59	49	0	0	0	66.2	66	36	34	30	45
Ervin Santana	12–8	4.65	23	23	1	0	133.2	139	73	69	47	99
Kevin Gregg	1–2	5.04	33	2	0	0	64.1	70	37	36	29	52

MINNESOTA TWINS

BATTING	G	AB	R	H	2B	3B	HR	RBI	TB	BB	SO	SB	OBP	SLG	BA
Jason Tyner	18	56	8	18	1	1	0	5	21	4	4	2	.367	.375	.321
Mike Redmond	45	148	17	46	9	0	1	26	58	6	14	0	.350	.392	.311
Joe Mauer	131	489	61	144	26	2	9	55	201	61	64	13	.372	.411	.294
Shannon Stewart	132	551	69	151	27	3	10	56	214	34	73	7	.323	.388	.274
Luis Rodriguez	79	175	21	47	10	2	2	20	67	18	23	2	.335	.383	.269
Lew Ford	147	522	70	138	30	4	7	53	197	45	85	13	.338	.377	.264
Michael Cuddyer	126	422	55	111	25	3	12	42	178	41	93	3	.330	.422	.263
Matthew LeCroy	101	304	33	79	5	0	17	50	135	41	85	0	.354	.444	.260
Juan Castro	97	272	27	70	18	1	5	33	105	9	39	0	.279	.386	.257
Luis Rivas	59	136	21	35	3	1	1	12	43	9	17	4	.311	.316	.257
Jacque Jones	142	523	74	130	22	4	23	73	229	51	120	13	.319	.438	.249
Jason Bartlett	74	224	33	54	10	1	3	16	75	21	37	4	.316	.335	.241
Brent Abernathy	24	67	5	16	1	0	1	6	20	7	9	2	.316	.299	.239
Justin Morneau	141	490	62	117	23	4	22	79	214	44	94	0	.304	.437	.239
Nick Punto	112	394	45	94	18	4	4	26	132	36	86	13	.301	.335	.239
Michael Ryan	57	117	7	27	5	0	2	13	38	9	22	1	.283	.325	.231
Terry Tiffee	54	150	9	31	8	1	1	15	44	8	15	1	.245	.293	.207

PITCHING	W–L	ERA	G	GS	CG	SV	INN	H	R	ER	BB	SO
Juan Rincon	6–6	2.45	75	0	0	0	77.0	63	26	21	30	84
Joe Nathan	7–4	2.70	69	0	0	43	70.0	46	22	21	22	94
Jesse Crain	12–5	2.71	75	0	0	1	79.2	61	28	24	29	25
Johan Santana	16–7	2.87	33	33	3	0	231.2	180	77	74	22	238
Scott Baker	3–3	3.35	10	9	0	0	53.2	48	21	20	14	32
Matt Guerrier	0–3	3.39	43	0	0	0	71.2	71	29	27	24	46
Carlos Silva	9–8	3.44	27	27	2	0	188.1	212	83	72	9	71
J.C. Romero	4–3	3.47	68	0	0	0	57.0	50	26	22	39	48
Brad Radke	9–12	4.04	31	31	3	0	200.2	214	98	90	23	117
Kyle Lohse	9–13	4.18	31	30	0	0	178.2	211	85	83	44	86
Terry Mulholland	0–2	4.27	49	0	0	0	59.0	61	30	28	17	18
Joe Mays	6–10	5.65	31	26	1	0	156.0	203	109	98	41	59

NEW YORK YANKEES

BATTING	G	AB	R	H	2B	3B	HR	RBI	TB	BB	SO	SB	OBP	SLG	BA
Alex Rodriguez	162	605	124	194	29	1	48	130	369	91	139	21	.421	.610	.321
Derek Jeter	159	654	122	202	25	5	19	70	294	77	117	14	.389	.450	.309
Hideki Matsui	162	629	108	192	45	3	23	116	312	63	78	2	.367	.496	.305
Robinson Cano	132	522	78	155	34	4	14	62	239	16	68	1	.320	.458	.297
Gary Sheffield	154	584	104	170	27	0	34	123	299	78	76	10	.379	.512	.291
Felix Escalona	10	14	0	4	1	0	0	2	5	1	4	0	.375	.357	.286
Bubba Crosby	76	98	15	27	0	1	1	6	32	4	14	4	.304	.327	.276
Jason Giambi	139	417	74	113	14	0	32	87	223	108	109	0	.440	.535	.271
Jorge Posada	142	474	67	124	23	0	19	71	204	66	94	1	.352	.430	.262
Bernie Williams	141	485	53	121	19	1	12	64	178	53	75	1	.321	.367	.249
Tony Womack	108	329	46	82	8	1	0	15	92	12	49	27	.276	.280	.249
Tino Martinez	131	303	43	73	9	0	17	49	133	38	54	2	.328	.439	.241
Ruben Sierra	61	170	14	39	12	0	4	29	63	9	41	0	.265	.371	.229
John Flaherty	47	127	10	21	5	0	2	11	32	6	26	0	.206	.252	.165
Andy Phillips	27	40	7	6	4	0	1	4	13	1	13	0	.171	.325	.150
Matt Lawton	21	48	6	6	0	0	2	4	12	7	8	1	.263	.250	.125
Mark Bellhorn	9	17	2	2	0	0	1	2	5	3	3	0	.250	.294	.118

PITCHING	W–L	ERA	G	GS	CG	SV	INN	H	R	ER	BB	SO
Mariano Rivera	7–4	1.38	71	0	0	43	78.1	50	18	12	18	80
Tom Gordon	5–4	2.57	79	0	0	2	80.2	59	25	23	29	69
Shawn Chacon	7–3	2.85	14	12	0	0	79.0	66	26	25	30	40
Aaron Small	10–0	3.20	15	9	1	0	76.0	71	27	27	24	37
Randy Johnson	17–8	3.79	34	34	4	0	225.2	207	102	95	47	211
Chien-Ming Wang	8–5	4.02	18	17	0	0	116.1	113	58	52	32	47
Mike Mussina	13–8	4.41	30	30	2	0	179.2	199	93	88	47	142
Tanyon Sturtze	5–3	4.73	64	1	0	1	78.0	76	43	41	27	45
Felix Rodriguez	0–0	5.01	34	0	0	0	32.1	33	18	18	20	18
Al Leiter	4–5	5.49	16	10	0	0	62.1	66	42	38	38	45
Scott Proctor	1–0	6.04	29	1	0	0	44.2	46	32	30	17	36
Jaret Wright	5–5	6.08	13	13	0	0	63.2	81	51	43	32	34

OAKLAND ATHLETICS

BATTING	G	AB	R	H	2B	3B	HR	RBI	TB	BB	SO	SB	OBP	SLG	BA
Mark Ellis	122	434	76	137	21	5	13	52	207	44	51	1	.384	.477	.316
Freddie Bynum	7	7	0	2	1	0	0	1	3	0	3	0	.286	.429	.286
Mark Kotsay	139	582	75	163	35	1	15	82	245	40	51	5	.325	.421	.280
Bobby Crosby	84	333	66	92	25	4	9	38	152	35	54	0	.346	.456	.276
Dan Johnson	109	375	54	103	21	0	15	58	169	50	52	0	.355	.451	.275
Jason Kendall	150	601	70	163	28	1	0	53	193	50	39	8	.345	.321	.271
Jay Payton	69	275	38	74	9	1	13	42	124	14	33	0	.302	.451	.269
Eric Chavez	160	625	92	168	40	1	27	101	291	58	129	6	.329	.466	.269
Bobby Kielty	116	377	55	99	20	0	10	57	149	50	67	3	.350	.395	.263
Scott Hatteberg	134	464	52	119	19	0	7	59	159	51	54	0	.334	.343	.256
Adam Melhuse	39	97	11	24	7	0	2	12	37	5	28	0	.284	.381	.247
Marco Scutaro	118	381	48	94	22	3	9	37	149	36	48	5	.310	.391	.247
Nick Swisher	131	462	66	109	32	1	21	74	206	55	110	0	.322	.446	.236
Matt Watson	19	48	4	9	3	0	0	5	12	2	4	0	.220	.250	.188
Keith Ginter	51	137	12	22	5	0	3	25	36	13	25	0	.234	.263	.161
Hiram Bocachica	9	19	2	2	0	0	0	0	2	0	7	0	.105	.105	.105

PITCHING	W–L	ERA	G	GS	CG	SV	INN	H	R	ER	BB	SO
Huston Street	5–1	1.72	67	0	0	23	78.1	53	17	15	26	72
Justin Duchscherer	7–4	2.21	65	0	0	5	85.2	67	25	21	19	85
Rich Harden	10–5	2.53	22	19	2	0	128.0	93	42	36	43	121
Kiko Calero	4–1	3.23	58	0	0	1	55.2	45	20	20	18	52
Jay Witasick	1–1	3.25	28	0	0	1	27.2	26	15	10	17	33
Joe Blanton	12–12	3.53	33	33	2	0	201.1	178	86	79	67	116
Dan Haren	14–12	3.73	34	34	3	0	217.0	212	101	90	53	163
Barry Zito	14–13	3.86	35	35	0	0	228.1	185	106	98	89	171
Kirk Saarloos	10–9	4.17	29	27	2	0	159.2	170	75	74	54	53
Ricrado Rincon	1–1	4.34	67	0	0	0	37.1	34	19	18	20	27
Joe Kennedy	4–5	4.45	19	8	0	0	60.2	64	33	30	20	45
Keiichi Yabu	4–0	4.50	40	0	0	1	58.0	64	34	29	26	44
Juan Cruz	0–3	7.44	28	0	0	0	32.2	38	33	27	22	34

BASEBALL

SEATTLE MARINERS

BATTING	G	AB	R	H	2B	3B	HR	RBI	TB	BB	SO	SB	OBP	SLG	BA
Rene Rivera	16	48	3	19	3	0	1	6	25	1	11	0	.408	.521	.396
Ichiro Suzuki	162	679	111	206	21	12	15	68	296	48	66	33	.350	.436	.303
Raul Ibanez	162	614	92	172	32	2	20	89	268	71	99	9	.355	.436	.280
Mike Morse	72	230	27	64	10	1	3	23	85	18	50	3	.349	.370	.278
Richie Sexson	156	558	99	147	36	1	39	121	302	89	167	1	.369	.541	.263
Yuniesky Betancourt	60	211	24	54	11	5	1	15	78	11	24	1	.296	.370	.256
Adrian Beltre	156	603	69	154	36	1	19	87	249	38	108	3	.303	.413	.255
Jimmy Reed	141	488	61	124	33	3	3	45	172	48	74	12	.322	.352	.254
Jose Lopez	54	190	18	47	19	0	2	25	72	6	25	4	.282	.379	.247
Greg Dobbs	59	142	8	35	7	1	1	20	47	9	25	1	.288	.331	.246
Yorvit Torrealba	42	108	14	26	4	0	2	8	36	7	25	0	.293	.333	.241
Dan Wilson	11	27	2	5	0	0	0	2	5	0	10	0	.214	.185	.185
Dave Hansen	60	75	5	13	0	0	2	11	19	9	19	0	.256	.253	.173
Miguel Ojeda	16	29	2	5	0	0	1	3	8	6	3	0	.314	.276	.172
Jaime Bubela	11	19	3	2	0	0	0	0	2	1	4	1	.150	.105	.105
Shin-Soo Choo	10	18	1	1	0	0	0	1	1	3	4	0	.190	.056	.056

PITCHING	W–L	ERA	G	GS	CG	SV	INN	H	R	ER	BB	SO
Felix Hernandez	4–4	2.67	12	12	0	0	84.1	61	26	25	23	77
Eddie Guardado	2–3	2.72	58	0	0	36	56.1	52	23	17	15	48
Julio Mateo	3–6	3.06	55	1	0	0	88.1	79	32	30	17	52
J.J. Putz	6–5	3.60	64	0	0	1	60.0	58	27	24	23	45
Jeff Nelson	1–3	3.93	49	0	0	1	36.2	32	17	16	22	34
Shigetoshi Hasegawa	1–3	4.19	46	0	0	0	66.2	66	31	31	16	30
Jeff Harris	2–5	4.19	11	8	0	0	53.2	48	27	25	20	25
Jamie Moyer	13–7	4.28	32	32	1	0	200.0	225	99	95	52	102
Gil Meche	10–8	5.09	29	26	0	0	143.1	153	92	81	72	83
Ryan Franklin	8–15	5.10	32	30	2	0	190.2	212	110	108	62	93
George Sherrill	4–3	5.21	29	0	0	0	19.0	13	12	11	7	24
Matt Thornton	0–4	5.21	55	0	0	0	57.0	54	33	33	42	57
Joel Pineiro	7–11	5.62	30	30	2	0	189.0	224	118	118	56	107

TAMPA BAY DEVIL RAYS

BATTING	G	AB	R	H	2B	3B	HR	RBI	TB	BB	SO	SB	OBP	SLG	BA
Carl Crawford	156	644	101	194	33	15	15	81	302	27	84	46	.331	.469	.301
Julio Logo	158	616	89	182	36	6	6	57	248	61	72	39	.362	.403	.295
Toby Hall	135	432	28	124	20	0	5	48	159	16	39	0	.315	.368	.287
Jorge Cantu	150	598	73	171	40	1	28	117	297	19	83	1	.311	.497	.286
Jonny Gomes	101	348	61	98	13	6	21	54	186	39	113	9	.372	.534	.282
Joey Gathright	76	203	29	56	7	3	0	13	69	10	39	20	.316	.340	.276
Travis Lee	129	404	54	110	22	2	12	49	172	35	66	7	.331	.426	.272
Alex S. Gonzalez	109	349	47	94	20	1	9	38	143	26	74	2	.323	.410	.269
Aubrey Huff	154	575	70	150	26	2	22	92	246	49	88	8	.321	.428	.261
Eduardo Perez	77	161	23	41	6	0	11	28	80	26	30	0	.368	.497	.255
Damon Hollins	120	342	44	85	17	1	13	46	143	23	63	8	.296	.418	.249
Nick Green	111	318	53	76	15	2	5	29	110	33	86	3	.329	.346	.239
Pete LaForest	25	64	5	11	3	0	1	4	17	6	23	0	.243	.266	.172
Eric Munson	11	18	2	3	1	0	0	2	4	4	3	0	.333	.222	.167

PITCHING	W–L	ERA	G	GS	CG	SV	INN	H	R	ER	BB	SO
Danys Baez	5–4	2.86	67	0	0	41	72.1	66	27	23	30	51
Joe Beimei	0–0	3.27	7	0	0	0	11.0	15	4	4	4	3
Chad Orvella	3–3	3.60	37	0	0	1	50.0	47	26	20	23	43
Scott Kazmir	10–9	3.77	32	32	0	0	186.0	172	90	78	100	174
Joe Borowski	1–5	3.82	32	0	0	0	35.1	26	15	15	11	16
Trever Miller	2–2	4.06	61	0	0	0	44.1	45	23	20	29	35
Jesus Colome	2–3	4.57	36	0	0	0	45.1	54	29	23	18	28
Lance Carter	1–2	4.89	39	0	0	1	57.0	61	31	31	15	22
Casey Fossum	8–12	4.92	36	25	0	0	162.2	170	100	89	60	128
Doug Waechter	5–12	5.62	29	25	0	0	157.0	191	109	98	38	87
Mark Hendrickson	11–8	5.90	31	31	1	0	178.1	227	126	117	49	89
Tim Corcoran	0–0	5.96	10	1	0	0	22.2	19	15	15	12	13
Seth McClung	7–11	6.59	34	17	0	0	109.1	106	85	80	62	92
Travis Harper	4–6	6.75	52	0	0	0	73.1	88	57	55	24	40
Dewon Brazelton	1–8	7.61	20	8	0	0	71.0	87	65	60	60	43

TEXAS RANGERS

BATTING

BATTING	G	AB	R	H	2B	3B	HR	RBI	TB	BB	SO	SB	OBP	SLG	BA
Esteban German	5	4	3	3	1	0	0	1	4	0	1	2	.750	1.000	.750
Michael Young	159	668	114	221	40	5	24	91	343	58	91	5	.385	.513	.331
Mark Teixeira	162	644	112	194	41	3	43	144	370	72	124	4	.379	.575	.301
Jason Botts	10	27	4	8	0	0	0	3	8	3	13	0	.367	.296	.296
Sandy Alomar Jr.	46	128	11	35	7	0	0	14	42	5	12	0	.306	.328	.273
Alfonso Soriano	156	637	102	171	43	2	36	104	326	33	125	30	.309	.512	.268
Kevin Mench	150	557	71	147	33	3	25	73	261	50	68	4	.328	.469	.264
Hank Blalock	161	647	80	170	34	0	25	92	279	51	132	1	.318	.431	.263
Gary Matthews Jr.	131	475	72	121	25	5	17	55	207	47	90	9	.320	.436	.255
Rod Barajas	120	410	53	104	24	0	21	60	191	26	70	0	.306	.466	.254
David Dellucci	128	435	97	109	17	5	29	65	223	76	121	5	.367	.513	.251
Mark DeRosa	66	148	26	36	5	0	8	20	65	16	35	1	.325	.439	.243
Adrian Gonzalez	43	150	17	34	7	1	6	17	61	10	37	0	.272	.407	.227
Gerald Laird	13	40	7	9	2	0	1	4	14	2	7	0	.262	.350	.225
Phil Nevin	29	99	15	18	5	0	3	8	32	8	30	2	.250	.323	.182
Marshall McDougall	18	18	3	3	1	0	0	0	4	0	10	0	.167	.222	.167

PITCHING

PITCHING	W–L	ERA	G	GS	CG	SV	INN	H	R	ER	BB	SO
Francisco Cordero	3–1	3.39	69	0	0	37	69.0	61	28	26	30	79
Kameron Loe	9–6	3.42	48	8	0	1	92.0	89	43	35	31	45
Kenny Rogers	14–8	3.46	30	30	1	0	195.1	205	86	75	53	87
Joaquin Benoit	4–4	3.72	32	9	0	0	87.0	69	39	36	38	78
Erasmo Ramirez	0–0	3.91	16	0	0	0	23.0	24	10	10	3	6
Juan Dominguez	4–6	4.22	22	10	0	0	70.1	78	37	33	25	45
Chris Young	12–7	4.26	31	31	0	0	164.2	162	84	78	45	137
John Wasdin	3–2	4.28	31	6	0	4	75.2	77	37	36	20	44
Brian Shouse	3–2	5.23	64	0	0	0	53.1	55	37	31	18	35
Doug Brocail	5–3	5.52	61	0	0	1	73.1	90	48	45	34	61
R.A. Dickey	1–2	6.67	9	4	0	0	29.2	29	23	22	17	15
C.J. Wilson	1–7	6.94	24	6	0	1	48.0	63	39	37	18	30
Edison Volquez	0–4	14.21	6	3	0	0	12.2	25	22	20	10	11

TORONTO BLUE JAYS

BATTING

BATTING	G	AB	R	H	2B	3B	HR	RBI	TB	BB	SO	SB	OBP	SLG	BA
John-Ford Griffin	7	13	3	4	2	0	1	6	9	0	4	0	.308	.692	.308
Frank Catalanotto	130	419	56	126	29	5	8	59	189	37	53	0	.367	.451	.301
Shea Hillenbrand	152	594	91	173	36	2	18	82	267	26	79	5	.343	.449	.291
Aaron Hill	105	361	49	99	25	3	3	40	139	34	41	2	.342	.385	.274
Orlando Hudson	131	461	62	125	25	5	10	63	190	30	65	7	.315	.412	.271
Vernon Wells	156	620	78	167	30	3	28	97	287	47	86	8	.320	.463	.269
Reed Johnson	142	398	55	107	21	6	8	58	164	22	82	5	.332	.412	.269
Eric Hinske	147	477	79	125	31	2	15	68	205	46	121	8	.333	.430	.262
Alex Rios	146	481	71	126	23	6	10	59	191	28	101	14	.306	.397	.262
Russ Adams	139	481	68	123	27	5	8	63	184	50	57	11	.325	.383	.256
Gregg Zaun	133	434	61	109	18	1	11	61	162	73	70	2	.355	.373	.251
Gabe Gross	40	92	11	23	4	1	1	7	32	10	21	1	.324	.348	.250
Corey Coskie	97	354	49	88	20	0	11	36	141	44	90	4	.337	.398	.249
Frank Menechino	70	148	22	32	7	0	4	13	51	25	33	0	.352	.345	.216
Ken Huckaby	35	87	8	18	4	0	18	6	22	5	19	0	.250	.253	.207
Guillermo Quiroz	12	36	3	7	2	0	0	4	9	2	13	0	.256	.250	.194

PITCHING

PITCHING	W–L	ERA	G	GS	CG	SV	INN	H	R	ER	BB	SO
Roy Halladay	12–4	2.41	19	19	5	0	141.2	118	39	38	18	108
Justin Speier	3–2	2.57	65	0	0	0	66.2	48	20	19	15	56
Jason Frasor	3–5	3.25	67	0	0	1	74.2	67	31	27	28	62
Scott Schoeneweis	3–4	3.32	80	0	0	1	57.0	54	23	21	25	43
Pete Walker	6–6	3.54	41	4	0	2	84.0	81	33	33	33	43
Josh Towers	13–12	3.71	33	33	2	0	208.2	237	101	86	29	112
Gustavo Chacin	13–9	3.72	34	34	0	0	203.0	213	93	84	70	121
Vinnie Chulk	0–1	3.88	62	0	0	0	72.0	68	33	31	26	39
Miguel Batista	5–8	4.10	71	0	0	31	74.2	80	39	34	27	54
Scott Downs	4–3	4.31	26	13	0	0	94.0	93	49	45	34	75
Dave Bush	5–11	4.49	25	24	2	0	136.1	142	73	68	29	75
Ted Lilly	10–11	5.56	25	25	0	0	126.1	135	79	78	58	96
Dustin McGowan	1–3	6.35	13	7	0	0	45.1	49	34	32	17	34
Brandon League	1–0	6.56	20	0	0	0	35.2	42	27	26	20	17

WORLD SERIES ALL-TIME RESULTS

Year	Result	Year	Result
2005	Chicago (A) 4, Houston (N) 0	1953	New York (A) 4, Brooklyn (N) 2
2004	Boston (A) 4, St. Louis (N) 0	1952	New York (A) 4, Brooklyn (N) 3
2003	Florida (N) 4, New York (A) 2	1951	New York (A) 4, New York (N) 2
2002	Anaheim (A) 4, San Francisco (N) 3	1950	New York (A) 4, Philadelphia (N) 0
2001	Arizona (N) 4, New York (A) 3	1949	New York (A) 4, Brooklyn (N) 1
2000	New York (A) 4, New York (N) 1	1948	Cleveland (A) 4, Boston (N) 2
1999	New York (A) 4, Atlanta (N) 0	1947	New York (A) 4, Brooklyn (N) 3
1998	New York (A) 4, San Diego (N) 0	1946	St. Louis (N) 4, Boston (A) 3
1997	Florida (N) 4, Cleveland (A) 3	1945	Detroit (A) 4, Chicago (N) 3
1996	New York (A) 4, Atlanta (N) 2	1944	St. Louis (N) 4, St. Louis (A) 2
1995	Atlanta (N) 4, Cleveland (A) 2	1943	New York (A) 4, St. Louis (N) 1
1994	Series canceled due to labor dispute.	1942	St. Louis (N) 4, New York (A) 1
1993	Toronto (A) 4, Philadelphia (N) 2	1941	New York (A) 4, Brooklyn (N) 1
1992	Toronto (A) 4, Atlanta (N) 2	1940	Cincinnati (N) 4, Detroit (A) 3
1991	Minnesota (A) 4, Atlanta (N) 3	1939	New York (A) 4, Cincinnati (N) 0
1990	Cincinnati (N) 4, Oakland (A) 0	1938	New York (A) 4, Chicago (N) 0
1989	Oakland (A) 4, San Francisco (N) 0	1937	New York (A) 4, New York (N) 1
1988	Los Angeles (N) 4, Oakland (A) 1	1936	New York (A) 4, New York (N) 2
1987	Minnesota (A) 4, St. Louis (N) 3	1935	Detroit (A) 4, Chicago (N) 2
1986	New York (N) 4, Boston (A) 3	1934	St. Louis (N) 4, Detroit (A) 3
1985	Kansas City (A) 4, St. Louis (N) 3	1933	New York (A) 4, Washington (A) 1
1984	Detroit (A) 4, San Diego (N) 1	1932	New York (A) 4, Chicago (N) 0
1983	Baltimore (A) 4, Philadelphia (N) 1	1931	St. Louis (N) 4, Philadelphia (A) 3
1982	St. Louis (N) 4, Milwaukee (A) 3	1930	Philadelphia (A) 4, St. Louis (N) 2
1981	Los Angeles (N) 4, New York (A) 2	1929	Philadelphia (A) 4, Chicago (N) 1
1980	Philadelphia (N) 4, Kansas City (A) 2	1928	New York (A) 4, St. Louis (N) 0
1979	Pittsburgh (N) 4, Baltimore (A) 3	1927	New York (A) 4, Pittsburgh (N) 0
1978	New York (A) 4, Los Angeles (N) 2	1926	St. Louis (N) 4, New York (A) 3
1977	New York (A) 4, Los Angeles (N) 2	1925	Pittsburgh (N) 4, Washington (A) 3
1976	Cincinnati (N) 4, New York (A) 0	1924	Washington (A) 4, New York (N) 3
1975	Cincinnati (N) 4, Boston (A) 3	1923	New York (A) 4, New York (N) 2
1974	Oakland (A) 4, Los Angeles (N) 1	1922	New York (N) 4, New York (A) 0; 1 tie
1973	Oakland (A) 4, New York (N) 3	1921	New York (N) 5, New York (A) 3
1972	Oakland (A) 4, Cincinnati (N) 3	1920	Cleveland (A) 5, Brooklyn (N) 2
1971	Pittsburgh (N) 4, Baltimore (A) 3	1919	Cincinnati (N) 5, Chicago (A) 3
1970	Baltimore (A) 4, Cincinnati (N) 1	1918	Boston (A) 4, Chicago (N) 2
1969	New York (N) 4, Baltimore (A) 1	1917	Chicago (A) 4, New York (N) 2
1968	Detroit (A) 4, St. Louis (N) 3	1916	Boston (A) 4, Brooklyn (N) 1
1967	St. Louis (N) 4, Boston (A) 3	1915	Boston (A) 4, Philadelphia (N) 1
1966	Baltimore (A) 4, Los Angeles (N) 0	1914	Boston (N) 4, Philadelphia (A) 0
1965	Los Angeles (N) 4, Minnesota (A) 3	1913	Philadelphia (A) 4, New York (N) 1
1964	St. Louis (N) 4, New York (A) 3	1912	Boston (A) 4, New York (N) 3; 1 tie
1963	Los Angeles (N) 4, New York (A) 0	1911	Philadelphia (A) 4, New York (N) 2
1962	New York (A) 4, San Francisco (N) 3	1910	Philadelphia (A) 4, Chicago (N) 1
1961	New York (A) 4, Cincinnati (N) 1	1909	Pittsburgh (N) 4, Detroit (A) 3
1960	Pittsburgh (N) 4, New York (A) 3	1908	Chicago (N) 4, Detroit (A) 1
1959	Los Angeles (N) 4, Chicago (A) 2	1907	Chicago (N) 4, Detroit (A) 0; 1 tie
1958	New York (A) 4, Milwaukee (N) 3	1906	Chicago (A) 4, Chicago (N) 2
1957	Milwaukee (N) 4, New York (A) 3	1905	New York (N) 4, Philadelphia (A) 1
1956	New York (A) 4, Brooklyn (N) 3	1904	No series
1955	Brooklyn (N) 4, New York (A) 3	1903	Boston (A) 5, Pittsburgh (N) 3
1954	New York (N) 4, Cleveland (A) 0		Note: A=American League; N=National League

WORLD SERIES – MOST VALUABLE PLAYERS

2005	Jermaine Dye, Chi (A)		1980	Mike Schmidt, Phil
2004	Manny Ramirez, Bos		1979	Willie Stargell, Pitt
2003	Josh Beckett, Fla		1978	Bucky Dent, NY (A)
2002	Troy Glaus, Ana		1977	Reggie Jackson, NY (A)
2001	Randy Johnson, Ari; Curt Schilling, Ari		1976	Johnny Bench, Cin
2000	Derek Jeter, NY (A)		1975	Pete Rose, Cin
1999	Mariano Rivera, NY (A)		1974	Rollie Fingers, Oak
1998	Scott Brosius, NY (A)		1973	Reggie Jackson, Oak
1997	Livan Hernandez, Fla		1972	Gene Tenace, Oak
1996	John Wetteland, NY (A)		1971	Roberto Clemente, Pitt
1995	Tom Glavine, Atl		1970	Brooks Robinson, Bal
1994	Series canceled due to labor dispute.		1969	Donn Clendenon, NY (N)
1993	Paul Molitor, Tor		1968	Mickey Lolich, Det
1992	Pat Borders, Tor		1967	Bob Gibson, StL
1991	Jack Morris, Min		1966	Frank Robinson, Bal
1990	Jose Rijo, Cin		1965	Sandy Koufax, LA
1989	Dave Stewart, Oak		1964	Bob Gibson, StL
1988	Orel Hershiser, LA		1963	Sandy Koufax, LA
1987	Frank Viola, Min		1962	Ralph Terry, NY (A)
1986	Ray Knight, NY (N)		1961	Whitey Ford, NY (A)
1985	Bret Saberhagen, KC		1960	Bobby Richardson, NY (A)
1984	Alan Trammell, Det		1959	Larry Sherry, LA
1983	Rick Dempsey, Bal		1958	Bob Turley, NY (A)
1982	Darrell Porter, StL		1957	Lew Burdette, Mil
1981	Ron Cey, LA; Steve Yeager, LA;		1956	Don Larsen, NY (A)
	Pedro Guerrero, LA		1955	Johnny Podres, Bklyn

LEAGUE CHAMPIONSHIP SERIES

	NATIONAL LEAGUE			AMERICAN LEAGUE
2005	Houston (WC) 4, St. Louis (C) 2		2005	Chicago (C) 4, Los Angeles (W) 1
2004	St. Louis (C) 4, Houston (WC) 3		2004	Boston (WC) 4, New York (E) 3
2003	Florida (WC) 4, Chicago (C) 3		2003	New York (E) 4, Boston (WC) 3
2002	San Francisco (WC) 4, St. Louis (C) 1		2002	Anaheim (WC) 4, Minnesota (C) 1
2001	Arizona (W) 4, Atlanta (E) 1		2001	New York (E) 4, Seattle (W) 1
2000	New York (WC) 4, St. Louis (C) 1		2000	New York (E) 4, Seattle (WC) 2
1999	Atlanta (E) 4, New York (WC) 2		1999	New York (E) 4, Boston (WC) 1
1998	San Diego (W) 4, Atlanta (E) 2		1998	New York (E) 4, Cleveland (C) 2
1997	Florida (WC) 4, Atlanta (E) 2		1997	Cleveland (C) 4, Baltimore (E) 2
1996	Atlanta (E) 4, St. Louis (C) 3		1996	New York (E) 4, Baltimore (WC) 1
1995	Atlanta (E) 4, Cincinnati (C) 0		1995	Cleveland (C) 4, Seattle (W) 2
1994	Playoffs canceled due to labor dispute.		1994	Playoffs canceled due to labor dispute.
1993	Philadelphia (E) 4, Atlanta (W) 2		1993	Toronto (E) 4, Chicago (W) 2
1992	Atlanta (W) 4, Pittsburgh (E) 3		1992	Toronto (E) 4, Oakland (W) 2
1991	Atlanta (W) 4, Pittsburgh (E) 3		1991	Minnesota (W) 4, Toronto (E) 1
1990	Cincinnati (W) 4, Pittsburgh (E) 2		1990	Oakland (W) 4, Boston (E) 0
1989	San Francisco (W) 4, Chicago (E) 1		1989	Oakland (W) 4, Toronto (E) 1
1988	Los Angeles (W) 4, New York (E) 3		1988	Oakland (W) 4, Boston (E) 0
1987	St. Louis (E) 4, San Francisco (W) 3		1987	Minnesota (W) 4, Detroit (E) 1
1986	New York (E) 4, Houston (W) 2		1986	Boston (E) 4, California (W) 3
1985	St. Louis (E) 4, Los Angeles (W) 2		1985	Kansas City (W) 4, Toronto (E) 3
1984	San Diego (W) 3, Chicago (E) 2		1984	Detroit (E) 3, Kansas City (W) 0
1983	Philadelphia (E) 3, Los Angeles (W) 1		1983	Baltimore (E) 3, Chicago (W) 1
1982	St. Louis (E) 3, Atlanta (W) 0		1982	Milwaukee (E) 3, California (W) 2
1981	Los Angeles (W) 3, Montreal (E) 2		1981	New York (E) 3, Oakland (W) 0
1980	Philadelphia (E) 3, Houston (W) 2		1980	Kansas City (W) 3, New York (E) 0
1979	Pittsburgh (E) 3, Cincinnati (W) 0		1979	Baltimore (E) 3, California (W) 1
1978	Los Angeles (W) 3, Philadelphia (E) 1		1978	New York (E) 3, Kansas City (W) 1
1977	Los Angeles (W) 3, Philadelphia (E) 1		1977	New York (E) 3, Kansas City (W) 2
1976	Cincinnati (W) 3, Philadelphia (E) 0		1976	New York (E) 3, Kansas City (W) 2
1975	Cincinnati (W) 3, Pittsburgh (E) 0		1975	Boston (E) 3, Oakland (W) 0
1974	Los Angeles (W) 3, Pittsburgh (E) 1		1974	Oakland (W) 3, Baltimore (E) 1
1973	New York (E) 3, Cincinnati (W) 2		1973	Oakland (W) 3, Baltimore (E) 2
1972	Cincinnati (W) 3, Pittsburgh (E) 2		1972	Oakland (W) 3, Detroit (E) 2
1971	Pittsburgh (E) 3, San Francisco (W) 1		1971	Baltimore (E) 3, Oakland (W) 0
1970	Cincinnati (W) 3, Pittsburgh (E) 0		1970	Baltimore (E) 3, Minnesota (W) 0
1969	New York (E) 3, Atlanta (W) 0		1969	Baltimore (E) 3, Minnesota (W) 0

Note: WC=wild-card team; W=Western Division; E=Eastern Division; C=Central Division

NLCS MOST VALUABLE PLAYER

2005	Roy Oswalt, Hou	1995	Mike Devereaux, Atl	1985	Ozzie Smith, StL
2004	Albert Pujols, StL	1994	Playoffs canceled	1984	Steve Garvey, SD
2003	Ivan Rodriguez, Fla	1993	Curt Schilling, Phil	1983	Gary Matthews, Phil
2002	Benito Santiago, SF	1992	John Smoltz, Atl	1982	Darrell Porter, StL
2001	Craig Counsell, Ari	1991	Steve Avery, Atl	1981	Burt Hooton, LA
2000	Mike Hampton, NY	1990	R. Myers/R. Dibble, Cin	1980	Manny Trillo, Phil
1999	Eddie Perez, Atl	1989	Will Clark, SF	1979	Willie Stargell, Pitt
1998	Sterling Hitchcock, SD	1988	Orel Hershiser, LA	1978	Steve Garvey, LA
1997	Livan Hernandez, Fla	1987	Jeffrey Leonard, SF	1977	Dusty Baker, LA
1996	Javier Lopez, Atl	1986	Mike Scott, Hou		

ALCS MOST VALUABLE PLAYER

2005	Paul Konerko, Chi	1996	Bernie Williams, NY	1987	Gary Gaetti, Min
2004	David Ortiz, Bos	1995	Orel Hershiser, Cle	1986	Marty Barrett, Bos
2003	Mariano Rivera, NY	1994	Playoffs canceled	1985	George Brett, KC
2002	Adam Kennedy, Ana	1993	Dave Stewart, Tor	1984	Kirk Gibson, Det
2001	Andy Pettitte, NY	1992	Roberto Alomar, Tor	1983	Mike Boddicker, Bal
2000	David Justice, NY	1991	Kirby Puckett, Min	1982	Fred Lynn, Cal
1999	Orlando Hernandez, NY	1990	Dave Stewart, Oak	1981	Graig Nettles, NY
1998	David Wells, NY	1989	Rickey Henderson, Oak	1980	Frank White, KC
1997	Marquis Grissom, Cle	1988	Dennis Eckersley, Oak		

ALL-STAR GAME

DATE	WINNER	SCORE	SITE	DATE	WINNER	SCORE	SITE
7-11-06	American	3-2	PNC Park, Pitt	7-11-67	National	2–1	Anaheim Stadium, Cal
7-12-05	American	7–5	Comerica Park, Det	7-12-66	National	2–1	Busch Stadium, StL
7-13-04	American	9–4	Minute Maid Park, Hou	7-13-65	National	6–5	Metropolitan Stadium, Min
7-15-03	American	7–6	U.S. Cellular Field, Chi				
7-9-02	Tie (11 inn)	7–7	Miller Park, Mil	7-7-64	National	7–4	Shea Stadium, NY
7-10-01	American	4–1	Safeco Field, Sea	7-9-63	National	5–3	Municipal Stadium, Cle
7-11-00	American	6–3	Turner Field, Atl	7-30-62	American	9–4	Wrigley Field, Chi
7-13-99	American	4–1	Fenway Park, Bos	7-10-62	National	3–1	D.C. Stadium, Wash
7-7-98	American	13–8	Coors Field, Col	7-31-61	Tie*	1–1	Fenway Park, Bos
7-8-97	American	3–1	Jacobs Field, Cle	7-11-61	National	5–4	Candlestick Park, SF
7-9-96	National	6–0	Veterans Stadium, Phil	7-13-60	National	6–0	Yankee Stadium, NY
7-11-95	National	3–2	The Ballpark in Arlington, Tex	7-11-60	National	5–3	Municipal Stadium, KC
				8-3-59	American	5–3	Memorial Coliseum, LA
7-12-94	National	8–7	Three Rivers Stadium, Pitt	7-7-59	National	5–4	Forbes Field, Pitt
7-13-93	American	9–3	Camden Yards, Bal	7-8-58	American	4–3	Memorial Stadium, Bal
7-14-92	American	13–6	Jack Murphy Stadium, SD	7-9-57	American	6–5	Sportsman's Park, StL
7-9-91	American	4–2	SkyDome, Tor	7-10-56	National	7–3	Griffith Stadium, Wash
7-10-90	American	2–0	Wrigley Field, Chi	7-12-55	National	6–5	County Stadium, Mil
7-11-89	American	5–3	Anaheim Stadium, Cal	7-13-54	American	11–9	Municipal Stadium, Cle
7-12-88	American	2–1	Riverfront Stadium, Cin	7-14-53	National	5–1	Crosley Field, Cin
7-14-87	National	2–0	Oakland Coliseum, Oak	7-8-52	National	3–2	Shibe Park, Phil
7-15-86	American	3–2	Astrodome, Hou	7-10-51	National	8–3	Briggs Stadium, Det
7-16-85	National	6–1	Metrodome, Min	7-11-50	National	4–3	Comiskey Park, Chi
7-10-84	National	3–1	Candlestick Park, SF	7-12-49	American	11–7	Ebbets Field, Bklyn
7-6-83	American	13–3	Comiskey Park, Chi	7-13-48	American	5–2	Sportsman's Park, StL
7-13-82	National	4–1	Olympic Stadium, Mon	7-8-47	American	2–1	Wrigley Field, Chi
8-9-81	National	5–4	Municipal Stadium, Cle	7-9-46	American	12–0	Fenway Park, Bos
7-8-80	National	4–2	Dodger Stadium, LA	1945	No game due to wartime travel restrictions.		
7-17-79	National	7–6	Kingdome, Sea	7-11-44	National	7–1	Forbes Field, Pitt
7-11-78	National	7–3	Jack Murphy Stadium, SD	7-13-43	American	5–3	Shibe Park, Phil
7-19-77	National	7–5	Yankee Stadium, NY	7-6-42	American	3–1	Polo Grounds, NY
7-13-76	National	7–1	Veterans Stadium, Phil	7-8-41	American	7–5	Briggs Stadium, Det
7-15-75	National	6–3	County Stadium, Mil	7-10-40	National	4–0	Sportsman's Park, StL
7-23-74	National	7–2	Three Rivers Stadium, Pitt	7-11-39	American	3–1	Yankee Stadium, NY
7-24-73	National	7–1	Royals Stadium, KC	7-6-38	National	4–1	Crosley Field, Cin
7-25-72	National	4–3	Atlanta Stadium, Atl	7-7-37	American	8–3	Griffith Stadium, Wash
7-13-71	American	6–4	Tiger Stadium, Det	7-7-36	National	4–3	Braves Field, Bos
7-14-70	National	5–4	Riverfront Stadium, Cin	7-8-35	American	4–1	Municipal Stadium, Cle
7-23-69	National	9–3	R.F.K. Memorial Stadium, Wash	7-10-34	American	9–7	Polo Grounds, NY
				7-6-33	American	4–2	Comiskey Park, Chi
7-9-68	National	1–0	Astrodome, Hou				

*Game called because of rain after nine innings.

ALL-STAR GAME – MOST VALUABLE PLAYERS

2006	Michael Young, Tex	AL	1988	Terry Steinbach, Oak	AL	1971	Frank Robinson, Bal	AL
2005	Miguel Tejada, Bal	AL	1987	Tim Raines, Mon	NL	1970	Carl Yastrzemski, Bos	AL
2004	Alfonso Soriano, Tex	AL	1986	Roger Clemens, Bos	AL	1969	Willie McCovey, SF	NL
2003	Garret Anderson, Ana	AL	1985	LaMarr Hoyt, SD	NL	1968	Willie Mays, SF	NL
2002	None selected		1984	Gary Carter, Mon	NL	1967	Tony Perez, Cin	NL
2001	Cal Ripken, Jr., Bal	AL	1983	Fred Lynn, Cal	AL	1966	Brooks Robinson, Bal	AL
2000	Derek Jeter, NY	AL	1982	Dave Concepcion, Cin	NL	1965	Juan Marichal, SF	NL
1999	Pedro Martinez, Bos	AL	1981	Gary Carter, Mon	NL	1964	Johnny Callison, Phil	NL
1998	Roberto Alomar, Bal	AL	1980	Ken Griffey, Cin	NL	1963	Willie Mays, SF	NL
1997	Sandy Alomar, Cle	AL	1979	Dave Parker, Pitt	NL	1962	Maury Wills, LA	NL
1996	Mike Piazza, LA	NL	1978	Steve Garvey, LA	NL		Leon Wagner, LA	AL
1995	Jeff Conine, Fla	NL	1977	Don Sutton, LA	NL			
1994	Fred McGriff, Atl	NL	1976	George Foster, Cin	NL			
1993	Kirby Puckett, Min	AL	1975	Bill Madlock, Chi	NL			
1992	Ken Griffey, Jr., Sea	AL		Jon Matlack, NY	NL			
1991	Cal Ripken, Jr., Bal	AL	1974	Steve Garvey, LA	NL			
1990	Julio Franco, Tex	AL	1973	Bobby Bonds, SF	NL			
1989	Bo Jackson, KC	AL	1972	Joe Morgan, Cin	NL			

Albert Pujols, Cardinals

TOM DIPACE

REGULAR SEASON – MOST VALUABLE PLAYERS

NATIONAL LEAGUE

YEAR	NAME AND TEAM	POSITION	YEAR	NAME AND TEAM	POSITION
2005	Albert Pujols, StL	First Base	1961	Frank Robinson, Cin	Outfield
2004	Barry Bonds, SF	Outfield	1960	Dick Groat, Pitt	Shortstop
2003	Barry Bonds, SF	Outfield	1959	Ernie Banks, Chi	Shortstop
2002	Barry Bonds, SF	Outfield	1958	Ernie Banks, Chi	Shortstop
2001	Barry Bonds, SF	Outfield	1957	Hank Aaron, Mil	Outfield
2000	Jeff Kent, SF	Second Base	1956	Don Newcombe, Bklyn	Pitcher
1999	Chipper Jones, Atl	Third Base	1955	Roy Campanella, Bklyn	Catcher
1998	Sammy Sosa, Chi	Outfield	1954	Willie Mays, NY	Outfield
1997	Larry Walker, Col	Outfield	1953	Roy Campanella, Bklyn	Catcher
1996	Ken Caminiti, SD	Third Base	1952	Hank Sauer, Chi	Outfield
1995	Barry Larkin, Cin	Shortstop	1951	Roy Campanella, Bklyn	Catcher
1994	Jeff Bagwell, Hou	First Base	1950	Jim Konstanty, Phil	Pitcher
1993	Barry Bonds, SF	Outfield	1949	Jackie Robinson, Bklyn	Second Base
1992	Barry Bonds, Pitt	Outfield	1948	Stan Musial, StL	Outfield
1991	Terry Pendleton, Atl	Third Base	1947	Bob Elliott, Bos	Third Base
1990	Barry Bonds, Pitt	Outfield	1946	Stan Musial, StL	First Base, Outfield
1989	Kevin Mitchell, SF	Outfield	1945	Phil Cavarretta, Chi	First Base
1988	Kirk Gibson, LA	Outfield	1944	Marty Marion, StL	Shortstop
1987	Andre Dawson, Chi	Outfield	1943	Stan Musial, StL	Outfield
1986	Mike Schmidt, Phil	Third Base	1942	Mort Cooper, StL	Pitcher
1985	Willie McGee, StL	Outfield	1941	Dolph Camilli, Bklyn	First Base
1984	Ryne Sandberg, Chi	Second Base	1940	Frank McCormick, Cin	First Base
1983	Dale Murphy, Atl	Outfield	1939	Bucky Walters, Cin	Pitcher
1982	Dale Murphy, Atl	Outfield	1938	Ernie Lombardi, Cin	Catcher
1981	Mike Schmidt, Phil	Third Base	1937	Joe Medwick, StL	Outfield
1980	Mike Schmidt, Phil	Third Base	1936	Carl Hubbell, NY	Pitcher
1979	Keith Hernandez, StL	First Base	1935	Gabby Hartnett, Chi	Catcher
	Willie Stargell, Pitt	First Base	1934	Dizzy Dean, StL	Pitcher
1978	Dave Parker, Pitt	Outfield	1933	Carl Hubbell, NY	Pitcher
1977	George Foster, Cin	Outfield	1932	Chuck Klein, Phil	Outfield
1976	Joe Morgan, Cin	Second Base	1931	Frankie Frisch, StL	Second Base
1975	Joe Morgan, Cin	Second Base	1930	No selection	
1974	Steve Garvey, LA	First Base	1929	Rogers Hornsby, Chi	Second Base
1973	Pete Rose, Cin	Outfield	1928	Jim Bottomley, StL	First Base
1972	Johnny Bench, Cin	Catcher	1927	Paul Waner, Pitt	Outfield
1971	Joe Torre, StL	Third Base	1926	Bob O'Farrell, StL	Catcher
1970	Johnny Bench, Cin	Catcher	1925	Rogers Hornsby, StL	Second Base, Manager
1969	Willie McCovey, SF	First Base			
1968	Bob Gibson, StL	Pitcher	1924	Dazzy Vance, Bklyn	Pitcher
1967	Orlando Cepeda, StL	First Base	1915-23	No selections	
1966	Roberto Clemente, Pitt	Outfield	1914	Johnny Evers, Bos	Second Base
1965	Willie Mays, SF	Outfield	1913	Jake Daubert, Bklyn	First Base
1964	Ken Boyer, StL	Third Base	1912	Larry Doyle, NY	Second Base
1963	Sandy Koufax, LA	Pitcher	1911	Wildfire Schulte, Chi	Outfield
1962	Maury Wills, LA	Shortstop			

REGULAR SEASON – MOST VALUABLE PLAYERS (cont.)

AMERICAN LEAGUE

Alex Rodriguez of the Yankees starred in the field and at bat.

EZRA SHAW/GETTY IMAGES

YEAR	NAME AND TEAM	POSITION
1966	Frank Robinson, Bal	Outfield
1965	Zoilo Versalles, Min	Shortstop
1964	Brooks Robinson, Bal	Third Base
1963	Elston Howard, NY	Catcher
1962	Mickey Mantle, NY	Outfield
1961	Roger Maris, NY	Outfield
1960	Roger Maris, NY	Outfield
1959	Nellie Fox, Chi	Second Base
1958	Jackie Jensen, Bos	Outfield
1957	Mickey Mantle, NY	Outfield
1956	Mickey Mantle, NY	Outfield
1955	Yogi Berra, NY	Catcher
1954	Yogi Berra, NY	Catcher
1953	Al Rosen, Cle	Third Base
1952	Bobby Shantz, Phil	Pitcher
1951	Yogi Berra, NY	Catcher
1950	Phil Rizzuto, NY	Shortstop
1949	Ted Williams, Bos	Outfield
1948	Lou Boudreau, Cle	Shortstop
1947	Joe DiMaggio, NY	Outfield
1946	Ted Williams, Bos	Outfield
1945	Hal Newhouser, Det	Pitcher
1944	Hal Newhouser, Det	Pitcher
1943	Spud Chandler, NY	Pitcher
1942	Joe Gordon, NY	Second Base
1941	Joe DiMaggio, NY	Outfield
1940	Hank Greenberg, Det	Outfield
1939	Joe DiMaggio, NY	Outfield
1938	Jimmie Foxx, Bos	First Base
1937	Charlie Gehringer, Det	Second Base
1936	Lou Gehrig, NY	First Base
1935	Hank Greenberg, Det	First Base
1934	Mickey Cochrane, Det	Catcher
1933	Jimmie Foxx, Phil	First Base
1932	Jimmie Foxx, Phil	First Base
1931	Lefty Grove, Phil	Pitcher
1930	No selection	
1929	No selection	
1928	Mickey Cochrane, Phil	Catcher
1927	Lou Gehrig, NY	First Base
1926	George Burns, Cle	First Base
1925	Roger Peckinpaugh, Wash	Shortstop
1924	Walter Johnson, Wash	Pitcher
1923	Babe Ruth, NY	Outfield
1922	George Sisler, StL	First Base
1915–21	No selections	
1914	Eddie Collins, Phil	Second Base
1913	Walter Johnson, Wash	Pitcher
1912	Tris Speaker, Bos	Outfield
1911	Ty Cobb, Det	Outfield

YEAR	NAME AND TEAM	POSITION
2005	Alex Rodriguez, NY	Third Base
2004	Vladimir Guerrero, Ana	Outfield
2003	Alex Rodriguez, Tex	Shortstop
2002	Miguel Tejada, Oak	Shortstop
2001	Ichiro Suzuki, Sea	Outfield
2000	Jason Giambi, Oak	First Base
1999	Ivan Rodriguez, Tex	Catcher
1998	Juan Gonzalez, Tex	Outfield
1997	Ken Griffey, Jr., Sea	Outfield
1996	Juan Gonzalez, Tex	Outfield
1995	Mo Vaughn, Bos	First Base
1994	Frank Thomas, Chi	First Base
1993	Frank Thomas, Chi	First Base
1992	Dennis Eckersley, Oak	Pitcher
1991	Cal Ripken, Jr., Bal	Shortstop
1990	Rickey Henderson, Oak	Outfield
1989	Robin Yount, Mil	Outfield
1988	Jose Canseco, Oak	Outfield
1987	George Bell, Tor	Outfield
1986	Roger Clemens, Bos	Pitcher
1985	Don Mattingly, NY	First Base
1984	Willie Hernandez, Det	Pitcher
1983	Cal Ripken, Jr., Bal	Shortstop
1982	Robin Yount, Mil	Shortstop
1981	Rollie Fingers, Mil	Pitcher
1980	George Brett, KC	Third Base
1979	Don Baylor, Cal	Outfield, DH
1978	Jim Rice, Bos	Outfield, DH
1977	Rod Carew, Min	First Base
1976	Thurman Munson, NY	Catcher
1975	Fred Lynn, Bos	Outfield
1974	Jeff Burroughs, Tex	Outfield
1973	Reggie Jackson, Oak	Outfield
1972	Dick Allen, Chi	First Base
1971	Vida Blue, Oak	Pitcher
1970	Boog Powell, Bal	First Base
1969	Harmon Killebrew, Min	Third Base, First Base
1968	Denny McLain, Det	Pitcher
1967	Carl Yastrzemski, Bos	Outfield

TRIVIA CHALLENGE

In 2005, the Nationals played their first season in Washington, D.C. The team moved there from Montreal, Canada, where they were known as the Expos. When was the last time a major-league team moved from one city to another?

The Texas Rangers, who started play in 1972 after moving from Washington, D.C., where they were known as the Senators.

REGULAR SEASON – ROOKIES OF THE YEAR

NATIONAL LEAGUE		AMERICAN LEAGUE	
2005	Ryan Howard, Phi (1B)	2005	Huston Street, Oak (P)
2004	Jason Bay, Pitt (OF)	2004	Bobby Crosby, Oak (SS)
2003	Dontrelle Willis, Fla (P)	2003	Angel Berroa, KC (SS)
2002	Jason Jennings, Col (P)	2002	Eric Hinske, Tor (3B)
2001	Albert Pujols, StL (OF)	2001	Ichiro Suzuki, Sea (OF)
2000	Rafael Furcal, Atl (SS)	2000	Kazuhiro Sasaki, Sea (P)
1999	Scott Williamson, Cin (P)	1999	Carlos Beltran, KC (OF)
1998	Kerry Wood, Chi (P)	1998	Ben Grieve, Oak (OF)
1997	Scott Rolen, Phil (3B)	1997	Nomar Garciaparra, Bos (SS)
1996	Todd Hollandsworth, LA (OF)	1996	Derek Jeter, NY (SS)
1995	Hideo Nomo, LA (P)	1995	Marty Cordova, Min (OF)
1994	Raul Mondesi, LA (OF)	1994	Bob Hamelin, KC (DH)
1993	Mike Piazza, LA (C)	1993	Tim Salmon, Cal (OF)
1992	Eric Karros, LA (1B)	1992	Pat Listach, Mil (SS)
1991	Jeff Bagwell, Hou (3B)	1991	Chuck Knoblauch, Min (2B)
1990	David Justice, Atl (OF)	1990	Sandy Alomar, Jr., Cle (C)
1989	Jerome Walton, Chi (OF)	1989	Gregg Olson, Bal (P)
1988	Chris Sabo, Cin (3B)	1988	Walt Weiss, Oak (SS)
1987	Benito Santiago, SD (C)	1987	Mark McGwire, Oak (1B)
1986	Todd Worrell, StL (P)	1986	Jose Canseco, Oak (OF)
1985	Vince Coleman, StL (OF)	1985	Ozzie Guillen, Chi (SS)
1984	Dwight Gooden, NY (P)	1984	Alvin Davis, Sea (1B)
1983	Darryl Strawberry, NY (OF)	1983	Ron Kittle, Chi (OF)
1982	Steve Sax, LA (2B)	1982	Cal Ripken, Jr., Bal (SS)
1981	Fernando Valenzuela, LA (P)	1981	Dave Righetti, NY (P)
1980	Steve Howe, LA (P)	1980	Joe Charboneau, Cle (OF)
1979	Rick Sutcliffe, LA (P)	1979	Alfredo Griffin, Tor (SS)
			John Castino, Min (3B)
1978	Bob Horner, Atl (3B)	1978	Lou Whitaker, Det (2B)
1977	Andre Dawson, Mon (OF)	1977	Eddie Murray, Bal (DH)
1976	Pat Zachry, Cin (P)	1976	Mark Fidrych, Det (P)
	Butch Metzger, SD (P)		
1975	John Montefusco, SF (P)	1975	Fred Lynn, Bos (OF)
1974	Bake McBride, StL (OF)	1974	Mike Hargrove, Tex (1B)
1973	Gary Matthews, SF (OF)	1973	Al Bumbry, Bal (OF)
1972	Jon Matlack, NY (P)	1972	Carlton Fisk, Bos (C)
1971	Earl Williams, Atl (C)	1971	Chris Chambliss, Cle (1B)
1970	Carl Morton, Mon (P)	1970	Thurman Munson, NY (C)
1969	Ted Sizemore, LA (2B)	1969	Lou Piniella, KC (OF)
1968	Johnny Bench, Cin (C)	1968	Stan Bahnsen, NY (P)
1967	Tom Seaver, NY (P)	1967	Rod Carew, Min (2B)
1966	Tommy Helms, Cin (2B)	1966	Tommie Agee, Chi (OF)
1965	Jim Lefebvre, LA (2B)	1965	Curt Blefary, Bal (OF)
1964	Dick Allen, Phil (3B)	1964	Tony Oliva, Min (OF)
1963	Pete Rose, Cin (2B)	1963	Gary Peters, Chi (P)
1962	Ken Hubbs, Chi (2B)	1962	Tom Tresh, NY (SS)
1961	Billy Williams, Chi (OF)	1961	Don Schwall, Bos (P)
1960	Frank Howard, LA (OF)	1960	Ron Hansen, Bal (SS)
1959	Willie McCovey, SF (1B)	1959	Bob Allison, Wash (OF)
1958	Orlando Cepeda, SF (1B)	1958	Albie Pearson, Wash (OF)
1957	Jack Sanford, Phil (P)	1957	Tony Kubek, NY (OF, SS)
1956	Frank Robinson, Cin (OF)	1956	Luis Aparicio, Chi (SS)
1955	Bill Virdon, StL (OF)	1955	Herb Score, Cle (P)
1954	Wally Moon, StL (OF)	1954	Bob Grim, NY (P)
1953	Junior Gilliam, Bklyn (2B)	1953	Harvey Kuenn, Det (SS)
1952	Joe Black, Bklyn (P)	1952	Harry Byrd, Phil (P)
1951	Willie Mays, NY (OF)	1951	Gil McDougald, NY (3B)
1950	Sam Jethroe, Bos (OF)	1950	Walt Dropo, Bos (1B)
1949	Don Newcombe, Bklyn (P)	1949	Roy Sievers, StL (OF)
1948*	Alvin Dark, Bos (SS)		
1947*	Jackie Robinson, Bklyn (1B)		

*One selection for both leagues

Chris Carpenter, Cardinals

REGULAR SEASON –
CY YOUNG AWARD WINNERS

Bartolo Colon of the Angels was the A.L.'s only 20-game winner.

DAVID E. KLUTHO (CARPENTER); ROBERT BECK (COLON)

NATIONAL LEAGUE

YEAR	PITCHER	W–L	SV	ERA
2005	Chris Carpenter, StL	21-5	0	2.83
2004	Roger Clemens, Hou	18–4	0	2.98
2003	Eric Gagne, LA	2–3	55	1.20
2002	Randy Johnson, Ari	24–5	0	2.32
2001	Randy Johnson, Ari	21–6	0	2.49
2000	Randy Johnson, Ari	19–7	0	2.64
1999	Randy Johnson, Ari	17–9	0	2.48
1998	Tom Glavine, Atl	20–6	0	2.47
1997	Pedro Martinez, Mon	17–8	0	1.90
1996	John Smoltz, Atl	24–8	0	2.94
1995	Greg Maddux, Atl	19–2	0	1.63
1994	Greg Maddux, Atl	16–6	0	1.56
1993	Greg Maddux, Atl	20–10	0	2.36
1992	Greg Maddux, Chi	20–11	0	2.18
1991	Tom Glavine, Atl	20–11	0	2.55
1990	Doug Drabek, Pitt	22–6	0	2.76
1989	Mark Davis, SD	4–3	44	1.85
1988	Orel Hershiser, LA	23–8	1	2.26
1987	Steve Bedrosian, Phil	5–3	40	2.83
1986	Mike Scott, Hou	18–10	0	2.22
1985	Dwight Gooden, NY	24–4	0	1.53
1984†	Rick Sutcliffe, Chi	16–1	0	2.69
1983	John Denny, Phil	19–6	0	2.37
1982	Steve Carlton, Phil	23–11	0	3.10
1981	Fernando Valenzuela, LA	13–7	0	2.48
1980	Steve Carlton, Phil	24–9	0	2.34
1979	Bruce Sutter, Chi	6–6	37	2.23
1978	Gaylord Perry, SD	21–6	0	2.72
1977	Steve Carlton, Phil	23–10	0	2.64
1976	Randy Jones, SD	22–14	0	2.74
1975	Tom Seaver, NY	22–9	0	2.38
1974	Mike Marshall, LA	15–12	21	2.42
1973	Tom Seaver, NY	19–10	0	2.08
1972	Steve Carlton, Phil	27–10	0	1.97
1971	Ferguson Jenkins, Chi	24–13	0	2.77
1970	Bob Gibson, StL	23–7	0	3.12
1969	Tom Seaver, NY	25–7	0	2.21
1968*	Bob Gibson, StL	22–9	0	1.12
1967	Mike McCormick, SF	22–10	0	2.85
1966	Sandy Koufax, LA (NL)	27–9	0	1.73
1965	Sandy Koufax, LA (NL)	26–8	2	2.04
1964	Dean Chance, LA (AL)	20–9	4	1.65
1963*	Sandy Koufax, LA (NL)	25–5	0	1.88
1962	Don Drysdale, LA (NL)	25–9	1	2.83
1961	Whitey Ford, NY (AL)	25–4	0	3.21
1960	Vernon Law, Pitt (NL)	20–9	0	3.08
1959	Early Wynn, Chi (AL)	22–10	0	3.17
1958	Bob Turley, NY (AL)	21–7	1	2.97
1957	Warren Spahn, Mil (NL)	21–11	3	2.69
1956*	Don Newcombe, Bklyn (NL)	27–7	0	3.06

* Won the MVP and Cy Young awards in the same season.
†NL games only. Sutcliffe pitched 15 games with Cleveland before being traded to the Cubs.
Note: One award was presented for both leagues from 1956-1966.

AMERICAN LEAGUE

YEAR	PITCHER	W–L	SV	ERA
2005	Bartolo Colon, LA	21–8	0	3.48
2004	Johan Santana, Min	20–6	0	2.61
2003	Roy Halladay, Tor	22–7	0	3.25
2002	Barry Zito, Oak	23–5	0	2.75
2001	Roger Clemens, NY	20–3	0	3.51
2000	Pedro Martinez, Bos	18–6	0	1.74
1999	Pedro Martinez, Bos	23–4	0	1.55
1998	Roger Clemens, Tor	20–6	0	2.65
1997	Roger Clemens, Tor	21–7	0	2.05
1996	Pat Hentgen, Tor	20–10	0	3.22
1995	Randy Johnson, Sea	18–2	0	2.48
1994	David Cone, KC	16–5	0	2.94
1993	Jack McDowell, Chi	22–10	0	3.37
1992*	Dennis Eckersley, Oak	7–1	51	1.91
1991	Roger Clemens, Bos	18–10	0	2.62
1990	Bob Welch, Oak	27–6	0	2.95
1989	Bret Saberhagen, KC	23–6	0	2.16
1988	Frank Viola, Min	24–7	0	2.64
1987	Roger Clemens, Bos	20–9	0	2.97
1986*	Roger Clemens, Bos	24–4	0	2.48
1985	Bret Saberhagen, KC	20–6	0	2.87
1984*	Willie Hernandez, Det	9–3	32	1.92
1983	LaMarr Hoyt, Chi	24–10	0	3.66
1982	Pete Vuckovich, Mil	18–6	0	3.34
1981*	Rollie Fingers, Mil	6–3	28	1.04
1980	Steve Stone, Bal	25–7	0	3.23
1979	Mike Flanagan, Bal	23–9	0	3.08
1978	Ron Guidry, NY	25–3	0	1.74
1977	Sparky Lyle, NY	13–5	26	2.17
1976	Jim Palmer, Bal	22–13	0	2.51
1975	Jim Palmer, Bal	23–11	1	2.09
1974	Catfish Hunter, Oak	25–12	0	2.49
1973	Jim Palmer, Bal	22–9	1	2.40
1972	Gaylord Perry, Cle	24–16	1	1.92
1971*	Vida Blue, Oak	24–8	0	1.82
1970	Jim Perry, Min	24–12	0	3.03
1969	Denny McLain, Det	24–9	0	2.80
	(tie) Mike Cuellar, Bal	23–11	0	2.38
1968*	Denny McLain, Det	31–6	0	1.96
1967	Jim Lonborg, Bos	22–9	0	3.16

REGULAR SEASON – CAREER INDIVIDUAL BATTING

GAMES

Pete Rose	3,562
Carl Yastrzemski	3,308
Hank Aaron	3,298
Rickey Henderson	3,081
Ty Cobb	3,035
Eddie Murray	3,026
Stan Musial	3,026
Cal Ripken, Jr.	3,001
Willie Mays	2,992
Dave Winfield	2,973
Rusty Staub	2,951
Brooks Robinson	2,896
Robin Yount	2,856
Al Kaline	2,834
*Rafael Palmeiro	2,831
Harold Baines	2,830
Eddie Collins	2,826
Reggie Jackson	2,820
Frank Robinson	2,808
Honus Wagner	2,792

AT-BATS

Pete Rose	14,053
Hank Aaron	12,364
Carl Yastrzemski	11,988
Cal Ripken, Jr.	11,551
Ty Cobb	11,429
Eddie Murray	11,336
Robin Yount	11,008
Dave Winfield	11,003
Stan Musial	10,972
Rickey Henderson	10,961
Willie Mays	10,881
Paul Molitor	10,835
Brooks Robinson	10,654
*Rafael Palmeiro	10,472
Honus Wagner	10,43
George Brett	10,349
Lou Brock	10,332
Cap Anson	10,278
Luis Aparicio	10,230
Tris Speaker	10,195

HOME RUNS

Hank Aaron	755
Babe Ruth	714
*Barry Bonds	708
Willie Mays	660
*Sammy Sosa	588
Frank Robinson	586
Mark McGwire	583
Harmon Killebrew	573
*Rafael Palmeiro	569
Reggie Jackson	563
Mike Schmidt	548
*Ken Griffey, Jr.	536
Mickey Mantle	536
Jimmie Foxx	534
Willie McCovey	521
Ted Williams	521
Eddie Mathews	512
Ernie Banks	512
Mel Ott	511
Eddie Murray	504

* Active in 2005.
Note: Stats were compiled after the 2005 season.

HITS

Pete Rose	4,256
Ty Cobb	4,191
Hank Aaron	3,771
Stan Musial	3,630
Tris Speaker	3,514
Carl Yastrzemski	3,419
Cap Anson	3,418
Honus Wagner	3,415
Paul Molitor	3,319
Eddie Collins	3,315
Willie Mays	3,283
Eddie Murray	3,255
Nap Lajoie	3,242
Cal Ripken, Jr.	3,184
George Brett	3,154
Paul Waner	3,152
Robin Yount	3,142
Tony Gwynn	3,141
Dave Winfield	3,110
Rickey Henderson	3,055

BATTING AVERAGE (5,000 AB)

Ty Cobb	.367
Rogers Hornsby	.358
Ed Delahanty	.346
Tris Speaker	.345
Ted Williams	.344
Billy Hamilton	.344
Dan Brouthers	.342
Harry Heilmann	.342
Babe Ruth	.342
Willie Keeler	.341
Bill Terry	.341
Lou Gehrig	.340
George Sisler	.340
Jesse Burkett	.338
Tony Gwynn	.338
Nap Lajoie	.338
Al Simmons	.334
Cap Anson	.333
Eddie Collins	.333
Paul Waner	.333

RUNS

Rickey Henderson	2,295
Ty Cobb	2,245
Hank Aaron	2,174
Babe Ruth	2,174
Pete Rose	2,165
*Barry Bonds	2,078
Willie Mays	2,062
Cap Anson	1,996
Stan Musial	1,949
Lou Gehrig	1,888
Tris Speaker	1,882
Mel Ott	1,859
Frank Robinson	1,829
Eddie Collins	1,821
Carl Yastrzemski	1,816
Ted Williams	1,798
Paul Molitor	1,782
Charlie Gehringer	1,774
Jimmie Foxx	1,751
Honus Wagner	1,736

DOUBLES

Tris Speaker	792
Pete Rose	746
Stan Musial	725
Ty Cobb	723
George Brett	665
Nap Lajoie	657
Carl Yastrzemski	646
Honus Wagner	640
Hank Aaron	624
Paul Molitor	605
Paul Waner	605
Craig Biggio	604
Cal Ripken, Jr.	603
*Rafael Palmeiro	585
Robin Yount	583
Cap Anson	581
Wade Boggs	578
Charlie Gehringer	574
*Barry Bonds	564
Eddie Murray	560

TRIPLES

Sam Crawford	309
Ty Cobb	297
Honus Wagner	252
Jake Beckley	243
Roger Connor	233
Tris Speaker	222
Fred Clarke	220
Dan Brouthers	205
Joe Kelley	194
Paul Waner	191
Bid McPhee	188
Eddie Collins	187
Ed Delahanty	185
Sam Rice	184
Jesse Burkett	182
Ed Konetchy	182
Edd Roush	182
Buck Ewing	178
Rabbit Maranville	177
Stan Musial	177

BASES ON BALLS

*Barry Bonds	2,311
Rickey Henderson	2,190
Babe Ruth	2,062
Ted Williams	2,019
Joe Morgan	1,865
Carl Yastrzemski	1,845
Mickey Mantle	1,733
Mel Ott	1,708
Eddie Yost	1,614
Darrell Evans	1,605
Stan Musial	1,599
Pete Rose	1,566
Harmon Killebrew	1,559
Lou Gehrig	1,508
Mike Schmidt	1,507
Eddie Collins	1,499
*Frank Thomas	1,466
Willie Mays	1,464
Jimmie Foxx	1,452
Eddie Mathews	1,444

REGULAR SEASON – CAREER INDIVIDUAL BATTING (CONT.)

RUNS BATTED IN

Hank Aaron	2,297
Babe Ruth	2,213
Cap Anson	2,076
Lou Gehrig	1,995
Stan Musial	1,951
Ty Cobb	1,938
Jimmie Foxx	1,922
Eddie Murray	1,917
Willie Mays	1,903
Mel Ott	1,860
*Barry Bonds	1,853
Carl Yastrzemski	1,844
Ted Williams	1,839
*Rafael Palmeiro	1,835
Dave Winfield	1,833
Al Simmons	1,827
Frank Robinson	1,812
Honus Wagner	1,732
Reggie Jackson	1,702
Cal Ripken, Jr.	1,695

SLUGGING PERCENTAGE (5,000 AB)

Babe Ruth	.690
Ted Williams	.634
Lou Gehrig	.632
*Barry Bonds	.611
Jimmie Foxx	.609
Hank Greenberg	.605
*Manny Ramirez	.599
Mark McGwire	.588
Joe DiMaggio	.579
Rogers Hornsby	.577
*Alex Rodriguez	.577
*Frank Thomas	.568
*Larry Walker	.565
Albert Belle	.564
Johnny Mize	.562
*Jim Thome	.562
*Juan Gonzalez	.561
*Ken Griffey, Jr.	.561
*Carlos Delgado	.559
Stan Musial	.559

STOLEN BASES

Rickey Henderson	1,406
Lou Brock	938
Billy Hamilton	912
Ty Cobb	892
Tim Raines	808
Vince Coleman	752
Eddie Collins	745
Max Carey	738
Honus Wagner	722
Joe Morgan	689
Willie Wilson	668
Bert Campaneris	649
Otis Nixon	620
George Davis	616
Tom Brown	615
Dummy Hoy	594
Maury Wills	586
George Van Haltren	583
Ozzie Smith	580
Hugh Duffy	574

* Active in 2005.

Hank Aaron is the all-time leader in home runs, RBIs, and total bases.

NEIL LEIFER

ON-BASE PERCENTAGE (5,000 AB)

Ted Williams	.482
Babe Ruth	.469
*Barry Bonds	.442
Lou Gehrig	.442
*Frank Thomas	.427
Jimmie Foxx	.425
Ty Cobb	.424
Rogers Hornsby	.424
Mickey Mantle	.422
Edgar Martinez	.418
Stan Musial	.417
Tris Speaker	.417
Wade Boggs	.415
*Jason Giambi	.413
Mel Ott	.410
Mickey Cochrane	.409
Hank Greenberg	.409
*Manny Ramirez	.409
*Jeff Bagwell	.408
Jim Thome	.408

TOTAL BASES

Hank Aaron	6,856
Stan Musial	6,134
Willie Mays	6,066
Ty Cobb	5,859
Babe Ruth	5,793
Pete Rose	5,752
*Barry Bonds	5,584
Carl Yastrzemski	5,539
Eddie Murray	5,397
*Rafael Palmeiro	5,388
Frank Robinson	5,373
Dave Winfield	5,221
Cal Ripken, Jr.	5,168
Tris Speaker	5,101
Lou Gehrig	5,060
George Brett	5,044
Mel Ott	5,041
Jimmie Foxx	4,956
Ted Williams	4,884
Honus Wagner	4,862

STRIKEOUTS

Reggie Jackson	2,597
*Sammy Sosa	2,194
Andres Galarraga	2,003
Jose Canseco	1,942
Willie Stargell	1,936
Mike Schmidt	1,883
*Fred McGriff	1,882
Tony Perez	1,867
Dave Kingman	1,816
*Jim Thome	1,762
Bobby Bonds	1,757
Dale Murphy	1,748
Lou Brock	1,730
Mickey Mantle	1,710
Harmon Killebrew	1,699
Chili Davis	1,698
Dwight Evans	1,697
Rickey Henderson	1,694
Dave Winfield	1,686
Gary Gaetti	1,602

REGULAR SEASON – CAREER INDIVIDUAL PITCHING

GAMES	
Jesse Orosco	1,251
*John Franco	1,119
Dennis Eckersley	1,071
Hoyt Wilhelm	1,070
Dan Plesac	1,064
Kent Tekulve	1,050
*Mike Stanton	1,027
Lee Smith	1,022
*Mike Jackson	1,005
Goose Gossage	1,002
Lindy McDaniel	987
Rollie Fingers	944
Gene Garber	931
Cy Young	906
Sparky Lyle	899
Jim Kaat	898
*Mike Timlin	893
*Roberto Hernandez	892
*Jose Mesa	887
Paul Assenmacher	884

LOSSES	
Cy Young	316
Jim Galvin	310
Nolan Ryan	292
Walter Johnson	279
Phil Niekro	274
Gaylord Perry	265
Don Sutton	256
Jack Powell	254
Eppa Rixey	251
Bert Blyleven	250
Bobby Mathews	248
Robin Roberts	245
Warren Spahn	245
Steve Carlton	244
Early Wynn	244
Jim Kaat	237
Frank Tanana	236
Gus Weyhing	232
Tommy John	231
Bob Friend	230

EARNED RUN AVERAGE	
Ed Walsh	1.82
Addie Joss	1.89
Al Spalding	2.04
Mordecai Brown	2.06
John Ward	2.10
Christy Mathewson	2.13
Tommy Bond	2.14
Rube Waddell	2.16
Walter Johnson	2.17
Ed Reulbach	2.28
Will White	2.28
Eddie Plank	2.35
Larry Corcoran	2.36
Eddie Cicotte	2.38
Candy Cummings	2.39
Doc White	2.39
Nap Rucker	2.42
George Bradley	2.43
Jim McCormick	2.43
Chief Bender	2.46

INNINGS PITCHED	
Cy Young	7,356.0
Jim Galvin	6,003.1
Walter Johnson	5,914.1
Phil Niekro	5,404.1
Nolan Ryan	5,386.0
Gaylord Perry	5,350.1
Don Sutton	5,282.1
Warren Spahn	5,243.2
Steve Carlton	5,217.1
Grover Alexander	5,190.0
Kid Nichols	5,056.1
Tim Keefe	5,049.2
Bert Blyleven	4,970.0
Bobby Mathews	4,956.0
Mickey Welch	4,802.0
Tom Seaver	4,782.2
Christy Mathewson	4,780.2
Tommy John	4,710.1
*Roger Clemens	4,704.1
Robin Roberts	4,688.2

WINNING PERCENTAGE**	
Al Spalding	.795
Spud Chandler	.717
*Pedro Martinez	.701
Whitey Ford	.690
Dave Foutz	.690
Bob Caruthers	.688
*Tim Hudson	.688
Don Gullett	.686
Lefty Grove	.680
Joe Wood	.672
Vic Raschi	.667
*Roger Clemens	.665
Larry Corcoran	.665
Christy Mathewson	.665
Sam Leever	.660
*Randy Johnson	.659
Sal Maglie	.657
Dick McBride	.656
Sandy Koufax	.655
Johnny Allen	.654

SHUTOUTS	
Walter Johnson	110
Grover Alexander	90
Christy Mathewson	79
Cy Young	76
Eddie Plank	69
Warren Spahn	63
Nolan Ryan	61
Tom Seaver	61
Bert Blyleven	60
Don Sutton	58
Pud Galvin	57
Ed Walsh	57
Bob Gibson	56
Three Finger Brown	55
Steve Carlton	55
Jim Palmer	53
Gaylord Perry	53
Juan Marichal	52
Rube Waddell	50
Vic Willis	50

WINS	
Cy Young	511
Walter Johnson	417
Grover Alexander	373
Christy Mathewson	373
Jim Galvin	365
Warren Spahn	363
Kid Nichols	361
Tim Keefe	342
*Roger Clemens	341
Steve Carlton	329
John Clarkson	328
Eddie Plank	326
Nolan Ryan	324
Don Sutton	324
*Greg Maddux	318
Phil Niekro	318
Gaylord Perry	314
Tom Seaver	311
Charley Radbourn	309
Mickey Welch	307

SAVES	
Lee Smith	478
*Trevor Hoffman	436
*John Franco	424
Dennis Eckersley	390
*Mariano Rivera	379
Jeff Reardon	367
Randy Myers	347
Rollie Fingers	341
John Wetteland	330
*Roberto Hernandez	324
*Troy Percival	324
*Jose Mesa	319
Rick Aguilera	318
Robb Nen	314
Tom Henke	311
Goose Gossage	310
Jeff Montgomery	304
Doug Jones	303
Bruce Sutter	300
*Rod Beck	286

COMPLETE GAMES	
Cy Young	749
Jim Galvin	646
Tim Keefe	554
Walter Johnson	531
Kid Nichols	531
Bobby Mathews	525
Mickey Welch	525
Charley Radbourn	489
John Clarkson	485
Tony Mullane	468
Jim McCormick	466
Gus Weyhing	448
Grover Alexander	437
Christy Mathewson	434
Jack Powell	422
Eddie Plank	410
Will White	394
Amos Rusie	393
Vic Willis	388
Tommy Bond	386

*Active in 2005. **Minimum 100 victories.

REGULAR SEASON – CAREER INDIVIDUAL PITCHING (CONT.)

STRIKEOUTS		BASES ON BALLS	
Nolan Ryan	5,714	Nolan Ryan	2,795
*Roger Clemens	4,502	Steve Carlton	1,833
*Randy Johnson	4,372	Phil Niekro	1,809
Steve Carlton	4,136	Early Wynn	1,775
Bert Blyleven	3,701	Bob Feller	1,764
Tom Seaver	3,640	Bobo Newsom	1,732
Don Sutton	3,574	Amos Rusie	1,707
Gaylord Perry	3,534	Charlie Hough	1,665
Walter Johnson	3,508	Gus Weyhing	1,566
Phil Niekro	3,342	Red Ruffing	1,541
Ferguson Jenkins	3,192	*Roger Clemens	1,520
Bob Gibson	3,117	Bump Hadley	1,442
*Greg Maddux	3,052	Warren Spahn	1,434
*Pedro Martinez	2,861	Earl Whitehill	1,431
Jim Bunning	2,855	Tony Mullane	1,408
Mickey Lolich	2,832	Sad Sam Jones	1,396
*Curt Schilling	2,832	Jack Morris	1,390
Cy Young	2,803	Tom Seaver	1,390
Frank Tanana	2,773	Gaylord Perry	1,379
David Cone	2,668	Bobby Witt	1,375

Barry Bonds

CHUCK SOLOMON

REGULAR SEASON – INDIVIDUAL BATTING, SINGLE SEASON

HITS		TRIPLES		RUNS BATTED IN	
Ichiro Suzuki, 2004	262	Chief Wilson, 1912	36	Hack Wilson, 1930	191
George Sisler, 1920	257	Dave Orr, 1886	31	Lou Gehrig, 1931	184
Lefty O'Doul, 1929	254	Heinie Reitz, 1894	31	Hank Greenberg, 1937	183
Bill Terry, 1930	254	Perry Werden, 1893	29	Lou Gehrig, 1927	175
Al Simmons, 1925	253	Harry Davis, 1897	28	Jimmie Foxx, 1938	175
Rogers Hornsby, 1922	250	Sam Thompson, 1894	28	Lou Gehrig, 1930	174
Chuck Klein, 1930	250	George Davis, 1893	27	Babe Ruth, 1921	171
Ty Cobb, 1911	248	Sam Thompson, 1894	27	Chuck Klein, 1930	170
George Sisler, 1922	246	Jimmy Williams, 1899	27	Hank Greenberg, 1935	170
Ichiro Suzuki, 2001	242	John Reilly, 1890	26	Jimmie Foxx, 1932	169
Heinie Manush, 1928	241	George Treadway, 1894	26		
Babe Herman, 1930	241	Joe Jackson, 1912	26	STRIKEOUTS	
		Sam Crawford, 1914	26	Adam Dunn, 2004	195
BATTING AVERAGE		Kiki Cuyler, 1925	26	Bobby Bonds, 1970	189
Hugh Duffy, 1894	.438			Jose Hernandez, 2002	188
Tip O'Neill, 1887	.435	HOME RUNS		Bobby Bonds, 1969	187
Willie Keeler, 1897	.432	Barry Bonds, 2001	73	Preston Wilson, 2000	187
Rogers Hornsby, 1924	.424	Mark McGwire, 1998	70	Rob Deer, 1987	186
Jesse Burkett, 1895	.423	Sammy Sosa, 1998	66	Jose Hernandez, 2001	185
Nap Lajoie, 1901	.422	Mark McGwire, 1999	65	Pete Incaviglia, 1986	185
Cap Anson, 1887	.421	Sammy Sosa, 2001	64	Cecil Fielder, 1990	182
Ty Cobb, 1911	.420	Sammy Sosa, 1999	63	*Jim Thome, 2003	182
George Sisler, 1922	.419	Roger Maris, 1961	61	Mo Vaughn, 2000	181
Ty Cobb, 1912	.410	Babe Ruth, 1927	60		
		Babe Ruth, 1921	59	RUNS	
DOUBLES		Jimmie Foxx, 1932	58	Billy Hamilton, 1894	198
Earl Webb, 1931	67	Hank Greenberg, 1938	58	Tom Brown, 1891	177
George Burns, 1926	64	Mark McGwire, 1997	58	Babe Ruth, 1921	177
Joe Medwick, 1936	64			Tip O'Neill, 1887	167
Hank Greenberg, 1934	63	TOTAL BASES		Lou Gehrig, 1936	167
Paul Waner, 1932	62	Babe Ruth, 1921	457	Billy Hamilton, 1895	166
Charlie Gehringer, 1936	60	Rogers Hornsby, 1922	450	Willie Keeler, 1894	165
Tris Speaker, 1923	59	Lou Gehrig, 1927	447	Joe Kelley, 1894	165
Chuck Klein, 1930	59	Chuck Klein, 1930	445	Arlie Latham, 1887	163
Todd Helton, 2000	59	Jimmie Foxx, 1932	438	Babe Ruth, 1928	163
Billy Herman, 1936	57	Stan Musial, 1948	429	Lou Gehrig, 1931	163
Billy Herman, 1935	57	Sammy Sosa, 2001	425		
Carlos Delgado, 2000	57	Hack Wilson, 1930	423		
		Chuck Klein, 1932	420		
		Luis Gonzalez, 2001	419		
		Lou Gehrig, 1930	419		

FAST FACT

Alex Rodriguez of the New York Yankees was the first American League MVP since 1995 to play in a division other than the A.L. West. That year, Mo Vaughn of the Boston Red Sox won the award.

REGULAR SEASON – INDIVIDUAL BATTING, SINGLE SEASON (CONT.)

STOLEN BASES	
Hugh Nicol, 1887	138
Rickey Henderson, 1982	130
Arlie Latham, 1887	129
Lou Brock, 1974	118
Charlie Comiskey, 1887	117
John Ward, 1887	111
Billy Hamilton, 1889	111
Billy Hamilton, 1891	111
Vince Coleman, 1985	110
Arlie Latham, 1888	109
Vince Coleman, 1987	109

BASES ON BALLS	
Barry Bonds, 2004	232
Barry Bonds, 2002	198
Barry Bonds, 2001	177
Babe Ruth, 1923	170
Ted Williams, 1947	162
Ted Williams, 1949	162
Mark McGwire, 1998	162
Ted Williams, 1946	156
Eddie Yost, 1956	151
Barry Bonds, 1996	151
Babe Ruth, 1920	150

SLUGGING PERCENTAGE	
Barry Bonds, 2001	.863
Babe Ruth, 1920	.847
Babe Ruth, 1921	.846
Barry Bonds, 2004	.812
Barry Bonds, 2002	.799
Babe Ruth, 1927	.772
Lou Gehrig, 1927	.765
Babe Ruth, 1923	.764
Rogers Hornsby, 1925	.756
Mark McGwire, 1998	.752
Jeff Bagwell, 1994	.750

REGULAR SEASON – INDIVIDUAL PITCHING, SINGLE SEASON

GAMES	
Mike Marshall, 1974	106
Kent Tekulve, 1979	94
Mike Marshall, 1973	92
Kent Tekulve, 1978	91
Wayne Granger, 1969	90
Mike Marshall, 1979	90
Kent Tekulve, 1987	90
*Jim Brower, 2004	89
Mark Eichhorn, 1987	89
Steve Kline, 2001	89
Paul Quantrill, 2003	89
Julian Tavarez, 1997	89

GAMES STARTED	
Will White, 1879	75
Jim Galvin, 1883	75
Jim McCormick, 1880	74
Charley Radbourn, 1884	73
Guy Hecker, 1884	73
Jim Galvin, 1884	72
John Clarkson, 1889	72
John Clarkson, 1885	70
Bill Hutchison, 1892	70
Matt Kilroy, 1887	69

INNINGS PITCHED	
Will White, 1878	680.0
Charley Radbourn, 1884	678.2
Guy Hecker, 1884	670.2
Jim McCormick, 1880	657.2
Jim Galvin, 1883	656.1
Jim Galvin, 1884	636.1
Charley Radbourn, 1883	632.1
John Clarkson, 1885	623.0
Jim Devlin, 1876	622.0
Bill Hutchison, 1892	622.0

WINS	
Charley Radbourn, 1884	59
John Clarkson, 1885	53
Guy Hecker, 1884	52
John Clarkson, 1889	49
Charley Radbourn, 1883	48
Charlie Buffinton, 1884	48
Al Spalding, 1876	47
John Ward, 1879	47
Jim Galvin, 1883	46
Jim Galvin, 1884	46
Matt Kilroy, 1887	46

LOSSES	
John Coleman, 1883	48
Will White, 1880	42
Larry McKeon, 1884	41
George Bradley, 1879	40
Jim McCormick, 1879	40
Henry Porter, 1888	37
Kid Carsey, 1891	37
George Cobb, 1892	37
Stump Weidman, 1886	36
Bill Hutchison, 1892	36

WINNING PERCENTAGE	
Roy Face, 1959	.947
Johnny Allen, 1937	.938
Phil Regan, 1966	.933
Perry Werden, 1884	.923
Larry Twitchell, 1887	.917
Greg Maddux, 1995	.905
Randy Johnson, 1995	.900
Ron Guidry, 1978	.893
Freddie Fitzsimmons, 1940	.889
Lefty Grove, 1931	.886
Bob Stanley, 1978	.882
Preacher Roe, 1951	.880

SAVES	
Bobby Thigpen, 1990	57
Eric Gagne, 2003	55
John Smoltz, 2002	55
Randy Myers, 1993	53
Trevor Hoffman, 1998	53
Mariano Rivera, 2004	53
Eric Gagne, 2002	52
Dennis Eckersley, 1992	51
Rod Beck, 1998	51
Mariano Rivera, 2001	50
Francisco Cordero, 2004	49
Dennis Eckersley, 1990	48
Rod Beck, 1993	48
Jeff Shaw, 1998	48

EARNED RUN AVERAGE	
Tim Keefe, 1880	0.86
Dutch Leonard, 1914	0.96
Three Finger Brown, 1906	1.04
Bob Gibson, 1968	1.12
Christy Mathewson, 1909	1.14
Walter Johnson, 1913	1.14
Jack Pfiester, 1907	1.15
Addie Joss, 1908	1.16
Carl Lundgren, 1907	1.17
Denny Driscoll, 1882	1.21

SHUTOUTS	
George Bradley, 1876	16
Grover Alexander, 1916	16
Jack Coombs, 1910	13
Bob Gibson, 1968	13
Jim Galvin, 1884	12
Ed Morris, 1886	12
Grover Alexander, 1915	12
Tommy Bond, 1879	11
Charley Radbourn, 1884	11
Dave Foutz, 1886	11
Christy Mathewson, 1908	11
Ed Walsh, 1908	11
Walter Johnson, 1913	11
Sandy Koufax, 1963	11
Dean Chance, 1964	11

COMPLETE GAMES	
Will White, 1879	75
Charley Radbourn, 1884	73
Jim McCormick, 1880	72
Jim Galvin, 1883	72
Guy Hecker, 1884	72
Jim Galvin, 1884	71
Tim Keefe, 1883	68
John Clarkson, 1885	68
John Clarkson, 1889	68
Bill Hutchison, 1892	67

STRIKEOUTS	
Matt Kilroy, 1886	513
Toad Ramsey, 1886	499
Hugh Daily, 1884	483
Dupee Shaw, 1884	451
Charley Radbourn, 1884	441
Charlie Buffinton, 1884	417
Guy Hecker, 1884	385
Nolan Ryan, 1973	383
Sandy Koufax, 1965	382
Bill Sweeney, 1884	374

BASES ON BALLS	
Amos Rusie, 1890	289
Mark Baldwin, 1889	274
Amos Rusie, 1892	270
Amos Rusie, 1891	262
Mark Baldwin, 1890	249
Jack Stivetts, 1891	232
Mark Baldwin, 1891	227
Phil Knell, 1891	226
Bob Barr, 1890	219
Amos Rusie, 1893	218

REGULAR SEASON – INDIVIDUAL BATTING, SINGLE GAME

MOST RUNS	
7 Guy Hecker, Lou	Aug. 15, 1886

MOST HITS	
7 Wilbert Robinson, Bal	June 10, 1892
Rennie Stennett, Pitt	Sept. 16, 1975

MOST HOME RUNS	
4 Bobby Lowe, Bos (N)	May 30, 1894
Ed Delahanty, Phil	July 13, 1896
Lou Gehrig, NY (A)	June 3, 1932
Gil Hodges, Bklyn	Aug. 31, 1950
Joe Adcock, Mil (N)	July 31, 1954
Rocky Colavito, Cle	June 10, 1959
Willie Mays, SF	April 30, 1961
Mike Schmidt, Phi	April 17, 1976
Bob Horner, Atl	July 6, 1986
Mark Whiten, StL	Sept. 7, 1993
Mike Cameron, Sea	May 2, 2002
Shawn Green, LA	May 23, 2002
Carlos Delgado, Tor	Sept. 25, 2003

MOST GRAND SLAMS	
2 Tony Lazzeri, NY (A)	May 24, 1936
Jim Tabor, Bos (A)	July 4, 1939
Rudy York, Bos (A)	July 27, 1946
Jim Gentile, Bal	May 9, 1961
Tony Cloninger, Atl	July 3, 1966
Jim Northrup, Det	June 24, 1968
Frank Robinson, Bal	June 26, 1970
Robin Ventura, Chi (A)	Sept. 4, 1995
Chris Hoiles, Bal	Aug. 14, 1998
Fernando Tatis, StL	April 23, 1999
Nomar Garciaparra, Bos	May 10, 1999
Bill Mueller, Bos	July 29, 2003

MOST RBIS	
12 Jim Bottomley, StL	Sept. 16, 1924
Mark Whiten, StL	Sept. 7, 1993

REGULAR SEASON – INDIVIDUAL PITCHING, SINGLE GAME

MOST INNINGS PITCHED	
26 Leon Cadore, Bklyn	May 1, 1920, tie 1–1
Joe Oeschger, Bos (N)	May 1, 1920, tie 1–1

MOST RUNS ALLOWED	
24 Al Travers, Det	May 18, 1912

MOST HITS ALLOWED	
36 Jack Wadsworth, Lou	Aug. 17, 1894

MOST STRIKEOUTS	
20 Roger Clemens, Bos	April 29, 1986
Roger Clemens, Bos	Sept. 18, 1996
Kerry Wood, Chi (N)	May 6, 1998
Randy Johnson, Ari	May 8, 2001

MOST WALKS ALLOWED	
16 Bill George, NY (N)	May 30, 1887
George Van Haltren, Chi (N)	June 27, 1887
Henry Gruber, Cle	April 19, 1890
Bruno Haas, Phil (A)	June 2, 1915

MOST WILD PITCHES	
6 J.R. Richard, Hou	April 10, 1979
Phil Niekro, Atl	Aug. 14, 1979
Bill Gullickson, Mon	April 10, 1982

NOTABLE ACHIEVEMENTS
NO-HIT GAMES, NINE INNINGS OR MORE

NATIONAL LEAGUE					
DATE		**PITCHER AND GAME**	**DATE**		**PITCHER AND GAME**
1876	July 15	George Bradley, StL vs. Hart 2–0	1893	Aug. 16	Bill Hawke, Bal vs. Wash 5–0
1880	June 12	John Richmond, Wor vs. Cle 1–0 (perfect game)	1897	Sept. 18	Cy Young, Cle vs. Cin 6–0
			1898	April 22	Ted Breitenstein, Cin vs. Pitt 11–0
	June 17	Monte Ward, Prov vs. Buf 5–0 (perfect game)		April 22	Jim Hughes, Bal vs. Bos 8–0
				July 8	Frank Donahue, Phil vs. Bos 5–0
	Aug. 19	Larry Corcoran, Chi vs. Bos 6–0		Aug. 21	Walter Thornton, Chi vs. Bklyn 2–0
	Aug. 20	Pud Galvin, Buff vs. Wor 1–0	1899	May 25	Deacon Phillippe, Lou vs. NY 7–0
1882	Sept. 20	Larry Corcoran, Chi vs. Wor 5–0		Aug. 7	Vic Willis, Bos vs. Wash 7–1
	Sept. 22	Tim Lovett, Bklyn vs. NY 4–0	1900	July 12	Noodles Hahn, Cin vs. Phil 4–0
1883	July 25	Hoss Radbourn, Prov vs. Cle 8–0	1901	July 15	Christy Mathewson, NY vs. StL 5–0
	Sept. 13	Hugh Daily, Cle vs. Phil 1–0	1903	Sept. 18	Chick Fraser, Phil vs. Chi 10–0
1884	June 27	Larry Corcoran, Chi vs. Prov 6–0	1904	June 11	Bob Wicker, Chi vs. NY 1–0 (hit in 10th; won in 12th)
	Aug. 4	Pud Galvin, Buf vs. Det 18–0			
1885	July 27	John Clarkson, Chi vs. Prov 4–0	1905	June 13	Christy Mathewson, NY vs. Chi 1–0
	Aug. 29	Charles Ferguson, Phil vs. Prov 1–0	1906	May 1	John Lush, Phil vs. Bklyn 6–0
1891	June 22	Tom Lovett, Bklyn vs. NY 4–0		July 20	Mal Eason, Bklyn vs. StL 2–0
	July 31	Amos Rusie, NY vs. Bklyn 6–0		Aug. 1	Harry McIntire, Bklyn vs. Pitt 0–1 (hit in 11th; lost in 13th)
1892	Aug. 6	Jack Stivetts, Bos vs. Bklyn 11–0			
	Aug. 22	Alex Sanders, Lou vs. Bal 6–2	1907	May 8	Frank Pfeffer, Bos vs. Cin 6–0
	Oct. 15	Bumpus Jones, Cin vs. Pitt 7–1 (first major league game)		Sept. 20	Nick Maddox, Pitt vs. Bklyn 2–1

NOTABLE ACHIEVEMENTS
NO-HIT GAMES, NINE INNINGS OR MORE (CONT.)

NATIONAL LEAGUE

DATE		PITCHER AND GAME	DATE		PITCHER AND GAME
1908	July 4	George Wiltse, NY vs. Phil 1–0 (10 innings)	1969	April 17	Bill Stoneman, Mon vs. Phil 7–0
	Sept. 5	Nap Rucker, Bklyn vs. Bos 6–0		April 30	Jim Maloney, Cin vs. Hou 10–0
1909	April 15	Leon Ames, NY vs. Bklyn 0–3 (hit in 10th; lost in 13th)		May 1	Don Wilson, Hou vs. Cin 4–0
1912	Sept. 6	Jeff Tesreau, NY vs. Phil 3–0		Aug. 19	Ken Holtzman, Chi vs. Atl 3–0
1914	Sept. 9	George Davis, Bos vs. Phil 7–0		Sept. 20	Bob Moose, Pitt vs. NY 4–0
1915	April 15	Rube Marquard, NY vs. Bklyn 2–0	1970	June 12	Dock Ellis, Pitt vs. SD 2–0
	Aug. 31	Jimmy Lavender, Chi vs. NY 2–0		July 20	Bill Singer, LA vs. Phil 5–0
1916	June 16	Tom Hughes, Bos vs. Pitt 2–0	1971	June 3	Ken Holtzman, Chi vs. Cin 1–0
1917	May 2	Jim Vaughn, Chi vs. Cin 0–1 (hit in 10th; lost in 10th)		June 23	Rick Wise, Phil vs. Cin 4–0
	May 2	Fred Toney, Cin vs. Chi 1–0 (10 innings)		Aug. 14	Bob Gibson, StL vs. Pitt 11–0
1919	May 11	Hod Eller, Cin vs. StL 6–0	1972	April 16	Burt Hooton, Chi vs. Phil 4–0
1922	May 7	Jesse Barnes, NY vs. Phil 6–0		Sept. 2	Milt Pappas, Chi vs. SD 8–0
1924	July 17	Jesse Haines, StL vs. Bos 5–0		Oct. 2	Bill Stoneman, Mon vs. NY 7–0
1925	Sept. 13	Dazzy Vance, Bklyn vs. Phil 10–1	1973	Aug. 5	Phil Niekro, Atl vs. SD 9–0
1929	May 8	Carl Hubbell, NY vs. Pitt 11–0	1975	Aug. 24	Ed Halicki, SF vs. NY 6–0
1934	Sept. 21	Paul Dean, StL vs. Bklyn 3–0	1976	July 9	Larry Dierker, Hou vs. Mon 6–0
1938	June 11	Johnny Vander Meer, Cin vs. Bos 3–0		Aug. 9	John Candelaria, Pitt vs. LA 2–0
	June 15	Johnny Vander Meer, Cin vs. Bklyn 6–0		Sept. 29	John Montefusco, SF vs. Atl 9–0
1940	April 30	Tex Carleton, Bklyn vs. Cin 3–0	1978	April 16	Bob Forsch, StL vs. Phil 5–0
1941	Aug. 30	Lon Warneke, StL vs. Cin 2–0		June 16	Tom Seaver, Cin vs. StL 4–0
1944	April 27	Jim Tobin, Bos vs. Bklyn 2–0	1979	April 7	Ken Forsch, Hou vs. Atl 6–0
	May 15	Clyde Shoun, Cin vs. Bos 1–0	1980	June 27	Jerry Reuss, LA vs. SF 8–0
1946	April 23	Ed Head, Bklyn vs. Bos 5–0	1981	May 10	Charlie Lea, Mon vs. SF 4–0
1947	June 18	Ewell Blackwell, Cin vs. Bos 6–0		Sept. 26	Nolan Ryan, Hou vs. LA 5–0
1948	Sept. 9	Rex Barney, Bklyn vs. NY 2–0	1983	Sept. 26	Bob Forsch, StL vs. Mon 3–0
1950	Aug. 11	Vern Bickford, Bos vs. Bklyn 7–0	1986	Sept. 25	Mike Scott, Hou vs. SF 2–0
1951	May 6	Cliff Chambers, Pitt vs. Bos 3–0	1988	Sept. 16	Tom Browning, Cin vs. LA 1–0 (perfect game)
1952	June 19	Carl Erskine, Bklyn vs. Chi 5–0	1990	June 29	Fernando Valenzuela, LA vs. StL 6–0
1954	June 12	Jim Wilson, Mil vs. Phil 2–0		Aug. 15	Terry Mulholland, Phil vs. SF 6–0
1955	May 12	Sam Jones, Chi vs. Pitt 4–0	1991	May 23	Tommy Greene, Phil vs. Mon 2–0
1956	May 12	Carl Erskine, Bklyn vs. NY 3–0		July 26	Mark Gardner, Mon vs. LA 0–1 (hit in 10th, lost in 10th)
	Sept. 25	Sal Maglie, Bklyn vs. Phil 5–0		July 28	Dennis Martinez, Mon vs. LA 2–0 (perfect game)
1959	May 26	Harvey Haddix, Pitt vs. Mil 0–1 (hit in 13th; lost in 13th)		Sept. 11	Kent Mercker (6), Mark Wohlers (2), and Alejandro Pena (1), Atl vs. SD 1–0
1960	May 15	Don Cardwell, Chi vs. StL 4–0	1992	Aug. 17	Kevin Gross, LA vs. SF 2–0
	Aug. 18	Lew Burdette, Mil vs. Phil 1–0	1993	Sept. 8	Darryl Kile, Hou vs. NY 7–1
	Sept. 16	Warren Spahn, Mil vs. Phil 4–0	1994	April 8	Kent Mercker, Atl vs. LA 6–0
1961	April 28	Warren Spahn, Mil vs. SF 1–0	1995	June 3	Pedro Martinez, Mon vs. SD 1–0 (perfect through nine, hit in 10th)
1962	June 30	Sandy Koufax, LA vs. NY 5–0		July 14	Ramon Martinez, LA vs. Fla 7–0
1963	May 11	Sandy Koufax, LA vs. SF 8–0	1996	May 11	Al Leiter, Fla vs. Col 11–0
	May 17	Don Nottebart, Hou vs. Phil 4–1		Sept. 17	Hideo Nomo, LA vs. Col 9–0
	June 15	Juan Marichal, SF vs. Hou 1–0	1997	June 10	Kevin Brown, Fla vs. SF 9–0
1964	April 23	Ken Johnson, Hou vs. Cin 0–1		July 12	Francisco Cordova (9) and Ricardo Rincon (1), Pitt vs. Col 3–0
	June 4	Sandy Koufax, LA vs. Phil 3–0	1999	June 25	Jose Jimenez, StL vs. Ari 1–0
	June 21	Jim Bunning, Phil vs. NY 6–0 (perfect game)	2001	May 12	A.J. Burnett, Fla vs. SD 3–0
1965	June 14	Jim Maloney, Cin vs. NY 0–1 (hit in 11th; lost in 11th)		Sept. 3	Bud Smith, StL vs. SD 4–0
	Aug. 19	Jim Maloney, Cin vs. Chi 1–0 (10 innings)	2003	April 27	Kevin Millwood, Phil vs. SF 1–0
	Sept. 9	Sandy Koufax, LA vs. Chi 1–0 (perfect game)		June 11	Roy Oswalt (1), Pete Munro (2⅔), Kirk Saarloos (1⅓), Brad Lidge (2), Octavio Dotel (1), and Billy Wagner (1), Hou vs. NY 8–0
1967	June 18	Don Wilson, Hou vs. Atl 2–0	2004	May 18	Randy Johnson, Ari vs. Atl 2–0 (perfect game)
1968	July 29	George Culver, Cin vs. Phil 6–1			
	Sept. 17	Gaylord Perry, SF vs. StL 1–0			
	Sept. 18	Ray Washburn, StL vs. SF 2–0			

FAST FACT

The San Diego Padres won the N.L. West in 2005 with an 82–80 record. Their .506 winning percentage was the lowest ever for a division champion.

NOTABLE ACHIEVEMENTS
NO-HIT GAMES, NINE INNINGS OR MORE (CONT.)

AMERICAN LEAGUE

DATE		PITCHER AND GAME	DATE		PITCHER AND GAME
1901	May 9	Earl Moore, Cle vs. Chi 2–4	1956	July 14	Mel Parnell, Bos vs. Chi 4–0
		(hit in 10th; lost in 10th)		Oct. 8	Don Larsen, NY (A) vs. Bklyn (N) 2–0
1902	Sept. 20	Jimmy Callahan, Chi vs. Det 3–0			(World Series, perfect game)
1904	May 5	Cy Young, Bos vs. Phil 3–0	1957	Aug. 20	Bob Keegan, Chi vs. Wash 6–0
		(perfect game)	1958	July 20	Jim Bunning, Det vs. Bos 3–0
	Aug. 17	Jesse Tannehill, Bos vs. Chi 6–0		Sept. 20	Hoyt Wilhelm, Bal vs. NY 1–0
1905	July 22	Weldon Henley, Phil vs. StL 6–0	1962	May 5	Bo Belinsky, LA vs. Bal 2–0
	Sept. 6	Frank Smith, Chi vs. Det 15–0		June 26	Earl Wilson, Bos vs. LA 2–0
	Sept. 27	Bill Dinneen, Bos vs. Chi 2–0		Aug. 1	Bill Monbouquette, Bos vs. Chi 1–0
1908	June 30	Cy Young, Bos vs. NY 8–0		Aug. 26	Jack Kralick, Min vs. KC 1–0
	Sept. 18	Bob Rhoades, Cle vs. Bos 2–1	1965	Sept. 16	Dave Morehead, Bos vs. Cle 2–0
	Sept. 20	Frank Smith, Chi vs. Phil 1–0	1966	June 10	Sonny Siebert, Cle vs. Wash 2–0
	Oct. 2	Addie Joss, Cle vs. Chi 1–0	1967	April 30	Steve Barber (8⅔) and Stu Miller (⅓),
		(perfect game)			Bal vs. Det 1–2
1910	April 20	Addie Joss, Cle vs. Chi 1–0		Aug. 25	Dean Chance, Min vs. Cle 2–1
	May 12	Chief Bender, Phil vs. Cle 4–0		Sept. 10	Joel Horlen, Chi vs. Det 6–0
	Aug. 30	Tom Hughes, NY vs. Cle 0–5	1968	April 27	Tom Phoebus, Bal vs. Bos 6–0
		(hit in 10th; lost in 11th)		May 8	Catfish Hunter, Oak vs. Min 4–0
1911	July 29	Joe Wood, Bos vs. StL 5–0			(perfect game)
	Aug. 27	Ed Walsh, Chi vs. Bos 5–0	1969	Aug. 13	Jim Palmer, Bal vs. Oak 8–0
1912	July 4	George Mullin, Det vs. StL 7–0	1970	July 3	Clyde Wright, Cal vs. Oak 4–0
	Aug. 30	Earl Hamilton, StL vs. Det 5–1		Sept. 21	Vida Blue, Oak vs. Min 6–0
1914	May 14	Jim Scott, Chi vs. Wash 0–1	1973	April 27	Steve Busby, KC vs. Det 3–0
		(hit in 10th; lost in 10th)		May 15	Nolan Ryan, Cal vs. KC 3–0
	May 31	Joe Benz, Chi vs. Cle 6–1		July 15	Nolan Ryan, Cal vs. Det 6–0
1916	June 21	George Foster, Bos vs. NY 2–0		July 30	Jim Bibby, Tex vs. Oak 6–0
	Aug. 26	Joe Bush, Phil vs. Cle 5–0	1974	June 19	Steve Busby, KC vs. Mil 2–0
	Aug. 30	Dutch Leonard, Bos vs. StL 4–0		July 19	Dick Bosman, Cle vs. Oak 4–0
1917	April 14	Ed Cicotte, Chi vs. StL 11–0		Sept. 28	Nolan Ryan, Cal vs. Min 4–0
	April 24	George Mogridge, NY vs. Bos 2–1	1975	June 1	Nolan Ryan, Cal vs. Bal 1–0
	May 5	Ernie Koob, StL vs. Chi 1–0		Sept. 28	Vida Blue (5), Glenn Abbott (1),
	May 6	Bob Groom, StL vs. Chi 3–0			Paul Lindblad (1), and Rollie Fingers (2),
	June 23	Ernie Shore, Bos vs. Wash 4–0			Oak vs. Cal 5–0
		(perfect game)	1976	July 28	John Odom (5) and Francisco
1918	June 3	Dutch Leonard, Bos vs. Det 5–0			Barrios (4), Chi vs. Oak 2–1
1919	Sept. 10	Ray Caldwell, Cle vs. NY 3–0	1977	May 14	Jim Colborn, KC vs. Tex 6–0
1920	July 1	Walter Johnson, Wash vs. Bos 1–0		May 30	Dennis Eckersley, Cle vs. Cal 1–0
1922	April 30	Charlie Robertson, Chi vs. Det 2–0		Sept. 22	Bert Blyleven, Tex vs. Cal 6–0
		(perfect game)	1981	May 15	Len Barker, Cle vs. Tor 3–0
1923	Sept. 4	Sam Jones, NY vs. Phil 2–0			(perfect game)
	Sept. 7	Howard Ehmke, Bos vs. Phil 4–0	1983	July 4	Dave Righetti, NY vs. Bos 4–0
1926	Aug. 21	Ted Lyons, Chi vs. Bos 6–0		Sept. 29	Mike Warren, Oak vs. Chi 3–0
1931	April 29	Wes Ferrell, Cle vs. StL 9–0	1984	April 7	Jack Morris, Det vs. Chi 4–0
	Aug. 8	Bob Burke, Wash vs. Bos 5–0		Sept. 30	Mike Witt, Cal vs. Tex 1–0
1934	Sept. 18	Bobo Newsom, StL vs. Bos 1–2			(perfect game)
		(hit in 10th; lost in 10th)	1986	Sept. 19	Joe Cowley, Chi vs. Cal 7–1
1935	Aug. 31	Vern Kennedy, Chi vs. Cle 5–0	1987	April 15	Juan Nieves, Mil vs. Bal 7–0
1937	June 1	Bill Dietrich, Chi vs. StL 8–0	1990	April 11	Mark Langston (7) and Mike Witt (2),
1938	Aug. 27	Monte Pearson, NY vs. Cle 13–0			Cal vs. Sea 1–0
1940	April 16	Bob Feller, Cle vs. Chi 1–0		June 2	Randy Johnson, Sea vs. Det 2–0
		(Opening Day)		June 11	Nolan Ryan, Tex vs. Oak 5–0
1945	Sept. 9	Dick Fowler, Phil vs. StL 1–0		June 29	Dave Stewart, Oak vs. Tor 5–0
1946	April 30	Bob Feller, Cle vs. NY 1–0		July 1	Andy Hawkins, NY vs. Chi 0–4 (pitched
1947	July 10	Don Black, Cle vs. Phil 3–0			eight innings of nine-inning game)
	Sept. 3	Bill McCahan, Phil vs. Wash 3–0		Sept. 2	Dave Stieb, Tor vs. Cle 3–0
1948	June 30	Bob Lemon, Cle vs. Det 2–0	1991	May 1	Nolan Ryan, Tex vs. Tor 3–0
1951	July 1	Bob Feller, Cle vs. Det 2–1		July 13	Bob Milacki (6), Mike Flanagan (1),
	July 12	Allie Reynolds, NY vs. Cle 1–0			Mark Williamson (1), and Gregg
	Sept. 28	Allie Reynolds, NY vs. Bos 8–0			Olson (1), Bal vs. Oak 2–0
1952	May 15	Virgil Trucks, Det vs. Wash 1–0		Aug. 11	Wilson Alvarez, Chi vs. Bal 7–0
	Aug. 25	Virgil Trucks, Det vs. NY 1–0		Aug. 26	Bret Saberhagen, KC vs. Chi 7–0
1953	May 6	Bobo Holloman, StL vs. Phil 6–0	1993	April 22	Chris Bosio, Sea vs. Bos 7–0
		(first major league start)		Sept. 4	Jim Abbott, NY vs. Cle 4–0

NOTABLE ACHIEVEMENTS
NO-HIT GAMES, NINE INNINGS OR MORE (cont.)

AMERICAN LEAGUE

DATE		PITCHER AND GAME
1994	April 27	Scott Erickson, Min vs. Mil 6–0
	July 28	Kenny Rogers, Tex vs. Cal 4–0
		(perfect game)
1996	May 14	Dwight Gooden, NY vs. Sea 2–0
1998	May 17	David Wells, NY vs. Min 4–0
		(perfect game)

DATE		PITCHER AND GAME
1999	July 18	David Cone, NY vs. Mon 6–0
		(perfect game)
	Sept. 11	Eric Milton, Min vs. Ana 7–0
2001	April 4	Hideo Nomo, Bos vs. Bal 3–0
2002	April 27	Derek Lowe, Bos vs. TB 10–0

LONGEST HITTING STREAKS

NATIONAL LEAGUE

PLAYER AND TEAM	YEAR	G
Willie Keeler, Bal	1897	44
Pete Rose, Cin	1978	44
Bill Dahlen, Chi	1894	42
Tommy Holmes, Bos	1945	37
Jimmy Rollins, Phil	2005-06	36
Billy Hamilton, Phil	1894	38
Luis Castillo, Fla	2002	35
Fred Clarke, Lou	1895	35
Benito Santiago, SD	1987	34
George Davis, NY	1893	33
Rogers Hornsby, StL	1922	32

AMERICAN LEAGUE

PLAYER AND TEAM	YEAR	G
Joe DiMaggio, NY	1941	56
George Sisler, StL	1922	41
Ty Cobb, Det	1911	40
Paul Molitor, Mil	1987	39
Ty Cobb, Det	1917	35
Ty Cobb, Det	1912	34
George Sisler, StL	1925	34
John Stone, Det	1930	34
George McQuinn, StL	1938	34
Dom DiMaggio, Bos	1949	34

TRIPLE CROWN WINNERS*

NATIONAL LEAGUE

PLAYER AND TEAM	YEAR	HR	RBI	BA
Paul Hines, Prov	1878	4	50	.358
Hugh Duffy, Bos	1894	18	145	.438
Heinie Zimmerman, Chi **	1912	14	103	.372
Rogers Hornsby, StL	1922	42	152	.401
Rogers Hornsby, StL	1925	39	143	.403
Chuck Klein, Phil	1933	28	120	.368
Joe Medwick, StL	1937	31	154	.374

* Player who leads in three categories: home runs, RBIs, and batting average.
** Zimmerman ranked first in RBIs as calculated by Ernie Lanigan, but only third as calculated by Information Concepts Inc.

AMERICAN LEAGUE

PLAYER AND TEAM	YEAR	HR	RBI	BA
Nap Lajoie, Phil	1901	14	125	.422
Ty Cobb, Det	1909	9	115	.377
Jimmie Foxx, Phil	1933	48	163	.356
Lou Gehrig, NY	1934	49	165	.363
Ted Williams, Bos	1942	36	137	.356
Ted Williams, Bos	1947	32	114	.343
Mickey Mantle, NY	1956	52	130	.353
Frank Robinson, Bal	1966	49	122	.316
Carl Yastrzemski, Bos	1967	44	121	.326

TRIPLE CROWN PITCHERS***

NATIONAL LEAGUE

PLAYER AND TEAM	YEAR	W	L	SO	ERA	PLAYER AND TEAM	YEAR	W	L	SO	ERA
Tommy Bond, Bos	1877	40	17	170	2.11	Hippo Vaughn, Chi	1918	22	10	148	1.74
Hoss Radbourn, Prov	1884	60	12	441	1.38	Grover Alexander, Chi	1920	27	14	173	1.91
Tim Keefe, NY	1888	35	12	333	1.74	Dazzy Vance, Bklyn	1924	28	6	262	2.16
John Clarkson, Bos	1889	49	19	284	2.73	Bucky Walters, Cin	1939	27	11	137	2.29
Amos Rusie, NY	1894	36	13	195	2.78	Sandy Koufax, LA	1963	25	5	306	1.88
Christy Mathewson, NY	1905	31	8	206	1.27	Sandy Koufax, LA	1965	26	8	382	2.04
Christy Mathewson, NY	1908	37	11	259	1.43	Sandy Koufax, LA	1966	27	9	317	1.73
Grover Alexander, Phil	1915	31	10	241	1.22	Steve Carlton, Phil	1972	27	10	310	1.97
Grover Alexander, Phil	1916	33	12	167	1.55	Dwight Gooden, NY	1985	24	4	268	1.53
Grover Alexander, Phil	1917	30	13	201	1.86	Randy Johnson, Ari	2002	24	5	334	2.32

AMERICAN LEAGUE

PLAYER AND TEAM	YEAR	W	L	SO	ERA	PLAYER AND TEAM	YEAR	W	L	SO	ERA
Cy Young, Bos	1901	33	10	158	1.62	Lefty Gomez, NY	1934	26	5	158	2.33
Rube Waddell, Phil	1905	26	11	287	1.48	Lefty Gomez, NY	1937	21	11	194	2.33
Walter Johnson, Wash	1913	36	7	303	1.09	Hal Newhouser, Det	1945	25	9	212	1.81
Walter Johnson, Wash	1918	23	13	162	1.27	Roger Clemens, Tor	1997	21	7	292	2.05
Walter Johnson, Wash	1924	23	7	158	2.72	Roger Clemens, Tor	1998	20	6	271	2.64
Lefty Grove, Phil	1930	28	5	209	2.54	Pedro Martinez, Bos	1999	23	4	313	2.07
Lefty Grove, Phil	1931	31	4	175	2.06						

***Pitcher who leads in three categories: wins, strikeouts, and ERA.

NOTABLE ACHIEVEMENTS
CONSECUTIVE GAMES PLAYED, 500 OR MORE GAMES

NATIONAL LEAGUE AND AMERICAN LEAGUE

Cal Ripken, Jr.	2,632	Frank McCormick	652
Lou Gehrig	2,130	Sandy Alomar, Sr.	648
Everett Scott	1,307	Eddie Brown	618
Steve Garvey	1,207	Roy McMillan	585
Billy Williams	1,117	George Pinckney	577
Joe Sewell	1,103	Steve Brodie	574
Miguel Tejada	918	Aaron Ward	565
Stan Musial	895	Alex Rodriguez	546
Eddie Yost	829	Candy LaChance	540
Gus Suhr	822	Buck Freeman	535
Nellie Fox	798	Fred Luderus	533
Pete Rose	745	Clyde Milan	511
Dale Murphy	740	Charlie Gehringer	511
Richie Ashburn	730	Vada Pinson	508
Ernie Banks	717	Tony Cuccinello	504
Pete Rose	678	Charlie Gehringer	504
Earl Averill	673	Omar Moreno	503

UNASSISTED TRIPLE PLAYS

PLAYER AND TEAM	DATE	POS	OPP	OPP BATTER
Neal Ball, Cle	7-19-09	SS	Bos	Amby McConnell
Bill Wambsganss, Cle	10-10-20	2B	Bklyn	Clarence Mitchell
George Burns, Bos	9-14-23	1B	Cle	Frank Brower
Ernie Padgett, Bos	10-6-23	SS	Phil	Walter Holke
Glenn Wright, Pitt	5-7-25	SS	StL	Jim Bottomley
Jimmy Cooney, Chi	5-30-27	SS	Pitt	Paul Waner
Johnny Neun, Det	5-31-27	1B	Cle	Homer Summa
Ron Hansen, Wash	7-30-68	SS	Cle	Joe Azcue
Mickey Morandini, Phil	9-20-92	2B	Pitt	Jeff King
John Valentin, Bos	7-15-94	SS	Min	Marc Newfield
Randy Velarde, Oak	5-29-00	2B	NYY	Shane Spencer
Rafael Furcal, Atl	5-10-03	SS	StL	Woody Williams

PENNANT WINNERS (PAST 50 YEARS)

NATIONAL LEAGUE

YEAR	TEAM	MANAGER	W	L	PCT	GA
2005	Houston Astros (WC)	Phil Garner	89	73	.549	-11
2004	St. Louis (C)	Tony LaRussa	105	57	.648	13
2003	Florida (WC)	Jack McKeon	91	71	.562	-10
2002	San Francisco (WC)	Dusty Baker	95	66	.590	-2.5
2001	Arizona (W)	Bob Brenly	92	70	.568	2
2000	New York (WC)	Bobby Valentine	94	68	.580	-6.5
1999	Atlanta (E)	Bobby Cox	103	59	.636	6.5
1998	San Diego (W)	Bruce Bochy	98	64	.605	9.5
1997	Florida (WC)	Jim Leyland	92	70	.568	-9
1996	Atlanta (E)	Bobby Cox	96	66	.593	8
1995	Atlanta (E)	Bobby Cox	90	54	.625	21
1994	Season ended Aug. 11 due to labor dispute.					
1993	Philadelphia (E)	Jim Fregosi	97	65	.599	3
1992	Atlanta (W)	Bobby Cox	98	64	.605	8
1991	Atlanta (W)	Bobby Cox	94	68	.580	1
1990	Cincinnati (W)	Lou Piniella	91	71	.562	5
1989	San Francisco (W)	Roger Craig	92	70	.568	3
1988	Los Angeles (W)	Tommy Lasorda	94	67	.584	7
1987	St. Louis (E)	Whitey Herzog	95	67	.586	3
1986	New York (E)	Dave Johnson	108	54	.667	21.5
1985	St. Louis (E)	Whitey Herzog	101	61	.623	3
1984	San Diego (W)	Dick Williams	92	70	.568	12
1983	Philadelphia (E)	Pat Corrales/Paul Owens	90	72	.556	6
1982	St. Louis (E)	Whitey Herzog	92	70	.568	3
1981**	Los Angeles (W)	Tommy Lasorda	63	47	.573	**
1980	Philadelphia (E)	Dallas Green	91	71	.562	1
1979	Pittsburgh (E)	Chuck Tanner	98	64	.605	2
1978	Los Angeles (W)	Tommy Lasorda	95	67	.586	2.5
1977	Los Angeles (W)	Tommy Lasorda	98	64	.605	10

GA = Games Ahead. **First half 36–21; second half 27–26, in season split by strike; defeated Houston in playoff for Western Division title.

LEGENDS

Roberto Clemente led Pittsburgh to the World Series in 1971.

WALTER IOOSS, JR.

■ **Roberto Clemente, outfielder,** b. August 18, 1934, Carolina, Puerto Rico; d. December 31, 1972, San Juan, Puerto Rico. Baseball's first Latino superstar, Clemente paved the way for dozens of stars who followed him to greatness from Latin America. He won 12 Gold Glove Awards and is considered by some the greatest rightfielder of all time. A four-time batting champion, 12-time All-Star, and the 1966 National League MVP, Clemente finished his career with exactly 3,000 hits. He died in a plane crash while flying emergency supplies to victims of an earthquake in Nicaragua. He was immediately inducted into the Baseball Hall of Fame.

■ **Hank Aaron, outfielder,** b. February 5, 1934, Mobile, Alabama. Aaron is the answer to trivia questions for his firsts and his lasts. He was first in the all-time alphabetical listing of major league baseball players when he retired and the last major leaguer to have played in the Negro Leagues. But he is most famous for his accomplishments with the bat: He is Number 1 in major league history in career home runs (755), RBIs (2,297), and total bases (6,856). Selected as an All-Star a record 25 times, he was the 1957 National League MVP and a member of baseball's All-Century Team.

■ **Ty Cobb, outfielder,** b. December 18, 1886, Narrows, Georgia; d. July 17, 1961, Atlanta, Georgia. Cobb's fiery temper and fierce competitiveness made him one of the game's most hated players, but there was no denying his greatness. He was baseball's first superstar of the modern era (post-1900), and his .366 lifetime average is by far the highest in major league history. He batted .300 or higher 23 years in a row, and topped .400 three times. He retired in 1928, but still ranks in the top five all-time in games played, at-bats, runs, hits, doubles, triples, total bases, batting average, and stolen bases.

PENNANT WINNERS (PAST 50 YEARS cont.)

NATIONAL LEAGUE

YEAR	TEAM	MANAGER	W	L	PCT	GA
1976	Cincinnati (W)	Sparky Anderson	102	60	.630	10
1975	Cincinnati (W)	Sparky Anderson	108	54	.667	20
1974	Los Angeles (W)	Walt Alston	102	60	.630	4
1973	New York (E)	Yogi Berra	82	79	.509	1.5
1972	Cincinnati (W)	Sparky Anderson	95	59	.617	10.5
1971	Pittsburgh (E)	Danny Murtaugh	97	65	.599	7
1970	Cincinnati (W)	Sparky Anderson	102	60	.630	14.5
1969	New York (E)	Gil Hodges	100	62	.617	8
1968	St. Louis	Red Schoendienst	97	65	.599	9
1967	St. Louis	Red Schoendienst	101	60	.627	10.5
1966	Los Angeles	Walt Alston	95	67	.586	1.5
1965	Los Angeles	Walt Alston	97	65	.599	2
1964	St. Louis	Johnny Keane	93	69	.574	1
1963	Los Angeles	Walt Alston	99	63	.611	6
1962#	San Francisco	Al Dark	103	62	.624	1
1961	Cincinnati	Fred Hutchinson	93	61	.604	4
1960	Pittsburgh	Danny Murtaugh	95	59	.617	7
1959‡	Los Angeles	Walt Alston	88	68	.564	2
1958	Milwaukee	Fred Haney	92	62	.597	8
1957	Milwaukee	Fred Haney	95	59	.617	8
1956	Brooklyn	Walt Alston	93	61	.604	1
1955	Brooklyn	Walt Alston	98	55	.641	13.5
1954	New York	Leo Durocher	97	57	.630	5

Note: League Championship Series playoffs began in 1969. #Defeated Los Angeles, two games to one, in playoff for pennant. ‡Defeated Milwaukee, two games to none, in playoff for pennant. WC=Wild-card team, E=East division champion, W=West division champion.

PENNANT WINNERS (PAST 50 YEARS)

AMERICAN LEAGUE

YEAR	TEAM	MANAGER	W	L	PCT	GA
2005	Chicago White Sox (C)	Ozzie Guillen	99	63	.611	6
2004	Boston (WC)	Terry Francona	98	64	.605	-3
2003	New York (E)	Joe Torre	101	61	.623	6
2002	Anaheim (WC)	Mike Scioscia	99	63	.611	-4
2001	New York (E)	Joe Torre	95	65	.594	13.5
2000	New York (E)	Joe Torre	87	74	.540	2.5
1999	New York (E)	Joe Torre	98	64	.605	4
1998	New York (E)	Joe Torre	114	48	.704	22
1997	Cleveland (C)	Mike Hargrove	86	75	.534	6
1996	New York (E)	Joe Torre	92	70	.568	4
1995	Cleveland (C)	Mike Hargrove	100	44	.694	30
1994	Season ended Aug. 11 due to labor dispute.					
1993	Toronto (E)	Cito Gaston	95	67	.586	7
1992	Toronto (E)	Cito Gaston	96	66	.593	4
1991	Minnesota (W)	Tom Kelly	95	67	.586	8
1990	Oakland (W)	Tony La Russa	103	59	.636	9
1989	Oakland (W)	Tony La Russa	99	63	.611	7
1988	Oakland (W)	Tony La Russa	104	58	.642	13
1987	Minnesota (W)	Tom Kelly	85	77	.525	2
1986	Boston (E)	John McNamara	95	66	.590	5.5
1985	Kansas City (W)	Dick Howser	91	71	.562	1
1984	Detroit (E)	Sparky Anderson	104	58	.642	15
1983	Baltimore (E)	Joe Altobelli	98	64	.605	6
1982	Milwaukee (E)	Buck Rodgers, Harvey Kuenn	95	67	.586	1
1981	New York (E)	Gene Michael, Bob Lemon	59	48	.551	#
1980	Kansas City (W)	Jim Frey	97	65	.599	14
1979	Baltimore (E)	Earl Weaver	102	57	.642	8
1978†	New York (E)	Billy Martin, Bob Lemon	100	63	.613	1
1977	New York (E)	Billy Martin	100	62	.617	2.5
1976	New York (E)	Billy Martin	97	62	.610	10.5
1975	Boston (E)	Darrell Johnson	95	65	.594	4.5
1974	Oakland (W)	Al Dark	90	72	.556	5
1973	Oakland (W)	Dick Williams	94	68	.580	6
1972	Oakland (W)	Dick Williams	93	62	.600	5.5
1971	Baltimore (E)	Earl Weaver	101	57	.639	12
1970	Baltimore (E)	Earl Weaver	108	54	.667	15
1969	Baltimore (E)	Earl Weaver	109	53	.673	19
1968	Detroit	Mayo Smith	103	59	.636	12
1967	Boston	Dick Williams	92	70	.568	1
1966	Baltimore	Hank Bauer	97	63	.606	9
1965	Minnesota	Sam Mele	102	60	.630	7
1964	New York	Yogi Berra	99	63	.611	1
1963	New York	Ralph Houk	104	57	.646	10.5
1962	New York	Ralph Houk	96	66	.593	5
1961	New York	Ralph Houk	109	53	.673	8
1960	New York	Casey Stengel	97	57	.630	8
1959	Chicago	Al Lopez	94	60	.610	5
1958	New York	Casey Stengel	92	62	.597	10
1957	New York	Casey Stengel	98	56	.636	8
1956	New York	Casey Stengel	97	57	.630	9
1955	New York	Casey Stengel	96	58	.623	3
1954	Cleveland	Al Lopez	111	43	.721	8

Note: League Championship Series playoffs began in 1969.
†Defeated Boston in a one-game playoff.
#First half 34–22; second half 25–26, in season split by strike; defeated Milwaukee in playoff for Eastern Division title.
WC=Wild-card team, E=East division champ, W=West division champ.

2005-06 OFF-SEASON TRANSACTIONS

The following is a list of big-time players who switched teams for the 2005 season.

■ Johnny Damon, centerfielder, New York Yankees

Damon, once the scruffy face of the Boston Red Sox, crossed enemy lines and became a Yankee with a four-year, $52 million contract in December.

Baseball's best leadoff hitter batted .316 with 18 stolen bases, 197 hits, and 117 runs scored in 2005. In four years with Boston, Damon ranked in the top 10 in the majors in runs and hits, and helped the Red Sox to three post-season appearances and the 2004 World Series title. His arrival in New York could mean the end of the Yankees' world championship drought.

TOM DIPACE

■ Alfonso Soriano, centerfielder, Washington Nationals

Soriano has a new home, in more ways than one. He went from being the second baseman in baseball's best infield in Texas to being an outfielder with the Nationals. In desperate need of offense, the Nats got one of the game's top offensive threats. Soriano has had three seasons of 36 or more home runs and four seasons of 30 or more stolen bases. He had 36 home runs, 104 RBIs and 30 steals in 2005 with the Rangers.

HARAZ N. GHANBARI/AP

■ Billy Wagner, pitcher, New York Mets

Billy the Kid is just 5'11" and weighs 201 pounds, but for 10 seasons he's been dominating hitters with a 100-mile-per-hour fastball. In November 2004, the left-handed closer left the Phillies and took his blazing heater to their N.L. East rivals, the Mets, for $43 million over four years. A four-time All-Star, Wagner has six 30-save seasons and has topped 100 strikeouts three times, despite pitching as many as 78 innings just once.

JOHN IACONO

■ A.J. Burnett, pitcher, Toronto Blue Jays

Burnett was considered the biggest prize among this year's free agents, and the Blue Jays bought his services for five years for $55 million. He was 12–12 with a 3.44 ERA in 2005 for the Florida Marlins, his third double-digit win season. Burnett lacks some polish, but he throws in the upper-90's and is still just 29 years old, two big reasons why Toronto made him the centerpiece of its rebuilding effort in the off-season.

CHRIS GRAYTHEN/GETTY IMAGES

2006 YOUNG STARS TO WATCH

■ **Felix Hernandez, pitcher, Seattle Mariners** The 19-year-old Hernandez was the youngest player in the majors when he made his debut in August 2005. He quickly showed why he'll soon be one of the best. Using a fastball that reaches the high 90's, the right-hander went 4–4 with a 2.67 ERA and 77 strikeouts against just 23 walks in 84 1/3 innings. Nine of his 12 starts were quality starts (at least six innings pitched, with three or fewer earned runs allowed). He's poised to become the ace of Seattle's rotation.

TED S. WARREN/AP

■ **Ryan Howard, first baseman, Philadelphia Phillies** That lefty-hitting first baseman slugging home runs for the Phillies in 2005 wasn't All-Star Jim Thome; it was the rookie Howard instead. He took over for the injured Thome and blasted 22 home runs (the most among

BOB ROSATO

rookies) and drove in 63 runs in just 88 games. Howard won N.L. Rookie of the Year honors and forced the Phillies to trade Thome to the White Sox, giving him the first baseman's job permanently.

■ **David Wright, third baseman, New York Mets** Wright's sparkling combination of offense and defense makes him one of the cornerstones of the Mets' revival. In his first full season in 2005, he batted .306 with 27 HRs and 102 RBIs. He might have made the defensive play of the year — a barehanded over-the-shoulder catch while falling, against the Padres.

JOHN IACONO

■ **Jeff Francoeur, outfielder, Atlanta Braves** Francouer was the most impressive of the 18 rookies who helped propel the Braves to a 14th straight division title in 2005. The Atlanta native was called up in July and batted .379 in his first six weeks. He finished at .300 with 14 home runs and 45 RBIs.

HEINZ KLUETMEIER

DID YOU KNOW?

In 2005, the Chicago White Sox won their first World Series since 1917. In 2006, the Boston Red Sox won their first World Series since 1918. Chicago Cubs fans are still waiting for their turn. The Cubs haven't won the Series since 1908, the longest championship drought for a big-league team.

2005-06 TIME LINE

■ **April 4, 2005:** Dmitri Young of the Detroit Tigers becomes the third major leaguer to hit three home runs on Opening Day, in an 11–2 win over the Kansas City Royals.

■ **April 14, 2005:** After President George W. Bush throws out the first pitch, the Washington Nationals play the first major-league baseball game in the nation's capital since 1971. They defeat the Arizona Diamondbacks, 5–3.

■ **June 5, 2005:** The Arizona Diamondbacks use the first pick in the draft to take high school shortstop Justin Upton, three years after the Tampa Bay Devil Rays selected his older brother B.J. with the second overall pick.

■ **July 12, 2005:** The American League wins its eighth straight All-Star Game (not counting a tie in 2002), beating the National League, 7–5.

■ **July 15, 2005:** Rafael Palmeiro of the Baltimore Orioles collects his 3,000th career hit, a double against the Seattle Mariners. Less than three weeks later, Palmeiro is suspended for testing positive for steroids. In all, 12 players will be suspended during baseball's first year of steroid testing.

■ **July 31, 2005:** Third baseman Wade Boggs and second baseman Ryne Sandberg are inducted into the Baseball Hall of Fame.

■ **August 20, 2005:** The Kansas City Royals snap a franchise-record 19-game losing streak by beating the Oakland A's. The Royals fall two defeats short of the American League record of 21 straight losses (by the 1988 Baltimore Orioles) and four short of the major league record of 23 (by the 1961 Philadelphia Phillies).

■ **September 22, 2005:** Pitcher Dontrelle Willis bats seventh in the Florida Marlins' lineup, the highest spot in the batting order for a pitcher in 32 years. Willis goes 1-for-4 and wins his 22nd game, 2–1, over the New York Mets.

■ **October 2, 2005:** Philadelphia Phillies shortstop Jimmy Rollins finishes the season on a 36-game hitting streak, baseball's longest in 18 years.

■ **October 9, 2005:** Chris Burke of the Houston Astros hits a walk-off home run in the 18th inning to give the Astros a 7–6, series-clinching win over the Atlanta Braves in their National League Division Series. Roger Clemens pitches three innings for Houston in his first relief appearance since 1984 to get the win.

■ **October 16, 2005:** Chicago White Sox pitcher Jose Contreras hurls the team's fourth straight complete game win over the Los Angeles Angels in the American League Championship Series. The White Sox clinch their first A.L. pennant since 1959 with the 6–3 win.

■ **October 26, 2005:** The White Sox win their first World Series since 1917 by beating the Astros, 1–0 , to conclude a four-game sweep.

■ **November 15, 2005:** Albert Pujols of the St. Louis Cardinals is voted National League MVP, stopping Barry Bonds' record streak of four straight MVP wins.

■ **March 20, 2006:** Japan defeats Cuba, 10–6, to win the first World Baseball Classic.

■ **May 28, 2006:** Barry Bonds hits the 715th home run of his major league career, off Colorado's Byung-Hyun Kim. He passes Babe Ruth and takes sole possession of second place behind Henry Aaron on the all-time home run list.

BASKETBALL MEN'S

After more than seven months of action-packed hoops, the 2005–2006 NBA season ended with a Flash. Miami Heat guard Dwyane Wade — nicknamed "Flash" by teammate Shaquille O'Neal — put on a superhero performance in the NBA Finals. Wade averaged 34.7 points per game as Miami beat the Dallas Mavericks in six games for its first championship.

Wade's heroics were a fitting finish to one of the most exciting postseasons in years. Superstars such as LeBron James of the Cleveland Cavaliers, Elton Brand of the Los Angeles Clippers, and Dirk Nowitzki of the Dallas Mavericks filled up the stat sheet and hit clutch shot after clutch shot. James had a triple-double in his first career playoff game and led a young Cavaliers squad to the

Eastern Conference semifinals. Brand was the main reason the Los Angeles Clippers won their first playoff series since 1976, when they were the Buffalo Braves. And Nowitzki's dominance helped the Dallas Mavericks defeat the defending champion San Antonio Spurs and scrappy Phoenix Suns in back-to-back nail-biting series.

The regular season had its "wow" moments too, starting

Dwyane Wade's explosive play against the Dallas Mavericks earned him the NBA Finals MVP award.

JOHN BIEVER

NBA TEAMS

EASTERN CONFERENCE
Atlanta Hawks
Boston Celtics
Charlotte Bobcats
Chicago Bulls
Cleveland Cavaliers
Detroit Pistons
Indiana Pacers
Miami Heat
Milwaukee Bucks
New Jersey Nets
New York Knicks
Orlando Magic
Philadelphia 76ers
Toronto Raptors
Washington Wizards

WESTERN CONFERENCE
Dallas Mavericks
Denver Nuggets
Golden State Warriors
Houston Rockets
Los Angeles Clippers
Los Angeles Lakers
Memphis Grizzlies
Minnesota Timberwolves
New Orleans Hornets
Phoenix Suns
Portland Trail Blazers
Sacramento Kings
San Antonio Spurs
Seattle SuperSonics
Utah Jazz

with an 81-point outburst by Kobe Bryant of the Los Angeles Lakers against the Toronto Raptors on January 22, 2006. Bryant's point total for the game was second in NBA history to the legendary Wilt Chamberlain's 100-point performance in 1962. Bryant finished the season with a league-leading 35.4 points per game — the highest scoring average in the NBA since Michael Jordan averaged 37.1 in 1986–1987.

Steve Nash of the Phoenix Suns won his second straight NBA MVP award by doing what he does best: pushing the pace and making his teammates better. He led Phoenix to its second-straight Pacific Division title even though the team had traded starters Joe Johnson and Quentin Richardson last summer and lost superstar big man Amaré

Stoudemire to a knee injury for most of the season. Nash averaged a career high 18.8 points and league-leading 10.5 assists per game.

The season's biggest surprise was the New Orleans/Oklahoma City Hornets. The team went 18-64 in 2004–2005 and had to be relocated to Oklahoma because of the damage to New Orleans caused by Hurricane Katrina. But the Hornets' luck changed when they found a gem in the 2005 NBA Draft: point guard Chris Paul, from Wake Forest University. With Paul running the show, the Hornets improved to 38-44 and were in the playoff hunt for most of the season. Paul (16.1

LeBron James averaged 31.4 points per game.

JOHN BIEVER

points, 7.8 assists) was the runaway winner of the NBA Rookie of the Year award.

2005-06 NBA FINAL STANDINGS

Eastern Conference

ATLANTIC	W	L	PCT	GB
a-Nets	49	33	.598	—
76ers	38	44	.463	11.0
Celtics	33	49	.402	16.0
Raptors	27	55	.329	22.0
Knicks	23	59	.280	26.0

CENTRAL	W	L	PCT	GB
e, c-Pistons	64	18	.780	—
x-Cavaliers	50	32	.610	14.0
x-Pacers	41	41	.500	23.0
x-Bulls	41	41	.500	23.0
x-Bucks	40	42	.488	24.0

SOUTHEAST	W	L	PCT	GB
se-Heat	52	30	.634	—
x-Wizards	42	40	.512	10.0
Magic	36	46	.439	16.0
Bobcats	26	56	.317	26.0
Hawks	26	56	.317	26.0

Western Conference

NORTHWEST	W	L	PCT	GB
nw-Nuggets	44	38	.537	—
Jazz	41	41	.500	3.0
SuperSonics	35	47	.427	9.0
Timberwolves	33	49	.402	11.0
Trail Blazers	21	61	.256	23.0

PACIFIC	W	L	PCT	GB
p-Suns	54	28	.659	—
x-Clippers	47	35	.573	7.0
x-Lakers	45	37	.549	9.0
x-Kings	44	38	.537	10.0
Warriors	34	48	.415	20.0

SOUTHWEST	W	L	PCT	GB
w, sw-Spurs	63	19	.768	—
x-Mavericks	60	22	.732	3.0
x-Grizzlies	49	33	.598	14.0
Hornets	38	44	.463	25.0
Rockets	34	48	.415	29.0

KEY x=clinched playoff berth; e=clinched Eastern Conference; a=clinched Atlantic Division; c=clinched Central Division; se=clinched Southeast Division; w=clinched Western Conference; sw=clinched Southwest Division; nw=clinched Northwest Division; p=clinched Pacific Division; W=wins; L=losses; PCT=winning percentage; GB=games back

2006 NBA PLAYOFFS

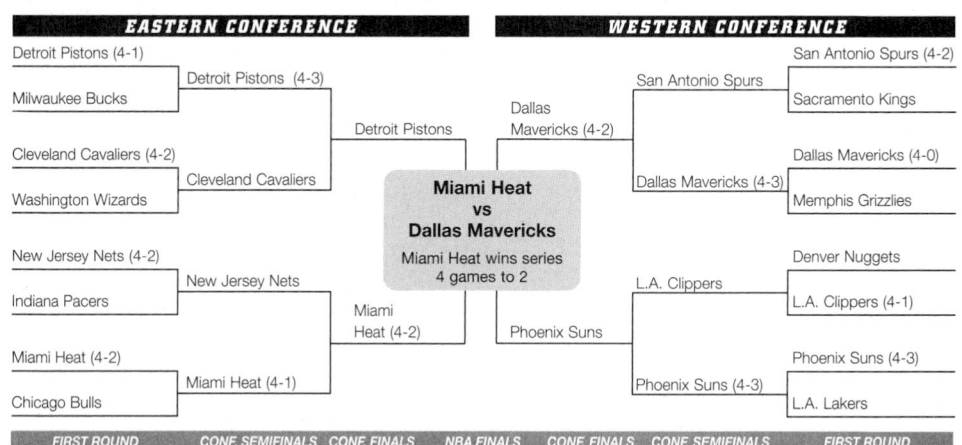

	EASTERN CONFERENCE					WESTERN CONFERENCE	
Detroit Pistons (4-1)							San Antonio Spurs (4-2)
	Detroit Pistons (4-3)				San Antonio Spurs		Sacramento Kings
Milwaukee Bucks				Dallas			
		Detroit Pistons		Mavericks (4-2)			
Cleveland Cavaliers (4-2)							Dallas Mavericks (4-0)
	Cleveland Cavaliers				Dallas Mavericks (4-3)		Memphis Grizzlies
Washington Wizards							
New Jersey Nets (4-2)							Denver Nuggets
	New Jersey Nets				L.A. Clippers		L.A. Clippers (4-1)
Indiana Pacers		Miami					
		Heat (4-2)		Phoenix Suns			
Miami Heat (4-2)							Phoenix Suns (4-3)
	Miami Heat (4-1)				Phoenix Suns (4-3)		L.A. Lakers
Chicago Bulls							

Miami Heat vs Dallas Mavericks
Miami Heat wins series 4 games to 2

FIRST ROUND   CONF. SEMIFINALS   CONF. FINALS   NBA FINALS   CONF. FINALS   CONF. SEMIFINALS   FIRST ROUND

NBA PLAYOFF RESULTS

FIRST ROUND
Eastern Conference
DETROIT PISTONS VS. MILWAUKEE BUCKS
GAME 1 April 23, 2006: Detroit 92, Milwaukee 74
GAME 2 April 26, 2006: Detroit 109, Milwaukee 98
GAME 3 April 29, 2006: Milwaukee 124, Detroit 104
GAME 4 May 1, 2006: Detroit 109, Milwaukee 99
GAME 5 May 3, 2006: Detroit 122, Milwaukee 93
DETROIT PISTONS WINS SERIES, 4–1

MIAMI HEAT VS. CHICAGO BULLS
GAME 1 April 22, 2006: Miami 111, Chicago 106
GAME 2 April 24, 2006: Miami 115, Chicago 108
GAME 3 April 27, 2006: Chicago 109, Miami 90
GAME 4 April 30, 2006: Chicago 93, Miami 87
GAME 5 May 2, 2006: Miami 92, Chicago 78
GAME 6 May 4, 2006: Miami 113, Chicago 96
MIAMI HEAT WIN SERIES, 4–2

NEW JERSEY NETS VS. INDIANA PACERS
GAME 1 April 23, 2006: Indiana 90, New Jersey 88
GAME 2 April 25, 2006: New Jersey 90, Indiana 75
GAME 3 April 27, 2006: Indiana 107, New Jersey 95
GAME 4 April 29, 2006: New Jersey 97, Indiana 88
GAME 5 May 2, 2006: New Jersey 92, Indiana 86
GAME 6 May 4, 2006: New Jersey 96, Indiana 90
NEW JERSEY NETS WIN SERIES, 4–2

CLEVELAND CAVALIERS VS. WASHINGTON WIZARDS
GAME 1 April 22, 2006: Cleveland 97, Washington 86
GAME 2 April 25, 2006: Washington 89, Cleveland 84
GAME 3 April 28, 2006: Cleveland 97, Washington 96
GAME 4 April 30, 2006: Washington 106, Cleveland 96
GAME 5 May 3, 2006: Cleveland 121, Washington 120 (OT)
GAME 6 May 5, 2006: Cleveland 114, Washington 113 (OT)
CLEVELAND CAVALIERS WIN SERIES, 4–1

Western Conference
SAN ANTONIO SPURS VS. SACRAMENTO KINGS
GAME 1 April 22, 2006: San Antonio 122, Sacramento 88
GAME 2 April 25, 2006: San Antonio 128, Sacramento 119 (OT)
GAME 3 April 28, 2006: Sacramento 94, San Antonio 93
GAME 4 April 30, 2006: Sacramento 102, San Antonio 84
GAME 5 May 2, 2006: San Antonio 109, Sacramento 98
GAME 6 May 5, 2006: San Antonio 105, Sacramento 83
SAN ANTONIO SPURS WIN SERIES, 4–2

PHOENIX SUNS VS. LOS ANGELES LAKERS
GAME 1 April 23, 2006: Phoenix 107, Los Angeles 102
GAME 2 April 26, 2006: Los Angeles 99, Phoenix 93
GAME 3 April 28, 2006: Los Angeles 99, Phoenix 92
GAME 4 April 30, 2006: Los Angeles 99, Phoenix 98 (OT)
GAME 5 May 2, 2006: Phoenix 114, Los Angeles 97
GAME 6 May 4, 2006: Phoenix 126, Los Angeles 118 (OT)
GAME 7 May 6, 2006: Phoenix 121, Los Angeles 90
PHOENIX SUNS WIN SERIES, 4–3

DENVER NUGGETS VS. LOS ANGELES CLIPPERS
GAME 1 April 22, 2006: Los Angeles 89, Denver 87
GAME 2 April 24, 2006: Los Angeles 98, Denver 87
GAME 3 April 27, 2006: Denver 94, Los Angeles 87
GAME 4 April 29, 2006: Los Angeles 100, Denver 86
GAME 5 May 1, 2006: Los Angeles 101, Denver 83
LOS ANGELES CLIPPERS WIN SERIES, 4–1

DALLAS MAVERICKS VS. MEMPHIS GRIZZLIES
GAME 1 April 23, 2006: Dallas 103, Memphis 93
GAME 2 April 26, 2006: Dallas 94, Memphis 79
GAME 3 April 29, 2006: Dallas 94, Memphis 89 (OT)
GAME 4 May 1, 2006: Dallas 102, Memphis 76
DALLAS MAVERICKS WIN SERIES, 4–0

CONFERENCE SEMIFINALS
Eastern Conference
DETROIT PISTONS VS. CLEVELAND CAVALIERS
GAME 1 May 7, 2006: Detroit 113, Cleveland 86
GAME 2 May 9, 2006: Detroit 97, Cleveland 91
GAME 3 May 13, 2006: Cleveland 86, Detroit 77
GAME 4 May 15, 2006: Cleveland 74, Detroit 72
GAME 5 May 17, 2006: Cleveland 86, Detroit 84
GAME 6 May 19, 2006: Detroit 84, Cleveland 82
GAME 7 May 21, 2006: Detroit 79, Cleveland 61
DETROIT PISTONS WINS SERIES, 4–3

MIAMI HEAT VS. NEW JERSEY NETS
GAME 1 May 8, 2006: New Jersey 100, Miami 88
GAME 2 May 10, 2006: Miami 111, New Jersey 89
GAME 3 May 12, 2006: Miami 103, New Jersey 92
GAME 4 May 14, 2006: Miami 102, New Jersey 92
GAME 5 May 16, 2006: Miami 106, New Jersey 105
MIAMI HEAT WIN SERIES, 4–1

NBA PLAYOFF RESULTS (cont.)

Western Conference
SAN ANTONIO SPURS VS. DALLAS MAVERICKS
GAME 1 May 7, 2006: San Antonio 87, Dallas 85
GAME 2 May 9, 2006: Dallas 113, San Antonio 91
GAME 3 May 13, 2006: Dallas 104, San Antonio 103
GAME 4 May 15, 2006: Dallas 123, San Antonio 118 (OT)
GAME 5 May 17, 2006: San Antonio 98, Dallas 97
GAME 6 May 19, 2006: San Antonio 91, Dallas 86
GAME 7 May 22, 2006: Dallas 119, San Antonio 111 (OT)
DALLAS MAVERICKS WIN SERIES, 4–3

PHOENIX SUNS VS. LOS ANGELES CLIPPERS
GAME 1 May 8, 2006: Phoenix 130, Los Angeles 123
GAME 2 May 10, 2006: Los Angeles 122, Phoenix 97
GAME 3 May 12, 2006: Phoenix 94, Los Angeles 91
GAME 4 May 14, 2006: Los Angeles 114, Phoenix 107
GAME 5 May 16, 2006: Phoenix 125, Los Angeles 118 (OT)
GAME 6 May 18, 2006: Los Angeles 118, Phoenix 106
GAME 7 May 22, 2006: Phoenix 127, Los Angeles 107
PHOENIX SUNS WIN SERIES, 4–3

CONFERENCE FINALS
Eastern Conference
DETROIT PISTONS VS. MIAMI HEAT
GAME 1 May 23, 2006: Miami 91, Detroit 86
GAME 2 May 25, 2006: Detroit 92, Miami 88

GAME 3 May 27, 2006: Miami 98, Detroit 83
GAME 4 May 29, 2006: Miami 89, Detroit 78
GAME 5 May 31, 2006: Detroit 91, Miami 78
GAME 6 June 2, 2006: Miami 95, Detroit 78
MIAMI HEAT WIN SERIES, 4–2

Western Conference
PHOENIX SUNS VS. DALLAS MAVERICKS
GAME 1 May 22, 2005: Phoenix 121, Dallas 118
GAME 2 May 24, 2005: Dallas 105, Phoenix 98
GAME 3 May 28, 2005: Dallas 95, Phoenix 88
GAME 4 May 30, 2005: Phoenix 106, Dallas 86
GAME 5 June 1, 2005: Dallas 117, Phoenix 101
GAME 6 June 3, 2006: Dallas 102, Phoenix 93
DALLAS MAVERICKS WIN SERIES, 4–2

FINALS
MIAMI HEAT VS. DALLAS MAVERICKS
GAME 1 June 8, 2006: Dallas 90, Miami 80
GAME 2 June 11, 2006: Dallas 99, Miami 85
GAME 3 June 13, 2006: Miami 98, Dallas 96
GAME 4 June 15, 2006: Miami 98, Dallas 74
GAME 5 June 18, 2005: Miami 101, Dallas 100 (OT)
GAME 6 June 20, 2005: Miami 95, Dallas 92
MIAMI HEAT WIN SERIES, 4–2

NBA FINALS COMPOSITE BOX SCORE

MIAMI HEAT

PLAYER	GP	Field Goals FGM	PCT	3-PT FG FGM	PCT	Free Throws FTM	PCT	Rebounds OFF	TOTAL	A	STL	TO	BLK	AVG
Dwyane Wade	6	65	46.8	3	27.3	75	77.3	12	47	23	16	22	6	34.7
Antoine Walker	6	43	39.1	10	27.0	5	55.6	4	33	13	4	12	3	13.8
Shaquille O'Neal	6	34	60.7	0	0.0	14	29.2	15	61	17	3	19	5	13.7
Jason Williams	6	18	36.0	10	34.5	7	63.6	0	11	28	3	8	0	8.8
James Posey	6	13	41.9	8	40.0	10	76.9	6	11	28	3	7	0	7.3
Udonis Haslem	6	18	50.0	0	0.0	3	30.0	17	37	2	7	14	6	6.5
Alonzo Mourning	6	9	69.2	0	0.0	8	66.7	4	19	0	2	4	9	4.3
Gary Payton	6	7	36.8	1	14.3	1	33.3	3	12	12	6	6	0	2.7
Shandon Anderson	4	2	33.3	0	0.0	2	50.0	2	7	12	6	6	0	1.5
Jason Kapono	1	0	0.0	0	0.0	0	0.0	0	0	0	0	0	0	0.0
Michael Doleac	1	0	0.0	0	0.0	0	0.0	0	0	0	0	0	0	0.0
TOTALS	**6**	**200**	**45.8**	**125**	**30.5**	**122**	**60.4**	**63**	**263**	**100**	**47**	**98**	**23**	**92.8**

DALLAS MAVERICKS

PLAYER	GP	Field Goals FGM	PCT	3-PT FG FGM	PCT	Free Throws FTM	PCT	Rebounds OFF	TOTAL	A	STL	TO	BLK	AVG
Dirk Nowitzki	6	41	39.0	6	25.0	49	89.1	9	65	15	4	13	4	22.8
Jason Terry	6	54	47.8	13	31.7	11	73.3	1	13	21	11	15	0	22.0
Josh Howard	6	31	38.8	5	26.2	21	80.0	10	49	11	7	15	4	14.7
Jerry Stackhouse	5	22	35.5	7	36.8	13	92.9	5	17	15	4	11	3	12.8
Devin Harris	6	16	36.4	0	0.0	12	75.0	3	5	17	5	11	0	7.3
Erick Dampier	6	13	72.2	0	0.0	8	50.0	16	49	2	6	8	4	5.7
Adrian Griffin	6	9	56.3	0	0.0	0	0.0	8	19	5	5	3	0	3.0
Marquis Daniels	6	6	54.5	1	33.3	4	80.0	2	3	8	0	4	0	2.8
DeSagana Diop	6	3	50.0	0	0.0	4	50.0	5	20	1	2	3	5	1.7
Keith Van Horn	5	3	27.3	1	16.7	0	0.0	1	6	0	0	3	0	1.4
Josh Powell	1	0	0.0	0	0.0	0	0.0	1	1	0	0	0	0	0.0
Didier Ilunga-Mbenga	2	0	0.0	0	0.0	0	0.0	0	3	0	0	1	0	0.0
Darrell Armstrong	1	0	0.0	0	0.0	0	0.0	0	1	0	0	0	0	0.0
TOTALS	**6**	**198**	**45.8**	**33**	**28.4**	**122**	**78.7**	**61**	**251**	**95**	**44**	**92**	**20**	**91.8**

KEY GP=games played; FGM=field goals made; PCT=percentage; FTM=free throws made; OFF=offensive; A=assists; STL=steals; TO=turnovers; BLK=blocks; AVG=average

NBA FINALS BOX SCORES

GAME 1

DALLAS MAVERICKS 90

	MIN	FG M-A	FT M-A	REB O-T	A	PF	STL	TO	PTS
A. Griffin	13	4-6	0-0	1-1	1	1	1	0	8
J. Terry	37	13-18	2-2	0-4	1	2	3	1	32
D. Nowitzki	39	4-14	6-6	2-10	4	2	3	2	16
J. Howard	43	3-14	4-6	0-12	4	4	1	5	10
D. Diop	16	0-0	0-0	1-2	0	2	1	2	0
J. Stackhouse	29	4-11	5-6	0-5	4	1	0	3	13
E. Dampier	27	3-4	2-4	3-7	0	4	0	0	8
D. Harris	17	0-3	1-2	0-0	2	1	0	1	1
K. Van Horn	10	1-2	0-0	0-2	0	0	0	0	2
M. Daniels	5	0-0	0-0	0-0	2	0	0	0	0
J. Powell									DNP
D. Armstrong									DNP
TOTALS	240	32-72	20-26	7-43	18	18	9	14	90

Percentages: Field Goals—44.4%, 3-Point Field Goals—6-18, 33%, (J. Terry 4-7, D. Nowitzki 2-4, J. Howard 0-4, J. Stackhouse 0-2, D. Harris 0-1). Free-Throws—76.9%. Team Rebounds: 4. Blocked Shots: 3 (D. Diop 2, J. Stackhouse 1)

MIAMI HEAT 80

	MIN	FG M-A	FT M-A	REB O-T	A	PF	STL	TO	PTS
J. Williams	34	5-11	0-0	0-4	4	3	1	1	12
D. Wade	43	11-25	6-10	3-6	6	4	4	5	28
U. Haslem	33	2-4	0-0	3-9	0	5	0	1	4
A. Walker	42	7-19	0-0	0-6	4	3	1	6	17
S. O'Neal	38	8-11	1-9	3-7	5	4	0	2	17
J. Posey	24	1-3	0-0	1-7	0	5	1	0	2
G. Payton	18	0-4	0-0	2-5	1	0	3	0	0
A. Mourning	5	0-1	0-0	0-1	0	1	0	0	0
D. Anderson									DNP
J. Kapono									DNP
M. Doleac									DNP
S. Anderson									DNP
TOTALS	240	34-78	7-19	12-45	20	25	10	15	80

Percentages: Field Goals—43.6%, 3-Point Field Goals—5-20, 25%, (J. Williams 2-5, D. Wade 0-2, A. Walker 3-9, S. O'Neal 0-0, J. Posey 0-1, G. Payton 0-3, A. Mourning 0-0). Free-Throws—36.8%. Team Rebounds: 10. Blocked Shots: 1 (D. Wade)

GAME 2

DALLAS MAVERICKS 99

	MIN	FG M-A	FT M-A	REB O-T	A	PF	STL	TO	PTS
A. Griffin	18	0-0	0-0	1-4	0	4	0	1	0
J. Terry	41	6-15	3-5	0-1	9	2	2	3	16
D. Nowitzki	41	8-16	10-11	1-16	4	2	0	1	26
J. Howard	28	6-12	1-1	1-3	1	5	0	4	15
D. Diop	12	0-0	1-2	1-4	0	5	1	1	1
J. Stackhouse	30	6-11	3-3	1-3	3	1	0	3	19
E. Dampier	28	2-3	2-3	4-13	1	2	1	2	6
D. Harris	23	4-10	3-3	0-1	4	4	1	1	11
K. Van Horn	10	2-3	0-0	0-0	0	1	0	1	5
M. Daniels	6	0-0	0-0	0-1	1	1	0	1	0
J. Powell									DNP
D. Armstrong									DNP
TOTALS	240	34-70	23-28	9-46	23	27	5	18	99

Percentages: Field Goals—48.6%, 3-Point Field Goals—8-19, 42.1% (J. Terry 1-6, D. Nowitzki 0-2, J. Howard 2-3, J. Stackhouse 4-5, D. Harris 0-1, K. Van Horn 1-2). Free-Throws—82.1%. Team Rebounds: 4. Blocked Shots: 5 (D. Nowitzki 2, J. Howard 2, E. Dampier 1)

MIAMI HEAT 85

	MIN	FG M-A	FT M-A	REB O-T	A	PF	STL	TO	PTS
J. Williams	30	3-10	4-5	0-2	4	2	1	0	11
D. Wade	40	6-19	11-14	4-8	3	4	2	4	23
U. Haslem	20	3-6	0-0	0-1	0	2	0	2	6
A. Walker	42	8-16	0-0	0-4	2	3	0	2	20
S. O'Neal	27	2-5	1-7	1-6	2	1	0	2	5
G. Payton	28	1-4	0-0	0-1	4	2	2	0	2
J. Posey	27	2-6	1-1	2-5	1	6	0	1	7
A. Mourning	20	4-4	3-5	1-4	0	3	0	1	11
S. Anderson	1	0-0	0-0	0-1	0	0	0	1	0
J. Kapono									DNP
M. Doleac									DNP
D. Anderson									DNP
TOTALS	240	29-70	20-32	8-32	16	23	5	13	85

Percentages: Field Goals—41.4%, 3-Point Field Goals—7-17, 41.2% (J. Williams 1-4, A. Walker 4-7, G. Payton 0-2, J. Posey 2-4). Free-Throws—62.5%. Team Rebounds: 12. Blocked Shots: 3 (D. Wade 1, A. Walker 1, A. Mourning 1)

GAME 3

MIAMI HEAT 98

	MIN	FG M-A	FT M-A	REB O-T	A	PF	STL	TO	PTS
D. Wade	43	14-26	13-18	2-13	2	5	2	1	42
J. Williams	34	5-11	0-0	0-1	3	3	0	3	12
U. Haslem	34	3-8	2-6	8-11	0	4	3	3	8
A. Walker	35	6-17	0-2	1-7	1	3	0	2	12
S. O'Neal	37	6-9	4-6	3-11	5	3	1	7	16
J. Posey	27	1-2	1-2	0-3	0	1	0	1	4
G. Payton	19	1-1	0-0	1-2	2	1	1	2	2
A. Mourning	8	1-2	0-0	1-1	0	3	2	1	2
D. Anderson									DNP
J. Kapono									DNP
M. Doleac									DNP
S. Anderson									DNP
TOTALS	240	37-76	20-34	16-49	13	23	9	20	98

Percentages: Field Goals—48.7%, 3-Point Field Goals—4-14, 28.6% (D. Wade 1-2, J. Williams 2-5, U. Haslem 0-0, A. Walker 0-5, S. O'Neal 0-0, J. Posey 1-2, G. Payton 0-1, A. Mourning 0-0). Free-Throws—58.8%. Team Rebounds: 13. Blocked Shots: 2 (S. O'Neal 2)

DALLAS MAVERICKS 96

	MIN	FG M-A	FT M-A	REB O-T	A	PF	STL	TO	PTS
A. Griffin	14	1-2	0-0	0-5	3	3	2	1	2
J. Terry	35	7-13	1-2	0-1	5	2	2	2	16
D. Nowitzki	44	9-21	10-12	0-6	1	5	0	3	30
J. Howard	42	8-15	2-2	0-5	1	4	0	1	21
D. Diop	10	0-0	0-0	1-4	0	4	0	0	0
J. Stackhouse	31	1-4	2-2	1-2	1	2	1	2	4
E. Dampier	29	6-11	2-5	5-9	0	4	3	1	14
D. Harris	18	4-7	1-3	0-0	4	3	1	2	9
K. Van Horn	8	0-2	0-0	0-2	0	2	0	2	0
M. Daniels	4	0-0	0-0	0-0	0	0	0	1	0
J. Powell									DNP
D. Armstrong									DNP
TOTALS	240	36-75	18-26	7-34	15	29	9	15	96

Percentages: Field Goals—48%, 3-Point Field Goals—6-16, 37.5% (J. Terry 1-3, D. Nowitzki 2-7, J. Howard 3-3, J. Stackhouse 0-1, K. Van Horn 0-2). Free-Throws—69.2%. Team Rebounds: 4. Blocked Shots: 2 (J. Howard 1, J. Stackhouse 1)

KEY MIN=minutes played; FG M-A=field goals made-attempted; FT M-A=free throws made-attempted; REB O-T=rebounds offensive-total; A=assists; PF=personal fouls; STL=steals; TO=turnovers; PTS=points; DNP=did not play

GAME 4

MIAMI HEAT 98

	MIN	FG M-A	FT M-A	REB O-T	A	PF	STL	TO	PTS
D. Wade	39	13-23	8-9	0-6	3	4	1	4	36
J. Williams	31	1-5	3-5	0-2	6	0	1	1	6
U. Haslem	17	1-2	0-0	0-2	1	5	2	4	2
A. Walker	39	5-11	2-2	0-3	2	2	2	0	14
S. O'Neal	29	6-8	5-10	3-13	3	4	0	3	17
J. Posey	26	5-9	3-4	1-10	1	3	1	1	15
S. Anderson	19	1-4	0-2	1-5	2	1	0	2	2
G. Payton	19	1-2	0-2	0-1	1	4	0	2	2
A. Mourning	13	1-2	2-2	1-6	0	3	0	1	4
J. Kapono	1	0-0	0-0	0-0	0	0	0	0	0
M. Doleac	1	0-0	0-0	0-0	0	0	0	0	0
D. Anderson									DNP
TOTALS	240	34-66	23-36	6-48	19	26	7	18	98

Percentages: Field Goals—51.5%, 3-Point Field Goals—7-19, 36.8%
(D. Wade 2-5, J. Williams 1-3, A. Walker 2-6, J. Posey 2-4, S. Anderson 0-1).
Free-Throws—63.9%. Team Rebounds: 13. Blocked Shots: 7 (D. Wade 1,
A. Walker 1, S. O'Neal 2, A. Mourning 3)

DALLAS MAVERICKS 74

	MIN	FG M-A	FT M-A	REB O-T	A	PF	STL	TO	PTS
D. Harris	27	4-8	3-3	0-0	2	3	0	3	11
J. Terry	32	8-18	0-1	0-1	0	2	1	3	17
D. Nowitzki	41	2-14	11-13	1-9	1	2	1	4	16
J. Howard	35	1-8	1-2	1-7	2	4	2	1	3
D. Diop	17	1-1	3-5	1-2	0	3	0	0	5
J. Stackhouse	30	6-18	3-3	3-4	4	1	1	0	16
E. Dampier	18	0-1	0-0	1-4	1	5	1	1	0
A. Griffin	16	3-3	0-0	3-6	0	2	0	0	6
D. Armstrong	6	0-2	0-0	0-1	0	0	0	0	0
K. Van Horn	4	0-3	0-0	0-1	0	0	0	0	0
M. Daniels	4	0-2	0-0	0-0	0	0	0	1	0
J. Powell	3	0-1	0-0	1-1	0	2	0	0	0
TOTALS	240	25-79	21-27	11-36	10	24	6	13	74

Percentages: Field Goals—31.6%, 3-Point Field Goals—3-22, 13.6% (J. Terry
1-5, D. Nowitzki 1-5, J. Howard 0-4, J. Stackhouse 1-5, D. Armstrong 0-1,
K. Van Horn 0-1, M. Daniels 0-1). Free-Throws—77.8%. Team Rebounds: 8.
Blocked Shots: 3 (D. Diop 1, J. Stackhouse 1, E. Dampier 1)

GAME 5

MIAMI HEAT 101

	MIN	FG M-A	FT M-A	REB O-T	A	PF	STL	TO	PTS
D. Wade	50	11-28	21-25	0-4	4	1	3	3	43
J. Williams	26	3-6	0-1	0-1	4	1	0	1	9
U. Haslem	29	1-3	0-0	2-4	0	6	0	1	2
A. Walker	36	2-7	1-2	0-2	2	4	0	2	6
S. O'Neal	47	8-12	2-12	2-12	1	5	2	3	18
J. Posey	44	2-6	4-4	2-6	0	5	2	1	10
G. Payton	30	3-5	1-1	0-2	2	4	0	0	8
S. Anderson	7	1-2	2-2	1-1	1	0	0	0	4
A. Mourning	4	0-0	1-2	0-1	0	0	0	0	1
D. Anderson									DNP
J. Kapono									DNP
M. Doleac									DNP
TOTALS	265	31-69	32-49	7-33	14	26	7	11	101

Percentages: Field Goals—44.9%, 3-Point Field Goals—7-17, 41.2%
(D. Wade 0-2, J. Williams 3-5, A. Walker 1-4, J. Posey 2-5, G. Payton 1-1).
Free-Throws—65.3%. Team Rebounds: 16. Blocked Shots: 0

DALLAS MAVERICKS 100

	MIN	FG M-A	FT M-A	REB O-T	A	PF	STL	TO	PTS
D. Harris	33	2-12	2-2	0-1	1	5	1	0	6
J. Terry	50	13-23	5-5	1-5	1	2	1	4	35
D. Nowitzki	49	8-19	4-5	2-8	3	4	0	2	20
J. Howard	50	8-17	9-11	5-10	3	4	0	3	25
D. Diop	20	1-2	0-0	1-4	0	6	0	0	2
E. Dampier	19	2-2	1-2	0-8	0	5	0	2	5
A. Griffin	15	1-2	0-0	1-2	1	3	1	1	2
M. Daniels	13	2-3	0-0	0-0	4	3	0	1	5
D. Mbenga	8	0-0	0-0	0-3	0	4	0	1	0
K. Van Horn	4	0-1	0-0	1-1	0	2	0	0	0
J. Stackhouse									DNP
D. Armstrong									DNP
TOTALS	265	37-81	21-25	11-42	13	38	3	14	100

Percentages: Field Goals—45.7%, 3-Point Field Goals—5-19, 26.3%
(D. Harris 0-1, J. Terry 4-9, D. Nowitzki 0-4, J. Howard 0-3, M. Daniels 1-1,
K. Van Horn 0-1). Free-Throws—84%. Team Rebounds: 12. Blocked Shots: 0

GAME 6

MIAMI HEAT 95

	MIN	FG M-A	FT M-A	REB O-T	A	PF	STL	TO	PTS
D. Wade	30	1-7	0-0	0-1	7	0	0	2	3
J. Williams	45	10-18	16-21	3-10	5	4	4	5	36
U. Haslem	40	8-13	1-4	4-10	1	3	2	0	17
A. Walker	33	6-17	2-3	3-11	2	2	1	0	14
S. O'Neal	30	4-11	1-4	3-12	1	5	0	2	9
J. Posey	25	2-5	1-2	0-5	0	2	3	6	6
G. Payton	17	1-3	0-0	0-1	2	3	0	2	2
A. Mourning	14	3-4	2-3	1-6	0	4	0	1	8
S. Anderson	2	0-0	0-0	0-0	0	0	0	1	0
D. Anderson									DNP
J. Kapono									DNP
M. Doleac									DNP
TOTALS	240	35-78	23-37	14-56	18	23	9	19	95

Percentages: Field Goals—44.9%, 3-Point Field Goals—2-18, 11.1%
(J. Williams 1-7, A. Walker 0-6, J. Posey 1-4, G. Payton 0-1).
Free-Throws—32.2%. Team Rebounds: 12. Blocked Shots: 10 (D. Wade 3,
A. Walker 1, S. O'Neal 1, A. Mourning 5)

DALLAS MAVERICKS 92

	MIN	FG M-A	FT M-A	REB O-T	A	PF	STL	TO	PTS
D. Harris	25	2-4	2-3	3-3	4	5	2	4	6
J. Terry	43	7-25	0-0	0-1	5	1	2	2	16
D. Nowitzki	47	10-22	8-8	3-15	2	5	0	1	29
J. Howard	30	5-16	4-4	3-12	0	5	4	1	14
D. Diop	16	1-3	0-1	0-4	1	3	0	0	2
J. Stackhouse	29	5-13	0-0	1-4	3	5	2	3	12
E. Dampier	24	0-1	1-2	3-8	0	2	1	2	1
M. Daniels	18	4-6	4-5	2-2	1	2	0	0	12
A. Griffin	4	0-2	0-0	1-1	0	0	1	0	0
D. Mbenga	1	0-0	0-0	0-0	0	0	0	0	0
K. Van Horn									DNP
D. Armstrong									DNP
TOTALS	240	34-92	19-23	16-50	16	28	12	13	92

Percentages: Field Goals—37%, 3-Point Field Goals—5-22, 22.7% (J. Terry
2-11, D. Nowitzki 1-2, J. Howard 0-2, J. Stackhouse 2-6, M. Daniels 0-1).
Free-Throws—82.6%. Team Rebounds: 1. Blocked Shots: 7 (D. Nowitzki 2,
J. Howard 1, D. Diop 2, J. Stackhouse 1, E. Dampier 1)

LEGENDS

■ **John Stockton, guard,** b. March 26, 1962, Spokane, Washington. Stockton is the NBA's all-time career leader in assists (15,806) and steals (3,265), and the single-season record-holder in assists per game (14.5). Stockton played his entire career with the Jazz, leading Utah to the playoffs in each of his 19 seasons. He missed only 22 games in his career. Stockton teamed with another legend, forward Karl Malone, to lead the Jazz to two NBA Finals (1997 and 1998). The old-school duo was famous for running the pick-and-roll play to perfection.

■ **Bill Russell, center,** b. February 12, 1934, Monroe, Louisiana. Russell was the NBA's ultimate winner. The 6'10"-tall center led the Boston Celtics to 11 NBA titles in 13 seasons, including eight in row from 1958–1959 through 1965–1966. Russell was an awkward high school player who blossomed in college at the University of San Francisco. He led the USF Dons to 56 consecutive victories and NCAA championships in 1955 and 1956. Russell's strength was his defense. With the Celtics, he would trigger their fast break with his amazing shot-blocking and rebounding skills. He averaged 22.5 rebounds for his career and once had 51 rebounds in a game. He was not a great shooter, and averaged only 15.1 points per game for his career. Russell won the NBA MVP award five times and was inducted to the Basketball Hall of Fame in 1974. He was player-coach on Boston's championship teams in 1967–1968 and 1968–1969, the first African-American coach in the NBA.

John Stockton is the NBA's all-time leader in assists.

■ **George Mikan, center,** b. June 18, 1924, Joliet, Illinois; d. June 1, 2005, Scottsdale, Arizona. How great was Mikan? When his Minneapolis Lakers played the New York Knicks in December 1949, the sign at Madison Square Garden read "Geo. Mikan vs. the Knicks." The 6'10"-tall Mikan was basketball's first superstar and the Lakers were the league's first dynasty. Mikan led the Lakers to four championships in the NBA's early years. He led the league in scoring three times and in rebounding average twice. He averaged 22.6 points per game over a nine-season career and won a total of seven championships, including three in two other pro leagues. Mikan was so dominant that the NCAA outlawed goaltending and the NBA widened the free throw lane because of him. Mikan's 10,156 points were the most in NBA history at the time of his retirement. He was named basketball's greatest player for the first half century by the Associated Press and was elected to the Basketball Hall of Fame in 1959.

2005–2006 NBA INDIVIDUAL LEADERS

Kobe Bryant

SCORING

	GP	PTS	AVG
Kobe Bryant, Los Angeles Lakers	80	2,832	35.4
Allen Iverson, Philadelphia 76ers	72	2,375	33.0
LeBron James, Cleveland Cavaliers	79	2,478	31.4
Gilbert Arenas, Washington Wizards	80	2,346	29.3
Dwyane Wade, Miami Heat	75	2,040	27.2

REBOUNDING

	GP	REB	AVG
Kevin Garnett, Minnesota Timberwolves	76	966	12.7
Dwight Howard, Orlando Magic	82	1,022	12.5
Shawn Marion, Phoenix Suns	81	959	11.8
Ben Wallace, Detroit Pistons	82	923	11.3
Tim Duncan, San Antonio Spurs	80	881	11.0
Troy Murphy, Golden State Warriors	74	743	10.0
Elton Brand, Los Angeles Clippers	79	790	10.0

ASSISTS

	GP	A	AVG
Steve Nash, Phoenix Suns	79	826	10.5
Baron Davis, Golden State Warriors	54	480	8.9
Brevin Knight, Charlotte Bobcats	69	610	8.8
Chauncey Billups, Detroit Pistons	81	699	8.6
Jason Kidd, New Jersey Nets	80	672	8.4

FIELD GOAL PERCENTAGE

	FGA	FGM	PCT
Shaquille O'Neal, Miami Heat	800	480	.600
Eddy Curry, New York Knicks	597	336	.563
Tony Parker, San Antonio Spurs	1,136	623	.548
Gerald Wallace, Charlotte Bobcats	589	317	.538
Andrew Bogut, Milwaukee Bucks	606	323	.533

FREE THROW PERCENTAGE

	FTA	FTM	PCT
Steve Nash, Phoenix Suns	279	257	.921
Peja Stojakovic, Sacramento Kings, Indiana Pacers	260	238	.915
Ray Allen, Seattle SuperSonics	359	324	.903
Dirk Nowitzki, Dallas Mavericks	598	539	.901
Wally Szczerbiak, Minnesota Timberwolves, Boston Celtics	310	278	.897

3-POINT FIELD GOAL PERCENTAGE

	FGA	FGM	PCT
Richard Hamilton, Detroit Pistons	120	55	.458
Tyronn Lue, Atlanta Hawks	127	58	.457
Leandro Barbosa, Phoenix Suns	196	87	.444
Mike James, Toronto Raptors	382	169	.442
Raja Bell, Phoenix Suns	446	197	.442

STEALS

	GP	STL	AVG
Gerald Wallace, Charlotte Bobcats	55	138	2.5
Brevin Knight, Charlotte Bobcats	69	157	2.3
Chris Paul, New Orleans/ Oklahoma City Hornets	78	175	2.2
Gilbert Arenas, Washington Wizards	80	161	2.0
Shawn Marion, Phoenix Suns	81	160	2.0

Marcus Camby

BLOCKS

	GP	BLK	AVG
Marcus Camby, Denver Nuggets	56	184	3.3
Andrei Kirilenko, Utah Jazz	69	220	3.2
Alonzo Mourning, Miami Heat	65	173	2.7
Josh Smith, Atlanta Hawks	80	208	2.6
Elton Brand, Los Angeles Clippers	79	201	2.5

KEY GP=games played; PTS=points; AVG=average; REB=rebounds; A=assists; FGA=field goals attempted; FGM=field goals made; PCT=percentage; FTA=free throw attempts; FTM=free throws made; STL=steals; BLK=blocks

TEAM-BY-TEAM STATS

ATLANTA HAWKS

PLAYER	GP	MIN	Field Goals FGM	PCT	3-PT FG FGA-FGM	Free Throws FTM	PCT	Rebounds OFF	TOTAL	A	STL	TO	BLK	AVG
Joe Johnson	82	3,340	632	45.3	360-128	261	79.1	98	335	536	103	267	31	20.2
Al Harrington	76	2,781	551	45.2	191-66	243	69.4	132	523	238	85	195	14	18.6
Zaza Pachulia	78	2,451	307	45.1	2-0	297	73.5	264	613	129	89	180	39	11.7
Josh Smith	80	2,542	329	42.5	110-34	210	71.9	176	531	191	64	162	208	11.3
Tyronn Lue	51	1,233	192	45.9	127-58	118	85.5	13	82	157	26	75	3	11.0
Josh Childress	74	2,250	278	55.2	65-32	154	76.6	134	387	131	86	101	39	10.0
Salim Stoudamire	61	1,234	204	41.5	216-82	99	90.0	12	116	75	27	82	3	9.7
Marvin Williams	79	1,955	235	44.3	53-13	189	74.7	122	383	63	48	83	24	8.5
Anthony Grundy	12	108	19	50.0	15-5	9	64.3	1	17	9	7	9	0	4.4
Royal Ivey	73	975	116	43.9	10-4	24	72.7	31	96	74	24	23	7	3.6
Tony Delk	1	7	0	0.0	0-0	2	100.0	1	2	0	0	0	0	2.0
Esteban Batista	57	498	34	42.5	1-0	33	62.3	61	144	7	15	38	11	1.8
John Edwards	40	297	31	48.4	0-0	8	72.7	18	48	5	3	12	15	1.8
Donta Smith	23	133	15	55.6	4-2	6	50.0	3	14	9	8	4	0	1.7
John Thomas	11	67	3	42.9	0-0	3	75.0	3	10	1	2	4	0	0.8
TEAM TOTALS	82	19,863	2,946	45.4	1,154-424	1,656	75.0	1,069	3,301	1,625	587	1,284	394	97.2
OPPONENTS	82	19,880	3,075	47.8	1,205-444	1,768	74.5	981	3,316	1,689	597	1,227	422	102.0

KEY GP=games played; MIN=minutes played; FGM=field goals made; PCT=percentage; FGA=field goals attempted; FTM=free throws made; OFF=offensive; A=assists; STL=steals; TO=turnovers; BLK=blocks; AVG=average

BOSTON CELTICS

PLAYER	GP	MIN	Field Goals		3-PT FG	Free Throws		Rebounds		A	STL	TO	BLK	AVG
			FGM	PCT	FGA-FGM	FTM	PCT	OFF	TOTAL					
Paul Pierce	79	3,087	689	47.1	314-111	627	77.2	77	530	375	107	273	34	26.8
Ricky Davis	42	1,752	329	46.4	125-40	129	78.7	40	187	221	49	115	9	19.7
Wally Szczerbiak	32	1,175	201	47.6	112-44	115	89.8	41	123	101	19	50	4	17.5
Mark Blount	39	1,085	194	51.1	0-0	127	76.4	36	162	66	15	120	36	12.4
Delonte West	71	2,418	333	48.7	218-84	86	85.1	57	289	329	84	133	46	11.8
Al Jefferson	59	1,062	189	49.9	4-0	86	64.2	97	299	30	30	62	46	7.9
Raef LaFrentz	82	2,031	238	43.1	286-112	51	68.0	80	406	115	29	65	72	7.8
Ryan Gomes	61	1,375	173	48.7	9-3	112	75.2	102	298	58	35	55	5	7.6
Tony Allen	51	980	129	47.1	34-11	100	74.6	32	111	67	51	67	18	7.2
Marcus Banks	18	268	33	41.3	19-6	27	90.0	4	19	32	7	23	0	5.5
Gerald Green	32	377	66	47.8	20-6	29	78.4	10	41	18	13	22	4	5.2
Kendrick Perkins	68	1,335	137	51.5	2-0	80	61.5	140	404	69	21	107	105	5.2
Dan Dickau	19	238	17	37.0	20-10	18	100.0	5	16	40	11	18	1	3.3
Orien Greene	80	1,236	100	39.5	40-9	45	66.2	37	145	129	77	109	10	3.2
Brian Scalabrine	71	941	74	38.3	87-31	26	72.2	27	114	51	21	50	19	2.9
Michael Olowokandi	16	168	20	44.4	0-0	5	62.5	5	41	6	3	14	6	2.8
Justin Reed	32	295	25	33.8	0-0	25	62.5	13	29	7	5	15	4	2.3
Dwayne Jones	14	90	4	40.0	0-0	6	46.2	10	31	2	1	3	3	1.0
TEAM TOTALS	82	19,879	2,951	46.7	1,290-467	1,664	75.5	813	3,245	1,716	578	1,359	422	98.0
OPPONENTS	82	19,880	2,944	45.6	1,265-446	1,825	74.3	910	3,279	1,763	688	1,210	404	99.5

CHARLOTTE BOBCATS

PLAYER	GP	MIN	Field Goals		3-PT FG	Free Throws		Rebounds		A	STL	TO	BLK	AVG
			FGM	PCT	FGA-FGM	FTM	PCT	OFF	TOTAL					
Gerald Wallace	55	1,897	317	53.8	50-14	188	61.4	123	412	96	138	99	115	15.2
Emeka Okafor	26	875	131	41.5	0-0	82	65.6	94	261	31	22	53	50	13.2
Brevin Knight	69	2,350	308	39.9	13-3	252	80.3	35	223	610	157	164	4	12.6
Primoz Brezec	79	2,170	409	51.7	0-0	164	73.2	181	440	45	19	85	32	12.4
Raymond Felton	80	2,402	345	39.1	271-90	161	72.5	77	265	446	102	182	8	11.9
Jumaine Jones	76	2,093	298	40.5	335-115	88	72.7	105	376	63	68	74	22	10.5
Kareem Rush	47	1,112	181	38.6	164-57	55	71.4	18	103	50	38	65	13	10.1
Melvin Ely	57	1,350	216	50.8	2-0	128	66.7	94	277	76	29	100	44	9.8
Keith Bogans	39	848	114	39.6	98-33	80	76.2	29	106	45	39	41	3	8.7
Sean May	23	399	70	40.9	5-0	49	76.6	42	109	22	17	33	12	8.2
Matt Carroll	78	1,275	192	40.3	185-72	138	82.1	34	157	35	47	48	11	7.6
Bernard Robinson	66	1,303	157	43.0	21-2	106	79.1	62	219	77	81	74	10	6.4
Alan Anderson	36	563	75	41.4	58-24	33	80.5	23	70	32	11	32	4	5.3
Jake Voskuhl	51	819	114	43.7	3-1	41	68.3	62	183	39	26	33	23	5.3
Lonny Baxter	18	120	12	37.5	0-0	12	75.0	7	33	2	2	7	1	2.0
Kevin Burleson	39	342	22	25.0	54-10	16	94.1	4	26	48	26	25	2	1.8
TEAM TOTALS	82	19,905	2,961	43.3	1,261-428	1,593	72.9	990	3,260	1,717	822	1,167	354	96.9
OPPONENTS	82	19,905	3,065	47.8	1,285-458	1,683	73.7	940	3,607	1,881	577	1,464	441	100.9

DID YOU KNOW?

Steve Nash and Hall of Famer Magic Johnson are the only point guards in history to win the NBA MVP award more than once. Nash has won the award twice and Johnson won it three times.

CHICAGO BULLS

PLAYER	GP	MIN	Field Goals FGM	PCT	3-PT FG FGA-FGM	Free Throws FTM	PCT	Rebounds OFF	TOTAL	A	STL	TO	BLK	AVG
Ben Gordon	80	2,483	486	42.2	382-166	211	78.7	43	219	240	75	180	5	16.9
Kirk Hinrich	81	2,955	451	41.8	341-126	256	81.5	29	288	514	94	188	21	15.9
Luol Deng	78	2,602	442	46.3	78-21	207	75.0	127	516	147	72	105	50	14.3
Andres Nocioni	82	2,238	383	46.1	238-93	204	84.3	89	500	117	40	120	52	13.0
Darius Songaila	62	1,330	236	48.1	5-2	94	81.7	76	246	88	35	85	16	9.2
Chris Duhon	74	2,157	215	40.0	278-100	117	81.8	28	220	373	70	117	3	8.7
Mike Sweetney	66	1,228	200	45.0	0-0	133	65.2	118	350	59	19	95	56	8.1
Tyson Chandler	79	2,119	160	56.5	1-0	97	50.3	265	714	81	41	123	104	5.3
Malik Allen	54	701	121	49.0	1-1	23	60.5	44	140	20	14	34	16	4.9
Othella Harrington	72	827	135	49.5	0-0	77	62.6	54	154	39	7	61	13	4.8
Jannero Pargo	57	643	109	37.3	103-39	17	81.0	8	61	94	24	61	2	4.8
Tim Thomas	3	31	6	37.5	6-1	0	0.0	0	4	2	0	1	1	4.3
Eddie Basden	19	144	15	40.5	7-1	8	80.0	7	28	8	9	9	2	2.1
Eric Piatkowski	29	228	24	39.3	33-9	2	40.0	4	23	13	6	11	1	2.0
Luke Schenscher	20	149	16	61.5	0-0	4	30.8	8	29	7	1	5	3	1.8
Stephen Graham	3	19	1	20.0	4-1	2	100.0	0	3	1	0	1	0	1.7
James Thomas	7	26	3	50.0	0-0	0	0.0	4	8	0	0	0	0	0.9
Randy Holcomb	4	11	1	100.0	0-0	0	0.0	1	1	0	0	0	0	0.5
Randy Livingston	5	22	0	0.0	0-0	0	0.0	1	4	1	1	0	1	0.0
TEAM TOTALS	82	19,906	3,004	44.6	1,477-560	1,452	73.8	906	3,508	1,804	508	1,224	345	97.8
OPPONENTS	82	19,906	2,773	42.6	1,428-501	1,921	77.7	881	3,422	1,652	611	1,228	420	97.2

CLEVELAND CAVALIERS

PLAYER	GP	MIN	Field Goals FGM	PCT	3-PT FG FGA-FGM	Free Throws FTM	PCT	Rebounds OFF	TOTAL	A	STL	TO	BLK	AVG
LeBron James	79	3,361	875	48.0	379-127	601	73.8	75	556	521	123	260	66	31.4
Zydrunas Ilgauskas	78	2,283	450	50.6	5-0	317	83.4	245	591	91	38	155	136	15.6
Larry Hughes	36	1,283	192	40.9	76-28	146	75.6	26	161	131	53	99	21	15.5
Flip Murray	28	1,027	142	44.8	65-20	73	70.2	15	67	77	38	56	7	13.5
Drew Gooden	79	2,176	334	51.2	3-1	176	68.2	237	665	56	52	106	49	10.7
Donyell Marshall	81	2,074	265	39.5	395-128	92	74.8	105	492	60	59	90	41	9.3
Damon Jones	82	2,090	190	38.7	371-140	32	64.0	14	133	169	37	55	1	6.7
Eric Snow	82	2,354	163	40.9	10-1	64	68.8	38	198	346	76	116	19	4.8
Anderson Varejao	48	763	79	52.7	1-0	61	51.3	77	235	19	31	27	19	4.6
Sasha Pavlovic	53	813	87	41.0	96-35	32	65.3	16	80	25	19	42	6	4.5
Stephen Graham	13	117	14	42.4	1-0	8	88.9	4	17	3	3	7	2	2.8
Luke Jackson	36	320	29	34.1	36-12	26	78.8	16	40	25	11	31	2	2.7
Alan Henderson	51	528	47	51.6	0-0	33	67.3	60	137	10	9	22	12	2.5
Zendon Hamilton	11	46	7	53.8	0-0	11	68.8	3	11	0	3	6	0	2.3
Ira Newble	36	358	17	29.8	13-3	11	68.8	21	56	9	5	12	10	1.3
Mike Wilks	37	250	17	28.8	14-2	6	50.0	6	27	18	8	15	1	1.1
Martynas Andriuskevicius	6	10	0	0.0	0-0	0	0.0	1	4	0	2	0	0	0.0
TEAM TOTALS	82	19,833	2,908	45.4	1,465-497	1,689	72.9	959	3,470	1,560	567	1,137	392	97.6
OPPONENTS	82	19,813	2,949	45.5	1,291-459	1,462	74.2	807	3,228	1,666	540	1,079	357	95.4

DALLAS MAVERICKS

PLAYER	GP	MIN	FGM	PCT	FGA-FGM	FTM	PCT	OFF	TOTAL	A	STL	TO	BLK	AVG
			Field Goals		3-PT FG	Free Throws		Rebounds						
Dirk Nowitzki	81	3,086	751	48.0	271-110	539	90.1	115	728	226	58	156	83	26.6
Jason Terry	80	2,800	516	47.0	416-171	168	80.0	31	158	306	100	135	27	17.1
Josh Howard	59	1,919	350	47.1	63-27	196	73.4	123	371	111	68	79	26	15.6
Jerry Stackhouse	55	1,524	242	40.1	130-36	195	88.2	32	153	160	37	121	10	13.0
Marquis Daniels	62	1,763	246	48.0	19-4	138	75.4	81	224	172	67	100	13	10.2
Devin Harris	56	1,273	190	46.9	21-5	169	71.6	26	125	177	53	84	16	9.9
Keith Van Horn	53	1,089	164	42.4	136-50	94	83.2	54	192	37	31	71	11	8.9
Erick Dampier	82	1,929	171	49.3	0-0	127	59.1	273	640	51	27	115	106	5.7
Adrian Griffin	52	1,247	98	48.0	2-0	41	77.4	75	227	89	51	39	9	4.6
Doug Christie	7	184	9	34.6	1-0	8	66.7	2	13	14	9	6	1	3.7
Rawle Marshall	23	244	24	40.0	3-1	22	75.9	8	31	10	8	15	7	3.1
Pavel Podkolzin	1	18	0	0.0	0-0	3	50.0	0	7	0	0	2	1	3.0
Josh Powell	37	430	37	45.7	0-0	36	80.0	28	81	9	7	22	4	3.0
DeSagana Diop	81	1,509	75	48.7	2-1	39	54.2	145	374	23	44	36	146	2.3
Darrell Armstrong	62	622	43	33.6	48-11	33	78.6	18	81	86	27	58	3	2.1
D.J. Mbenga	43	240	32	53.3	1-0	10	50.0	19	56	2	6	16	25	1.7
TEAM TOTALS	82	19,883	2,948	46.2	1,113-416	1,818	78.3	1,030	3,461	1,473	593	1,112	488	99.1
OPPONENTS	82	19,881	2,801	44.3	1,120-404	1,626	75.2	935	3,144	1,433	536	1,151	400	93.1

DENVER NUGGETS

PLAYER	GP	MIN	FGM	PCT	FGA-FGM	FTM	PCT	OFF	TOTAL	A	STL	TO	BLK	AVG
			Field Goals		3-PT FG	Free Throws		Rebounds						
Carmelo Anthony	80	2,940	756	48.1	152-37	573	80.8	122	394	216	88	218	42	26.5
Andre Miller	82	2,940	404	46.3	27-5	313	73.8	92	351	674	106	256	18	13.7
Ruben Patterson	26	736	139	54.3	6-1	65	58.0	45	90	67	34	68	9	13.2
Kenyon Martin	56	1,548	297	49.5	22-5	121	71.2	93	353	79	43	72	52	12.9
Marcus Camby	56	1,854	302	46.5	11-1	111	71.2	132	668	115	79	92	184	12.8
Earl Boykins	60	1,545	271	41.0	179-62	152	87.4	21	81	230	48	83	4	12.6
Voshon Lenard	12	238	42	40.8	35-10	5	38.5	2	28	18	8	11	2	8.3
Earl Watson	46	980	121	42.9	172-68	37	62.7	17	86	160	37	75	7	7.5
Greg Buckner	73	1,755	181	43.4	243-86	43	78.2	31	209	127	87	52	20	6.7
DerMarr Johnson	58	925	132	43.1	160-56	34	81.0	19	96	55	25	46	26	6.1
Eduardo Najera	64	1,451	127	42.2	12-4	89	78.1	128	325	52	53	54	34	5.4
Reggie Evans	26	604	43	45.3	0-0	49	50.5	57	226	15	16	44	5	5.2
Francisco Elson	72	1,578	151	53.2	5-1	49	66.2	99	339	47	54	65	45	4.9
Howard Eisley	19	281	30	34.9	38-12	20	83.3	2	19	44	8	18	2	4.8
Linas Kleiza	61	522	77	44.5	13-2	57	70.4	38	116	15	10	16	13	3.5
Julius Hodge	14	35	5	38.5	0-0	3	37.5	5	7	6	2	8	0	0.9
Nene Hilario	1	3	0	0.0	0-0	0	0.0	0	0	0	0	2	0	0.0
Bryon Russell	1	3	0	0.0	0-0	0	0.0	0	1	1	0	0	0	0.0
Charles Smith	1	2	0	0.0	1-0	0	0.0	0	0	0	0	0	0	0.0
TEAM TOTALS	82	19,930	3,078	46.1	1,076-350	1,721	74.4	903	3,389	1,921	698	1,216	463	100.3
OPPONENTS	82	19,935	3,070	45.4	1,480-530	1,538	73.6	965	3,434	1,959	586	1,323	436	100.1

DETROIT PISTONS

| PLAYER | GP | MIN | Field Goals | | 3-PT FG | Free Throws | | Rebounds | | A | STL | TO | BLK | AVG |
			FGM	PCT	FGA-FGM	FTM	PCT	OFF	TOTAL					
Richard Hamilton	80	2,823	649	49.1	120-55	256	84.5	84	256	275	52	173	16	20.1
Chauncey Billups	81	2,928	423	41.8	425-184	465	89.4	41	252	699	71	170	8	18.5
Rasheed Wallace	80	2,778	459	43.0	434-155	136	74.3	90	547	182	82	85	130	15.1
Tayshaun Prince	82	2,895	455	45.5	183-64	182	76.5	104	346	186	62	91	39	14.1
Tony Delk	23	375	71	44.4	47-20	18	72.0	13	51	33	13	19	1	7.8
Antonio McDyess	82	1,736	285	50.9	2-0	68	55.7	156	436	90	46	76	48	7.8
Ben Wallace	82	2,886	237	51.0	4-0	123	41.6	301	923	158	146	88	181	7.3
Amir Johnson	3	39	7	70.0	3-2	4	100.0	3	4	3	0	4	2	6.7
Maurice Evans	80	1,138	154	45.2	116-43	52	80.0	76	163	60	41	39	15	5.0
Carlos Delfino	68	729	91	40.3	60-20	45	67.2	28	113	44	21	36	15	3.6
Carlos Arroyo	50	599	57	36.3	6-2	42	72.4	24	70	155	19	45	3	3.2
Lindsey Hunter	30	356	37	37.0	43-11	2	50.0	10	40	62	19	20	1	2.9
Kelvin Cato	4	34	5	41.7	0-0	0	0.0	1	7	2	0	2	2	2.5
Jason Maxiell	26	157	23	42.6	0-0	14	33.3	12	28	3	4	11	5	2.3
Alex Acker	5	35	4	25.0	5-1	0	0.0	1	5	4	1	4	0	1.8
Darko Milicic	25	139	17	51.5	2-0	3	37.5	10	28	9	3	15	15	1.5
Dale Davis	28	179	9	37.5	1-0	8	53.3	21	53	6	0	4	9	0.9
TEAM TOTALS	82	19,831	2,983	45.5	1,451-557	1,418	72.7	975	3,322	1,971	580	931	490	96.8
OPPONENTS	82	19,830	2,915	45.2	1,012-329	1,235	73.6	951	3,350	1,541	481	1,145	285	90.2

GOLDEN STATE WARRIORS

| PLAYER | GP | MIN | Field Goals | | 3-PT FG | Free Throws | | Rebounds | | A | STL | TO | BLK | AVG |
			FGM	PCT	FGA-FGM	FTM	PCT	OFF	TOTAL					
Jason Richardson	75	2,877	641	44.6	477-183	276	67.3	105	438	232	97	37	167	23.2
Baron Davis	54	1,974	335	38.9	324-102	195	67.5	45	236	480	89	14	159	17.9
Troy Murphy	74	2,515	363	43.3	181-58	251	78.7	195	743	101	47	108	26	14.0
Derek Fisher	82	2,589	364	41.0	295-117	244	83.3	36	211	352	125	156	8	13.3
Mike Dunleavy	81	2,581	331	40.6	260-74	196	77.8	78	399	237	60	120	32	11.5
Mickael Pietrus	52	1,181	169	40.4	176-56	87	60.8	58	163	44	33	78	10	9.3
Ike Diogu	69	1,035	175	52.4	0-0	136	81.0	95	229	29	15	78	30	7.0
Monta Ellis	49	889	132	41.5	82-28	42	71.2	22	105	78	32	58	11	6.8
Adonal Foyle	77	1,825	152	50.7	0-0	41	61.2	143	424	33	44	80	125	4.5
Andris Biedrins	68	996	118	63.8	0-0	22	30.6	124	283	24	23	34	47	3.8
Will Bynum	15	162	21	40.4	9-2	10	62.5	3	12	19	7	14	0	3.6
Zarko Cabarkapa	61	507	67	38.5	20-5	60	71.4	37	111	20	13	35	7	3.3
Chris Taft	17	143	23	60.5	0-0	1	16.7	19	36	2	2	7	2	2.8
Calbert Cheaney	42	449	42	38.9	8-0	8	100.0	20	61	19	13	17	2	2.2
Aaron Miles	19	120	6	33.3	0-0	4	100.0	0	14	24	4	11	1	0.8
TEAM TOTALS	82	19,830	2,939	43.3	1,832-625	1,573	71.8	980	3,465	1,694	604	1,156	357	98.5
OPPONENTS	82	19,830	3,047	45.7	1,335-469	1,624	74.3	985	3,647	1,828	576	1,258	409	99.8

HOUSTON ROCKETS

PLAYER	GP	MIN	FGM	PCT	FGA-FGM	FTM	PCT	OFF	TOTAL	A	STL	TO	BLK	AVG
			Field Goals		3-PT FG	Free Throws		Rebounds						
Tracy McGrady	47	1,746	410	40.6	234-73	254	74.7	46	307	225	59	120	41	24.4
Yao Ming	57	1,946	467	51.9	1-0	337	85.3	148	581	85	30	147	94	22.3
Rafer Alston	63	2,432	280	37.9	312-102	99	69.2	36	255	425	101	157	15	12.1
Juwan Howard	80	2,538	394	45.9	4-0	154	80.6	168	535	112	49	133	8	11.8
Derek Anderson	20	582	68	39.3	67-19	61	83.6	12	83	53	15	37	4	10.8
David Wesley	71	2,378	226	40.3	271-99	151	80.7	24	178	204	59	120	6	9.9
Stromile Swift	66	1,342	225	49.1	2-0	136	65.1	103	291	25	38	91	50	8.9
Luther Head	80	2,308	254	40.3	313-113	86	69.9	33	266	215	89	119	9	8.8
Keith Bogans	33	1,064	101	39.5	102-32	47	58.0	26	149	83	32	49	6	8.5
Richie Frahm	8	116	15	42.9	22-8	4	80.0	0	10	6	1	4	0	5.3
Jon Barry	20	342	25	38.5	32-12	24	82.8	1	31	26	13	22	1	4.3
Chuck Hayes	40	534	59	56.2	1-0	29	64.4	67	179	14	26	12	14	3.7
Lonny Baxter	23	281	33	45.8	0-0	16	84.2	38	84	2	9	13	7	3.6
Stephen Graham	6	40	6	37.5	5-1	4	100.0	1	7	3	2	5	0	2.8
Dikembe Mutombo	64	956	50	52.6	0-0	69	75.8	100	306	4	17	35	57	2.6
John Lucas	13	106	14	38.9	9-2	0	0.0	2	5	12	5	7	0	2.3
Moochie Norris	29	243	26	40.0	5-0	13	76.5	9	34	29	14	16	1	2.2
Rick Brunson	23	218	16	34.8	12-5	7	58.3	1	20	33	8	19	1	1.9
Ryan Bowen	68	661	37	29.8	22-3	11	78.6	31	88	24	21	13	6	1.3
Maciej Lampe	4	13	2	28.6	0-0	0	0.0	3	5	0	0	2	0	1.0
Josh Davis	1	1	0	0.0	0-0	0	0.0	0	0	0	0	0	0	0.0
TEAM TOTALS	82	19,830	2,708	43.3	1,414-469	1,502	75.9	849	3,414	1,580	588	1,193	320	90.1
OPPONENTS	82	19,830	2,708	42.9	1,465-541	1,560	73.1	874	3,351	1,647	582	1,094	373	91.7

INDIANA PACERS

PLAYER	GP	MIN	FGM	PCT	FGA-FGM	FTM	PCT	OFF	TOTAL	A	STL	TO	BLK	AVG
			Field Goals		3-PT FG	Free Throws		Rebounds						
Jermaine O'Neal	51	1,802	380	47.2	10-3	261	70.9	102	476	133	27	151	117	20.1
Peja Stojakovic	40	1,454	274	46.1	225-91	140	90.3	45	250	68	26	8	52	19.5
Ron Artest	16	605	109	46.0	54-18	74	61.2	26	78	35	42	43	11	19.4
Stephen Jackson	81	2,911	472	41.1	339-117	268	78.6	48	312	225	104	203	43	16.4
Fred Jones	68	1,838	233	41.7	187-63	122	76.3	18	170	154	55	107	20	9.6
Jamaal Tinsley	42	1,123	158	40.9	70-16	58	63.7	35	133	211	49	109	6	9.3
Anthony Johnson	75	1,981	267	44.3	155-51	106	75.2	31	168	324	63	115	22	9.2
Austin Croshere	50	1,147	132	46.3	140-54	90	88.2	62	265	62	22	48	7	8.2
Danny Granger	78	1,762	221	46.2	93-30	115	77.7	131	384	90	58	80	62	7.5
Sarunas Jasikevicius	75	1,560	170	39.6	236-86	121	91.0	19	153	227	40	116	4	7.3
Jeff Foster	63	1,583	138	55.2	4-0	96	60.4	224	574	50	41	64	27	5.9
David Harrison	67	1,031	148	50.3	0-0	89	51.1	84	254	14	23	79	59	5.7
Jonathan Bender	2	21	4	80.0	0-0	2	100.0	0	4	2	0	0	1	5.0
Scot Pollard	45	774	70	45.5	0-0	29	76.3	73	218	24	37	26	20	3.8
Eddie Gill	41	132	10	22.2	23-7	18	78.3	0	15	12	11	9	1	1.1
Samaki Walker	7	23	0	0.0	0-0	2	100.0	0	3	0	0	2	1	0.3
TEAM TOTALS	82	19,730	2,786	44.4	1,536-536	1,591	73.7	898	3,457	1,631	598	1,254	409	93.9
OPPONENTS	82	19,730	2,831	43.5	1,083-371	1,511	73.3	968	3,384	1,520	661	1,112	399	92.0

LOS ANGELES CLIPPERS

PLAYER	GP	MIN	Field Goals FGM	PCT	3-PT FG FGA-FGM	Free Throws FTM	PCT	Rebounds OFF	TOTAL	A	STL	TO	BLK	AVG
Elton Brand	79	3,096	756	52.7	3-1	440	77.5	236	790	208	81	173	201	24.7
Corey Maggette	32	946	167	44.5	71-24	212	82.8	28	169	66	19	78	4	17.8
Sam Cassell	78	2,654	493	44.3	190-70	289	86.3	40	287	491	74	175	11	17.2
Cuttino Mobley	79	2,978	429	42.6	245-83	229	83.9	50	341	238	93	145	36	14.8
Chris Kaman	78	2,562	369	52.3	2-0	194	77.0	187	750	79	45	176	108	11.9
Vladimir Radmanovic	30	886	108	41.7	158-66	38	73.1	25	171	64	29	40	14	10.7
Shaun Livingston	61	1,524	149	42.7	8-1	53	68.8	41	183	273	46	111	32	5.8
Quinton Ross	67	1,519	130	42.2	7-0	57	76.0	38	170	79	51	47	16	4.7
Zeljko Rebraca	29	413	52	54.2	0-0	31	75.6	13	64	9	5	24	19	4.7
Chris Wilcox	48	658	90	53.6	2-0	38	64.4	46	173	18	15	32	21	4.5
Daniel Ewing	66	973	97	38.0	78-22	36	78.3	23	85	84	37	57	6	3.8
James Singleton	59	758	77	51.0	20-10	39	78.0	63	197	29	19	21	28	3.4
Vin Baker	8	84	7	46.7	0-0	13	72.2	2	19	4	4	9	4	3.4
Walter McCarty	36	352	33	33.3	45-10	12	57.1	15	68	23	8	19	5	2.4
Boniface N'Dong	23	153	22	41.5	1-0	6	66.7	15	37	7	2	6	5	2.2
Yaroslav Korolev	24	128	9	30.0	7-2	7	70.0	5	13	9	3	9	4	1.1
Howard Eisley	13	113	4	23.5	4-1	0	0.0	1	14	25	3	3	0	0.7
Anthony Goldwire	3	22	1	14.3	2-0	0	0.0	0	1	2	0	1	0	0.7
TEAM TOTALS	82	19,806	2,993	46.5	843-290	1,694	79.1	828	3,532	1,708	534	1,185	503	97.2
OPPONENTS	82	19,805	2,887	43.5	1,367-474	1,593	73.2	858	3,290	1,765	570	1,053	355	95.6

LOS ANGELES LAKERS

PLAYER	GP	MIN	Field Goals FGM	PCT	3-PT FG FGA-FGM	Free Throws FTM	PCT	Rebounds OFF	TOTAL	A	STL	TO	BLK	AVG
Kobe Bryant	80	3,273	978	45.0	518-180	696	85.0	71	425	360	147	250	30	35.4
Lamar Odom	80	3,221	445	48.1	215-80	216	69.0	181	738	443	75	213	64	14.8
Smush Parker	82	2,776	348	44.7	328-120	125	69.4	37	271	302	140	147	16	11.5
Chris Mihm	59	1,545	230	50.1	0-0	144	71.6	137	373	61	16	83	73	10.2
Brian Cook	81	1,532	261	51.1	84-36	84	83.2	88	274	74	37	61	32	7.9
Kwame Brown	72	1,979	204	52.6	1-0	128	54.5	182	473	72	27	100	46	7.4
Devean George	71	1,541	170	40.0	160-50	58	67.4	82	274	68	66	54	34	6.3
Luke Walton	69	1,332	135	41.2	55-18	57	75.0	88	247	156	41	178	5	5.0
Laron Profit	25	277	40	47.6	18-3	21	87.5	8	43	15	11	24	5	4.2
Sasha Vujacic	82	1,454	108	34.6	172-59	46	88.5	33	159	139	48	50	3	3.9
Ronny Turiaf	23	160	15	50.0	0-0	15	55.6	11	37	8	3	7	10	2.0
Jim Jackson	13	91	9	29.0	11-4	0	0.0	0	12	4	2	5	0	1.7
Andrew Bynum	46	340	33	40.2	0-0	8	29.6	34	80	9	4	17	22	1.6
Von Wafer	16	74	6	15.8	17-2	6	75.0	5	8	4	3	1	0	1.3
Stanislav Medvedenko	2	7	1	50.0	0-0	0	0.0	0	0	1	0	0	0	1.0
Devin Green	27	137	6	21.4	2-0	13	61.9	10	24	7	3	5	0	0.9
Aaron McKie	14	121	3	25.0	2-0	1	50.0	3	20	11	5	2	0	0.5
TEAM TOTALS	82	19,854	2,992	45.3	1,583-552	1,618	74.5	970	3,458	1,734	628	1,143	350	99.4
OPPONENTS	82	19,856	2,945	45.0	1,342-474	1,585	74.7	893	3,292	1,730	536	1,158	354	96.9

MEMPHIS GRIZZLIES

| PLAYER | GP | MIN | Field Goals | | 3-PT FG | Free Throws | | Rebounds | | | | | | | |
			FGM	PCT	FGA-FGM	FTM	PCT	OFF	TOTAL	A	STL	TO	BLK	AVG
Pau Gasol	80	3,132	600	50.3	12-3	425	68.9	191	713	371	46	235	153	20.4
Mike Miller	74	2,267	354	46.6	339-138	168	80.0	42	397	200	52	140	27	13.7
Eddie Jones	75	2,439	292	40.4	374-133	168	78.1	35	279	177	131	93	27	11.8
Damon Stoudamire	27	861	114	39.7	104-36	53	85.5	23	95	128	19	55	1	11.7
Chucky Atkins	43	1,158	160	40.1	182-64	107	81.1	11	75	129	29	57	2	11.4
Bobby Jackson	71	1,777	286	38.2	332-129	107	73.3	44	223	195	61	101	1	11.4
Shane Battier	81	2,844	303	48.8	165-65	147	70.7	164	429	136	92	90	114	10.1
Lorenzen Wright	78	1,693	194	47.8	2-0	66	56.4	142	395	48	52	67	46	5.8
Jake Tsakalidis	51	733	100	60.6	0-0	57	65.5	78	212	13	14	39	32	5.0
Hakim Warrick	68	724	101	44.3	0-0	76	66.1	43	144	30	14	56	21	4.1
Dahntay Jones	71	969	109	41.4	21-3	60	64.5	20	104	39	38	50	15	4.0
Brian Cardinal	36	402	46	41.4	29-13	19	70.4	11	55	33	23	27	0	3.4
Anthony Roberson	16	91	14	45.2	10-5	2	100.0	0	6	5	1	3	0	2.2
Antonio Burks	57	572	51	35.4	6-1	10	43.5	4	37	76	20	36	0	2.0
Lawrence Roberts	33	185	20	45.5	2-0	11	47.8	26	49	5	8	5	2	1.5
John Thomas	3	25	2	100.0	0-0	0	0.0	0	0	1	0	2	1	1.3
TEAM TOTALS	82	19,855	2,746	44.8	1,578-590	1,476	71.1	834	3,213	1,586	600	1,134	442	92.2
OPPONENTS	82	19,855	2,691	43.6	1,223-408	1,465	75.4	927	3,331	1,605	597	1,213	456	88.5

MIAMI HEAT

| PLAYER | GP | MIN | Field Goals | | 3-PT FG | Free Throws | | Rebounds | | | | | | | |
			FGM	PCT	FGA-FGM	FTM	PCT	OFF	TOTAL	A	STL	TO	BLK	AVG
Dwyane Wade	75	2,897	699	49.5	76-13	629	78.3	107	430	503	146	268	58	27.2
Shaquille O'Neal	59	1,805	480	60.0	0-0	221	46.9	172	541	113	23	168	104	20.0
Jason Williams	59	1,876	268	44.2	288-107	85	86.7	6	139	287	53	100	5	12.3
Antoine Walker	82	2,201	391	43.5	383-137	81	62.8	103	421	166	47	150	30	12.2
Udonis Haslem	81	2,494	300	50.8	2-0	157	78.9	167	634	95	50	80	17	9.3
Alonzo Mourning	65	1,303	188	59.7	1-0	133	59.4	125	359	11	13	79	173	7.8
Gary Payton	81	2,305	230	42.0	230-66	100	79.4	34	233	257	71	102	10	7.7
James Posey	67	1,912	159	40.3	290-117	48	78.7	33	319	89	54	58	20	7.2
Derek Anderson	23	466	40	30.8	67-21	32	84.2	9	60	48	8	17	2	5.8
Gerald Fitch	18	239	30	33.7	26-7	17	73.9	7	30	33	7	15	5	4.7
Jason Kapono	51	667	79	44.6	53-21	28	84.8	12	71	37	7	20	3	4.1
Wayne Simien	43	416	58	48.3	0-0	30	88.2	38	88	7	13	24	1	3.4
Michael Doleac	31	371	37	42.0	0-0	24	80.0	23	85	8	10	14	7	3.2
Dorell Wright	20	133	20	46.5	6-3	15	88.2	2	32	8	3	14	1	2.9
Shandon Anderson	48	640	54	42.9	19-5	13	72.2	18	81	30	17	24	6	2.6
Earl Barron	8	46	5	31.3	0-0	3	75.0	2	10	0	0	5	0	1.6
Matt Walsh	2	3	1	100.0	0-0	0	0.0	0	0	0	0	1	0	1.0
TEAM TOTALS	82	19,757	3,039	47.8	1,441-497	1,616	70.0	858	3,533	1,692	522	1,186	442	99.9
OPPONENTS	82	19,749	2,871	44.0	1,359-490	1,642	73.9	826	3,185	1,596	560	1,063	298	96.0

MILWAUKEE BUCKS

PLAYER	GP	MIN	FGM	PCT	FGA-FGM	FTM	PCT	OFF	TOTAL	A	STL	TO	BLK	AVG
Michael Redd	80	3,127	682	45.0	413-163	501	87.7	78	342	229	95	170	5	25.4
Bobby Simmons	75	2,533	366	45.3	250-105	165	82.5	91	333	172	86	123	21	13.4
T.J. Ford	72	2,558	328	41.6	104-35	187	75.4	63	311	473	104	219	7	12.2
Mo Williams	58	1,534	267	42.4	191-73	96	85.0	30	143	230	52	105	7	12.1
Andrew Bogut	82	2,348	323	53.3	3-0	122	62.9	189	573	192	49	125	68	9.4
Jamaal Magloire	82	2,467	287	46.7	0-0	178	53.5	220	778	56	29	166	80	9.2
Joe Smith	44	886	145	47.5	2-0	89	77.4	83	230	31	24	40	13	8.6
Charlie Bell	59	1,281	180	43.9	168-71	63	70.8	21	120	130	59	41	5	8.4
Dan Gadzuric	74	886	171	55.3	1-0	41	46.1	91	232	24	25	35	43	5.2
Toni Kukoc	65	1,020	116	38.9	147-45	40	71.4	26	150	139	33	66	17	4.9
Jiri Welsch	58	863	86	38.7	49-14	65	74.7	22	111	62	34	41	1	4.3
Jermaine Jackson	30	207	11	42.3	4-1	12	85.7	8	27	25	4	13	1	1.2
Reece Gaines	12	52	6	50.0	2-0	1	25.0	0	0	3	1	1	0	1.1
Ervin Johnson	18	80	7	41.2	0-0	1	50.0	5	24	2	1	5	2	0.8
Josh Davis	4	12	1	25.0	1-0	0	0.0	2	3	1	1	1	0	0.5
TEAM TOTALS	82	19,855	2,976	45.3	1,335-507	1,561	73.8	929	3,377	1,769	597	1,197	270	97.8
OPPONENTS	82	19,854	2,972	46.6	1,385-490	1,671	74.7	832	3,307	1,847	606	1,182	414	98.8

MINNESOTA TIMBERWOLVES

PLAYER	GP	MIN	FGM	PCT	FGA-FGM	FTM	PCT	OFF	TOTAL	A	STL	TO	BLK	AVG
Kevin Garnett	76	2,960	626	52.6	30-8	396	81.0	214	966	308	104	180	107	21.8
Wally Szczerbiak	40	1,558	292	49.5	143-58	163	89.6	36	190	112	21	86	15	20.1
Ricky Davis	36	1,463	255	42.9	117-33	146	80.7	25	164	173	42	98	8	19.1
Marcus Banks	40	1,227	186	47.9	44-16	91	77.8	19	116	188	47	96	11	12.0
Mark Blount	42	1,157	179	50.6	0-0	71	74.7	60	203	33	25	74	40	10.2
Troy Hudson	36	794	127	38.1	101-40	48	92.3	8	44	106	12	40	4	9.5
Trenton Hassell	77	2,513	286	46.4	23-7	131	74.4	82	216	203	43	124	29	9.2
Bracey Wright	7	136	21	41.2	17-6	14	87.5	3	18	5	1	8	0	8.9
Rashad McCants	79	1,365	241	45.0	180-67	78	73.6	29	143	63	44	86	22	7.9
Marko Jaric	75	2,105	226	39.9	133-40	95	68.8	60	233	293	108	127	21	7.8
Justin Reed	40	704	94	42.5	1-0	62	77.5	40	116	34	18	37	11	6.3
Michael Olowokandi	32	751	87	44.6	0-0	19	48.7	45	179	17	19	41	27	6.0
Eddie Griffin	70	1,360	130	35.1	82-16	44	59.5	107	389	40	13	43	148	4.6
Anthony Carter	45	592	53	38.7	15-4	40	72.7	9	62	101	24	40	9	3.3
Richie Frahm	25	229	24	36.9	48-15	3	60.0	3	23	15	3	4	2	2.6
Ronald Dupree	36	268	33	52.4	1-0	14	34.1	21	49	14	12	14	0	2.2
Mark Madsen	62	678	27	40.9	7-0	20	42.6	50	141	11	23	26	17	1.2
Nikoloz Tskitishvili	5	13	1	25.0	0-0	1	50.0	0	2	0	0	2	0	0.6
TEAM TOTALS	82	19,855	2,888	45.6	942-310	1,436	75.8	811	3,233	1,716	559	1,189	471	91.7
OPPONENTS	82	19,854	2,852	44.1	1,229-447	1,525	73.6	974	3,385	1,554	539	1,139	374	93.6

Visit our website for the latest
stats and sports info.

NEW JERSEY NETS

PLAYER	GP	MIN	FGM	PCT	FGA-FGM	FTM	PCT	OFF	TOTAL	A	STL	TO	BLK	AVG
			Field Goals		**3-PT FG**	**Free Throws**		**Rebounds**						
Vince Carter	79	2,907	653	43.0	367-125	480	79.9	135	462	338	94	213	53	24.2
Richard Jefferson	78	3,057	495	49.3	188-60	471	81.2	95	534	297	59	174	17	19.5
Nenad Krstic	80	2,467	447	50.7	4-1	185	69.8	182	513	88	32	133	63	13.5
Jason Kidd	80	2,980	366	40.4	395-139	194	79.5	86	580	672	150	192	29	13.3
Clifford Robinson	80	1,861	219	42.7	175-60	52	65.8	55	267	89	44	62	40	6.9
Jeff McInnis	28	489	63	44.1	16-3	20	69.0	11	50	52	11	29	2	5.3
Marc Jackson	37	431	66	44.6	0-0	38	79.2	30	89	22	5	28	6	4.6
Jason Collins	71	1,894	104	39.7	12-3	44	51.2	93	342	70	46	61	40	3.6
Lamond Murray	57	577	72	39.8	78-27	25	62.5	29	132	13	17	22	7	3.4
Jacque Vaughn	80	1,231	107	43.7	6-1	59	72.8	15	91	123	42	52	1	3.4
Zoran Planinic	56	596	66	36.1	56-13	46	69.7	14	74	53	20	43	4	3.4
Scott Padgett	62	721	71	35.3	121-42	27	79.4	56	165	41	28	21	12	3.4
Bostjan Nachbar	11	98	12	37.5	14-2	5	62.5	4	11	5	3	4	0	2.8
Derrick Zimmerman	2	32	2	66.7	0-0	0	0.0	1	4	7	0	4	0	2.0
Antoine Wright	39	369	29	35.8	15-1	11	50.0	8	30	12	4	21	3	1.8
Linton Johnson	9	36	5	50.0	0-0	1	25.0	0	7	2	2	4	0	1.2
John Thomas	2	36	1	16.7	0-0	0	0.0	7	10	0	1	2	1	1.0
TEAM TOTALS	82	19,780	2,778	44.0	1,447-477	1,658	75.8	822	3,361	1,884	558	1,119	278	93.8
OPPONENTS	82	19,783	2,730	43.9	1,336-465	1,654	74.1	787	3,386	1,641	589	1,177	329	92.4

NEW ORLEANS/OKLAHOMA CITY HORNETS

PLAYER	GP	MIN	FGM	PCT	FGA-FGM	FTM	PCT	OFF	TOTAL	A	STL	TO	BLK	AVG
			Field Goals		**3-PT FG**	**Free Throws**		**Rebounds**						
David West	74	2,526	530	51.2	11-3	199	84.3	168	548	92	61	105	64	17.1
Chris Paul	78	2,809	407	43.0	177-50	394	84.7	61	400	611	175	183	6	16.1
Speedy Claxton	71	2,020	304	41.3	63-17	246	76.9	39	193	339	108	154	6	12.3
Desmond Mason	70	2,104	275	39.9	6-1	206	68.2	64	298	66	42	113	17	10.8
Marc Jackson	27	594	108	48.9	2-1	28	82.4	56	128	22	8	37	2	9.1
P.J. Brown	75	2,382	269	46.1	0-0	139	82.7	182	547	90	46	90	50	9.0
Rasual Butler	79	1,875	257	40.6	242-92	79	69.3	51	232	40	33	65	45	8.7
Kirk Snyder	68	1,309	205	45.3	129-46	86	73.5	55	161	102	29	7	23	8.0
J.R. Smith	55	990	144	39.3	140-52	83	82.2	19	110	58	37	54	4	7.7
Marcus Fizer	3	39	9	52.9	1-1	1	50.0	1	7	1	0	2	0	6.7
Aaron Williams	34	691	81	51.6	0-0	35	67.3	59	166	16	13	25	18	5.8
Linton Johnson	27	491	56	40.3	36-13	17	73.9	40	115	12	10	24	12	5.3
Bostjan Nachbar	25	409	42	33.9	57-17	25	69.4	4	49	22	13	20	5	5.0
Chris Andersen	32	569	56	57.1	0-0	49	47.6	61	155	6	8	26	41	5.0
Moochie Norris	16	183	20	42.6	9-4	16	64.0	3	20	21	6	17	0	3.8
Brandon Bass	29	266	28	40.0	0-0	12	63.2	18	68	3	3	11	7	2.3
Arvydas Macijauskas	19	136	14	34.1	12-3	13	86.7	3	10	5	7	8	0	2.3
Jackson Vroman	41	410	26	39.4	0-0	21	47.7	33	86	11	12	21	11	1.8
Maciej Lampe	2	15	0	0.0	0-0	0	0.0	1	4	2	0	0	1	0.0
TEAM TOTALS	82	19,804	2,831	44.0	885-300	1,649	75.8	918	3,297	1,519	611	1,095	311	92.8
OPPONENTS	82	19,805	2,883	45.9	1,486-546	1,530	76.0	860	3,358	1,584	527	1,197	432	95.6

NEW YORK KNICKS

PLAYER	GP	MIN	FGM	PCT	FGA-FGM	FTM	PCT	OFF	TOTAL	A	STL	TO	BLK	AVG
Stephon Marbury	60	2,188	349	45.1	104-33	246	75.5	25	175	382	63	157	4	16.3
Jamal Crawford	79	2,555	366	41.6	293-101	295	82.6	36	248	301	87	175	15	14.3
Eddy Curry	72	1,869	336	56.3	0-0	307	63.2	145	432	19	28	179	56	13.6
Jalen Rose	26	744	110	46.0	57-28	82	81.2	13	82	68	10	3	50	12.7
Channing Frye	65	1,572	305	47.7	9-3	189	82.5	138	374	53	30	97	47	12.3
Steve Francis	24	659	84	44.2	13-7	83	76.1	14	71	83	23	58	6	10.8
Nate Robinson	72	1,542	230	40.7	146-58	152	75.2	56	167	147	59	114	1	9.3
Quentin Richardson	55	1,443	163	35.5	188-64	61	67.0	65	230	88	39	56	6	8.2
Qyntel Woods	49	1,015	129	50.8	60-22	49	64.5	44	190	47	32	61	13	6.7
Maurice Taylor	67	1,209	182	46.8	1-0	58	69.9	65	229	53	21	103	14	6.3
Jackie Butler	55	742	117	54.4	0-0	58	75.3	67	183	25	17	62	31	5.3
David Lee	67	1,129	137	59.6	0-0	71	57.7	109	303	43	30	51	20	5.1
Antonio Davis	36	753	68	42.8	1-0	45	73.8	75	172	14	20	43	9	5.0
Trevor Ariza	36	712	61	41.8	3-1	42	54.5	49	137	46	43	46	9	4.6
Malik Rose	72	1,117	105	37.4	1-1	107	78.1	84	259	67	43	80	14	4.4
Matt Barnes	6	92	11	36.7	4-1	3	75.0	7	24	6	4	6	0	4.3
Jerome James	44	404	56	46.3	0-0	25	62.5	39	91	12	3	51	23	3.1
Ime Udoka	8	115	9	37.5	3-1	3	50.0	3	17	6	1	2	0	2.8
Anfernee Hardaway	4	72	4	28.6	1-0	2	100.0	0	10	8	2	6	0	2.5
TEAM TOTALS	82	19,923	2,822	45.5	884-320	1,878	72.6	1,034	3,394	1,468	555	1,449	271	95.6
OPPONENTS	82	19,929	2,967	46.7	1,495-565	1,868	75.3	883	3,163	1,744	674	1,154	437	102.0

ORLANDO MAGIC

PLAYER	GP	MIN	FGM	PCT	FGA-FGM	FTM	PCT	OFF	TOTAL	A	STL	TO	BLK	AVG
Steve Francis	46	1,733	249	43.3	70-18	231	79.7	60	219	262	51	156	11	16.2
Dwight Howard	82	3,025	468	53.1	2-0	356	59.5	288	1,022	125	65	217	115	15.8
Grant Hill	21	612	119	49.0	8-2	78	76.5	15	80	48	24	35	6	15.1
Hedo Turkoglu	78	2,611	398	45.4	283-114	255	86.1	70	333	216	70	130	21	14.9
Jameer Nelson	62	1,786	347	48.3	165-70	141	77.9	39	180	302	70	148	9	14.6
DeShawn Stevenson	82	2,649	359	46.0	15-2	180	74.4	59	241	160	58	123	17	11.0
Carlos Arroyo	27	596	111	50.2	14-5	64	81.0	9	60	77	19	38	1	10.8
Keyon Dooling	50	1,139	178	44.0	43-13	101	83.5	11	78	109	49	82	4	9.4
Tony Battie	82	2,217	280	50.7	6-0	89	66.4	145	457	49	46	88	69	7.9
Darko Milicic	30	628	102	50.7	0-0	25	59.5	34	123	32	11	36	62	7.6
Pat Garrity	57	943	101	41.7	129-50	30	81.1	31	108	38	12	38	9	4.9
Trevor Ariza	21	290	32	40.0	2-0	35	70.0	29	81	15	14	16	2	4.7
Kelvin Cato	23	300	31	43.1	0-0	26	74.3	19	63	2	6	16	10	3.8
Travis Diener	23	246	29	42.0	57-25	5	83.3	4	21	16	7	10	0	3.8
Mario Kasun	28	213	31	44.9	0-0	18	78.3	24	60	3	2	15	3	2.9
Bo Outlaw	32	355	35	60.3	0-0	5	62.5	31	77	14	10	17	12	2.3
Stacey Augmon	36	389	25	34.2	0-0	21	70.0	18	53	23	12	11	6	2.0
Terence Morris	22	194	16	32.7	2-0	3	100.0	6	38	4	6	7	5	1.6
TEAM TOTALS	82	19,903	2,911	47.2	796-299	1,663	73.0	892	3,294	1,495	532	1,240	362	94.9
OPPONENTS	82	19,905	2,870	45.4	1,287-460	1,672	73.2	911	3,150	1,644	615	1,099	386	96.0

PHILADELPHIA 76ERS

PLAYER	GP	MIN	Field Goals		3-PT FG	Free Throws		Rebounds		A	STL	TO	BLK	AVG
			FGM	PCT	FGA-FGM	FTM	PCT	OFF	TOTAL					
Allen Iverson	72	3,100	815	44.7	223-72	675	81.4	44	232	532	140	248	10	33.0
Chris Webber	75	2,893	617	43.4	77-21	263	75.6	184	741	256	103	182	62	20.2
Andre Iguodala	82	3,088	344	50.0	158-56	263	75.4	117	481	255	135	153	21	12.3
Kyle Korver	82	2,565	327	43.0	438-184	101	84.9	27	270	163	65	98	26	11.5
John Salmons	82	2,063	219	42.0	87-26	155	77.5	48	220	223	73	125	13	7.5
Samuel Dalembert	66	1,759	196	53.1	11-0	93	70.5	159	541	25	34	107	160	7.3
Willie Green	10	153	28	42.4	19-10	4	80.0	1	15	5	2	12	0	7.0
Steven Hunter	69	1,315	175	60.1	0-0	71	51.4	110	271	17	12	64	76	6.1
Lee Nailon	22	236	40	50.0	0-0	13	86.7	23	42	7	8	10	4	4.2
Matt Barnes	50	540	59	53.6	11-2	29	67.4	41	97	22	16	24	7	3.0
Kevin Ollie	70	1,073	75	43.1	3-1	41	83.7	13	98	101	33	29	3	2.7
Shavlik Randolph	57	489	44	45.4	0-0	43	60.6	55	133	19	19	21	12	2.3
Louis Williams	30	150	23	44.2	9-2	8	61.5	3	19	10	5	13	0	1.9
James Thomas	15	126	7	53.8	0-0	8	57.1	8	31	1	0	7	3	1.5
Michael Bradley	46	369	32	40.5	5-1	2	66.7	40	107	17	5	19	7	1.5
Zendon Hamilton	1	3	0	0.0	0-0	1	50.0	0	0	0	1	0	0	1.0
Deng Gai	2	5	0	0.0	0-0	0	0.0	0	0	0	0	0	0	0.0
TEAM TOTALS	82	19,905	3,001	45.8	1,031-375	1,770	76.0	873	3,298	1,653	651	1,159	404	99.4
OPPONENTS	82	19,904	3,100	46.3	1,420-498	1,609	76.2	974	3,507	1,882	630	1,269	386	101.3

PHOENIX SUNS

PLAYER	GP	MIN	Field Goals		3-PT FG	Free Throws		Rebounds		A	STL	TO	BLK	AVG
			FGM	PCT	FGA-FGM	FTM	PCT	OFF	TOTAL					
Shawn Marion	81	3,268	716	52.5	290-96	241	80.9	249	959	143	160	125	137	21.8
Steve Nash	79	2,801	541	51.2	342-150	257	92.1	47	333	826	61	276	12	18.8
Raja Bell	79	2,959	425	45.7	446-197	115	78.8	44	253	207	76	89	22	14.7
Boris Diaw	81	2,875	449	52.6	30-8	174	73.1	159	558	503	58	85	189	13.3
Leandro Barbosa	57	1,590	273	48.1	196-87	111	75.5	31	150	158	48	89	6	13.1
Tim Thomas	26	637	107	43.5	105-45	28	66.7	22	127	18	16	32	6	11.0
Eddie House	81	1,418	320	42.2	316-123	33	80.5	15	132	148	42	76	12	9.8
James Jones	75	1,773	243	41.8	285-110	103	85.1	44	253	57	38	35	49	9.3
Amare Stoudemire	3	50	9	33.3	1-0	8	88.9	6	16	2	1	1	3	8.7
Kurt Thomas	53	1,411	190	48.6	0-0	75	81.5	102	415	57	23	57	54	8.6
Andre Barrett	2	21	3	42.9	1-0	3	100.0	1	3	2	0	1	0	4.5
Josh Davis	1	5	1	33.3	1-0	2	66.7	1	1	0	1	0	0	4.0
Jim Jackson	27	420	38	29.5	63-14	9	69.2	11	64	31	10	30	6	3.7
Pat Burke	42	347	63	49.6	7-2	13	61.9	21	73	16	6	33	13	3.4
Brian Grant	21	248	27	41.5	0-0	7	87.5	11	57	7	5	7	3	2.9
Dijon Thompson	10	44	11	44.0	11-4	2	100.0	4	11	1	3	2	1	2.8
Nikoloz Tskitishvili	12	85	12	36.4	3-1	8	66.7	9	20	3	1	4	2	2.8
Sharrod Ford	3	13	2	66.7	0-0	0	0.0	1	3	0	0	2	1	1.3
TEAM TOTALS	82	19,955	3,430	47.9	2,097-837	1,189	80.6	778	3,428	2,179	549	1,088	412	108.4
OPPONENTS	82	19,952	3,243	45.4	1,423-516	1,429	73.1	1,028	3,763	1,546	591	1,218	282	102.8

FAST FACT

The New Orleans/Oklahoma City Hornets were the NBA's most improved team. They went from an 18–64 record in 2004–2005 to 38–44 in 2005-2006.

PORTLAND TRAIL BLAZERS

PLAYER	GP	MIN	Field Goals		3-PT FG	Free Throws		Rebounds		A	STL	TO	BLK	AVG
			FGM	PCT	FGA-FGM	FTM	PCT	OFF	TOTAL					
Zach Randolph	74	2,546	536	43.6	55-16	245	71.4	193	592	144	57	165	14	18.0
Darius Miles	40	1,288	235	46.1	10-2	87	53.4	24	182	73	42	99	39	14.0
Juan Dixon	76	1,923	357	43.5	170-65	156	80.4	30	177	149	58	6	113	12.3
Ruben Patterson	45	1,057	188	49.6	7-0	138	61.1	73	154	60	42	82	12	11.4
Sebastian Telfair	68	1,644	228	39.4	162-57	130	74.3	19	120	247	66	115	6	9.5
Steve Blake	68	1,781	206	43.8	184-76	72	79.1	26	146	306	42	83	5	8.2
Jarrett Jack	79	1,597	189	44.2	76-20	128	80.0	18	160	219	41	102	2	6.7
Martell Webster	61	1,064	139	42.3	182-65	61	85.9	29	130	34	21	43	14	6.6
Voshon Lenard	14	220	33	37.5	43-15	11	61.1	3	19	23	13	20	2	6.6
Joel Przybilla	56	1,395	131	54.8	0-0	82	53.2	146	391	43	20	76	130	6.1
Viktor Khryapa	69	1,490	158	46.2	30-10	77	69.4	114	307	88	50	84	29	5.8
Travis Outlaw	69	1,155	162	44.0	53-14	62	69.7	48	189	34	31	37	46	5.8
Theo Ratliff	55	1,304	108	57.1	0-0	54	65.1	89	279	28	18	47	88	4.9
Brian Skinner	27	516	44	48.4	0-0	15	51.7	46	127	13	14	27	23	3.8
Charles Smith	21	209	30	42.3	37-15	5	62.5	3	16	9	5	4	6	3.8
Sergei Monia	23	338	29	34.1	33-9	8	66.7	11	51	19	6	12	5	3.3
Ha Seung-Jin	27	213	18	58.1	0-0	8	47.1	14	49	1	3	14	8	1.6
TEAM TOTALS	82	19,729	2,791	44.5	1,042-364	1,339	68.9	886	3,089	1,490	529	1,205	435	88.8
OPPONENTS	82	19,730	3,032	46.8	1,306-498	1,498	76.0	1,029	3,474	1,737	592	1,060	403	98.3

SACRAMENTO KINGS

PLAYER	GP	MIN	Field Goals		3-PT FG	Free Throws		Rebounds		A	STL	TO	BLK	AVG
			FGM	PCT	FGA-FGM	FTM	PCT	OFF	TOTAL					
Mike Bibby	82	3,167	597	43.2	497-192	342	84.9	29	240	444	82	199	10	21.1
Ron Artest	40	1,604	241	38.3	199-60	132	71.7	49	208	168	80	88	30	16.9
Peja Stojakovic	31	1,148	171	40.3	179-71	98	93.3	34	165	68	19	51	2	16.5
Brad Miller	79	2,925	434	49.5	88-34	280	82.8	122	615	374	61	180	62	15.0
Bonzi Wells	52	1,683	284	46.3	45-10	129	67.9	142	401	144	94	126	25	13.6
Shareef Abdur-Rahim	72	1,958	332	52.5	22-5	218	78.4	106	357	149	48	108	42	12.3
Kevin Martin	72	1,910	262	48.0	179-66	188	84.7	58	261	97	55	81	9	10.8
Kenny Thomas	82	2,292	305	50.5	1-0	138	67.6	199	618	168	72	135	39	9.1
Francisco Garcia	67	1,302	130	40.0	137-39	78	77.2	39	185	94	41	75	47	5.6
Corliss Williamson	37	362	43	41.7	2-2	38	77.6	21	67	14	7	30	4	3.4
Jason Hart	66	818	86	38.9	31-9	37	66.1	12	71	70	31	43	5	3.3
Brian Skinner	38	431	38	55.1	0-0	12	44.4	30	101	17	11	18	20	2.3
Ronnie Price	29	150	21	36.2	27-6	12	100.0	5	15	11	6	10	0	2.1
Vitaly Potapenko	9	31	5	71.4	0-0	0	0.0	1	2	2	0	2	0	1.1
Jamal Sampson	12	39	5	71.4	0-0	0	0.0	5	18	5	0	0	4	0.8
Sergei Monia	3	7	0	0.0	1-0	2	100.0	0	1	0	1	0	0	0.7
TEAM TOTALS	82	19,830	2,954	45.4	1,408-494	1,704	78.4	852	3,325	1,825	608	1,199	299	98.9
OPPONENTS	82	19,830	3,053	45.4	1,316-462	1,412	74.7	953	3,456	1,733	656	1,199	403	97.3

SAN ANTONIO SPURS

PLAYER	GP	MIN	FGM	PCT	FGA-FGM	FTM	PCT	OFF	TOTAL	A	STL	TO	BLK	AVG
			Field Goals		3-PT FG	Free Throws		Rebounds						
Tony Parker	80	2,715	623	54.8	36-11	253	70.7	38	261	460	83	249	4	18.9
Tim Duncan	80	2,787	574	48.4	5-2	335	62.9	231	881	253	70	198	162	18.6
Manu Ginobili	65	1,816	309	46.2	217-83	280	77.8	42	230	235	101	121	26	15.1
Michael Finley	77	2,037	286	41.2	279-110	98	85.2	31	247	116	37	62	7	10.1
Bruce Bowen	82	2,755	232	43.3	245-104	51	60.7	35	320	126	79	67	30	7.5
Nazr Mohammed	80	1,390	190	50.4	0-0	113	78.5	163	418	40	21	91	49	6.2
Brent Barry	74	1,257	156	45.2	202-80	39	66.1	29	159	123	39	52	27	5.8
Nick Van Exel	65	989	136	39.7	154-55	28	68.3	6	91	123	16	57	3	5.5
Robert Horry	63	1,182	112	38.4	144-53	44	64.7	71	242	79	43	41	51	5.1
Beno Udrih	54	590	106	45.5	70-24	39	78.0	18	52	92	14	53	2	5.1
Rasho Nesterovic	80	1,521	172	51.5	2-0	18	60.0	114	309	33	21	53	88	4.5
Sean Marks	25	180	37	52.1	3-0	7	58.3	12	43	7	5	7	7	3.2
Melvin Sanders	16	111	16	48.5	3-2	7	70.0	4	23	3	5	8	0	2.6
Fabricio Oberto	59	492	44	47.3	2-0	15	55.6	57	123	27	9	28	11	1.7
Alex Scales	1	1	0	0.0	0-0	0	0.0	0	0	0	0	0	0	0.0
TEAM TOTALS	82	19,805	2,993	47.2	1,362-524	1,327	70.2	851	3,399	1,717	543	1,126	467	95.6
OPPONENTS	82	19,806	2,782	43.3	886-300	1,414	74.0	886	3,303	1,336	599	1,136	343	88.8

SEATTLE SUPERSONICS

PLAYER	GP	MIN	FGM	PCT	FGA-FGM	FTM	PCT	OFF	TOTAL	A	STL	TO	BLK	AVG
			Field Goals		3-PT FG	Free Throws		Rebounds						
Ray Allen	78	3,022	681	45.4	653-269	324	90.3	71	332	286	105	188	16	25.1
Rashard Lewis	78	2,879	538	46.7	370-142	350	81.8	111	390	182	102	141	50	20.1
Chris Wilcox	29	873	167	59.2	0-0	74	78.7	72	237	34	18	40	13	14.1
Luke Ridnour	79	2,629	334	41.8	149-43	199	87.7	47	235	550	123	162	22	11.5
Earl Watson	24	603	98	43.2	100-42	38	73.1	7	72	129	31	61	3	11.5
Flip Murray	48	1,082	179	39.7	76-17	99	71.7	18	86	120	30	79	4	9.9
Vladimir Radmanovic	47	1,088	154	40.1	196-72	55	88.7	39	187	72	32	53	15	9.3
Nick Collison	66	1,448	207	52.5	3-0	79	69.9	143	368	74	21	77	35	7.5
Damien Wilkins	82	1,523	193	44.4	56-14	136	84.0	79	192	107	72	85	12	6.5
Robert Swift	47	985	124	51.5	0-0	53	58.2	94	264	8	15	49	56	6.4
Reggie Evans	41	788	88	50.9	1-0	66	55.0	114	276	23	24	41	5	6.4
Johan Petro	68	1,287	153	51.0	0-0	47	62.7	109	296	15	25	60	51	5.2
Mike Wilks	10	107	12	38.7	5-1	19	65.5	3	12	14	6	9	0	4.4
Danny Fortson	23	275	27	52.9	0-0	33	76.7	31	78	2	4	26	2	3.8
Mikki Moore	47	585	54	43.5	2-0	46	74.2	44	130	27	7	40	15	3.3
Vitaly Potapenko	24	318	32	50.0	0-0	10	58.8	26	62	7	2	14	2	3.1
Mateen Cleaves	27	232	25	35.2	16-4	19	79.2	2	14	42	3	14	2	2.7
Rick Brunson	4	31	5	62.5	1-0	0	0.0	0	2	2	0	3	0	2.5
Noel Felix	12	82	6	24.0	3-1	5	62.5	3	13	2	2	8	3	1.5
TEAM TOTALS	82	19,831	3,077	45.9	1,631-605	1,652	78.5	1,013	3,246	1,696	622	1,208	306	102.6
OPPONENTS	82	19,830	3,202	48.5	1,445-542	1,713	76.0	1,003	3,319	1,973	598	1,194	399	105.6

TORONTO RAPTORS

| PLAYER | GP | MIN | Field Goals | | 3-PT FG | Free Throws | | Rebounds | | | | | | |
			FGM	PCT	FGA-FGM	FTM	PCT	OFF	TOTAL	A	STL	TO	BLK	AVG
Chris Bosh	70	2,751	549	50.5	13-0	474	81.6	204	647	181	50	157	79	22.5
Mike James	79	2,921	576	46.9	382-169	283	83.7	45	262	460	72	206	3	20.3
Morris Peterson	82	3,139	478	43.6	448-177	241	82.0	65	381	190	104	126	15	16.8
Charlie Villanueva	81	2,364	435	46.3	214-70	113	70.6	181	521	88	60	99	63	13.0
Jalen Rose	46	1,237	180	40.4	115-31	166	76.5	15	129	113	20	65	10	12.1
Matt Bonner	78	1,711	209	44.8	243-102	63	82.9	86	284	56	49	32	31	7.5
Joey Graham	80	1,579	198	47.8	87-29	108	81.2	57	244	60	37	92	13	6.7
Jose Calderon	64	1,487	132	42.3	43-7	78	84.8	30	141	288	42	101	4	5.5
Andre Barrett	17	261	35	36.1	13-2	6	66.7	8	22	50	10	14	0	4.6
Antonio Davis	8	191	14	45.2	0-0	7	35.0	15	36	7	3	8	1	4.4
Pape Sow	42	592	53	43.1	0-0	41	71.9	54	146	8	21	30	19	3.5
Eric Williams	28	355	29	38.7	18-5	28	73.7	10	50	15	7	15	2	3.3
Darrick Martin	40	343	34	35.1	40-16	18	75.0	2	20	57	17	15	0	2.6
Rafael Araujo	52	605	53	36.6	1-0	15	53.6	43	144	15	24	42	6	2.3
Loren Woods	27	324	28	47.5	1-0	6	42.9	44	110	4	9	16	23	2.3
Aaron Williams	14	100	10	52.6	0-0	5	83.3	5	15	1	4	5	3	1.8
Alvin Williams	1	10	0	0.0	2-0	1	50.0	0	3	0	0	0	0	1.0
TEAM TOTALS	82	19,955	3,013	45.4	1,620-608	1,653	79.1	864	3,155	1,593	529	1,071	272	101.1
OPPONENTS	82	19,956	3,164	49.1	1,363-508	1,696	74.8	835	3,374	1,938	518	1,165	359	104.0

UTAH JAZZ

| PLAYER | GP | MIN | Field Goals | | 3-PT FG | Free Throws | | Rebounds | | | | | | |
			FGM	PCT	FGA-FGM	FTM	PCT	OFF	TOTAL	A	STL	TO	BLK	AVG
Mehmet Okur	82	2,942	519	46.0	234-80	354	78.0	211	746	194	40	163	73	18.0
Carlos Boozer	33	1,026	219	54.9	0-0	99	72.3	73	285	88	30	69	8	16.3
Andrei Kirilenko	69	2,606	336	46.0	117-36	346	69.9	161	552	299	102	203	220	15.3
Matt Harpring	71	1,946	322	47.5	39-14	227	72.5	158	368	98	59	109	14	12.5
Deron Williams	80	2,309	339	42.1	219-91	95	70.4	35	194	359	60	145	17	10.8
Gordan Giricek	37	955	166	43.3	59-18	43	75.4	15	70	63	16	63	4	10.6
Devin Brown	81	1,709	207	39.3	118-39	158	74.5	73	207	104	44	99	14	7.5
Milt Palacio	71	1,374	171	42.4	16-1	98	65.3	17	134	190	47	110	14	6.2
Keith McLeod	66	1,231	120	35.3	82-24	106	79.7	11	78	151	42	76	9	5.6
Jarron Collins	79	1,731	129	46.1	0-0	157	71.7	134	333	97	36	61	27	5.3
C.J. Miles	23	205	28	36.8	20-5	18	75.0	18	38	16	7	9	2	3.4
Kris Humphries	62	621	77	37.9	5-0	34	52.3	56	157	30	23	31	16	3.0
Andre Owens	23	210	27	36.5	16-3	12	66.7	11	21	8	5	13	0	3.0
Greg Ostertag	60	807	61	49.2	0-0	24	50.0	82	225	58	6	46	66	2.4
Robert Whaley	23	212	23	40.4	0-0	3	50.0	16	43	17	7	14	8	2.1
TEAM TOTALS	82	19,880	2,744	44.2	925-311	1,774	71.9	1,071	3,451	1,772	524	1,290	492	92.4
OPPONENTS	82	19,880	2,730	44.9	1,297-490	1,839	74.6	871	3,108	1,511	663	1,166	463	95.0

TRIVIA CHALLENGE

Which of the following players did *not* make the 2005–2006 All-NBA First Team: Dwyane Wade, Dirk Nowitzki, or Shaquille O'Neal?

Dwyane Wade

WASHINGTON WIZARDS

PLAYER	GP	MIN	Field Goals		3-PT FG	Free Throws		Rebounds		A	STL	TO	BLK	AVG
			FGM	PCT	FGA-FGM	FTM	PCT	OFF	TOTAL					
Gilbert Arenas	80	3,383	746	44.7	540-199	655	82.0	59	280	484	161	297	25	29.3
Antawn Jamison	82	3,287	660	44.2	373-147	217	73.1	167	765	158	90	137	12	20.5
Caron Butler	75	2,706	494	45.5	120-41	289	87.0	114	466	186	127	175	18	17.6
Antonio Daniels	80	2,284	230	41.8	101-23	284	84.5	19	172	284	52	89	8	9.6
Jarvis Hayes	21	517	77	42.1	47-17	25	83.3	19	76	27	16	22	1	9.3
Brendan Haywood	79	1,876	222	51.4	0-0	131	58.5	200	467	46	30	97	104	7.3
Chucky Atkins	28	552	66	37.9	92-33	22	71.0	12	45	69	14	30	0	6.7
Jared Jeffries	77	1,952	187	45.1	50-16	99	58.9	164	379	148	58	99	50	6.4
Etan Thomas	71	1,116	131	53.3	0-0	75	60.0	99	279	14	20	51	68	4.7
Donell Taylor	51	465	53	39.0	17-4	30	69.8	16	53	45	30	34	4	2.7
Andray Blatche	29	178	26	38.8	13-3	10	83.3	12	38	10	5	12	7	2.2
Billy Thomas	17	132	13	32.5	30-10	2	100.0	5	14	9	10	6	1	2.2
Awvee Storey	25	118	16	39.0	7-3	8	57.1	8	22	4	3	5	1	1.7
Calvin Booth	33	252	20	42.6	2-1	5	55.6	19	52	12	9	8	9	1.4
Michael Ruffin	76	1,013	34	44.2	2-0	37	50.0	122	271	27	33	38	31	1.4
TEAM TOTALS	82	19,831	2,975	44.7	1,394-497	1,889	75.7	1,035	3,379	1,523	658	1,143	339	101.7
OPPONENTS	82	19,830	3,014	46.5	1,379-501	1,655	74.5	964	3441	1,766	537	1,326	341	99.8

TODAY'S STARS

GREG NELSON

Elton Brand turned the Clippers into winners.

■ **Elton Brand, forward,** b. March 11, 1979, Peekskill, New York. Brand used to be known as a good player who played on bad teams, but that changed in 2005–2006. Brand led the Clippers to a 47–35 record and their first playoff series win in 20 seasons. The reason: He became quicker by losing 20 pounds in the off-season and extended the range of his jump shot to 16 feet from the basket. Brand averaged 24.7 points, nearly five points more than his previous career high.

■ **Steve Nash, guard,** b. February 7, 1974, Johannesburg, South Africa. Nash won his second straight NBA MVP in 2005–2006. The 6'3"-tall playmaker led the NBA with 10.5 assists per game and averaged a career-high 18.8 points. Nash is terrific at pushing the pace and making his teammates better. He led the Suns to a 54–28 record even though the team lost starters Joe Johnson and Quentin Richardson in the offseason and was without star forward Amaré Stoudemire (knee injury) for most of the season.

■ **Dwight Howard, forward,** b. December 8, 1985, Atlanta, Georgia. Howard is the NBA's next great big man. At age 20, he is already a dominant rebounder (12.5 per game, second in the league), and his offensive game is rapidly improving. On April 15, the 6'11"-tall Howard gave hoops fans a glimpse of the future: He had a monster 28-point, 26-rebound performance against the Philadelphia 76ers.

NBA CHAMPIONS

SEASON	CHAMPION	SERIES	RUNNER-UP	WINNING COACH	FINALS MVP
2005–06	Miami	4-2	Dallas Mavericks	Pat Riley	Dwyane Wade
2004–05	San Antonio	4-3	Detroit Pistons	Gregg Popovich	Tim Duncan, SA
2003–04	Detroit	4-1	L.A. Lakers	Larry Brown	Chauncey Billups, Det
2002–03	San Antonio	4-2	New Jersey	Gregg Popovich	Tim Duncan, SA
2001–02	L.A. Lakers	4-0	New Jersey	Phil Jackson	Shaquille O'Neal, L.A.
2000–01	L.A. Lakers	4-1	Philadelphia	Phil Jackson	Shaquille O'Neal, L.A.
1999–00	L.A. Lakers	4-2	Indiana	Phil Jackson	Shaquille O'Neal, L.A.
1998–99	San Antonio	4-1	New York	Gregg Popovich	Tim Duncan, SA
1997–98	Chicago	4-2	Utah	Phil Jackson	Michael Jordan, Chi
1996–97	Chicago	4-2	Utah	Phil Jackson	Michael Jordan, Chi
1995–96	Chicago	4-2	Seattle	Phil Jackson	Michael Jordan, Chi
1994–95	Houston	4-0	Orlando	Rudy Tomjanovich	Hakeem Olajuwon, Hou
1993–94	Houston	4-3	New York	Rudy Tomjanovich	Hakeem Olajuwon, Hou
1992–93	Chicago	4-2	Phoenix	Phil Jackson	Michael Jordan, Chi
1991–92	Chicago	4-2	Portland	Phil Jackson	Michael Jordan, Chi
1990–91	Chicago	4-1	L.A. Lakers	Phil Jackson	Michael Jordan, Chi
1989–90	Detroit	4-1	Portland	Chuck Daly	Isiah Thomas, Det
1988–89	Detroit	4-0	L.A. Lakers	Chuck Daly	Joe Dumars, Det
1987–88	L.A. Lakers	4-3	Detroit	Pat Riley	James Worthy, L.A.
1986–87	L.A. Lakers	4-2	Boston	Pat Riley	Magic Johnson, L.A.
1985–86	Boston	4-2	Houston	K.C. Jones	Larry Bird, Bos
1984–85	L.A. Lakers	4-2	Boston	Pat Riley	Kareem Abdul-Jabbar, L.A.
1983–84	Boston	4-3	L.A. Lakers	K.C. Jones	Larry Bird, Bos
1982–83	Philadelphia	4-0	L.A. Lakers	Billy Cunningham	Moses Malone, Phil
1981–82	L.A. Lakers	4-2	Philadelphia	Pat Riley	Magic Johnson, L.A.
1980–81	Boston	4-2	Houston	Bill Fitch	Cedric Maxwell, Bos
1979–80	L.A. Lakers	4-2	Philadelphia	Paul Westhead	Magic Johnson, L.A.
1978–79	Seattle	4-1	Washington	Lenny Wilkens	Dennis Johnson, Sea
1977–78	Washington	4-3	Seattle	Dick Motta	Wes Unseld, Wash
1976–77	Portland	4-2	Philadelphia	Jack Ramsay	Bill Walton, Port
1975–76	Boston	4-2	Phoenix	Tom Heinsohn	Jo Jo White, Bos
1974–75	Golden State	4-0	Washington	Al Attles	Rick Barry, GS
1973–74	Boston	4-3	Milwaukee	Tom Heinsohn	John Havlicek, Bos
1972–73	New York	4-1	L.A. Lakers	Red Holzman	Willis Reed, N.Y.
1971–72	L.A. Lakers	4-1	New York	Bill Sharman	Wilt Chamberlain, L.A.
1970–71	Milwaukee	4-0	Baltimore	Larry Costello	Kareem Abdul-Jabbar, Mil
1969–70	New York	4-3	L.A. Lakers	Red Holzman	Willis Reed, N.Y.
1968–69	Boston	4-3	L.A. Lakers	Bill Russell	Jerry West, L.A.
1967–68	Boston	4-2	L.A. Lakers	Bill Russell	—
1966–67	Philadelphia	4-2	San Francisco	Alex Hannum	—
1965–66	Boston	4-3	L.A. Lakers	Red Auerbach	—
1964–65	Boston	4-1	L.A. Lakers	Red Auerbach	—
1963–64	Boston	4-1	San Francisco	Red Auerbach	—
1962–63	Boston	4-2	L.A. Lakers	Red Auerbach	—
1961–62	Boston	4-3	L.A. Lakers	Red Auerbach	—
1960–61	Boston	4-1	St. Louis	Red Auerbach	—
1959–60	Boston	4-3	St. Louis	Red Auerbach	—
1958–59	Boston	4-0	Minneapolis	Red Auerbach	—
1957–58	St. Louis	4-2	Boston	Alex Hannum	—
1956–57	Boston	4-3	St. Louis	Red Auerbach	—
1955–56	Philadelphia	4-1	Ft. Wayne	George Senesky	—
1954–55	Syracuse	4-3	Ft. Wayne	Al Cervi	—
1953–54	Minneapolis	4-3	Syracuse	John Kundla	—
1952–53	Minneapolis	4-1	New York	John Kundla	—
1951–52	Minneapolis	4-3	New York	John Kundla	—
1950–51	Rochester	4-3	New York	Les Harrison	—
1949–50	Minneapolis	4-2	Syracuse	John Kundla	—
1948–49	Minneapolis	4-2	Washington	John Kundla	—
1947–48	Baltimore	4-2	Philadelphia	Buddy Jeannette	—
1946–47	Philadelphia	4-1	Chicago	Ed Gottlieb	—

Note: The NBA did not name a Finals MVP from 1946–47 to 1967–68.

ALL-TIME INDIVIDUAL LEADERS

SCORING

MOST POINTS, CAREER	PTS	AVG
Kareem Abdul-Jabbar	38,387	24.6
Karl Malone	36,928	25.0
Michael Jordan	32,292	30.1
Wilt Chamberlain	31,419	30.1
Moses Malone	27,409	20.6
Elvin Hayes	27,313	21.0
Hakeem Olajuwon	26,946	21.8
Oscar Robertson	26,710	25.7
Dominique Wilkins	26,668	24.8
John Havlicek	26,395	20.8

HIGHEST SCORING AVERAGE, CAREER		
Michael Jordan	30.1	1,072 games
Wilt Chamberlain	30.1	1,045 games
Allen Iverson	27.4	610 games
Elgin Baylor	27.4	846 games
Jerry West	27.0	932 games
Bob Pettit	26.4	792 games
Shaquille O'Neal	26.3	941 games
George Gervin	26.2	791 games
Oscar Robertson	25.7	1,040 games
Karl Malone	25.0	1,476 games

Note: Minimum 400 games or 10,000 points.

MOST POINTS, GAME		OPPONENT	DATE
100	Wilt Chamberlain, Phil	N.Y.	3/2/62
81	Kobe Bryant, LAL	Tor	1/22/06
73	Wilt Chamberlain, Phil	Chi	1/13/62
73	Wilt Chamberlain, SF	N.Y.	11/16/62
73	David Thompson, Den	Det	4/9/78
72	Wilt Chamberlain, SF	L.A.	11/3/62
71	Elgin Baylor, L.A.	N.Y.	11/15/60
71	David Robinson, SA	LAC	4/24/94
70	Wilt Chamberlain, SF	Syr	3/10/63
69	Michael Jordan, Chi	Clev	3/28/90

HIGHEST FIELD-GOAL PERCENTAGE, CAREER
.599 Artis Gilmore

Note: Minimum 2,000 field goals made.

HIGHEST FREE-THROW PERCENTAGE, CAREER
.904 Mark Price

Note: Minimum 1,200 free throws made.

3-POINT FIELD GOALS
Most 3-point Field Goals, Career:
2,560 Reggie Miller, Indiana
Highest 3-point Field-goal Percentage, Career:
.454 Steve Kerr, San Antonio
Most 3-point Field Goals, Game:
12 Kobe Bryant, L.A. Lakers vs. Seattle, 1/7/03
Note: First year of shot: 1979–80.

*Steals have only been an official stat since the 1973–74 season.

Michael Jordan averaged 30.1 points per game for his career.

JOHN BIEVER

STEALS*

Most Steals, Career: 3,265 John Stockton, Utah
Most Steals, Game: 11 Kendall Gill, New Jersey vs. Miami, 4/3/99; Larry Kenon, San Antonio vs. Kansas City, 12/26/76

REBOUNDS

MOST REBOUNDS, CAREER

PLAYER	REBOUNDS	YRS	AVG
Wilt Chamberlain	23,924	14	22.9
Bill Russell	21,620	13	22.5
Kareem Abdul-Jabbar	17,440	20	11.2
Elvin Hayes	16,279	16	12.5
Moses Malone	16,212	19	12.2
Karl Malone	14,968	19	10.1
Robert Parish	14,715	21	9.1
Nate Thurmond	14,464	14	15.0
Walt Bellamy	14,241	14	13.7
Wes Unseld	13,769	13	14.0

MOST REBOUNDS, GAME

NO.	PLAYER, TEAM	OPPONENT	DATE
55	Wilt Chamberlain, Phil	Bos	11/24/60
51	Bill Russell, Bos	Syr	2/5/60
49	Bill Russell, Bos	Phil	11/16/57
49	Bill Russell, Bos	Det	3/11/65
45	Wilt Chamberlain, Phil	Syr	2/6/60
45	Wilt Chamberlain, Phil	L.A.	1/21/61

KEY PTS=points; AVG=average; NO.=number; YRS=years

ASSISTS

MOST ASSISTS, CAREER

John Stockton	15,806
Mark Jackson	10,334
Magic Johnson	10,141
Oscar Robertson	9,887
Isiah Thomas	9,061

MOST ASSISTS, GAME

30 Scott Skiles, Orlando vs. Denver, 12/30/90

BLOCKS*

MOST BLOCKS, CAREER

Hakeem Olajuwon	3,830
Kareem Abdul-Jabbar	3,189
Dikembe Mutombo	3,154
Mark Eaton	3,064
David Robinson	2,954

MOST BLOCKS, GAME

17 Elmore Smith, L.A. Lakers vs. Portland, 10/28/73

*Blocks have only been an official stat since the 1973–74 season.

Magic Johnson's 10,141 assists led to five Laker titles.

JOHN W. MCDONOUGH (2)

DID YOU KNOW?

The 2006 NBA Finals were the first since 1998 in which a team other than the San Antonio Spurs or the Los Angeles Lakers represented the Western Conference.

MOST VALUABLE PLAYER: MAURICE PODOLOFF TROPHY

Steve Nash, Phoenix Suns

SEASON	PLAYER, TEAM
2005–06	Steve Nash, Phoenix
2004–05	Steve Nash, Phoenix
2003–04	Kevin Garnett, Minnesota
2002–03	Tim Duncan, San Antonio
2001–02	Tim Duncan, San Antonio
2000–01	Allen Iverson, Philadelphia
1999–00	Shaquille O'Neal, L.A. Lakers
1998–99	Karl Malone, Utah
1997–98	Michael Jordan, Chicago
1996–97	Karl Malone, Utah
1995–96	Michael Jordan, Chicago
1994–95	David Robinson, San Antonio
1993–94	Hakeem Olajuwon, Houston
1992–93	Charles Barkley, Phoenix
1991–92	Michael Jordan, Chicago
1990–91	Michael Jordan, Chicago
1989–90	Magic Johnson, L.A. Lakers
1988–89	Magic Johnson, L.A. Lakers
1987–88	Michael Jordan, Chicago
1986–87	Magic Johnson, L.A. Lakers
1985–86	Larry Bird, Boston
1984–85	Larry Bird, Boston
1983–84	Larry Bird, Boston
1982–83	Moses Malone, Philadelphia
1981–82	Moses Malone, Houston
1980–81	Julius Erving, Philadelphia

SEASON	PLAYER, TEAM
1979–80	Kareem Abdul-Jabbar, L.A. Lakers
1978–79	Moses Malone, Houston
1977–78	Bill Walton, Portland
1976–77	Kareem Abdul-Jabbar, L.A. Lakers
1975–76	Kareem Abdul-Jabbar, L.A. Lakers
1974–75	Bob McAdoo, Buffalo
1973–74	Kareem Abdul-Jabbar, Milwaukee
1972–73	Dave Cowens, Boston
1971–72	Kareem Abdul-Jabbar, Milwaukee
1970–71	Kareem Abdul-Jabbar, Milwaukee
1969–70	Willis Reed, New York
1968–69	Wes Unseld, Baltimore
1967–68	Wilt Chamberlain, Philadelphia
1966–67	Wilt Chamberlain, Philadelphia
1965–66	Wilt Chamberlain, Philadelphia
1964–65	Bill Russell, Boston
1963–64	Oscar Robertson, Cincinnati
1962–63	Bill Russell, Boston
1961–62	Bill Russell, Boston
1960–61	Bill Russell, Boston
1959–60	Wilt Chamberlain, Philadelphia
1958–59	Bob Pettit, St. Louis
1957–58	Bill Russell, Boston
1956–57	Bob Cousy, Boston
1955–56	Bob Pettit, St. Louis

ROOKIE OF THE YEAR: EDDIE GOTTLIEB TROPHY

SEASON	PLAYER, TEAM
2005–06	Chris Paul, New Orleans
2004–05	Emeka Okafor, Charlotte
2003–04	LeBron James, Cleveland
2002–03	Amare Stoudemire, Phoenix
2001–02	Pau Gasol, Memphis
2000–01	Mike Miller, Orlando
1999–00	Steve Francis, Houston
	Elton Brand, Chicago
1998–99	Vince Carter, Toronto
1997–98	Tim Duncan, San Antonio
1996–97	Allen Iverson, Philadelphia
1995–96	Damon Stoudamire, Toronto
1994–95	Jason Kidd, Dallas
	Grant Hill, Detroit
1993–94	Chris Webber, Golden State
1992–93	Shaquille O'Neal, Orlando
1991–92	Larry Johnson, Charlotte
1990–91	Derrick Coleman, New Jersey
1989–90	David Robinson, San Antonio
1988–89	Mitch Richmond, Golden State
1987–88	Mark Jackson, New York
1986–87	Chuck Person, Indiana
1985–86	Patrick Ewing, New York
1984–85	Michael Jordan, Chicago
1983–84	Ralph Sampson, Houston
1982–83	Terry Cummings, San Diego
1981–82	Buck Williams, New Jersey
1980–81	Darrell Griffith, Utah
1979–80	Larry Bird, Boston
1978–79	Phil Ford, Kansas City
1977–78	Walter Davis, Phoenix
1976–77	Adrian Dantley, Buffalo
1975–76	Alvan Adams, Phoenix
1974–75	Keith Wilkes, Golden State
1973–74	Ernie DiGregorio, Buffalo
1972–73	Bob McAdoo, Buffalo
1971–72	Sidney Wicks, Portland
1970–71	Dave Cowens, Boston
	Geoff Petrie, Portland
1969–70	Kareem Abdul-Jabbar, Milwaukee
1968–69	Wes Unseld, Baltimore
1967–68	Earl Monroe, Baltimore
1966–67	Dave Bing, Detroit
1965–66	Rick Barry, San Francisco

Chris Paul scored 16.1 points and dished out 7.8 assists per game.

GREG NELSON

SEASON	PLAYER, TEAM
1964–65	Willis Reed, New York
1963–64	Jerry Lucas, Cincinnati
1962–63	Terry Dischinger, Chicago
1961–62	Walt Bellamy, Chicago
1960–61	Oscar Robertson, Cincinnati
1959–60	Wilt Chamberlain, Philadelphia
1958–59	Elgin Baylor, Minneapolis
1957–58	Woody Sauldsberry, Philadelphia
1956–57	Tom Heinsohn, Boston
1955–56	Maurice Stokes, Rochester
1954–55	Bob Pettit, Milwaukee
1953–54	Ray Felix, Baltimore
1952–53	Don Meineke, Ft. Wayne

Note: There were co-winners in 1999–00, 1994–95, and 1970–71.

DEFENSIVE PLAYER OF THE YEAR

SEASON	PLAYER, TEAM	SEASON	PLAYER, TEAM
2005–06	Ben Wallace, Detroit	1993–94	Hakeem Olajuwon, Houston
2004–05	Ben Wallace, Detroit	1992–93	Hakeem Olajuwon, Houston
2003–04	Ron Artest, Indiana	1991–92	David Robinson, San Antonio
2002–03	Ben Wallace, Detroit	1990–91	Dennis Rodman, Detroit
2001–02	Ben Wallace, Detroit	1989–90	Dennis Rodman, Detroit
2000–01	Dikembe Mutombo, Philadelphia/Atlanta	1988–89	Mark Eaton, Utah
1999–00	Alonzo Mourning, Miami	1987–88	Michael Jordan, Chicago
1998–99	Alonzo Mourning, Miami	1986–87	Michael Cooper, L.A. Lakers
1997–98	Dikembe Mutombo, Atlanta	1985–86	Alvin Robertson, San Antonio
1996–97	Dikembe Mutombo, Atlanta	1984–85	Mark Eaton, Utah
1995–96	Gary Payton, Seattle	1983–84	Sidney Moncrief, Milwaukee
1994–95	Dikembe Mutombo, Denver	1982–83	Sidney Moncrief, Milwaukee

SIXTH MAN AWARD

SEASON	PLAYER, TEAM
2005–06	Mike Miller, Memphis
2004–05	Ben Gordon, Chicago
2003–04	Antawn Jamison, Dallas
2002–03	Bobby Jackson, Sacramento
2001–02	Corliss Williamson, Detroit
2000–01	Aaron McKie, Philadelphia
1999–00	Rodney Rogers, Phoenix
1998–99	Darrell Armstrong, Orlando
1997–98	Danny Manning, Phoenix
1996–97	John Starks, New York
1995–96	Toni Kukoc, Chicago
1994–95	Anthony Mason, New York
1993–94	Dell Curry, Charlotte
1992–93	Clifford Robinson, Portland
1991–92	Detlef Schrempf, Indiana
1990–91	Detlef Schrempf, Indiana
1989–90	Ricky Pierce, Milwaukee
1988–89	Eddie Johnson, Phoenix
1987–88	Roy Tarpley, Dallas
1986–87	Ricky Pierce, Milwaukee
1985–86	Bill Walton, Boston
1984–85	Kevin McHale, Boston
1983–84	Kevin McHale, Boston
1982–83	Bobby Jones, Philadelphia

JOHN W. MCDONOUGH

Mike Miller averaged 13.7 points off the bench.

MOST IMPROVED PLAYER

SEASON	PLAYER, TEAM
2005–06	Boris Diaw, Phoenix Suns
2004–05	Bobby Simmons, L.A. Clippers
2003–04	Zach Randolph, Portland
2002–03	Gilbert Arenas, Golden State
2001–02	Jermaine O'Neal, Indiana
2000–01	Tracy McGrady, Orlando
1999–00	Jalen Rose, Indiana
1998–99	Darrell Armstrong, Orlando
1997–98	Alan Henderson, Atlanta
1996–97	Isaac Austin, Miami
1995–96	Gheorghe Muresan, Washington

SEASON	PLAYER, TEAM
1994–95	Dana Barros, Philadelphia
1993–94	Don MacLean, Washington
1992–93	Mahmoud Abdul-Rauf, Denver
1991–92	Pervis Ellison, Washington
1990–91	Scott Skiles, Orlando
1989–90	Rony Seikaly, Miami
1988–89	Kevin Johnson, Phoenix
1987–88	Kevin Duckworth, Portland
1986–87	Dale Ellis, Seattle
1985–86	Alvin Robertson, San Antonio

2006 NBA DRAFT – FIRST ROUND

June 28, 2006, New York, NY

1. Andrea Bargnani, Toronto
2. LaMarcus Aldridge, Chicago
3. Adam Morrison, Charlotte
4. Tyrus Thomas, Portland
5. Shelden Williams, Atlanta
6. Brandon Roy, Minnesota
7. Randy Foye, Boston
8. Rudy Gay, Houston
9. Patrick O'Bryant, Golden State
10. Mouhamed Saer Sene, Seattle

11. J.J. Redick, Orlando
12. Hilton Armstrong, New Orleans
13. Thabo Sefolosha, Philadelphia (traded to Chicago)
14. Ronnie Brewer, Utah
15. Cedric Simmons, New Orleans
16. Rodney Carney, Chicago (traded to Philadelphia)
17. Shawne Williams, Indiana
18. Olexsiy Pecherov, Washington
19. Quincy Douby, Sacramento

20. Renaldo Balkman, New York
21. Rajon Rondo, Phoenix
22. Marcus Williams, New Jersey
23. Josh Boone, New Jersey
24. Kyle Lowry, Memphis
25. Shannon Brown, Cleveland
26. Jordan Farmar, Lakers
27. Sergio Rodriguez, Phoenix
28. Maurice Ager, Dallas
29. Mardy Collins, New York
30. Joel Freeland, Portland

ALL-STAR GAME RESULTS

YEAR	RESULT	SITE	WINNING COACH	MOST VALUABLE PLAYER
2006	East 122, West 120	Houston, TX	Flip Saunders	LeBron James, Cleveland
2005	East 125, West 115	Denver, CO	Stan Van Gundy	Allen Iverson, Philadelphia
2004	West 136, East 132	Los Angeles, CA	Flip Saunders	Shaquille O'Neal, L.A. Lakers
2003	West 155, East 145 (2 OT)	Atlanta, GA	Rick Adelman	Kevin Garnett, Minnesota
2002	West 135, East 120	Philadelphia, PA	Don Nelson	Kobe Bryant, L.A. Lakers
2001	East 111, West 110	Washington, DC	Larry Brown	Allen Iverson, Philadelphia
2000	West 137, East 126	Oakland, CA	Phil Jackson	Shaquille O'Neal, L.A. Lakers/ Tim Duncan, San Antonio
1999	Canceled due to lockout			
1998	East 135, West 114	New York, NY	Larry Bird	Michael Jordan, Chicago
1997	East 132, West 120	Cleveland, OH	Doug Collins	Glen Rice, Charlotte
1996	East 129, West 118	San Antonio, TX	Phil Jackson	Michael Jordan, Chicago
1995	West 139, East 112	Phoenix, AZ	Paul Westphal	Mitch Richmond, Sacramento
1994	East 127, West 118	Minneapolis, MN	Lenny Wilkens	Scottie Pippen, Chicago
1993	West 135, East 132	Salt Lake City, UT	Paul Westphal	Karl Malone/John Stockton,Utah
1992	West 153, East 113	Orlando, FL	Don Nelson	Magic Johnson, L.A. Lakers
1991	East 116, West 114	Charlotte, NC	Chris Ford	Charles Barkley, Philadelphia
1990	East 130, West 113	Miami, FL	Chuck Daly	Magic Johnson, L.A. Lakers
1989	West 143, East 134	Houston, TX	Pat Riley	Karl Malone, Utah
1988	East 138, West 133	Chicago, IL	Mike Fratello	Michael Jordan, Chicago
1987	West 154, East 149 (OT)	Seattle, WA	Pat Riley	Tom Chambers, Seattle
1986	West 139, East 132	Dallas, TX	K.C. Jones	Isiah Thomas, Detroit
1985	West 140, East 129	Indianapolis, IN	Pat Riley	Ralph Sampson, Houston
1984	East 154, West 145 (OT)	Denver, CO	K.C. Jones	Isiah Thomas, Detroit
1983	East 132, West 123	Los Angeles, CA	Billy Cunningham	Julius Erving, Philadelphia
1982	East 120, West 118	East Rutherford, NJ	Bill Fitch	Larry Bird, Boston
1981	East 123, West 120	Cleveland, OH	Billy Cunningham	Nate Archibald, Boston
1980	East 144, West 135 (OT)	Washington, DC	Billy Cunningham	George Gervin, San Antonio
1979	West 134, East 129	Detroit, MI	Lenny Wilkens	David Thompson, Denver
1978	West 133, East 125	Atlanta, GA	Billy Cunningham	Randy Smith, Buffalo
1977	West 125, East 124	Milwaukee, WI	Larry Brown	Julius Erving, Philadelphia
1976	East 123, West 109	Philadelphia, PA	Tom Heinsohn	Dave Bing, Washington
1975	East 108, West 102	Phoenix, AZ	K.C. Jones	Walt Frazier, New York
1974	West 134, East 123	Seattle, WA	Larry Costello	Bob Lanier, Detroit
1973	East 104, West 84	Chicago, IL	Tom Heinsohn	Dave Cowens, Boston
1972	West 112, East 110	Los Angeles, CA	Bill Sharman	Jerry West, L.A. Lakers
1971	West 108, East 107	San Diego, CA	Larry Costello	Lenny Wilkens, Seattle
1970	East 142, West 135	Philadelphia, PA	Red Holzman	Willis Reed, New York
1969	East 123, West 112	Baltimore, MD	Gene Shue	Oscar Robertson, Cincinnati
1968	East 144, West 124	New York, NY	Alex Hannum	Hal Greer, Philadelphia
1967	West 135, East 120	San Francisco, CA	Fred Schaus	Rick Barry, San Francisco
1966	East 137, West 94	Cincinnati, OH	Red Auerbach	Adrian Smith, Cincinnati
1965	East 124, West 123	St. Louis, MO	Red Auerbach	Jerry Lucas, Cincinnati
1964	East 111, West 107	Boston, MA	Red Auerbach	Oscar Robertson, Cincinnati
1963	East 115, West 108	Los Angeles, CA	Red Auerbach	Bill Russell, Boston
1962	West 150, East 130	St. Louis, MO	Fred Schaus	Bob Pettit, St. Louis
1961	West 153, East 131	Syracuse, NY	Paul Seymour	Oscar Robertson, Cincinnati
1960	East 125, West 115	Philadelphia, PA	Red Auerbach	Wilt Chamberlain, Philadelphia
1959	West 124, East 108	Detroit, MI	Ed Macauley	Bob Pettit, St. Louis/ Elgin Baylor, Minnesota
1958	East 130, West 118	St. Louis, MO	Red Auerbach	Bob Pettit, St. Louis
1957	East 109, West 97	Boston, MA	Red Auerbach	Bob Cousy, Boston
1956	West 108, East 94	Rochester, NY	Charley Eckman	Bob Pettit, St. Louis
1955	East 100, West 91	New York, NY	Al Cervi	Bill Sharman, Boston
1954	East 98, West 93 (OT)	New York, NY	Joe Lapchick	Bob Cousy, Boston
1953	West 79, East 75	Ft. Wayne, IN	John Kundla	George Mikan, Minnesota
1952	East 108, West 91	Boston, MA	Al Cervi	Paul Arizin, Philadelphia
1951	East 111, West 94	Boston, MA	Joe Lapchick	Ed Macauley, Boston

FAST FACT

The 2007 NBA All-Star Weekend will take place in Las Vegas, Nevada. It will be the first time that the event is held in a city that does not have an NBA team.

TRIVIA CHALLENGE

Which player led the NBA in 3-pointers made (269) in 2005–2006: Gilbert Arenas, Raja Bell, or Ray Allen?

Ray Allen

2005-06 TIME LINE

■ **October 15, 2005:** Center Jason Collier of the Atlanta Hawks (age 28) dies after having trouble breathing while at his home. The cause of death is determined to be an enlarged heart.

■ **December 12, 2005:** Stan Van Gundy resigns as coach of the Miami Heat. Team president Pat Riley, who led the Los Angeles Lakers to four titles in the 1980's, takes over as head coach.

■ **January 22, 2006:** Guard Kobe Bryant of the Los Angeles Lakers scores 81 points in a 122-104 win over the Toronto Raptors. It is second-highest single-game point total in NBA history. Bryant scores 55 points in the second half, 14 more than the entire Raptors team.

■ **February 18, 2006:** Knicks guard Nate Robinson (5'9" tall) wins the NBA slam dunk contest, beating 76ers forward Andre Iguodala in the final. Forward Dirk Nowitzki of the Dallas Mavericks wins the 3-point shootout.

■ **February 19, 2006:** The Eastern Conference All-Stars defeat the Western Conference All-Stars, 122-120. Cleveland Cavaliers swingman LeBron James (age 21) becomes the youngest All-Star MVP in history.

■ **March 8, 2006:** The Hornets play the Los Angeles Lakers in the first professional sports event held in New Orleans since Hurricane Katrina hit the city on August 29, 2005. A sell-out crowd of 17,744 watches the Lakers beat the Hornets, 113-107.

■ **April 22, 2006:** In his first career play-off game, LeBron James scorches the Washington Wizards with a triple-double (32 points, 11 rebounds, 11 assists). The Cavs win the game, 97-86, and the series four games to two. They lose to the Detroit Pistons in seven games in the Eastern Conference semifinals.

■ **May 1, 2006:** The Los Angeles Clippers beat the Denver Nuggets, 4-1, in the first round of the playoffs. It is the franchise's first playoff series win since 1976, when they were the Buffalo Braves.

■ **June 20, 2006:** The Miami Heat beat the Dallas Mavericks in six games to win its first NBA championship. Guard Dwyane Wade is named Finals MVP after averaging 34.7 points in the series.

■ **June 22, 2006:** After a disastrous 23-59 season, the New York Knicks fire Hall of Fame coach Larry Brown. Team president and general manager Isiah Thomas is named as Brown's replacement.

■ **June 28, 2006:** The Toronto Raptors select Andrea Bargnani of Italy with the first pick in the NBA draft.

WORLD CHAMPIONSHIP OF BASKETBALL

YEAR	WINNER	RUNNER-UP	SCORE	SITE
2002	Yugoslavia	Argentina	84-77 (OT)	Indianapolis, Indiana
1998	Yugoslavia	Russia	64-62	Athens, Greece
1994*	United States	Russia	137-91	Toronto, Ontario, Canada
1990	Yugoslavia	Soviet Union	92-75	Buenos Aires, Argentina
1986	United States	Soviet Union	87-85	Madrid, Spain
1982	Soviet Union	United States	95-94	Cali, Colombia
1978	Yugoslavia	Soviet Union	82-81 (OT)	Manila, Philippines
1974	Soviet Union	Yugoslavia	†	San Juan, Puerto Rico
1970	Yugoslavia	Brazil	†	Ljubljana, Yugoslavia
1967	Soviet Union	Yugoslavia	†	Montevideo, Uruguay
1963	Brazil	Yugoslavia	†	Rio de Janeiro, Brazil
1959	Brazil	United States	†	Santiago, Chile
1954	United States	Brazil	†	Rio de Janeiro, Brazil
1950	Argentina	United States	†	Rio de Janeiro, Brazil

* U.S. professionals began competing in 1994. In 1998, an NBA labor dispute resulted in a boycott of the World Championship by NBA stars. Players from the Continental Basketball Association, European professional leagues, and U.S. colleges were used to fill the U.S. team's roster.
† Result determined by overall record in final round of competition.

BASKETBALL

The Sacramento Monarchs won their city's first professional basketball title in 2005. The Monarchs beat the Connecticut Sun, 3–1, in the best-of-five final-round series to win the 2005 WNBA Championship. It was the second-straight championship series loss for the Sun. In 2004, they lost to the Seattle Storm in a best-of-three series.

The Monarchs marched into the Finals without having lost a game in the playoffs. They defeated the Los Angeles Sparks, 2–0, and the Houston Comets, 2–0. Sacramento forward/center Yolanda Griffith was named the MVP of the championship round. The four-time All-Star averaged 18.5 points and 9.8 rebounds during the Finals.

There were plenty of all-star performances during the regular season as well. Forward Sheryl Swoopes of the Houston Comets led the league in scoring (18.6 points per game) and was named the league MVP. The MVP race was the closest in WNBA history. Swoopes edged center Lauren Jackson (17.6 points per game) of the Seattle Storm by just two points in the voting. The 6' 5"-tall Jackson was the 2003 MVP. Forward Tamika Catchings of the Indiana Fever was named the Defensive Player of the Year, and guard Temeka Johnson of the Washington Mystics was the Rookie of the Year. Catchings led the league in steals (2.6 per game). Johnson led all rookies in scoring (9.3 points per game), assists (5.2), and steals (1.29).

The WNBA expanded from 13 to 14 teams for the 2006 season. The new franchise, the Chicago Sky, was set to play its first game on May 20, 2006.

Yolanda Griffith (left) of the Sacramento Monarchs put the crowning touch on a championship season by winning MVP honors in the WNBA Finals.

BOB CHILD/AP

FAST FACT

Forward Sheryl Swoopes of the Houston Comets is the only player to win the WNBA's Most Valuable Player award three times (2000, 2002, and 2005).

Sheryl Swoopes was the MVP of the All-Star Game and the regular season.

TINA FINEBERG/AP

2005 WNBA FINAL STANDINGS

EASTERN CONFERENCE					WESTERN CONFERENCE				
TEAM	W	L	PCT	GB	TEAM	W	L	PCT	GB
Sun	26	8	.765	—	Monarchs	25	9	.735	—
Fever	21	13	.618	5.0	Storm	20	14	.588	5.0
Liberty	18	16	.529	8.0	Comets	19	15	.559	6.0
Shock	16	18	.471	10.0	Sparks	18	16	.529	7.0
Mystics	16	18	.471	10.0	Mercury	16	18	.471	9.0
Sting	6	28	.176	20.0	Lynx	14	20	.412	11.0
					Silver Stars	7	27	.206	18.0

2005 WNBA Playoffs

EASTERN CONFERENCE			WESTERN CONFERENCE	

Connecticut Sun (2-0)
Detroit Shock
Connecticut Sun (2-0)

Indiana Fever (2-0)
New York Liberty
Indiana Fever

SACRAMENTO MONARCHS (3-1)

Connecticut Sun

Sacramento Monarchs (2-0)
Houston Comets

Sacramento Monarchs (2-1)
Los Angeles Sparks

Seattle Storm
Houston Comets (2-1)

| CONF. SEMIFINALS | CONF. FINALS | FINALS | CONF. FINALS | CONF. SEMIFINALS |

2005 WNBA PLAYOFF RESULTS

EASTERN CONFERENCE SEMIFINALS

August 30: Fever 63, Liberty 51
September 1: Fever 58, Liberty 50
Indiana Fever won series, 2–0

August 31: Sun 73, Shock 62
September 2: Sun 75, Shock 67
Connecticut Sun won series, 2–0

WESTERN CONFERENCE SEMIFINALS

August 30: Storm 75, Comets 67
September 1: Comets 67, Storm 64
September 3: Comets 75, Storm 58
Houston Comets won series, 2–1

August 31: Monarchs 75, Sparks 72
September 2: Monarchs 81, Sparks 63
Sacramento Monarchs won series, 2–0

EASTERN CONFERENCE FINALS

September 8: Sun 73, Fever 68
September 10: Sun 77, Fever 67 (OT)
Connecticut Sun won series, 2–0

WESTERN CONFERENCE FINALS

September 8: Monarchs 73, Comets 69
September 10: Monarchs 74, Comets 65
Sacramento Monarchs won series, 2–0

WNBA FINALS

September 14: Monarchs 69, Sun 65
September 15: Sun 77, Monarchs 70 (OT)
September 18: Monarchs 66, Sun 55
September 20: Monarchs 62, Sun 59
Sacramento Monarchs won series, 3–1

WNBA FINALS COMPOSITE BOX SCORE

SACRAMENTO MONARCHS

PLAYER	GP	MPG	FG%	3P%	FT%	REBOUNDS OFF	DEF	TOTAL	APG	SPG	BPG	TO	PF	PPG
Yolanda Griffith	4	30.8	.491	.000	.667	4.25	5.50	9.75	1.3	1.25	.50	1.75	2.75	18.5
Nicole Powell	4	34.0	.375	.520	.500	.25	2.75	3.00	1.3	1.00	.25	.75	1.25	12.8
Kara Lawson	4	25.8	.414	.500	1.000	.00	2.25	2.25	1.5	1.00	.25	.50	.75	10.3
DeMya Walker	4	28.0	.447	.000	.750	.50	2.00	2.50	3.5	.75	.00	2.50	3.00	9.3
Rebekkah Brunson	4	22.3	.370	.000	.750	1.50	3.50	5.00	1.3	.50	.25	1.00	3.50	5.8
Chelsea Newton	4	18.8	.389	.000	.750	.50	1.50	2.00	1.0	.25	.00	1.00	2.50	4.3
Ticha Penicheiro	4	24.5	.167	.000	.667	.25	3.50	3.75	4.0	.50	.25	2.25	1.00	2.5
Kristin Haynie	4	13.0	.200	.000	1.000	.75	1.25	2.00	1.5	1.25	.00	.25	.75	1.5
Olympia Scott-Richardson	3	2.3	.500	.000	.000	.33	.33	.67	.0	.00	.00	.00	.00	1.3
Hamchetou Maiga	4	7.0	.286	.000	.000	.50	.50	1.00	.3	.75	.00	.50	1.00	1.0
TEAM AVERAGES	4	206.2	.395	.462	.746	8.80	23.20	32.00	15.5	7.20	1.50	10.80	16.00	66.8

CONNECTICUT SUN

PLAYER	GP	MPG	FG%	3P%	FT%	REBOUNDS OFF	DEF	TOTAL	APG	SPG	BPG	TO	PF	PPG
Nykesha Sales	4	35.0	.365	.417	.765	1.00	1.75	2.75	3.0	1.75	.75	2.50	2.25	17.3
Taj McWilliams-Franklin	4	35.5	.500	.000	.667	3.50	8.75	12.25	1.5	.75	1.50	2.00	2.50	14.5
Katie Douglas	4	34.5	.452	.316	.636	1.25	3.25	4.50	2.3	1.75	.25	1.00	2.50	12.8
Asjha Jones	4	23.0	.462	.000	.600	1.25	2.25	3.50	.5	.50	.75	2.00	3.50	8.3
Lindsay Whalen	3	24.7	.263	.000	.500	.67	1.33	2.00	3.0	1.00	.33	3.00	1.00	4.0
Margo Dydek	4	15.8	.313	.000	1.000	.75	4.25	5.00	.8	.50	1.75	2.00	2.25	2.8
Brooke Wyckoff	4	15.0	.400	.375	.000	.00	1.50	1.50	.5	.00	.50	.75	1.25	2.8
Jennifer Derevjanik	4	14.0	.500	.000	.500	.00	.50	.50	1.3	1.00	.00	1.25	.50	1.5
Le'Coe Willingham	2	4.5	.000	.000	1.000	.00	.50	.50	.0	.00	.00	.50	.00	1.0
Jaime Carey	4	12.5	.143	.200	.000	.00	.50	.50	1.8	.25	.00	.75	1.25	.8
Laura Summerton	1	1.0	.000	.000	.000	.00	.00	.00	.0	.00	.00	.00	.00	.0
TEAM AVERAGES	4	206.2	.401	.317	.667	8.20	24.00	32.20	13.8	7.20	5.80	15.20	16.00	64.0

Note: Players with fewest minutes are not necessarily included in the boxscore. Team totals may not match the sum of listed players' totals.

KEY GP=games played; MPG=minutes per game; FG%=field-goal percentage; 3P%=3-point percentage; FT%=free-throw percentage; OFF=offensive; DEF=defensive; APG=assists per game; SPG=steals per game; BPG=blocks per game; TO=turnovers; PF=personal fouls; PPG=points per game

WNBA FINALS GAME 1 MONARCHS 69, SUN 65 Time of Game: 1:51 Attendance: 8,157

9/14/2005 Mohegan Sun Arena, Uncasville, CT   Officials: Daryl Humphrey, Michael Price, Tina Napier

SACRAMENTO MONARCHS

PLAYER	POS	MIN	FGM-A	3GM-A	FTM-A	REBOUNDS OFF	DEF	TOT	A	STL	BLK	TO	PF	PTS
Ticha Penicheiro	G	21	0-1	0-0	2-2	0	1	1	8	1	0	3	1	2
Chelsea Newton	G	20	2-4	0-0	2-2	1	1	2	0	0	0	0	1	6
Nicole Powell	F	32	4-9	2-3	0-0	1	4	5	2	1	1	0	1	10
Rebekkah Brunson	F	26	2-10	0-0	1-1	2	4	6	0	2	0	0	2	5
Yolanda Griffith	C	28	11-17	0-0	3-5	3	6	9	0	0	0	2	2	25
Kara Lawson		24	3-9	1-4	2-2	0	0	0	1	1	0	0	0	9
DeMya Walker		24	4-10	0-0	0-0	0	1	1	3	1	0	2	2	8
Kristin Haynie		15	1-4	0-0	0-0	1	1	2	3	1	0	0	0	2
Hamchetou Maiga		8	1-3	0-0	0-0	2	0	2	0	1	0	0	0	2
Olympia Scott-Richardson		2	0-0	0-0	0-0	0	1	1	0	0	0	0	0	0
TOTAL		200	28-67 (41.8%)	3-7 (42.9%)	10-12 (83.3%)	10	19	29	17	8	1	7	10	69

CONNECTICUT SUN

PLAYER	POS	MIN	FGM-A	3GM-A	FTM-A	REBOUNDS OFF	DEF	TOT	A	STL	BLK	TO	PF	PTS
Katie Douglas	G	33	6-10	2-4	0-0	0	5	5	2	1	0	1	1	14
Lindsay Whalen	G	25	3-9	0-3	1-2	0	0	0	2	1	0	0	1	7
Nykesha Sales	F	33	7-17	4-7	5-5	0	2	2	4	1	0	3	2	23
Taj McWilliams-Franklin	F	31	4-6	0-0	0-0	3	7	10	2	1	1	3	2	8
Margo Dydek	C	24	2-6	0-0	1-1	3	4	7	2	0	4	3	2	5
Asjha Jones		18	1-2	0-0	0-0	1	2	3	2	2	2	1	3	2
Brooke Wyckoff		12	1-3	0-2	0-0	0	0	0	1	0	0	1	0	2
Jennifer Derevjanik		11	1-1	0-0	0-0	0	1	1	0	0	0	1	1	2
Le'Coe Willingham		7	0-2	0-0	2-2	0	1	1	0	0	0	1	0	2
Jaime Carey		6	0-0	0-0	0-0	0	0	0	0	0	0	1	0	0
Laura Summerton														DNP
TOTAL		200	25-56 (44.6%)	6-16 (37.5%)	9-10 (90%)	7	22	29	15	6	7	15	12	65

WNBA FINALS GAME 2 SUN 77, MONARCHS 70 Time of Game: 2:22 Attendance: 8,444

9/15/2005 Mohegan Sun Arena, Uncasville, CT   Officials: Lisa Mattingly, Sue Blauch, Bryan Enterline

SACRAMENTO MONARCHS

PLAYER	POS	MIN	FGM-A	3GM-A	FTM-A	REBOUNDS OFF	DEF	TOT	A	STL	BLK	TO	PF	PTS
Chelsea Newton	G	23	4-8	0-2	1-2	1	1	2	3	0	0	2	4	9
Ticha Penicheiro	G	21	0-2	0-1	0-0	0	2	2	2	0	0	4	0	0
Nicole Powell	F	39	5-15	4-9	2-4	0	5	5	2	2	0	1	2	16
Rebekkah Brunson	F	16	0-3	0-0	0-0	0	3	3	1	0	0	1	4	0
Yolanda Griffith	C	37	7-17	0-0	2-4	6	3	9	3	1	1	0	4	16
DeMya Walker		34	6-10	0-0	2-2	0	6	6	2	2	0	4	1	14
Kara Lawson		29	4-7	1-2	2-2	0	4	4	2	0	1	0	4	11
Kristin Haynie		15	0-2	0-0	2-2	1	1	2	1	2	0	1	0	2
Hamchetou Maiga		5	0-0	0-0	0-0	0	0	0	0	0	0	1	3	0
Erin Buescher		2	0-0	0-0	0-0	0	1	1	0	0	0	0	0	0
TOTAL		225	27-67 (40.3%)	5-14 (35.7%)	11-16 (68.8%)	9	26	35	16	7	2	14	22	70

CONNECTICUT SUN

PLAYER	POS	MIN	FGM-A	3GM-A	FTM-A	REBOUNDS OFF	DEF	TOT	A	STL	BLK	TO	PF	PTS
Katie Douglas	G	41	7-15	1-5	1-4	1	2	3	3	3	1	1	3	16
Jennifer Derevjanik	G	24	1-2	0-1	1-2	0	0	0	4	2	0	2	0	3
Taj McWilliams-Franklin	F	41	8-17	0-1	8-11	4	12	16	2	1	1	1	2	24
Nykesha Sales	F	37	7-16	3-5	2-2	3	0	3	4	3	2	2	3	19
Margo Dydek	C	11	0-3	0-0	0-0	0	6	6	1	1	1	1	0	0
Brooke Wyckoff		27	3-5	3-4	0-0	0	2	2	1	0	0	1	0	9
Asjha Jones		23	1-5	0-0	1-2	1	4	5	0	0	0	4	4	3
Jaime Carey		21	1-3	1-2	0-0	0	0	0	4	0	0	2	2	3
TOTAL		225	28-66 (42.4%)	8-18 (44.4%)	13-21 (61.9%)	9	26	35	19	10	4	14	14	77

KEY POS=position; MIN=minutes; FGM-A=field goals made-attempts; 3GM-A=3-point field goals made-attempts; FTM-A=free throws made-attempts; TOT=total; A=assists; STL=steals; BLK=blocks; PTS=points

WNBA FINALS GAME 3 MONARCHS 66, SUN 55 Time of Game: 2:08 Attendance 14,073
9/18/2005 ARCO Arena, Sacramento, CA   Officials: Bob Trammell, June Courteau, Kurt Walker

CONNECTICUT SUN

PLAYER	POS	MIN	FGM-A	3GM-A	FTM-A	REBOUNDS OFF	DEF	TOT	A	STL	BLK	TO	PF	PTS
Katie Douglas	G	31	2-7	1-5	1-1	1	2	3	0	0	0	2	5	6
Lindsay Whalen	G	23	1-4	0-1	0-0	0	0	0	2	1	1	5	1	2
Nykesha Sales	F	36	6-16	2-6	3-6	0	4	4	2	2	1	2	2	17
Taj McWilliams-Franklin	F	35	7-11	0-0	2-4	3	10	13	2	0	3	2	3	16
Margo Dydek	C	19	3-4	0-0	0-0	0	6	6	0	1	2	2	4	6
Asjha Jones		24	2-7	0-1	3-6	1	0	1	0	0	0	1	2	7
Jennifer Derevjanik		12	0-0	0-0	1-2	0	1	1	1	1	0	1	0	1
Jaime Carey		11	0-3	0-2	0-0	0	1	1	0	0	0	0	2	0
Brooke Wyckoff		9	0-0	0-0	0-0	0	1	1	0	0	1	0	1	0
TOTAL		200	21-52 (32.8%)	3-15 (18.8%)	10-19 (77.3%)	5	25	30	7	5	8	15	20	55

SACRAMENTO MONARCHS

PLAYER	POS	MIN	FGM-A	3GM-A	FTM-A	REBOUNDS OFF	DEF	TOT	A	STL	BLK	TO	PF	PTS
Ticha Penicheiro	G	31	1-7	0-1	1-2	1	5	6	3	1	0	1	2	3
Chelsea Newton	G	16	1-3	0-0	0-0	0	1	1	0	1	0	1	4	2
Nicole Powell	F	35	4-14	4-8	0-0	0	1	1	1	1	0	0	0	12
Rebekkah Brunson	F	22	3-6	0-0	0-0	2	3	5	3	0	0	0	5	6
Yolanda Griffith	C	30	7-12	0-0	5-8	5	6	11	2	2	1	3	2	19
DeMya Walker		28	3-11	0-0	0-0	1	1	2	4	1	0	0	2	6
Kara Lawson		24	4-7	2-2	6-6	0	4	4	0	0	0	1	1	16
Kristin Haynie		9	1-1	0-0	0-0	0	2	2	2	0	0	0	1	2
Hamchetou Maiga		5	0-3	0-0	0-0	0	0	0	0	1	0	0	1	0
TOTAL		200	24-64 (37.5%)	6-11 (54.5%)	12-16 (75.0%)	9	23	32	15	7	1	6	18	66

WNBA FINALS GAME 4 MONARCHS 62, SUN 59 Time of Game: 2:09 Attendance 15,002
9/20/2005 ARCO Arena, Sacramento, CA   Officials: Michael Price, Bryan Enterline, Tina Napier

CONNECTICUT SUN

PLAYER	POS	MIN	FGM-A	3GM-A	FTM-A	REBOUNDS OFF	DEF	TOT	A	STL	BLK	TO	PF	PTS
Katie Douglas	G	33	4-10	2-5	5-6	3	4	7	4	3	0	0	1	15
Lindsay Whalen	G	26	1-6	0-0	1-2	2	4	6	5	1	0	4	1	3
Taj McWilliams-Franklin	F	35	5-14	0-0	0-0	4	6	10	0	1	1	2	3	10
Nykesha Sales	F	34	3-14	1-6	3-4	1	1	2	2	1	0	3	2	10
Margo Dydek	C	9	0-3	0-0	0-0	0	1	1	0	0	1	2	3	0
Asjha Jones		27	8-12	0-0	5-7	2	3	5	0	0	1	2	5	21
Jaime Carey		12	0-1	0-1	0-0	0	1	1	3	1	0	1	0	0
Brooke Wyckoff		12	0-2	0-2	0-0	0	3	3	0	0	1	1	4	0
Jennifer Derevjanik		9	0-1	0-0	0-0	0	0	0	0	1	0	1	1	0
Le'Coe Willingham		2	0-0	0-0	0-0	0	0	0	0	0	0	0	0	0
Laura Summerton		1	0-0	0-0	0-0	0	0	0	0	0	0	0	0	0
TOTAL		200	21-63 (33.3%)	3-14 (21.4%)	14-19 (73.7%)	12	23	35	14	8	4	15	21	59

SACRAMENTO MONARCHS

PLAYER	POS	MIN	FGM-A	3GM-A	FTM-A	REBOUNDS OFF	DEF	TOT	A	STL	BLK	TO	PF	PTS
Ticha Penicheiro	G	25	2-8	0-0	1-2	0	6	6	3	0	1	1	1	5
Chelsea Newton	G	16	0-3	0-0	0-0	0	3	3	1	0	0	1	1	0
Nicole Powell	F	30	5-10	3-5	0-0	0	1	1	0	0	0	2	2	13
Rebekkah Brunson	F	25	5-8	0-0	2-3	2	4	6	1	0	1	3	3	12
Yolanda Griffith	C	28	3-11	0-0	8-10	3	7	10	0	2	0	2	3	14
Kara Lawson		26	1-6	1-2	2-2	0	1	1	3	1	0	1	1	5
DeMya Walker		26	4-7	0-0	1-2	1	0	1	5	1	0	4	4	9
Kristin Haynie		13	0-3	0-0	0-0	1	1	2	0	2	0	0	1	0
Hamchetou Maiga		10	1-1	0-0	0-0	0	2	2	1	1	0	1	0	2
Olympia Scott-Richardson		1	1-1	0-0	0-0	0	0	0	0	0	0	0	0	2
Erin Buescher														DNP
TOTAL		200	22-58 (37.9%)	4-7 (57.1%)	14-19 (73.7%)	7	25	32	14	7	2	15	16	62

WNBA CHAMPIONS

YEAR	CHAMPION	RUNNER-UP	MVP
2005	Sacramento Monarchs	Connecticut Sun	Yolanda Griffith
2004	Seattle Storm	Connecticut Sun	Betty Lennox
2003	Detroit Shock	Los Angeles Sparks	Ruth Riley
2002	Los Angeles Sparks	New York Liberty	Lisa Leslie
2001	Los Angeles Sparks	Charlotte Sting	Lisa Leslie
2000	Houston Comets	New York Liberty	Cynthia Cooper
1999	Houston Comets	New York Liberty	Cynthia Cooper
1998	Houston Comets	Phoenix Mercury	Cynthia Cooper
1997	Houston Comets	New York Liberty	Cynthia Cooper

TEAM-BY-TEAM STATS

CHARLOTTE STING

PLAYER	GP	MIN	FIELD GOALS		3-PT FG		FREE THROWS		REBOUNDS		A	STL	TO	BLK	PPG
			FGM	PCT	FGA	FGM	FTM	PCT	OFF	TOTAL					
Tangela Smith	31	1,063	169	.417	7	0	83	.798	45	162	41	51	84	32	13.6
Sheri Sam	34	1,075	146	.387	56	18	77	.713	53	145	91	44	100	2	11.4
Tammy Sutton-Brown	34	887	111	.509	0	0	96	.681	64	179	14	30	69	37	9.4
Allison Feaster	21	666	61	.377	86	37	33	.846	9	37	51	14	38	2	9.1
Jia Perkins	30	464	64	.424	9	3	19	.633	24	44	32	29	32	9	5.0
Adrienne Goodson	33	486	144	.410	3	2	22	.611	33	71	21	11	34	1	4.3
Teana Miller	31	362	44	.484	0	0	25	.694	29	65	7	14	26	18	3.6
Helen Darling	31	600	27	.307	32	10	43	.741	5	47	83	41	51	0	3.5
Ayana Walker	21	333	29	.426	0	0	13	.650	20	65	19	8	19	12	3.4
Kelly Mazzante	27	226	21	.292	46	14	8	.800	14	31	7	9	7	0	2.4
Janel McCarville	28	311	17	.340	0	0	16	.640	32	76	11	12	22	7	1.8
Caity Matter	10	56	3	.231	7	1	2	1.000	3	6	1	0	4	2	0.9
Kristen Rasmussen	27	551	49	.480	18	7	22	.733	28	81	24	14	20	16	4.7
STING	34	6,925	772	.404	301	104	1447	.716	316	925	493	284	535	113	61.6
OPPONENTS	34	–	851	.451	339	124	509	.714	355	1,055	496	269	534	146	68.7

Note: Players with fewest minutes are not necessarily included in the boxscore. Team totals may not match the sum of listed players' totals.

KEY	FGM=field goals made; PCT=percentage; FGA=field-goal attempts; FTM=free throws made; A=assists; STL=steals; BLK=blocks

FAST FACT

Center Cheryl Ford of the Detroit Shock is the daughter of NBA great Karl Malone. Malone played 19 seasons in the NBA with the Utah Jazz (1985-2003) and the Los Angeles Lakers (2003-04).

CONNECTICUT SUN

| PLAYER | GP | MIN | FIELD GOALS | | 3-PT FG | | FREE THROWS | | REBOUNDS | | | | | | |
			FGM	PCT	FGA	FGM	FTM	PCT	OFF	TOTAL	A	STL	TO	BLK	PPG
Nykesha Sales	34	1,074	201	.417	116	49	108	.750	36	124	74	61	64	10	15.6
Taj McWilliams-Franklin	34	1,083	180	.495	18	4	107	.787	78	248	65	37	59	25	13.9
Lindsay Whalen	34	1,047	135	.466	46	16	125	.801	29	128	172	42	89	2	12.1
Katie Douglas	32	998	119	.413	110	31	82	.774	45	130	94	48	54	4	11.0
Asjha Jones	33	705	133	.484	5	2	56	.589	54	121	40	10	51	7	9.1
Margo Dydek	31	671	87	.537	2	1	50	.769	27	195	38	8	47	71	7.3
Brooke Wyckoff	34	596	35	.398	52	22	13	.650	25	95	35	13	28	9	3.1
Le'Coe Willingham	18	91	7	.412	0	0	10	.500	10	17	3	2	14	0	1.3
Jennifer Derevjanik	34	359	8	.364	7	1	7	.438	10	30	40	11	26	2	0.7
Jaime Carey	15	86	7	.368	13	4	0	.000	2	6	7	2	4	0	1.2
Laura Summerton	11	43	3	.333	0	0	4	.800	5	10	3	2	4	0	0.9
Jessica Brungo	12	47	1	.111	4	0	0	.000	1	6	2	0	2	0	0.2
SUN	34	6,800	916	.452	373	130	512	.744	322	1,100	573	236	452	130	72.8
OPPONENTS	34	–	835	.398	400	122	452	.755	350	1,078	495	258	442	79	66.0

DETROIT SHOCK

| PLAYER | GP | MIN | FIELD GOALS | | 3-PT FG | | FREE THROWS | | REBOUNDS | | | | | | |
			FGM	PCT	FGA	FGM	FTM	PCT	OFF	TOTAL	A	STL	TO	BLK	PPG
Deanna Nolan	33	1,213	184	.398	90	28	128	.800	31	156	121	55	100	14	15.9
Cheryl Ford	33	932	120	.430	0	0	73	.487	113	322	26	33	69	46	9.5
Ruth Riley	33	855	100	.375	12	3	48	.800	43	156	39	23	68	46	7.6
Kara Braxton	33	455	97	.462	1	0	33	.550	42	100	14	18	52	13	6.9
Plenette Pierson	35	762	91	.394	2	1	87	.696	46	121	34	24	74	19	7.7
Elaine Powell	29	671	62	.437	2	0	39	.600	25	80	77	29	51	4	5.6
Katie Smith	36	1,160	140	.380	159	53	97	.782	23	83	87	30	71	5	11.9
Swin Cash	21	458	48	.381	10	2	21	.656	42	88	43	12	47	6	5.7
Barbara Farris	34	444	25	.342	0	0	33	.611	31	84	19	8	43	1	2.4
Sheila Lambert	12	152	14	.311	7	1	4	.800	2	17	21	8	24	1	2.8
Andrea Stinson	18	102	8	.348	10	2	4	.667	6	12	13	3	4	0	1.2
SHOCK	34	6,925	831	.403	238	76	509	.658	412	1,215	474	241	571	155	66.1
OPPONENTS	34	–	784	.403	456	154	565	.749	273	1,018	473	272	520	136	67.3

PLAYER	GP	MIN	FIELD GOALS		3-PT FG		FREE THROWS		REBOUNDS		A	STL	TO	BLK	PPG
			FGM	PCT	FGA	FGM	FTM	PCT	OFF	TOTAL					
Sheryl Swoopes	33	1,225	217	.447	75	27	153	.850	27	119	141	66	72	26	18.6
Michelle Snow	33	966	152	.551	0	0	92	.708	68	225	40	20	65	38	12.0
Tari Phillips	32	366	40	.426	0	0	31	.646	30	79	14	11	30	8	3.5
Janeth Arcain	34	1,079	128	.421	16	3	83	.883	20	93	53	55	56	6	10.1
Tina Thompson	15	439	62	.413	40	12	16	.762	17	57	22	12	32	4	10.1
Dominique Canty	33	997	95	.399	4	80	110	.727	25	108	101	29	67	2	8.2
Dawn Staley	33	905	63	.396	56	21	32	.800	9	70	149	36	54	1	5.4
Sancho Lyttle	33	460	59	.584	0	0	22	.550	35	125	17	20	23	3	4.2
Edwige Lawson	19	126	8	.286	15	5	6	1.000	1	9	4	2	12	1	1.4
Roneeka Hodges	26	188	13	.277	26	5	2	1.000	9	17	7	3	3	0	1.3
Kiesha Brown	6	32	1	.500	1	0	0	.000	0	1	2	3	4	0	0.3
Felicia Ragland	4	9	0	.000	0	0	0	.000	0	0	1	0	0	0	0.0
COMETS	34	6,875	860	.448	205	62	527	.764	276	960	467	246	425	105	67.9
OPPONENTS	34	–	848	.436	423	148	419	.750	274	961	541	197	481	111	66.6

PLAYER	GP	MIN	FIELD GOALS		3-PT FG		FREE THROWS		REBOUNDS		A	STL	TO	BLK	PPG
			FGM	PCT	FGA	FGM	FTM	PCT	OFF	TOTAL					
Tamika Catchings	34	1,174	157	.388	123	35	152	.788	69	264	143	90	91	16	14.7
Kelly Miller	34	1,057	122	.439	114	37	67	.848	26	86	81	40	53	2	10.2
Natalie Williams	34	804	103	.415	0	0	45	.672	74	186	31	35	56	12	7.4
Tan White	34	693	85	.335	81	25	47	.810	21	53	53	30	70	7	7.1
Tully Bevilaqua	31	873	63	.389	116	44	24	.545	12	63	80	60	51	0	6.3
Jurgita Streimikyte	34	686	82	.461	6	3	19	.704	37	101	32	29	36	11	5.5
Deanna Jackson	34	472	56	.403	3	0	50	.735	37	77	23	17	32	12	4.8
Kelly Schumacher	34	516	58	.420	11	2	17	.810	26	68	14	10	33	24	4.0
Ebony Hoffman	33	497	47	.405	2	1	25	.833	34	97	16	21	23	10	3.6
Yolanda Paige	13	78	6	.273	5	1	3	.750	2	9	13	2	6	0	1.2
Coretta Brown	6	23	2	.400	5	2	0	.000	0	2	3	1	3	0	1.0
Jennifer Benningfield	10	52	3	.375	2	0	3	.750	3	6	4	1	4	1	0.9
FEVER	34	6,925	784	.400	468	150	452	.760	341	1,012	493	336	477	95	63.8
OPPONENTS	34	–	775	.431	367	123	460	.717	279	990	435	234	558	113	62.7

LOS ANGELES SPARKS

PLAYER	GP	MIN	FIELD GOALS FGM	PCT	3-PT FG FGA	FGM	FREE THROWS FTM	PCT	REBOUNDS OFF	TOTAL	A	STL	TO	BLK	PPG
Chamique Holdsclaw	33	1,183	216	.480	13	3	126	.788	86	223	104	38	99	16	17.0
Lisa Leslie	34	1,096	204	.440	34	7	102	.586	70	248	87	67	100	71	15.2
Tamika Whitmore	34	917	115	.434	19	5	92	.868	54	143	42	33	57	14	9.6
Nikki Teasley	19	551	45	.333	94	29	22	.846	6	53	70	23	47	4	7.4
Mwadi Mabika	17	367	39	.320	49	11	10	.500	8	27	29	15	14	0	5.8
Doneeka Hodges	32	669	65	.414	69	31	17	.680	8	47	77	18	48	7	5.6
Tamecka Dixon	30	607	63	.409	5	0	34	.850	24	67	77	24	40	2	5.3
Laura Macchi	13	148	21	.396	28	9	12	.706	6	18	7	8	13	1	4.8
Christi Thomas	32	520	48	.500	12	4	22	.688	28	104	17	11	25	19	3.8
Raffaella Masciadri	33	463	44	.423	46	19	15	.750	20	47	23	15	21	1	3.7
Edniesha Curry	13	113	7	.304	16	6	3	.500	4	11	12	7	10	1	1.8
Marlous Nieuwveen	7	16	2	.667	0	0	0	.000	2	2	0	0	2	0	0.6
Jessica Moore	15	109	4	.500	0	0	0	.000	4	8	1	4	5	0	0.5
SPARKS	**34**	**6,800**	**873**	**.428**	**387**	**124**	**456**	**.724**	**321**	**1,004**	**551**	**264**	**492**	**136**	**68.4**
OPPONENTS	**34**	**—**	**818**	**.418**	**519**	**182**	**527**	**.743**	**332**	**1,041**	**567**	**247**	**544**	**115**	**69.0**

MINNESOTA LYNX

PLAYER	GP	MIN	FIELD GOALS FGM	PCT	3-PT FG FGA	FGM	FREE THROWS FTM	PCT	REBOUNDS OFF	TOTAL	A	STL	TO	BLK	PPG
Katie Smith	23	766	100	.383	104	35	71	.789	12	55	61	25	54	2	13.3
Nicole Ohlde	34	1,038	133	.455	2	0	116	.817	63	194	78	21	84	22	11.2
Svetlana Abrosimova	31	777	109	.395	82	33	53	.726	29	107	60	48	80	6	9.8
Chandi Jones	10	281	29	.349	32	11	12	.632	10	33	30	13	17	3	8.1
Vanessa Hayden	31	595	103	.433	0	0	40	.556	48	163	23	15	63	68	7.9
Stacey Lovelace	34	594	70	.405	63	26	43	.796	35	107	31	24	37	11	6.1
Tamika Williams	34	758	86	.551	3	0	25	.543	76	171	39	30	41	2	5.8
Kristi Harrower	34	832	53	.351	68	22	28	.778	11	82	96	38	54	1	4.6
Amber Jacobs	33	478	40	.385	53	20	21	.724	4	19	68	19	46	4	3.7
Amanda Lassiter	31	388	38	.330	72	24	7	.636	10	46	23	14	29	4	3.5
Kristen Mann	24	185	30	.500	9	0	11	.688	11	35	11	8	7	1	3.0
Tynesha Lewis	11	90	10	.370	3	1	7	.778	0	5	7	3	11	1	2.5
Susan King Borchardt	3	17	0	.000	0	0	3	.750	0	1	1	0	0	1	1.0
LYNX	**34**	**6,850**	**801**	**.412**	**492**	**172**	**437**	**.727**	**310**	**1,025**	**531**	**258**	**536**	**127**	**65.0**
OPPONENTS	**34**	**—**	**862**	**.427**	**376**	**129**	**435**	**.735**	**344**	**1,055**	**537**	**275**	**487**	**144**	**67.3**

NEW YORK LIBERTY

PLAYER	GP	MIN	FIELD GOALS		3-PT FG		FREE THROWS		REBOUNDS						
			FGM	PCT	FGA	FGM	FTM	PCT	OFF	TOTAL	A	STL	TO	BLK	PPG
Becky Hammon	34	1,180	145	.432	178	65	118	.901	20	114	146	60	107	2	13.9
Ann Wauters	28	879	151	.541	2	2	79	.752	47	184	41	18	71	23	13.7
Vickie Johnson	34	1,023	129	.474	84	30	65	.774	37	118	92	23	44	2	10.4
Shameka Christon	34	809	111	.411	89	24	65	.855	25	92	41	33	50	19	9.1
Elena Baranova	33	953	104	.441	85	33	47	.855	39	227	59	25	59	46	8.7
Crystal Robinson	32	969	85	.379	107	34	30	.789	29	100	58	21	38	5	7.3
Cathrine Kraayeveld	17	196	23	.418	24	9	14	.933	13	27	5	4	17	8	4.1
La'Keshia Frett	33	361	42	.477	0	0	14	.737	15	38	18	12	18	4	3.0
Erin Thorn	21	203	21	.389	29	10	4	1.000	4	14	13	4	7	0	2.7
Tamara Moore	7	48	4	.667	3	1	2	1.000	0	7	6	0	4	0	1.6
DeTrina White	13	90	4	.364	0	0	8	.667	9	22	0	4	3	3	1.2
Edwige Lawson	2	12	0	.000	2	0	2	1.000	0	2	0	0	0	0	1.0
LIBERTY	34	6,925	828	.445	605	208	452	.819	242	974	498	214	462	112	68.1
OPPONENTS	34	—	859	.427	398	125	442	.727	345	1,030	473	275	411	86	67.2

PHOENIX MERCURY

PLAYER	GP	MIN	FIELD GOALS		3-PT FG		FREE THROWS		REBOUNDS						
			FGM	PCT	FGA	FGM	FTM	PCT	OFF	TOTAL	A	STL	TO	BLK	PPG
Diana Taurasi	33	1,089	175	.410	179	56	121	.801	22	138	150	38	112	28	16.0
Penny Taylor	29	852	121	.464	94	38	102	.864	38	120	94	38	77	11	13.2
Anna DeForge	33	1,131	142	.390	144	47	102	.850	31	114	80	41	81	7	13.1
Kamila Vodichkova	28	821	127	.494	7	3	48	.667	60	196	63	28	58	22	10.9
Maria Stepanova	15	409	68	.472	0	0	26	.650	29	80	23	20	22	38	10.8
Plenette Pierson	12	318	36	.343	1	0	20	.690	19	59	13	10	32	13	7.7
Shereka Wright	25	346	24	.407	35	11	35	.673	18	50	23	14	28	3	3.8
Sandora Irvin	12	122	14	.800	8	4	12	.800	16	34	5	5	2	6	3.7
Belinda Snell	20	226	19	.345	37	11	16	.889	19	36	18	7	11	1	3.3
Ashley Robinson	34	659	42	.326	1	0	19	.500	48	118	31	20	38	34	3.0
Gwen Jackson	11	121	13	.500	4	2	3	.500	8	23	3	0	10	3	2.8
Angelina Williams	16	149	15	.300	18	4	6	.857	9	23	9	4	11	7	2.5
Niele Ivey	14	152	8	.333	10	2	6	1.000	3	10	20	6	6	0	1.7
MERCURY	34	6,800	826	.414	539	178	531	.766	342	1,062	549	243	517	179	69.4
OPPONENTS	34	—	855	.429	332	121	523	.726	319	1,024	470	265	483	112	69.2

SACRAMENTO MONARCHS

PLAYER	GP	MIN	FIELD GOALS FGM	PCT	3-PT FG FGA	FGM	FREE THROWS FTM	PCT	REBOUNDS OFF	TOTAL	A	STL	TO	BLK	PPG
DeMya Walker	22	598	125	.534	1	1	60	.645	47	117	48	28	69	13	14.1
Yolanda Griffith	34	962	173	.485	0	0	123	.707	87	223	52	42	68	31	13.8
Nicole Powell	34	988	120	.379	159	66	58	.806	32	124	62	39	44	16	10.7
Kara Lawson	24	508	65	.439	81	36	26	.839	7	33	37	13	22	3	8.0
Rebekkah Brunson	34	722	105	.427	0	0	55	.598	75	187	16	28	42	15	7.8
Ticha Penicheiro	34	927	54	.314	41	8	79	.790	8	97	149	48	67	6	5.7
Chelsea Newton	34	715	60	.403	25	6	22	.611	32	66	55	24	37	9	4.4
Hamchetou Maiga	34	408	59	.450	0	0	11	.314	31	67	30	24	42	6	3.8
Kristin Haynie	30	434	40	.342	32	5	19	.826	19	62	43	33	35	1	3.5
Erin Buescher	23	209	28	.700	0	0	20	.588	14	29	14	16	26	5	3.3
Olympia Scott-Richardson	18	170	14	.359	0	0	10	.500	17	33	5	4	22	2	2.1
Li jie Miao	18	135	9	.300	20	6	7	1.000	0	4	13	5	15	1	1.7
MONARCHS	34	6,800	853	.430	360	129	494	.685	369	1,043	527	304	500	108	68.5
OPPONENTS	34	—	751	.412	376	113	478	.732	273	967	463	235	622	132	61.6

SAN ANTONIO SILVER STARS

PLAYER	GP	MIN	FIELD GOALS FGM	PCT	3-PT FG FGA	FGM	FREE THROWS FTM	PCT	REBOUNDS OFF	TOTAL	A	STL	TO	BLK	PPG
Marie Ferdinand	31	999	132	.369	65	20	104	.776	40	116	68	46	70	5	12.5
Wendy Palmer-Daniel	34	882	125	.517	56	24	52	.743	53	193	33	20	42	7	9.6
Shannon Johnson	34	1,104	88	.365	90	28	113	.831	17	91	158	46	113	5	9.3
LaToya Thomas	21	505	69	.429	7	3	44	.898	18	68	22	7	33	8	8.8
Katie Feenstra	34	673	104	.468	0	0	90	.703	57	175	6	9	62	44	8.8
Chantelle Anderson	34	669	83	.466	0	0	37	.804	28	90	11	8	55	15	6.0
Shyra Ely	31	528	50	.379	31	9	30	.769	11	62	27	7	33	4	4.5
Bernadette Ngoyisa	26	251	46	.568	0	0	19	.731	17	61	5	5	25	2	4.3
Kendra Wecker	1	11	2	.333	3	0	0	.000	0	0	2	1	1	0	4.0
Dalma Ivanyi	30	577	25	.373	45	20	5	.625	5	50	68	26	53	0	2.5
Nikki McCray	23	302	15	.242	20	1	7	.636	7	20	16	11	18	0	1.7
Edna Campbell	28	248	21	.313	19	5	1	1.000	2	14	14	7	15	0	1.7
Tai Dillard	10	51	2	.250	3	0	1	.250	1	6	3	2	3	0	0.9
SILVER STARS	34	6,800	764	.417	339	110	503	.771	256	946	433	195	535	90	63.0
OPPONENTS	34	—	898	.436	408	142	463	.758	351	1,055	563	283	429	148	70.6

SEATTLE STORM

PLAYER	GP	MIN	FIELD GOALS FGM	PCT	3-PT FG FGA	FGM	FREE THROWS FTM	PCT	REBOUNDS OFF	TOTAL	A	STL	TO	BLK	PPG
Lauren Jackson	34	1,176	206	.458	118	34	151	.834	96	313	57	36	59	67	17.6
Betty Lennox	28	800	123	.392	78	24	76	.874	21	124	57	35	75	5	12.4
Sue Bird	30	1,020	130	.442	103	45	59	.855	21	72	176	29	87	6	12.1
Janell Burse	34	859	127	.523	0	0	86	.699	81	199	23	19	78	40	10.0
Iziane Castro Marques	33	879	93	.384	72	24	59	.808	23	97	49	18	59	4	8.2
Suzy Batkovic	29	461	76	.437	7	2	45	.776	26	94	26	17	32	24	6.9
Tanisha Wright	34	528	49	.462	1	0	24	.667	20	57	53	18	40	3	3.6
Alicia Thompson	30	329	32	.395	22	7	12	.750	10	45	14	4	18	4	2.8
Francesca Zara	34	413	34	.400	22	5	17	.810	11	39	51	16	41	1	2.6
Simone Edwards	28	201	24	.585	0	0	7	.583	9	31	3	4	4	2	2.0
Mandisa Stevenson	4	53	3	.250	1	0	0	.000	2	6	1	2	4	0	1.5
Natalia Vodopyanova	17	98	8	.364	5	1	8	.667	3	20	10	3	8	2	1.5
STORM	34	6,825	906	.439	429	142	544	.791	323	1,099	520	201	516	158	73.5
OPPONENTS	34	—	892	.412	419	133	490	.759	334	1,020	568	267	438	154	70.8

WASHINGTON MYSTICS

PLAYER	GP	MIN	FIELD GOALS FGM	PCT	3-PT FG FGA	FGM	FREE THROWS FTM	PCT	REBOUNDS OFF	TOTAL	A	STL	TO	BLK	PPG
Alana Beard	30	1,015	155	.380	101	32	80	.762	25	130	90	45	63	9	14.1
DeLisha Milton-Jones	33	1,069	138	.417	119	39	79	.798	45	172	58	57	75	18	11.9
Chasity Melvin	34	1,051	150	.492	16	4	93	.674	82	199	25	31	61	14	11.7
Temeka Johnson	34	973	125	.458	43	13	52	.788	13	104	177	44	88	1	9.3
Charlotte Smith-Taylor	34	1,036	87	.458	100	42	30	.652	34	128	71	22	46	11	7.2
Coco Miller	34	500	68	.425	24	9	8	.800	24	59	44	26	28	3	4.5
Laurie Koehn	30	230	37	.468	75	35	4	.800	4	11	10	2	6	0	3.8
Nakia Sanford	27	293	29	.483	0	0	30	.484	15	45	6	10	17	11	3.3
Murriel Page	34	589	47	.395	22	6	8	1.000	21	83	25	15	23	9	3.2
Kaayla Chones	12	61	6	.429	0	0	2	.667	2	6	1	1	4	0	1.2
Tamicha Jackson	8	66	4	.154	9	1	0	.000	1	6	10	5	4	0	1.1
Mactabene Amachree	3	3	0	.000	0	0	2	1.000	0	0	0	0	0	0	0.7
MYSTICS	34	6,900	847	.430	510	181	388	.711	266	943	517	260	435	76	66.6
OPPONENTS	34	—	833	.445	433	150	489	.755	267	1,024	545	205	504	108	67.8

TRIVIA CHALLENGE

Which of these teams was not part of the WNBA when the league began play in 1997: the New York Liberty, the Los Angeles Sparks, or the Indiana Fever?

The Indiana Fever joined the WNBA in 2000.

JERRY S. MENDOZA/AP

2005 WNBA INDIVIDUAL LEADERS

POINTS	GP	PTS	AVG
Sheryl Swoopes, Houston Comets	33	614	18.6
Lauren Jackson, Seattle Storm	34	597	17.6
Chamique Holdsclaw, L.A. Sparks	33	561	17.0
Diana Taurasi, Phoenix Mercury	33	527	16.0
Deanna Nolan, Detroit Shock	33	524	15.9

REBOUNDS	GP	REB	AVG
Cheryl Ford, Detroit Shock	33	322	9.8
Lauren Jackson, Seattle Storm	34	313	9.2
Tamika Catchings, Indiana Fever	34	264	7.8
Lisa Leslie, L.A. Sparks	34	248	7.3
Taj McWilliams-Franklin, Conn. Sun	34	248	7.3

ASSISTS	GP	A	AVG
Sue Bird, Seattle Storm	30	176	5.9
Temeka Johnson, Wash. Mystics	34	177	5.2
Lindsay Whalen, Conn. Sun	34	172	5.1
Shannon Johnson, S.A. Silver Stars	34	158	4.6
Diana Taurasi, Phoenix Mercury	33	150	4.5

FIELD-GOAL PERCENTAGE	FGA	FGM	PCT
Michelle Snow, Houston Comets	276	152	.551
Ann Wauters, New York Liberty	279	151	.541
DeMya Walker, Sac. Monarchs	234	125	.534
Janell Burse, Seattle Storm	243	127	.523
W. Palmer-Daniel, S.A. Silver Stars	242	125	.517

FREE-THROW PERCENTAGE	FTA	FTM	PCT
Becky Hammon, New York Liberty	131	118	.901
Janeth Arcain, Houston Comets	94	83	.883
Betty Lennox, Seattle Storm	87	76	.874
Tamika Whitmore, L.A. Sparks	106	92	.868
Penny Taylor, Phoenix Mercury	118	102	.864

3-POINT FIELD-GOAL PERCENTAGE	FGA	FGM	PCT
Laurie Koehn, Wash. Mystics	75	35	.467
Doneeka Hodges, L.A. Sparks	69	31	.449
Kara Lawson, Sac. Monarchs	81	36	.444
Sue Bird, Seattle Storm	103	45	.437
Allison Feaster, Charlotte Sting	86	37	.430

STEALS	GP	STL	AVG
Tamika Catchings, Indiana Fever	34	90	2.65
Sheryl Swoopes, Houston Comets	33	66	2.00
Lisa Leslie, L.A. Sparks	34	67	1.97
Tully Bevilaqua, Indiana Fever	31	60	1.94
Nykesha Sales, Conn. Sun	34	61	1.79

BLOCKS	GP	BLK	AVG
Margo Dydek, Conn. Sun	31	71	2.29
Vanessa Hayden, Minnesota Lynx	31	68	2.19
Lisa Leslie, L.A. Sparks	34	71	2.09
Lauren Jackson, Seattle Storm	34	67	1.97
Ruth Riley, Detroit Shock	33	46	1.39

Note: L.A.=Los Angeles, Conn.=Connecticut, Wash.=Washington, S.A.=San Antonio, Sac.=Sacramento

TODAY'S STARS

■ **Chamique Holdsclaw, forward,** b. August 9, 1977, Flushing, New York. Holdsclaw has been an All-Star four times in her seven-season WNBA career. She ranked third in the league in scoring (17 points per game) and ninth in rebounds (6.8) in 2005. The first overall pick in the 1999 WNBA Draft, Holdsclaw was named the Rookie of the Year in her first season. She was a two-time Naismith Player of the Year at Tennessee (1997-98, 1998-99) and led the Lady Volunteers to three national titles (1995-96, 1996-97, and 1997-98). Holdsclaw played her first six WNBA seasons with the Washington Mystics. She was traded to the Los Angeles Sparks in the spring of 2005.

■ **Nykesha Sales, guard,** b. May 10, 1976, Bloomfield, Connecticut. Sales led the Connecticut Sun in scoring (15.6 points per game) and steals (1.79) in 2005. She also helped the Sun reach the WNBA Finals for the second season in a row. Sales was tops on her team in scoring (17.2 points per game) in the championship series. The 6'-tall guard is a five-time WNBA All-Star.

■ **Temeka Johnson, guard,** b. September 6, 1982, Kenner, Louisiana. Johnson was named the 2005 WNBA Rookie of the Year. Playing for the Washington Mystics, she led all rookies in scoring (9.3 points per game) and was second in the league in assists (5.2). Johnson was the sixth overall selection in the 2005 WNBA Draft. She was a three-time All-America honorable mention at Louisiana State University, where she set the school's all-time career assist record (945).

Chamique Holdsclaw added her electricity to the Los Angeles Sparks in 2005.

ROBERT BECK

DID YOU KNOW?

Detroit Shock coach Bill Laimbeer played in the NBA for 14 seasons. He played 12$\frac{1}{2}$ seasons with the Detroit Pistons (1982-94), and was the starting center on two championship teams.

WNBA ALL-STAR GAME RESULTS

YEAR	RESULT	SITE	WINNING COACH	MVP
2005	West 122, East 99	Uncasville, CT	Anne Donovan	Sheryl Swoopes, Houston Comets
2004	U.S. National Team 74, WNBA All-Stars 58	New York, NY	Van Chancellor	Yolanda Griffith, Sacramento Monarchs
2003	West 84, East 75	New York, NY	Michael Cooper	Nikki Teasley, Los Angeles Sparks
2002	West 81, East 76	Washington, D.C.	Michael Cooper	Lisa Leslie, Los Angeles Sparks
2001	West 80, East 72	Orlando, FL	Van Chancellor	Lisa Leslie, Los Angeles Sparks
2000	West 73, East 61	Phoenix, AZ	Van Chancellor	Tina Thompson, Houston Comets
1999	West 79, East 61	New York, NY	Van Chancellor	Lisa Leslie, Los Angeles Sparks

2006 WNBA DRAFT

APRIL 5, 2006, BOSTON, MASS

FIRST ROUND PICK TEAM	NAME/POSITION	SCHOOL	FIRST ROUND PICK TEAM	NAME/POSITION	SCHOOL
1. Minnesota	Seimone Augustus, G	LSU	8. Washington	Tamara James (from L.A.), G	Miami
2. Phoenix	Cappie Pondexter, G	Rutgers	9. Indiana	La'Tangela Atkinson, G	Miami
3. Charlotte	Monique Currie, G-F	Duke	10. Charlotte	Tye'sha Fluker, C	Tennessee
4. San Antonio	Sophia Young, F	Baylor	11. Seattle	Barbara Turner, G	Connecticut
5. Los Angeles	Lisa Willis, G	UCLA	12. New York	Sherill Baker, G	Georgia
6. Chicago	Candice Dupree, G	Temple	13. Sacramento	Kim Smith, F	Utah
7. Minnesota	Shona Thorburn, G	Utah	14. Sacramento	Scholanda Hudson, G	LSU

KEY G=guard; F=forward; C=center

LEGENDS

Ruthie Bolton (right) was one of the WNBA's first All-Stars.

ROCKY WIDNER/WNBAE/GETTY IMAGES

■ **Ruthie Bolton, guard,** b. May 25, 1967, McClain, Mississippi. Bolton played eight seasons in the WNBA (1997–2004) and was selected to the All-WNBA First Team in 1997 and 1999. She averaged 10.0 points and 1.6 assists per game during her pro career. Bolton is a two-time Olympic gold medalist (1996 and 2000). She is currently the women's basketball coach at William Jessup University in Rocklin, California.

■ **Teresa Weatherspoon, guard,** b. December 8, 1965, Jasper, Texas. Known as a defensive wizard, T-Spoon was named the WNBA's Defensive Player of the Year in 1997 and 1998. The 5' 8" guard led the league in steals both seasons (3.04 per game in 1997 and 3.33 in 1998). Weatherspoon played college ball at Louisiana Tech. She led the Lady Techsters to an NCAA title in 1988, and won an Olympic gold medal that same year.

■ **Katrina McClain, forward,** b. September 19, 1965, Wichita, Kansas. A two-time All-America at Georgia (1985–86, 1986–87), McClain averaged 17.6 points per game during her four-year college career (1984–1987). She helped lead the U.S. Women's Olympic team to a gold medal in 1988 and 1996. McClain played professionally in the United States for one season with the Atlanta Glory of the American Basketball League (1997–98). She averaged a team-high 7.8 rebounds per game. Before that, she played pro ball overseas for nine seasons: in Japan, Italy, and Spain.

DID YOU KNOW?

The Western Conference has won eight of the nine WNBA championships. The Detroit Shock is the only Eastern team to win the title (2003).

2005-06 TIME LINE

■ **May 21, 2005:** Opening night of the WNBA season. In her first game with the Los Angeles Sparks, forward Chamique Holdsclaw scores 16 points and grabs 14 rebounds to lead the team over the defending champion Seattle Storm, 68–50.

■ **July 9, 2005:** The Western Conference wins the WNBA All-Star Game for the sixth straight season, defeating the Eastern Conference, 122–99. Forward Sheryl Swoopes of the Houston Comets scores 15 points for the West and is named the game's MVP.

■ **September 20, 2005:** The Sacramento Monarchs win their first WNBA championship by beating the Connecticut Sun, 62–59, in Game 4 of the Finals. Monarch forward/center Yolanda

Griffith scores 14 points and grabs 10 rebounds and is named MVP of the championship series.

■ **November 16, 2005:** The Chicago Sky, the WNBA's newest franchise, holds its expansion draft. The Sky selects one player from each of the 13 existing teams.

■ **April 5, 2006:** The Minnesota Lynx choose Seimone Augustus as the Number 1 pick in the WNBA Draft.

■ **May 3, 2006:** The WNBA tips off its 10th regular season with 14 teams.

TRIVIA CHALLENGE

True or False: Diana Taurasi of the Phoenix Mercury is the only player from the University of Connecticut to be selected with the first overall pick in the WNBA Draft.

False. Two Connecticut players have been picked first in the WNBA Draft: Diana Taurasi by the Phoenix Mercury (2004) and Sue Bird by the Seattle Storm (2002).

AWARD WINNERS

YEAR	MVP	ROOKIE	DEFENSIVE	IMPROVED	SPORTSMANSHIP	COACH
2005	Sheryl Swoopes	Temeka Johnson	Tamika Catchings	Nicole Powell	Taj McWilliams-Franklin	John Whisenant
2004	Lisa Leslie	Diana Taurasi	Lisa Leslie	Kelly Miller/ Wendy Palmer	Teresa Edwards	Susie McConnell Serio
2003	Lauren Jackson	Cheryl Ford	Sheryl Swoopes	Michelle Snow	Edna Campbell	Bill Laimbeer
2002	Sheryl Swoopes	Tamika Catchings	Sheryl Swoopes	Coco Miller	Jennifer Gillom	Marianne Stanley
2001	Lisa Leslie	Jackie Stiles	Debbie Black	Janeth Arcain	Sue Wicks	Dan Hughes
2000	Sheryl Swoopes	Betty Lennox	Sheryl Swoopes	Tari Phillips	Susie McConnell Serio	Michael Cooper
1999	Yolanda Griffith	Chamique Holdsclaw	Yolanda Griffith	N/A	Dawn Staley	Van Chancellor
1998	Cynthia Cooper	Tracy Reid	Teresa Weatherspoon	N/A	Susie McConnell Serio	Van Chancellor
1997	Cynthia Cooper	N/A	Teresa Weatherspoon	N/A	Haixia Zheng	Van Chancellor

NEWCOMER*

1998   Susie McConnell Serio

1999   Yolanda Griffith

*No longer awarded

Visit our website for the latest stats and sports info.

When the 2005-06 season began, the Florida Gators seemed to have as much chance of winning the national championship as a pack of real Florida alligators. But what the Gators lacked in talent, they more than made up for in teamwork. They shared the ball, shot 50 percent for the season, and played a defense that proved as fearsome as their nickname would suggest. They started the season by winning their first 17 games. They would finish the season winning 11 straight games, including six in the NCAA Tournament, and finish Number 1.

The Gators proved they were the best team the country in the post-season. But it was the debate over who was the best *player* in the country that dominated regular-season headlines. Duke's J.J. Redick and Gonzaga's Adam Morrison waged a back-and-forth, cross-country battle for both the scoring crown and National Player of the Year honors. Morrison won the scoring title at 28.1 points per game, besting Redicks's 26.8. Redick, however, was named National Player of the Year. He finished his career as the NCAA all-time leader in three-pointers.

Both players' teams went into the tournament ranked in the Top 5 in the nation. But neither reached the Final Four showdown many fans had been waiting for. Redick and the Blue Devils were upended in the Sweet 16 by Louisiana State. Morrison and the Bulldogs lost on the same night to UCLA, which stormed back from a 17-point deficit to win, 74–71.

George Mason University

Joakim Noah of Florida was named the Most Outstanding Player of the NCAA Tournament.

JOHN BIEVER

emerged as the Cinderella team of the tournament. The Patriots pulled some extra-large upsets. First, they picked off Final Four regular Michigan State and then toppled defending national champion North Carolina to reach the Sweet 16. After beating Wichita State, the undersized Patriots dumped tourney favorite Connecticut and its lineup of future NBA players.

For the first time since 1980 and only the second time ever, none of the four regional Number 1 seeds (Connecticut, Villanova, Duke, and Memphis) advanced to the Final Four.

Once the tournament moved on to the Final Four in Indianapolis, Indiana, some of the drama disappeared. Florida turned the Cinderella Patriots back into pumpkins, routing them, 73–58. UCLA reached its first final in 11 years with an easy win over the LSU Tigers. But the Bruins were no match for Florida's athleticism, stifling defense, and team play in the final. Florida jumped to a double-digit lead in the first half and coasted to a 73–57 victory. The Gators' remarkable journey from a team that was unranked to one that was unbeatable was complete.

NCAA MEN'S DIVISION I CHAMPIONSHIP BOX SCORE

FLORIDA GATORS: 73

PLAYER	POS	MIN	FG M-A	3-PT M-A	FT M-A	PF	PTS
Corey Brewer	F	37	4-12	2-3	1-3	3	11
Joakim Noah	F	33	7-9	0-0	2-2	2	16
Al Horford	C	24	5-8	0-0	4-5	2	14
Taurean Green	G	36	1-9	0-7	0-1	1	2
Lee Humphrey	G	36	4-8	4-8	3-3	1	15
Adrian Moss		10	3-6	0-0	3-4	0	9
Walter Hodge		12	0-3	0-1	0-0	1	0
Chris Richard		12	2-3	0-0	2-2	3	6
TOTALS			**26-58**	**6-19**	**15-20**	**13**	**73**
			(44.8%)	(75.0%)	(31.6%)		

UCLA BRUINS: 57

PLAYER	POS	MIN	FG M-A	3-PT M-A	FT M-A	PF	PTS
Cedric Bozeman	F	25	2-3	0-0	5-6	2	9
Luc Richard Mbah a Moute	F	32	3-9	0-2	0-0	4	6
Ryan Hollins	C	26	4-10	0-0	2-2	2	10
Jordan Farmar	G	34	8-21	1-8	1-2	2	18
Arron Afflalo	G	32	3-10	2-7	2-2	2	10
Darren Collison		21	0-3	0-0	0-0	3	0
Alfred Aboya		14	1-1	0-0	0-2	2	2
Lorenzo Mata		9	1-4	0-0	0-0	3	2
Michael Roll		7	0-0	0-0	0-0	2	0
TOTALS			**22-61**	**3-17**	**10-14**	**22**	**57**
			(36.1%)	(71.4%)	(17.6%)		

 KEY POS=position; MIN=minutes played; FG M-A=field goals made-attempted; 3-PT M-A=3-point field goals made-attempted; FT M-A=free throws made-attempted; PF=personal fouls; PTS=points; F=forward; G=guard; C=center

Guard Jordan Farmar led UCLA to the championship game.

DAVID GONZALES

USA TODAY/ESPN Coaches Top 25 Final Poll

RANK	SCHOOL	FINAL RECORD	POINTS
1	Florida	33-6	775
2	UCLA	32-7	739
3	LSU	27-9	666
4	Connecticut	30-4	658
5	Villanova	28-5	620
6	Memphis	33-4	607
7	Duke	32-4	585
8	George Mason	27-8	564
9	Texas	30-7	542
10	Gonzaga	29-4	503
11	Boston College	28-8	463
12	Washington	26-7	403
13	Ohio State	26-6	354
14	North Carolina	23-8	312
15	West Virginia	22-11	300
16	Georgetown	23-10	296
17	Illinois	26-7	261
18	Pittsburgh	25-8	247
19	George Washington	27-3	221
20	Tennessee	22-8	198
21	Wichita State	26-9	169
22	Kansas	25-8	155
23	Iowa	25-9	109
24	Bradley	22-11	106
25	Bucknell	27-5	51

TRIVIA CHALLENGE

At Number 11, George Mason tied for the lowest seed to reach a Final Four, matching the record set in 1986 by a team that also made the 2006 Final Four. Which team was it?

LSU

NCAA MEN'S DIVISION I INDIVIDUAL LEADERS

SCORING

PLAYER	CLASS	GP	FG	3FG	FT	PTS	AVG
Adam Morrison, Gonzaga	Jr.	33	306	74	240	926	28.1
J.J. Redick, Duke	Sr.	36	302	139	221	964	26.8
Keydren Clark, St. Peter's	Sr.	32	273	105	189	840	26.3
Andre Collins, Loyola	Sr.	28	256	118	101	731	26.1
Brion Rush, Grambling State	Sr.	21	189	54	109	541	25.8
Quincy Douby, Rutgers	Jr.	33	287	116	149	839	25.4
Steve Burtt, Iona	Sr.	31	258	96	168	780	25.2
Rodney Stuckey, Eastern Washington	So.	30	250	55	171	726	24.2
Alan Daniels, Lamar	Sr.	31	250	75	155	730	23.5
Trey Johnson, Jackson State	Sr.	32	255	67	174	751	23.5

KEY GP=games played; FG=field goals; 3FG=3-point field goals; FT=free throws; PTS=points; AVG=average; So.=sophomore; Jr.=junior; Sr.=senior

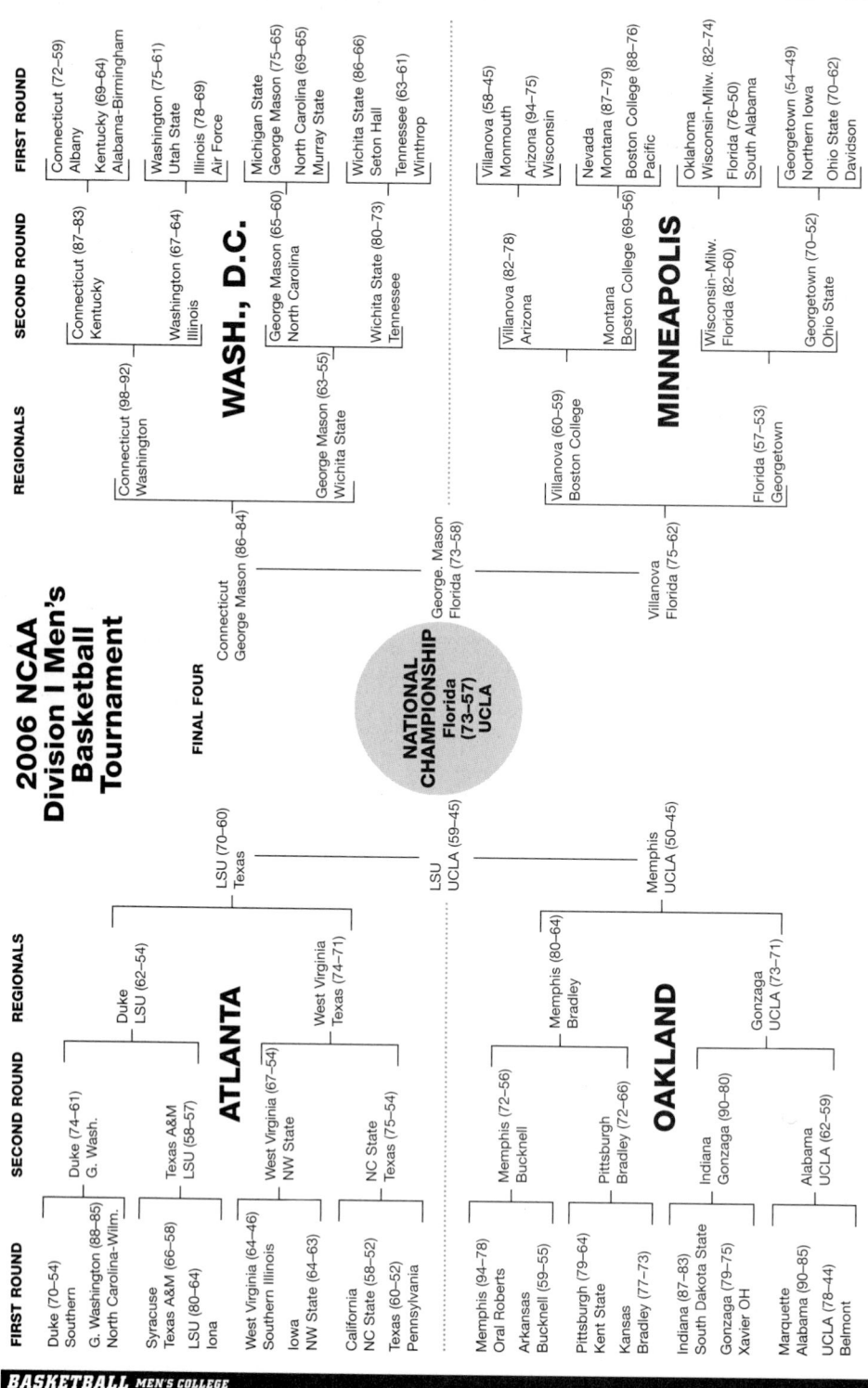

2006 NCAA Division I Men's Basketball Tournament

CHICAGO'S FINEST

The Chicago White Sox celebrated their first World Series championship since 1917. The Sox won 99 games in the regular season, breezed through the playoffs, and finished with a sweep of the Houston Astros in the World Series. Outfielder Jermaine Dye was named the Series' MVP.

DARREN CARROLL

MICHELLE'S MOVE

Michelle Wie showed that she could compete with the best women golfers in the world, and challenge the men, too. In June 2005, she finished second to Annika Sorenstam at the LPGA Championship. In July, she just missed the cut in the PGA's John Deere Classic (she also had just missed the cut in the men's Sony Open in January). On October 5, Wie turned pro — six days before her 16th birthday. Since then, she's signed endorsement contracts worth more than $10 million a year.

DUNKIN' DUNCAN

Forward/center Tim Duncan led the San Antonio Spurs to their second title in three years. Duncan was MVP of the NBA Finals, as the Spurs defeated the defending champion Detroit Pistons in seven games. For the regular season, Duncan averaged 20.3 points and 11.1 rebounds, and was voted an NBA All-Star for the seventh time in eight seasons.

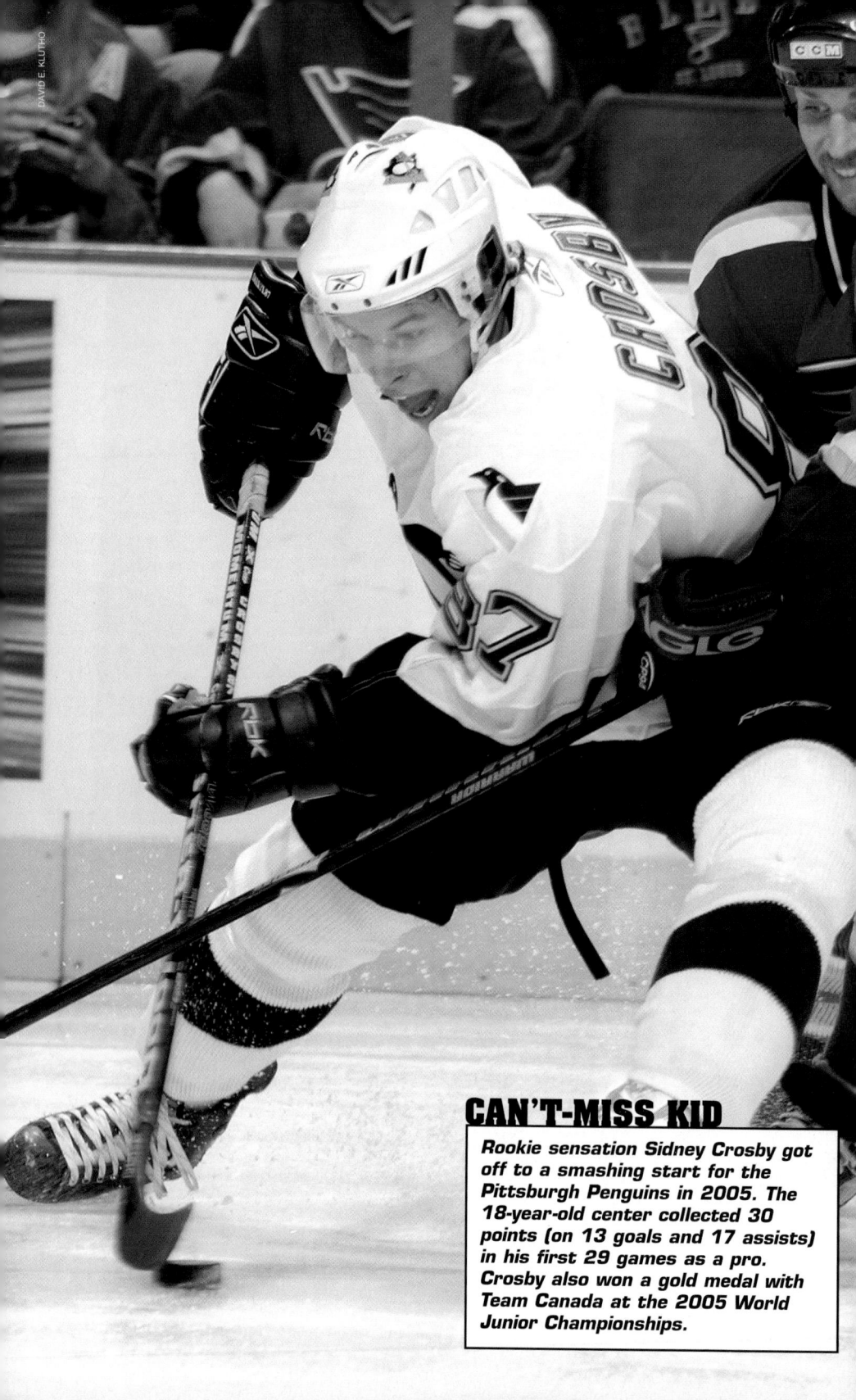

CAN'T-MISS KID

Rookie sensation Sidney Crosby got off to a smashing start for the Pittsburgh Penguins in 2005. The 18-year-old center collected 30 points (on 13 goals and 17 assists) in his first 29 games as a pro. Crosby also won a gold medal with Team Canada at the 2005 World Junior Championships.

MAKING WAVES

In 2004, 22-year-old Sofia Mulanovich became the first South American to be named world champion of the Association of Surfing Professionals (ASP). In 2005, the 5' 3" native of Peru kept up her winning ways, finishing second to Chelsea Georgeson of Australia for the ASP crown.

HAPPY LANDON

Landon Donovan led the
Los Angeles Galaxy to their
second Major League
Soccer championship in
2005. Donovan had
returned to play in the U.S.
after a year with Bayer
Leverkusen in the German
Bundesliga. He led the
Galaxy in the regular
season in both goals and
assists, despite missing 10
games because of national
team duty and illness.
Donovan led the league in
game-winning goals, with
seven.

TIGER'S TALE

Tiger Woods was named PGA Tour Player of the Year in 2005 for the seventh time in his nine-year career. He won six tournaments, including his fourth Masters and his second British Open. He had the lowest scoring average on the tour, 68.66 strokes per round.

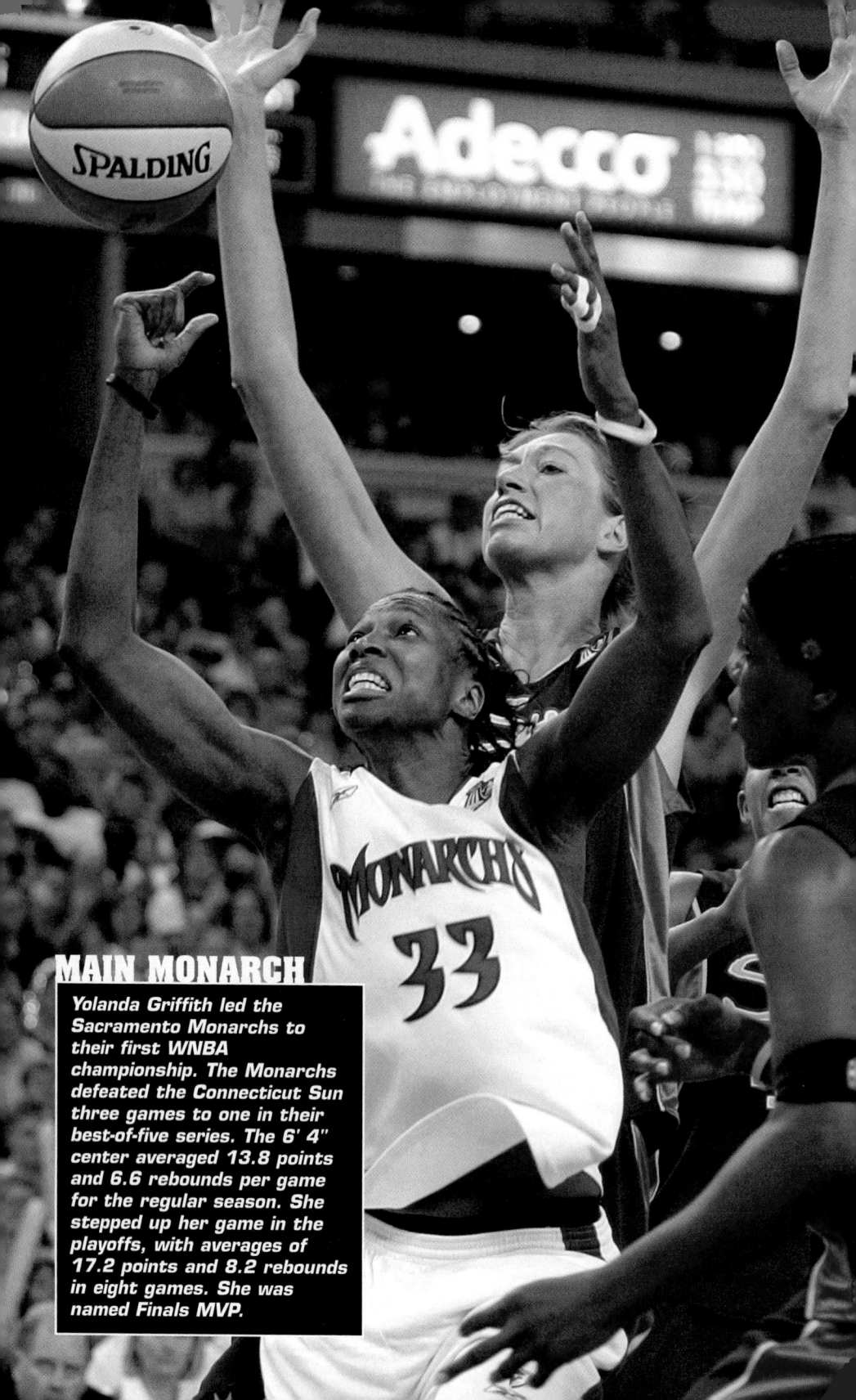

MAIN MONARCH

Yolanda Griffith led the Sacramento Monarchs to their first WNBA championship. The Monarchs defeated the Connecticut Sun three games to one in their best-of-five series. The 6' 4" center averaged 13.8 points and 6.6 rebounds per game for the regular season. She stepped up her game in the playoffs, with averages of 17.2 points and 8.2 rebounds in eight games. She was named Finals MVP.

TROJAN HORSE

University of Southern California running back Reggie Bush took home the Heisman Trophy in 2005 as the best player in college football. Bush ran up 1,740 yards on 8.7 yards per carry. He caught 37 passes for another 478 yards, and scored a total of 18 touchdowns. Bush led the Trojans to a 12-1 record. Their only loss came in the national championship game to the University of Texas in the Rose Bowl.

SUPER SENIOR

After leading the University of Illinois to the Final Four in 2004-05, guard Dee Brown returned to school for his senior year and played even better. The 6' 0" guard averaged 14.1 points and 4.8 assists per game as the Illini jumped out to nine straight wins to start the 2005-06 season.

RARE AIR

Skateboarder Danny Way made history in July 2005, getting major air over the Ju Yong Guan Gate of the Great Wall of China. Dropping in from a 65-foot-high super ramp, Way landed five jumps across the 70-foot gap, including three backside 360s. In August, he successfully defended his X Games gold medal in Skateboard Big Air.

CHAIRMAN OF THE BOARD

Already the only athlete to medal at both the Summer and Winter X Games, Shaun White added an Olympic medal to his collection in 2006. The 19-year-old snowboarder (and skateboarder) won the gold medal in Halfpipe at the Winter Olympics in Turin, Italy. In January, White won his fourth straight gold medal in Slopestyle and his second gold medal in Superpipe at the 2006 Winter X Games.

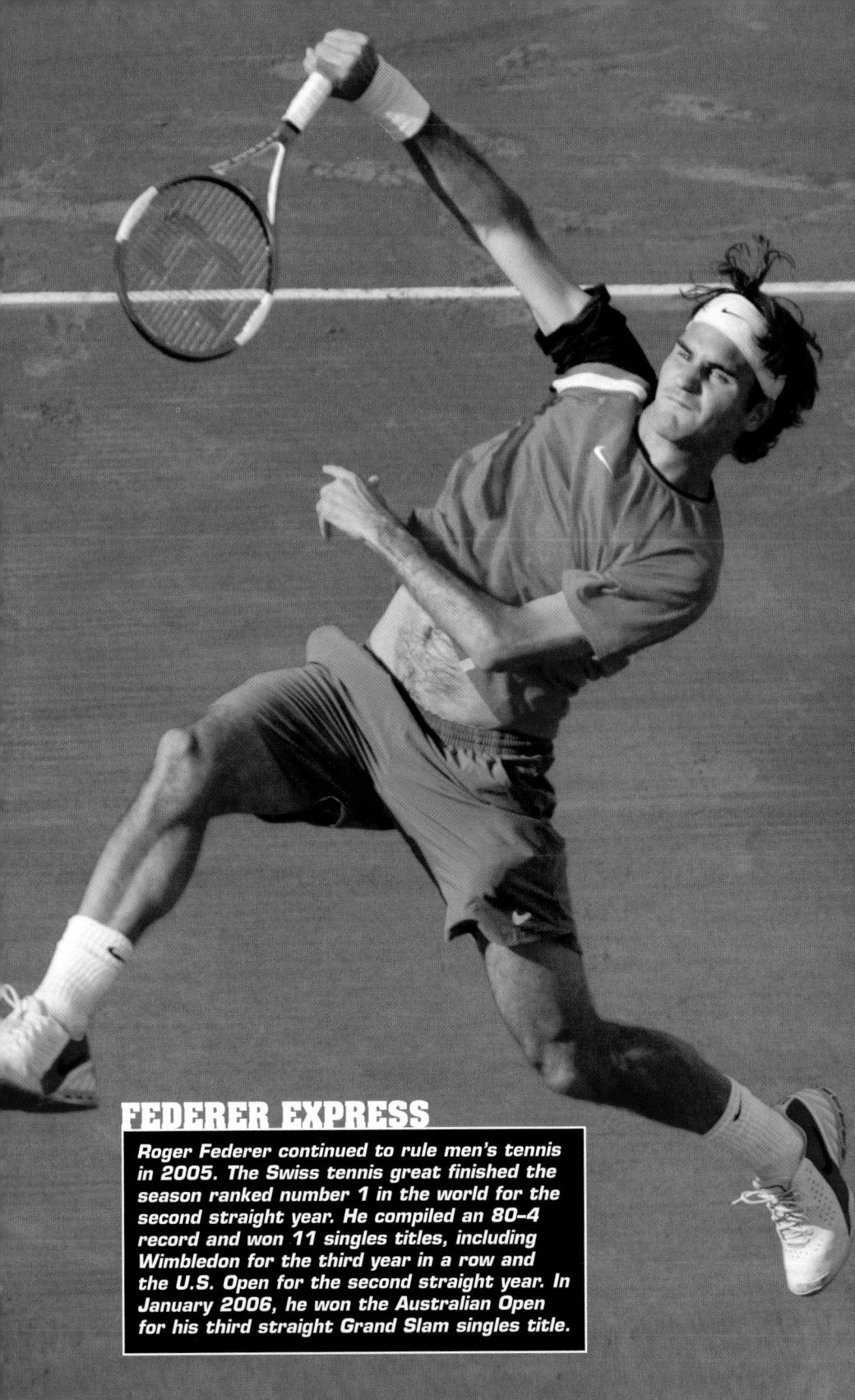

FEDERER EXPRESS

Roger Federer continued to rule men's tennis in 2005. The Swiss tennis great finished the season ranked number 1 in the world for the second straight year. He compiled an 80–4 record and won 11 singles titles, including Wimbledon for the third year in a row and the U.S. Open for the second straight year. In January 2006, he won the Australian Open for his third straight Grand Slam singles title.

SHE'S ALL THAT

Candace Parker was the only two-time USA Today National High School Player of the Year in the award's history. She enrolled at the University of Tennessee, but missed the 2004-05 college basketball season because of knee surgery. As a redshirt freshman, the 6' 3" forward has been magical for the Lady Volunteers. Through the first eight games of the 2005-06 season, she was averaging 16.3 points and 9.8 rebounds per game.

STEADY STEWART

Tony Stewart captured his second career Nextel Cup Championship in 2005, becoming the 14th driver in NASCAR history to win the season title more than once. Stewart won five races during the year, but it was his overall consistency that won him the second-ever Chase for the Championship. In the final 22 races on the schedule, he finished in the top 10 a whopping 19 times.

POOL SHARK

In 2004, Katie Hoff was the youngest member of the U.S. Olympic swimming team (age 15). In 2005, she became one of the U.S. team's brightest stars. Hoff won three gold medals at the World Championships, in Montreal, Canada. She set an American record in the 200-meter individual medley and championship records in the 400-meter individual medley and as a member of the 800-meter freestyle relay team.

MAN OF STEEL

Led by wide receiver Hines Ward, the Pittsburgh Steelers defeated the Seattle Seahawks, 21–10, in Super Bowl XL. Ward was the game's MVP. He caught five passes for 123 yards and this touchdown — on a trick-play from fellow receiver Antwaan Randle El. The victory capped an amazing late-season drive by the Steelers, who looked like they would miss the playoffs as late as December.

NCAA MEN'S DIVISION I INDIVIDUAL LEADERS (cont.)

FIELD GOAL PERCENTAGE

PLAYER	CLASS	GP	FGM	FGA	PCT
Randall Hanke, Providence	So.	27	149	220	67.7
Cedric Smith, Texas A&M-Corpus Christi	Jr.	27	139	210	66.2
Brian Thornton, Xavier	Sr.	21	114	178	64.0
Joakim Noah, Florida	So.	39	202	322	62.7
James Augustine, Illinois	Sr.	33	174	279	62.4
Michael Harrison, Colorado State	Jr.	31	160	257	62.3
Kyle Hines, North Carolina-Greensboro	So.	30	239	384	62.2
Nate Harris, Utah State	Sr.	32	215	346	62.1
Eric Williams, Wake Forest	Sr.	34	223	360	61.9
Kibwe Trim, Sacred Heart	Sr.	28	194	314	61.8

Note: Minimum five field goals made per game.

FREE THROW PERCENTAGE

PLAYER	CLASS	GP	FTM	FTA	PCT
Blake Ahearn, Missouri State	Jr.	31	117	125	93.6
Jermaine Anderson, New Hampshire	Jr.	26	68	74	91.9
Shawan Robinson, Clemson	Sr.	32	84	92	91.3
Derek Raivio, Gonzaga	Jr.	31	83	91	91.2
Adam Vogelsberg, Middle Tennessee State	Jr.	28	108	119	90.8
Gerry McNamara, Syracuse	Sr.	35	111	123	90.2
Andre Collins, Loyola (Maryland)	Sr.	28	101	112	90.2
Chris Hernandez, Stanford	Sr.	30	109	121	90.1
Daniel Horton, Michigan	Sr.	33	136	151	90.1
Walker Russell, Jacksonville State	Sr.	29	112	125	89.6

Note: Minimum 2.5 free throws made per game.

REBOUNDING

PLAYER	CLASS	GP	REB	AVG
Paul Millsap, Louisiana Tech	Jr.	33	438	13.3
Kenny Adeleke, Hartford	Sr.	28	366	13.1
Curtis Withers, Charlotte	Sr.	32	362	11.3
Yemi Nicholson, Denver	Sr.	31	339	10.9
Shelden Williams, Duke	Sr.	33	384	10.7
Aaron Gray, Pittsburgh	Jr.	33	345	10.5
Nick Fazekas, Nevada	Jr.	33	342	10.4
Glen Davis, LSU	So.	36	350	9.7
P.J. Tucker, Texas	Jr.	37	353	9.5
LaMarcus Aldridge, Texas	So.	37	339	9.2

ASSISTS

PLAYER	CLASS	GP	A	APG
Marcus Williams, Connecticut	Jr.	23	198	8.6
Jared Jordan, Marist	Jr.	29	247	8.5
Jose Juan Barea, Northeastern	Sr.	29	244	8.4
Terrell Everett, Oklahoma	Sr.	29	199	6.9
Walker Russell, Jacksonville State	Sr.	29	197	6.8
Kenny Grant, Davidson	Sr.	31	208	6.7
Bobby Dixon, Troy	Sr.	29	192	6.6

Marcus Williams, Connecticut

3-POINT FIELD GOAL PERCENTAGE

PLAYER	CLASS	GP	3FGM	3FGA	PCT
Juma Kamara, Portland State	Sr.	28	48	91	52.7
Steven Sir, Northern Arizona	Sr.	32	93	190	48.9
Steve Barnes, Southern Utah	Jr.	30	45	92	48.9
Dan Nwaelele, Air Force	Jr.	31	67	139	48.2
Brock Reichner, Brigham Young	Sr.	29	53	110	48.2

Note: Minimum 2.5 three-point field goals made per game.

KEY GP=games played; FGM=field goals made; FGA=field goals attempted; PCT=percentage; FTM=free throws made; FTA=free throws attempted; REB=rebounds; AVG=average; A=assists; APG=assists per game; 3FGM=3-point field goals made; 3FGA=3-point field goals attempted

NCAA MEN'S DIVISION I INDIVIDUAL LEADERS (cont.)

STEALS

PLAYER	CLASS	GP	STL	SPG
Tim Smith, East Tennessee State	Sr.	28	95	3.4
Oliver Lafayette, Houston	Jr.	31	105	3.4
Obie Trotter, Alabama A&M	Sr.	26	87	3.3
Ibrahim Jaaber, Pennsylvania	Jr.	29	96	3.3
Kevin Hamilton, Holy Cross	Sr.	31	102	3.3

BLOCKS

Oliver Lafayette, Houston

PLAYER	CLASS	GP	BLK	BPG
Shawn James, Northeastern	So.	30	196	6.5
Justin Williams, Wyoming	Sr.	30	163	5.4
Stephane Lasme, Massachusetts	Jr.	28	108	3.9
Shelden Williams, Duke	Sr.	36	137	3.8

NELSON CHENAULT/US PRESSWIRE

KEY GP=games played; STL=steals; SPG=steals per game; BLK=blocks; BPG=blocks per game

DID YOU KNOW?

Florida became just the seventh school to have won a national championship in both football and men's basketball. The others are Maryland, Michigan, Michigan State, Ohio State, Syracuse, and UCLA.

2005-06 TIME LINE

■ **November 22, 2005:** In the year's best regular-season game, Number 8 Gonzaga needs three overtimes to defeat Number 12 Michigan State at the Maui Invitational in Hawaii. Adam Morrison scores 43 points in the Bulldogs' 109–106 win.

■ **December 10, 2005:** The National Player of the Year race between Morrison and Duke senior guard J.J. Redick takes off. Hours after Redick scores 41 points to lead Duke to a 97–66 romp over Texas, Morrison banks in a three-pointer with 2.5 seconds left to beat Oklahoma State, 64–62.

■ **January 21, 2006:** The nation's three remaining unbeaten teams all lose on the same day to unranked teams. Number 1 Duke is stunned at Georgetown, Number 2 Florida falls at Tennessee, and Number 9 Pittsburgh loses at St. John's.

■ **February 14, 2006:** : Redick sets the NCAA record by making his 414th career three-pointer in the Blue Devils' 93–70 win over Wake Forest. He finishes his career with 457 threes.

■ **March 11, 2006:** Behind the spectacular play of tournament MVP Gerry McNamara, Syracuse wins the Big East tournament by toppling Pittsburgh, 65–61. The Orange entered the tournament unlikely to receive an invitation to the NCAA Tournament, but win four games in four days to capture the league's automatic bid.

■ **March 26, 2006:** George Mason continues its Cinderella run through the NCAA Tournament, beating top seed Connecticut, 86–84, in overtime to win the Washington, D.C. Region. The Patriots are the first team from a mid-major conference to reach the Final Four since 1979.

■ **March 30, 2006:** South Carolina defeats Michigan, 76–64, to win the National Invitation Tournament (NIT). The Gamecocks become the first team since St. John's in 1943-1944 to win back-to-back NIT championships.

■ **April 1, 2006:** UCLA advances to its record 13th national championship game by beating LSU, 59–45. The Bruins will play Florida, who stop George Mason, 73–58.

■ **April 3, 2006:** Led by Most Outstanding Player Joakim Noah (16 points, 9 rebounds, and a championship-game record 6 blocks), the Florida Gators win their first national championship in men's basketball, cruising past UCLA, 73–57. The Gators win their six tournament games by an average of 16 points.

NCAA MEN'S DIVISION I CHAMPIONSHIP RESULTS

YEAR	WINNER	SCORE	RUNNER-UP	THIRD PLACE	FOURTH PLACE	WINNING COACH
2006	Florida	75-57	UCLA	* George Mason	* LSU	Billy Donovan
2005	North Carolina	75-70	Illinois	* Michigan State	* Louisville	Roy Williams
2004	Connecticut	82-73	Georgia Tech	* Duke	* Oklahoma State	Jim Calhoun
2003	Syracuse	81-78	Kansas	* Texas	* Marquette	Jim Boeheim
2002	Maryland	64-52	Indiana	* Kansas	* Oklahoma	Gary Williams
2001	Duke	82-72	Arizona	* Maryland	* Michigan State	Mike Krzyzewski
2000	Michigan St.	89-76	Florida	* Wisconsin	* North Carolina	Tom Izzo
1999	Connecticut	77-74	Duke	* Michigan St.	* Ohio State	Jim Calhoun
1998	Kentucky	78-69	Utah	* Stanford	* North Carolina	Tubby Smith
1997	Arizona	84-79 (OT)	Kentucky	* Minnesota	* North Carolina	Lute Olson
1996	Kentucky	76-67	Syracuse	‡ Vacated	Mississippi State	Rick Pitino
1995	UCLA	89-78	Arkansas	* North Carolina	* Oklahoma State	Jim Harrick
1994	Arkansas	76-72	Duke	* Arizona	* Florida	Nolan Richardson
1993	North Carolina	77-71	‡Vacated	* Kansas	* Kentucky	Dean Smith
1992	Duke	71-51	‡Vacated	* Cincinnati	* Indiana	Mike Krzyzewski
1991	Duke	72-65	Kansas	* Nevada-Las Vegas	* North Carolina	Mike Krzyzewski
1990	Nevada-Las Vegas	103-73	Duke	* Arkansas	* Georgia Tech	Jerry Tarkanian
1989	Michigan	80-79 (OT)	Seton Hall	* Duke	* Illinois	Steve Fisher
1988	Kansas	83-79	Oklahoma	* Arizona	* Duke	Larry Brown
1987	Indiana	74-73	Syracuse	* Nevada-Las Vegas	* Providence	Bobby Knight
1986	Louisville	72-69	Duke	* Kansas	* Louisiana State	Denny Crum
1985	Villanova	66-64	Georgetown	St. John's (N.Y.)	‡ Vacated	Rollie Massimino
1984	Georgetown	84-75	Houston	* Kentucky	* Virginia	John Thompson
1983	North Carolina State	54-52	Houston	* Georgia	* Louisville	Jim Valvano
1982	North Carolina	63-62	Georgetown	* Houston	* Louisville	Dean Smith
1981	Indiana	63-50	North Carolina	Virginia	Louisiana State	Bobby Knight
1980	Louisville	59-54	‡Vacated	Purdue	Iowa	Denny Crum
1979	Michigan State	75-64	Indiana St.	DePaul	Penn	Jud Heathcote
1978	Kentucky	94-88	Duke	Arkansas	Notre Dame	Joe Hall
1977	Marquette	67-59	North Carolina	Nevada-Las Vegas	North Carolina-Charlotte	Al McGuire
1976	Indiana	86-68	Michigan	UCLA	Rutgers	Bobby Knight
1975	UCLA	92-85	Kentucky	Louisville	Syracuse	John Wooden
1974	North Carolina State	76-64	Marquette	UCLA	Kansas	Norm Sloan
1973	UCLA	87-66	Memphis St.	Indiana	Providence	John Wooden
1972	UCLA	81-76	Florida St.	North Carolina	Louisville	John Wooden
1971	UCLA	68-62	‡Vacated	‡Vacated	Kansas	John Wooden
1970	UCLA	80-69	Jacksonville	New Mexico State	St. Bonaventure	John Wooden
1969	UCLA	92-72	Purdue	Drake	North Carolina	John Wooden
1968	UCLA	78-55	North Carolina	Ohio State	Houston	John Wooden
1967	UCLA	79-64	Dayton	Houston	North Carolina	John Wooden
1966	Texas Western	72-65	Kentucky	Duke	Utah	Don Haskins
1965	UCLA	91-80	Michigan	Princeton	Wichita State	John Wooden
1964	UCLA	98-83	Duke	Michigan	Kansas State	John Wooden
1963	Loyola (Illinois)	60-58 (OT)	Cincinnati	Duke	Oregon State	George Ireland
1962	Cincinnati	71-59	Ohio St.	Wake Forest	UCLA	Edwin Jucker
1961	Cincinnati	70-65 (OT)	Ohio St.	‡Vacated	Utah	Edwin Jucker
1960	Ohio State	75-55	California	Cincinnati	NYU	Fred Taylor
1959	California	71-70	West Virginia	Cincinnati	Louisville	Pete Newell
1958	Kentucky	84-72	Seattle	Temple	Kansas State	Adolph Rupp
1957	North Carolina	54-53 (3 OT)	Kansas	San Francisco	Michigan State	Frank McGuire
1956	San Francisco	83-71	Iowa	Temple	SMU	Phil Woolpert
1955	San Francisco	77-63	La Salle	Colorado	Iowa	Phil Woolpert
1954	La Salle	92-76	Bradley	Penn State	USC	Kenneth Loeffler
1953	Indiana	69-68	Kansas	Washington	Louisiana State	Branch McCracken
1952	Kansas	80-63	St. John's (N.Y.)	Illinois	Santa Clara	Forrest Allen
1951	Kentucky	68-58	Kansas St.	Illinois	Oklahoma State	Adolph Rupp
1950	City College of N.Y.	71-68	Bradley	North Carolina State	Baylor	Nat Holman
1949	Kentucky	46-36	Oklahoma St.	Illinois	Oregon State	Adolph Rupp
1948	Kentucky	58-42	Baylor	Holy Cross	Kansas State	Adolph Rupp
1947	Holy Cross	58-47	Oklahoma	Texas	City College of N.Y.	Alvin Julian
1946	Oklahoma A&M	43-40	North Carolina	Ohio St.	California	Hank Iba
1945	Oklahoma A&M	49-45	NYU	* Arkansas	* Ohio State	Hank Iba
1944	Utah	42-40 (OT)	Dartmouth	* Iowa State	* Ohio State	Vadal Peterson
1943	Wyoming	46-34	Georgetown	* Texas	* DePaul	Everett Shelton
1942	Stanford	53-38	Dartmouth	* Colorado	* Kentucky	Everett Dean
1941	Wisconsin	39-34	Washington St.	* Pittsburgh	* Arkansas	Harold Foster
1940	Indiana	60-42	Kansas	* Duquesne	* USC	Branch McCracken
1939	Oregon	46-33	Ohio St.	* Oklahoma	* Villanova	Howard Hobson

* Tied for third place. ‡Student-athletes representing St. Joseph's (Pennsylvania) in 1961, Villanova in 1971, Western Kentucky in 1971, UCLA in 1980, Memphis State in 1985, Michigan in 1992 and 1993, and Massachusetts in 1996 were declared ineligible subsequent to the tournament. Under NCAA rules, the teams' and ineligible student-athletes' records were deleted, and the teams' places in the standings were vacated.

TODAY'S STARS

■ **Tyler Hansbrough, forward,** b. November 3, 1985, Poplar Bluff, Missouri. This freshman helped keep the Tar Heels among the nation's elite in 2006, despite losing their top seven scorers from the 2005 title team. Known for his furious playing style, Hansbrough became a first-team All-ACC and third-team All-America performer. He was named National Freshman of the Year after becoming the first frosh to lead the Tar Heels in both scoring (18.9 points per game) and rebounding (7.8 per game). He helped the Heels to a second place finish in the Atlantic Coast Conference and a Top 10 final ranking

Tyler Hansbrough was an All-America as a freshman.

BOB ROSATO

■ **Joakim Noah, forward,** b. February 25, 1985, New York, New York. In his freshman season, Noah was best known as the ponytail-wearing son of tennis Hall of Famer Yannick Noah. But he became a starter as a sophomore and emerged as a force. Entering the NCAA Tournament, he led the team in points (13.8) and blocks (2.0) and was second in rebounds (6.7). But in the Big Dance, no one was bigger than Noah. His numbers spiked to 16.1 points, 9.5 rebounds, and 4.8 blocks. He was an easy choice for the tounament's Most Outstanding Player award.

■ **Glen Davis, forward,** b. January 1, 1986, Baton Rouge, Louisiana. Davis spent most of his sophomore season insisting he was not another Shaquille O'Neal but playing like him anyway. However, Davis did something Shaq never did: He took the Tigers to the Final Four. At 6'9", 315 pounds, "Big Baby" used his size and strength to lead the Southeast Conference in scoring (18.6) and rebounding (9.7) per game. He was voted the SEC Player of the Year one season after being named the league's Freshman of the Year.

NCAA FINAL FOUR MOST OUTSTANDING PLAYERS

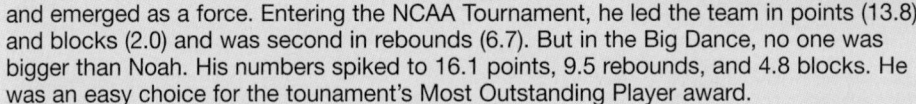

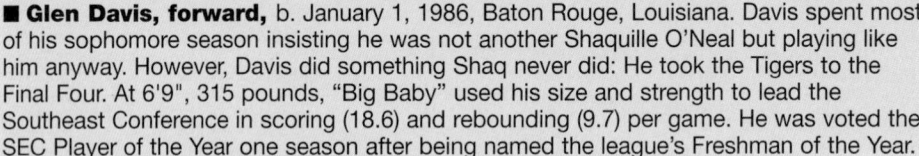

YEAR	WINNER, SCHOOL	YEAR	WINNER, SCHOOL	YEAR	WINNER, SCHOOL
2006	Joakim Noah, Florida	1982	James Worthy, North Carolina	1958	* Elgin Baylor, Seattle
2005	Sean May, North Carolina	1981	Isiah Thomas, Indiana	1957	* Wilt Chamberlain, Kansas
2004	Emeka Okafor, Connecticut	1980	Darrell Griffith, Louisville	1956	* Hal Lear, Temple
2003	Carmelo Anthony, Syracuse	1979	Earvin Johnson, Michigan State	1955	Bill Russell, San Francisco
2002	Juan Dixon, Maryland	1978	Jack Givens, Kentucky	1954	Tom Gola, La Salle
2001	Shane Battier, Duke	1977	Butch Lee, Marquette	1953	* B.H. Born, Kansas
2000	Mateen Cleaves, Michigan State	1976	Kent Benson, Indiana	1952	Clyde Lovellette, Kansas
1999	Richard Hamilton, Connecticut	1975	Richard Washington, UCLA	1951	Bill Spivey, Kentucky
1998	Jeff Sheppard, Kentucky	1974	David Thompson, North Carolina State	1950	Irwin Dambrot, CCNY
1997	Miles Simon, Arizona	1973	Bill Walton, UCLA	1949	Alex Groza, Kentucky
1996	Tony Delk, Kentucky	1972	Bill Walton, UCLA	1948	Alex Groza, Kentucky
1995	Ed O'Bannon, UCLA	1971	*† Howard Porter, Villanova	1947	George Kaftan, Holy Cross
1994	Corliss Williamson, Arkansas	1970	Sidney Wicks, UCLA	1946	Bob Kurland, Oklahoma A&M
1993	Donald Williams, North Carolina	1969	** Lew Alcindor, UCLA	1945	Bob Kurland, Oklahoma A&M
1992	Bobby Hurley, Duke	1968	** Lew Alcindor, UCLA	1944	Arnie Ferrin, Utah
1991	Christian Laettner, Duke	1967	** Lew Alcindor, UCLA	1943	Ken Sailors, Wyoming
1990	Anderson Hunt, UNLV	1966	* Jerry Chambers, Utah	1942	Howard Dallmar, Stanford
1989	Glen Rice, Michigan	1965	* Bill Bradley, Princeton	1941	John Kotz, Wisconsin
1988	Danny Manning, Kansas	1964	Walt Hazzard, UCLA	1940	Marv Huffman, Indiana
1987	Keith Smart, Indiana	1963	Art Heyman, Duke	1939	* Jimmy Hull, Ohio State
1986	Pervis Ellison, Louisville	1962	Paul Hogue, Cincinnati		
1985	Ed Pinckney, Villanova	1961	* Jerry Lucas, Ohio State		* Not a member of the championship-winning team.
1984	Patrick Ewing, Georgetown	1960	Jerry Lucas, Ohio State		† Record later vacated.
1983	* Akeem Olajuwon, Houston	1959	* Jerry West, West Virginia		** Now known as Kareem Abdul-Jabbar.

FAST FACT

In 2006, Florida and LSU of the Southeastern Conference both advanced to Indianapolis. That made eight straight years that at least two teams from the same conference reached the Final Four.

YEAR	WINNER	SCORE	RUNNER-UP	YEAR	WINNER	SCORE	RUNNER-UP
2006	South Carolina	76–64	Michigan	1971	North Carolina	84–66	Georgia Tech
2005	South Carolina	60–57	St. Joseph's	1970	Marquette	65–53	St. John's (N.Y.)
2004	Michigan	62–55	Rutgers	1969	Temple	89–76	Boston College
2003	St. John's (N.Y.)	70–67	Georgetown	1968	Dayton	61–48	Kansas
2002	Memphis	72–62	South Carolina	1967	Southern Illinois	71–56	Marquette
2001	Tulsa	79–60	Alabama	1966	Brigham Young	97–84	NYU
2000	Wake Forest	71–61	Notre Dame	1965	St. John's (N.Y.)	55–51	Villanova
1999	California	61–60	Clemson	1964	Bradley	86–54	New Mexico
1998	Minnesota	79–72	Penn State	1963	Providence	81–66	Canisius
1997	Michigan	82–73	Florida State	1962	Dayton	73–67	St. John's (N.Y.)
1996	Nebraska	60–56	St. Joseph's	1961	Providence	62–59	St. Louis
1995	Virginia Tech	65–64 (OT)	Marquette	1960	Bradley	88–72	Providence
1994	Villanova	80–73	Vanderbilt	1959	St. John's (N.Y.)	76–71 (OT)	Bradley
1993	Minnesota	62–61	Georgetown	1958	Xavier	78–74 (OT)	Dayton
1992	Virginia	81–76	Notre Dame	1957	Bradley	84–83	Memphis State
1991	Stanford	78–72	Oklahoma	1956	Louisville	93–80	Dayton
1990	Vanderbilt	74–72	St. Louis	1955	Duquesne	70–58	Dayton
1989	St. John's (N.Y.)	73–65	St. Louis	1954	Holy Cross	71–62	Duquesne
1988	Connecticut	72–67	Ohio State	1953	Seton Hall	58–46	St. John's (N.Y.)
1987	Southern Miss.	84–80	La Salle	1952	La Salle	75–64	Dayton
1986	Ohio State	73–63	Wyoming	1951	BYU	62–43	Dayton
1985	UCLA	65–62	Indiana	1950	CCNY	69–61	Bradley
1984	Michigan	83–63	Notre Dame	1949	San Francisco	48–47	Loyola (Illinois)
1983	Fresno State	69–60	DePaul	1948	St. Louis	65–52	NYU
1982	Bradley	67–58	Purdue	1947	Utah	49–45	Kentucky
1981	Tulsa	86–84 (OT)	Syracuse	1946	Kentucky	46–45	Rhode Island
1980	Virginia	58–55	Minnesota	1945	DePaul	71–54	Bowling Green
1979	Indiana	53–52	Purdue	1944	St. John's (N.Y.)	47–39	DePaul
1978	Texas	101–93	North Carolina State	1943	St. John's (N.Y.)	48–27	Toledo
1977	St. Bonaventure	94–91	Houston	1942	West Virginia	47–45	Western Kentucky
1976	Kentucky	71–67	North Carolina-Charlotte	1941	Long Island Univ.	56–42	Ohio University
1975	Princeton	80–69	Providence	1940	Colorado	51–40	Duquesne
1974	Purdue	87–81	Utah	1939	Long Island Univ.	44–32	Loyola (Illinois)
1973	Virginia Tech	92–91 (OT)	Notre Dame	1938	Temple	60–36	Colorado
1972	Maryland	100–69	Niagara				

POINTS

PLAYER	YEAR	GP	FG	3FG	FT	PTS
Pete Maravich, LSU	1970	31	522	—	337	1,381
Elvin Hayes, Houston	1968	33	519	—	176	1,214
Frank Selvy, Furman	1954	29	427	—	355	1,209
Pete Maravich, LSU	1969	26	433	—	282	1,148
Pete Maravich, LSU	1968	26	432	—	274	1,138
Bo Kimble, Loyola Marymount	1990	32	404	92	231	1,131
Hersey Hawkins, Bradley	1988	31	377	87	284	1,125
Austin Carr, Notre Dame	1970	29	444	—	218	1,106
Austin Carr, Notre Dame	1971	29	430	—	241	1,101
Otis Birdsong, Houston	1977	36	452	—	186	1,090

**Bo Kimble,
Loyola Marymount**

SCORING AVERAGE

PLAYER	YEAR	GP	FG	FT	PTS	AVG
Pete Maravich, LSU	1970	31	522	337	1,381	44.5
Pete Maravich, LSU	1969	26	433	282	1,148	44.2
Pete Maravich, LSU	1968	26	432	274	1,138	43.8
Frank Selvy, Furman	1954	29	427	355	1,209	41.7
Johnny Neumann, Mississippi	1971	23	366	191	923	40.1

ANDY HAYT

KEY GP=games played; FG=field goals; 3FG=3-point field goals; FT=free throws; PTS=points; AVG=average

DID YOU KNOW?

J.J. Redick became the fourth Duke player in the past eight seasons to be named National Player of the Year. The others are Elton Brand (1999), Shane Battier (2001), and Jason Williams (2002).

NCAA MEN'S DIVISION I SINGLE-SEASON LEADERS (cont.)

SCORING AVERAGE (CONT.)

PLAYER	YEAR	GP	FG	FT	PTS	AVG
Freeman Williams, Portland State	1977	26	417	176	1,010	38.8
Billy McGill, Utah	1962	26	394	221	1,009	38.8
Calvin Murphy, Niagara	1968	24	337	242	916	38.2
Austin Carr, Notre Dame	1970	29	444	218	1,106	38.1
Austin Carr, Notre Dame	1971	29	430	241	1,101	38.0

REBOUND AVERAGE (BEFORE 1973)

PLAYER	YEAR	GP	REB	AVG
Charlie Slack, Marshall	1955	21	538	25.6
Leroy Wright, Pacific	1959	26	652	25.1
Art Quimby, Connecticut	1955	25	611	24.4
Charlie Slack, Marshall	1956	22	520	23.6
Ed Conlin, Fordham	1953	26	612	23.5

REBOUND AVERAGE (SINCE 1973*)

PLAYER	YEAR	GP	REB	AVG
Kermit Washington, American	1973	25	511	20.4
Marvin Barnes, Providence	1973	30	571	19.0
Marvin Barnes, Providence	1974	32	597	18.7
Pete Padgett, Nevada	1973	26	462	17.8
Jim Bradley, Northern Illinois	1973	24	426	17.8

*Freshmen became eligible for varsity play before the 1972-73 season.

ASSISTS

PLAYER	YEAR	GP	A
Mark Wade, Nevada-Las Vegas	1987	38	406
Avery Johnson, Southern University	1988	30	399
Anthony Manuel, Bradley	1988	31	373
Avery Johnson, Southern University	1987	31	333
Mark Jackson, St. John's (N.Y.)	1986	32	328

FIELD GOAL PERCENTAGE

PLAYER	YEAR	FGM	FGA	PCT
Steve Johnson, Oregon State	1981	235	315	74.6
Dwayne Davis, Florida	1989	179	248	72.2
Keith Walker, Utica	1985	154	216	71.3
Steve Johnson, Oregon State	1980	211	297	71.0
Adam Mark, Belmont	2002	150	212	70.8

Steve Kerr, Arizona

FREE THROW PERCENTAGE

PLAYER	YEAR	FTM	FTA	PCT
Blake Ahearn, Southwest Missouri State	2004	117	120	97.5
Craig Collins, Penn State	1985	94	98	95.9
J.J. Redick, Duke	2004	143	150	95.3
Steve Drabyn, Belmont	2003	78	82	95.1
Rod Foster, UCLA	1982	95	100	95.0

3-POINT FIELD GOAL PERCENTAGE

PLAYER	YEAR	3FGM	3FGA	PCT
Glenn Tropf, Holy Cross	1988	52	82	63.4
Sean Wightman, Western Michigan	1992	48	76	63.2
Keith Jennings, East Tennessee State	1991	84	142	59.2
Dave Calloway, Monmouth	1989	48	82	58.5
Steve Kerr, Arizona	1988	114	199	57.3

BOB ROSATO

KEY GP=games played; FG=field goals; FT=free throws; PTS=points; AVG=average; REB=rebounds; A=assists; FGM=field goals made; FGA=field goals attempted; PCT=percentage; FTM=free throws made; FTA=free throws attempted; 3FGM=3-point field goals made; 3FGA=3-point field goals attempted

FAST FACT

Adam Morrison of Gonzaga led the nation in scoring, but fell short of winning a national championship. Only one player has ever pulled off that impressive double feat in the same season: Clyde Lovelette of Kansas in the 1951-1952 season.

NCAA MEN'S DIVISION I SINGLE-SEASON LEADERS (cont.)

STEALS

PLAYER	YEAR	GP	STL
Desmond Cambridge, Alabama A&M	2002	29	160
Mookie Blaylock, Oklahoma	1988	39	150
Aldwin Ware, Florida A&M	1988	29	142
Darron Brittman, Chicago State	1986	28	139
John Linehan, Providence	2002	31	139

Shawn James, Northeastern

BLOCKS

PLAYER	YEAR	GP	BLK
David Robinson, Navy	1986	35	207
Shawn James, Northeastern	2006	30	196
Adonal Foyle, Colgate	1997	28	180
Keith Closs, Central Connecticut State	1996	28	178
Shawn Bradley, BYU	1991	34	177

BOB BREIDENBACH/PROVIDENCE JOURNAL/AP

TRIVIA CHALLENGE

KEY GP=games played; STL=steals; BLK=blocks

How many different schools has Louisville head coach Rick Pitino directed to the Final Four?

An NCAA-record three (Providence in 1987; Kentucky in 1993, 1996, and 1997; and Louisville in 2005)

LEGENDS

Danny Manning carried Kansas to a national title.

■ **Danny Manning, forward,** b. May 17, 1966, Hattiesburg, Mississippi. As a senior in 1988, Manning carried the sixth-seeded Jayhawks to the national championship. Manning was named Most Outstanding Player after dominating the title game with 31 points, 18 rebounds and 5 steals. He averaged 24.8 points and 9.0 rebounds on his way to 1988 National Player of the Year honors. He left Kansas as a two-time All-America and the sixth-leading scorer in NCAA history. The Los Angeles Clippers selected him with the first pick in the 1988 NBA Draft. He made two All-Star teams before retiring in 2003.

■ **Ralph Sampson, center,** b. July 7, 1960, Harrisonburg, Virginia. From 1980-1983, Sampson was a four-time All-America and a three-time ACC and National Player of the Year. He led the Cavaliers to three ACC regular-season championships and an NIT title as a freshman, and to the Final Four as a sophomore. At 7'4", Sampson easily finished as Virginia's all-time leader in both rebounding (899) and blocked shots (462). In 1983, he was the Number 1 pick in the NBA Draft and became an All-Star before injuries shortened his career.

ANDY HAYT

■ **David Thompson, forward,** b. July 13, 1954, Shelby, North Carolina. The high-flying small forward was a three-time ACC Player of the Year, a three-time All-America, and a two-time National Player of the Year. The Wolfpack lost just one game in his sophomore and junior seasons combined. In 1974, N.C. State dethroned seven-time national champ UCLA to win the NCAA Tournament thanks largely to Thompson's Most Outstanding Player performance. He averaged 26.8 points for his college career.

Crystal Langhorne (1) and her Maryland teammates celebrate their championship.

BILL FRAKES

No team in the 2006 NCAA Women's Basketball Tournament was younger than Maryland. No team was better, either.

The Terrapins, who started two freshman, two sophomores, and a junior, seemed to be a year ahead of schedule in winning their first national championship. Even 35-year-old head coach Brenda Frese was part of the youth movement that took the Terrapins to the best season in school history. Led by second-team All-America forward Crystal Langhorne — who averaged team-highs in points (17.2) and rebounds (8.6) while leading the nation by shooting 67 percent — Maryland spent the regular-season proving they belonged among the nation's elite teams.

The Terps finished the year 34–4, and were rarely outside the Top 5. Their four losses came to Number 2 Tennessee in November, Number 2 Duke in early January (their only home loss), at Number 1 Duke in February (their only road loss) and to Number 1 North Carolina in the finals of the Atlantic Coast Conference (ACC) Tournament before embarking on their championship run.

With three teams in the Final Four, the ACC stole the headlines from the SEC, which before the season boasted the nation's pre-season top team (Tennessee), top player (Louisiana State's Seimone Augustus, who would go on to win a second straight National Player of the Year award) and top freshman (Candace Parker of Tennessee). The Lady Vols, in the midst of their longest national championship drought ever, won their first 18 games, including head coach Pat Summitt's 900th career win.

But Duke topped Tennessee in a Number 1 vs. Number 2 showdown in January, and the Lady Vols struggled to regain their intimidating form

the rest of the way. They would go on to lose in the Elite Eight to North Carolina. Duke, meanwhile, lost the Number 1 ranking the next week, to the arch-rival Tar Heels. Sparked by speedy All-America point guard Ivory Latta, UNC employed a fast-breaking offense and pressure defense that carried them to the best record in the country. Carolina lost just one game entering the NCAAs, an overtime defeat to Maryland in Chapel Hill, North Carolina.

The Tar Heels stormed to the Final Four in Boston, Massachusetts, only to run into ACC foes Duke and Maryland. The two teams had combined for nine losses entering the weekend and eight had been to one another. In one semifinal, Maryland took advantage of Latta's injured knee and handed the Tar Heels their second loss of the season. In the other, Duke ended Augustus's great college career by dealing the LSU guard her third straight national semifinal defeat.

In the title game, the Terps rallied from a 13-point deficit to defeat Duke in overtime. Fresh-

TRIVIA CHALLENGE

Three straight Number 2 seeds have won the national title. Do you know the last Number 1 seed to win the national championship?

Connecticut in 2003.

man point guard Kristi Toliver nailed a three-pointer to force the OT, and the excited Terrapins ran back to their huddle before the extra session shouting, "Overtime is our time!" They were right. Maryland outplayed the Blue Devils in overtime. Toliver's free throws with 35 seconds left put them in front for good, and they held on to win their sixth OT game of the year against no defeats.

In 2006, it wasn't just overtime that was the Terps' time. As it turned out, any time was their time.

Seimone Augustus was named Player of the Year.

MILES KENNEDY/AP

FAST FACT

To celebrate the 25th anniversary of women's basketball being sponsored by the NCAA, a Silver Anniversary team was announced during the 2006 season. The five players named were Cheryl Miller (Southern California, 1982–1986), Chamique Holdsclaw (Tennessee, 1995–1999), Diana Taurasi (Connecticut, 2000–2004), Bridgette Gordon (Tennessee, 1985–1989) and Sheryl Swoopes (Texas Tech, 1991–1993). Pat Summitt of Tennessee was named the team's coach.

NCAA WOMEN'S DIVISION I CHAMPIONSHIP BOX SCORE

MARYLAND TERRAPINS: 78

PLAYER	MIN	FG M-A	FT M-A	OFF	TOT	A	PF	PTS
Laura Harper	37	6–14	4–6	4	7	0	4	16
Marissa Coleman	36	4–12	2–2	1	14	2	2	10
Crystal Langhorne	38	4–6	4–6	2	7	4	4	12
Kristi Toliver	43	6–18	2–2	1	3	4	2	16
Shay Doron	36	4–9	6–6	0	3	1	4	16
Ashleigh Newman	17	1–3	1–2	0	0	0	3	4
Charmine Carr	3	0–0	0–0	1	1	0	0	0
Jade Perry	15	2–3	0–0	0	2	0	1	4
TOTALS		**27–65** **(41.5%)**	**19–24** **(79.2%)**	**9**	**37**	**11**	**20**	**78**

DUKE BLUE DEVILS: 75

PLAYER	MIN	FG M-A	FT M-A	OFF	TOT	A	PF	PTS
Mistie Williams	36	1–8	1–3	0	3	3	3	3
Wanisha Smith	8	0–2	0–0	1	4	0	1	0
Alison Bales	41	7–11	5–6	3	12	1	4	19
Lindsey Harding	38	6–14	4–5	0	3	1	5	16
Monique Currie	37	7–16	8–9	3	6	4	4	22
Abby Waner	37	1–6	2–3	3	4	4	1	5
Chante Black	13	0–2	0–0	0	3	1	3	0
Jessica Foley	15	3–6	2–2	1	1	0	0	10
TOTALS		**25–65** **(38.5%)**	**22–28** **(78.6%)**	**11**	**36**	**14**	**21**	**75**

KEY
MIN=minutes played; FG M-A=field goals made-attempted; FT M-A=free throws made-attempted; REB=rebounds; OFF=offensive; TOT=total; A=assists; PF=personal fouls; PTS=points

USA TODAY/ESPN TOP 25 FINAL POLL

RANK	TEAM	RECORD	POINTS
1.	Maryland	34–4	775
2.	Duke	31–4	744
3.	North Carolina	33–2	689
4.	LSU	31–4	679
5.	Tennessee	31–5	641
6.	Connecticut	32–5	619
7.	Stanford	26–8	536
8.	Oklahoma	31–5	499
9.	Rutgers	27–5	494
10.	Ohio State	29–3	463
11.	Purdue	26–7	460
12.	Utah	27–7	447
13.	Georgia	23–9	437
14.	Baylor	26–7	436
15.	DePaul	27–7	356
16.	Michigan State	24–10	289
17.	Arizona State	25–7	228
18.	UCLA	21–11	173
19.	Boston College	21–12	162
20.	Brigham Young	26–6	161
21.	New Mexico	22–10	108
22.	Vanderbilt	21–11	103
23.	Temple	24–8	81
24.	Louisiana Tech	26–5	79
25.	George Washington	23–9	64

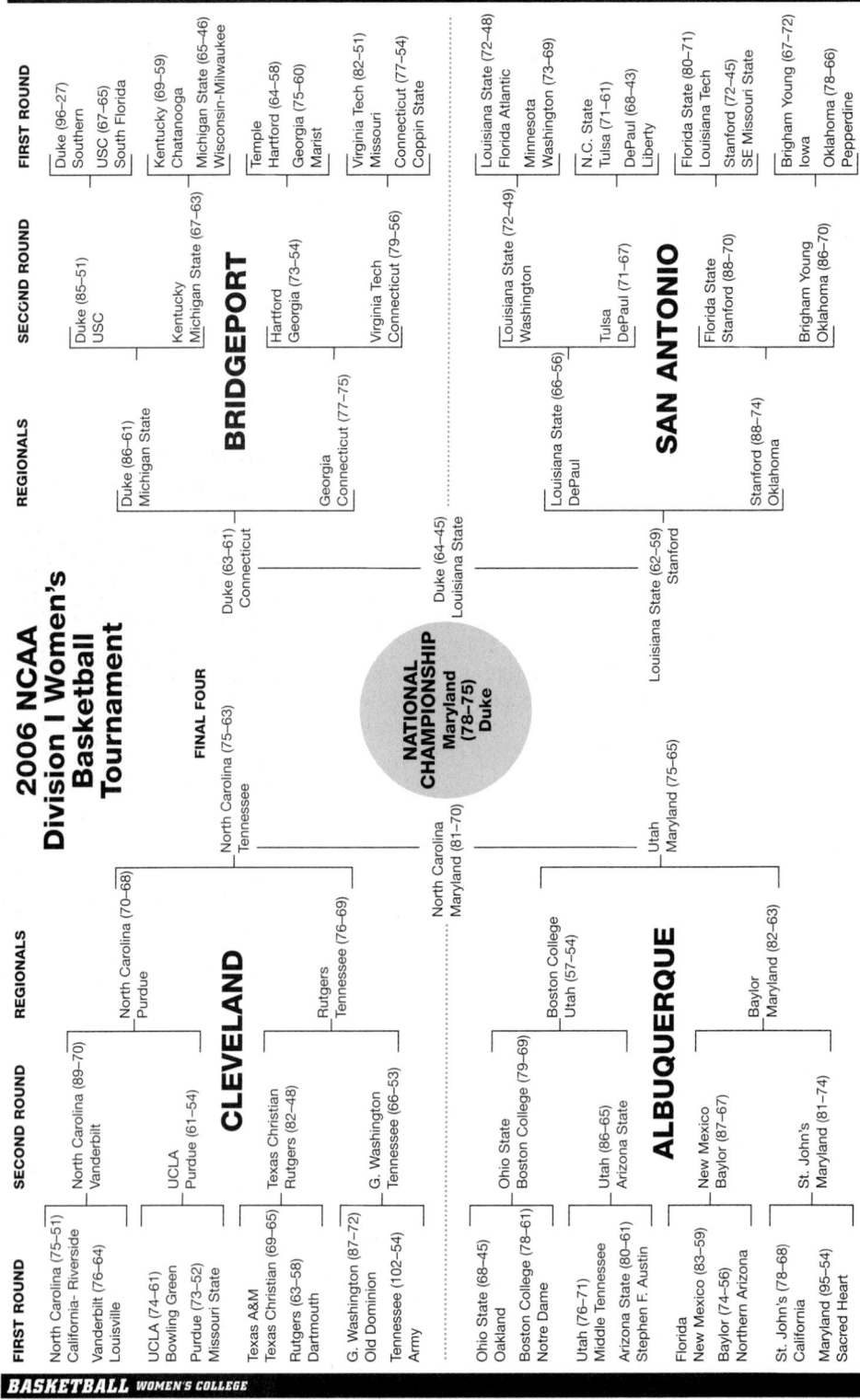

2006 NCAA Division I Women's Basketball Tournament

FIRST ROUND

SECOND ROUND

REGIONALS

BRIDGEPORT

Duke (96–27)
Southern
USC (67–65)
South Florida
Kentucky (69–59)
Chatanooga
Michigan State (67–63)
Wisconsin–Milwaukee
Temple
Hartford (64–58)
Georgia (75–60)
Marist
Virginia Tech (82–51)
Missouri
Connecticut (77–54)
Coppin State

Duke (85–51)
USC
Kentucky
Michigan State (67–63)
Hartford
Georgia (73–54)
Virginia Tech
Connecticut (79–56)

Duke (86–61)
Michigan State
Georgia
Connecticut (77–75)

Duke (63–61)
Connecticut

SAN ANTONIO

Louisiana State (72–48)
Florida Atlantic
Minnesota
Washington (73–69)
N.C. State
Tulsa (71–61)
DePaul (68–43)
Liberty
Florida State (80–71)
Louisiana Tech
Stanford (72–45)
SE Missouri State
Brigham Young (67–72)
Iowa
Oklahoma (78–66)
Pepperdine

Louisiana State (72–49)
Washington
Tulsa
DePaul (71–67)
Florida State
Stanford (88–70)
Brigham Young
Oklahoma (86–70)

Louisiana State (66–56)
DePaul
Stanford (88–74)
Oklahoma

Duke (64–45)
Louisiana State

FINAL FOUR

North Carolina (75–63)
Tennessee

NATIONAL CHAMPIONSHIP
Maryland (78–75)
Duke

Louisiana State (62–59)
Stanford

Utah
Maryland (75–65)

North Carolina
Maryland (81–70)

CLEVELAND

REGIONALS

North Carolina (70–68)
Purdue

Rutgers
Tennessee (76–69)

SECOND ROUND

North Carolina (89–70)
Vanderbilt
UCLA
Purdue (61–54)
Texas Christian
Rutgers (82–48)
G. Washington
Tennessee (66–53)

FIRST ROUND

North Carolina (75–51)
California– Riverside
Vanderbilt (76–64)
Louisville
UCLA (74–61)
Bowling Green
Purdue (73–52)
Missouri State
Texas A&M
Texas Christian (69–65)
Rutgers (63–58)
Dartmouth
G. Washington (87–72)
Old Dominion
Tennessee (102–54)
Army

ALBUQUERQUE

Boston College
Utah (57–54)

Baylor
Maryland (82–63)

Ohio State
Boston College (79–69)
Utah (86–65)
Arizona State
New Mexico
Baylor (87–67)
St. John's
Maryland (81–74)

Florida
New Mexico (83–59)
Baylor (74–56)
Northern Arizona
St. John's (78–68)
California
Maryland (95–54)
Sacred Heart

Ohio State (68–45)
Oakland
Boston College (78–61)
Notre Dame
Utah (76–71)
Middle Tennessee
Arizona State (80–61)
Stephen F. Austin

NCAA WOMEN'S DIVISION I INDIVIDUAL LEADERS

SCORING

PLAYER	CLASS	GP	FG	3FG	FT	PTS	AVG
Seimone Augustus, LSU	Sr.	32	310	17	100	737	23.0
Sophia Young, Baylor	Sr.	32	290	0	130	710	22.2
Jessica Dickson, South Florida	Jr.	31	243	68	128	682	22.0
Courtney Paris, Oklahoma	Fr.	35	320	0	122	762	21.8
Candice Wiggins, Stanford	So.	32	233	84	141	691	21.6
Cappie Pondexter, Rutgers	Sr.	31	239	59	131	668	21.5
Nefertiti Walker, Stetson	Sr.	27	192	80	117	581	21.5
Chrissy Givens, Middle Tennessee	Jr.	31	246	46	129	667	21.5
Tara Boothe, Xavier	Sr.	30	250	23	121	644	21.5
Emily Christian, Tennessee Tech	Sr.	32	259	24	144	686	21.4
Tamara James, Miami (Florida)	Sr.	29	208	52	146	614	21.2

KEY GP=games played; FG=field goals; 3FG=3-point field goals; FT=free throws; PTS=points; AVG=average

LEGENDS

Ann Meyers made hoops history in high school, college, and the pros.

■ **Ann Meyers, guard,** b. March 26, 1955, San Diego, California. The first high school player to make the U.S. National Team, Meyers arrived at UCLA as the school's first female full-scholarship athlete in 1974. She was the first four-time All-America in the country, and led the Bruins to the 1978 Association of Intercollegiate Athletes for Women (AIAW) national championship. She finished her career with averages of 17.4 points and 8.4 rebounds, and is the UCLA career record-holder in assists (544) and steals (403). A U.S. Olympian in the first women's basketball competition at the Games in 1976 (and a silver-medal winner), Meyers went on to become the first woman to have a tryout with an NBA team (the Indiana Pacers). She didn't make it, but she did make her mark in basketball history.

■ **Cheryl Miller, forward,** b. January 3, 1964, Riverside, California. Miller was the dominant college player of her time. She arrived at the University of Southern California as a four-time high school All-America who had once scored 105 points in a game and left as a four-time college All-America who scored over 3,000 points in her career. Along the way, she won three National Player of the Year awards, helped USC to two national championships, and set school records in scoring (3,018 career points and 23.6 per game) and rebounding (1,534 career rebounds and 12.0 per game).

■ **Sue Bird, guard,** b. October 16, 1980, Syosset, New York. Bird dominated on the court while playing at the University of Connecticut from 1998-2002. The 2002 National Player of the Year and a two-time All-America, Bird directed the Huskies to national titles in 2000 and 2002, when the team went a perfect 39–0. She was named the nation's best point guard three times. She finished second in career assists (585) at UConn, but likely would have been first had she not hurt her knee eight games into her freshman year and missed the rest of the season. She may have been the best shooter in UConn women's basketball history, setting school records for 3-point percentage (45.9 percent) and free-throw percentage (89.2 percent).

NCAA WOMEN'S DIVISION I INDIVIDUAL LEADERS (cont.)

FIELD GOAL PERCENTAGE

PLAYER	CLASS	GP	FGM	FGA	PCT
Crystal Langhorne, Maryland	So.	34	213	324	65.7
Liz Sherwood, Vanderbilt	So.	32	172	268	64.2
Rebecca Brown, Princeton	Sr.	28	178	281	63.3
Courtney Paris, Oklahoma	Fr.	35	320	515	62.1
Jessica Davenport, Ohio State	Jr.	32	241	390	61.8
Sylvia Fowles, Louisiana State University	So.	32	201	328	61.3
Heather Turner, Buffalo	So.	28	157	257	61.1
Crystal Kelly, Western Kentucky	So.	32	221	364	60.7
Kristen Kovesdy, Arizona State	Sr.	32	165	275	60.0
Traci Edwards, Wisconsin-Milwaukee	Fr.	31	182	304	59.9

Note: Minimum 5 field goals made per game.

FREE THROW PERCENTAGE

PLAYER	CLASS	GP	FTM	FTA	PCT
Adrienne Squire, Penn State	So.	29	80	83	96.4
Tommi Paris, Furman	Sr.	30	102	110	92.7
Chelsi Welch, Oklahoma	Jr.	35	88	95	92.6
Nefertiti Walker, Stetson	Sr.	27	117	128	91.4
Cyndi Valentin, Indiana	Sr.	32	144	159	90.6
Laura Shelton, Eastern Kentucky	Sr.	27	126	140	90.0
Jami Montagnino, Tulane	Jr.	27	80	89	89.9
Julie Briody, New Mexico	Jr.	29	77	86	89.5
Sara Ellis, Lehigh	Jr.	28	94	105	89.5
Megan Duffy, Notre Dame	Sr.	30	135	152	88.8

Note: Minimum 2.5 free throws made per game.

Courtney Paris, Oklahoma

REBOUNDING

PLAYER	CLASS	GP	REB	AVG
Courtney Paris, Oklahoma	Fr.	35	523	14.9
Ashley Haynes, Austin Peay	Sr.	28	374	13.4
Jillian Robbins, Tulsa	Jr.	32	409	12.8
Kyra Kaylor, William Mary	So.	28	334	11.9
LaKrisha Brown, Morehead State	Sr.	29	336	11.6
Sylvia Fowles, Louisiana State University	So.	32	358	11.2
Quanitra Hollingsworth, Virginia Comm.	Fr.	28	311	11.1
Khara Smith, DePaul	Sr.	33	365	11.1
Meredith Alexis, James Madison	Jr.	31	339	10.9
Jenny Callan, Lehigh	Sr.	28	306	10.9

ASSISTS

PLAYER	CLASS	GP	A	APG
Lyndsey Medders, Iowa State	Jr.	28	215	7.7
Shona Thorburn, Utah	Sr.	32	233	7.3
Sally Skeldon, Mercer	Jr.	26	179	6.9
Dee Davis, Vanderbilt	Jr.	31	212	6.8
Ashley Langford, Tulane	Fr.	26	171	6.6
Melanie Boeglin, Indiana State	Sr.	33	217	6.6
Carolyn Kieger, Marquette	Sr.	29	188	6.5
Claire Sullivan, Lehigh	So.	28	180	6.4
Erin Grant, Texas Tech	Sr.	29	183	6.3
Iva Milevoj, Winthrop	Sr.	29	179	6.2

DARREN CARROLL

KEY GP=games played; FGM=field goals made; FGA=field goals attempted; PCT=percentage; FTM=free throws made; FTA=free throws attempted; REB=rebounds; AVG=average; A=assists; APG=assists per game

DID YOU KNOW?

For the first time ever, three teams from the same conference advanced to the Final Four. North Carolina, Duke and Maryland from the ACC all made it to Boston, Massachusetts for the big showdown.

3-POINT FIELD GOAL PERCENTAGE

PLAYER	CLASS	GP	3FGM	3FGA	PCT
Julie Larsen, Utah	Sr.	17	35	67	52.2
Carlynn Savant, Missouri	Jr.	18	39	77	50.6
Mel Thomas, Connecticut	So.	19	54	107	50.5
Kristi Woodard, Creighton	Sr.	14	34	70	48.6
Chelsea Wagner, Oregon	Sr.	17	41	86	47.7
Ellen Hamilton, Butler	Jr.	17	48	101	47.5
Katie Montgomery, New Mexico	Jr.	18	38	80	47.5
Amanda Cavo, Canisius	Fr.	18	36	76	47.4
Jodi Bolerjack, Wyoming	So.	16	40	85	47.1
Ivory Latta, North Carolina	Jr.	18	47	100	47.0

Note: Minimum 2 3-point field goals made per game.

Julie Larsen, Utah

(left margin) COURTESY UTAH SPORTS INFORMATION

STEALS

PLAYER	CLASS	GP	STL	SPG
Sherill Baker, Georgia	Sr.	31	146	4.7
Leilani Mitchell, Idaho	Jr.	29	115	4.0
Kristen Boone, North Carolina-Greensboro	So.	26	101	3.9
Tanya Rhodes, Rhode Island	Sr.	26	99	3.8
Megan Ballard, Colgate	Sr.	29	106	3.7
Lisa Willis, UCLA	Sr.	32	115	3.6
Amanda Rego, San Diego	So.	21	75	3.6

BLOCKS

PLAYER	CLASS	GP	BLK	BPG
Brooke McAfee, Indiana/Purdue-Indianapolis	Sr.	28	137	4.9
Cassie Hager, Northern Iowa	Sr.	30	128	4.3
Zane Teilane, Western Illinois	Sr.	30	125	4.2
Marita Payne, Auburn	Sr.	29	107	3.7
Sarah Beato, Columbia	Sr.	27	96	3.6
Courtney Paris, Oklahoma	Fr.	35	116	3.3
Hope Foster, Bucknell	So.	29	95	3.3
Alison Bales, Duke	Jr.	31	98	3.2
Katie Beth Pate, Lipscomb	Sr.	21	66	3.1
Jessica Davenport, Ohio State	Jr.	32	98	3.1

KEY GP=games played; 3FGM=3-point field goals made; 3FGA=3-point field goals attempted; PCT=percentage; STL=steals; SPG=steals per game; BLK=blocks; BPG=blocks per game

NCAA WOMEN'S DIVISION I CHAMPIONSHIP RESULTS

YEAR	WINNER	SCORE	RUNNER-UP	WINNING COACH
2006	Maryland	78–75 (OT)	Duke	Brenda Frese
2005	Baylor	84–62	Michigan State	Kim Mulkey-Robertson
2004	Connecticut	70–61	Tennessee	Geno Auriemma
2003	Connecticut	73–68	Tennessee	Geno Auriemma
2002	Connecticut	82–70	Oklahoma	Geno Auriemma
2001	Notre Dame	68–66	Purdue	Muffet McGraw
2000	Connecticut	71–52	Tennessee	Geno Auriemma
1999	Purdue	62–45	Duke	Carolyn Peck
1998	Tennessee	93–75	Louisiana Tech	Pat Summitt
1997	Tennessee	68–59	Old Dominion	Pat Summitt
1996	Tennessee	83–65	Georgia	Pat Summitt
1995	Connecticut	70–64	Tennessee	Geno Auriemma
1994	North Carolina	60–59	Louisiana Tech	Sylvia Hatchell
1993	Texas Tech	84–82	Ohio State	Marsha Sharp
1992	Stanford	78–62	Western Kentucky	Tara VanDerveer
1991	Tennessee	70–67 (OT)	Virginia	Pat Summitt
1990	Stanford	88–81	Auburn	Tara VanDerveer
1989	Tennessee	76–60	Auburn	Pat Summitt
1988	Louisiana Tech	56–54	Auburn	Leon Barmore
1987	Tennessee	67–44	Louisiana Tech	Pat Summitt
1986	Texas	97–81	USC	Jody Conradt
1985	Old Dominion	70–65	Georgia	Marianne Stanley
1984	USC	72–61	Tennessee	Linda Sharp
1983	USC	69–67	Louisiana Tech	Linda Sharp
1982	Louisiana Tech	76–62	Cheyney	Sonja Hogg

2005-06 TIME LINE

■ **January 7, 2006:** Renewing the best rivalry in the sport, Number 1 Tennessee defeats Number 7 Connecticut, 89–80, in Knoxville, Tennessee, before the biggest regular-season crowd (24,635) in Thompson-Boling Arena history.

■ **January 19, 2006:** Pat Summitt of Tennessee becomes the first Division I coach to win 900 games, as the Lady Vols top Vanderbilt, 80–68. But, Tennessee loses its next two games, a 95–73 blowout to Number 2 Duke in Durham, North Carolina, and a 66–63 loss at home to Kentucky. It is the first time in nine years the Lady Vols have lost consecutive games.

■ **January 29, 2006:** Number 2 North Carolina overcomes a 13-point second-half deficit to beat Number 1 Duke, 74–70, in Durham. The Tar Heels take over the Number 1 ranking for the first time in school history. In the rematch in Chapel Hill, North Carolina, less than a month later, UNC rolls over Duke, 77–65.

■ **February 24, 2006:** Texas Tech's Hall of Fame coach Marsha Sharp announces her retirement, effective at the end of the season.

■ **March 19, 2006:** Tennessee's Candace Parker becomes the first player to dunk twice in one game, and the first to do it in an NCAA Tournament game, as the Lady Vols roll over Army, 102–54.

■ **April 1, 2006:** Kansas State wins the National Invitation Tournament (NIT). Shalee Lehning posts a triple-double with 14 points, 10 rebounds, and 10 assists as the Wildcats beats Marquette, 77–65.

■ **April 2, 2006:** For the second time this year, Maryland defeats North Carolina, giving the Tar Heels their only two losses of the season. The Terps win their NCAA tournament semifinal, 81–70, advancing to their first-ever championship game, where they will meet Duke. The Blue Devils defeat Louisiana State, 64–45.

■ **April 4, 2006:** Maryland rallies from 13 points down and beats Duke, 78–75, to win its first national championship. Freshman Kristi Toliver ties the game with a three-pointer at the end of regulation. Her free throws in the final minutes of overtime give the Terps the lead for good.

■ **April 6, 2006:** Army coach Maggie Dixon, who led the Cadets to their first-ever NCAA Tournament, dies suddenly from a heart problem at age 28.

TRIVIA CHALLENGE

In the 2006 NCAA Tournament, Candace Parker of Tennessee became the first woman to dunk twice in one game. Three other players in women's history have dunked in a college game: Georgeann Wells of West Virginia, Charlotte Smith of North Carolina, and Michelle Snow of Tennessee. Only one of them did it three times in her career. Can you guess who?

Snow, who did it in 2000, 2001, and 2002.

FAST FACT

Southern scored just 27 points in its first round NCAA Tournament loss to Duke, the fewest points ever scored by a team in a tournament game.

Visit our website for the latest stats and sports info.

NCAA WOMEN'S DIVISION I SINGLE-SEASON LEADERS

POINTS

PLAYER	YEAR	GP	PTS
Jackie Stiles, Southwest Missouri State	2001	35	1,062
Cindy Brown, Long Beach State	1987	35	974
Genia Miller, California State-Fullerton	1991	33	969
Sheryl Swoopes, Texas Tech	1993	34	955
Andrea Congreaves, Mercer	1992	28	925
Wanda Ford, Drake	1986	30	919
Chamique Holdsclaw, Tennessee	1998	39	915
Barbara Kennedy, Clemson	1982	31	908
Patricia Hoskins, Mississippi Valley State	1989	27	908
LaTaunya Pollard, Long Beach State	1983	31	907

SCORING AVERAGE

PLAYER	YEAR	GP	FG	3FG	FT	PTS	AVG
Patricia Hoskins, Mississippi Valley State	1989	27	345	13	205	908	33.6
Andrea Congreaves, Mercer	1992	28	353	77	142	925	33.0
Deborah Temple, Delta State	1984	28	373	—	127	873	31.2
Andrea Congreaves, Mercer	1993	26	302	51	150	805	31.0
Wanda Ford, Drake	1986	30	390	—	139	919	30.6
Anucha Brown, Northwestern	1985	28	341	—	173	855	30.5
LeChandra LeDay, Grambling	1988	28	334	36	146	850	30.4
Jackie Stiles, Southwest Missouri State	2001	35	365	65	267	1,062	30.3
Kim Perrot, Louisiana-Lafayette	1990	28	309	95	128	841	30.0

TODAY'S STARS

Little Ivory Latta became a big star in 2005–2006.

■ **Ivory Latta, guard,** b. September 24, 1984, Rock Hill, South Carolina. The Tar Heels 5'6"-tall point guard won All-America and National Player of the Year honors while leading UNC to the best season in school history. The Tar Heels went 33–2, won the ACC regular-season and tournament titles, claimed their first-ever Number 1 ranking, and advanced to their first Final Four since they won the national championship in 1994. The lightning-quick Latta won the ACC Player of the Year award after leading the team in points (18.4), assists (5.1), and steals (2.29).

■ **Candace Parker, forward,** b. April 19, 1986, St. Louis, Missouri. A two-time National Player of the Year in high school, Parker became the first woman to win the slam dunk contest at the McDonald's All-American game in 2004. After red-shirting in 2004–2005 because of a knee injury, Parker finally took the court as a freshman in 2005–2006 and quickly took off. She led the Lady Vols to the Southeast Conference (SEC) title, was named SEC Freshman of the Year and MVP of the SEC tournament. A second-team All-America, Parker averaged 17.3 points and 8.3 rebounds.

■ **Courtney Paris, center,** b. September 1, 1987, San Jose, California. As a freshman, the 6'4"-tall center averaged 21.9 points, 15 rebounds, and 3.3 blocks. Her 539 rebounds were a single-season NCAA record. She was a first-team All-America and was named first-team All-Big 12, co-Big 12 Defensive Player of the Year, Big 12 Freshman of the Year, Big 12 Tournament MVP, and National Freshman of the Year. Oklahoma finished the season at 31-5, including a perfect 16–0 in the Big 12 Conference, and reached the Sweet 16 in the NCAA tournament.

HOCKEY

BILL WIPPERT

Joe Thornton of the San Jose Sharks was the league's scoring champ and most valuable player.

7,443 goals, plus the 145 goals awarded during shootouts. An average of 6.1 goals were scored per game, up 18 percent from 2003–2004, when teams averaged only 5.1 goals — the biggest jump in goal scoring in 75 years. And for the first time in a decade, five players scored at least 50 goals and seven players tallied at least 100 points, led by San Jose Sharks forward Joe Thornton (125 points).

The Detroit Red Wings once again won the President's Trophy for having the league's best regular season record (58 wins, 124 points). But the mighty

Following a season lost to a lockout over a new collective bargaining agreement, the NHL returned on October 5, 2005. For the first time in league history, all 30 teams were in action on the same day, highlighted by the debuts of rookies Sidney Crosby of the Pittsburgh Penguins and Alexander Ovechkin of the Washington Capitals. And despite the lockout, the NHL returned with a stellar season that included attendance records at many arenas, thanks largely to some bright, young stars.

Besides signing a new, six-year agreement with the players that put a $39 million cap on team salaries, the league introduced a series of rule changes aimed at increasing scoring. A shootout was added to settle games that weren't decided after a five-minute overtime. The league decided to ignore the red line at center ice, allowing players to make long two-line passes and open up the game. The NHL also cracked down on defensive tactics that had kept offensive players from maneuvering freely in the past. The last major rule change put a limit on the size of a goaltender's pads, with the hope that players would find more openings to score.

The rule changes had a huge impact on play. At season's end, teams had scored a total of

NHL TEAMS

EASTERN CONFERENCE
Atlanta Thrashers
Boston Bruins
Buffalo Sabres
Carolina Hurricanes
Florida Panthers
Montreal Canadiens
New Jersey Devils
New York Islanders
New York Rangers
Ottawa Senators
Philadelphia Flyers
Pittsburgh Penguins
Tampa Bay Lightning
Toronto Maple Leafs
Washington Capitals

WESTERN CONFERENCE
Anaheim Ducks
Calgary Flames
Chicago Blackhawks
Colorado Avalanche
Columbus Blue Jackets
Dallas Stars
Detroit Red Wings
Edmonton Oilers
Los Angeles Kings
Minnesota Wild
Nashville Predators
Phoenix Coyotes
San Jose Sharks
St. Louis Blues
Vancouver Canucks

DAVID E. KLUTHO

Oiler Fernando Pisani scored a league-high 14 playoff goals.

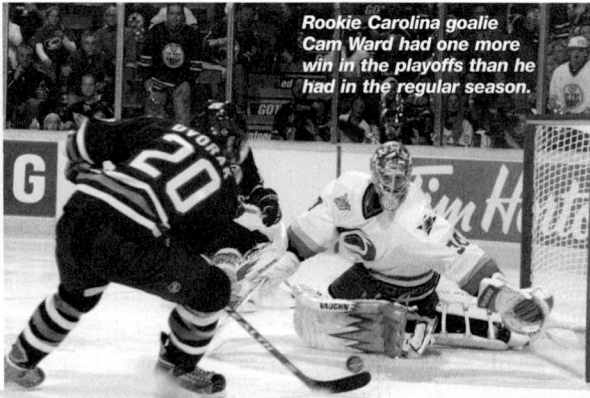

LOU CAPOZZOLA

Rookie Carolina goalie Cam Ward had one more win in the playoffs than he had in the regular season.

Wings were ousted by the Edmonton Oilers in the opening round of the playoffs. The red-hot Oilers then rang up series victories against the San Jose Sharks and Anaheim Mighty Ducks and reach their first Stanley Cup final since 1990. They became the first eighth-seeded playoff team to reach the finals.

In the Eastern Conference, the Carolina Hurricanes came from behind in the first and third rounds against the Montreal Canadiens and the Buffalo Sabres to make the second finals appearance in their history.

In the Stanley Cup finals, Carolina jumped out to a 3–1 series lead against Edmonton.

But the Oilers responded, eventually tying the series at 3–3.

The Oilers' Cinderella story ended in Game 7, when rookie goaltender Cam Ward backstopped the Hurricanes to their first Stanley Cup, 3–1. Ward won 15 games in the playoffs, and won the Conn Smythe Trophy as the post-season MVP.

NHL 2005-2006 FINAL STANDINGS

Atlantic Division

	GP	W	L	OTL	GF	GA	PTS
y-Devils	82	46	27	9	242	229	101
x-Flyers	82	45	26	11	267	259	101
x-Rangers	82	44	26	12	257	215	100
Islanders	82	36	40	6	230	278	78
Penguins	82	22	46	14	244	316	58

Central Division

	GP	W	L	OTL	GF	GA	PTS
z-Red Wings	82	58	16	8	305	209	124
x-Predators	82	49	25	8	259	227	106
Blue Jackets	82	35	43	4	223	279	74
Blackhawks	82	26	43	13	211	285	65
Blues	82	21	46	15	197	292	57

Northeast Division

	GP	W	L	OTL	GF	GA	PTS
z-Senators	82	52	21	9	314	211	113
x-Sabres	82	52	24	6	281	239	110
x-Canadiens	82	42	31	9	243	247	93
Maple Leafs	82	41	33	8	257	270	90
Bruins	82	29	37	16	230	266	74

Northwest Division

	GP	W	L	OTL	GF	GA	PTS
y-Flames	82	46	25	11	218	200	103
x-Avalanche	82	43	30	9	283	257	95
x-Oilers	82	41	28	13	256	251	95
Canucks	82	42	32	8	256	255	92
Wild	82	38	36	8	231	215	84

Southeast Division

	GP	W	L	OTL	GF	GA	PTS
y-Hurricanes	82	52	22	8	294	260	112
x-Lightning	82	43	33	6	252	260	92
Thrashers	82	41	33	8	281	275	90
Panthers	82	37	34	11	240	257	85
Capitals	82	29	41	12	237	306	70

Pacific Division

	GP	W	L	OTL	GF	GA	PTS
y-Stars	82	53	23	6	265	218	112
x-Sharks	82	44	27	11	266	242	99
x-Mighty Ducks	82	43	27	12	254	229	98
Kings	82	42	35	5	249	270	89
Coyotes	82	38	39	5	246	271	81

KEY GP=games played; W=win; L=loss; OTL=overtime loss; GF=goals for; GA=goals against; PTS=points; GF/GA include team goals awarded in shootout victories; x=clinched playoff spot; y=clinched division title; z=clinched best record in conference

2006 STANLEY CUP CHAMPIONSHIP

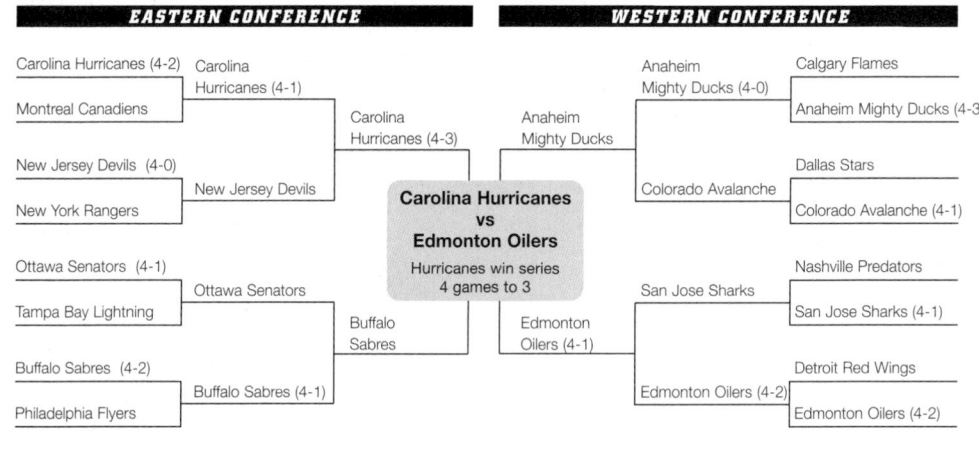

EASTERN CONFERENCE | **WESTERN CONFERENCE**

Carolina Hurricanes (4-2)
Carolina Hurricanes (4-1)
Montreal Canadiens
Carolina Hurricanes (4-3)

New Jersey Devils (4-0)
New Jersey Devils
New York Rangers

Ottawa Senators (4-1)
Ottawa Senators
Tampa Bay Lightning
Buffalo Sabres

Buffalo Sabres (4-2)
Buffalo Sabres (4-1)
Philadelphia Flyers

Carolina Hurricanes vs Edmonton Oilers
Hurricanes win series 4 games to 3

Anaheim Mighty Ducks
Edmonton Oilers (4-1)

Anaheim Mighty Ducks (4-0)
Calgary Flames
Anaheim Mighty Ducks (4-3)

Colorado Avalanche
Dallas Stars
Colorado Avalanche (4-1)

San Jose Sharks
Nashville Predators
San Jose Sharks (4-1)

Edmonton Oilers (4-2)
Detroit Red Wings
Edmonton Oilers (4-2)

QUARTERFINALS SEMIFINALS FINALS STANLEY CUP FINALS SEMIFINALS QUARTERFINALS

2006 STANLEY CUP PLAYOFF RESULTS

Conference Quarterfinals
EASTERN CONFERENCE
Tampa Bay Lightning vs. Ottawa Senators
GAME 1. April 21 – Ottawa 4, Tampa Bay 1
GAME 2. April 23 – Tampa Bay 4, Ottawa 3
GAME 3. April 25 – Ottawa 8, Tampa Bay 4
GAME 4. April 27 – Ottawa 5, Tampa Bay 2
GAME 5. April 29 – Ottawa 3, Tampa Bay 2
Senators win series 4-1

Montreal Canadiens vs. Carolina Hurricanes
GAME 1. April 22 – Montreal 6, Carolina 1
GAME 2. April 24 – Montreal 6, Carolina 5 (2OT)
GAME 3. April 26 – Carolina 2, Montreal 1 (OT)
GAME 4. April 28 – Carolina 3, Montreal 2
GAME 5. April 30 – Carolina 2, Montreal 1
GAME 6. May 2 – Carolina 2, Montreal 1 (OT)
Hurricanes win series 4-2

New York Rangers vs. New Jersey Devils
GAME 1. April 22 – New Jersey 6, NY Rangers 1
GAME 2. April 24 – New Jersey 4, NY Rangers 1
GAME 3. April 26 – New Jersey 3, NY Rangers 0
GAME 4. April 29 – New Jersey 4, NY Rangers 2
Devils win series 4-0

Philadelphia Flyers vs. Buffalo Sabres
GAME 1. April 22 – Buffalo 3, Philadelphia 2 (2OT)
GAME 2. April 24 – Buffalo 8, Philadelphia 2
GAME 3. April 26 – Philadelphia 4, Buffalo 2
GAME 4. April 28 – Philadelphia 5, Buffalo 4
GAME 5. April 30 – Buffalo 3, Philadelphia 0
GAME 6. May 2 – Buffalo 7, Philadelphia 1
Sabres win series 4-2

WESTERN CONFERENCE
Edmonton Oilers vs. Detroit Red Wings
GAME 1. April 21 – Detroit 3, Edmonton 2 (2OT)
GAME 2. April 23 – Edmonton 4, Detroit 2
GAME 3. April 25 – Edmonton 4, Detroit 3 (2OT)
GAME 4. April 27 – Detroit 4, Edmonton 2
GAME 5. April 29 – Edmonton 3, Detroit 2
GAME 6. May 1 – Edmonton 4, Detroit 3
Oilers win series 4-2

Colorado Avalanche vs. Dallas Stars
GAME 1. April 22 – Colorado 5, Dallas 2
GAME 2. April 24 – Colorado 5, Dallas 4 (OT)
GAME 3. April 26 – Colorado 4, Dallas 3 (OT)
GAME 4. April 28 – Dallas 4, Colorado 1
GAME 5. April 30 – Colorado 3, Dallas 2 (OT)
Avalanche win series 4-1

Anaheim Ducks vs. Calgary Flames
GAME 1. April 21 – Calgary 2, Anaheim 1 (OT)
GAME 2. April 23 – Anaheim 4, Calgary 3
GAME 3. April 25 – Calgary 5, Anaheim 2
GAME 4. April 27 – Anaheim 3, Calgary 2 (OT)
GAME 5. April 29 – Calgary 3, Anaheim 2
GAME 6. May 1 – Anaheim 2, Calgary 1
GAME 7. May 3 – Anaheim 3, Calgary 0
Mighty Ducks win series 4-3

San Jose Sharks vs. Nashville Predators
GAME 1. Apr 21 – Nashville 4, San Jose 3
GAME 2. Apr 23 – San Jose 3, Nashville 0
GAME 3. Apr 25 – San Jose 4, Nashville 1
GAME 4. Apr 27 – San Jose 5, Nashville 4
GAME 5. Apr 30 – San Jose 2, Nashville 1
Sharks win series 4-1

Conference Semifinals

EASTERN CONFERENCE

Buffalo Sabres vs. Ottawa Senators
GAME 1. May 5 – Buffalo 7, Ottawa 6 (OT)
GAME 2. May 8 – Buffalo 2, Ottawa 1
GAME 3. May 10 – Buffalo 3, Ottawa 2 (OT)
GAME 4. May 11 – Ottawa 2, Buffalo 1
GAME 5. May 13 – Buffalo 3, Ottawa 2 (OT)
Sabres win series 4-1

New Jersey Devils vs. Carolina Hurricanes
GAME 1. May 6 – Carolina 6, New Jersey 0
GAME 2. May 8 – Carolina 3, New Jersey 2 (OT)
GAME 3. May 10 – Carolina 3, New Jersey 1
GAME 4. May 13 – New Jersey 5, Carolina 1
GAME 5. May 14 – Carolina 4, New Jersey 1
Hurricanes win series 4-1

WESTERN CONFERENCE

Edmonton Oilers vs. San Jose Sharks
GAME 1. May 7 – San Jose 2, Edmonton 1
GAME 2. May 8 – San Jose 2, Edmonton 1
GAME 3. May 10 – Edmonton 3, San Jose 2 (3OT)
GAME 4. May 12 – Edmonton 6, San Jose 3
GAME 5. May 14 – Edmonton 6, San Jose 3
GAME 6. May 17 – Edmonton 2, San Jose 0
Oilers win series 4-2

Anaheim Ducks vs. Colorado Avalanche
GAME 1. May 5 – Anaheim 5, Colorado 0
GAME 2. May 7 – Anaheim 3, Colorado 0
GAME 3. May 9 – Anaheim 4, Colorado 3 (OT)
GAME 4. May 11 – Anaheim 4, Colorado 1
Mighty Ducks win series 4-0

EASTERN CONFERENCE FINALS

Buffalo Sabres vs. Carolina Hurricanes
GAME 1. May 20 – Buffalo 3, Carolina 2
GAME 2. May 22 – Carolina 4, Buffalo 3
GAME 3. May 24 – Buffalo 4, Carolina 3
GAME 4. May 26 – Carolina 4, Buffalo 0
GAME 5. May 28 – Carolina 4, Buffalo 3 (OT)
GAME 6. May 30 – Buffalo 2, Carolina 1 (OT)
GAME 7. Jun 1 – Carolina 4, Buffalo 2
Hurricanes win series 4-3

WESTERN CONFERENCE FINALS

Edmonton Oilers vs. Anaheim Ducks
GAME 1. May 19 – Edmonton 3, Anaheim 1
GAME 2. May 21 – Edmonton 3, Anaheim 1
GAME 3. May 23 – Edmonton 5, Anaheim 4
GAME 4. May 25 – Anaheim 6, Edmonton 3
GAME 5. May 27 – Edmonton 2, Anaheim 1
Oilers win series 4-1

Stanley Cup Finals

Edmonton Oilers vs. Carolina Hurricanes
GAME 1. June 5 – Carolina 5, Edmonton 4
GAME 2. June 7 – Carolina 5, Edmonton 0
GAME 3. June 10 – Edmonton 2, Carolina 1
GAME 4. June 12 – Carolina 2, Edmonton 1
GAME 5. June 14 – Edmonton 4, Carolina 3 (OT)
GAME 6. June 17 – Edmonton 4, Carolina 0
GAME 7. June 19 – Carolina 3, Edmonton 1
Hurricanes win series 4-3

STANLEY CUP CHAMPIONSHIP BOX SCORES

Game 1: June 5, 2006 — Carolina 5, Edmonton 4

	1st	2nd	3rd	Total
Edmonton	1	2	1	4
Carolina	0	1	4	5

1st Period Scoring
Edmonton 8:18, Fernando Pisani (Raffi Torres, Jaroslav Spacek)
2nd Period Scoring
Edmonton 10:36, Chris Pronger (penalty shot)
Edmonton 16:23, Ethan Moreau (Matt Greene)
Carolina 17:17, Rod Brind'Amour (Justin Williams, Cory Stillman)
3rd Period Scoring
Carolina 1:40, Ray Whitney (Doug Weight, Andrew Ladd)
Carolina 5:09, Ray Whitney (power play) (Mark Recchi, Eric Staal)
Carolina 10:02, Justin Williams (shorthanded) (Chad LaRose, Aaron Ward)
Edmonton 13:31, Ales Hemsky (power play) (Jarret Stoll, Chris Pronger)
Carolina 19:28, Rod Brind'Amour (unassisted)

Game 2: June 7, 2006 — Carolina 5, Edmonton 0

	1st	2nd	3rd	Total
Edmonton	0	0	0	0
Carolina	1	2	2	5

1st Period Scoring
Carolina 6:21, Andrew Ladd (Eric Staal, Frantisek Kaberle)
2nd Period Scoring
Carolina 10:28, Frantisek Kaberle (power play) (Ray Whitney, Matt Cullen)
Carolina 19:57, Cory Stillman (Niclas Wallin, Justin Williams)
3rd Period Scoring
Carolina 2:21, Doug Weight (power play) (Mark Recchi, Matt Cullen)
Carolina 4:12, Mark Recchi (power play) (Frantisek Kaberle, Matt Cullen)

Game 3: June 10, 2006 — Edmonton 2, Carolina 1

	1st	2nd	3rd	Total
Edmonton	0	0	1	1
Carolina	1	0	1	2

1st Period Scoring
Edmonton 2:31, Shawn Horcoff (Jaroslav Spacek, Ales Hemsky)
2nd Period Scoring None
3rd Period Scoring
Carolina 9:09, Rod Brind'Amour (Cory Stillman)
Edmonton 17:45, Ryan Smyth (Ales Hemsky, Jaroslav Spacek)

STANLEY CUP CHAMPIONSHIP BOX SCORES (cont.)

Game 4: June 12, 2006 — Carolina 2, Edmonton 1

	1st	2nd	3rd	Total
Edmonton	1	0	0	1
Carolina	1	1	0	2

1st Period Scoring
Edmonton 8:40, Sergei Samsonov (Radek Dvorak, Jarret Stoll)
Carolina 9:09, Cory Stillman (power play) (Frantisek Kaberle, Eric Staal)
2nd Period Scoring
Carolina 15:56, Mark Recchi (Eric Staal, Cory Stillman)
3rd Period Scoring
None

Game 5: June 14, 2006 — Edmonton 4, Carolina 3, OT

	1st	2nd	3rd	OT	Total
Edmonton	3	0	0	1	4
Carolina	2	1	0	0	3

1st Period Scoring
Edmonton 0:16, Fernando Pisani (Chris Pronger, Raffi Torres)
Carolina 5:54, Eric Staal (power play) (Doug Weight, Bret Hedican)
Carolina 10:16, Ray Whitney (power play) (Eric Staal, Mark Recchi)
Edmonton 13:25, Ales Hemsky (power play) (Dick Tarnstrom, Steve Staios)
Edmonton 19:42, Michael Peca (Ales Hemsky, Chris Pronger)
2nd Period Scoring
Carolina 9:56, Eric Staal (power play) (Ray Whitney, Cory Stillman)
3rd Period Scoring
None
OT Period Scoring
Edmonton 0:00, Fernando Pisani (shorthanded) (unassisted)

Game 6: June 10, 2006 — Edmonton 4, Carolina 0

	1st	2nd	3rd	Total
Edmonton	0	2	2	4
Carolina	0	0	0	0

1st Period Scoring
None
2nd Period Scoring
Edmonton 1:45, Fernando Pisani (power play) (Ales Hemsky, Jaroslav Spacek)
Edmonton 9:54, Raffi Torres (Steve Staios, Fernando Pisani)
3rd Period Scoring
Edmonton 3:04, Ryan Smyth 7 (power play) (Michael Peca, Jaroslav Spacek)
Edmonton 13:05, Shawn Horcoff 7 (power play) (Radek Dvorak, Dick Tarnstrom)

Game 7: June 19, 2006 — Carolina 3, Edmonton 1

	1st	2nd	3rd	Total
Edmonton	0	0	1	1
Carolina	1	1	1	3

1st Period Scoring
Carolina 1:26, Aaron Ward (Mark Recchi, Matt Cullen)
2nd Period Scoring
Carolina 4:18, Frantisek Kaberle (power play) (Cory Stillman, Matt Cullen)
3rd Period Scoring
Edmonton 1:03, Fernando Pisani (Rem Murray, Raffi Torres)
Carolina 18:59, Justin Williams (empty net) (Eric Staal, Bret Hedican)

2005–2006 NHL INDIVIDUAL LEADERS

SCORING

Points

PLAYER	GP	PTS
Joe Thornton, Bruins-Sharks	81	125
Jaromir Jagr, Rangers	82	123
Alexander Ovechkin, Capitals	81	106
Daniel Alfredsson, Senators	77	103
Dany Heatley, Senators	82	103
Sidney Crosby, Penguins	81	102
Eric Staal, Hurricanes	82	100
Ilya Kovalchuk, Thrashers	78	98
Marc Savard, Thrashers	82	97
Jonathan Cheechoo, Sharks	82	93
Marian Hossa, Thrashers	80	92
Brad Richards, Lightning	82	91
Teemu Selanne, Mighty Ducks	80	90
Jason Spezza, Senators	68	90
Brian Gionta, Devils	82	89
Olli Jokinen, Panthers	82	89
Pavel Datsyuk, Red Wings	75	87
Joe Sakic, Avalanche	82	87
Patrick Marleau, Sharks	82	86
Paul Kariya, Predators	82	85

Goals

PLAYER	GP	G
Jonathan Cheechoo, Sharks	82	56
Jaromir Jagr, Rangers	82	54
Ilya Kovalchuk, Thrashers	78	52
Alexander Ovechkin, Capitals	81	52
Dany Heatley, Senators	82	50
Brian Gionta, Devils	82	48
Simon Gagne, Flyers	72	47
Eric Staal, Hurricanes	82	45
Daniel Alfredsson, Senators	77	43
Teemu Selanne, Mighty Ducks	80	40
Brendan Shanahan, Red Wings	82	40
Sidney Crosby, Penguins	81	39
Marian Hossa, Thrashers	80	39
Henrik Zetterberg, Red Wings	77	39
Marian Gaborik, Wild	65	38
Olli Jokinen, Panthers	82	38
Ryan Smyth, Oilers	75	36
Jarome Iginla, Flames	82	35
Vincent Lecavalier, Lightning	80	35
Miroslav Satan, Islanders	82	35

SCORING (cont'd)

Assists

PLAYER	GP	A
Joe Thornton, Bruins/Sharks	81	96
Jason Spezza, Senators	68	71
Jaromir Jagr, Rangers	82	69
Marc Savard, Thrashers	82	69
Brad Richards, Lightning	82	68
Nicklas Lidstrom, Red Wings	80	64
Sidney Crosby, Penguins	81	63
Daniel Alfredsson, Senators	77	60
Pavel Datsyuk, Red Wings	75	59
Ales Hemsky, Oilers	81	58
Tomas Kaberle, Maple Leafs	82	58
Sergei Zubov, Stars	78	58
Henrik Sedin, Canucks	82	57
Peter Forsberg, Flyers	60	56
Michael Nylander, Rangers	81	56
Vaclav Prospal, Lightning	81	55
Joe Sakic, Avalanche	82	55
Eric Staal, Hurricanes	82	55
Cory Stillman, Hurricanes	72	55
Paul Kariya, Predators	82	54

Plus/Minus

PLAYER	GP	+/-
Wade Redden, Senators	65	35
Michal Rozsival, Rangers	82	35
Jaromir Jagr, Rangers	82	34
Andrej Meszaros, Senators	82	34
Mathieu Schneider, Red Wings	72	33
Simon Gagne, Flyers	72	31
Michael Nylander, Rangers	81	31
Joe Thornton, Bruins/Sharks	81	31
Brenden Morrow, Stars	81	30
Daniel Alfredsson, Senators	77	29
Dany Heatley, Senators	82	29
Brian Pothier, Senators	77	29
Brendan Shanahan, Red Wings	82	29
Henrik Zetterberg, Red Wings	77	29
Philippe Boucher, Stars	66	28
Marek Malik, Rangers	74	28
Teemu Selanne, Mighty Ducks	80	28
Martin Gelinas, Panthers	82	27
Mikael Samuelsson, Red Wings	71	27
Pavel Datsyuk, Red Wings	75	26

Note: +/- = plus minus rating (A player is awarded a plus (+1) each time he is on the ice when his team scores an even-strength or shorthanded goal. He receives a minus (-1) each time he is on the ice when the opposing team scores an even-strength or short-handed goal. Power-play goals are not included in the rating.)

KEY	A=assists; G=goals; GP=games played; GA=goals allowed; GAA=goals-against average; OTL=overtime loss; +/-=plus/minus; PTS=points; SA=shots allowed; SV=saves; SV%=save percentage; SO=shutouts

GOALTENDING

Goals Against Average

PLAYER	GP	GAA
Miikka Kiprusoff, Flames	74	2.07
Dominik Hasek, Senators	43	2.09
Manny Legace, Red Wings	51	2.19
Cristobal Huet, Canadiens	36	2.20
Henrik Lundqvist, Rangers	53	2.24
Manny Fernandez, Wild	58	2.29
Ilya Bryzgalov, Mighty Ducks	31	2.51
Marty Turco, Stars	68	2.55
Vesa Toskala, Sharks	37	2.56
Martin Brodeur, Devils	73	2.57
Ryan Miller, Sabres	48	2.60
Curtis Sanford, Blues	34	2.66
Jean-Sebastien Giguere, Mighty Ducks	60	2.66
Tomas Vokoun, Predators	61	2.67
Dwayne Roloson, Wild/Oilers	43	2.73
Chris Osgood, Red Wings	32	2.76
Tim Thomas, Bruins	38	2.77
Martin Gerber, Car	60	2.78
Sean Burke, Lightning	35	2.80
Ray Emery, Senators	39	2.82

Shutouts

PLAYER	GP	W	L	OTL	SO
Miikka Kiprusoff, Flames	74	42	20	11	10
Cristobal Huet, Canadiens	36	18	11	4	7
Manny Legace, Red Wings	51	37	8	3	7
Martin Brodeur, Devils	73	43	23	7	5
John Grahame, Lightning	57	29	22	1	5
Dominik Hasek, Senators	43	28	10	4	5
Mathieu Garon, Kings	63	31	26	3	4
Curtis Joseph, Coyotes	60	32	21	3	4
Roberto Luongo, Panthers	75	35	30	9	4
Tomas Vokoun, Predators	61	36	18	7	4

Save Percentage

PLAYER	GP	GA	SA	SAVE PCT	W	L	OTL
Cristobal Huet, Canadiens	36	77	1,085	.929	18	11	4
Dominik Hasek, Senators	43	90	1,202	.925	28	10	4
Miikka Kiprusoff, Flames	74	151	1,951	.923	42	20	11
Henrik Lundqvist, Rangers	53	116	1,485	.922	30	12	9
Manny Fernandez, Wild	58	130	1,612	.919	30	18	7
Tomas Vokoun, Predators	61	160	1,984	.919	36	18	7
Tim Thomas, Bruins	38	101	1,213	.917	12	13	10
Manny Legace, Red Wings	51	106	1,244	.915	37	8	3
Roberto Luongo, Panthers	75	213	2,488	.914	35	30	9
Ryan Miller, Sabres	48	124	1,440	.914	30	14	3

Wins

PLAYER	GP	W	L	OTL
Martin Brodeur, Devils	73	43	23	7
Miikka Kiprusoff, Flames	74	42	20	11
Marty Turco, Stars	68	41	19	5
Martin Gerber, Hurricanes	60	38	14	6
Manny Legace, Red Wings	51	37	8	3
Tomas Vokoun, Predators	61	36	18	7
Roberto Luongo, Panthers	75	35	30	9
Alexander Auld, Canucks	67	33	26	6
Curtis Joseph, Coyotes	60	32	21	3
Mathieu Garon, Kings	63	31	26	3

NHL TEAM-BY-TEAM STATS

ANAHEIM MIGHTY DUCKS

PLAYER	GP	G	A	PTS	+/-	PIM
Teemu Selanne	80	40	50	90	28	44
Andy McDonald	82	34	51	85	24	32
Scott Niedermayer	82	13	50	63	8	96
Joffrey Lupul	81	28	25	53	-13	48
Chris Kunitz	67	19	22	41	19	69
Ryan Getzlaf	57	14	25	39	6	22
Rob Niedermayer	76	15	24	39	-5	89
Francois Beauchemin	61	8	26	34	8	41
Jonathan Hedstrom	79	13	14	27	2	48
Todd Marchant	61	6	19	25	3	46
Corey Perry	56	13	12	25	1	50
Todd Fedoruk	76	4	19	23	6	174
Samuel Pahlsson	82	11	10	21	-1	34
Petr Sykora	34	7	13	20	1	28
Ruslan Salei	78	1	18	19	17	114
Keith Carney	61	2	16	18	13	48
Joe DiPenta	72	2	6	8	8	46
Vitaly Vishnevski	82	1	7	8	8	91
Zenon Konopka	23	4	3	7	-4	48
Dustin Penner	19	4	3	7	3	14

GOALTENDER	GP	GA	SA	GAA	SV	SV%	SO
Ilya Bryzgalov	31	66	733	2.51	667	.910	1
Jean-Sebastien Giguere	60	150	1,692	2.66	1,542	.911	2

ATLANTA THRASHERS

PLAYER	GP	G	A	PTS	+/-	PIM
Ilya Kovalchuk	78	52	46	98	-6	68
Marc Savard	82	28	69	97	7	100
Marian Hossa	80	39	53	92	17	67
Slava Kozlov	82	25	46	71	14	33
Peter Bondra	60	21	18	39	-3	40
Jaroslav Modry	79	7	31	38	-9	76
Greg de Vries	82	7	28	35	1	76
Scott Mellanby	71	12	22	34	5	55
Bobby Holik	64	15	18	33	-6	79
Niclas Havelid	82	4	28	32	9	48
Andy Sutton	76	8	17	25	13	144
Serge Aubin	74	7	17	24	-4	79
Patrik Stefan	64	10	14	24	3	36
Ronald Petrovicky	60	8	12	20	-8	62
Jim Slater	71	10	10	20	1	46
Brad Larsen	62	7	8	15	-3	21
Garnet Exelby	75	1	9	10	11	75
Steve McCarthy	16	7	3	10	0	8
J.P. Vigier	41	4	6	10	-4	40

GOALTENDER	GP	GA	SA	GAA	SV	SV%	SO
Mike Dunham	17	36	336	2.77	300	.893	1
Kari Lehtonen	38	106	1,123	2.94	1,017	.906	2
Michael Garnett	24	73	634	3.45	561	.885	2

KEY — GP=games played; G=goals; A=assists; PTS=points; +/-=plus/minus; PIM=penalty minutes; GA=goals allowed; SA=shots allowed; GAA=goals-against average; SV=saves; SV%=save percentage; SO=shutouts

BOSTON BRUINS

PLAYER	GP	G	A	PTS	+/-	PIM
Patrice Bergeron	81	31	42	73	3	22
Brad Boyes	82	26	43	69	11	30
Glen Murray	64	24	29	53	-8	52
Marco Sturm	51	23	20	43	14	32
Sergei Samsonov	55	18	19	37	-3	22
Joe Thornton	23	9	24	33	0	6
Brian Leetch	61	5	27	32	-10	36
Brad Stuart	55	10	21	31	-6	38
P.J. Axelsson	59	10	18	28	-3	4
Brad Isbister	58	6	17	23	-2	46
Travis Green	82	10	12	22	-2	79
Jiri Slegr	32	5	11	16	-2	56
David Tanabe	54	4	12	16	0	48
Wayne Primeau	50	6	8	14	-10	40
Nick Boynton	54	5	7	12	-7	93
Milan Jurcina	51	6	5	11	3	54
Tom Fitzgerald	71	4	6	10	-10	40
Hal Gill	80	1	9	10	-4	124
Dave Scatchard	16	4	6	10	-2	28
Alexei Zhamnov	24	1	9	10	-4	30

GOALTENDER	GP	GA	SA	GAA	SV	SV%	SO
Hannu Toivonen	20	51	590	2.63	539	.914	1
Tim Thomas	38	101	1,213	2.77	1,112	.917	1
Andrew Raycroft	30	100	824	3.71	724	.879	0

BUFFALO SABRES

PLAYER	GP	G	A	PTS	+/-	PIM
Maxim Afinogenov	77	22	51	73	6	84
Chris Drury	81	30	37	67	-11	32
Ales Kotalik	82	25	37	62	-3	62
Daniel Briere	48	25	33	58	3	48
Tim Connolly	63	16	39	55	5	28
Thomas Vanek	81	25	23	48	-11	72
Derek Roy	70	18	28	46	1	57
Brian Campbell	79	12	32	44	-14	16
Jochen Hecht	64	18	24	42	10	34
J.P. Dumont	54	20	20	40	-1	38
Teppo Numminen	75	2	38	40	6	36
Jason Pominville	57	18	12	30	-4	22
Paul Gaustad	78	9	15	24	4	65
Mike Grier	81	7	16	23	-7	28
Henrik Tallinder	82	6	15	21	10	74
Dmitri Kalinin	55	2	16	18	14	54
Toni Lydman	75	1	16	17	9	82
Jay McKee	75	5	11	16	0	57
Taylor Pyatt	41	6	6	12	-1	33
Rory Fitzpatrick	56	4	5	9	-18	50

GOALTENDER	GP	GA	SA	GAA	SV	SV%	SO
Ryan Miller	48	124	1,440	2.60	1,316	.914	1
Martin Biron	35	93	980	2.89	887	.905	1
Mika Noronen	4	12	77	4.26	65	.844	0

CALGARY FLAMES

PLAYER	GP	G	A	PTS	+/-	PIM
Jarome Iginla	82	35	32	67	5	86
Daymond Langkow	82	25	34	59	2	46
Dion Phaneuf	82	20	29	49	5	93
Tony Amonte	80	14	28	42	3	43
Kristian Huselius	54	15	24	39	2	36
Andrew Ference	82	4	27	31	-12	85
Chuck Kobasew	77	20	11	31	-10	64
Steve Reinprecht	52	10	19	29	10	24
Roman Hamrlik	51	7	19	26	8	56
Matthew Lombardi	55	6	20	26	-1	48
Robyn Regehr	68	6	20	26	6	67
Chris Simon	72	8	14	22	0	94
Shean Donovan	80	9	11	20	9	82
Jordan Leopold	74	2	18	20	6	68
Stephane Yelle	74	4	14	18	10	48
Marcus Nilson	70	6	11	17	13	32
Darren McCarty	67	7	6	13	-1	117
Jamie Lundmark	12	4	6	10	2	20
Byron Ritchie	45	4	2	6	-2	69
Rhett Warrener	61	3	3	6	7	54

GOALTENDER	GP	GA	SA	GAA	SV	SV%	SO
Miikka Kiprusoff	74	151	1,951	2.07	1,800	.923	10
Philippe Sauve	8	22	202	3.28	180	.891	0
Brian Boucher	3	15	103	4.95	88	.854	0

CAROLINA HURRICANES

PLAYER	GP	G	A	PTS	+/-	PIM
Eric Staal	82	45	55	100	-8	81
Cory Stillman	72	21	55	76	-9	32
Justin Williams	82	31	45	76	1	60
Rod Brind'Amour	78	31	39	70	8	68
Erik Cole	60	30	29	59	19	54
Ray Whitney	63	17	38	55	0	42
Matt Cullen	78	25	24	49	4	40
Frantisek Kaberle	77	6	38	44	8	46
Bret Hedican	74	5	22	27	11	58
Aaron Ward	71	6	19	25	2	62
Kevyn Adams	82	15	8	23	0	36
Oleg Tverdovsky	72	3	20	23	-1	37
Craig Adams	67	10	11	21	1	51
Mike Commodore	72	3	10	13	12	138
Chad LaRose	49	1	12	13	7	35
Doug Weight	23	4	9	13	-6	25
Andrew Hutchinson	36	3	8	11	-2	18
Andrew Ladd	29	6	5	11	0	4
Glen Wesley	64	2	8	10	10	46
Josef Vasicek	23	4	5	9	3	8

GOALTENDER	GP	GA	SA	GAA	SV	SV%	SO
Martin Gerber	60	162	1,719	2.78	1,557	.906	3
Cam Ward	28	91	773	3.68	682	.882	0

CHICAGO BLACKHAWKS

PLAYER	GP	G	A	PTS	+/-	PIM
Kyle Calder	79	26	33	59	-4	52
Mark Bell	82	25	23	48	-14	107
Tyler Arnason	60	13	28	41	5	40
Rene Bourque	77	16	18	34	3	56
Radim Vrbata	45	13	21	34	4	16
Brent Seabrook	69	5	27	32	5	60
Martin Lapointe	82	14	17	31	-30	106
Matthew Barnaby	82	8	20	28	-11	178
Jaroslav Spacek	45	7	17	24	8	72
Jim Vandermeer	76	6	18	24	-2	116
Patrick Sharp	50	9	14	23	1	36
Duncan Keith	81	9	12	21	-11	79
Pavel Vorobiev	39	9	12	21	-2	34
Mikael Holmqvist	72	10	10	20	-14	16
Mark Cullen	29	7	9	16	7	2
Curtis Brown	71	5	10	15	-9	38
Jim Dowd	60	3	12	15	-5	38
Matt Ellison	26	3	9	12	-4	17
Andy Hilbert	28	5	4	9	-4	22
Milan Bartovic	24	1	6	7	0	8

GOALTENDER	GP	GA	SA	GAA	SV	SV%	SO
Adam Munro	10	25	234	2.99	209	.893	1
Craig Anderson	29	86	757	3.32	671	.886	1
Nikolai Khabibulin	50	157	1,379	3.35	1,222	.886	0

COLORADO AVALANCHE

PLAYER	GP	G	A	PTS	+/-	PIM
Joe Sakic	82	32	55	87	10	60
Alex Tanguay	71	29	49	78	8	46
Andrew Brunette	82	24	39	63	9	48
Milan Hejduk	74	24	34	58	13	24
Rob Blake	81	14	37	51	2	94
Marek Svatos	61	32	18	50	0	60
John-Michael Liles	82	14	35	49	5	44
Pierre Turgeon	62	16	30	46	1	32
Ian Laperriere	82	21	24	45	3	116
Brett McLean	82	9	31	40	-7	51
Patrice Brisebois	80	10	28	38	1	55
Brett Clark	80	9	27	36	3	56
Antti Laaksonen	81	16	18	34	-2	40
Steve Konowalchuk	21	6	9	15	5	14
Karlis Skrastins	82	3	11	14	-7	65
Dan Hinote	73	5	8	13	-5	48
Brad Richardson	41	3	10	13	0	12
Cody McCormick	45	4	4	8	1	29
Bob Boughner	41	1	6	7	2	54
Brad May	54	3	3	6	-14	82

GOALTENDER	GP	GA	SA	GAA	SV	SV%	SO
Peter Budaj	34	86	864	2.86	778	.900	2
David Aebischer	43	123	1,233	2.98	1,110	.900	3

HOCKEY

COLUMBUS BLUE JACKETS

PLAYER	GP	G	A	PTS	+/-	PIM
David Vyborny	80	22	43	65	-9	50
Rick Nash	54	31	23	54	5	51
Nikolai Zherdev	73	27	27	54	-13	50
Sergei Fedorov	62	12	31	43	-1	64
Jan Hrdina	75	10	23	33	-8	78
Bryan Berard	44	12	20	32	-29	32
Manny Malhotra	58	10	21	31	1	41
Jason Chimera	80	17	13	30	-10	95
Trevor Letowski	81	10	18	28	-2	36
Duvie Westcott	78	6	22	28	1	133
Jaroslav Balastik	66	12	10	22	-1	26
Adam Foote	65	6	16	22	-16	89
Rostislav Klesla	51	6	13	19	-4	75
Ron Hainsey	55	2	15	17	13	43
Dan Fritsche	59	6	7	13	-14	22
Mark Hartigan	33	9	3	12	-1	22
Jody Shelley	80	3	7	10	-4	163
Todd Marchant	18	3	6	9	-1	20
Aaron Johnson	26	2	6	8	9	23
Radoslav Suchy	79	1	7	8	-8	30

GOALTENDER	GP	GA	SA	GAA	SV	SV%	SO
Martin Prusek	9	20	165	3.22	145	.879	0
Pascal Leclaire	33	97	1,084	3.23	987	.911	0
Marc Denis	49	151	1,505	3.25	1,354	.900	1

DALLAS STARS

PLAYER	GP	G	A	PTS	+/-	PIM
Mike Modano	78	27	50	77	23	58
Jason Arnott	81	32	44	76	13	102
Sergei Zubov	78	13	58	71	20	46
Brenden Morrow	81	23	42	65	30	183
Jussi Jokinen	81	17	38	55	2	30
Jere Lehtinen	80	33	19	52	9	30
Philippe Boucher	66	16	27	43	28	77
Bill Guerin	70	13	27	40	0	115
Stu Barnes	78	15	21	36	9	44
Niko Kapanen	81	14	21	35	-10	36
Antti Miettinen	79	11	20	31	0	46
Steve Ott	82	5	17	22	1	178
Stephane Robidas	75	5	15	20	15	67
Niklas Hagman	54	6	9	15	-2	16
Martin Skoula	61	4	11	15	6	36
Trevor Daley	81	3	11	14	-2	87
Jon Klemm	76	4	7	11	-3	60
Jaroslav Svoboda	43	4	3	7	-3	22
Janne Niinimaa	22	2	4	6	-5	24
Mathias Tjarnqvist	33	2	4	6	4	18

GOALTENDER	GP	GA	SA	GAA	SV	SV%	SO
Marty Turco	68	166	1,624	2.55	1,458	.898	3
Johan Hedberg	19	48	472	2.67	424	.898	0

DETROIT RED WINGS

PLAYER	GP	G	A	PTS	+/-	PIM
Pavel Datsyuk	75	28	59	87	26	22
Henrik Zetterberg	77	39	46	85	29	30
Brendan Shanahan	82	40	41	81	29	105
Nicklas Lidstrom	80	16	64	80	21	50
Robert Lang	72	20	42	62	17	72
Tomas Holmstrom	81	29	30	59	14	66
Mathieu Schneider	72	21	38	59	33	86
Jason Williams	80	21	37	58	4	26
Mikael Samuelsson	71	23	22	45	27	42
Steve Yzerman	61	14	20	34	8	18
Kris Draper	80	10	22	32	3	58
Jason Woolley	53	1	18	19	3	28
Johan Franzen	80	12	4	16	4	36
Daniel Cleary	77	3	12	15	5	40
Andreas Lilja	82	2	13	15	18	98
Mark Mowers	46	4	11	15	13	16
Brett Lebda	46	3	9	12	9	20
Chris Chelios	81	4	7	11	22	108
Kirk Maltby	82	5	6	11	-9	80
Niklas Kronwall	27	1	8	9	11	28

GOALTENDER	GP	GA	SA	GAA	SV	SV%	SO
Manny Legace	51	106	1,244	2.19	1,138	.915	7
Chris Osgood	32	85	828	2.76	743	.897	2
Jimmy Howard	4	10	104	2.99	94	.904	0

EDMONTON OILERS

PLAYER	GP	G	A	PTS	+/-	PIM
Ales Hemsky	81	19	58	77	-5	64
Shawn Horcoff	79	22	51	73	0	85
Jarret Stoll	82	22	46	68	4	74
Ryan Smyth	75	36	30	66	-5	58
Chris Pronger	80	12	44	56	2	74
Raffi Torres	82	27	14	41	4	50
Fernando Pisani	80	18	19	37	5	42
Marc-Andre Bergeron	75	15	20	35	3	38
Radek Dvorak	64	8	20	28	-2	26
Steve Staios	82	8	20	28	10	84
Ethan Moreau	74	11	16	27	6	87
Marty Reasoner	58	9	17	26	-12	20
Michael Peca	71	9	14	23	-4	56
Jaroslav Spacek	31	5	14	19	3	24
Jason Smith	76	4	13	17	1	84
Sergei Samsonov	19	5	11	16	0	6
Georges Laraque	72	2	10	12	-5	73
Igor Ulanov	37	3	6	9	-11	29
Todd Harvey	63	5	2	7	-7	32
Cory Cross	34	2	3	5	-5	38

GOALTENDER	GP	GA	SA	GAA	SV	SV%	SO
Dwayne Roloson	19	47	497	2.42	450	.905	1
Ty Conklin	18	43	359	2.80	316	.880	1
Michael Morrison	21	42	361	2.83	319	.884	0
Jussi Markkanen	37	105	873	3.13	768	.880	0

HOCKEY

FLORIDA PANTHERS

PLAYER	GP	G	A	PTS	+/-	PIM
Olli Jokinen	82	38	51	89	14	88
Joe Nieuwendyk	65	26	30	56	-2	46
Jozef Stumpel	74	15	37	52	11	26
Nathan Horton	71	28	19	47	8	89
Jay Bouwmeester	82	5	41	46	1	79
Martin Gelinas	82	17	24	41	27	80
Gary Roberts	58	14	26	40	4	51
Chris Gratton	76	17	22	39	6	104
Mike Van Ryn	80	8	29	37	15	90
Juraj Kolnik	77	15	20	35	1	40
Rostislav Olesz	59	8	13	21	-4	24
Stephen Weiss	41	9	12	21	-2	22
Sean Hill	78	2	18	20	3	80
Jon Sim	33	10	8	18	-1	26
Lukas Krajicek	67	2	14	16	1	50
Joel Kwiatkowski	73	4	8	12	3	86
Gregory Campbell	64	3	6	9	-11	40
Kristian Huselius	24	5	3	8	-11	4
Niklas Hagman	30	2	4	6	-8	2
Steve Montador	51	1	5	6	4	68

GOALTENDER	GP	GA	SA	GAA	SV	SV%	SO
Roberto Luongo	75	213	2,488	2.97	2,275	.914	4
Jamie McLennan	17	34	360	3.01	326	.906	0

LOS ANGELES KINGS

PLAYER	GP	G	A	PTS	+/-	PIM
Lubomir Visnovsky	80	17	50	67	7	50
Craig Conroy	78	22	44	66	13	78
Pavol Demitra	58	25	37	62	21	42
Michael Cammalleri	80	26	29	55	-14	50
Alexander Frolov	69	21	33	54	17	40
Derek Armstrong	62	13	28	41	-2	46
Joe Corvo	81	14	26	40	16	38
Sean Avery	75	15	24	39	-5	257
Eric Belanger	65	17	20	37	-5	62
Dustin Brown	79	14	14	28	-10	80
Mattias Norstrom	77	4	23	27	-3	58
Luc Robitaille	65	15	9	24	-6	52
Tom Kostopoulos	76	8	14	22	-8	100
Jeremy Roenick	58	9	13	22	-5	36
Tim Gleason	78	2	19	21	0	77
Nathan Dempsey	53	2	11	13	0	48
Jeff Cowan	46	8	1	9	-8	73
Mike Weaver	53	0	9	9	-3	14
Aaron Miller	56	0	8	8	-6	27
Mark Parrish	19	5	3	8	-9	4

GOALTENDER	GP	GA	SA	GAA	SV	SV%	SO
Jason LaBarbera	29	69	688	2.89	619	.900	1
Mathieu Garon	63	185	1,738	3.22	1,553	.894	4

MINNESOTA WILD

PLAYER	GP	G	A	PTS	+/-	PIM
Brian Rolston	82	34	45	79	14	50
Marian Gaborik	65	38	28	66	6	64
Pierre-Marc Bouchard	80	17	42	59	3	28
Randy Robitaille	67	12	28	40	-5	54
Todd White	61	19	21	40	-1	18
Wes Walz	82	19	18	37	7	61
Marc Chouinard	74	14	16	30	1	34
Alexandre Daigle	46	5	23	28	-6	12
Kurtis Foster	58	10	18	28	-3	60
Pascal Dupuis	67	10	16	26	-10	40
Filip Kuba	65	6	19	25	0	44
Mikko Koivu	64	6	15	21	-9	40
Daniel Tjarnqvist	60	3	15	18	-11	32
Andrei Zyuzin	57	7	11	18	-12	50
Brent Burns	72	4	12	16	-7	32
Stephane Veilleux	71	7	9	16	-13	63
Nick Schultz	79	2	12	14	2	43
Kyle Wanvig	51	4	8	12	-8	64
Willie Mitchell	64	2	6	8	15	87
Derek Boogaard	65	2	4	6	2	158

GOALTENDER	GP	GA	SA	GAA	SV	SV%	SO
Manny Fernandez	58	130	1,612	2.29	1,482	.919	1
Josh Harding	3	8	83	2.59	75	.904	1
Dwayne Roloson	24	68	759	3.00	691	.910	1

MONTREAL CANADIENS

PLAYER	GP	G	A	PTS	+/-	PIM
Alexei Kovalev	69	23	42	65	-1	76
Saku Koivu	72	17	45	62	1	70
Michael Ryder	81	30	25	55	-5	40
Mike Ribeiro	79	16	35	51	-6	36
Andrei Markov	67	10	36	46	13	74
Jan Bulis	73	20	20	40	2	50
Sheldon Souray	75	12	27	39	-11	116
Christopher Higgins	80	23	15	38	-1	26
Craig Rivet	82	7	27	34	-5	109
Richard Zednik	67	16	14	30	-2	48
Tomas Plekanec	67	9	20	29	4	32
Steve Begin	76	11	12	23	9	113
Francis Bouillon	67	3	19	22	-6	34
Radek Bonk	61	6	15	21	-3	52
Mathieu Dandenault	82	5	15	20	8	83
Alexander Perezhogin	67	9	10	19	5	38
Niklas Sundstrom	55	6	9	15	-6	30
Pierre Dagenais	32	5	7	12	-5	16
Mark Streit	48	2	9	11	-6	28
Mike Komisarek	71	2	4	6	-1	116

GOALTENDER	GP	GA	SA	GAA	SV	SV%	SO
Cristobal Huet	36	77	1,085	2.20	1,008	.929	7
Yann Danis	6	14	152	2.69	138	.908	1
Jose Theodore	38	122	1,025	3.46	903	.881	0
David Aebischer	7	26	240	3.73	214	.892	0

HOCKEY

NASHVILLE PREDATORS

PLAYER	GP	G	A	PTS	+/-	PIM
Paul Kariya	82	31	54	85	-6	40
Steve Sullivan	69	31	37	68	2	50
Yanic Perreault	69	22	35	57	-3	30
Kimmo Timonen	79	11	39	50	-3	74
Martin Erat	80	20	29	49	0	76
Marek Zidlicky	67	12	37	49	8	82
Scott Hartnell	81	25	23	48	8	101
Dan Hamhuis	82	7	31	38	11	70
Adam Hall	75	14	15	29	0	40
David Legwand	44	7	19	26	3	34
Scottie Upshall	48	8	16	24	14	34
Mike Sillinger	31	10	12	22	0	14
Greg Johnson	68	11	8	19	5	10
Ryan Suter	71	1	15	16	7	66
Scott Walker	33	5	11	16	2	36
Jerred Smithson	66	5	9	14	9	54
Darcy Hordichuk	74	7	6	13	9	163
Vernon Fiddler	40	8	4	12	-2	42
Danny Markov	58	0	11	11	9	62
Jordin Tootoo	34	4	6	10	9	55

GOALTENDER	GP	GA	SA	GAA	SV	SV%	SO
Chris Mason	23	52	597	2.54	545	.913	2
Tomas Vokoun	61	160	1,984	2.67	1,824	.919	4

NEW JERSEY DEVILS

PLAYER	GP	G	A	PTS	+/-	PIM
Brian Gionta	82	48	41	89	18	46
Scott Gomez	82	33	51	84	8	42
Jamie Langenbrunner	80	19	34	53	-1	74
Brian Rafalski	82	6	43	49	0	36
Patrik Elias	38	16	29	45	11	20
Sergei Brylin	82	15	22	37	-4	46
Paul Martin	80	5	32	37	1	32
John Madden	82	16	20	36	-7	36
Zach Parise	81	14	18	32	-1	28
Viktor Kozlov	69	12	13	25	0	16
Grant Marshall	76	8	17	25	-18	70
Alexander Mogilny	34	12	13	25	-7	6
Jay Pandolfo	82	10	10	20	2	16
Colin White	73	3	14	17	-2	91
Sean Brown	35	1	11	12	-14	27
Richard Matvichuk	62	1	10	11	2	40
Erik Rasmussen	67	5	5	10	-4	32
Vladimir Malakhov	29	4	5	9	-9	26
Brad Lukowich	18	1	7	8	3	8
Tommy Albelin	36	0	6	6	4	2

GOALTENDER	GP	GA	SA	GAA	SV	SV%	SO
Martin Brodeur	73	187	2,105	2.57	1,918	.911	5
Scott Clemmensen	13	35	295	3.35	260	.881	0

NEW YORK ISLANDERS

PLAYER	GP	G	A	PTS	+/-	PIM
Miroslav Satan	82	35	31	66	-8	54
Alexei Yashin	82	28	38	66	-14	68
Jason Blake	76	28	29	57	0	60
Mike York	75	13	39	52	-9	30
Mark Parrish	57	24	17	41	-14	16
Trent Hunter	82	16	19	35	-9	34
Shawn Bates	66	15	19	34	-11	60
Chris Campoli	80	9	25	34	-16	46
Alexei Zhitnik	59	5	24	29	4	88
Brent Sopel	57	2	25	27	-9	64
Arron Asham	63	9	15	24	-5	103
Oleg Kvasha	49	9	12	21	-2	32
Robert Nilsson	53	6	14	20	-6	26
Radek Martinek	74	1	16	17	-9	32
Brad Lukowich	57	1	12	13	-3	32
Janne Niinimaa	41	1	9	10	-7	62
Sean Bergenheim	28	4	5	9	-11	20
Joel Bouchard	25	1	8	9	5	23
Jeff Hamilton	13	2	6	8	0	8
Wyatt Smith	42	0	8	8	-7	26

GOALTENDER	GP	GA	SA	GAA	SV	SV%	SO
Wade Dubielewicz	7	15	145	2.90	130	.897	0
Rick DiPietro	63	180	1,797	3.02	1,617	.900	1
Garth Snow	20	68	595	3.72	527	.886	0

NEW YORK RANGERS

PLAYER	GP	G	A	PTS	+/-	PIM
Jaromir Jagr	82	54	69	123	34	72
Michael Nylander	81	23	56	79	31	76
Martin Straka	82	22	54	76	17	42
Martin Rucinsky	52	16	39	55	10	56
Petr Prucha	68	30	17	47	3	32
Steve Rucchin	72	13	23	36	6	10
Petr Sykora	40	16	15	31	5	22
Michal Rozsival	82	5	25	30	35	90
Jason Ward	81	10	18	28	-4	44
Fedor Tyutin	77	6	19	25	1	58
Tom Poti	73	3	20	23	16	70
Marek Malik	74	2	16	18	28	78
Dominic Moore	82	9	9	18	4	28
Ville Nieminen	48	5	12	17	10	53
Marcel Hossa	64	10	6	16	-6	28
Sandis Ozolinsh	19	3	11	14	2	20
Blair Betts	66	8	2	10	-10	24
Jed Ortmeyer	78	5	2	7	2	38
Jason Strudwick	65	3	4	7	-10	66
Darius Kasparaitis	67	0	6	6	7	97

GOALTENDER	GP	GA	SA	GAA	SV	SV%	SO
Henrik Lundqvist	53	116	1,485	2.24	1,369	.922	2
Kevin Weekes	32	91	867	2.95	776	.895	0

OTTAWA SENATORS

PLAYER	GP	G	A	PTS	+/-	PIM
Daniel Alfredsson	77	43	60	103	29	50
Dany Heatley	82	50	53	103	29	86
Jason Spezza	68	19	71	90	23	33
Wade Redden	65	10	40	50	35	63
Peter Schaefer	82	20	30	50	16	40
Bryan Smolinski	81	17	31	48	8	46
Mike Fisher	68	22	22	44	23	64
Zdeno Chara	71	16	27	43	17	135
Andrej Meszaros	82	10	29	39	34	61
Brian Pothier	77	5	30	35	29	59
Chris Neil	79	16	17	33	9	204
Antoine Vermette	82	21	12	33	17	44
Chris Kelly	82	10	20	30	21	76
Patrick Eaves	58	20	9	29	7	22
Vaclav Varada	76	5	16	21	2	50
Chris Phillips	69	1	18	19	19	90
Anton Volchenkov	75	4	13	17	21	53
Martin Havlat	18	9	7	16	6	4
Brandon Bochenski	20	6	7	13	7	14
Christoph Schubert	56	4	6	10	4	48

GOALTENDER	GP	GA	SA	GAA	SV	SV%	SO
Dominik Hasek	43	90	1,202	2.09	1,112	.925	5
Ray Emery	39	102	1,045	2.82	943	.902	3
Michael Morrison	4	12	96	3.48	84	.875	0

PHILADELPHIA FLYERS

PLAYER	GP	G	A	PTS	+/-	PIM
Simon Gagne	72	47	32	79	31	38
Peter Forsberg	60	19	56	75	21	46
Mike Knuble	82	34	31	65	25	80
Joni Pitkanen	58	13	33	46	22	78
Michal Handzus	73	11	33	44	-2	38
Jeff Carter	81	23	19	42	10	40
R.J. Umberger	73	20	18	38	9	18
Sami Kapanen	58	12	22	34	-9	12
Mike Richards	79	11	23	34	6	65
Freddy Meyer	57	6	21	27	10	33
Kim Johnsson	47	6	19	25	5	34
Eric Desjardins	45	4	20	24	3	56
Mike Rathje	79	3	21	24	22	46
Derian Hatcher	77	4	13	17	2	93
Petr Nedved	28	5	9	14	-8	36
Branko Radivojevic	64	8	6	14	-6	44
Brian Savage	66	9	5	14	-18	28
Jon Sim	39	7	7	14	-6	28
Donald Brashear	76	4	5	9	-2	166
Niko Dimitrakos	19	5	4	9	4	6

GOALTENDER	GP	GA	SA	GAA	SV	SV%	SO
Robert Esche	40	113	1,099	2.97	986	.897	1
Antero Niittymaki	46	133	1,266	2.97	1,133	.895	2

PHOENIX COYOTES

PLAYER	GP	G	A	PTS	+/-	PIM
Shane Doan	82	30	36	66	-9	123
Mike Comrie	80	30	30	60	2	55
Ladislav Nagy	51	15	41	56	8	74
Mike Johnson	80	16	38	54	7	50
Paul Mara	78	15	32	47	-12	70
Geoff Sanderson	75	25	21	46	-14	58
Keith Ballard	82	8	31	39	-18	99
Derek Morris	53	6	21	27	-7	54
Oleg Saprykin	67	11	14	25	-16	50
Zbynek Michalek	82	9	15	24	4	62
Steve Reinprecht	28	12	11	23	1	8
Dave Scatchard	47	11	12	23	-11	84
Fredrik Sjostrom	75	6	17	23	1	42
Boyd Devereaux	78	8	14	22	-13	44
Mike Leclerc	35	9	12	21	0	29
Jamie Lundmark	38	5	13	18	-1	36
Mike Ricci	78	10	6	16	-22	69
Denis Gauthier	45	2	9	11	-4	61
Oleg Kvasha	15	4	7	11	5	6
Petr Nedved	25	2	9	11	-6	34

GOALTENDER	GP	GA	SA	GAA	SV	SV%	SO
Curtis Joseph	60	166	1,690	2.91	1,524	.902	4
David LeNeveu	15	44	386	3.24	342	.886	0
Brian Boucher	11	33	268	3.87	235	.877	0
Philippe Sauve	5	17	128	5.45	111	.867	0

PITTSBURGH PENGUINS

PLAYER	GP	G	A	PTS	+/-	PIM
Sidney Crosby	81	39	63	102	-1	110
Sergei Gonchar	75	12	46	58	-13	100
Mark Recchi	63	24	33	57	-28	56
John LeClair	73	22	29	51	-24	61
Ryan Malone	77	22	22	44	-22	63
Zigmund Palffy	42	11	31	42	5	12
Colby Armstrong	47	16	24	40	15	58
Ryan Whitney	68	6	32	38	-7	85
Michel Ouellet	50	16	16	32	-13	16
Ric Jackman	49	6	22	28	-20	46
Tomas Surovy	53	12	13	25	-13	45
Mario Lemieux	26	7	15	22	-16	16
Andy Hilbert	19	7	11	18	8	16
Josef Melichar	72	3	12	15	-2	66
Erik Christensen	33	6	7	13	-3	34
Eric Boguniecki	38	5	6	11	-2	29
Dick Tarnstrom	33	5	5	10	-10	52
Konstantin Koltsov	60	3	6	9	-10	20

GOALTENDER	GP	GA	SA	GAA	SV	SV%	SO
Marc-Andre Fleury	50	152	1,485	3.25	1,333	.898	1
Sebastien Caron	26	87	733	3.98	646	.881	1
Jocelyn Thibault	16	60	484	4.46	424	.876	0

SAN JOSE SHARKS

PLAYER	GP	G	A	PTS	+/-	PIM
Jonathan Cheechoo	82	56	37	93	23	58
Joe Thornton	58	20	72	92	31	55
Patrick Marleau	82	34	52	86	-12	26
Nils Ekman	77	21	36	57	20	54
Tom Preissing	74	11	32	43	17	26
Milan Michalek	81	17	18	35	1	45
Steve Bernier	39	14	13	27	4	35
Alyn McCauley	76	12	14	26	-3	30
Scott Hannan	81	6	18	24	7	58
Mark Smith	80	9	15	24	3	97
Christian Ehrhoff	64	5	18	23	10	32
Kyle McLaren	77	2	21	23	6	66
Marcel Goc	81	8	14	22	-7	22
Grant Stevenson	47	10	12	22	-7	14
Scott Thornton	71	10	11	21	-8	84
Niko Dimitrakos	45	4	12	16	0	26
Marco Sturm	23	6	10	16	-8	16
Brad Stuart	23	2	10	12	-2	14
Josh Langfeld	39	2	9	11	4	16
Wayne Primeau	21	5	3	8	-6	17
GOALTENDER	**GP**	**GA**	**SA**	**GAA**	**SV**	**SV%**	**SO**
Nolan Schaefer	7	11	138	1.88	127	.920	1
Vesa Toskala	37	87	878	2.56	791	.901	2
Evgeni Nabokov	45	133	1,160	3.10	1,027	.885	1

ST. LOUIS BLUES

PLAYER	GP	G	A	PTS	+/-	PIM
Scott Young	79	18	31	49	-32	52
Doug Weight	47	11	33	44	-11	50
Petr Cajanek	71	10	31	41	-22	54
Mike Sillinger	48	22	19	41	-17	49
Dean McAmmond	78	15	22	37	-25	32
Keith Tkachuk	41	15	21	36	-15	46
Jay McClement	67	6	21	27	-23	30
Lee Stempniak	57	14	13	27	-10	22
Dallas Drake	62	2	24	26	-13	59
Jamal Mayers	67	15	11	26	-22	129
Dennis Wideman	67	8	16	24	-31	83
Christian Backman	52	6	12	18	-15	48
Eric Weinrich	59	1	16	17	-10	44
Kevin Dallman	46	4	9	13	-15	21
Mike Glumac	33	7	5	12	-8	33
Barret Jackman	63	4	6	10	-6	156
Mark Rycroft	80	6	4	10	-14	46
Eric Brewer	32	6	3	9	-17	45
Ryan Johnson	65	3	6	9	-21	33
Vladimir Orszagh	16	4	5	9	-2	14
GOALTENDER	**GP**	**GA**	**SA**	**GAA**	**SV**	**SV%**	**SO**
Curtis Sanford	34	81	885	2.66	804	.908	3
Jason Bacashihua	19	52	515	3.23	463	.899	0
Patrick Lalime	31	103	868	3.64	765	.881	0
Reinhard Divis	12	37	231	4.67	194	.840	0

TAMPA BAY LIGHTNING

PLAYER	GP	G	A	PTS	+/-	PIM
Brad Richards	82	23	68	91	0	32
Vaclav Prospal	81	25	55	80	-3	50
Vincent Lecavalier	80	35	40	75	0	90
Martin St. Louis	80	31	30	61	-3	38
Fredrik Modin	77	31	23	54	5	56
Dan Boyle	79	15	38	53	-8	38
Ruslan Fedotenko	80	26	15	41	-4	44
Pavel Kubina	76	5	33	38	-12	96
Ryan Craig	48	15	13	28	-4	6
Darryl Sydor	80	4	19	23	-18	30
Dave Andreychuk	42	6	12	18	-13	16
Paul Ranger	76	1	17	18	5	58
Evgeny Artyukhin	72	4	13	17	-4	90
Rob DiMaio	61	4	13	17	-7	30
Dmitry Afanasenkov	68	9	6	15	-7	16
Cory Sarich	82	1	14	15	-2	79
Tim Taylor	82	7	6	13	-12	22
Nolan Pratt	82	0	9	9	7	60
Martin Cibak	65	2	6	8	-9	22
Norm Milley	14	2	1	3	-2	4

GOALTENDER	GP	GA	SA	GAA	SV	SV%	SO
Gerald Coleman	2	2	17	2.79	15	.882	0
Sean Burke	35	80	764	2.80	684	.895	2
John Grahame	57	161	1,450	3.06	1,289	.889	5

TORONTO MAPLE LEAFS

PLAYER	GP	G	A	PTS	+/-	PIM
Mats Sundin	70	31	47	78	7	58
Bryan McCabe	73	19	49	68	-1	116
Tomas Kaberle	82	9	58	67	-1	46
Darcy Tucker	74	28	33	61	-12	100
Jason Allison	66	17	43	60	-18	76
Alexander Steen	75	18	27	45	-9	42
Kyle Wellwood	81	11	34	45	0	14
Jeff O'Neill	74	19	19	38	-19	64
Alexei Ponikarovsky	81	21	17	38	15	68
Nik Antropov	57	12	19	31	13	56
Chad Kilger	79	17	11	28	-6	63
Matthew Stajan	80	15	12	27	5	50
Eric Lindros	33	11	11	22	-3	43
Tie Domi	77	5	11	16	-10	109
Ken Klee	56	3	12	15	-1	66
Alexander Khavanov	64	6	6	12	-11	60
Aki Berg	75	0	8	8	-5	56
Clarke Wilm	60	1	7	8	-15	43
Carlo Colaiacovo	21	2	5	7	0	17
Ian White	12	1	5	6	2	10

GOALTENDER	GP	GA	SA	GAA	SV	SV%	SO
Jean-Sebastien Aubin	11	25	330	2.22	305	.924	1
Mikael Tellqvist	25	73	697	3.13	624	.895	2
Ed Belfour	49	159	1,476	3.29	1,317	.892	0

VANCOUVER CANUCKS

PLAYER	GP	G	A	PTS	+/-	PIM
Markus Naslund	81	32	47	79	-19	66
Henrik Sedin	82	18	57	75	11	56
Todd Bertuzzi	82	25	46	71	-17	120
Daniel Sedin	82	22	49	71	7	34
Brendan Morrison	82	19	37	56	-1	84
Anson Carter	81	33	22	55	-1	41
Nolan Baumgartner	70	5	29	34	11	30
Ed Jovanovski	44	8	25	33	-8	58
Mattias Ohlund	78	13	20	33	-6	92
Sami Salo	59	10	23	33	9	38
Ryan Kesler	82	10	13	23	1	79
Matt Cooke	45	8	10	18	-8	71
Richard Park	60	8	10	18	-2	29
Bryan Allen	77	7	10	17	4	115
Jarkko Ruutu	82	10	7	17	1	142
Trevor Linden	82	7	9	16	3	15
Alex Burrows	43	7	5	12	5	61
Kevin Bieksa	39	0	6	6	-1	77
Josh Green	33	4	2	6	2	14
Steve McCarthy	51	2	4	6	3	43

GOALTENDER	GP	GA	SA	GAA	SV	SV%	SO
Alexander Auld	67	189	1,938	2.94	1,749	.902	0
Dan Cloutier	13	36	334	3.17	298	.892	0
Maxime Ouellet	4	12	113	3.24	101	.894	0
Mika Noronen	4	10	77	3.53	67	.870	0

WASHINGTON CAPITALS

PLAYER	GP	G	A	PTS	+/-	PIM
Alexander Ovechkin	81	52	54	106	2	52
Dainius Zubrus	71	23	34	57	3	84
Jeff Halpern	70	11	33	44	-8	79
Brian Willsie	82	19	22	41	-19	77
Chris Clark	78	20	19	39	9	110
Matt Pettinger	71	20	18	38	-2	39
Ben Clymer	77	16	17	33	-7	72
Brian Sutherby	76	14	16	30	-17	73
Jamie Heward	71	7	21	28	-5	54
Bryan Muir	72	8	18	26	-9	72
Brooks Laich	73	7	14	21	-9	26
Matt Bradley	74	7	12	19	-8	72
Steve Eminger	66	5	13	18	-12	81
Shaone Morrisonn	80	1	13	14	7	91
Mathieu Biron	52	4	9	13	-11	50
Andrew Cassels	31	4	8	12	-3	14
Brendan Witt	58	1	10	11	-5	141
Ivan Majesky	57	1	8	9	-2	66
Jeff Friesen	33	3	4	7	-11	24
Nolan Yonkman	38	0	7	7	1	86

GOALTENDER	GP	GA	SA	GAA	SV	SV%	SO
Brent Johnson	26	81	854	3.44	773	.905	1
Olaf Kolzig	59	206	1,987	3.53	1,781	.896	0

LEGENDS

Mike Bossy scored at least 50 goals in nine straight seasons.

■ **Mike Bossy, right wing,** b. January 22, 1957, Montreal, Quebec. Bossy was one of the best pure goal scorers in NHL history. He scored at least 50 goals in nine consecutive seasons from the start of his career, and topped 60 goals five times. Only Bossy and Wayne Gretzky have accomplished that feat. Bossy led the Islanders to five consecutive Stanley Cup finals appearances (1980–1984), raising the Cup four times. In his five finals appearances, Bossy registered 69 goals and won the Conn Smythe Trophy in 1982 as the finals' most valuable player. Nagging back injuries forced Bossy to retire early. He was inducted into the Hockey Hall of Fame in 1991 and had his jersey retired by the Islanders in 1992.

■ **Paul Coffey, defenseman,** b. June 1, 1961, Weston, Ontario, Canada. Coffey is considered one of the best defensemen in NHL history, partly because of his tremendous offensive skills. In 1,409 career games, Coffey tallied 396 goals and 1,135 assists. In 1986, he set the single-season record for goals by a defenseman (46). Coffey spent seven seasons with the Edmonton Oilers, where he won three Stanley Cups while playing alongside Wayne Gretzky. Coffey added his fourth Cup with Mario Lemieux and the Pittsburgh Penguins in 1991. He scored 196 points in 194 career playoff games. Coffey won the Norris Trophy as the league's top defenseman three times — twice with Edmonton and once with the Detroit Red Wings.

■ **Glenn Hall, goaltender,** b. October 3, 1931, Humboldt, Saskatchewan, Canada. Nicknamed "Mr. Goalie," Hall won three Vezina Trophies as the league's top netminder during his tremendous career with the Detroit Red Wings, Chicago Blackhawks, and St. Louis Blues. In 1954, Hall replaced the legendary Terry Sawchuk as the starting goalie in Detroit, and went on to win the Calder Trophy as the league's top rookie in 1955–1956. Over a span of eight seasons, he played in 502 consecutive games, an NHL record for goalies. In 1961, Hall led the Blackhawks to their first Stanley Cup championship in 23 years. During the 1967–1968 season, he helped the St. Louis Blues reach the Cup finals. Although they fell to Edmonton, Hall was awarded the Conn Smythe Trophy as the playoff MVP. Hall retired at age 40, after the 1970–1971 season, and was elected to the Hockey Hall of Fame in 1975.

THE STANLEY CUP

Awarded annually to the team that wins the NHL's best-of-seven final-round playoffs. The Stanley Cup is the oldest trophy for which professional athletes in North America compete. It was donated in 1893 by Frederick Arthur, Lord Stanley of Preston.

SEASON	CHAMPION	FINALIST	GAMES PLAYED IN FINAL
2005–06	Carolina Hurricanes	Edmonton Oilers	7
2003–04	Tampa Bay Lightning	Calgary Flames	7
2002–03	New Jersey Devils	Anaheim Mighty Ducks	7
2001–02	Detroit Red Wings	Carolina Hurricanes	5
2000–01	Colorado Avalanche	New Jersey Devils	7
1999–00	New Jersey Devils	Dallas Stars	6
1998–99	Dallas Stars	Buffalo Sabres	6
1997–98	Detroit Red Wings	Washington Capitals	4
1996–97	Detroit Red Wings	Philadelphia Flyers	4
1995–96	Colorado Avalanche	Florida Panthers	4
1994–95	New Jersey Devils	Detroit Red Wings	4
1993–94	New York Rangers	Vancouver Canucks	7
1992–93	Montreal Canadiens	Los Angeles Kings	5
1991–92	Pittsburgh Penguins	Chicago Blackhawks	4
1990–91	Pittsburgh Penguins	Minnesota North Stars	6
1989–90	Edmonton Oilers	Boston Bruins	5
1988–89	Calgary Flames	Montreal Canadiens	6
1987–88	Edmonton Oilers	Boston Bruins	4
1986–87	Edmonton Oilers	Philadelphia Flyers	7
1985–86	Montreal Canadiens	Calgary Flames	5
1984–85	Edmonton Oilers	Philadelphia Flyers	5
1983–84	Edmonton Oilers	New York Islanders	5
1982–83	New York Islanders	Edmonton Oilers	4
1981–82	New York Islanders	Vancouver Canucks	4
1980–81	New York Islanders	Minnesota North Stars	5
1979–80	New York Islanders	Philadelphia Flyers	6
1978–79	Montreal Canadiens	New York Rangers	5
1977–78	Montreal Canadiens	Boston Bruins	6
1976–77	Montreal Canadiens	Boston Bruins	4
1975–76	Montreal Canadiens	Philadelphia Flyers	4
1974–75	Philadelphia Flyers	Buffalo Sabres	6
1973–74	Philadelphia Flyers	Boston Bruins	6
1972–73	Montreal Canadiens	Chicago Blackhawks	6
1971–72	Boston Bruins	New York Rangers	6
1970–71	Montreal Canadiens	Chicago Blackhawks	7
1969–70	Boston Bruins	St. Louis Blues	4
1968–69	Montreal Canadiens	St. Louis Blues	4
1967–68	Montreal Canadiens	St. Louis Blues	4
1966–67	Toronto Maple Leafs	Montreal Canadiens	6
1965–66	Montreal Canadiens	Detroit Red Wings	6
1964–65	Montreal Canadiens	Chicago Blackhawks	7
1963–64	Toronto Maple Leafs	Detroit Red Wings	7
1962–63	Toronto Maple Leafs	Detroit Red Wings	5
1961–62	Toronto Maple Leafs	Chicago Blackhawks	6
1960–61	Chicago Blackhawks	Detroit Red Wings	6
1959–60	Montreal Canadiens	Toronto Maple Leafs	4
1958–59	Montreal Canadiens	Toronto Maple Leafs	5
1957–58	Montreal Canadiens	Boston Bruins	6
1956–57	Montreal Canadiens	Boston Bruins	5
1955–56	Montreal Canadiens	Detroit Red Wings	5
1954–55	Detroit Red Wings	Montreal Canadiens	7
1953–54	Detroit Red Wings	Montreal Canadiens	7
1952–53	Montreal Canadiens	Boston Bruins	5
1951–52	Detroit Red Wings	Montreal Canadiens	4

Note: The 2004–2005 season was cancelled because of a lockout.

GAMES PLAYED

SEASON	CHAMPION	FINALIST	IN FINAL
1950–51	Toronto Maple Leafs	Montreal Canadiens	5
1949–50	Detroit Red Wings	New York Rangers	7
1948–49	Toronto Maple Leafs	Detroit Red Wings	4
1947–48	Toronto Maple Leafs	Detroit Red Wings	4
1946–47	Toronto Maple Leafs	Montreal Canadiens	6
1945–46	Montreal Canadiens	Boston Bruins	5
1944–45	Toronto Maple Leafs	Detroit Red Wings	7
1943–44	Montreal Canadiens	Chicago Blackhawks	4
1942–43	Detroit Red Wings	Boston Bruins	4
1941–42	Toronto Maple Leafs	Detroit Red Wings	7
1940–41	Boston Bruins	Detroit Red Wings	4
1939–40	New York Rangers	Toronto Maple Leafs	6
1938–39	Boston Bruins	Toronto Maple Leafs	5
1937–38	Chicago Blackhawks	Toronto Maple Leafs	4
1936–37	Detroit Red Wings	New York Rangers	5
1935–36	Detroit Red Wings	Toronto Maple Leafs	4
1934–35	Montreal Maroons	Toronto Maple Leafs	3
1933–34	Chicago Blackhawks	Detroit Red Wings	4
1932–33	New York Rangers	Toronto Maple Leafs	4
1931–32	Toronto Maple Leafs	New York Rangers	3
1930–31	Montreal Canadiens	Chicago Blackhawks	5
1929–30	Montreal Canadiens	Boston Bruins	2
1928–29	Boston Bruins	New York Rangers	2
1927–28	New York Rangers	Montreal Maroons	5
1926–27	Ottawa Senators	Boston Bruins	4
1925–26	Montreal Maroons	Victoria Cougars	4
1924–25	Victoria Cougars	Montreal Canadiens	4
1923–24	Montreal Canadiens	Vancouver Maroons, Calgary Tigers	2, 2*
1922–23	Ottawa Senators	Edmonton Eskimos, Vancouver Maroons	2, 4*
1921–22	Toronto St. Pats	Vancouver Millionaires	5
1920–21	Ottawa Senators	Vancouver Millionaires	5
1919–20	Ottawa Senators	Seattle Metropolitans	5
1918–19	No decision*	No decision*	5
1917–18	Toronto Arenas	Vancouver Millionaires	5
1916–17	Seattle Metropolitans	—	—
1915–16	Montreal Canadiens	—	—
1914–15	Vancouver Millionaires	—	—
1913–14	Toronto Blueshirts	—	—
1912–13	Quebec Bulldogs	—	—
1911–12	Quebec Bulldogs	—	—
1910–11	Ottawa Senators	—	—
1909–10	Montreal Wanderers	—	—
1908–09	Ottawa Senators	—	—
1907–08	Montreal Wanderers	—	—
1906–07	Montreal Wanderers (Mar.)	—	—
1906–07	Kenora Thistles (Jan.)	—	—
1905–06	Montreal Wanderers (Mar.)	—	—
1905–06	Ottawa Silver Seven (Feb.)	—	—
1904–05	Ottawa Silver Seven	—	—
1903–04	Ottawa Silver Seven	—	—
1902–03	Ottawa Silver Seven (Mar.)	—	—
1902–03	Montreal A.A.A. (Feb.)	—	—
1901–02	Montreal A.A.A. (Mar.)	—	—
1901–02	Winnipeg Victorias (Jan.)	—	—

*In 1923–24, the Montreal Canadiens beat the Vancouver Maroons in two games and the Calgary Tigers in two games. In 1922–23, the Ottawa Senators beat the Edmonton Eskimos in two games and the Vancouver Maroons in four games. In 1918–19, the Montreal Canadiens traveled to meet the Seattle Metropolitans. After five games had been played — the teams were tied at two wins apiece and one tie — the series was called off by the local Department of Health because of an influenza epidemic and the death of Canadien defenseman Joe Hall from influenza.

THE STANLEY CUP (cont.)

SEASON	CHAMPION	FINALIST	GAMES PLAYED IN FINAL
1900–01	Winnipeg Victorias	—	—
1899–00	Montreal Shamrocks	—	—
1898–99	Montreal Shamrocks (Mar.)	—	—
1898–99	Montreal Victorias (Feb.)	—	—
1897–98	Montreal Victorias	—	—
1896–97	Montreal Victorias	—	—
1895–96	Montreal Victorias (Dec.)	—	—
1895–96	Winnipeg Victorias (Feb.)	—	—
1894–95	Montreal Victorias	—	—
1893–94	Montreal A.A.A.	—	—
1892–93	Montreal A.A.A.	—	—

2005-06 TIME LINE

■ **July 13, 2005:** The lockout that cancelled the 2004–2005 NHL season ends, after 301 days. The owners and players union agree on a new six-year labor contract.

■ **July 22, 2005:** The NHL Board of Governors approves a series of rule changes for the 2005–2006 season, led by a new shootout format to decide games that remain tied after overtime.

■ **July 30, 2005:** Junior hockey phenom Sydney Crosby is selected first overall in the 2005 NHL Entry Draft by the Pittsburgh Penguins. Crosby, a 5'11"-tall center, turns 18 eight days later.

■ **October 5, 2005:** The first regular-season NHL games are played since the Stanley Cup finals in June 2004. All 30 teams are in action, and the first-ever overtime shootout takes place, between the Ottawa Senators and the Toronto Maple Leafs. Dany Heatley scores the tie-breaking goal for the Senators.

■ **October 8, 2005:** In his first home game, Sidney Crosby, scores his first NHL goal and posts his first multi-point game (3 points) as the Pittsburgh Penguins lose to the Boston Bruins, 7–6, in overtime.

■ **October 15, 2005:** Just five games into the season, future Hall of Famer Brett Hull retires from the Phoenix Coyotes after 19 stellar seasons in the NHL. Hull finishes his career with 741 goals, second only to Wayne Gretzky and Gordie Howe, and two Stanley Cup titles.

■ **January 24, 2006:** Pittsburgh Penguins legendary center Mario Lemieux retires from the NHL for a second time. Lemieux ends his career with 1,723 points, seventh all-time, and two Stanley Cup titles.

■ **February 26, 2006:** Sweden edges Finland, 3–2, to win the gold medal in men's hockey at the 2006 Olympics in Turin, Italy.

■ **April 17, 2006:** San Jose Sharks center Joe Thornton clinches his first scoring title with 125 points (29 goals, 96 assists) to edge New York Rangers forward Jaromir Jagr by two points.

■ **May 1, 2006:** Ales Hemsky scores two goals as the eighth-seeded Edmonton Oilers beat the top-seeded Detroit Red Wings, 4–3, to win their first-round Stanley Cup playoff series in six games.

■ **June 19, 2006:** For the third straight season, the Stanley Cup Finals reach a seventh game. And for the second straight season, a team from Canada comes up short. Behind stellar goaltending by Conn Smythe winner Cam Ward, the Carolina Hurricanes beat the Edmonton Oilers, 3–1, to win their first Cup in franchise history.

CONN SMYTHE TROPHY

Awarded to the Most Valuable Player of the Stanley Cup playoffs, as selected by the Professional Hockey Writers Association. The trophy was named for the former coach, general manager, president, and owner of the Toronto Maple Leafs.

SEASON	PLAYER	SEASON	PLAYER
2005–06	Cam Ward, Carolina Hurricanes	1994–95	Claude Lemieux, New Jersey Devils
2003–04	Brad Richards, Tampa Bay Lightning	1993–94	Brian Leetch, New York Rangers
2002–03	Jean-Sebastien Giguere, Anaheim Mighty Ducks	1992–93	Patrick Roy, Montreal Canadiens
		1991–92	Mario Lemieux, Pittsburgh Penguins
2001–02	Nicklas Lidstrom, Detroit Red Wings	1990–91	Mario Lemieux, Pittsburgh Penguins
2000–01	Patrick Roy, Colorado Avalanche	1989–90	Bill Ranford, Edmonton Oilers
1999–00	Scott Stevens, New Jersey Devils	1988–89	Al MacInnis, Calgary Flames
1998–99	Joe Nieuwendyk, Dallas Stars	1987–88	Wayne Gretzky, Edmonton Oilers
1997–98	Steve Yzerman, Detroit Red Wings	1986–87	Ron Hextall, Philadelphia Flyers
1996–97	Mike Vernon, Detroit Red Wings	1985–86	Patrick Roy, Montreal Canadiens
1995–96	Joe Sakic, Colorado Avalanche	1984–85	Wayne Gretzky, Edmonton Oilers

HART MEMORIAL TROPHY

Awarded annually "to the player adjudged to be the most valuable to his team." The original trophy was donated by Dr. David A. Hart, father of Cecil Hart, former manager-coach of the Montreal Canadiens.

SEASON	WINNER	SEASON	WINNER
2005–06	Joe Thornton, San Jose Sharks	1993–94	Sergei Fedorov, Detroit Red Wings
2003–04	Martin St. Louis, Tampa Bay Lightning	1992–93	Mario Lemieux, Pittsburgh Penguins
2002–03	Peter Forsberg, Colorado Avalanche	1991–92	Mark Messier, New York Rangers
2001–02	Jose Theodore, Montreal Canadiens	1990–91	Brett Hull, St. Louis Blues
2000–01	Joe Sakic, Colorado Avalanche	1989–90	Mark Messier, Edmonton Oilers
1999–00	Chris Pronger, St. Louis Blues	1988–89	Wayne Gretzky, Los Angeles Kings
1998–99	Jaromir Jagr, Pittsburgh Penguins	1987–88	Mario Lemieux, Pittsburgh Penguins
1997–98	Dominik Hasek, Buffalo Sabres	1986–87	Wayne Gretzky, Edmonton Oilers
1996–97	Dominik Hasek, Buffalo Sabres	1985–86	Wayne Gretzky, Edmonton Oilers
1995–96	Mario Lemieux, Pittsburgh Penguins	1984–85	Wayne Gretzky, Edmonton Oilers
1994–95	Eric Lindros, Philadelphia Flyers		

ART ROSS TROPHY

Awarded annually "to the player who leads the league in scoring points at the end of the regular season." The trophy was presented to the NHL in 1947 by Arthur Howie Ross, former manager-coach of the Boston Bruins. If two or more players are tied, the tie-breakers, in order, are: (1) player with most goals, (2) player with fewer games played, (3) player who scored the first goal of the season.

SEASON	WINNER	POINTS	SEASON	WINNER	POINTS
2005–06	Joe Thornton, San Jose Sharks	125	1993–94	Wayne Gretzky, Los Angeles Kings	130
2003–04	Martin St. Louis, Tampa Bay Lightning	94	1992–93	Mario Lemieux, Pittsburgh Penguins	160
2002–03	Peter Forsberg, Colorado Avalanche	106	1991–92	Mario Lemieux, Pittsburgh Penguins	131
2001–02	Jarome Iginla, Calgary Flames	96	1990–91	Wayne Gretzky, Los Angeles Kings	163
2000–01	Jaromir Jagr, Pittsburgh Penguins	121	1989–90	Wayne Gretzky, Los Angeles Kings	142
1999–00	Jaromir Jagr, Pittsburgh Penguins	96	1988–89	Mario Lemieux, Pittsburgh Penguins	199
1998–99	Jaromir Jagr, Pittsburgh Penguins	127	1987–88	Mario Lemieux, Pittsburgh Penguins	168
1997–98	Jaromir Jagr, Pittsburgh Penguins	102	1986–87	Wayne Gretzky, Edmonton Oilers	183
1996–97	Mario Lemieux, Pittsburgh Penguins	122	1985–86	Wayne Gretzky, Edmonton Oilers	215
1995–96	Mario Lemieux, Pittsburgh Penguins	161	1984–85	Wayne Gretzky, Edmonton Oilers	208
1994–95	Jaromir Jagr, Pittsburgh Penguins	70			

Note: The 2004–2005 season was cancelled because of a lockout.

LADY BYNG MEMORIAL TROPHY

Awarded annually "to the player adjudged to have exhibited the best type of sportsmanship and gentlemanly conduct combined with a high standard of playing ability." Lady Byng, who first presented the trophy in 1925, was the wife of Canada's Governor-General. She donated a second trophy in 1936 because the first one was given permanently to Frank Boucher of the New York Rangers, who had won it seven times in eight seasons.

SEASON	WINNER	SEASON	WINNER
2005–06	Pavel Datsyuk, Detroit Red Wings	1993–94	Wayne Gretzky, Los Angeles Kings
2003–04	Brad Richards, Tampa Bay Lightning	1992–93	Pierre Turgeon, New York Islanders
2002–03	Alexander Mogilny, Toronto Maple Leafs	1991–92	Wayne Gretzky, Los Angeles Kings
2001–02	Ron Francis, Carolina Hurricanes	1990–91	Wayne Gretzky, Los Angeles Kings
2000–01	Joe Sakic, Colorado Avalanche	1989–90	Brett Hull, St. Louis Blues
1999–00	Pavol Demitra, St. Louis Blues	1988–89	Joe Mullen, Calgary Flames
1998–99	Wayne Gretzky, New York Rangers	1987–88	Mats Naslund, Montreal Canadiens
1997–98	Ron Francis, Pittsburgh Penguins	1986–87	Joe Mullen, Calgary Flames
1996–97	Paul Kariya, Anaheim Mighty Ducks	1985–86	Mike Bossy, New York Islanders
1995–96	Paul Kariya, Anaheim Mighty Ducks	1984–85	Jari Kurri, Edmonton Oilers
1994–95	Ron Francis, Pittsburgh Penguins		

JAMES NORRIS MEMORIAL TROPHY

Awarded annually "to the defense player who demonstrates throughout the season the greatest all-around ability in the position." James Norris was the former owner-president of the Detroit Red Wings.

SEASON	WINNER	SEASON	WINNER
2005–06	Niklas Lidstrom, Detroit Red Wings	1993–94	Ray Bourque, Boston Bruins
2003–04	Scott Niedermayer, New Jersey Devils	1992–93	Chris Chelios, Chicago Blackhawks
2002–03	Nicklas Lidstrom, Detroit Red Wings	1991–92	Brian Leetch, New York Rangers
2001–02	Nicklas Lidstrom, Detroit Red Wings	1990–91	Ray Bourque, Boston Bruins
2000–01	Nicklas Lidstrom, Detroit Red Wings	1989–90	Ray Bourque, Boston Bruins
1999–00	Chris Pronger, St. Louis Blues	1988–89	Chris Chelios, Montreal Canadiens
1998–99	Al MacInnis, St. Louis Blues	1987–88	Ray Bourque, Boston Bruins
1997–98	Rob Blake, Los Angeles Kings	1986–87	Ray Bourque, Boston Bruins
1996–97	Brian Leetch, New York Rangers	1985–86	Paul Coffey, Edmonton Oilers
1995–96	Chris Chelios, Chicago Blackhawks	1984–85	Paul Coffey, Edmonton Oilers
1994–95	Paul Coffey, Detroit Red Wings		

CALDER MEMORIAL TROPHY

Awarded annually "to the player selected as the most proficient in his first year of competition in the National Hockey League." Frank Calder was a former NHL president. Sergei Makarov, who won the award in 1989-90, was the oldest recipient of the trophy, at 31. If a player is 26 or older as of September 15 of a season, he is not eligible to win the award.

SEASON	WINNER	SEASON	WINNER
2005–06	Alexander Ovechkin, Washington Capitals	1993–94	Martin Brodeur, New Jersey Devils
2003–04	Andrew Raycroft, Boston Bruins	1992–93	Teemu Selanne, Winnipeg Jets
2002–03	Barret Jackman, St. Louis Blues	1991–92	Pavel Bure, Vancouver Canucks
2001–02	Dany Heatley, Atlanta Thrashers	1990–91	Ed Belfour, Chicago Blackhawks
2000–01	Evgeni Nabokov, San Jose Sharks	1989–90	Sergei Makarov, Calgary Flames
1999–00	Scott Gomez, New Jersey Devils	1988–89	Brian Leetch, New York Rangers
1998–99	Chris Drury, Colorado Avalanche	1987–88	Joe Nieuwendyk, Calgary Flames
1997–98	Sergei Samsonov, Boston Bruins	1986–87	Luc Robitaille, Los Angeles Kings
1996–97	Bryan Berard, New York Islanders	1985–86	Gary Suter, Calgary Flames
1995–96	Daniel Alfredsson, Ottawa Senators	1984–85	Mario Lemieux, Pittsburgh Penguins
1994–95	Peter Forsberg, Quebec Nordiques		

VEZINA TROPHY

Awarded annually "to the goalkeeper adjudged to be the best at his position." The trophy was named for Georges Vezina, an outstanding goalie for the Montreal Canadiens who collapsed during a game on November 28, 1925, and died four months later of tuberculosis. The general managers of the NHL teams vote on the award.

SEASON	WINNER	SEASON	WINNER
2005–06	Miikka Kiprusoff, Calgary Flames	1993–94	Dominik Hasek, Buffalo Sabres
2003–04	Martin Brodeur, New Jersey Devils	1992–93	Ed Belfour, Chicago Blackhawks
2002–03	Martin Brodeur, New Jersey Devils	1991–92	Patrick Roy, Montreal Canadiens
2001–02	Jose Theodore, Montreal Canadiens	1990–91	Ed Belfour, Chicago Blackhawks
2000–01	Dominik Hasek, Buffalo Sabres	1989–90	Patrick Roy, Montreal Canadiens
1999–00	Olaf Kolzig, Washington Capitals	1988–89	Patrick Roy, Montreal Canadiens
1998–99	Dominik Hasek, Buffalo Sabres	1987–88	Grant Fuhr, Edmonton Oilers
1997–98	Dominik Hasek, Buffalo Sabres	1986–87	Ron Hextall, Philadelphia Flyers
1996–97	Dominik Hasek, Buffalo Sabres	1985–86	John Vanbiesbrouck, New York Rangers
1995–96	Jim Carey, Washington Capitals	1984–85	Pelle Lindbergh, Philadelphia Flyers
1994–95	Dominik Hasek, Buffalo Sabres		

SELKE TROPHY

Awarded annually "to the forward who best excels in the defensive aspects of the game." The trophy was named for Frank J. Selke, the architect of the Montreal Canadiens dynasty that won the Stanley Cup five consecutive times in the late 1950's. The winner is selected by a vote of the Professional Hockey Writers Association.

SEASON	WINNER	SEASON	WINNER
2005–06	Rod Brind'Amour, Carolina Hurricanes	1993–94	Sergei Fedorov, Detroit Red Wings
2003–04	Kris Draper, Detroit Red Wings	1992–93	Doug Gilmour, Toronto Maple Leafs
2002–03	Jere Lehtinen, Dallas Stars	1991–92	Guy Carbonneau, Montreal Canadiens
2001–02	Michael Peca, New York Islanders	1990–91	Dirk Graham, Chicago Blackhawks
2000–01	John Madden, New Jersey Devils	1989–90	Rick Meagher, St. Louis Blues
1999–00	Steve Yzerman, Detroit Red Wings	1988–89	Guy Carbonneau, Montreal Canadiens
1998–99	Jere Lehtinen, Dallas Stars	1987–88	Guy Carbonneau, Montreal Canadiens
1997–98	Jere Lehtinen, Dallas Stars	1986–87	Dave Poulin, Philadelphia Flyers
1996–97	Michael Peca, Buffalo Sabres	1985–86	Troy Murray, Chicago Blackhawks
1995–96	Sergei Fedorov, Detroit Red Wings	1984–85	Craig Ramsay, Buffalo Sabres
1994–95	Ron Francis, Pittsburgh Penguins		

ALL-TIME CAREER RECORDS

Points

PLAYER	YRS	GP	G	A	PTS	PTS/GAME
Wayne Gretzky, Edm, LA, StL, NYR	20	1,487	894	1,963	2,857	1.921
Mark Messier, Edm, Van, NYR	25	1,756	694	1,193	1,887	1.075
Gordie Howe, Det, Hart	26	1,767	801	1,049	1,850	1.047
Ron Francis, Hart, Pitt, Car, Tor	23	1,731	549	1,249	1,798	1.039
Marcel Dionne, Det, LA, NYR	18	1,348	731	1,040	1,771	1.314

Goal-Scoring

PLAYER	YRS	GP	G	G/GAME
Wayne Gretzky, Edm, LA, StL, NYR	20	1,487	894	.601
Gordie Howe, Det, Hart	26	1,767	801	.453
Brett Hull, Cal, StL, Dal, Det	19	1,264	741	.586
Marcel Dionne, Det, LA, NYR	18	1,348	731	.542
Phil Esposito, Chi, Bos, NYR	18	1,282	717	.559

KEY YRS=years; GP=games played; G=goals; A=assists; PTS=points; PTS/GAME=points per game; G/Game=goals per game

Wayne Gretzky

RICHARD MACKSON

CAREER RECORDS (cont.)

Assists

PLAYER	YRS	GP	A	A/GAME
Wayne Gretzky, Edm, LA, StL, NYR	20	1,487	1,963	1.320
Ron Francis, Hart, Pitt, Car, Tor	23	1,731	1,249	.721
Mark Messier, Edm, NYR, Van	25	1,756	1,193	.679
Ray Bourque, Bos, Col	22	1,612	1,169	.725
Paul Coffey, Edm, Pitt, LA, Det, Hart, Phi, Chi, Car, Bos	21	1,409	1,135	.806

GOALTENDING

Wins

Patrick Roy

GOALTENDER	W	L	T
Patrick Roy, Mtl, Col	551	315	131
Ed Belfour, Chi, SJ, Dal, Tor	457	303	111
Terry Sawchuk, Det, Bos, Tor, LA, NYR	447	330	172
Martin Brodeur, NJ	446	240	105
Jacques Plante, Mtl, NYR, StL, Tor, Bos	435	247	145

Shutouts

GOALTENDER	TEAM	YRS	GP	SO
Terry Sawchuk	Det, Bos, Tor, LA, NYR	21	971	103
George Hainsworth	Mtl, Tor	11	465	94
Glenn Hall	Det, Chi, StL	18	906	84
Jacques Plante	Mtl, NYR, StL, Tor, Bos	18	837	82
Tiny Thompson	Bos, Det	12	553	81
Alex Connell	Ott, Det, NYA, Mtl M	12	417	81

Goals-Against Average (Pre-1950)

GOALTENDER	TEAM	YRS	GP	GA	GAA
George Hainsworth	Mtl, Tor	11	465	937	1.91
Alex Connell	Ott, Det, NYA, Mtl M	12	417	830	1.91
Chuck Gardiner	Chi	7	316	664	2.02
Lorne Chabot	NYR, Tor, Mtl, Chi, Mtl M, NYA	11	411	861	2.04
Tiny Thompson	Bos, Det	12	553	1,183	2.08

Goals-Against Average (Post-1950)

GOALTENDER	TEAM	YRS	GP	GA	GAA
Martin Brodeur	NJ	13	813	1,760	2.21
Dominik Hasek	Chi, Buf, Det, Ott	14	638	1,374	2.22
Ken Dryden	Mtl	8	397	870	2.24
Jacques Plante	Mtl, NYR, StL, Tor, Bos	18	837	1,965	2.38
Chris Osgood	Det, NYI, StL	12	600	1,409	2.45

Note: Minimum 350 games played. Goals-against average equals goals against per 60 minutes played.

KEY YRS=years; GP=games played; A/GAME=assists per game; W=win; L=loss; T=tie; SO=shutout; GA=goals allowed; GAA=goals-against average

FAST FACT

Between the 1980–1981 season and the 2000–2001 season, only three players won the Art Ross Trophy for most points: Wayne Gretzky (10 times), Mario Lemieux (6), and Jaromir Jagr (5). But since then, four different players have won the honor: Jarome Iginla, Peter Forsberg, Martin St. Louis, and Joe Thornton. In 2005–2006, Thornton edged Jagr by two points.

TRIVIA CHALLENGE

Carolina's Cam Ward of the Carolina Hurricanes became the fourth rookie goaltender to win the Conn Smythe trophy as postseason MVP. Who are the other three?

Ken Dryden (Montreal, 1971), Patrick Roy (Montreal, 1986), Ron Hextall (Philadelphia, 1987).

TODAY'S STARS

■ **Alexander Ovechkin, left wing,** b. September 17, 1985, Moscow, Russia. The 6'2" left-winger was drafted in 2004, but he spent one more season playing in Russia for Dynamo Moscow before making his debut with the Washington Capitals following the lockout. Ovechkin began his NHL career with two goals against Columbus and registered points in his first eight games, on his way to finishing third in the league in points (106) and third in goals (52). Ovechkin is the second player in NHL history to score at least 50 goals and 100 points in his first season, joining Teemu Selanne of the Anaheim Ducks. Ovechkin won the Calder Trophy as the NHL's rookie of the year.

BILL WIPPERT

Alexander Ovechkin scored 50 goals in his rookie season.

■ **Sidney Crosby, center,** b. August 7, 1987, Cole Harbour, Nova Scotia, Canada. Crosby was selected by the Pittsburgh Penguins with the first pick in the 2005 Entry Draft, and his NHL debut was the most anticipated since Mario Lemieux entered the league in 1984. Crosby had dominated his junior hockey league in Canada, winning the scoring title at age 16. His transition to the NHL at age 18 was seamless. He earned an assist in his first pro game and scored his first goal in his third contest. He finished the season sixth in points (102), and was a finalist for rookie of the year honors.

■ **Ilya Kovalchuk, left wing,** b. April 15, 1983, Tver, Russia. In 2001, the Atlanta Thrashers made Kovalchuk the first Russian-born player to be taken first in the NHL Entry Draft. In just his third season, Kovalchuk tied for the league-lead in goals (41) with Jarome Iginla and Rick Nash. After playing in Russia during the lockout, Kovalchuk returned to the Thrashers and posted career highs in goals (52) and points (98) while leading Atlanta to a franchise-best 90 points, just two shy of a spot in the playoffs.

DID YOU KNOW?

Defenseman Chris Chelios won his first Stanley Cup in 1986 with the Montreal Canadiens. He didn't raise the Cup again until 2002, with the Detroit Red Wings. The span — 16 years — is the longest in NHL history between two individual Cup victories.

SOCCER

The Italian team celebrates its World Cup title.

In the end, the 2006 version of the Cup may be best remembered for the record number of disciplinary cards issued by referees. Zidane's red was the 28th of the tournament, six more than the previous high in 1998. Yellow cards were everywhere: 310 were shown, passing the 2002 record of 272. But for American soccer fans, the biggest disappointment was their team's dismal performance. After

The year 2006 meant only one thing to soccer fans around the globe: World Cup! The biggest sports event on earth, played every four years, kicked off in Germany on June 9 with 32 nations battling to win the coveted golden trophy. An estimated 1 billion TV viewers watched the final between Italy and France on July 9. The two teams were tied, 1–1, after 90 minutes of regulation time and two 15-minute overtimes, before Italy won, 5–3, in a penalty kick shootout. It was Italy's fourth World Cup title and its first since 1982. Host nation Germany beat Portugal, 3–1, in the third place match.

Unlike past World Cups, no single player dominated the tournament. The Golden Shoe Award, given to the top scorer in the World Cup, was awarded to forward Miroslav Klose of Germany, who booted in five goals. It was the lowest winning total since the 1962 Cup. Brazil's great striker Ronaldo scored just three goals in the 2006 tournament, but it was enough to make him the all-time leading goal scorer (15) in Cup history. France's midfielder Zinedine Zidane won the Golden Ball award as the tournament's best all-around player and retired from international competition afterwards. But his reputation as a classy player took a serious hit when he was sent off from the pitch after receiving a red card in the final for head-butting Italy's Marco Materazzi.

reaching the quarterfinals of the 2002 Cup, big things were expected from Team USA. Instead, the Yanks were eliminated in the first round after losses to the Czech Republic and Ghana, and a tie with Italy. The team played with little spirit, scoring just two goals (one an own-goal by Italy) and managed a tournament low of four shots on goal.

Many of the players on the Team USA roster came from Major League Soccer, which celebrated its 10th season in 2005. The league added two new teams for its anniversary year—Chivas USA (Los Angeles, California) and Real Salt Lake (Salt Lake City, Utah). In the 10th MLS Cup Championship, the Los Angeles Galaxy and the New England Revolution played to a scoreless tie through regulation, and the Galaxy's Guiller-

MLS TEAMS
EASTERN CONFERENCE
Chicago Fire
Columbus Crew
D.C. United
Kansas City Wizards
MetroStars
New England Revolution
WESTERN CONFERENCE
Club Deportivo Chivas USA
Colorado Rapids
FC Dallas
Los Angeles Galaxy
Real Salt Lake
San Jose Earthquakes

mo Ramirez scored the winner in overtime. In the regular season, forward Taylor Twellman of the New England Revolution scored a league-high 17 goals, while Pat Onstad of the San Jose Earthquakes led all goalkeepers in shutouts (12).

The 2006 MLS season opened with two big moves: the San Jose Earthquakes relocated to Houston and changed their name to the Dynamo and the MetroStars were sold to the Red Bull Company of Austria. The company, makers of an energy drink, renamed the team the New York Red Bulls and promised to help pay construction costs for a new soccer-only stadium. Rumors flew throughout the season about Zidane joining the squad, but nothing had been con-

firmed. David Beckham, who stepped down as captain of England's national team after the World Cup, was also mentioned as a possible addition to an MLS team.

Taylor Twellman led MLS in scoring, with 17 goals.

CHRIS ADUAMA/SPORTSSTOCKIMAGES.COM

JIM ROGASH/WIREIMAGE.COM

Landon Donovan led the Los Angeles Galaxy to the 2005 MLS championship.

2005 MLS FINAL STANDINGS

EASTERN CONFERENCE

TEAM	GP	W	L	T	PTS	GF	GA
y-New England	32	17	7	8	59	55	37
x-D.C. United	32	16	10	6	54	58	37
x-Chicago	32	15	13	4	49	49	50
x-Metrostars	32	12	9	11	47	53	49
Kansas City	32	11	9	12	45	52	44
Columbus	32	11	16	5	38	34	45

WESTERN CONFERENCE

TEAM	GP	W	L	T	PTS	GF	GA
y-San Jose	32	18	4	10	64	53	31
x-FC Dallas	32	13	10	9	48	52	44
x-Colorado	32	13	13	6	45	40	37
x-Los Angeles	32	13	13	6	45	44	45
Real Salt Lake	32	5	22	5	20	30	65
Chivas USA	32	4	22	6	18	31	67

Note: Three points for a win. One point for a tie.
x=clinched playoffs; y=conference champion

KEY GP=games played; W=win; L=loss; T=tie; PTS=points; GF=goals for; GA=goals against

SOCCER

MLS CUP 2005

Pizza Hut Park, Frisco, Texas
November 13, 2005
Attendance: 21,193

	1st Half	2nd Half	Final
Los Angeles Galaxy	0	1	1
New England Revolution	0	0	0

Scoring Summary:
LA: Guillermo Ramirez (unassisted) 107

Galaxy: Kevin Hartman, Chris Albright, Ugo Ihemelu, Tyrone Marshall, Todd Dunivant, Cobi Jones (Ednaldo de Conceicao 11), Paulo Nagamura, Peter Vagenas, Ned Grabavoy (Guillermo Ramirez 66), Landon Donovan, Herculez Gomez (Alan Gordon 12)

Wizards: Matt Reis, Jay Heaps, Michael Parkhurst, Joe Franchino, James Riley (Ryan Latham 11), Clint Dempsey, Daniel Hernandez (Andy Dorman 91+), Shalrie Joseph, Steve Ralston, Taylor Twellman, Pat Noonan (Jose Cancela 64)

Note: Numbers next to player names indicate time of game.

2005 MLS PLAYOFFS

Revolution							Earthquakes
Revolution	Revolution					Galaxy	
MetroStars							Galaxy
		Revolution	**GALAXY**	Galaxy			
Fire		(1–0)	**1 – 0**	(2–0)			Rapids
	Fire				Rapids		
United							FC Dallas

PLAYOFF LEADERS

GOALS	GP	G
Landon Donovan, Galaxy	4	4
Ivan Guerrero, Fire	3	2
Carlos Ruiz, Dallas	2	2
15 players tied with 1		

ASSISTS	GP	A
Terry Cooke, Rapids	3	2
Thiago, Fire	3	2
Cobi Jones, Galaxy	4	2
18 players tied with 1		

SHOTS	GP	SH
Herculez Gomez, Galaxy	4	15
Landon Donovan, Galaxy	4	12
Ramon Nunez, Dallas	2	12
Ricardo Clark, Earthquakes	2	11
Carlos Ruiz, Dallas	2	11
Chris Rolfe, Fire	3	10
Pat Noonan, Revolution	4	9
Jovan Kirovski, Rapids	3	7
Jack Stewart, Fire	2	7
5 players tied with 6		

GOALS-AGAINST AVERAGE	GP	GAA
Zach Thornton, CHI	3	0.33
Kevin Hartman, LA	4	0.46
Matt Reis, NE	4	0.69
Scott Garlick, DAL	2	0.86
Joe Cannon, COL	3	1.20
Tony Meola, MET	2	1.50
Pat Onstad, SJ	2	2.00
Nick Rimando, DC	2	2.00
Minimum: 75 minutes played		

KEY GP=games played; G=goals; A=assists; SH=shots; GAA=goals-against average

TRIVIA CHALLENGE

Name the year in which the first World Cup was played, the host country, and the winning team.

The first World Cup was played in 1930 in Uruguay and was won by Uruguay.

MLS STARS

Pat Onstad of the San Jose Earthquakes

KYLE RYAN/ICON SMI

■ **Pat Onstad, goalkeeper,** b. January 13, 1968, Rochester, New York. Onstad is the MLS's all-time leader in goals-against average (1.12, as of June 1, 2006). After signing with the San Jose Earthquakes (now the Houston Dynamo) in 2003, he established his reputation for steady backstopping as a rookie by helping the 'Quakes win the MLS Cup championship, 4–2, over the Chicago Fire. In 2005, Onstad led MLS in goals against average (0.97) and tallied a league best 12 shutouts.

■ **Clint Dempsey, midfielder/forward,** b. March 9, 1983, Nacogdoches, Texas. The 2004 MLS Rookie of the Year plays with a spirit that makes soccer fans smile. Dempsey was drafted out of Furman University by the New England Revolution in 2004, and scored seven goals and one assist in his first year in MLS. In 2005, he finished eighth in goals (10) and sixth in assists (9) as the Revs reached the Cup Final for the first time. New England lost to the Los Angeles Galaxy, 1–0.

■ **Jaime Moreno, forward,** b. January 19, 1974, Santa Cruz, Bolivia. Moreno is a living legend, having been named to the All-Time MLS Best XI in 2005 while still active. Moreno joined D.C. United in 1996 and has played all but one of his 11 seasons with the Red and Black. In 1997, he led MLS in goals (16). As of June 1, 2006, he was the league's second all-time leading goal scorer (100).

2005 MLS STATISTICAL LEADERS

SCORING	GP	G	A
Taylor Twellman, Revolution	29	17	8
Landon Donovan, Galaxy	26	16	11
Jaime Moreno, United	31	16	7
Carlos Ruiz, Dallas	21	13	2
Jeff Cunningham, Rapids	29	13	3
Herculez Gomez, Galaxy	26	12	2
Amado Guevara, Metrostars	28	12	11
Clint Dempsey, Revolution	30	11	10
Christian Gomez, United	33	11	9
Youri Djorkaeff, Metrostars	26	11	8
Josh Wolff, Wizards	22	10	10

GOALS	GP	G
Taylor Twellman, Revolution	25	17
Jaime Moreno, United	29	16
Jeff Cunningham, Rapids	26	12
Landon Donovan, Galaxy	22	12
Christian Gomez, United	31	11
Herculez Gomez, Galaxy	22	11
Amado Guevara, Metrostars	26	11
Carlos Ruiz, Dallas	19	11
Clint Dempsey, Revolution	26	10
Youri Djorkaeff, Metrostars	24	10
Josh Wolff, Wizards	22	10

ASSISTS	GP	A
Dwayne De Rosario, Earthquakes	28	13
Ronnie O'Brien, Dallas	28	12
Simon Elliott, Crew	32	11
Amado Guevara, Metrostars	26	11
Landon Donovan, Galaxy	22	10
Josh Wolff, Wizards	22	10
Ronald Cerritos, Earthquakes	30	9
Clint Dempsey, Revolution	26	9
Christian Gomez, United	31	9
Chris Klein, Wizards	31	9

GOALS-AGAINST AVERAGE	G
Pat Onstad, Earthquakes	0.97
Jonny Walker, Crew	1.13
Matt Reis, Revolution	1.13
Nick Rimando, United	1.17
Joe Cannon, Rapids	1.20
Zach Wells, Metrostars	1.24
Scott Garlick, Dallas	1.36
Bo Oshoniyi, Wizards	1.38
Kevin Hartman, Galaxy	1.39
Zach Thornton, Fire	1.64
Tony Meola, Metrostars	1.87
Brad Guzan, Chivas	1.99
D.J. Countess, RSL	2.01

KEY GP=games played; G=goals; A=assists; PTS=points; GAA=goals-against average; W=win; L=loss; T=tie

SOCCER

TEAM-BY-TEAM STATS

CHICAGO FIRE

PLAYER	GP	MIN	G	A	C	SHOTS	SOG
Chris Rolfe	29	1,942	8	5	1	61	32
Nate Jaqua	18	1,361	7	3	4	45	24
Thiago	27	2,220	6	7	3	45	20
Jesse Marsch	28	1,947	5	2	4	25	15
Justin Mapp	29	2,356	3	8	3	48	19
Lubos Reiter	14	772	3	2	1	22	16
Gonzalo Segares	21	1,864	3	2	5	10	5
Chris Armas	22	1,879	2	2	0	17	5
Ivan Guerrero	26	2,314	2	5	1	15	3
Andy Herron	20	983	2	2	1	22	12
Chad Barrett	20	597	1	4	0	25	9
Samuel Caballero	17	1,440	1	1	2	11	4
Jim Curtin	27	2,144	1	3	3	12	6
*Kelly Gray	6	508	1	0	2	6	2
Will Johnson	6	162	1	0	1	4	2
Jack Stewart	9	401	1	0	1	10	5
John Thorrington	8	368	1	0	1	2	1
C.J. Brown	20	1,658	0	2	6	2	0
Scott Buete	8	365	0	0	0	2	1
Leonard Griffin	3	152	0	0	1	0	0
Will John	6	200	0	1	0	2	0
Logan Pause	27	2,094	0	2	2	2	1
Tony Sanneh	12	989	0	1	1	1	1
FIRE	**32**	**2,880**	**49**	**52**	**45**	**389**	**183**
OPPONENTS	**32**	**2,880**	**50**	**59**	**56**	**335**	**152**

GOALKEEPER	GP	MIN	SHTS	SVS	SHO	GA	GAA
Zach Thornton	27	2,310	126	82	6	42	1.64
Matt Pickens	5	300	15	10	0	4	1.20
David Mahoney	3	270	11	7	1	4	1.33
TOTALS	**32**	**2,880**	**183**	**99**	**7**	**50**	**1.56**

CHIVAS USA

PLAYER	GP	MIN	G	A	C	SHOTS	SOG
Hector Cuadros	26	1,694	4	4	6	30	9
Ezra Hendrickson	31	2,745	3	1	4	30	10
Thiago Martins	22	1,779	3	1	5	46	16
Juan Francisco Palencia	9	810	3	1	4	28	15
Isaac Romo	25	1,190	3	1	4	33	15
Antonio Martinez	25	1,602	2	3	5	24	11
Ramon Ramirez	31	2,573	2	6	7	25	8
Douglas Sequeira	23	2,070	2	1	5	19	5
Matt Taylor	21	1,304	2	2	1	24	7
Arturo Torres	23	1,367	2	2	3	16	5
Esteban Arias	15	1,141	1	0	4	3	2
Juan Pablo Garcia	9	771	1	0	2	23	14
*Ryan Suarez	15	1,168	1	0	2	3	1
Armando Begines	22	1,659	0	0	3	2	1
Milton Blanco	5	43	0	0	0	0	0
Sergio Garcia	5	441	0	0	0	0	0
Francisco Gomez	12	648	0	1	2	6	0
*Alfonso Loera	12	877	0	0	2	1	1
Rodrigo Lopez	1	6	0	0	0	0	0
*Aaron Lopez	4	238	0	0	1	1	1
Francisco Mendoza	24	1,878	0	2	5	26	11
Mike Munoz	1	15	0	0	0	0	0
Jesus Ochoa	16	1,030	0	0	2	7	2
Orlando Perez	27	2,070	0	3	2	8	4
CHIVAS USA	**32**	**2,880**	**31**	**28**	**70**	**355**	**138**
OPPONENTS	**32**	**2,880**	**67**	**66**	**58**	**480**	**218**

GOALKEEPER	GP	MIN	SHTS	SVS	SHO	GA	GAA
Brad Guzan	24	2,079	156	104	2	46	1.99
Sergio Garcia	5	441	30	19	1	8	1.63
Martin Zuniga	4	360	32	18	0	13	3.25
TOTALS	**32**	**2,880**	**138**	**141**	**3**	**67**	**2.09**

*Player no longer with team

KEY GP=games played; MIN=minutes played; G=goals; A=assists; C=corner kick; SHTS=shots SOG=shots on goal; SHO=shutouts; SVS=saves; C/P=catches/punches; GA=goals allowed; GAA=goals-against average

COLORADO RAPIDS

PLAYER	GP	MIN	G	A	C	SHOTS	SOG
Jeff Cunningham	26	1,670	12	3	4	55	31
Jean Philippe Peguero	26	1,842	7	6	6	48	20
Alain Nkong	28	1,732	5	4	9	48	18
Dedi Ben Dayan	8	358	4	2	0	12	8
Terry Cooke	20	1,492	2	2	3	18	6
Luchi Gonzalez	20	1,449	2	2	1	22	14
Kyle Beckerman	30	2,343	1	4	5	24	8
*Mark Chung	6	434	1	0	0	7	4
Eric Denton	31	2,693	1	5	5	23	4
Wolde Harris	10	505	1	0	0	7	4
*Chris Henderson	8	661	1	5	0	5	2
Jovan Kirovski	7	630	1	1	2	14	5
Pablo Mastroeni	14	943	1	0	3	5	3
Fabrice Noel	7	125	1	0	0	5	3
Nat Borchers	31	2,721	0	1	7	13	2
Matt Crawford	4	256	0	0	0	1	0
Leo Cullen	15	750	0	1	3	1	0
Hunter Freeman	20	1,217	0	1	4	5	2
Dan Gargan	12	512	0	2	1	2	0
Sasha Gotsmanov	1	21	0	0	0	0	0
Ritchie Kotschau	28	2,272	0	2	2	8	1
Ricky Lewis	16	1,298	0	0	2	1	1
Amir Lowery	1	1	0	0	0	0	0
*Guy Melamed	14	911	0	1	4	10	2
*Martin Morales	1	61	0	0	0	1	0
Mike Petke	19	1,623	0	0	6	3	2
*Eugene Sepuya	1	18	0	0	0	0	0
Diego Serna	1	13	0	0	1	1	1
RAPIDS	**32**	**2,880**	**40**	**42**	**72**	**339**	**141**
OPPONENTS	**32**	**2,880**	**37**	**33**	**45**	**390**	**165**

GOALKEEPER	GP	MIN	SHTS	SVS	SHO	GA	GAA
Joe Cannon	27	2,399	139	100	8	32	1.20
Byron Foss	6	481	26	21	2	5	0.94
TOTALS	**32**	**2,880**	**141**	**121**	**10**	**37**	**1.16**

COLUMBUS CREW

PLAYER	GP	MIN	G	A	C	SHOTS	SOG
Edson Buddle	23	1,762	9	2	0	70	24
Knox Cameron	20	804	4	1	0	15	7
Cornell Glen	22	1,241	4	4	5	52	20
Frankie Hejduk	18	1,396	3	0	5	16	7
John Wolyniec	17	890	3	1	0	18	8
Chris Henderson	21	1,767	2	3	2	28	9
Eric Vasquez	11	703	2	0	0	9	5
Simon Elliott	32	2,880	1	11	5	31	9
Chad Marshall	30	2,655	1	3	1	25	10
Domenic Mediate	11	478	1	0	0	12	7
*Ante Razov	7	505	1	1	0	16	5
Mario Rodriguez	19	1,310	1	0	2	22	9
Jamal Sutton	8	330	1	1	1	7	2
David Testo	17	1,031	1	3	4	7	2
Stephen Armstrong	7	246	0	0	0	5	1
Devin Barclay	1	19	0	0	0	0	0
Robin Fraser	29	2,607	0	0	7	0	0
Stephen Herdsman	7	467	0	0	0	0	0
Ryan Kelly	7	296	0	0	0	0	0
*Manny Lagos	5	187	0	1	1	0	0
Kyle Martino	27	2,248	0	8	6	24	9
Mark Schulte	19	1,540	0	1	3	2	0
Marcus Storey	12	382	0	1	0	6	1
Danny Szetela	16	1,117	0	1	3	16	1
Chris Wingert	27	1,896	0	0	8	10	1
CREW	**32**	**2,880**	**34**	**42**	**53**	**391**	**137**
OPPONENTS	**32**	**2,880**	**45**	**49**	**49**	**443**	**186**

GOALKEEPER	GP	MIN	SHTS	SVS	SHO	GA	GAA
Jonny Walker	16	1,440	87	66	5	18	1.12
Jon Busch	9	765	50	34	3	14	1.65
Bill Gaudette	6	495	33	21	1	10	1.82
Matt Jordan	2	180	16	13	0	3	1.50
TOTALS	**32**	**2,880**	**137**	**134**	**9**	**45**	**1.41**

D.C. UNITED

PLAYER	GP	MIN	G	A	C	SHOTS	SOG
Jaime Moreno	29	2,445	16	7	2	77	46
Christian Gomez	31	2,419	11	9	6	64	37
Santino Quaranta	18	1,185	5	5	2	30	17
Freddy Adu	25	1,487	4	6	4	37	16
Joshua Gros	30	2,563	4	4	6	29	12
Dema Kovalenko	26	2,057	4	4	3	41	13
Bobby Boswell	27	2,344	3	1	6	12	6
Ben Olsen	23	1,874	2	4	7	23	12
Jamil Walker	22	732	2	7	0	21	11
Brian Carroll	32	2,567	1	3	4	10	4
Facundo Erpen	8	696	1	0	4	5	4
Nana Kuffour	3	181	1	0	0	3	1
Bryan Namoff	17	1,348	1	1	4	8	3
*Mike Petke	7	627	1	0	1	4	2
Alecko Eskandarian	12	661	0	1	1	21	8
Lucio Filomeno	1	22	0	0	0	0	0
*Steve Guppy	5	286	0	1	1	1	0
Shawn Kuykendall	2	10	0	0	1	0	0
Matt Nickell	4	31	0	0	0	1	1
Brandon Prideaux	29	2,455	0	0	4	3	2
Clyde Simms	26	1,263	0	1	1	13	3
David Stokes	10	390	0	1	0	2	1
Jason Thompson	1	1	0	0	0	0	0
John Wilson	17	1,099	0	2	2	5	2
D.C. UNITED	**32**	**2,880**	**58**	**58**	**61**	**410**	**201**
OPPONENTS	**32**	**2,880**	**37**	**31**	**72**	**308**	**136**

GOALKEEPER	GP	MIN	SHTS	SVS	SHO	GA	GAA
Nick Rimando	30	2,700	128	92	11	35	1.17
Troy Perkins	2	180	8	5	0	2	1.00
TOTALS	**32**	**2,880**	**201**	**97**	**11**	**37**	**1.16**

FC DALLAS

PLAYER	GP	MIN	G	A	C	SHOTS	SOG
Carlos Ruiz	19	1,549	11	2	2	63	30
Roberto Mina	21	1,270	7	4	2	35	13
Ronnie O'Brien	28	2,512	6	12	8	83	37
Eddie Johnson	15	1,180	5	2	1	30	12
Ramon Nunez	21	1,141	5	3	1	49	22
Abe Thompson	18	674	4	0	0	19	10
Aaron Pitchkolan	20	1,442	3	1	3	16	7
Arturo Alvarez	24	1,285	2	4	2	31	14
Clarence Goodson	29	2,488	2	1	9	18	9
Richard Mulrooney	7	574	2	2	1	7	2
Bobby Rhine	28	2,438	2	8	4	25	9
Chris Gbandi	17	1,519	1	1	7	14	7
Oscar Pareja	18	646	1	1	3	9	6
Steve Jolley	13	1,057	0	0	1	4	2
*Ty Maurin	3	17	0	0	0	0	0
Drew Moor	20	936	0	0	0	7	4
*Philip Salyer	2	180	0	0	0	0	0
Carey Talley	20	1,092	0	3	2	11	4
Simo Valakari	28	2,471	0	1	8	8	1
Greg Vanney	25	2,210	0	1	4	8	5
David Wagenfuhr	19	1,369	0	2	1	8	2
Mark Wilson	8	615	0	0	2	14	3
Alex Yi	1	66	0	0	1	1	0
DALLAS	**32**	**2,880**	**52**	**48**	**63**	**460**	**199**
OPPONENTS	**32**	**2,880**	**44**	**47**	**48**	**367**	**158**

GOALKEEPER	GP	MIN	SHTS	SVS	SHO	GA	GAA
Scott Garlick	28	2,457	135	98	6	37	1.36
Jeff Cassar	4	333	21	13	0	7	1.89
Dario Sala	1	90	2	2	1	0	0.00
TOTALS	**32**	**2,880**	**199**	**113**	**7**	**44**	**1.38**

KANSAS CITY WIZARDS

PLAYER	GP	MIN	G	A	C	SHOTS	SOG
Josh Wolff	22	1,910	10	10	0	51	29
Scott Sealy	28	1,669	9	2	0	31	20
Chris Klein	31	2,765	7	9	0	84	34
Sasha Victorine	30	2,658	7	4	0	35	15
Davy Arnaud	31	2,527	5	4	6	64	25
Jack Jewsbury	29	1,001	4	0	1	26	14
Jose Burciaga Jr.	31	2,667	2	4	9	36	10
Jimmy Conrad	25	2,241	2	2	4	11	5
Preki	16	478	2	2	1	13	5
Ryan Pore	8	285	1	1	0	6	1
Alex Zotinca	16	1,061	1	1	1	15	8
Dustin Branan	1	1	0	0	0	0	0
*Justin Detter	4	41	0	0	0	1	0
Nick Garcia	30	2,678	0	0	3	7	3
Diego Gutierrez	21	1,701	0	2	5	13	3
Jermaine Hue	3	55	0	0	0	2	0
Ryan Raybould	1	11	0	0	0	0	0
Brian Roberts	11	338	0	1	1	3	0
*Khari Stephenson	6	146	0	0	1	6	1
Antti Sumiala	2	116	0	1	0	2	1
Shavar Thomas	25	2,012	0	0	4	3	0
*Diego Walsh *	1	16	0	0	0	0	0
Kerry Zavagnin	28	2,421	0	4	5	13	4
WIZARDS	**32**	**2,880**	**52**	**48**	**42**	**422**	**178**
OPPONENTS	**32**	**2,880**	**44**	**52**	**52**	**357**	**163**

GOALKEEPER	GP	MIN	SHTS	SVS	SHO	GA	GAA
Bo Oshoniyi	32	2,880	163	112	7	44	1.38
TOTALS	**32**	**2,880**	**178**	**112**	**7**	**44**	**1.38**

LOS ANGELES GALAXY

PLAYER	GP	MIN	G	A	C	SHOTS	SOG
Landon Donovan	22	1,887	12	10	3	49	32
Herculez Gomez	22	1,508	11	2	5	54	25
Peter Vagenas	29	2,478	5	4	3	29	12
*Jovan Kirovski	24	1,704	4	4	2	48	20
Cobi Jones	31	2,397	3	6	3	28	15
Chris Albright	22	1,773	1	2	7	29	12
Pablo Chinchilla	19	1,400	1	0	2	7	2
Ednaldo da Conceicao	19	951	1	3	4	14	7
Michael Enfield	6	249	1	0	0	4	2
Tyrone Marshall	25	2,085	1	2	7	15	4
Guillermo Ramirez	24	1,593	1	1	2	62	30
Marcelo Saragosa	4	256	1	0	0	1	1
Benjamin Benditson	1	21	0	0	0	0	0
*Paul Broome	3	84	0	0	0	0	0
Mubarike Chisoni	11	308	0	0	1	4	2
Todd Dunivant	32	2,880	0	2	3	14	3
Josh Gardner	1	13	0	0	0	0	0
Alan Gordon	5	200	0	0	1	1	0
Ned Grabavoy	12	656	0	3	0	8	0
Ugo Ihemelu	25	2,031	0	1	4	1	0
Paulo Nagamura	25	2,028	0	2	7	21	8
Joseph Ngwenya	16	620	0	0	0	10	6
Troy Roberts	14	822	0	0	3	2	0
Michael Umana	15	756	0	0	2	4	2
GALAXY	**32**	**2,880**	**44**	**42**	**59**	**405**	**183**
OPPONENTS	**32**	**2,880**	**45**	**36**	**72**	**321**	**143**

GOALKEEPER	GP	MIN	SHTS	SVS	SHO	GA	GAA
Kevin Hartman	31	2,790	138	94	6	43	1.39
Steve Cronin	1	90	5	3	0	2	2.00
TOTALS	**32**	**2,880**	**183**	**97**	**6**	**45**	**1.41**

METROSTARS

PLAYER	GP	MIN	G	A	C	SHOTS	SOG
Jeff Agoos	25	2,150	0	0	9	9	4
Michael Bradley	30	2,628	1	4	3	17	5
Danilo da Silva	5	62	0	0	0	1	1
Youri Djorkaeff	24	1,986	10	7	2	76	33
*Gilberto Flores	3	39	0	0	2	1	0
Sergio Galvan Rey	27	1,598	7	0	2	44	23
Eddie Gaven	28	2,257	8	4	3	34	19
Amado Guevara	26	2,284	11	11	0	67	31
Jason Hernandez	3	268	0	0	9	0	0
Abbe Ibrahim	16	577	2	3	3	15	8
Chris Leitch	28	2,344	0	1	0	8	2
Mark Lisi	28	1,971	0	5	0	19	6
Mike Magee	29	1,835	5	5	1	27	13
Carlos Mendes	24	1,916	0	0	7	1	0
Jeff Parke	21	1,632	0	1	3	6	1
Eric Quill	2	11	0	0	5	0	0
Ante Razov	18	1,431	6	5	4	46	17
Tim Regan	20	1,643	0	0	0	3	1
Seth Stammler	10	361	0	1	5	2	2
Ryan Suarez	4	141	0	0	2	0	0
Tim Ward	13	1,034	0	3	0	6	2
*John Wolyniec	8	527	2	3	4	9	5
METROSTARS	**32**	**2,880**	**53**	**53**	**65**	**391**	**173**
OPPONENTS	**32**	**2,880**	**49**	**55**	**57**	**485**	**212**

GOALKEEPER	GP	MIN	SHTS	SVS	SHO	GA	GAA
Zach Wells	17	1,530	95	69	4	21	1.24
Tony Meola	15	1,350	117	83	2	28	1.87
TOTALS	**32**	**2,880**	**173**	**152**	**6**	**49**	**1.53**

NEW ENGLAND REVOLUTION

PLAYER	GP	MIN	G	A	C	SHOTS	SOG
Jose Cancela	25	1,643	2	5	1	23	11
*Cassio	3	112	0	0	7	1	1
Clint Dempsey	26	2,319	10	9	4	60	27
Andy Dorman	30	1,960	2	5	8	21	9
Connally Edozien	9	220	0	0	4	6	4
Joe Franchino	24	2,011	0	3	0	10	4
Jay Heaps	31	2,790	1	5	4	17	10
Daniel Hernandez	7	557	0	0	7	8	0
Jamie Holmes	1	20	0	0	5	0	0
Avery John	14	1,167	0	1	1	0	0
Shalrie Joseph	31	2,788	6	5	3	32	18
Jeff Larentowicz	1	1	0	0	0	0	0
Ryan Latham	6	157	0	0	1	3	2
Marshall Leonard	27	1,923	1	1	2	15	8
Pat Noonan	21	1,843	8	7	2	57	29
Michael Parkhurst	32	2,880	0	0	0	0	0
Ricardo Phillips	4	34	0	0	2	0	0
Steve Ralston	21	1,857	1	6	0	29	14
James Riley	23	1,294	1	3	0	9	4
Khano Smith	23	928	3	2	2	27	8
Taylor Twellman	25	2,226	17	7	0	82	51
Luke Vercollone	3	35	0	0	0	0	0
REVOLUTION	**32**	**2,880**	**55**	**59**	**55**	**400**	**200**
OPPONENTS	**32**	**2,880**	**37**	**44**	**61**	**374**	**169**

GOALKEEPER	GP	MIN	SHTS	SVS	SHO	GA	GAA
Matt Reis	31	2,784	162	115	10	35	1.13
Doug Warren	2	96	7	4	0	2	1.88
TOTALS	**32**	**2,880**	**200**	**119**	**10**	**37**	**1.16**

SIKIDS.com
Visit our website for the latest stats and sports info.

REAL SALT LAKE

PLAYER	GP	MIN	G	A	C	SHOTS	SOG
Jason Kreis	24	2,160	9	4	6	65	31
Andy Williams	26	2,102	5	3	5	46	18
Jordan Cila	12	646	3	1	1	6	4
Clint Mathis	27	2,123	3	4	7	45	17
Brian Dunseth	24	2,011	2	0	3	8	5
Seth Trembly	22	1,176	2	0	8	25	13
Jamie Watson	19	818	2	1	1	16	10
Chris Brown	29	2,125	1	1	0	30	10
Kevin Novak	3	221	1	0	0	4	2
Eddie Pope	20	1,756	1	0	0	8	4
Melvin Tarley	9	729	1	1	0	22	12
Nelson Akwari	23	1,887	0	0	5	3	1
*Matt Behncke	8	587	0	0	0	6	2
Nikolas Besagno	2	69	0	0	1	1	0
Paul Broome	11	917	0	0	4	1	0
Gustavo Cabrera	4	360	0	1	2	0	0
Kenny Cutler	19	1,699	0	0	5	5	2
Leslie Fitzpatrick	18	716	0	2	0	8	6
Adolfo Gregorio	6	359	0	0	0	4	2
Brian Kamler	28	2,028	0	0	3	11	3
Cameron Knowles	4	346	0	0	1	0	0
Luke Kreamalmeyer	6	249	0	1	0	6	2
Michael Lookingland	1	90	0	0	0	0	0
*Leighton O'Brien	6	236	0	0	1	2	1
Rusty Pierce	15	1,200	0	1	3	3	1
*Marlon Rojas	7	507	0	0	1	0	0
Robert Scarlett	9	720	0	2	0	8	3
*Dipsy Selolwane	8	401	0	0	0	10	4
Dante Washington	9	282	0	1	0	7	3
*Evan Whitfield	5	135	0	0	1	2	1
REAL SALT LAKE	**32**	**2,880**	**30**	**23**	**60**	**352**	**157**
OPPONENTS	**32**	**2,880**	**65**	**60**	**48**	**443**	**216**

GOALKEEPER	GP	MIN	SHTS	SVS	SHO	GA	GAA
D.J. Countess	27	2,422	170	112	4	54	2.01
Brian Kamler	1	8	0	0	0	0	0.00
Jay Nolly	5	450	46	34	0	11	2.20
TOTALS	**32**	**2,880**	**157**	**146**	**4**	**65**	**2.03**

SAN JOSE EARTHQUAKES

PLAYER	GP	MIN	G	A	C	SHOTS	SOG
Chris Aloisi	6	495	0	0	4	3	1
Wade Barrett	30	2,664	1	2	3	4	2
Danny Califf	20	1,742	2	0	3	9	5
Ronald Cerritos	30	2,308	6	9	0	50	29
Brian Ching	16	990	7	5	2	25	17
Mark Chung	24	2,053	6	7	6	32	16
Ricardo Clark	30	2,492	3	2	4	31	6
Ryan Cochrane	14	776	0	0	7	2	0
Brad Davis	18	1,408	2	8	4	23	11
Troy Dayak	7	551	1	0	2	5	1
Dwayne De Rosario	28	2,375	9	13	0	70	34
Kevin Goldthwaite	3	147	0	1	1	1	1
Kelly Gray	20	1,773	1	2	0	10	2
*Wes Hart	7	178	0	0	6	0	0
Roger Levesque	1	12	0	0	2	0	0
Alejandro Moreno	31	2,167	8	4	3	42	20
Brian Mullan	25	1,996	3	6	1	22	11
Julian Nash	10	233	1	1	0	3	3
Danny O'Rourke	13	1,050	0	0	0	4	2
Eddie Robinson	29	2,450	1	1	3	5	2
Ian Russell	13	235	0	0	1	2	1
Craig Waibel	6	527	0	1	0	1	0
Chris Wondolowski	2	5	0	0	1	0	0
EARTHQUAKES	**32**	**2,880**	**53**	**62**	**54**	**344**	**164**
OPPONENTS	**32**	**2,880**	**31**	**25**	**81**	**355**	**136**

GOALKEEPER	GP	MIN	SHTS	SVS	SHO	GA	GAA
Pat Onstad	32	2,880	136	105	12	31	0.97
TOTALS	**32**	**2,880**	**164**	**105**	**12**	**31**	**0.97**

ALL-TIME MLS CUP RESULTS

YEAR	CHAMPION	SCORE	RUNNER-UP
2005	Los Angeles Galaxy	1–0	New England Revolution
2004	D.C. United	3–2	Kansas City Wizards
2003	San Jose Earthquakes	4–2	Chicago Fire
2002	Los Angeles Galaxy	1–0 (OT)	New England Revolution
2001	San Jose Earthquakes	2–1 (OT)	Los Angeles Galaxy
2000	Kansas City Wizards	1–0	Chicago Fire
1999	D.C. United	2–0	Los Angeles Galaxy
1998	Chicago Fire	2–0	D.C. United
1997	D.C. United	2–1	Colorado Rapids
1996	D.C. United	3–2 (OT)	Los Angeles Galaxy

FAST FACT

FC Dallas is an original member of MLS. The team joined the league in 1996 as the Dallas Burn and changed its name before the 2005 season. The initials "FC" stand for Football Club.

MLS AWARD WINNERS

YEAR	MVP	SCORING CHAMPION	GOAL OF THE YEAR	COACH
2005	Taylor Twellman, Revolution	Taylor Twellman, Revolution	Dwayne De Rosario, Earthquakes	Dominic Kinnear, Earthquakes
2004	Amado Guevara, MetroStars	Amado Guevara, MetroStars	Dwayne De Rosario, Earthquakes	Greg Andrulis, Crew
2003	Preki, Wizards	Preki, Wizards	Damani Ralph, Fire	Dave Sarachan, Fire
2002	Carlos Ruiz, Galaxy	Taylor Twellman, Revolution	Carlos Ruiz, Galaxy	Steve Nicol, Revolution
2001	Alex Pineda Chacon, Fusion	Alex Pineda Chacon, Fusion	Clint Mathis, MetroStars	Frank Yallop, Earthquakes
2000	Tony Meola, Wizards	Mamadou Diallo, Mutiny	Marcelo Balboa, Rapids	Bob Gansler, Wizards
1999	Jason Kreis, Burn	Jason Kreis, Burn	Marco Etcheverry, United	Sigi Schmid, Galaxy
1998	Marco Etcheverry, United	Stern John, Crew	Brian McBride, Crew	Bob Bradley, Fire
1997	Preki, Wizards	Preki, Wizards	Marco Etcheverry, United	Bruce Arena, United
1996	Carlos Valderrama, Mutiny	Roy Lassiter, Mutiny	Eric Wynalda, Clash	Thomas Rongen, Mutiny

YEAR	GOALKEEPER	DEFENDER	ROOKIE	COMEBACK PLAYER
2005	Pat Onstad, Earthquakes	Jimmy Conrad, Wizards	Michael Parkhurst, Revolution	Chris Klein, Wizards
2004	Joe Cannon, Rapids	Robin Fraser, Crew	Clint Dempsey, Revolution	Brian Ching, Earthquakes
2003	Pat Onstad, Earthquakes	Carlos Bocanegra, Fire	Damani Ralph, Fire	Chris Armas, Fire
2002	Joe Cannon, Earthquakes	Carlos Bocanegra, Fire	Kyle Martino, Crew	Chris Klein, Wizards
2001	Tim Howard, MetroStars	Jeff Agoos, Earthquakes	Rodrigo Faria, MetroStars	Troy Dayak, Earthquakes
2000	Tony Meola, Wizards	Peter Vermes, Wizards	Carlos Bocanegra, Fire	Tony Meola, Wizards
1999	Kevin Hartman, Galaxy	Robin Fraser, Galaxy	Jay Heaps, Fusion	Not awarded
1998	Zach Thornton, Fire	Lubos Kubik, Fire	Ben Olsen, United	Not awarded
1997	Brad Friedel, Crew	Eddie Pope, United	Mike Duhaney, Mutiny	Not awarded
1996	Mark Dodd, Burn	John Doyle, Clash	Steve Ralston, Mutiny	Not awarded

MLS LEGENDS

Carlos Valderrama was the first MVP of MLS.

■ Carlos Valderrama, midfielder,
b. September 2, 1961, Santa Marta, Colombia. Known as *El Pibe,* or "The Kid" in his native Colombia, Valderrama played professionally in Spain and France before joining the Tampa Bay Mutiny in Major League Soccer's first season (1996). The floppy-haired wonder earned the league's first MVP award in '96, and went on to rack up an MLS record 114 assists in seven seasons with the Mutiny, Miami Fusion, and Colorado Rapids. He retired after the 2002 season, and was named to the All-Time MLS Best XI in 2005.

■ Marco Etcheverry, midfielder,
b. September 26, 1970, Santa Cruz, Bolivia. Perhaps the best player ever in MLS, Etcheverry joined D.C. United in the league's inaugural season (1996) and led the Black and Red to the league's first two championships (1996, 1997). The Bolivian won the league MVP award in 1998, and one year later led United to the 1999 title. Etcheverry retired from MLS after the 2003 season. He was named to the All-Time MLS Best XI in 2005.

■ Jorge Campos, goalkeeper, b. October 15, 1966, Acapulco, Mexico. At 5'7"-tall, Campos was short for a goalkeeper. But he made up for his lack of size with his aggressive game (and the eye-popping goalkeeper jerseys he designed himself). Campos joined the Los Angeles Galaxy in 1996 and led MLS in goals-against average (1.20) that year. He played one more season in L.A. before being traded to the Chicago Fire. Campos retired from the league after the 1998 season. He still holds the MLS record for best career winning percentage (64.4).

MLS ALL-STAR GAME RESULTS

YEAR	RESULT	SITE	MVP
2005	MLS 4, Fulham FC 1	Columbus, Ohio	Taylor Twellman, New England Revolution
2004	East 3, West 2	Washington, D.C.	Amado Guevara, MetroStars
2003	MLS 3, Guadalajara Chivas 1	Carson, California	Carlos Ruiz, Los Angeles Galaxy
2002	MLS 3, USA 2	Washington, D.C.	Marco Etcheverry, D.C. United
2001	East 6, West 6	San Jose, California	Landon Donovan, San Jose Earthquakes
2000	East 9, West 4	Columbus, Ohio	Mamadou Diallo, Tampa Bay Mutiny
1999	West 6, East 4	San Diego, California	Preki, Kansas City Wizards
1998	MLS USA 6, World 1	Orlando, Florida	Brian McBride, Columbus Crew
1997	East 5, West 4	East Rutherford, New Jersey	Carlos Valderrama, Tampa Bay Mutiny
1996	East 3, West 2	East Rutherford, New Jersey	Carlos Valderrama, Tampa Bay Mutiny

SOCCER

UNITED SOCCER LEAGUE FIRST DIVISION* CHAMPIONS

YEAR	CHAMPION	SCORE	RUNNER-UP
2005	Seattle Sounders	1–1 (4-3 on PKs)	Richmond Kickers
2004	Montreal Impact	2–0	Seattle Sounders
2003	Charleston Battery	3–0	Minnesota Thunder
2002	Milwaukee Rampage	2–1 (2 OT)	Richmond Kickers
2001	Rochester Raging Rhinos	2–0	Hershey Wildcats
2000	Rochester Raging Rhinos	3–1	Minnesota Thunder
1999	Minnesota Thunder	2–1	Rochester Raging Rhinos
1998	Rochester Raging Rhinos	3–1	Minnesota Thunder
1997	Milwaukee Rampage	2–1 (SO)	Carolina Dynamo
1996	Seattle Sounders	2–0	Rochester Raging Rhinos
1995	Seattle Sounders	1–2 (SO), 3–0, 2–1 (SO)	Atlanta Ruckus
1994	Montreal Impact	1–0	Colorado Foxes
1993	Colorado Foxes	3–1 (OT)	Los Angeles Salsa
1992	Colorado Foxes	1–0	Tampa Bay Rowdies
1991	San Francisco Bay Blackhawks	1–3, 2–0 (1–0 on PKs)	Albany Capitals

*United Soccer League serves as a minor league system for Major League Soccer.

UNITED SOCCER LEAGUE RESULTS

2005 FIRST DIVISION FINAL STANDINGS

Team	GP	W	L	T
Montreal Impact	28	18	3	7
Rochester Raging Rhinos	28	15	7	6
Vancouver Whitecaps	28	12	7	9
Seattle Sounders	28	11	6	11
Portland Timbers	28	10	9	9
Richmond Kickers	28	10	9	9
Puerto Rico Islanders	28	10	10	8
Atlanta Silverbacks	28	10	15	3
Charleston Battery	28	9	14	5
Minnesota Thunder	28	7	11	10
Virginia Beach Mariners	28	7	14	7
Toronto Lynx	28	3	17	8

2005 FIRST DIVISION CHAMPIONSHIP

Qwest Field, Seattle, Washington
Saturday, October 1, 2005

Seattle Sounders 1*, Richmond Kickers 1

Scoring Summary

Richmond: Sascha Gorres 24

Seattle: Maykel Galindo (Ryan Edwards) 73

*Seattle won on penalty kicks.

DID YOU KNOW?

On March 22, 2006, Kasey Keller earned the first point ever scored in a match by a U.S. goalkeeper since assists became an official stat in 1991. Keller picked up his point when he assisted on a goal during Team USA's 4–1 loss to Germany.

2005 LAMAR HUNT U.S. OPEN CUP RESULTS

The annual Lamar Hunt U.S. Open Cup is open to all amateur and professional teams in the United States. The tournament is a single-elimination event running at the same time as the MLS season. The winner advances to the CONCACAF (Confederation of North, Central American, and Caribbean Association Football) Cup, a tournament of the top club teams from North and Central America and the Caribbean.

QUARTERFINALS
MetroStars 1, Rochester Rhinos 3
Colorado Rapids 1, Minnesota Thunder 4
DC United 3, Richmond Kickers 1
Des Moines Menace 1, Kansas City Wizards 6
San Jose Earthquakes 2, Portland Timbers 0
FC Dallas 3, Columbus Crew 1
Chicago Fire 3, New England Revolution 2 (OT)
Chivas USA 2, Los Angeles Galaxy 5

SEMI-FINALS
Minnesota Thunder 2, Los Angeles Galaxy 5
Chicago Fire 0, FC Dallas 1

2005 LAMAR HUNT
U.S. OPEN CUP FINAL RESULTS
September 28, 2005, Los Angeles, California
FC Dallas 0, Los Angeles Galaxy 1
Scoring summary: Herculez Gomez 1 (Chris Albright) 25

LAMAR HUNT U.S. OPEN CUP RESULTS

YEAR	CHAMPION	YEAR	CHAMPION
2005	Los Angeles Galaxy (MLS)	1959	McIlvaine Canvasbacks (Los Angeles, CA)
2004	Kansas City Wizards (MLS)	1958	Los Angeles Kickers (CA)
2003	Chicago Fire (MLS)	1957	Kutis SC (St. Louis, MO)
2002	Columbus Crew (MLS)	1956	Harmarville SC (PA)
2001	Los Angeles Galaxy (MLS)	1955	Eintracht Sport Club (New York City)
2000	Chicago Fire (MLS)	1954	New York Americans (New York City)
1999	Rochester Rhinos (A-League)	1953	Falcons SC (Chicago, IL)
1998	Chicago Fire (MLS)	1952	Harmarville SC (PA)
1997	Dallas Burn (MLS)	1951	German Hungarian SC (New York City)
1996	D.C. United (MLS)	1950	Simpkins-Ford SC (St. Louis, MO)
1995	Richmond Kickers (VA)	1949	Morgan SC (PA)
1994	Greek American AC (San Francisco, CA)	1948	Simpkins-Ford SC (St. Louis, MO)
1993	Club Deportivo Mexico (San Francisco, CA)	1947	Ponta Delgada SC (Fall River, MA)
1992	San Jose Oaks (CA)	1946	Chicago Viking FC (IL)
1991	Brooklyn Italians SC (East New York, NY)	1945	Brookhattan FC (New York City)
1990	AAC Eagles (Chicago, IL)	1944	Brooklyn Hispano SC (New York City)
1989	HRC Kickers (St. Petersburg, FL)	1943	Brooklyn Hispano SC (New York City)
1988	Busch SC (St. Louis, MO)	1942	Gallatin SC (PA)
1987	Club Espana (Washington, D.C.)	1941	Pawtucket FC (RI)
1986	Kutis SC (St. Louis, MO)	1940	No winner
1985	Greek American AC (San Francisco, CA)	1939	St. Mary's Celtic SC (Brooklyn, NY)
1984	AO Krete (New York City)	1938	Sparta A and BA (Chicago, IL)
1983	NY Pancyprian-Freedoms (New York City)	1937	New York American FC (New York City)
1982	NY Pancyprian-Freedoms (New York City)	1936	German-Americans (Philadelphia, PA)
1981	Maccabee SC (Los Angeles, CA)	1935	Central Breweries FC (Chicago, IL)
1980	NY Pancyprian-Freedoms (New York City)	1934	Stix, Baer and Fuller FC (St. Louis, MO)
1979	Brooklyn Dodgers SC (New York City)	1933	Stix, Baer and Fuller FC (St. Louis, MO)
1978	Maccabee SC (Los Angeles, CA)	1932	New Bedford FC (MA)
1977	Maccabee SC (Los Angeles, CA)	1931	Fall River FC (MA)
1976	San Francisco AC (CA)	1930	Fall River FC (MA)
1975	Maccabee SC (Los Angeles, CA)	1929	Hakoah All Stars SC (New York City)
1974	Greek American AA (New York City)	1928	New York National FC (New York City)
1973	Maccabee SC (Los Angeles, CA)	1927	Fall River FC (MA)
1972	Elizabeth SC (Union, NJ)	1926	Bethlehem Steel FC (PA)
1971	Hota SC (New York City)	1925	Shawsheen FC (Andover, MA)
1970	Elizabeth SC (Union, NJ)	1924	Fall River FC (MA)
1969	Greek American AA (New York City)	1923	Paterson FC (NJ)
1968	Greek American AA (New York City)	1922	Scullin Steel FC (St. Louis, MO)
1967	Greek American AA (New York City)	1921	Robbins Dry Dock FC (Brooklyn, NY)
1966	Ukrainian Nationals (Philadelphia, PA)	1920	Ben Miller FC (St. Louis, MO)
1965	New York Hungaria (New York City)	1919	Bethlehem Steel FC (PA)
1964	Los Angeles Kickers (CA)	1918	Bethlehem Steel FC (PA)
1963	Ukrainian Nationals (Philadelphia, PA)	1917	Fall River Rovers (MA)
1962	New York Hungaria (New York City)	1916	Bethlehem Steel FC (PA)
1961	Ukrainian Nationals (Philadelphia, PA)	1915	Bethlehem Steel FC (PA)
1960	Ukrainian Nationals (Philadelphia, PA)	1914	Brooklyn Field Club (New York City)

2006 WORLD CUP GROUP STANDINGS

GROUP A

Country	GP	W	L	T	GF	GA	Pts
*Germany	3	3	0	0	8	2	9
*Ecuador	3	2	1	0	5	3	6
Poland	3	1	2	0	2	4	3
Costa Rica	3	0	3	0	3	9	0

GROUP B

Country	GP	W	L	T	GF	GA	Pts
*England	3	2	0	1	5	2	7
*Sweden	3	1	0	2	3	2	5
Paraguay	3	1	2	0	2	2	3
Trinidad-Tobago	3	0	2	1	0	4	1

GROUP C

Country	GP	W	L	T	GF	GA	Pts
*Argentina	3	2	0	1	8	1	7
*Netherlands	3	2	0	1	3	1	7
Cote D'Ivoire	3	1	2	0	5	6	3
Serbia-Montenegro	3	0	3	0	2	10	0

GROUP D

Country	GP	W	L	T	GF	GA	Pts
*Portugal	3	3	0	0	5	1	9
*Mexico	3	1	1	1	4	3	4
Angola	3	0	1	2	1	2	2
Iran	3	0	2	1	2	6	1

GROUP E

Country	GP	W	L	T	GF	GA	Pts
*Italy	3	2	0	1	5	1	7
*Ghana	3	2	1	0	4	3	6
Czech Republic	3	1	2	0	3	4	3
United States	3	0	2	1	2	6	1

GROUP F

Country	GP	W	L	T	GF	GA	Pts
*Brazil	3	3	0	0	7	1	9
*Australia	3	1	1	1	5	5	4
Croatia	3	0	1	2	2	3	2
Japan	3	0	2	1	2	7	1

GROUP G

Country	GP	W	L	T	GF	GA	Pts
*Switzerland	3	2	0	1	4	0	7
*France	3	1	0	2	3	1	5
South Korea	3	1	1	1	3	4	4
Togo	3	0	3	0	1	6	0

GROUP H

Country	GP	W	L	T	GF	GA	Pts
*Spain	3	3	0	0	8	1	9
*Ukraine	3	2	1	0	5	4	6
Tunisia	3	0	2	1	3	6	1
Saudi Arabia	3	0	2	1	2	7	1

*Advanced to second round.
Note: In group play, teams are awarded three points for a victory, one for a tie. The top two in each group advance to the Round of 16.

2006 WORLD CUP FINAL

	1st half	2nd half	Total	OT	PK
ITALY	1	0	1	0	5
FRANCE	1	0	1	0	3

First-half Scoring: 1, France, Zidane (6:05 on penalty kick); 1, Italy, Materazzi (18:44)

Penalty Kicks: 5, Italy: Pirlo, Materazzi, De Rossi, Del Piero, Grosso; 3, France: Wiltford, Abidal, Sagnol

KEY: OT=overtime; PK=penalty kicks

2006 WORLD CUP FINAL BRACKET

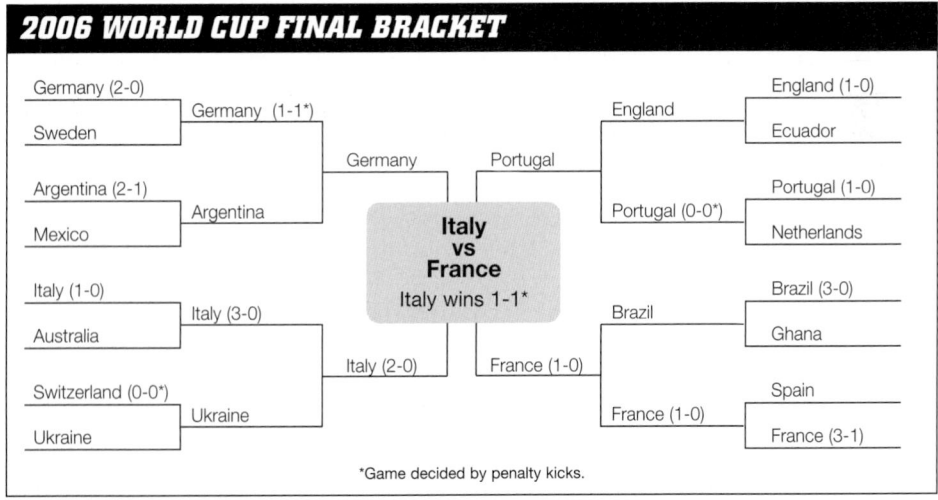

- Germany (2-0)
- Sweden
- Germany (1-1*)
- Argentina (2-1)
- Mexico
- Argentina
- Germany
- Italy (1-0)
- Australia
- Italy (3-0)
- Switzerland (0-0*)
- Ukraine
- Ukraine
- Italy (2-0)

Italy vs France — Italy wins 1-1*

- England
- Portugal
- England (1-0)
- Ecuador
- Portugal (1-0)
- Netherlands
- Portugal (0-0*)
- Brazil
- Brazil (3-0)
- Ghana
- France (1-0)
- France (1-0)
- Spain
- France (3-1)

*Game decided by penalty kicks.

WORLD CUP STARS

■ **Miroslav Klose, forward,** b. June 9, 1978, Opole, Poland. Klose scored five goals during the 2006 World Cup, making him the leading scorer and Golden Shoe winner. He helped the German team to a third-place finish in the tournament before their countrymen. Klose first made his mark in 2002, scoring five goals in his debut World Cup. He is now the only player to have scored five or more goals in back-to-back World Cup tournaments, and is only five goals away from matching Brazilian forward Ronaldo as the all-time World Cup top scorer. In his two seasons with the German club, Werder Bremen, Klose has scored an impressive 40 goals. He is 28 years old and figures to be a member of the German team in the 2010 World Cup, in South Africa.

Miroslav Klose was the leading scorer in the 2006 World Cup.

SHAUN BOTTERILL/GETTY IMAGES

■ **Thierry Henry, forward,** b. August 17, 1977, Paris, France. Henry, a striker for both the French national team and the English club Arsenal is one of the top players in the world. He was the runner-up in both 2003 and 2004 for the FIFA World Player of the Year award. He scored three goals for France in both the 1998 and 2006 World Cups. In 2005, Henry became Arsenal's top goal-scorer of all time, surpassing Ian Wright's record of 185 goals.

■ **Fabio Cannavaro, defender,** b. September 13, 1973, Naples, Italy. As captain of his national team, Cannavaro led Italy to its 2006 World Cup victory, the first in 24 years. He is regarded as one of the best central defenders in the world, known for making countless interceptions at the right times. Since his debut with the national team in 1997, Cannavaro has played in 100 international games for Italy. Following the World Cup, he left the Italian club Juventus to join the Spanish superclub Real Madrid, which already boasts such stars as Ronaldo and David Beckham.

ALL-TIME WORLD CUP SCORING LEADERS

PLAYER, NATION	TOURNAMENTS	GOALS
Ronaldo, Brazil	1998, 2002, 2006	15
Gerd Müller, West Germany	1970, 1974	14
Just Fontaine, France	1958	13
Pelé, Brazil	1958, 1962, 1966, 1970	12
Jürgen Klinsman, Germany	1990, 1994, 1998	11
Sandor Kocsis, Hungary	1954	11
Teofilo Cubillas, Peru	1970, 1978	10
Miroslav Klose, Germany	2002, 2006	10
Gregorz Lato, Poland	1974, 1978, 1982	10
Helmut Rahn, West Germany	1954, 1958	10
Gary Lineker, England	1986, 1990	10

WORLD CUP LEGENDS

RICHARD MACKSON

■ Roberto Baggio, striker, b. February 18, 1967, Caldogno, Italy. Flair and artistry were major ingredients of Baggio's game. He scored nine goals (tied for seventh all-time) in three Cup appearances (1990, 1994, 1998) with Italy. In 1990, he netted two goals, including one in Italy's 2–1 victory over England in the third-place match. But Baggio cemented his name into Cup annals forever in 1994 with his brilliant play — and a single moment of despair. Baggio scored five goals in the tournament, and Italy reached the championship match against Brazil. The final was decided on penalty kicks but Baggio missed Italy's chance to tie, and Brazil won, 3–2. Baggio scored two more goals in the 1998 Cup before Italy was eliminated in the quarterfinals by eventual champion France.

Roberto Baggio led Italy to the World Cup final in 1994.

■ Bobby Charlton, midfielder, b. October 11, 1937, Ashington, England. Charlton was voted Best Player in the 1966 World Cup. Playing on his home soil, Charlton's speed and booming shot led England to its first and only World Cup championship. He scored both goals in England's 2–1 semifinal win over powerhouse Portugal, while also shutting down forward Eusebio, the Cup's eventual top scorer. In the final against West Germany, Charlton was marked by the equally dangerous midfielder Franz Beckenbauer. The West German held Charlton scoreless, but the Englishman also shut down Beckenbauer, and England won, 4–2. Charlton was knighted by England's Queen Elizabeth II in 1994 for his contributions to his country's soccer history. Today he's called Sir Bobby.

■ Jürgen Klinsmann, forward, b. July 30, 1964, Göppingen, West Germany. Tied for fifth place on the all-time World Cup scoring list (11 goals), Klinsman was Germany's top attacker throughout the 1990's. He played in three World Cup tournaments (1990, 1994, 1998). His three goals in '90 helped lead his home country to the final against Argentina, which West Germany won, 1–0. In the 1994 Cup, he finished with five goals (tied for third most in the tournament) though West Germany was upset by Bulgaria in the quarterfinals. Klinsmann retired from soccer in 1999. He was manager (head coach) of Germany's 2006 World Cup team, which finished third.

ALL-TIME WORLD CUP RESULTS

YEAR	CHAMPION	SCORE	RUNNER-UP	WINNING COACH
2006	Italy	1–1 (5-3)	France	Marcello Lippi
2002	Brazil	2–0	Germany	Luiz Felipe Scolari
1998	France	3–0	Brazil	Aime Jacquet
1994	Brazil	0–0 (3–2)	Italy	Carlos Alberto Parreira
1990	West Germany	1–0	Argentina	Franz Beckenbauer
1986	Argentina	3–2	West Germany	Carlos Bilardo
1982	Italy	3–1	West Germany	Enzo Bearzot
1978	Argentina	3–1	Netherlands	César Menotti
1974	West Germany	2–1	Netherlands	Helmut Schön
1970	Brazil	4–1	Italy	Mario Zagallo
1966	England	4–2	West Germany	Alf Ramsey
1962	Brazil	3–1	Czechoslovakia	Aymore Moreira
1958	Brazil	5–2	Sweden	Vicente Feola
1954	West Germany	3–2	Hungary	Sepp Herberger
1950	Uruguay	2–1	Brazil	Juan Lopez
1938	Italy	4–2	Hungary	Vittorio Pozzo
1934	Italy	2–1	Czechoslovakia	Vittorio Pozzo
1930	Uruguay	4–2	Argentina	Alberto Supicci

2005-06 TIME LINE

■ **March 15, 2005:** The U.S. women's team wins the final of the Algarve Cup, defeating Germany, 1–0. Forward Christie Welsh scores the winner. The annual tournament is played in Faro, Portugal.

■ **April 2, 2005:** Major League Soccer kicks off its tenth season. With two new clubs, Real Salt Lake (Utah) and Chivas USA (Los Angeles), the league expands to 12 teams.

■ **July 30, 2005:** The tenth MLS All-Star game is played in Columbus, Ohio. The MLS stars defeats F.C. Fulham, a team from England's Premier League, 4–1.

■ **August 14, 2005:** Forward Jason Kreis of Real Salt Lake becomes the first MLS player to score 100 career goals when he tallies in the 72nd minute against the Kansas City Wizards. Kreis does a backflip on the pitch to celebrate.

■ **September 5, 2005:** The U.S. men's national team qualifies for its fifth World Cup in a row with a 2–0 win against Mexico in a match in Columbus, Ohio.

■ **September 29, 2005:** The Los Angeles Galaxy defeats F.C. Dallas, 1–0, in the final of the U.S. Open Cup, an annual tournament open to all amateur and pro teams in the U.S. Galaxy forward Herculez Gomez scores the game's only goal.

■ **October 23, 2005:** The U.S. women's national team beats Mexico, 3–0, and finishes the 2005 season with a record of 8-0-1. The team allows no goals in 2005.

■ **November 10, 2005:** Forward Taylor Twellman of the New England Revolution wins the 2005 MLS MVP award. The 25-year-old also wins the Golden Shoe as the league's top goal scorer. Twellman finishes with 17 goals.

■ **November 13, 2005:** The Los Angeles Galaxy defeat the New England Revolution, 1–0, to win the MLS Cup. It is the second championship for Los Angeles. Galaxy forward Pando Ramirez scores the winner in overtime and is named MVP of the match.

■ **November 30, 2005:** Goalkeeper Kasey Keller wins the Honda Award as the best player on the U.S. national team. Keller set a record of eight shutouts for Team USA in 2005.

■ **January 22, 2006:** The U.S. women's national team wins the Four Nations Cup tournament, defeating host nation China in the final, 2–0. Forward Christine Lilly nets both goals for Team USA.

■ **March 9, 2006:** The MetroStars are sold to the Red Bull Company of Austria, makers of an energy drink. The team is renamed the New York Red Bulls.

■ **March 15, 2006:** Team USA is ranked Number 5 in the world by FIFA. It is the highest ranking ever for the United States men's team.

■ **March 16, 2006:** The defending champion United States women's national team loses the final of the Algarve Cup to Germany, 4–3, in a penalty kick shootout.

■ **July 9, 2006:** Italy defeats France on penalty kicks in the final to win the 2006 World Cup, in Germany.

TRIVIA CHALLENGE

Which of these three active MLS stars has not played in every season since the league began in 1996: Tony Meola, Taylor Twellman, or Eddie Pope?

Twellman. He was drafted by the New England Revolution in 2002 at age 22.

DID YOU KNOW?

The United States hosted the World Cup in 1994. More than 3.5 million fans turned out for the 52 matches. The final was played in California's Rose Bowl, where Brazil beat Italy, 3–2, in a penalty-kick shootout.

ACTION SPORTS

Over the past year, action sports, especially snowboarding, have taken off across the globe. They now might just be the most popular individual sporting events in the world. Even at the 2006 Winter Olympic Games in Turin, Italy — where snowboarding appeared for only the second time — the sport was one of the main draws.

United States athletes won seven medals, including three gold medals, out of a possible 18 in snowboarding in Turin. The highlights came in the Halfpipe events. Americans Hannah Teter and Gretchen Bleiler finished first and second in the women's competition, while countrymen Shaun White and Danny Kass pulled the same feat in the men's event.

White's gold medal on the second day of Olympic competition came less than two weeks after he dominated the Winter X Games, in Aspen, Colorado. White ran away with the gold medals in the snowboard Slopestyle and Superpipe. It was White's fourth straight Slopestyle gold.

But perhaps the most memorable story of the 2006 Winter X Games was the return of skier Tanner Hall. In March of 2005, Hall crashed while skiing, breaking both his ankles and heels. He was told he would never ski again. But he returned to the slopes at the X Games in January to win the gold medal in the Ski Superpipe event.

At the 2005 Summer X Games in Los Angeles, California, skateboarder Danny Way continued a remarkable year by winning gold in the Big Air event. Way helped bring Big Air

Dave Mirra has won more X Games medals (19) than anyone.

to the X Games the year before, but struggled with his first three runs because of a broken ankle. But on his fourth run, Way launched a full 50 feet into the air and pulled off a 70-plus foot frontside 360 to climb from fifth to first place, and win his second straight gold medal. Less than a month earlier, Way became the first athlete to jump the Great Wall of China without the use of a motorized device. He cleared the 61-foot gap four times.

Dave Mirra, the king of the X Games, added another medal to his collection in 2005, winning gold in the BMX Park event, despite strong competition from Scotty Cranmer, the youngest rider in the field. Cranmer, age 18, took the silver. Mirra now has 19 total X Games medals, the most in competition history.

Teen wakeboarding sensation Dallas Friday kicked off 2005 with a bang, and never slowed up. After winning on her first three stops on the Pro Wakeboard Tour, Friday took gold in the Wakeboarding event at the X Games. It was her fourth X Games gold medal, and third in a row.

Elsewhere on the water, the East Coast surfing team took a hit when the world's top-ranked surfer, Kelly Slater, decided to skip the event at the last moment. But despite having to compete with nine surfers to the West Coast's 10, the East team pulled out the gold medal for the third consecutive year. Slater won the Association of Surfing Professionals (ASP) men's championship in 2005. Chelsea Georgeson of Australia won the ASP women's championship.

WINTER X GAMES RESULTS

MOTO X

YEAR	EVENT	GOLD	SILVER	BRONZE
2006	Best Trick	Jeremy Stenberg, U.S.	Mat Rebeaud, U.S.	Ronnie Faisst, U.S.
2005	Best Trick	Brian Deegan, U.S.	Jeff Kargola, U.S.	Dustin Miller, U.S.
2004	Best Trick	Caleb Wyatt, U.S.	Mike Metzger, U.S.	Nate Adams, U.S.
2003	Big Air	Mike Metzger, U.S.	Dane Kinnaird, Australia	Caleb Wyatt, U.S.
2002	Big Air	Brian Deegan, U.S.	Mike Jones, U.S.	Tommy Clowers, U.S.
2001	Big Air	Mike Jones, U.S.	Tommy Clowers, U.S.	Clifford Adoptante, U.S.

SKIING — MEN

YEAR	EVENT	GOLD	SILVER	BRONZE
2006	Skier X	Lars Lewen, Sweden	Reggie Crist, U.S.	Chris Del Bosco, U.S.
2005	Skier X	Reggie Crist, U.S.	Zach Crist, U.S.	Enak Gavaggio, France
2004	Skier X	Casey Puckett, U.S.	Lars Lewen, Sweden	Reggie Crist, U.S.
2003	Skier X	Lars Lewen, Sweden	Reggie Crist, U.S.	Enak Gavaggio, France
2002	Skier X	Reggie Crist, U.S.	Peter Lind, Sweden	Enak Gavaggio, France
2001	Skier X	Zach Crist, U.S.	Tomas Andersson, Sweden	Enak Gavaggio, France
2000	Skier X	Shaun Palmer, U.S.	Bill Hudson, U.S.	Zach Crist, U.S.
1999	Skier X	Enak Gavaggio, France	Shane McConkey, U.S.	Jeremy Nobis, U.S.
1998	Skier X	Denis Rey, France	Kent Kreitler, U.S.	Chris Davenport, U.S.
2006*	Best Trick	T.J. Schiller, Canada	Charles Gagnier, Canada	Andrea Hatveit, Norway
2005	Slopestyle	Charles Gagnier, Canada	Tanner Hall, U.S.	Jon Olsson, Sweden
2004	Slopestyle	Tanner Hall, U.S.	Peter Olenick, U.S.	Jon Olsson, Sweden
2003	Slopestyle	Tanner Hall, U.S.	Pep Fujas, U.S.	Jon Olsson, Sweden
2002	Slopestyle	Tanner Hall, U.S.	C.R. Johnson, U.S.	Jon Olsson, Sweden
2006	Superpipe	Tanner Hall, U.S.	Laurent Favre, France	Simon Dumont, U.S.
2005	Superpipe	Simon Dumont, U.S.	Tanner Hall, U.S.	Jon Olsson, Sweden
2004	Superpipe	Simon Dumont, U.S.	Jon Olsson, Sweden	Peter Olenick, U.S.
2003	Superpipe	Candide Thovex, France	Tanner Hall, U.S.	Jon Olsson, Sweden
2002	Superpipe	Jon Olsson, Sweden	Philippe Larose, Canada	Philippe Poirier, Canada
2001	Big Air	Tanner Hall, U.S.	Evan Raps, U.S.	C.R. Johnson, U.S.
2000	Big Air	Candide Thovex, France	Skogen Sprang, U.S.	Evan Raps, U.S.
1999	Big Air	J.F. Cusson, Canada	Jonny Moseley, U.S.	Vincent Dorion, Canada

SKIING — WOMEN

YEAR	EVENT	GOLD	SILVER	BRONZE
2006	Skier X	Karin Huttary, Austria	Gro Kvinlog, Norway	Ophelie David, France
2005	Skier X	Sanna Tidstrand, Sweden	Karin Huttary, Austria	Magdalena Jonsson, Sweden
2004	Skier X	Karin Huttary, Austria	Aleisha Cline, Canada	Sanna Tidstrand, Sweden
2003	Skier X	Aleisha Cline, Canada	Karin Huttary, Austria	Cecilie Larsen, Norway
2002	Skier X	Aleisha Cline, Canada	Magdalena Jonsson, Sweden	Patti Sherman-Kauf, U.S.
2001	Skier X	Aleisha Cline, Canada	Magdalena Jonsson, Sweden	Chiara Lawrence, U.S.
2000	Skier X	Anik Demers, Canada	Chiara Lawrence, U.S.	Patti Sherman-Kauf, U.S.
1999	Skier X	Aleisha Cline, Canada	Darian Boyle, U.S.	Patti Sherman-Kauf, U.S.
2006	Superpipe	Grete Eliassen, Norway	Sarah Burke, Canada	Marie Martinod-Routin, France
2005	Superpipe	Grete Eliassen, Norway	Sarah Burke, Canada	Kristi Leskinen, U.S.

SNOWBOARDING — MEN

YEAR	EVENT	GOLD	SILVER	BRONZE
2006	Slopestyle	Shaun White, U.S.	Andreas Wiig, Norway	Danny Kass, U.S.
2005	Slopestyle	Shaun White, U.S.	Danny Kass, U.S.	Travis Rice, U.S.
2004	Slopestyle	Shaun White, U.S.	Danny Kass, U.S.	Andreas Wiig, Norway
2003	Slopestyle	Shaun White, U.S.	Jussi Oksanen, Finland	Jimi Tomer, U.S.
2002	Slopestyle	Travis Rice, U.S.	Shaun White, U.S.	Todd Richards, U.S.
2001	Slopestyle	Kevin Jones, U.S.	Todd Richards, U.S.	Jussi Oksanen, Finland

* Ski Slopestyle was turned into Ski Best Trick due to time considerations.

WINTER X GAMES RESULTS (cont.)

SNOWBOARDING — MEN (cont.)

YEAR	EVENT	GOLD	SILVER	BRONZE
2000	Slopestyle	Kevin Jones, U.S.	Todd Richards, U.S.	Peter Line, U.S.
1999	Slopestyle	Peter Line, U.S.	Kevin Jones, U.S.	Jimmy Halopoff, U.S.
1998	Slopestyle	Ross Powers, U.S.	Kevin Jones, U.S.	Rob Kingwill, U.S.
1997	Slopestyle	Daniel Franck, Norway	Jimmy Halopoff, U.S.	Bryan Iguchi, U.S.
2006	Snowboarder X	Nate Holland, U.S.	Marco Huser, Switzerland	Jayson Hale, U.S.
2005	Snowboarder X	Xavier de le Rue, France	Seth Wescott, U.S.	Marco Huser, Switzerland
2004	Snowboarder X	Ueli Kestenholz, Switzerland	Seth Wescott, U.S.	Xavier de le Rue, France
2003	Snowboarder X	Ueli Kestenholz, Switzerland	Xavier de le Rue, France	Michael Rosengren, U.S.
2002	Snowboarder X	Philippe Conte, Switzerland	Seth Wescott, U.S.	Berti Denervaud, Switzerland
2001	Snowboarder X	Scott Gaffney, Canada	Mark Schulz, U.S.	Seth Wescott, U.S.
2000	Snowboarder X	Drew Neilson, Canada	Scott Gaffney, Canada	Jason Ford, U.S.
1999	Snowboarder X	Shaun Palmer, U.S.	Drew Neilson, Canada	Scott Gaffney, Canada
1998	Snowboarder X	Shaun Palmer, U.S.	Jason Brown, U.S.	Seth Wescott, U.S.
1997	Snowboarder X	Shaun Palmer, U.S.	Berti Denervaud, Switzerland	Mike Basich, U.S.
2006	Superpipe	Shaun White, U.S.	Mason Aguirre, U.S.	Scotty Lago, U.S.
2005	Superpipe	Antti Autti, Finland	Andy Finch, U.S.	Danny Kass, U.S.
2004	Superpipe	Steve Fisher, U.S.	Danny Kass, U.S.	Keir Dillon, U.S.
2003	Superpipe	Shaun White, U.S.	Danny Kass, U.S.	Markku Koski, Finland
2002	Superpipe	J.J. Thomas, U.S.	Shaun White, U.S.	Keir Dillon, U.S.
2001	Superpipe	Danny Kass, U.S.	Tommy Czeschin, U.S.	Ross Powers, U.S.
2000	Superpipe	Todd Richards, U.S.	Ross Powers, U.S.	Tommy Czeschin, U.S.
1999	Halfpipe	Jimi Scott, U.S.	Mike Michalchuk, Canada	Luke Wynen, U.S.
1998	Halfpipe	Ross Powers, U.S.	Guillaume Chastagnol, France	Todd Richards, U.S.
1997	Halfpipe	Todd Richards, U.S.	Daniel Franck, Norway	Fabien Rohrer, Switzerland
2001	Big Air	Jussi Oksanen, Finland	Todd Richards, U.S.	Josh Dirksen, U.S.
2000	Big Air	Peter Line, U.S.	Jason Borgstede, U.S.	Kevin Jones, U.S.
1999	Big Air	Kevin Sansalone, Canada	Peter Line, U.S.	Kevin Jones, U.S.
1998	Big Air	Jason Borgstede, U.S.	Ryan W. Williams, U.S.	Kevin Jones, U.S.
1997	Big Air	Jimmy Halopoff, U.S.	Steve Adkins, U.S.	Bjorn Leines, U.S.

SNOWBOARDING — WOMEN

YEAR	EVENT	GOLD	SILVER	BRONZE
2006	Slopestyle	Janna Meyen, U.S.	Hana Beaman, U.S.	Jamie Anderson, U.S.
2005	Slopestyle	Janna Meyen, U.S.	Silvia Mittermueller, Germany	Natasza Zurek, Canada
2004	Slopestyle	Janna Meyen, U.S.	Tara Dakides, U.S.	Jessica Dalpiaz, U.S.
2003	Slopestyle	Janna Meyen, U.S.	Hana Beaman, U.S.	Lindsey Jacobellis, U.S.
2002	Slopestyle	Tara Dakides, U.S.	Janna Meyen, U.S.	Barrett Christy, U.S.
2001	Slopestyle	Jaime MacLeod, U.S.	Shannon Dunn, U.S.	Marni Yamada, U.S.
2000	Slopestyle	Tara Dakides, U.S.	Jaime MacLeod, U.S.	Barrett Christy, U.S.
1999	Slopestyle	Tara Dakides, U.S.	Barrett Christy, U.S.	Jaime MacLeod, U.S.
1998	Slopestyle	Jennie Waara, Sweden	Barrett Christy, U.S.	Aurelie Sayres, U.S.
1997	Slopestyle	Barrett Christy, U.S.	Cara-Beth Burnside, U.S.	Jennie Waara, Sweden
2006	Snowboarder X	Maelle Ricker, Canada	Joanie Anderson, U.S.	Claudia Haeusermann, Switzerland
2005	Snowboarder X	Lindsey Jacobellis, U.S.	Erin Simmons, Canada	Karine Ruby, France
2004	Snowboarder X	Lindsey Jacobellis, U.S.	Karine Ruby, France	Yvonne Mueller, Switzerland
2003	Snowboarder X	Lindsey Jacobellis, U.S.	Tanja Frieden, Switzerland	Yvonne Mueller, Switzerland
2002	Snowboarder X	Ine Poetzl, Austria	Erin Simmons, Canada	Tanja Frieden, Switzerland
2001	Snowboarder X	Line Oestvold, Norway	Erin Simmons, Canada	Amy Johnson, U.S.
2000	Snowboarder X	Leslee Olson, U.S.	Carlee Baker, Canada	Line Oestvold, Norway
1999	Snowboarder X	Maelle Ricker, Canada	Leslee Olson, U.S.	Candice Drouin, Canada
1998	Snowboarder X	Tina Dixon, U.S.	Corrie Rudishauser, U.S.	Katrina Warnick, U.S.
1997	Snowboarder X	Jennie Waara, Sweden	Hillary Maybery, U.S.	Aurelie Sayres, U.S.
2006	Superpipe	Kelly Clark, U.S.	Torah Bright, Australia	Soko Yamaoka, Japan
2005	Superpipe	Gretchen Bleiler, U.S.	Doriane Vidal, France	Hannah Teter, U.S.
2004	Superpipe	Hannah Teter, U.S.	Kelly Clark, U.S.	Doriane Vidal, France

WINTER X GAMES RESULTS (cont.)

SNOWBOARDING — WOMEN (cont.)

YEAR	EVENT	GOLD	SILVER	BRONZE
2003	Superpipe	Gretchen Bleiler, U.S.	Kelly Clark, U.S.	Hannah Teter, U.S.
2002	Superpipe	Kelly Clark, U.S.	Stine Brun Kjeldaas, Norway	Natasza Zurek, Canada
2001	Superpipe	Shannon Dunn, U.S.	Natasza Zurek, Canada	Fabienne Reuteler, Switzerland
2000	Superpipe	Stine Brun Kjeldaas, Norway	Barrett Christy, U.S.	Natasza Zurek, Canada
1999	Halfpipe	Michelle Taggart, U.S.	Shannon Dunn, U.S.	Cara-Beth Burnside, U.S.
1998	Halfpipe	Cara-Beth Burnside, U.S.	Michelle Taggart, U.S.	Nicola Thost, Germany
1997	Halfpipe	Shannon Dunn, U.S.	Jennie Waara, Sweden	Nicole Angelrath, Switzerland
2001	Big Air	Tara Dakides, U.S.	Barrett Christy, U.S.	Jenna Murano, U.S.
2000	Big Air	Tara Dakides, U.S.	Leah Wagner, Canada	Jessica Dalpiaz, U.S.
1999	Big Air	Barrett Christy, U.S.	Tara Dakides, U.S.	Janet Matthews, Canada
1998	Big Air	Tina Basich, U.S.	Barrett Christy, U.S.	Tara Zwink, U.S.
1997	Big Air	Barrett Christy, U.S.	Tara Zwink, U.S.	Tina Basich, U.S.

SNOWMOBILING

YEAR	EVENT	GOLD	SILVER	BRONZE
2006	SnoCross	Blair Morgan, Canada	Levi LaVallee, U.S.	Ross Martin, U.S.
2005	SnoCross	Blair Morgan, Canada	Tucker Hibbert, U.S.	Steve Martin, Canada
2004	SnoCross	Michael Island, Canada	Tucker Hibbert, U.S.	Blair Morgan, Canada
2003	SnoCross	Blair Morgan, Canada	D.J. Eckstrom, U.S.	Tucker Hibbert, U.S.
2002	SnoCross	Blair Morgan, Canada	Tucker Hibbert, U.S.	Tomi Ahmasalo, Finland
2001	SnoCross	Blair Morgan, Canada	Kent Ipsen, U.S.	D.J. Eckstrom, U.S.
2000	SnoCross	Tucker Hibbert, U.S.	Blair Morgan, Canada	T.J. Gulla, U.S.
1999	SnoCross	Chris Vincent, U.S.	Blair Morgan, Canada	Trevor John, U.S.
1998	SnoCross	Toni Haikonen, Finland	Dennis Burks, U.S.	Per Berggren, Sweden
2004	HillCross	Levi LaVallee, U.S.	Justin Tate, U.S.	Carl Kuster, Canada
2003	HillCross	T.J. Gulla, U.S.	Carl Kuster, Canada	Steve Martin, Canada
2002	HillCross	Carl Kuster, Canada	Steve Martin, Canada	Rick Ward, U.S.
2001	HillCross	Carl Kuster, Canada	Vinny Clark, Canada	Matt Luczynski, U.S.

ULTRACROSS*

YEAR	GOLD	SILVER	BRONZE
2005	Marco Huser, Switzerland	Xavier de le Rue, France	Nate Holland, U.S.
	Eric Andersson, Sweden	Davey Barr, Canada	Eric Archer, U.S.
2004	Nate Holland, U.S.	Lars Lewen, Sweden	Xavier Kuhn, France
	Reggie Crist, U.S.	Xavier de le Rue, France	Drew Neilson, Canada
2003	Xavier de le Rue, France	Seth Wescott, U.S.	Ben Jacobellis, U.S.
	Kaj Zackrisson, Sweden	Peter Lind, Sweden	Lars Lewen, Sweden
2002	Seth Wescott, U.S.	Scott Gaffney, Canada	Rob Fagan, Canada
	Peter Lind, Sweden	Eric Archer, U.S.	Enak Gavaggio, France
2001	Shaun Palmer, U.S.	Jason Evans, U.S.	Pontus Staahlkloo, Sweden
	Hiroomi Takizawa, Japan	Isidor Gruener, Austria	Matt Murphy, U.S.
2000	Travis McLain, U.S.	Scott Gaffney, Canada	Terry Plum, U.S.
	Peter Lind, Sweden	Sverre Liliequist, Sweden	Mike Dill, U.S.

*First athlete listed in each category is a snowboarder; the second athlete is a skier.

U.S. OPEN SNOWBOARDING CHAMPIONSHIPS RESULTS

HALFPIPE — MEN

YEAR	GOLD	SILVER	BRONZE
2006	Shaun White, U.S.	Danny Davis, U.S.	Mason Aguirre, U.S.
2005	Danny Kass, U.S.	Steve Fisher, U.S.	Antti Autti, Finland
2004	Danny Kass, U.S.	Steve Fisher, U.S.	Keir Dillon, U.S.
2003	Ross Powers, U.S.	Kazuhiro Kokubo, Japan	Daniel Franck, Norway

U.S. OPEN SNOWBOARDING CHAMPIONSHIPS RESULTS (cont.)

HALFPIPE — MEN (cont.)

YEAR	GOLD	SILVER	BRONZE
2002	Danny Kass, U.S.	Markku Koski, Finland	Keir Dillon, U.S.
2001	Danny Kass, U.S.	Abe Teter, U.S.	Daniel Franck, Norway
2000	Guillaume Morisset, Canada	Ross Powers, U.S.	Xavier Hoffman, Germany
1999	Ross Powers, U.S.	Xavier Hoffman, Germany	Tommy Czeschin, U.S.
1998	Rob Kingwill, U.S.	Terje Haakonsen, Norway	Todd Richards, U.S.
1997	Todd Richards, U.S.	Terje Haakonsen, Norway	Sebu Kuhlberg, Finland
1996	Jimi Scott, U.S.	Sami Hyry, Finland	Max Ploetzender, Austria
1995	Terje Haakonsen, Norway	Jason Evans, U.S.	J.J. Collier, U.S.
1994	Todd Richards, U.S.	Lael Gregory, U.S.	Jason Evans, U.S.
1993	Terje Haakonsen, Norway	Keith Wallace, U.S.	Sebu Kuhlberg, Finland
1992	Terje Haakonsen, Norway	Jeff Brushie, U.S.	Todd Richards, U.S.
1991	Jimi Scott, U.S.	Craig Kelly, U.S.	Shaun Palmer, U.S.
1990	Craig Kelly, U.S.	Shaun Palmer, U.S.	Jeff Brushie, U.S.
1989	Craig Kelly, U.S.	Bert Lamar, U.S.	Terry Kidwell, U.S.
1988	Terry Kidwell, U.S.	Bert Lamar, U.S.	Craig Kelly, U.S.

HALFPIPE — WOMEN

YEAR	GOLD	SILVER	BRONZE
2006	Torah Bright, Australia	Gretchen Bleiler, U.S.	Elena Hight, U.S.
2005	Gretchen Bleiler, U.S.	Torah Bright, Australia	Hannah Teter, U.S.
2004	Kelly Clark, U.S.	Tricia Byrnes, U.S.	Stine Brun Kjeldaas, Norway
2003	Gretchen Bleiler, U.S.	Natasza Zurek, Canada	Hannah Teter, U.S.
2002	Kelly Clark, U.S.	Tricia Byrnes, U.S.	Stine Brun Kjeldaas, Norway
2001	Natasza Zurek, Canada	Shannon Dunn, U.S.	Gretchen Bleiler, U.S.
2000	Natasza Zurek, Canada	Shannon Dunn, U.S.	Barrett Christy, U.S.
1999	Nicola Thost, Germany	Tricia Byrnes, U.S.	Shannon Dunn, U.S.
1998	Nicola Thost, Germany	Tricia Byrnes, U.S.	Tara Teigen, Canada
1997	Barrett Christy, U.S.	Tricia Byrnes, U.S.	Michelle Taggart, U.S.
1996	Satu Jarvela, Finland	Michelle Taggart, U.S.	Jennie Waara, Sweden
1995	Satu Jarvela, Finland	Nicole Angelrath, Switzerland	Jennie Waara, Sweden
1994	Shannon Dunn, U.S	Tina Basich, U.S.	Sandra Farmand, Germany
1993	Shannon Dunn, U.S.	Janna Meyen, U.S.	Tricia Byrnes, U.S.
1992	Tricia Byrnes, U.S.	Nicole Angelrath, Switzerland	Tina Basich, U.S.
1991	Janna Meyen, U.S.	Tina Basich, U.S.	Michelle Taggart, U.S.
1990	Tina Basich, U.S.	Lisa Vinciguerra, U.S.	Jean Higgins, U.S.
1989	Jean Higgins, U.S.	Tara Eberhard, U.S.	Ashild Lofthus, Norway
1988	Petra Mussig, Germany	Jean Higgins, U.S.	Gayle Guerin, U.S.

QUARTERPIPE — MEN

YEAR	GOLD	SILVER	BRONZE
2005	Danny Davis, U.S.	Risto Matilla, Finland	Kevin Peirce, U.S.

QUARTERPIPE — WOMEN

YEAR	GOLD	SILVER	BRONZE
2005	Hana Beaman, U.S.	Junko Asazuma, Japan	Molly Aguirre, U.S.

RAIL JAM — MEN

YEAR	GOLD	SILVER	BRONZE
2005	Eddie Wall, U.S.	Yale Cousino, U.S.	Jed Anderson, U.S.
2004	Rahm Klampert, U.S.	Travis Rice, U.S.	Chris Rotax, U.S.
2003	Travis Rice, U.S.	Shaun White, U.S.	Zach Leach, U.S.

RAIL JAM — WOMEN

YEAR	GOLD	SILVER	BRONZE
2005	Leanne Pelosi, Canada	Hana Beaman, U.S.	Spencer O'Brien, Canada
2004	Leanne Pelosi, Canada	Erin Comstock, U.S.	Natasza Zurek, Canada

U.S. OPEN SNOWBOARDING CHAMPIONSHIPS RESULTS (cont.)

SLOPESTYLE — MEN

YEAR	GOLD	SILVER	BRONZE
2006	Shaun White, U.S.	Chas Guidemond, U.S.	Jussi Oksanen, Finland
2005	Risto Mattila, Finland	Jussi Oksanen, Finland	Andreas Wiig, Norway
2004	Jake Blauvelt, U.S.	Travis Rice, U.S.	Christopher Schmidt, Germany
2003	Shaun White, U.S.	Travis Rice, U.S.	Nate Sheehan, U.S.
2002	Rahm Klampert, U.S.	Travis Rice, U.S.	Ryan Paris, U.S.

Hana Beaman

SLOPESTYLE — WOMEN

YEAR	GOLD	SILVER	BRONZE
2006	Hana Beaman, U.S.	Spencer O'Brien, U.S.	Jaime Anderson, U.S.
2005	Janna Meyen, U.S.	Leanne Pelosi, Canada	Natasza Zurek, Canada
2004	Priscilla Levac, Canada	Kelly Clark, U.S.	Hana Beaman, U.S.
2003	Hana Beaman, U.S.	Priscilla Levac, Canada	Hannah Teter, U.S.
2002	Annie Boulanger, Canada	Hannah Teter, U.S.	Jaime MacLeod, U.S.

SUMMER X GAMES RESULTS

AGGRESSIVE IN-LINE — MEN

YEAR	EVENT	GOLD	SILVER	BRONZE
2003	Park	Bruno Lowe, Germany	Stephane Alfano, France	Sven Boekhorst, Netherlands
2002	Park	Jaren Grob, U.S.	Bruno Lowe, Germany	Blake Dennis, Australia
2001	Park	Jaren Grob, U.S.	Louie Zamora, U.S.	Franky Morales, U.S.
2000	Park	Sven Boekhorst, Netherlands	Jaren Grob, U.S.	Sam Fogarty, Australia
1999	Street	Nicky Adams, Canada	Blake Dennis, Australia	Aaron Feinberg, U.S.
1998	Street	Jonathan Bergeron, Canada	Marco Hintze, Mexico	Aaron Feinberg, U.S.
1997	Street	Aaron Feinberg, U.S.	Tim Ward, Australia	Chris Edwards, U.S.
1996	Street	Arlo Eisenberg, U.S.	Matt Mantz, U.S.	Chris Edwards, U.S.
1995	Street	Matt Salerno, Australia	Scott Bentley, New Zealand	Ryan Jacklone, U.S.
2004	Vert	Takeshi Yasutoko, Japan	Marco De Santi, Brazil	Eito Yasutoko, Japan
2003	Vert	Eito Yasutoko, Japan	Takeshi Yasutoko, Japan	Nel Martin, Spain
2002	Vert	Takeshi Yasutoko, Japan	Eito Yasutoko, Japan	Marc Englehart, U.S.
2001	Vert	Taig Khris, France	Takeshi Yasutoko, Japan	Shane Yost, Australia
2000	Vert	Eito Yasutoko, Japan	Takeshi Yasutoko, Japan	Cesar Mora, Australia
1999	Vert	Eito Yasutoko, Japan	Cesar Mora, Australia	Matt Salerno, Australia
1998	Vert	Cesar Mora, Australia	Matt Salerno, Australia	Taig Khris, France
1997	Vert	Tim Ward, Australia	Taig Khris, France	Chris Edwards, U.S.
1996	Vert	Rene Hulgreen, Denmark	Tom Fry, Australia	Chris Edwards, U.S.
1995	Vert	Tom Fry, Australia	Cesar Mora, Australia	Manuel Billiris, Australia
1999	Vert Triples	Sven Boekhorst, Netherlands	Mike Budnik, U.S.	Maki Komori, Japan
		Javier Bujanda, Spain	Cesar Mora, Australia	Eito Yasutoko, Japan
		Taig Khris, France	Matt Salerno, Australia	Takeshi Yasutoko, Japan
1998	Vert Triples	Paul Malina, Australia	Mike Budnik, U.S.	Sven Boekhorst, Netherlands
		Viorel Popa, U.S.	Cesar Mora, Australia	Javier Bujanda, Spain
		Sam Fogarty, Australia	Matt Salerno, Australia	Taig Khris, France

SUMMER X GAMES RESULTS (cont.)

AGGRESSIVE IN-LINE — MEN (cont.)

YEAR	EVENT	GOLD	SILVER	BRONZE
1996	Best Trick	Dion Antony, Australia	Ryan Jacklone, U.S.	Eric Schrijn, U.S.
1995	Best Trick	B. Hardin, U.S.	Ryan Jacklone, U.S.	Brooke Howard-Smith, New Zealand
1995	High Air	Chris Edwards, U.S.	Manuel Billiris, Australia	Ichi Komori, Japan

Fabiola da Silva

TONY DONALDSON/ICON SMI

FAST FACT

In June 2005, in-line skater Fabiola da Silva of Brazil became the first woman to land a double backflip on a vert ramp. Competing against men, she finished fourth in Vert at the 2005 World Championships.

AGGRESSIVE IN-LINE — WOMEN

YEAR	EVENT	GOLD	SILVER	BRONZE
2003	Park	Fabiola da Silva, Brazil	Jenny Logue, Great Britain	Martina Svobodova, Slovakia
2002	Park	Martina Svobodova, Slovakia	Jenna Downing, Great Britain	Fallon Heffernan, U.S.
2001	Park	Martina Svobodova, Slovakia	Fallon Heffernan, U.S.	Anneke Winter, Germany
2000	Park	Fabiola da Silva, Brazil	Martina Svobodova, Slovakia	Kelly Matthews, U.S.
1999	Street	Sayaka Yabe, Japan	Kelly Matthews, U.S.	Jenny Curry, U.S.
1998	Street	Jenny Curry, U.S.	Salima Sanga, Switzerland	Sayaka Yabe, Japan
1997	Street	Sayaka Yabe, Japan	Katie Brown, U.S.	True Otis, U.S.
2001	Vert	Fabiola da Silva, Brazil	Ayumi Kawasaki, Japan	N/A
2000	Vert	Fabiola da Silva, Brazil	Ayumi Kawasaki, Japan	Merce Borrull, Spain
1999	Vert	Ayumi Kawasaki, Japan	Fabiola da Silva, Brazil	Maki Komori, Japan
1998	Vert	Fabiola da Silva, Brazil	Ayumi Kawasaki, Japan	Maki Komori, Japan
1997	Vert	Fabiola da Silva, Brazil	Claudia Trachsel, Switzerland	Ayumi Kawasaki, Japan
1996	Vert	Fabiola da Silva, Brazil	Jodie Tyler, Australia	Tasha Hodgson, Australia
1995	Vert	Tasha Hodgson, Australia	Angie Walton, New Zealand	Laura Connery, U.S.

BAREFOOT JUMPING

YEAR	GOLD	SILVER	BRONZE
1998	Peter Fleck, U.S.	Ron Scarpa, U.S.	Massimiliano Colosio, Italy
1997	Peter Fleck, U.S.	Evan Berger, South Africa	Warren Fine, South Africa
1996	Ron Scarpa, U.S.	Jon Kretchman, U.S.	Rael Nurick, South Africa
1995	Justin Seers, Australia	Ron Scarpa, U.S.	Rael Nurick, South Africa

BIKE STUNT

YEAR	EVENT	GOLD	SILVER	BRONZE
2005	Dirt	Corey Bohan, Australia	Chris Doyle, U.S.	Ryan Guettler, U.S.
2004	Dirt	Corey Bohan, Australia	Chris Doyle, U.S.	T.J. Lavin, U.S.
2003	Dirt	Ryan Nyquist, U.S.	Corey Bohan, Australia	Chris Doyle, U.S.
2002	Dirt	Allan Cooke, U.S.	Ryan Nyquist, U.S.	Chris Doyle, U.S.
2001	Dirt	Stephen Murray, Great Britain	Ryan Nyquist, U.S.	T.J. Lavin, U.S.
2000	Dirt	Ryan Nyquist, U.S.	Cory Nastazio, U.S.	T.J. Lavin, U.S.
1999	Dirt	T.J. Lavin, U.S.	Brian Foster, U.S.	Ryan Nyquist, U.S.
1998	Dirt	Brian Foster, U.S.	Ryan Nyquist, U.S.	Joey Garcia, U.S.
1997	Dirt	T.J. Lavin, U.S.	Brian Foster, U.S.	Ryan Nyquist, U.S.

TODAY'S STARS

■ **Danny Harf, wakeboarding,**
b. October 15, 1984, Visalia, California.
Harf is the only wakeboarder in X Games
history to win three straight gold medals
(2001, 2002, and 2003). He missed out on
a medal in 2004, but won his fourth gold
medal in five years in 2005. In addition to
his gold at the Summer X Games in 2005,
Harf also finished first in three other major
competitions: the Portland and Fort Worth
championships on the Pro Wakeboard
Tour, and the World Wakeboarding
Association National Championship. He is
best known for his aggressive style and
his switch heelside 900.

Danny Harf has won gold medals in four of the past five X Games.

■ **Jamie Bestwick, BMX,** b. July 8, 1971, Great Britain. After an off-year in 2004,
when he finished sixth in the BMX Vert event at the X Games, Bestwick returned to form
in 2005. He won gold medals in the Vert event at the Bike Show in his native United
Kingdom and at the Gravity Games, and also took home two gold medals at the
Summer X Games. Bestwick dominated the Vert event with runs of 94.33 and 95.00.
Two days later, he won the Best Trick event, edging out the legendary Dave Mirra.

■ **Danny Way, skateboarding,** b. April 15, 1974, Portland, Oregon. Way may be best
known for skating at the top of the sport while injured. In 2000, he underwent several
shoulder and knee surgeries, but still returned to dominate the sport. In 2004, he helped
bring the Big Air event to the X Games, which sends skateboarders off a massive ramp
into a bone-shaking 70-foot jump. Way won the event in 2004, and then defended his
title in 2005, despite skating on a broken ankle. He broke the ankle in early July, before
becoming the first athlete to jump the Great Wall of China without the use of a motorized device.

SUMMER X GAMES RESULTS (cont.)

BIKE STUNT (cont.)

YEAR	EVENT	GOLD	SILVER	BRONZE
1996	Dirt	Joey Garcia, U.S.	T.J. Lavin, U.S.	Brian Foster, U.S.
1995	Dirt	Jay Miron, Canada	Taj Mihelich, U.S.	Joey Garcia, U.S.
2003	Flatland	Simon O'Brien, Australia	Nathan Penonzek, Canada	Trevor Meyer, U.S.
2002	Flatland	Martti Kuoppa, Finland	Michael Steingraeber, Germany	Phil Dolan, Great Britain
2001	Flatland	Martti Kuoppa, Finland	Phil Dolan, Great Britain	Matt Wilhelm, U.S.
2000	Flatland	Martti Kuoppa, Finland	Michael Steingraeber, Germany	Phil Dolan, Great Britain
1999	Flatland	Trevor Meyer, U.S.	Phil Dolan, Great Britain	Nathan Penonzek, Canada
1998	Flatland	Trevor Meyer, U.S.	Andrew Faris, Canada	Martti Kuoppa, Finland
1997	Flatland	Trevor Meyer, U.S.	Nate Hanson, U.S.	Andrew Faris, Canada
2005	Park	Dave Mirra, U.S.	Scotty Cranmer, U.S.	Ryan Nyquist, U.S.
2004	Park	Dave Mirra, U.S.	Ryan Nyquist, U.S.	Ryan Guettler, Australia
2003	Park	Ryan Nyquist, U.S.	Gary Young, U.S.	Dave Mirra, U.S.
2002	Park	Ryan Nyquist, U.S.	Alistair Whitton, Great Britain	Chad Kagy, U.S.
2001	Park	Bruce Crisman, U.S.	Alistair Whitton, Great Britain	Jay Miron, Canada
2000	Park	Dave Mirra, U.S.	Markus Wilke, Germany	Ryan Nyquist, U.S.

SUMMER X GAMES RESULTS (cont.)

BIKE STUNT (cont.)

YEAR	EVENT	GOLD	SILVER	BRONZE
1999	Street	Dave Mirra, U.S.	Jay Miron, Canada	Chad Kagy, U.S.
1998	Street	Dave Mirra, U.S.	Jay Miron, Canada	Dennis McCoy, U.S.
1997	Street	Dave Mirra, U.S.	Dennis McCoy, U.S.	Dave Voelker, U.S.
1996	Street	Dave Mirra, U.S.	Jay Miron, Canada	Rob Nolli, U.S.
2005	Vert	Jamie Bestwick, Great Britain	Chad Kagy, U.S.	Kevin Robinson, U.S.
2004	Vert	Dave Mirra, U.S.	Simon Tabron, Great Britain	Kevin Robinson, U.S.
2003	Vert	Jamie Bestwick, Great Britain	Dave Mirra, U.S.	Kevin Robinson, U.S.
2002	Vert	Dave Mirra, U.S.	Mat Hoffman, U.S.	Simon Tabron, Great Britain
2001	Vert	Dave Mirra, U.S.	Jay Miron, Canada	Mat Hoffman, U.S.
2000	Vert	Jamie Bestwick, Great Britain	Dave Mirra, U.S.	Mat Hoffman, U.S.
1999	Vert	Dave Mirra, U.S.	Jay Miron, Canada	Simon Tabron, Great Britain
1998	Vert	Dave Mirra, U.S.	Dennis McCoy, U.S.	Simon Tabron, Great Britain
1997	Vert	Dave Mirra, U.S.	Dennis McCoy, U.S.	Mat Hoffman, U.S.
1996	Vert	Mat Hoffman, U.S.	Dave Mirra, U.S.	Jamie Bestwick, Great Britain
1995	Vert	Mat Hoffman, U.S.	Dave Mirra, U.S.	Jay Miron, Canada
1998	Vert Doubles	Dave Mirra, U.S. Dennis McCoy, U.S.	Jay Miron, Canada Dave Osato, Canada	Jason Davies, Great Britain John Parker, U.S.

BUNGY

YEAR	GOLD	SILVER	BRONZE
1996	Peter Bihun, Canada	Doug Anderson, Canada	Carolyn Anderson, Canada
1995	Doug Anderson, Canada	Mark Baldwin, U.S.	Todd Watkins, U.S.

DOWNHILL BMX

YEAR	GOLD	SILVER	BRONZE
2003	Brandon Meadows, U.S.	Kyle Bennett, U.S.	Michael Day, U.S.
2002	Robbie Miranda, U.S.	Kyle Bennett, U.S.	Robert de Wilde, Netherlands
2001	Brandon Meadows, U.S.	Brian Foster, U.S.	John Whipperman, U.S.

DOWNHILL IN-LINE — MEN

YEAR	EVENT	GOLD	SILVER	BRONZE
1998		Patrick Naylor, U.S.	Jeremy Anderson, U.S.	Dane Lewis, U.S.
1997		Derek Downing, U.S.	Keith Turner, U.S.	B.J. Steketee, U.S.
1996		Dante Muse, U.S.	Derek Parra, U.S.	Jim Wiederhold, U.S.
1995	Combined	Derek Downing, U.S.	Jim Wiederhold, U.S.	Jondon Trevena, U.S.

DOWNHILL IN-LINE — WOMEN

YEAR	GOLD	SILVER	BRONZE
1998	Julie Brandt, U.S.	Aimee Sanderson, U.S.	Theresa Cliff, U.S.
1997	Gypsy Tidwell, U.S.	Julie Brandt, U.S.	Jessica Apgar, U.S.
1996	Gypsy Tidwell, U.S.	Jennifer Jones, U.S.	Desly Hill, Australia

KITESKIING

YEAR	GOLD	SILVER	BRONZE
1995	Cory Roessler, U.S.	Clarin Mustad, Norway	Thomas Jeltsch, Germany

MOUNTAIN BIKING — MEN

YEAR	EVENT	GOLD	SILVER	BRONZE
1995	Dual Downhill	Robert Naughton, U.S.	Jurgen Beneke, Germany	Todd Tanner, U.S.
1995	Dual Slalom	Jimmy Knight, U.S.	Myles Rockwell, U.S.	Mike King, U.S.
1995	Observed Trials	Libor Karas, Czech Republic	Hans Rey, Germany	Marc Brooks, U.S.

MOUNTAIN BIKING — WOMEN

YEAR	EVENT	GOLD	SILVER	BRONZE
1995	Dual Downhill	Cheri Elliott, U.S.	Kim Sonier, U.S.	Leigh Donovan, U.S.
1995	Dual Slalom	Leigh Donovan, U.S.	Cheri Elliott, U.S.	Giovanna Bonazzi, Italy

MOTO X

YEAR	EVENT	GOLD	SILVER	BRONZE
2003	Big Air	Brian Deegan, U.S.	Nate Adams, U.S.	Kenny Bartram, U.S.
2002	Big Air	Mike Metzger, U.S.	Carey Hart, U.S.	Brian Deegan, U.S.
2001	Big Air	Kenny Bartram, U.S.	Dustin Miller, U.S.	Brian Deegan, U.S.

Travis Pastrana

ALLEN KEE/WIREIMAGE.COM

SIKIDS.COM
Visit our website for the latest stats and sports info.

2005	Freestyle	Travis Pastrana, U.S.	Kenny Bartram, U.S.	Nate Adams, U.S.
2004	Freestyle	Nate Adams, U.S.	Travis Pastrana, U.S.	Adam Jones, U.S.
2003	Freestyle	Travis Pastrana, U.S.	Nate Adams, U.S.	Brian Deegan, U.S.
2002	Freestyle	Mike Metzger, U.S.	Kenny Bartram, U.S.	Drake McElroy, U.S.
2001	Freestyle	Travis Pastrana, U.S.	Clifford Adoptante, U.S.	Jake Windham, U.S.
2000	Freestyle	Travis Pastrana, U.S.	Tommy Clowers, U.S.	Brian Deegan, U.S.
1999	Freestyle	Travis Pastrana, U.S.	Mike Cinqmars, U.S.	Brian Deegan, U.S.
2005	Step Up	Tommy Clowers, U.S.	Matt Buyten, U.S.	Jeremy McGrath, U.S.
2004	Step Up	Jeremy McGrath, U.S.	Matt Buyten, U.S.	Tommy Clowers, U.S.
2003	Step Up	Matt Buyten, U.S.	Tommy Clowers, U.S.	Ronnie Renner, U.S.
2002	Step Up	Tommy Clowers, U.S.	Mike Metzger, U.S.	Brian Deegan, U.S.
2001	Step Up	Tommy Clowers, U.S.	Travis Pastrana, U.S.	Colin Morrison, U.S. (tie)
				Ronnie Renner, U.S.
				Kris Rourke, U.S.
				Jeremy Stenberg, U.S.
2000	Step Up	Tommy Clowers, U.S.	Kris Rourke, U.S.	Brian Deegan, U.S.
2005	Super Moto	Doug Henry, U.S.	Jeremy McGrath, U.S.	Chad Reed, Australia
2004	Super Moto	Ben Bostrom, U.S.	Eddy Seel, Belgium	Jeremy McGrath, U.S.
2005	Best Trick	Jeremy Stenberg, U.S.	Travis Pastrana, U.S.	Nate Adams, U.S.
2004	Best Trick	Chuck Carothers, U.S.	Nate Adams, U.S.	Travis Pastrana, U.S.

SUMMER X GAMES RESULTS (cont.)

SKATEBOARDING — MEN

YEAR	EVENT	GOLD	SILVER	BRONZE
2003	Park	Ryan Sheckler, U.S.	Rodil de Araujo, Jr., Brazil	Chad Bartie, Australia
2002	Park	Rodil de Araujo, Jr., Brazil	Wagner Ramos, Brazil	Eric Koston, U.S.
2001	Park	Rodil de Araujo, Jr., Brazil	Kerry Getz, U.S.	Caine Gayle, U.S.
2000	Park	Eric Koston, U.S.	Rodil de Araujo, Jr., Brazil	Kerry Getz, U.S.
2005	Street	Paul Rodriguez, U.S.	Greg Lutzka, U.S.	Chris Cole, U.S.
2004	Street	Paul Rodriguez, U.S.	Andrew Reynolds, U.S.	Bastien Salabanzi, France
2003	Street	Eric Koston, U.S.	Rodil de Araujo, Jr., Brazil	Paul Rodriguez, U.S.
2002	Street	Rodil de Araujo, Jr., Brazil	Wagner Ramos, Brazil	Kyle Berard, U.S.
2001	Street	Kerry Getz, U.S.	Eric Koston, U.S.	Chris Senn, U.S.
1999	Street	Chris Senn, U.S.	Pat Channita, U.S.	Chad Fernandez, U.S.
1998	Street	Rodil de Araujo, Jr., Brazil	Andy Macdonald, U.S.	Chris Senn, U.S.
1997	Street	Chris Senn, U.S.	Andy Macdonald, U.S.	Brian Patch, U.S.
1996	Street	Rodil de Araujo, Jr., Brazil	Chris Senn, U.S.	Brian Patch, U.S.
1995	Street	Chris Senn, U.S.	Tony Hawk, U.S.	Willy Santos, U.S.
2003	Street Best Trick	Chad Muska, U.S.	Rodil de Araujo, Jr., Brazil	Wagner Ramos, Brazil
2002	Street Best Trick	Rodil de Araujo, Jr., Brazil	Wagner Ramos, Brazil	Dayne Brummet, U.S.
2001	Street Best Trick	Rick McCrank, Canada	Kerry Getz, U.S.	Eric Koston, U.S.
1996	Street Best Trick	Gershon Mosley, U.S.	Chris Senn, U.S.	Brian Patch, U.S.
1995	Street Best Trick	Jamie Thomas, U.S.	Gershon Mosley, U.S.	Kareem Campbell, U.S.
2005	Vert	Pierre-Luc Gagnon, Canada	Shaun White, U.S.	Sandro Dias, Brazil
2004	Vert	Bucky Lasek, U.S.	Pierre-Luc Gagnon, Canada	Rune Glifberg, Denmark
2003	Vert	Bucky Lasek, U.S.	Andy Macdonald, U.S.	Rune Glifberg, Denmark
2002	Vert	Pierre-Luc Gagnon, Canada	Bob Burnquist, Brazil	Rune Glifberg, Denmark
2001	Vert	Bob Burnquist, Brazil	Bucky Lasek, U.S.	Tas Pappas, Australia
2000	Vert	Bucky Lasek, U.S.	Pierre-Luc Gagnon, Canada	Colin McKay, Canada
1999	Vert	Bucky Lasek, U.S.	Andy Macdonald, U.S.	Tony Hawk, U.S.
1998	Vert	Andy Macdonald, U.S.	Giorgio Zattoni, Italy	Tony Hawk, U.S.
1997	Vert	Tony Hawk, U.S.	Rune Glifberg, Denmark	Bob Burnquist, Brazil
1996	Vert	Andy Macdonald, U.S.	Tony Hawk, U.S.	Tas Pappas, Australia
1995	Vert	Tony Hawk, U.S.	Neal Hendrix, U.S.	Rune Glifberg, Denmark
2005	Vert Best Trick	Bob Burnquist, Brazil	Colin McKay, Canada	Pierre-Luc Gagnon, Canada
2004	Vert Best Trick	Sandro Dias, Brazil	Pierre-Luc Gagnon, Canada	Danny Mayer, U.S.
2003	Vert Best Trick	Tony Hawk, U.S.	Sandro Dias, Brazil	Andy Macdonald, U.S.
2002	Vert Best Trick	Pierre-Luc Gagnon, Canada	Sandro Dias, Brazil	Tony Hawk, U.S.
2001	Vert Best Trick	Matt Dove, U.S.	Tony Hawk, U.S.	Bob Burnquist, Brazil
2000	Vert Best Trick	Bob Burnquist, Brazil	Colin McKay, Canada	Andy Macdonald, U.S.
1999	Vert Best Trick	Tony Hawk, U.S.	Colin McKay, Canada	Bob Burnquist, Brazil
2005	Big Air	Danny Way, U.S.	Pierre-Luc Gagnon, Canada	Andy Macdonald, U.S.
2004	Big Air	Danny Way, U.S.	Pierre-Luc Gagnon, Canada	Andy Macdonald, U.S.
2003	Vert Doubles	Bucky Lasek, U.S. Bob Burnquist, Brazil	Rune Glifberg, Denmark Mike Crum, U.S.	Neal Hendrix, U.S. Buster Halterman, U.S.
2002	Vert Doubles	Tony Hawk, U.S. Andy Macdonald, U.S.	Bob Burnquist, Brazil Bucky Lasek, U.S.	Mike Crum, U.S. Rune Glifberg, Denmark
2001	Vert Doubles	Tony Hawk, U.S. Andy Macdonald, U.S.	Mike Crum, U.S. Chris Gentry, U.S.	Mike Frazier, U.S. Neal Hendrix, U.S.
2000	Vert Doubles	Tony Hawk, U.S. Andy Macdonald, U.S.	Pierre-Luc Gagnon, Canada Max Dufour, Canada	Sandro Dias, Brazil Cristiano Mateus, Brazil
1999	Vert Doubles	Tony Hawk, U.S. Andy Macdonald, U.S.	Bucky Lasek, U.S. Brian Patch, U.S.	Mike Crum, U.S. Rune Glifberg, Denmark
1998	Vert Doubles	Tony Hawk, U.S. Andy Macdonald, U.S.	Bucky Lasek, U.S. Brian Patch, U.S.	Bob Burnquist, Brazil Lincoln Ueda, Brazil
1997	Vert Doubles	Tony Hawk, U.S. Andy Macdonald, U.S.	Mike Frazier, U.S. Neal Hendrix, U.S.	Max Dufour, Canada Mathias Ringstrom, Sweden
1995	High Air	Danny Way, U.S.	Neal Hendrix, U.S.	Tas Pappas, Australia

Cara-Beth Burnside

DESIREE ASTORGA

DID YOU KNOW?

When the X Games debuted in June 1995 in Rhode Island, the official title of the event was the Extreme Games. The first X Games gold medal was awarded to Justin Sears in the Barefoot Waterski Jumping competition.

SKATEBOARDING — WOMEN

YEAR	EVENT	GOLD	SILVER	BRONZE
2005	Street	Elissa Steamer, U.S.	Evelien Bouilliart, Belgium	Marissa Del Santo, U.S.
2004	Street	Elissa Steamer, U.S.	Vanessa Torres, U.S.	Lauren Perkins, U.S.
2005	Vert	Cara-Beth Burnside, U.S.	Lyn-Z Adams Hawkins, U.S.	Mimi Knoop, U.S.
2004	Vert	Lyn-Z Adams Hawkins, U.S.	Cara-Beth Burnside, U.S.	Mimi Knoop, U.S.

SPORT CLIMBING — MEN

YEAR	EVENT	GOLD	SILVER	BRONZE
2002	Speed	Maxim Stenkovoy, Ukraine	Alexandre Pechekhonov, Russia	Serguei Sinitsyn, Russia
2001	Speed	Maxim Stenkovoy, Ukraine	Vladimir Zakharov, Ukraine	Chris Bloch, U.S.
2000	Speed	Vladimir Zakharov, Ukraine	Chris Bloch, U.S.	Tomasz Oleksy, Poland
1999	Speed	Aaron Shamy, U.S.	Chris Bloch, U.S.	Vladimir Netsvetaev, Russia
1998	Speed	Vladimir Netsvetaev, Russia	Aaron Shamy, U.S.	Chris Bloch, U.S.
1997	Speed	Hans Florine, U.S.	Chris Bloch, U.S.	Jason Campbell, U.S.
1996	Speed	Hans Florine, U.S.	Chris Bloch, U.S.	Tim Fairfield, U.S.
1995	Speed	Hans Florine, U.S.	Salavat Rakhmetov, Russia	Yuji Hirayama, Japan
1999	Bouldering	Chris Sharma, U.S.	Francois Petit, France	Stephane Julien, France
1998	Difficulty	Christian Core, Italy	Francois Legrand, France	Vadim Vinokur, U.S.
1997	Difficulty	Francois Legrand, France	Yuji Hirayama, Japan	Chris Sharma, U.S.
1996	Difficulty	Arnaud Petit, France	Francois Lombard, France	Cristian Brenna, Italy
1995	Difficulty	Ian Vickers, Great Britain	Arnaud Petit, France	Francois Petit, France

2005-06 TIME LINE

■ **January 29, 2005:** Snowboarder Shaun White takes the gold medal in the Slopestyle event at the X Games for the third straight year. White blew out his knee while competing in the Superpipe event at the X Games in 2004, and underwent reconstructive surgery before returning to win his sixth career X Games gold medal.

■ **January 29, 2005:** White isn't the only snowboarder to three-peat at the X Games. On the same Saturday afternoon, Lindsey Jacobellis edges out Erin Simmons by half the length of a snow-board to win the women's Snowboard X event for the third consecutive year.

■ **July 9, 2005:** Danny Way jumps the Great Wall of China, becoming the first skateboarder to clear the wall without the use of a motorized aid. He drops in from a massive ramp, reaching a speed of 50 miles per hour before clearing the 61-foot gap four times. On his final three runs, Way adds several tricks to the routine, including 360-degree spins.

■ **August 5, 2005:** After years of disap-pointing finishes in the Skateboard Vert event at the X Games, Pierre-Luc Gagnon wins gold, beating out snowboard specialist Shaun White and Sandro Diaz. Four-time Vert winner Bucky Lasek fails to medal.

■ **August 6, 2005:** After failing to win the gold medal in the Moto X Freestyle event at the 2004 Summer X Games for the first time in his career, Travis Pastrana takes back the top spot, thanks to a superb backflip Saran Wrap that helps clinch the title. In six appearances in the event, Pastrana has won the gold medal five times.

■ **August 6, 2005:** BMX king Dave Mirra adds to his record X games medal count by winning the BMX Park event. It is his 19th overall medal, and 14th gold medal.

■ **January 31, 2006:** After fracturing both ankles and heel bones during a ski-ing accident in March 2005, Tanner Hall wins gold in the Ski Superpipe event at the Winter X Games, edging out Simon Dumont. Hall had finished second to Dumont at each of the last two X Games.

■ **February 12, 2006:** Shaun White wins the gold medal in Halfpipe at the 2006 Winter Olympics, while teammate Danny Kass takes the silver medal. On the next day, the U.S. snowboarders achieve another one-two punch in the women's Halfpipe, with Hannah Teter winning the gold medal and Gretchen Bleiler the silver.

SUMMER X GAMES RESULTS (cont.)

SPORT CLIMBING — WOMEN

YEAR	EVENT	GOLD	SILVER	BRONZE
2002	Speed	Tori Allen, U.S.	Olga Zakharova, Ukraine	Etti Hendrawati, Indonesia
2001	Speed	Elena Repko, Ukraine	Olga Zakharova, Ukraine	Alena Ostapenko, Ukraine
2000	Speed	Etti Hendrawati, Indonesia	Elena Repko, Ukraine	Olga Zakharova, Ukraine
1999	Speed	Renata Piszczek, Poland	Olga Zakharova, Ukraine	Etti Hendrawati, Indonesia
1998	Speed	Elena Ovchinnikova, U.S.	Yuyun Yuniar, Indonesia	Venera Tchereshneva, Russia
1997	Speed	Elena Ovchinnikova, U.S.	Abby Watkins, Australia	Mi Sun Go, South Korea
1996	Speed	Cecile Le Flem, France	Elena Choumilova, Russia	Natalie Richer, France
1995	Speed	Elena Ovchinnikova, Russia	Diane Russell, U.S.	Georgia Phipps-Franklin, U.S.
1999	Bouldering	Stephanie Bodet, France	Liv Sansoz, France	Elena Choumilova, Russia
1998	Difficulty	Katie Brown, U.S.	Mi Sun Go, South Korea	Elena Choumilova, Russia
1997	Difficulty	Katie Brown, U.S.	Liv Sansoz, France	Muriel Sarkany, Belgium
1996	Difficulty	Katie Brown, U.S.	Laurence Guyon, France	Liv Sansoz, France
1995	Difficulty	Robyn Erbesfield, U.S.	Elena Ovchinnikova, Russia	Mia Axon, U.S.

SUMMER X GAMES RESULTS (cont.)

STREET LUGE

YEAR	EVENT	GOLD	SILVER	BRONZE
2001	Super Mass	Brent DeKeyser, U.S.	David Rogers, U.S.	Dave Auld, U.S.
2000	Super Mass	Bob Pereyra, U.S.	Lee Dansie, Great Britain	John Rogers, U.S.
1999	Super Mass	David Rogers, U.S.	Biker Sherlock, U.S.	Sean Slate, U.S.
1998	Super Mass	Rat Sult, U.S.	Bob Pereyra, U.S.	Todd Lehr, U.S.
1997	Super Mass	Chris Ponseti, U.S.	Biker Sherlock, U.S.	Rat Sult, U.S.
2000	Dual	Bob Ozman, U.S.	Wade Sokol, U.S.	Bob Pereyra, U.S.
1999	Dual	Dennis Derammelaere, U.S.	Lee Dansie, Great Britain	Biker Sherlock, U.S.
1998	Dual	Biker Sherlock, U.S.	Stefan Wagner, Germany	Dave Auld, U.S.
1997	Dual	Biker Sherlock, U.S.	Dennis Derammelaere, U.S.	Darren Lott, U.S.
1996	Dual	Shawn Goulart, U.S.	Stefan Wagner, Germany	Dennis Derammelaere, U.S.
1995	Dual	Bob Pereyra, U.S.	Stefan Wagner, Germany	Shawn Goulart, U.S.
1998	Mass	Rat Sult, U.S.	Sean Slate, U.S.	Steve Fernando, U.S.
1997	Mass	Biker Sherlock, U.S.	Dennis Derammelaere, U.S.	Lee Dansie, Great Britain
1996	Mass	Biker Sherlock, U.S.	Daryl Thompson, U.S.	Dennis Derammelaere, U.S.
1995	Mass	Shawn Goulart, U.S.	Lee Dansie, Great Britain	Stefan Wagner, Germany

SURFING — MEN

YEAR	GOLD	SILVER	BRONZE
2005	East Coast	West Coast	N/A
2004	East Coast	West Coast	N/A
2003	East Coast	West Coast	N/A

WAKEBOARDING — MEN

YEAR	GOLD	SILVER	BRONZE
2005	Danny Harf, U.S.	Phillip Soven, U.S.	Josh Sanders, Australia
2004	Phillip Soven, U.S.	Chad Sharpe, Canada	Parks Bonifay, U.S.
2003	Danny Harf, U.S.	Parks Bonifay, U.S.	Daniel Watkins, U.S.
2002	Danny Harf, U.S.	Darin Shapiro, U.S.	Shaun Murray, U.S.
2001	Danny Harf, U.S.	Darin Shapiro, U.S.	Erik Ruck, U.S.
2000	Darin Shapiro, U.S.	Shaun Murray, U.S.	Shane Bonifay, U.S.
1999	Parks Bonifay, U.S.	Darin Shapiro, U.S.	Brannan Johnson, U.S.
1998	Darin Shapiro, U.S.	Shaun Murray, U.S.	Zane Schwenk, U.S.
1997	Jeremy Kovak, Canada	Darin Shapiro, U.S.	Parks Bonifay, U.S.
1996	Parks Bonifay, U.S.	Jeremy Kovak, Canada	Scott Byerly, U.S.

WAKEBOARDING — WOMEN

YEAR	GOLD	SILVER	BRONZE
2005	Dallas Friday, U.S.	Emily Copeland, U.S.	Tara Hamilton, U.S.
2004	Dallas Friday, U.S.	Tara Hamilton, U.S.	Maeghan Major, U.S.
2003	Dallas Friday, U.S.	Melissa Marquardt, U.S.	Emily Copeland, U.S.
2002	Emily Copeland, U.S.	Dallas Friday, U.S.	Leslie Kent, U.S.
2001	Dallas Friday, U.S.	Emily Copeland, U.S.	Tara Hamilton, U.S.
2000	Tara Hamilton, U.S.	Dallas Friday, U.S.	Maeghan Major, U.S.
1999	Maeghan Major, U.S.	Emily Copeland, U.S.	Andrea Gaytan, Mexico
1998	Andrea Gaytan, Mexico	Dana Preble, U.S.	Tara Hamilton, U.S.
1997	Tara Hamilton, U.S.	Andrea Gaytan, Mexico	Jaime Necrason, U.S.

WINDSURFING — MEN

YEAR	GOLD	SILVER	BRONZE
1995	Bjorn Dunkerbeck, Spain	Micah Buzianis, U.S.	Al Aguera, U.S.

WINDSURFING — WOMEN

YEAR	GOLD	SILVER	BRONZE
1995	Angela Cochran, U.S.	Jayne Fenner-Benedict, U.S.	Jutta Mueller, Germany

SUMMER X GAMES RESULTS (cont.)

X VENTURE RACE

YEAR	GOLD	SILVER	BRONZE
1997	Team Presidio	Team Endeavour	Team Red Hot
	Ian Adamson, Australia	Louise Cooper-Lovelace, U.S.	Sharyn Davis, Australia
	John Howard, New Zealand	Neil Jones, New Zealand	John Jacoby, Australia
	Andrea Spitzer, Germany	Jeff Mitchell, New Zealand	Tim Smallwood, Australia
1996	Team Kobeer	Team Eco-Internet	Team Mirage
	Angelika Castaneda, U.S.	Ian Adamson, Australia	Kirk Boylston, U.S.
	John Howard, New Zealand	Robert Nagle, Ireland	Nancy Bristow, U.S.
	Keith Murray, New Zealand	Vivienne Prince, U.S.	Steve Gurney, New Zealand
1995	Team Thredbo	Twin Team	Team Eco-Internet
	Jane Hall, Australia	Angelika Castaneda, U.S.	Ian Adamson, Australia
	Andrew Hislop, Australia	Adrian Crane, U.S.	John Howard, New Zealand
	Rod Hislop, Australia	Tom Possert, U.S.	Keith Murray, New Zealand
	John Jacoby, Australia	Robert Rambach, U.S.	Robert Nagle, Ireland
	Novak Thompson, Australia	Marshall Ulrich, U.S.	Cathy Sassin-Smith, U.S.

WINTER GRAVITY GAMES RESULTS

SNOWBOARDING — MEN

YEAR	EVENT	GOLD	SILVER	BRONZE
2005	Snowboardcross	Xavier de le Rue, France	Jason Smith, U.S.	Mike Rosengren, U.S.
2005	Slopestyle	Chad Otterstrom, U.S.	Antti Autti, Finland	Wyatt Caldwell, U.S.
2005	Superpipe	Crispin Lipscomb, Canada	Danny Davis, U.S.	Risto Mattila, Finland
2005	Rail Jam	Chad Otterstrom, U.S.	N/A	N/A

SNOWBOARDING — WOMEN

YEAR	EVENT	GOLD	SILVER	BRONZE
2005	Snowboardcross	Leslee Olson, U.S.	Marni Yamada, U.S.	Jordan Karlinski, U.S.
2005	Slopestyle	Janna Meyen, U.S.	Silvia Mittermueller, Germany	Izumi Amaike, Japan
2005	Superpipe	Gretchen Bleiler, U.S.	Hannah Teter, U.S.	Elena Hight, U.S.
2005	Rail Jam	Leanne Pelosi, Canada	N/A	N/A

SKIING — MEN

YEAR	EVENT	GOLD	SILVER	BRONZE
2005	Skiercross	Casey Puckett, U.S.	Zach Crist, U.S.	Jakub Fiala, U.S.
2005	Slopestyle	TJ Schiller, Canada	Simon Dumont, U.S.	Charles Gagnier, Canada
2005	Superpipe	Corey Vanular, U.S.	Andrew Woods, U.S.	Simon Dumont, U.S.
2005	Rail Jam	Tim Russell, U.S.	N/A	N/A

SKIING — WOMEN

YEAR	EVENT	GOLD	SILVER	BRONZE
2005	Skiercross	Brett Buckles, U.S.	Valentine Scuotto, France	Sara-Maude Boucher, Canada
2005	Superpipe	Kristi Leskinen, U.S.	Sarah Burke, Canada	Grete Eliassen, Norway
2005	Rail Jam	Grete Eliassen, Norway	N/A	N/A

Note: Winter Gravity Games were not held in 2006 because of the Winter Olympics.

LEGENDS

STEVE BOYLE/NEWSPORT

Bucky Lasek has been at the top of the Vert world since 1999.

■ **Bucky Lasek, skateboarding,** b. December 3, 1972, in Baltimore, Maryland. Lasek made his first statement on the skateboarding scene by taking the gold medal in the Vert event at the 1999 Summer X Games. He won the title again a year later, and that was only the beginning. In 2004, Lasek became the first skateboarder to win the Vans Triple Crown, the Gravity Games, and the Slam City Jam in the same year. He wrapped up his season by winning the Vert event at the Summer X Games for a record fourth time.

■ **Dave Mirra, BMX,** b. April 4, 1974, in Syracuse, New York. Mirra has competed in and medaled in every X Games competition since 1995, the first year of the event. He broke the record for most X Games medals in 2004, passing Tony Hawk, who had 16. After taking gold in the Freestyle Park event at the 2005 Games, Mirra's medal count is now 19, including 14 golds. Besides dominating the competition, Mirra is known for bringing style to the BMX event. He is always breaking out a few new tricks to entertain the crowd.

■ **Janna Meyen, snowboarding,** b. February 12, 1977 in Torrance, California. Meyen became the first athlete in Summer or Winter X Games history to win one event four times in a row when she won the 2006 women's Slopestyle title. Despite falling into last place after the first run of the finals, Meyen rebounded to score a 91.33 in her second run. The highlight of that run was a 55-foot channel-gap jump, something no other competitor landed. In addition to her X Games four-peat, Meyen went undefeated in Slopestyle and Rail events between March 2003 and March 2005.

TRIVIA CHALLENGE

How old was Dallas Friday when she won the silver medal at X Games Six to become the youngest wakeboarder to ever medal?

She was 13 years old.

DID YOU KNOW?

At Summer X Games Nine in 2003, skateboarder Jake Brown attempted to compete a 900 in the Skateboard Vert Best trick event more than 20 times, but never successfully landed it. Tony Hawk landed the first 900 in skateboard competition at the X Games in 1999.

SUMMER GRAVITY GAMES RESULTS

BIKE

YEAR	EVENT	GOLD	SILVER	BRONZE
2004	Street	Morgan Wade, U.S.	Ryan Nyquist, U.S.	Steven McCann, Australia
2003	Street	Dave Mirra, U.S.	Ryan Nyquist, U.S.	Steven McCann, Australia
2002	Street	Dave Mirra, U.S.	Ryan Nyquist, U.S.	Tom Haugen, U.S.
2001	Street	Ryan Nyquist, U.S.	Dave Osato, Canada	Chad Kagy, U.S.
2000	Street	Dave Osato, Canada	Ryan Nyquist, U.S.	Mike Laird, U.S.
1999	Street	Dave Mirra, U.S.	Ryan Nyquist, U.S.	Jay Miron, Canada
2005	Dirt	Ryan Guettler, U.S.	Luke Parslow, U.S.	Joey Marks, U.S.
2004	Dirt	Ryan Nyquist, U.S.	Steven McCann, Australia	Stephen Murray, Great Britain
2003	Dirt	Ryan Nyquist, U.S.	Chris Doyle, U.S.	Steven McCann, Australia
2002	Dirt	Stephen Murray, Great Britain	Allan Cooke, U.S.	Chris Doyle, U.S.
2001	Dirt	Stephen Murray, Great Britain	Todd Walkowiak, U.S.	Chris Doyle, U.S.
2000	Dirt	T.J. Lavin, U.S.	Chris Doyle, U.S.	Ryan Jordan, U.S.
1999	Dirt	Ryan Nyquist, U.S.	Todd Walkowiak, U.S.	T.J. Lavin, U.S.

Ryan Guettler

2005	Vert	Jamie Bestwick, Great Britain	Dennis McCoy, U.S.	Kevin Robinson, U.S.
2004	Vert	Jamie Bestwick, Great Britain	Chad Kagy, U.S.	Kevin Robinson, U.S.
2003	Vert	Dave Mirra, U.S.	Kevin Robinson, U.S.	Simon Tabron, Great Britain
2002	Vert	Simon Tabron, Great Britain	Dave Mirra, U.S.	Jay Miron, Canada
2001	Vert	Jamie Bestwick, Great Britain	Kevin Robinson, U.S.	Simon Tabron, Great Britain
2000	Vert	Dave Mirra, U.S.	Jamie Bestwick, Great Britain	Jay Miron, Canada
1999	Vert	Jamie Bestwick, Great Britain	Jay Miron, Canada	John Parker, U.S.

FREESTYLE MOTOCROSS

YEAR	GOLD	SILVER	BRONZE
2005	Kenny Bartram, U.S.	Jeremy Stenberg, U.S.	Ronnie Renner, U.S.
2004	Nate Adams, U.S.	Jeremy Stenberg, U.S.	Ronnie Faisst, U.S.
2003	Nate Adams, U.S.	Travis Pastrana, U.S.	Ronnie Renner, U.S.
2002	Travis Pastrana, U.S.	Mike Metzger, U.S.	Kenny Bartram, U.S.
2001	Travis Pastrana, U.S.	Clifford Adoptante, U.S.	Tommy Clowers, U.S.
2000	Brian Deegan, U.S.	Mike Metzger, U.S.	Kenny Bartram, U.S.
1999	Travis Pastrana, U.S.	Brian Deegan, U.S.	Carey Hart, U.S.

Chris Cole

TONY DONALDSON/ICON SMI

TRIVIA CHALLENGE

In 2005, one athlete finished first in the Dew Action Sports Tour final standings in two different events. Who was it?

Ryan Guettler. The BMX rider finished first on the Dew Action Sports Tour standings in both the Dirt and Park disciplines.

FAST FACT

At age 15, motocross rider Travis Pastrana posted a nearly perfect 99.0 in Moto X Freestyle in the first year of the sport's competition, at the 1999 X Games. No one has topped the score since.

SKATEBOARDING — MEN

YEAR	EVENT	GOLD	SILVER	BRONZE
2005	Vert	Bucky Lasek, U.S	Andy Macdonald, U.S.	Sandro Dias, Brazil
2004	Vert	Rune Glifberg, Denmark	Andy Macdonald, U.S.	Pierre-Luc Gagnon, Canada
2003	Vert	Bucky Lasek, U.S.	Andy Macdonald, U.S.	Rune Glifberg, Denmark
2002	Vert	Bucky Lasek, U.S.	Bob Burnquist, Brazil	Pierre-Luc Gagnon, Canada
2001	Vert	Rune Glifberg, Denmark	Bucky Lasek, U.S.	Andy Macdonald, U.S.
2000	Vert	Andy Macdonald, U.S.	Bob Burnquist, Brazil	Pierre-Luc Gagnon, Canada
1999	Vert	Bob Burnquist, Brazil	Bucky Lasek, U.S.	Andy Macdonald, U.S.
2004	Vert Best Trick	Sandro Diaz, Brazil	Danny Mayer, U.S.	Pierre-Luc Gagnon, Canada
2003	Vert Best Trick	Mathias Ringstrom, Sweden	Danny Mayer, U.S.	Sandro Diaz, Brazil
2002	Vert Best Trick	Pierre-Luc Gagnon, Canada	Bob Burnquist, Brazil	Sandro Diaz, Brazil
2005	Street	Chris Cole, U.S.	Wagner Ramos, Brazil	Andre Genovesi, Brazil
2004	Street	Rodil de Araujo, Jr., Brazil	Greg Lutzka, U.S.	Ryan Sheckler, U.S.
2003	Street	Ryan Sheckler, U.S.	Rick McCrank, Canada	Chris Senn, U.S.
2002	Street	Eric Koston, U.S.	Pat Channita, U.S.	Kerry Getz, U.S.
2001	Street	Eric Koston, U.S.	Rick McCrank, Canada	Kyle Berard, U.S.
2000	Street	Eric Koston, U.S.	Brian Anderson, U.S.	Kerry Getz, U.S.
1999	Street	Brian Anderson, U.S.	Rodil de Araujo, Jr., Brazil	Eric Koston, U.S.
2004	Street Best Trick	Paul Machnau, Canada	Nilton Neves, Brazil	Josh Evin, Canada
2003	Street Best Trick	Chris Haslam, Canada	Daniel Vieira, Brazil	Chad Bartie, Australia
2002	Downhill, 2-person	Mark Golter, U.S.	Dane Van Bommel, U.S.	Alex Wenk, Switzerland
2001	Downhill, 2-person	Dane Van Bommel, U.S.	Gary Hardwick, U.S.	Mark Golter, U.S.
2000	Downhill, 2-person	Dane Van Bommel, U.S.	John Gwiazdowski, U.S.	Alex Wenk, Switzerland
1999	Downhill, 2-person	Lee Dansie, Great Britain	Biker Sherlock, U.S.	Dane Van Bommel, U.S.
2002	Downhill, 4-person	Darryl Freeman, U.S.	Mark Golter, U.S.	Dane Van Bommel, U.S.
2001	Downhill, 4-person	Dane Van Bommel, U.S.	Alex Wenk, Switzerland	Lee Dansie, Great Britain
2000	Downhill, 4-person	Dane Van Bommel, U.S.	John Gwiazdowski, U.S.	Alex Wenk, Switzerland
1999	Downhill, 4-person	Biker Sherlock, U.S.	Dane Van Bommel, U.S.	Emanuel Antuna, France

SUMMER GRAVITY GAMES RESULTS (cont.)

SKATEBOARDING — WOMEN

YEAR	EVENT	GOLD	SILVER	BRONZE
2004	Street	Elissa Steamer, U.S.	Lauren Perkins, U.S.	Lyn-Z Adams Hawkins, U.S.

AGGRESSIVE IN-LINE — MEN

YEAR	EVENT	GOLD	SILVER	BRONZE
2001	Street	Blake Dennis, Australia	Louie Zamora, U.S.	Aaron Feinberg, U.S.
2000	Street	Sven Boekhorst, Netherlands	Blake Dennis, Australia	Wilfried Rossignol, France
1999	Street	Sven Boekhorst, Netherlands	Den Bosch, Netherlands	Louie Zamora, U.S.
2003	Street Best Trick	Richie Velasquez, U.S.	Stephane Alfano, France	Brian Aragon, U.S.
2003	Vert	Eito Yasutoko, Japan	Marco de Santi, Brazil	Marc Englehart, U.S.
2002	Vert	Marc Englehart, U.S.	Takeshi Yasutoko, Japan	Shane Yost, Tasmania
2001	Vert	Taig Khris, France	Takeshi Yasutoko, Japan	Matt Lindenmuth, U.S.
2000	Vert	Matt Salerno, Australia	Taig Khris, France	Eito Yasutoko, Japan
1999	Vert	Taig Khris, France	Shane Yost, Australia	Cesar Mora, Australia

AGGRESSIVE IN-LINE — WOMEN

YEAR	EVENT	GOLD	SILVER	BRONZE
2001	Street	Martina Svobodova, Slovakia	Fabiola da Silva, Brazil	Deborah West, U.S.
2000	Street	Martina Svobodova, Slovakia	Fabiola da Silva, Brazil	Kelly Matthews, U.S.
1999	Street	Fabiola da Silva, Brazil	Anneke Winter, Germany	Kelly Matthews, U.S.
2001	Vert	Ayumi Kawasaki, Japan	Fabiola da Silva, Brazil	N/A
2000	Vert	Fabiola da Silva, Brazil	Ayumi Kawasaki, Japan	Merce Borrull, Spain
1999	Vert	Fabiola da Silva, Brazil	Merce Borrull, Spain	Maki Komori, Japan

WAKEBOARDING — MEN

YEAR	GOLD	SILVER	BRONZE
2005	Phillip Sloven, U.S.	Daniel Watkins, U.S.	Rusty Malinoski, Canada
2004	Trevor Hansen, U.S.	Andrew Adkinson, U.S.	Brett Eisenhauer, Australia
2003	Parks Bonifay, U.S.	Shane Bonifay, U.S.	Brett Eisenhauer, Australia
2002	Mark Kenney, U.S.	Danny Harf, U.S.	Darin Shapiro, U.S.
2001	Darin Shapiro, U.S.	Parks Bonifay, U.S.	Daniel Watkins, Australia
2000	Parks Bonifay, U.S.	Darin Shapiro, U.S.	Ryan Wynne, U.S.
1999	Shaun Murray, U.S.	Parks Bonifay, U.S.	Rob Struharik, U.S.

WAKEBOARDING — WOMEN

YEAR	GOLD	SILVER	BRONZE
2005	Emily Copeland, U.S.	Lauren Loe, U.S.	Dallas Friday, U.S.
2004	Dallas Friday, U.S.	Emily Copeland, U.S.	Lauren Loe, U.S.
2003	Emily Copeland, U.S.	Tara Hamilton, U.S.	Leslie Kent, U.S.
2002	Emily Copeland, U.S.	Melissa Marquardt, U.S.	Dallas Friday, U.S.
2001	Dallas Friday, U.S.	Tara Hamilton, U.S.	Christy Smith, U.S.
2000	Maeghan Major, U.S.	Tara Hamilton, U.S.	Lauren Loe, U.S.
1999	Andrea Gaytan, Mexico	Tara Hamilton, U.S.	Christy Smith, U.S.

STREET LUGE

YEAR	EVENT	GOLD	SILVER	BRONZE
2002	4-person	Mike McIntyre, U.S.	John Rogers, U.S.	Dave Rogers, U.S.
2001	4-person	Rat Sult, U.S.	Biker Sherlock, U.S.	John Fryer, U.S.
1999	4-person	Sean Mallard, U.S.	Biker Sherlock, U.S.	George Orton, U.S.
2002	6-person	Dave Rogers, U.S.	Mike McIntyre, U.S.	John Rogers, U.S.
2001	6-person	Rat Sult, U.S.	Kurtis Head, U.S.	David Kelly, U.S.
1999	6-person	Biker Sherlock, U.S.	Sean Slate, U.S.	Wade Sokol, U.S.

SURFING — ALL-TIME RESULTS

Kelly Slater

FRANCK FAUGERE/DPPI/ICON SMI

YEAR	MEN	YEAR	LONGBOARD
2005	Kelly Slater, U.S.	2005	*Longboard cancelled in 2005*
2004	Andy Irons, U.S.	2004	Joel Tudor, U.S.
2003	Andy Irons, U.S.	2003	Beau Young, Australia
2002	Andy Irons, U.S.	2002	Colin McPhillips, U.S.
2001	C.J. Hobgood, U.S.	2001	Colin McPhillips, U.S.
2000	Sunny Garcia, U.S.	2000	Beau Young, Australia
1999	Mark Occhilupo, Australia	1999	Colin McPhillips, U.S.
1998	Kelly Slater, U.S.	1998	Joel Tudor, U.S.
1997	Kelly Slater, U.S.	1997	Dino Miranda, U.S.
1996	Kelly Slater, U.S.	1996	Bonga Perkins, U.S.
1995	Kelly Slater, U.S.	1995	Rusty Keaulana, U.S.
1994	Kelly Slater, U.S.	1994	Rusty Keaulana, U.S.
1993	Derek Ho, U.S.	1993	Rusty Keaulana, U.S.
1992	Kelly Slater, U.S.	1992	Joey Hawkins, U.S.
1991	Damien Hardman, Australia	1991	Martin McMillan, Australia
1990	Tom Curren, U.S.	1990	Nat Young, Australia
1989	Martin Potter, Great Britain	1989	Nat Young, Australia
1988	Barton Lynch, Australia	1988	Nat Young, Australia
1987	Damien Hardman, Australia	1987	Stuart Entwistle, Australia
1986	Tom Curren, U.S.	1986	Nat Young, Australia
1985	Tom Curren, U.S.		
1984	Tom Carroll, Australia		
1983	Tom Carroll, Australia		
1982	Mark Richards, Australia		
1981	Mark Richards, Australia		
1980	Mark Richards, Australia		
1979	Mark Richards, Australia		
1978	Wayne Bartholomew, Australia		
1977	Shaun Tomson, South Africa		
1976	Peter Townend, Australia		

SURFING — ALL-TIME RESULTS (cont.)

ASSOCIATION OF SURFING PROFESSIONALS (ASP) WORLD CHAMPIONS (cont.)

Chelsea Georgeson

YEAR	WOMEN	YEAR	WOMEN
2005	Chelsea Georgeson, Australia	1990	Pam Burridge, Australia
2004	Sofia Mulanovich, Peru	1989	Wendy Botha, Australia
2003	Layne Beachley, Australia	1988	Freida Zamba, U.S.
2002	Layne Beachley, Australia	1987	Wendy Botha, South Africa
2001	Layne Beachley, Australia	1986	Freida Zamba, U.S.
2000	Layne Beachley, Australia	1985	Freida Zamba, U.S.
1999	Layne Beachley, Australia	1984	Freida Zamba, U.S.
1998	Layne Beachley, Australia	1983	Kim Mearig, U.S.
1997	Lisa Andersen, U.S.	1982	Debbie Beacham, U.S.
1996	Lisa Andersen, U.S.	1981	Margo Oberg, U.S.
1995	Lisa Andersen, U.S.	1980	Margo Oberg, U.S.
1994	Lisa Andersen, U.S.	1979	Lynne Boyer, U.S.
1993	Pauline Menczer, Australia	1978	Lynne Boyer, U.S.
1992	Wendy Botha, Australia	1977	Margo Oberg, U.S
1991	Wendy Botha, Australia		

MOTOCROSS — ALL-TIME RESULTS

250CC SUPERCROSS

YEAR	CHAMPION	HOMETOWN	YEAR	CHAMPION	HOMETOWN
2005	Ricky Carmichael	Havana, Florida	1989	Jeff Stanton	Sherwood, Michigan
2004	Chad Reed	Kurri Kurri, Australia	1988	Rick Johnson	El Cajon, California
2003	Ricky Carmichael	Havana, Florida	1987	Jeff Ward	Mission Viejo, California
2002	Ricky Carmichael	Havana, Florida	1986	Rick Johnson	El Cajon, California
2001	Ricky Carmichael	Havana, Florida	1985	Jeff Ward	Mission Viejo, California
2000	Jeremy McGrath	Menifee, California	1984	Johnny O'Mara	Simi Valley, California
1999	Jeremy McGrath	Menifee, California	1983	David Bailey	Axton, Virginia
1998	Jeremy McGrath	Menifee, California	1982	Donnie Hansen	Canyon Country, California
1997	Jeff Emig	Riverside, California	1981	Mark Barnett	Bridgeview, Illinois
1996	Jeremy McGrath	Menifee, California	1980	Mike Bell	Lakewood, California
1995	Jeremy McGrath	Murrieta, California	1979	Bob Hannah	Carson, Nevada
1994	Jeremy McGrath	Murrieta, California	1978	Bob Hannah	Whittier, California
1993	Jeremy McGrath	Murrieta, California	1977	Bob Hannah	Whittier, California
1992	Jeff Stanton	Sherwood, Michigan	1976	Jim Weinert	Laguna Beach, California
1991	Jean-Michel Bayle	Manosque, France	1975	Jim Ellis	Cobalt, Connecticut
1990	Jeff Stanton	Sherwood, Michigan	1974	Pierre Karsmakers	Netherlands

MOTOCROSS — ALL-TIME RESULTS (cont.)

250CC MOTOCROSS

YEAR	CHAMPION	HOMETOWN	YEAR	CHAMPION	HOMETOWN
2005	Ricky Carmichael	Havana, Florida	1992	Jeff Stanton	Sherwood, Michigan
2004	Ricky Carmichael	Havana, Florida	1991	Jean-Michel Bayle	Manosque, France
2003	Ricky Carmichael	Havana, Florida	1990	Jeff Stanton	Sherwood, Michigan
2002	Ricky Carmichael	Havana, Florida	1989	Jeff Stanton	Sherwood, Michigan
2001	Ricky Carmichael	Havana, Florida	1988	Jeff Ward	Mission Viejo, California
2000	Ricky Carmichael	Havana, Florida	1987	Rick Johnson	El Cajon, California
1999	Greg Albertyn	Johannesburg, South Africa	1986	Rick Johnson	El Cajon, California
1998	Doug Henry	Oxford, Connecticut	1985	Jeff Ward	Mission Viejo, California
1997	Jeff Emig	Riverside, California	1984	Rick Johnson	El Cajon, California
1996	Jeff Emig	Riverside, California	1983	David Bailey	Axton, Virginia
1995	Jeremy McGrath	Murrieta, California	1982	Donnie Hansen	Canyon Country, California
1994	Mike LaRocco	South Bend, Indiana	1981	Kent Howerton	San Antonio, Texas
1993	Mike Kiedrowski	Acton, California	1980	Kent Howerton	San Antonio, Texas
			1979	Bob Hannah	Carson City, Nevada
			1978	Bob Hannah	Whittier, California
			1977	Tony DiStefano	Morrisville, Pennsylvania
			1976	Tony DiStefano	Morrisville, Pennsylvania
			1975	Tony DiStefano	Morrisville, Pennsylvania
			1974	Gary Jones	Hacienda Heights, California
			1973	Gary Jones	Hacienda Heights, California
			1972	Gary Jones	Hacienda Heights, California

Ricky Carmichael

ROB TRINGALI/SPORTSCHROME

125CC MOTOCROSS

YEAR	CHAMPION	HOMETOWN	YEAR	CHAMPION	HOMETOWN
2005	Ivan Tedesco	Temecula, California	1989	Mike Kiedrowski	Canyon Country, California
2004	James Stewart, Jr.	Haines City, Florida	1988	George Holland	Kerman, California
2003	Grant Langston	Durban, South Africa	1987	Micky Dymond	Yorba Linda, California
2002	James Stewart, Jr.	Haines City, Florida	1986	Micky Dymond	Yorba Linda, California
2001	Michael Brown	Piney Flats, Tennessee	1985	Ron Lechien	El Cajon, California
2000	Travis Pastrana	Annapolis, Maryland	1984	Jeff Ward	Mission Viejo, California
1999	Ricky Carmichael	Havana, Florida	1983	Johnny O'Mara	Simi Valley, California
1998	Ricky Carmichael	Havana, Florida	1982	Mark Barnett	Bridgeview, Illinois
1997	Ricky Carmichael	Havana, Florida	1981	Mark Barnett	Bridgeview, Illinois
1996	Steve Lamson	Pollock Pines, California	1980	Mark Barnett	Bridgeview, Illinois
1995	Steve Lamson	Pollock Pines, California	1979	Broc Glover	El Cajon, California
1994	Doug Henry	Oxford, Connecticut	1978	Broc Glover	El Cajon, California
1993	Doug Henry	Oxford, Connecticut	1977	Broc Glover	El Cajon, California
1992	Jeff Emig	Highland, California	1976	Bob Hannah	Whittier, California
1991	Mike Kiedrowski	Canyon Country, California	1975	Marty Smith	San Diego, California
1990	Guy Cooper	Stillwater, Oklahoma	1974	Marty Smith	San Diego, California

GOLF

ollowing a disappointing season on the PGA Tour in 2004, Tiger Woods reclaimed his spot atop the world rankings in 2005. After wins at the Buick Invitational, Ford Championship, and the Masters, Woods finished fourth or higher in seven tournaments between June and August, including a win at the British Open, the 10th major championship victory of his career. A second place finish at the season-ending Tour Championship helped Woods clinch Player of the Year honors and top $10 million in annual earnings for the first time. He added his 11th major by winning the British Open again in 2006.

But Woods wasn't the only player making news on the PGA Tour in 2005. Michael Campbell, of New Zealand, won the 105th U.S. Open with a final-round 69, edging Woods by two strokes. Woods birdied four holes on the back nine, but bogeys at the 16th and 17th holes kept him from winning the U.S. Open for a third time.

After finally breaking through to win a major (the Masters) in 2004, Phil Mickelson rode a hot putter to win the PGA Championship in August. Mickelson took charge of the tournament with two superb rounds to open the tournament, before holding on over the weekend for his fourth win of the season. And Mickelson wasn't content to stop there. In April 2006, Mickelson won the Masters for the second time in three years by holding off the best players in the world with a final round that included only one bogey. The top five players in the world — Woods, Mickelson, Vijay Singh, Retief Goosen, and Ernie Els — all be-

Tiger Woods won back-to-back British Open championships in 2005 and 2006.

FRED VUICH

gan the final round in the Top 10. The week before, Mickelson won the BellSouth Classic at 28-under par, 13 strokes ahead of the second-place finisher. Woods couldn't get his putter going in the final round, and finished in third place, his fifth straight Top 10 finish in a major.

On the LPGA Tour in 2005, Annika Sorenstam was once again leaps and bounds ahead of her competition. She entered just 20 tournaments and won 10 of them, while finishing in the Top 10 in five others. Sorenstam posted the lowest scoring average on the tour for the sixth straight season. Three of her 10 victories came consecutively in March, concluding with an eight-shot win at the first major of the season, the Kraft Nabisco Championship.

Although she continued to dominate, Sorenstam saw several young challengers step up and play well, including Rookie of the Year Paula Creamer. The 19-year-old won two tournaments, becoming the youngest

player to win on the LPGA Tour in 52 years. Creamer finished in the Top 10 11 times, led the tour in putting average, and finished second on the money list to Sorenstam with $1.5 million. Creamer's top win came at the Evian Masters, where she blew away the field, beating Michelle Wie by eight shots.

Despite not winning, Wie made news by turning pro on October 5, 2005, a week before she turned 16. She made her professional debut on October 13, at the Samsung World Championship at Bighorn Golf Club in Palm Desert, California. Sorenstam won the event, and Wie was in fourth place before she was disqualified from the tournament for a suspected rules violation in the third round. Early in 2006, Wie finished third at the Fields Open in Hawaii and third at the Kraft Nabsico Championship. She also competed against the men in the PGA Tour's Sony Open for the third straight year, but failed to make the cut.

Annika Sorenstam entered 20 tournaments in 2005 and won 10 of them.

ROBERT BECK

Phil Mickelson won his second Masters in 2006.

ROBERT BECK

ALL-TIME CHAMPIONS — MEN

THE MASTERS

YEAR	WINNER	YEAR	WINNER	YEAR	WINNER
2006	Phil Mickelson	1982	*Craig Stadler	1958	Arnold Palmer
2005	*Tiger Woods	1981	Tom Watson	1957	Doug Ford
2004	Phil Mickelson	1980	Seve Ballesteros	1956	Jack Burke, Jr.
2003	*Mike Weir	1979†	*Fuzzy Zoeller	1955	Cary Middlecoff
2002	Tiger Woods	1978	Gary Player	1954	*Sam Snead
2001	Tiger Woods	1977	Tom Watson	1953	Ben Hogan
2000	Vijay Singh	1976	Ray Floyd	1952	Sam Snead
1999	Jose Maria Olazabal	1975	Jack Nicklaus	1951	Ben Hogan
1998	Mark O'Meara	1974	Gary Player	1950	Jimmy Demaret
1997	Tiger Woods	1973	Tommy Aaron	1949	Sam Snead
1996	Nick Faldo	1972	Jack Nicklaus	1948	Claude Harmon
1995	Ben Crenshaw	1971	Charles Coody	1947	Jimmy Demaret
1994	Jose Maria Olazabal	1970	*Billy Casper	1946	Herman Keiser
1993	Bernhard Langer	1969	George Archer	1943–45	No tournament
1992	Fred Couples	1968	Bob Goalby	1942	*Byron Nelson
1991	Ian Woosnam	1967	Gay Brewer, Jr.	1941	Craig Wood
1990	*Nick Faldo	1966	*Jack Nicklaus	1940	Jimmy Demaret
1989	*Nick Faldo	1965	Jack Nicklaus	1939	Ralph Guldahl
1988	Sandy Lyle	1964	Arnold Palmer	1938	Henry Picard
1987	*Larry Mize	1963	Jack Nicklaus	1937	Byron Nelson
1986	Jack Nicklaus	1962	Arnold Palmer	1936	Horton Smith
1985	Bernhard Langer	1961	Gary Player	1935	*Gene Sarazen
1984	Ben Crenshaw	1960	Arnold Palmer	1934	Horton Smith
1983	Seve Ballesteros	1959	Art Wall, Jr.		

*Winner in playoff. †Playoff cut from 18 holes to sudden death. Note: Played at Augusta National Golf Club, Augusta, Georgia.

GOLF

ALL-TIME CHAMPIONS – MEN (cont.)

U.S. OPEN

YEAR	WINNER	YEAR	WINNER	YEAR	WINNER
2006	Geoff Ogilvy	1970	Tony Jacklin	1931	*Billy Burke
2005	Michael Campbell	1969	Orville Moody	1930	Bobby Jones
2004	Retief Goosen	1968	Lee Trevino	1929	*Bobby Jones
2003	Jim Furyk	1967	Jack Nicklaus	1928	*Johnny Farrell
2002	Tiger Woods	1966	*Billy Casper	1927	*Tommy Armour
2001	*Retief Goosen	1965	*Gary Player	1926	Bobby Jones
2000	Tiger Woods	1964	Ken Venturi	1925	*Willie MacFarlane
1999	Payne Stewart	1963	*Julius Boros	1924	Cyril Walker
1998	Lee Janzen	1962	*Jack Nicklaus	1923	*Bobby Jones
1997	Ernie Els	1961	Gene Littler	1922	Gene Sarazen
1996	Steve Jones	1960	Arnold Palmer	1921	Jim Barnes
1995	Corey Pavin	1959	Billy Casper	1920	Edward Ray
1994	*Ernie Els	1958	Tommy Bolt	1919	*Walter Hagen
1993	Lee Janzen	1957	*Dick Mayer	1917–18	No tournament
1992	Tom Kite	1956	Cary Middlecoff	1916	Chick Evans
1991	*Payne Stewart	1955	*Jack Fleck	1915	Jerry Travers
1990	*Hale Irwin	1954	Ed Furgol	1914	Walter Hagen
1989	Curtis Strange	1953	Ben Hogan	1913	*Francis Ouimet
1988	*Curtis Strange	1952	Julius Boros	1912	John McDermott
1987	Scott Simpson	1951	Ben Hogan	1911	*John McDermott
1986	Ray Floyd	1950	*Ben Hogan	1910	*Alex Smith
1985	Andy North	1949	Cary Middlecoff	1909	George Sargent
1984	*Fuzzy Zoeller	1948	Ben Hogan	1908	*Fred McLeod
1983	Larry Nelson	1947	*Lew Worsham	1907	Alex Ross
1982	Tom Watson	1946	*Lloyd Mangrum	1906	Alex Smith
1981	David Graham	1942–45	No tournament	1905	Willie Anderson
1980	Jack Nicklaus	1941	Craig Wood	1904	Willie Anderson
1979	Hale Irwin	1940	*Lawson Little	1903	*Willie Anderson
1978	Andy North	1939	*Byron Nelson	1902	Laurie Auchterlonie
1977	Hubert Green	1938	Ralph Guldahl	1901	*Willie Anderson
1976	Jerry Pate	1937	Ralph Guldahl	1900	Harry Vardon
1975	*Lou Graham	1936	Tony Manero	1899	Willie Smith
1974	Hale Irwin	1935	Sam Parks, Jr.	1898	Fred Herd
1973	Johnny Miller	1934	Olin Dutra	1897†	Joe Lloyd
1972	Jack Nicklaus	1933	Johnny Goodman	1896†	James Foulis
1971	*Lee Trevino	1932	Gene Sarazen	1895†	Horace Rawlins

*Winner in playoff. The 1990 playoff went to one hole of sudden death after an 18-hole playoff.
In the 1994 playoff, Montgomerie was eliminated after 18 playoff holes, and Els beat Roberts on the 20th. †Before 1898, 36 holes; from 1898 on, 72 holes.

BRITISH OPEN

YEAR	WINNER	YEAR	WINNER	YEAR	WINNER
2006	Tiger Woods	1985	Sandy Lyle	1964	Tony Lema
2005	Tiger Woods	1984	Seve Ballesteros	1963	*Bob Charles
2004	*Todd Hamilton	1983	Tom Watson	1962	Arnold Palmer
2003	Ben Curtis	1982	Tom Watson	1961	Arnold Palmer
2002	*Ernie Els	1981	Bill Rogers	1960	Kel Nagle
2001	David Duval	1980	Tom Watson	1959	Gary Player
2000	Tiger Woods	1979	Seve Ballesteros	1958	*Peter Thomson
1999	*Paul Lawrie	1978	Jack Nicklaus	1957	Bobby Locke
1998	*Mark O'Meara	1977	Tom Watson	1956	Peter Thomson
1997	Justin Leonard	1976	Johnny Miller	1955	Peter Thomson
1996	Tom Lehman	1975	*Tom Watson	1954	Peter Thomson
1995	*John Daly	1974	Gary Player	1953	Ben Hogan
1994	Nick Price	1973	Tom Weiskopf	1952	Bobby Locke
1993	Greg Norman	1972	Lee Trevino	1951	Max Faulkner
1992	Nick Faldo	1971	Lee Trevino	1950	Bobby Locke
1991	Ian Baker-Finch	1970	*Jack Nicklaus	1949	*Bobby Locke
1990	Nick Faldo	1969	Tony Jacklin	1948	Henry Cotton
1989††	*Mark Calcavecchia	1968	Gary Player	1947	Fred Daly
1988	Seve Ballesteros	1967	Robert DeVicenzo	1946	Sam Snead
1987	Nick Faldo	1966	Jack Nicklaus	1940–45	No tournament
1986	Greg Norman	1965	Peter Thomson	1939	Richard Burton

*Winner in playoff. †† Playoff cut from 18 holes to 4 holes.

ALL-TIME CHAMPIONS — MEN (cont.)

BRITISH OPEN (cont.)

YEAR	WINNER	YEAR	WINNER	YEAR	WINNER
1938	Reginald A. Whitcombe	1915–19	No tournament	1898	Harry Vardon
1937	Henry Cotton	1914	Harry Vardon	1897	Harold Hilton
1936	Alfred Padgham	1913	John H. Taylor	1896	*Harry Vardon
1935	Alfred Perry	1912	Ted Ray	1895	John H. Taylor
1934	Henry Cotton	1911	Harry Vardon	1894	John H. Taylor
1933	*Denny Shute	1910	James Braid	1893	William Auchterlonie
1932	Gene Sarazen	1909	John H. Taylor	1892**	Harold Hilton
1931	Tommy Armour	1908	James Braid	1891	Hugh Kirkaldy
1930	Bobby Jones	1907	Arnaud Massy	1890	John Ball
1929	Walter Hagen	1906	James Braid	1889	*Willie Park, Jr.
1928	Walter Hagen	1905	James Braid	1888	Jack Burns
1927	Bobby Jones	1904	Jack White	1887	Willie Park, Jr.
1926	Bobby Jones	1903	Harry Vardon	1886	David Brown
1925	Jim Barnes	1902	Alexander Herd	1885	Bob Martin
1924	Walter Hagen	1901	James Braid	1884	Jack Simpson
1923	Arthur G. Havers	1900	John H. Taylor	1883	*Willie Fernie
1922	Walter Hagen	1899	Harry Vardon	1882	Robert Ferguson
1921	*Jock Hutchison				
1920	George Duncan				

*Winner in playoff.
**Championship extended from 36 to 72 holes.

TRIVIA CHALLENGE

What is the record for the largest victory in LPGA Tour history?

11 shots. Annika Sorenstam won the 2002 Kellogg-Keebler Classic by 11 shots, tying Jan Stephenson for the record. Stephenson won the 1981 Mary Kay Classic by the same margin.

LEGENDS

Gary Player won the British Open in three different decades.

■ **Gary Player,** b. November 1, 1935, Johannesburg, South Africa. Player is one of the most successful golfers in history. He ranks fourth all-time in major championship victories with nine. Only Player, Gene Sarazen, Ben Hogan, Jack Nicklaus, and Tiger Woods have won all four major championships at least once in their careers. Player dominated in the difficult conditions at the British Open, becoming the only player in the 20th century to win the tournament in three different decades. His most notable win on U.S. soil came in 1978 at the Masters. He started the final round seven shots off the lead, but rallied late, posting birdies on seven of his last 10 holes to win by a single shot.

■ **Walter Hagen,** b. December 21, 1892, Rochester, New York; d. October 6, 1969, Traverse City, Michigan. Long before Jack Nicklaus and Tiger Woods ruled major championships, Hagen won 11 majors between 1914 and 1927, highlighted by four consecutive PGA Championships (1924–1927). In addition to his major victories, Hagen won the Western Open five times and was the captain of the Ryder Cup team six times. He retired from the tour with 40 career victories.

■ **Byron Nelson,** b. February 4, 1912, Dallas, Texas. Nelson ruled the PGA Tour for 11 years, during which time he won 52 events, including four major championships. Only World War II kept him from winning more. In 1945, Nelson turned in the greatest season in golf history. He won 18 times, highlighted by a victory at the PGA Championship. At one point, he reeled off 11 consecutive tournament wins. During his career, Nelson made 113 straight cuts, which is second in PGA history only to Tiger Woods's 142 straight cuts. In 1968, the annual PGA Tour stop in Nelson's hometown of Dallas was renamed the Byron Nelson Golf Classic and remains the only official tournament named after a player.

CARL IWASAKI

ALL-TIME CHAMPIONS — MEN (cont.)

BRITISH OPEN (cont.)

YEAR	WINNER	YEAR	WINNER	YEAR	WINNER
1881	Robert Ferguson	1873	Tom Kidd	1865	Andrew Strath
1880	Robert Ferguson	1872	Tom Morris, Jr.	1864	Tom Morris, Sr.
1879	Jamie Anderson	1871	No tournament	1863	Willie Park
1878	Jamie Anderson	1870	Tom Morris, Jr.	1862	Tom Morris, Sr.
1877	Jamie Anderson	1869	Tom Morris, Jr.	1861‡	Tom Morris, Sr.
1876	*Bob Martin	1868	Tom Morris, Jr.	1860†	Willie Park
1875	Willie Park	1867	Tom Morris, Sr.		
1874	Mungo Park	1866	Willie Park		

*Tied, but opponent refused playoff. ‡The second annual Open was open to amateurs and pros. †The first event was open only to pro golfers.

TODAY'S STARS

Sergio Garcia finished 2005 ranked eighth in the world.

DAVID WALBERG

■ **Sergio Garcia,** b. January 9, 1980, Castellon, Spain. Garcia burst onto the PGA Tour in 1999 at the age of 19. He shot a 10-under-par 62 in his first professional round, and in August of that year dueled with Tiger Woods down the stretch of the PGA Championship, (he lost by two strokes). Garcia's booming drives and warm personality immediately made him one of the most popular golfers in the world. After struggling with his swing, he finally cracked through in 2001, winning the MasterCard Colonial and Buick Championship. After capturing the Booz Allen Classic in 2005, Garcia now has six PGA Tour victories and 10 more worldwide. He finished 2005 eighth in the world rankings, the highest year-end finish of his career.

■ **Justin Leonard,** b. June 15, 1972, Dallas, Texas. Despite being one of the shorter hitters on the PGA Tour, Leonard has earned a reputation as one of its best iron players. His accuracy from the fairway has helped him to 10 career victories, including the British Open Championship in 1997. After winning just four tournaments between 1999 and 2004, Leonard revitalized his career with two wins in 2005. In addition to his individual success on the PGA Tour, he had the most memorable moment of his career at the Ryder Cup in 1999. Leonard birdied four consecutive holes before sinking a 45-foot putt on the 17th hole to beat Jose Maria Olazabal and clinch the Cup for the U.S. team.

■ **Chris DiMarco,** b. August 23, 1968, Huntington, New York. DiMarco finished a career-high seventh on the money list in 2005, despite not winning a single event. He made the cut in 17 of his 24 tournaments, including six Top 10 finishes. He lost in the finals at the WGC-Accenture Match Play Championships to David Toms, and also finished second to Tiger Woods at the Masters and at the WGC-NEC Invitational. He wrapped up his career-year with an undefeated 4-0-1 record at the President's Cup in September, helping lead the U.S. squad to victory over the International team.

2005-06 MEN'S TIME LINE

■ **June 19, 2005:** Michael Campbell holds off a late charge by Tiger Woods to become the first player from New Zealand to win the U.S. Open. Campbell fires a 1-under-par 69 to finish at even par for the tournament, two strokes ahead of Woods.

■ **July 17, 2005:** Tiger Woods wins the British Open at the Old Course at St. Andrews. Woods runs away with the title, posting a 14-under-par total, good for a five-stroke victory over Colin Montgomerie.

■ **August 15, 2005:** Phil Mickelson returns on Monday morning to birdie the 18th hole and win the PGA Championship over Thomas Bjorn and Steve Elkington. After failing to win a major championship in his first 47 appearances, Mickelson has now won two in a 16-month span.

■ **August 21, 2005:** Tiger Woods continues his dominance in the state of Ohio by sinking a clutch birdie putt on the 16th hole to edge Chris DiMarco at the World Golf Championship NEC Invitational. Including his three titles at the Memorial Tournament, played in Columbus, Ohio, Woods has won seven times in 16 starts in Ohio.

■ **September 25, 2005:** Chris DiMarco sinks a putt from 12 feet away to clinch the President's Cup for the United States. The U.S. team wins 18 1/2 points to 15 1/2, thanks to wins in four out of the first five matches in Sunday's singles showdown.

■ **October 9, 2005:** Tiger Woods defeats John Daly on the second playoff hole to win the World Golf Championships American Express Championship. His sixth victory of the 2005 season clinches the money title as well as Player of the Year honors.

■ **January 8, 2006:** Stuart Appleby makes a birdie on the first playoff hole to defeat Vijay Singh at the season-opening Mercedes Championship. Appleby joins Gene Littler (in 1957) as the only players to win the tournament three times in a row.

■ **March 5, 2006:** Tiger Woods cards a 3-under-par 69 in the final round of the Doral Championship to win the tournament for the second consecutive season. The win is Woods' second of the season and 48th overall on the PGA Tour.

■ **April 9, 2006:** A week after winning the BellSouth Classic by 13 strokes, Phil Mickelson wins his second Masters tournament in three years. Due to rain delays, Mickelson plays 24 holes on Sunday for his second straight major championship.

ALL-TIME CHAMPIONS — MEN (cont.)

PGA CHAMPIONSHIP

YEAR	WINNER	YEAR	WINNER	YEAR	WINNER
2005	Phil Mickelson	1988	Jeff Sluman	1971	Jack Nicklaus
2004	Vijay Singh	1987	*Larry Nelson	1970	Dave Stockton
2003	Shaun Micheel	1986	Bob Tway	1969	Ray Floyd
2002	Rich Beem	1985	Hubert Green	1968	Julius Boros
2001	David Toms	1984	Lee Trevino	1967	*Don January
2000	*Tiger Woods	1983	Hal Sutton	1966	Al Geiberger
1999	Tiger Woods	1982	Raymond Floyd	1965	Dave Marr
1998	Vijay Singh	1981	Larry Nelson	1964	Bobby Nichols
1997	Davis Love III	1980	Jack Nicklaus	1963	Jack Nicklaus
1996	*Mark Brooks	1979	*David Graham	1962	Gary Player
1995	*Steve Elkington	1978	*John Mahaffey	1961	*Jerry Barber
1994	Nick Price	1977†	*Lanny Wadkins	1960	Jay Hebert
1993	*Paul Azinger	1976	Dave Stockton	1959	Bob Rosburg
1992	Nick Price	1975	Jack Nicklaus	1958	Dow Finsterwald
1991	John Daly	1974	Lee Trevino	1957	Lionel Hebert
1990	Wayne Grady	1973	Jack Nicklaus	1956	Jack Burke
1989	Payne Stewart	1972	Gary Player	1955	Doug Ford

*Winner in playoff. †Playoff changed from 18 holes to sudden death.

ALL-TIME CHAMPIONS – MEN (cont.)

PGA CHAMPIONSHIP (cont.)

YEAR	WINNER	YEAR	WINNER	YEAR	WINNER
1954	Chick Harbert	1941	Vic Ghezzi	1928	Leo Diegel
1953	Walter Burkemo	1940	Byron Nelson	1927	Walter Hagen
1952	Jim Turnesa	1939	Henry Picard	1926	Walter Hagen
1951	Sam Snead	1938	Paul Runyan	1925	Walter Hagen
1950	Chandler Harper	1937	Denny Shute	1924	Walter Hagen
1949	Sam Snead	1936	Denny Shute	1923	Gene Sarazen
1948	Ben Hogan	1935	Johnny Revolta	1922	Gene Sarazen
1947	Jim Ferrier	1934	Paul Runyan	1921	Walter Hagen
1946	Ben Hogan	1933	Gene Sarazen	1920	Jock Hutchison
1945	Byron Nelson	1932	Olin Dutra	1919	Jim Barnes
1944	Bob Hamilton	1931	Tom Creavy	1917–18	No tournament
1943	No tournament	1930	Tommy Armour	1916	Jim Barnes
1942	Sam Snead	1929	Leo Diegel		

ALL-TIME CHAMPIONS – WOMEN

LPGA CHAMPIONSHIP

YEAR	WINNER	YEAR	WINNER	YEAR	WINNER
2006	Se Ri Pak	1988	Sherri Turner	1970	*Shirley Englehorn
2005	Annika Sorenstam	1987	Jane Geddes	1969	Betsy Rawls
2004	Annika Sorenstam	1986	Pat Bradley	1968	*Sandra Post
2003	Annika Sorenstam	1985	Nancy Lopez	1967	Kathy Whitworth
2002	Se Ri Pak	1984	Patty Sheehan	1966	Gloria Ehret
2001	Karrie Webb	1983	Patty Sheehan	1965	Sandra Haynie
2000	*Juli Inkster	1982	Jan Stephenson	1964	Mary Mills
1999	Juli Inkster	1981	Donna Caponi	1963	Mickey Wright
1998	Se Ri Pak	1980	Sally Little	1962	Judy Kimball
1997	*Chris Johnson	1979	Donna Caponi	1961	Mickey Wright
1996	Laura Davies	1978	Nancy Lopez	1960	Mickey Wright
1995	Kelly Robbins	1977	Chako Higuchi	1959	Betsy Rawls
1994	Laura Davies	1976	Betty Burfeindt	1958	Mickey Wright
1993	Patty Sheehan	1975	Kathy Whitworth	1957	Louise Suggs
1992	Betsy King	1974	Sandra Haynie	1956	*Marlene Hagge
1991	Meg Mallon	1973	Mary Mills	1955	†Beverly Hanson
1990	Beth Daniel	1972	Kathy Ahern		
1989	Nancy Lopez	1971	Kathy Whitworth		

*Won in playoff. The 1956 and 1997 titles were decided in sudden death; 1968 and 1970 were 18-hole playoffs. †Won match-play final.

U.S. WOMEN'S OPEN

YEAR	WINNER	YEAR	WINNER	YEAR	WINNER
2006	Annika Sorenstam	1985	Kathy Baker	1964	*Mickey Wright
2005	Birdie Kim	1984	Hollis Stacy	1963	Mary Mills
2004	Meg Mallon	1983	Jan Stephenson	1962	Murle Breer
2003	*Hilary Lunke	1982	Janet Anderson	1961	Mickey Wright
2002	Juli Inkster	1981	Pat Bradley	1960	Betsy Rawls
2001	Karrie Webb	1980	Amy Alcott	1959	Mickey Wright
2000	Karrie Webb	1979	Jerilyn Britz	1958	Mickey Wright
1999	Juli Inkster	1978	Hollis Stacy	1957	Betsy Rawls
1998	†Se Ri Pak	1977	Hollis Stacy	1956	*Kathy Cornelius
1997	Alison Nicholas	1976	*JoAnne Carner	1955	Fay Crocker
1996	Annika Sorenstam	1975	Sandra Palmer	1954	Babe Zaharias
1995	Annika Sorenstam	1974	Sandra Haynie	1953	*Betsy Rawls
1994	Patty Sheehan	1973	Susie Berning	1952	Louise Suggs
1993	Lauri Merten	1972	Susie Berning	1951	Betsy Rawls
1992	*Patty Sheehan	1971	JoAnne Carner	1950	Babe Zaharias
1991	Meg Mallon	1970	Donna Caponi	1949	Louise Suggs
1990	Betsy King	1969	Donna Caponi	1948	Babe Zaharias
1989	Betsy King	1968	Susie Berning	1947	Betty Jameson
1988	Liselotte Neumann	1967	Catherine LaCoste	1946	Patty Berg
1987	*Laura Davies	1966	Sandra Spuzich		
1986	*Jane Geddes	1965	Carol Mann		

*Winner in playoff. †Winner on second hole of sudden death after 18-hole playoff ended in a tie.

LEGENDS

■ **Nancy Lopez,** b. January 6, 1957, Torrance, California. At the age of 12, Lopez won the New Mexico Women's Amateur. In 1972 and 1974, she won the USGA Junior Girls Championship. As a rookie in 1978, Lopez won nine tournaments, including a record-setting five in a row, on her way to Rookie of the Year and Player of the Year honors. Her top victory of the season came at the LPGA Championship, an event she would win two more times. By 1987, Lopez had posted 35 career victories, which qualified her for the LPGA's Hall of Fame. She was inducted on July 20th as its 11th member. Lopez never won the U.S. Women's Open, but in 1997 she became the first woman to ever shoot four rounds in the 60's at the tournament, only to finish one stroke behind the winner. Lopez posted her final victory — the 48th of her career — at the 1997 Chick-fil-A Charity Championship.

Nancy Lopez won the LPGA Championship three times.

BILL LUSTER

■ **Babe Didrikson Zaharias,** b. June 26, 1911, Port Arthur, Texas, d. September 27, 1956.
Before Annika Sorenstam, Suzy Whaley, and Michelle Wie competed on the PGA Tour, Zaharias was the first to play against men. Just three years after seriously picking up the game of golf, Zaharias competed in the 1938 Los Angeles Open. She began to dominate on the LPGA Tour the following decade. By 1948, she had already won five major championships, and in 1950, she won the season's three majors: the U.S. Women's Open, the Titleholders Championship, and the Western Open. She was the leading money winner on the tour for two straight seasons (1950–1951), before having to cut back on her schedule because of cancer. Following surgery, she made a comeback in 1954, when she won her 10th and final major championship.

■ **Amy Alcott,** b. February 22, 1956, Kansas City, Missouri. After qualifying for the LPGA Tour in 1975, Alcott won her first event at the Orange Blossom Classic. It was only her third career start as a pro. She went on to win the Rookie of the Year award. For her career, Alcott won 29 events, including five major championships. She won ever major except for the LPGA Championship, where she finished second twice and third once. Her final victory came at the Nabisco Dinah Shore in 1991. Eight years later, she was inducted into the LPGA Tour and World Golf halls of fame.

DID YOU KNOW?

Annika Sorenstam in the only player in LPGA Tour history to top $2 million in earnings in a single season. After her impressive 2005 campaign, Sorenstam has now reached that milestone in five straight seasons. Entering 2006, she had notched 66 victories on the tour for over $18 million in career earnings.

SIKIDS.com

Visit our website for the latest stats and sports info.

TODAY'S STARS

Paula Creamer became the youngest LPGA tournament winner in history.

■ **Paula Creamer,** b. August 5, 1986, Mountain View, California. Michelle Wie may have the edge when it comes to popularity, but Creamer has had even more success on the LPGA Tour over the past two years. Four days after graduating from high school in 2005, Creamer sank a 17-foot birdie putt on the final hole to win the Sybase Classic. At 18 years, 9 months, and 17 days, she became the youngest winner in tour history. Later in 2005, she won the Evian Masters by eight shots, becoming the youngest player to reach $1 million in career earnings. She finished the season ranked in the Top 5 in four statistical categories, including first in putts per green (1.75). Through eight starts in 2006, she had already posted three Top 10 finishes.

■ **Michelle Wie,** b. October 11, 1989, Honolulu, Hawaii. In 2000, at the age of 10, Wie became the youngest player to qualify for an USGA amateur championship when she made the field at the Women's Public Links Championship. She went on to win the event in 2003. That same year, she shot a 66 in the third round of the Kraft Nabisco Championship, the lowest round ever by an amateur. In 2004, she competed in the men's Sony Open on the PGA Tour. She finished at even par over the first two rounds and missed the cut by a single stroke. Wie turned professional in October 2005, and in February 2006 she was ranked third in the women's world rankings.

■ **Cristie Kerr,** b. October 12, 1977, Miami, Florida. Kerr turned pro after finishing as the low amateur at the 1996 U.S. Women's Open. Since then, she has won more than $5 million on tour, which ranks her 18th on the all-time list. In 2002, she led wire-to-wire to win her first tournament, the Long Drugs Challenge. In the first round, she carded a career-low 62. Her best season on tour was 2005, when she posted 11 Top 10 finishes, including wins at Kingsmill and the Wendy's Championship for Children. She has six career victories.

ALL-TIME CHAMPIONS — WOMEN (cont.)

KRAFT NABISCO CHAMPIONSHIP

YEAR	WINNER	YEAR	WINNER	YEAR	WINNER
2006	Karrie Webb	1994	Donna Andrews	1982	Sally Little
2005	Annika Sorenstam	1993	Helen Alfredsson	1981	Nancy Lopez
2004	Grace Park	1992	*Dottie Mochrie	1980	Donna Caponi
2003	Patricia Meunier-Lebouc	1991	Amy Alcott	1979	Sandra Post
2002	Annika Sorenstam	1990	Betsy King	1978	*Sandra Post
2001	Annika Sorenstam	1989	Juli Inkster	1977	Kathy Whitworth
2000	Karrie Webb	1988	Amy Alcott	1976	Judy Rankin
1999	Dottie Pepper	1987	*Betsy King	1975	Sandra Palmer
1998	Pat Hurst	1986	Pat Bradley	1974	*Jo Ann Prentice
1997	Betsy King	1985	Alice Miller	1973	Mickey Wright
1996	Patti Sheehan	1984	*Juli Inkster	1972	Jane Blalock
1995	Nanci Bowen	1983	Amy Alcott		

*Winner in sudden-death playoff. Note: Designated fourth major in 1983; played at Mission Hills Country Club, Rancho Mirage, California.

DU MAURIER CLASSIC

YEAR	WINNER	YEAR	WINNER	YEAR	WINNER
2000	Meg Mallon	1990	Cathy Johnston	1980	Pat Bradley
1999	Karrie Webb	1989	Tammie Green	1979	Amy Alcott
1998	Brandie Burton	1988	Sally Little	1978	JoAnne Carner
1997	Colleen Walker	1987	Jody Rosenthal	1977	Judy Rankin
1996	Laura Davies	1986	*Pat Bradley	1976	*Donna Caponi
1995	Jenny Lidback	1985	Pat Bradley	1975	*JoAnne Carner
1994	Martha Nause	1984	Juli Inkster	1974	Carole Jo Callison
1993	Brandie Burton	1983	Hollis Stacy	1973	*Jocelyne Bourassa
1992	Sherri Steinhauer	1982	Sandra Haynie		
1991	Nancy Scranton	1981	Jan Stephenson		

*Winner in sudden-death playoff. Note: Designated third major in 1979; discontinued in 2001.

WOMEN'S BRITISH OPEN

YEAR	WINNER
2006	Sherri Steinhauer
2005	Jeong Jang
2004	Karen Stupples
2003	Annika Sorenstam
2002	Karrie Webb
2001	Se Ri Pak

Note: Designated fourth major in 2001.

FAST FACT

Lorena Ochoa won the Franklin American Mortgage Championship in 2004 to become the first Mexican-born player to win on the LPGA Tour. She won once more in 2004, once in 2005, and again early in 2006.

2005-06 WOMEN'S TIME LINE

■ **March 27, 2005:** Annika Sorenstam wins the Kraft Nabisco Championship, the first LPGA major tournament of the season. The win is Sorenstam's third straight victory of 2005 and fifth straight overall.

■ **May 22, 2005:** Four days before her high school graduation, Paula Creamer sinks a 17-foot putt to win the Sybase Classic. She is the youngest winner of a multi-round event in tour history.

■ **June 12, 2005:** Annika Sorenstam beats Michelle Wie by three strokes at the McDonald's LPGA Championship. She becomes the first player in LPGA history to win the same major championship three years in a row.

■ **June 26, 2005:** Birdie Kim conquers a brutally tough course to win the U.S. Women's Open by two strokes.

■ **July 23, 2005:** In a duel between three of the youngest stars in women's golf, 19-year-old Paula Creamer pulls away for an eight-shot victory at the Evian Masters in France over Lorena Ochoa, age 23, and amateur Michelle Wie, age 15.

■ **July 31, 2005:** In the LPGA's final major championship of the season, South Korea's Jeong Jang goes wire-to-wire to win the Weetabix Women's British Open. Jang becomes the eighth first-time winner on the tour in 2005.

■ **October 5, 2005:** Less than a week before her 16th birthday, Michelle Wie turns pro at a news conference in her home state of Hawaii.

■ **October 16, 2005:** After finishing her first professional tournament in a tie for fourth place, Michelle Wie is disqualified from the Samsung World Championship because of a rules violation during Saturday's third round.

■ **November 20, 2005:** Annika Sorenstam wraps up one of the best seasons in LPGA history by winning the ADT Championship. Sorenstam clinches Player of the Year honors and the money title.

■ **April 2, 2006:** Karrie Webb makes a remarkable comeback to win her second Kraft Nabisco Championship, in a playoff over third-round leader Lorena Ochoa.

MOTOR SPORTS

The breathtaking finish of the 90th Indianapolis 500 in May was the highlight of the 2005–2006 year in the world of motor sports. Sam Hornish, Jr., won his first Indianapolis 500 by edging 19-year-old rookie Marco Andretti on the final lap of the race. It was the second-closest finish in race history, with only .0635 of a second separating the two drivers.

Marco, the son of IndyCar champion Michael Andretti and the grandson of racing legend Mario Andretti, would have become the first Andretti to be crowned Indy 500 champion since Mario won the big race in 1969.

His father, Michael, attempting to win his first Indianapolis 500 in 15 career starts, came out of retirement just for this year's race and led during a caution with four laps to go. But when the green flag waved both his son and Hornish quickly passed him. The younger Andretti appeared to have the race won as he came down the front

stretch on lap 200, but Hornish sped past him only 250 yards from the finish line.

Elsewhere in the Indy Racing League (IRL), Dan Wheldon, winner of the 2005 Indy 500, won the 2005 IndyCar Series Driver's Championship. In addition, talks began that were aimed at unifying the IRL and Champ Car, the two open-wheel series of American racing. However, it was unlikely that the two organizations would be merged in time for the 2007 racing season.

In NASCAR, the 2006 running of the Daytona 500 in February was marked by controversy. Jimmie Johnson won the race, but his victory was tainted. Seven days before the race, his crew chief, Chad Knaus, was banned for illegally tampering with Johnson's car after a pre-race inspection. NASCAR ruled that

Johnson's car had an illegal aerodynamic advantage over his competitors' vehicles because the rear window had been raised. As a result, he was sent to the back of the field for a qualifying race and Knaus was suspended for four races.

In the overall driver standings, Tony Stewart won the 2005 NASCAR Nextel Cup

Tony Stewart drove his Number 20 Chevrolet Monte Carlo to his second points title in four years.

points championship. He led all drivers in Top 5 (17) and Top 10 (25) finishes and was second in wins (5). Stewart became the 14th driver in NASCAR history — and the second active driver (with four-time winner Jeff Gordon) — to win the points championships more than once. Stewart also won the championship in 2002.

Dan Wheldon was the first driver to win the Indy 500 and the IndyCar championship in the same year (2005).

J.P. MOCZULSKI/REUTERS

INDY RACING LEAGUE (IRL) ALL-TIME RESULTS

INDIANAPOLIS 500 WINNERS

FRED VUICH

Sam Hornish, Jr.

YEAR	DRIVER	MILES PER HOUR (M.P.H.)
2006	Sam Hornish, Jr.	157.085
2005	Dan Wheldon	157.603
2004	Buddy Rice (450*)	138.518
2003	Gil de Ferran	156.291
2002	Helio Castroneves	166.499
2001	Helio Castroneves	141.574
2000	Juan Montoya	167.607
1999	Kenny Brack	153.176
1998	Eddie Cheever, Jr.	145.155
1997	Arie Luyendyk	145.827
1996	Buddy Lazier	147.956
1995	Jacques Villeneuve	153.616
1994	Al Unser, Jr.	160.872
1993	Emerson Fittipaldi	157.207
1992	Al Unser, Jr.	134.477
1991	Rick Mears	176.457
1990	Arie Luyendyk	185.981
1989	Emerson Fittipaldi	167.581
1988	Rick Mears	144.809
1987	Al Unser	162.175
1986	Bobby Rahal	170.722
1985	Danny Sullivan	152.982
1984	Rick Mears	163.612
1983	Tom Sneva	162.117
1982	Gordon Johncock	162.029
1981	Bobby Unser	139.084

YEAR	DRIVER	M.P.H.
1980	Johnny Rutherford	142.862
1979	Rick Mears	158.899
1978	Al Unser	161.363
1977	A.J. Foyt, Jr.	161.331
1976	Johnny Rutherford (255*)	148.725
1975	Bobby Unser (435*)	149.213
1974	Johnny Rutherford	158.589
1973	Gordon Johncock (332.5*)	159.036
1972	Mark Donohue	162.962
1971	Al Unser	157.735
1970	Al Unser	155.749
1969	Mario Andretti	156.867
1968	Bobby Unser	152.882
1967	A.J. Foyt, Jr.	151.207
1966	Graham Hill	144.317
1965	Jim Clark	150.686
1964	A.J. Foyt, Jr.	147.350
1963	Parnelli Jones	143.137
1962	Rodger Ward	140.293
1961	A.J. Foyt, Jr.	139.130
1960	Jim Rathmann	138.767
1959	Rodger Ward	135.857
1958	Jimmy Bryan	133.791
1957	Sam Hanks	135.601
1956	Pat Flaherty	128.490
1955	Bob Sweikert	128.213
1954	Bill Vukovich	130.840
1953	Bill Vukovich	128.740
1952	Troy Ruttman	128.922
1951	Lee Wallard	126.244
1950	Johnnie Parsons (345*)	124.002
1949	Bill Holland	121.327
1948	Mauri Rose	119.814
1947	Mauri Rose	116.338
1946	George Robson	114.820
1942–45	No races held during World War II	
1941	Floyd Davis/Mauri Rose	115.117
1940	Wilbur Shaw	114.277

Note: Miles per hour (M.P.H.) denotes average race speed. *Miles completed before race was called because of rain.

INDY RACING LEAGUE ALL-TIME RESULTS (cont.)

INDIANAPOLIS 500 WINNERS (cont.)

YEAR	DRIVER	MILES PER HOUR (M.P.H.)	YEAR	DRIVER	M.P.H.
1939	Wilbur Shaw	115.035	1925	Peter DePaolo	101.127
1938	Floyd Roberts	117.200	1924	L.L. Corum/Joe Boyer	98.234
1937	Wilbur Shaw	113.580	1923	Tommy Milton	90.954
1936	Louis Meyer	109.069	1922	Jimmy Murphy	94.484
1935	Kelly Petillo	106.240	1921	Tommy Milton	89.621
1934	Bill Cummings	104.863	1920	Gaston Chevrolet	88.618
1933	Louis Meyer	104.162	1919	Howdy Wilcox	88.050
1932	Fred Fame	104.144	1917–18	No races held during World War I	
1931	Louis Schneider	96.629	1916	Dario Resta (scheduled for 300 miles)	84.001
1930	Billy Arnold	100.448	1915	Ralph DePalma	89.840
1929	Ray Keech	97.585	1914	Rene Thomas	82.474
1928	Louis Meyer	99.482	1913	Jules Goux	75.933
1927	George Souders	97.545	1912	Joe Dawson	78.719
1926	Frank Lockhart (400*)	95.904	1911	Ray Harroun	74.602

*Miles completed before race was called because of rain.

IRL CHAMPIONS

YEAR	DRIVER
2005	Dan Wheldon
2004	Tony Kanaan
2003	Scott Dixon
2002	Sam Hornish, Jr.
2001	Sam Hornish, Jr.
2000	Buddy Lazier
1999	Greg Ray
1998	Kenny Brack
1996–97*	Tony Stewart
1996 (Series' first year)	Buzz Calkins and Scott Sharp (co-champions)

Danica Patrick

IRL ROOKIES OF THE YEAR

YEAR	DRIVER
2005	Danica Patrick
2004	Kosuke Matsuura
2003	Dan Wheldon
2002	Laurent Redon
2001	Felipe Giaffone
2000	Airton Dare
1999	Scott Harrington
1998	Robby Unser
1996–97*	Jim Guthrie
1996 (Series' first year)	No award

*This season started in 1996 and ended in 1997.

CHAMPIONSHIP AUTO RACING TEAMS (CART)

ALL-TIME CART CHAMPIONSHIP SERIES CHAMPIONS

YEAR	DRIVER	YEAR	DRIVER
2005	Sebastien Bourdais	1985	Al Unser
2004	Sebastien Bourdais	1984	Mario Andretti
2003	Paul Tracy	1983	Al Unser
2002	Cristiano da Matta	1982	Rick Mears
2001	Gil de Ferran	1981	Rick Mears
2000	Gil de Ferran	1980	Johnny Rutherford
1999	Juan Montoya	1979	Rick Mears
1998	Alex Zanardi		
1997	Alex Zanardi		
1996	Jimmy Vasser		
1995	Jacques Villeneuve		
1994	Al Unser, Jr.		
1993	Nigel Mansell		
1992	Bobby Rahal		
1991	Michael Andretti		
1990	Al Unser, Jr.		
1989	Emerson Fittipaldi		
1988	Danny Sullivan		
1987	Bobby Rahal		
1986	Bobby Rahal		

Sebastien Bourdais

DID YOU KNOW?

In 2005, Dan Wheldon set IRL single-season records for races won (6) and races led (15), on his way to winning the series championship.

TODAY'S STARS

Kasey Kahne won four of the first 15 races on the 2006 schedule.

NIGEL KINRADE

■ **Kasey Kahne,** b. April 10, 1980, Enumclaw, Washington. In 2004, the rookie Kahne replaced NASCAR legend Bill Elliott in his Number 9 Dodge. After finishing second five times as a rookie, Kahne was proclaimed as NASCAR's next great driver. That season he had 13 Top 5 finishes and 14 Top 10's. He broke through the next season with his first career Nextel Cup victory at the Chevy American Revolution 400. He was one of the series' hottest drivers early in the 2006 season, winning four of the first 15 races on the schedule. He also had six Top 5 finishes and 10 Top 10's.

■ **Dan Wheldon,** b. June 22, 1978, Emberton, England. Wheldon is currently the dominant driver in the IRL. After finishing second in 2004, he won the 2005 points championship and won three times as many races (6) as his next closest competitor. While Danica Patrick got most of the headlines in 2005 for being the first woman to finish as high as fourth in the Indianapolis 500, Wheldon won the race. By doing so, he became the first driver to win the IndyCar championship and the Indianapolis 500 in the same season. Over the 17-race schedule, he led all drivers in Top 10 finishes (15) and tied for first in Top 5 finishes (12).

■ **Kyle Busch,** b. May 2, 1985, Las Vegas, Nevada. Racing is in Busch's genes. His older brother Kurt was the 2004 Nextel Cup champion and their father, Tom, raced cars near the family home in Las Vegas. As a rookie in 2005, Kyle became the youngest driver in Nextel Cup history to win both the pole for a race (19 years, 9 months, 24 days) and to win a race (20 years, 4 months, 2 days). He finished the season with two victories and was named Rookie of the Year. In 2004 he won the same honor in the NASCAR Busch Series.

FAST FACT

Tony Stewart competed twice in the Indy 500 and the Coca-Cola 600 on the same day, driving a total of 1,100 miles each day. He finished no worse than ninth in any of the races.

TRIVIA CHALLENGE

Which owner has won the most Indianapolis 500 winners in the history of the race?

Roger Penske. The victory by Sam Hornish, Jr., in 2006 gave Penske his 14th win, nine more than any other owner.

SIKIDS.COM
Visit our website for the latest stats and sports info.

2005-06 TIME LINE

■ **July 2, 2005:** Danica Patrick becomes the second woman in IRL history to win the pole position for a race when she qualifies for the Argent Mortgage Indy 300.

■ **August 7, 2005:** Tony Stewart wins the Allstate 400 at the Brickyard. It is the Indiana native's first career victory at the historic Indianapolis Motor Speedway.

■ **September 25, 2005:** Dan Wheldon clinches the 2005 IRL championship at the Watkins Glen Indy Grand Prix.

■ **November 20, 2005:** Tony Stewart clinches the NASCAR Nextel Cup championship at the Ford 400.

■ **November 28, 2005:** Target Chip Ganassi Racing announces that it has signed IRL champion Dan Wheldon, beginning in 2006. Wheldon won the 2005 IRL championship while driving for Andretti Green Racing.

■ **January 23, 2006:** Toyota announces that it plans to start competing in the Nextel Cup for the first time, starting in 2007.

■ **February 19, 2006:** Jimmie Johnson wins the Daytona 500 amid controversy that his crew chief illegally tampered with the car after the pre-race inspection.

■ **May 20, 2006:** Jimmie Johnson wins the NASCAR Nextel All-Star Challenge, NASCAR's All-Star race, and earns more than $1 million in prize money.

■ **May 28, 2006:** Sam Hornish, Jr., wins the Indianapolis 500.

DID YOU KNOW?

Former Boston Red Sox outfielder Mike Greenwell finished 26th in his first NASCAR Craftsman Truck Series race, the City of Mansfield (Ohio) 250, on May 27, 2005. During his 12 years with Boston, the left-handed hitter batted .303 and had 726 RBIs.

NASCAR ALL-TIME RESULTS

NASCAR CHAMPIONS

YEAR	DRIVER	YEAR	DRIVER	YEAR	DRIVER
2005	Tony Stewart	1986	Dale Earnhardt	1967	Richard Petty
2004	Kurt Busch	1985	Darrell Waltrip	1966	David Pearson
2003	Matt Kenseth	1984	Terry Labonte	1965	Ned Jarrett
2002	Tony Stewart	1983	Bobby Allison	1964	Richard Petty
2001	Jeff Gordon	1982	Darrell Waltrip	1963	Joe Weatherly
2000	Bobby Labonte	1981	Darrell Waltrip	1962	Joe Weatherly
1999	Dale Jarrett	1980	Dale Earnhardt	1961	Ned Jarrett
1998	Jeff Gordon	1979	Richard Petty	1960	Rex White
1997	Jeff Gordon	1978	Cale Yarborough	1959	Lee Petty
1996	Terry Labonte	1977	Cale Yarborough	1958	Lee Petty
1995	Jeff Gordon	1976	Cale Yarborough	1957	Buck Baker
1994	Dale Earnhardt	1975	Richard Petty	1956	Buck Baker
1993	Dale Earnhardt	1974	Richard Petty	1955	Tim Flock
1992	Alan Kulwicki	1973	Benny Parsons	1954	Lee Petty
1991	Dale Earnhardt	1972	Richard Petty	1953	Herb Thomas
1990	Dale Earnhardt	1971	Richard Petty	1952	Tim Flock
1989	Rusty Wallace	1970	Bobby Isaac	1951	Herb Thomas
1988	Bill Elliott	1969	David Pearson	1950	Bill Rexford
1987	Dale Earnhardt	1968	David Pearson	1949	Red Byron

WINS LEADERS*

RANK	DRIVER
1.	Richard Petty (200)
2.	David Pearson (105)
3.	Bobby Allison** (84)
	Darrell Waltrip** (84)
5.	Cale Yarborough (83)
6.	Dale Earnhardt (76)
7.	Jeff Gordon (74)
8.	Rusty Wallace (55)
9.	Lee Petty (54)
10.	Ned Jarrett** (50)
	Junior Johnson** (50)
12.	Herb Thomas (48)
13.	Buck Baker (46)
14.	Bill Elliott (44)
15.	Tim Flock (39)
16.	Bobby Isaac (37)
17.	Mark Martin (35)
18.	Fireball Roberts (33)
19.	Dale Jarrett (32)
20.	Rex White (28)
21.	Fred Lorenzen (26)

*Through June 2006
**Tie

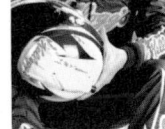

Kyle Busch

ROOKIES OF THE YEAR

YEAR	DRIVER	YEAR	DRIVER
2005	Kyle Busch	1981	Ron Bouchard
2004	Kasey Kahne	1980	Jody Ridley
2003	Jamie McMurray	1979	Dale Earnhardt
2002	Ryan Newman	1978	Ronnie Thomas
2001	Kevin Harvick	1977	Ricky Rudd
2000	Matt Kenseth	1976	Skip Manning
1999	Tony Stewart	1975	Bruce Hill
1998	Kenny Irwin	1974	Earl Ross
1997	Mike Skinner	1973	Lennie Pond
1996	Johnny Benson	1972	Larry Smith
1995	Ricky Craven	1971	Walter Ballard
1994	Jeff Burton	1970	Bill Dennis
1993	Jeff Gordon	1969	Dick Brooks
1992	Jimmy Hensley	1968	Pete Hamilton
1991	Bobby Hamilton	1967	Donnie Allison
1990	Rob Moroso	1966	James Hylton
1989	Dick Trickle	1965	Sam McQuagg
1988	Ken Bouchard	1964	Doug Cooper
1987	Davey Allison	1963	Billy Wade
1986	Alan Kulwicki	1962	Tom Cox
1985	Ken Schrader	1961	Woodie Wilson
1984	Rusty Wallace	1960	David Pearson
1983	Sterling Marlin	1959	Richard Petty
1982	Geoffrey Bodine	1958	Shorty Rollins

GREG FOSTER

DAYTONA 500 WINNERS

YEAR	DRIVER	M.P.H.	YEAR	DRIVER	M.P.H.	YEAR	DRIVER	M.P.H.
2006	Jimmie Johnson	142.667	1990	Derrike Cope	165.761	1974	Richard Petty	140.894
2005	Jeff Gordon	135.173	1989	Darrell Waltrip	148.466	1973	Richard Petty	157.205
2004	Dale Earnhardt, Jr.	156.345	1988	Bobby Allison	137.531	1972	A.J. Foyt, Jr.	161.550
2003	Michael Waltrip	133.870	1987	Bill Elliott	176.263	1971	Richard Petty	144.462
2002	Ward Burton	142.971	1986	Geoffrey Bodine	148.124	1970	Pete Hamilton	149.601
2001	Michael Waltrip	161.783	1985	Bill Elliott	172.265	1969	Lee Roy Yarbrough	157.950
2000	Dale Jarrett	155.669	1984	Cale Yarborough	150.994	1968	Cale Yarborough	143.251
1999	Jeff Gordon	161.551	1983	Cale Yarborough	155.979	1967	Mario Andretti	146.926
1998	Dale Earnhardt	172.712	1982	Bobby Allison	153.991	1966	Richard Petty	160.627
1997	Jeff Gordon	148.295	1981	Richard Petty	169.651	1965	Fred Lorenzen	141.539
1996	Dale Jarrett	154.308	1980	Buddy Baker	177.602	1964	Richard Petty	154.334
1995	Sterling Marlin	141.710	1979	Richard Petty	143.977	1963	Tiny Lund	151.566
1994	Sterling Marlin	156.931	1978	Bobby Allison	159.730	1962	Fireball Roberts	152.529
1993	Dale Jarrett	154.972	1977	Cale Yarborough	153.218	1961	Marvin Panch	149.601
1992	Davey Allison	168.256	1976	David Pearson	152.181	1960	Junior Johnson	124.740
1991	Ernie Irvan	148.148	1975	Benny Parsons	153.649	1959	Lee Petty	135.521

TALLADEGA 500* WINNERS

YEAR	DRIVER	M.P.H.	YEAR	DRIVER	M.P.H.	YEAR	DRIVER	M.P.H.
2006	Jimmie Johnson	142.880	1993	Dale Earnhardt	153.858	1980	Neil Bonnett	166.894
2005	Jeff Gordon	146.904	1992	Ernie Irvan	176.309	1979	Darrell Waltrip	161.229
2004	Jeff Gordon	129.396	1991	Dale Earnhardt	147.383	1978	Lennie Pond	174.700
2003	Dale Earnhardt, Jr.	144.625	1990	Dale Earnhardt	174.430	1977	Donnie Allison	162.524
2002	Dale Earnhardt, Jr.	159.022	1989	Terry Labonte	157.354	1976	Dave Marcis	157.547
2001	Bobby Hamilton	184.003	1988	Ken Schrader	154.505	1975	Buddy Baker	130.892
2000	Jeff Gordon	161.157	1987	Bill Elliott	171.293	1974	Richard Petty	148.637
1999	Dale Earnhardt	163.395	1986	Bobby Hillin	151.552	1973	Dick Brooks	145.454
1998	Bobby Labonte	163.439	1985	Cale Yarborough	148.772	1972	James Hylton	148.728
1997	Terry Labonte	156.601	1984	Dale Earnhardt	155.485	1971	Bobby Allison	145.945
1996	Jeff Gordon	133.387	1983	Dale Earnhardt	170.611	1970	Pete Hamilton	158.517
1995	Sterling Marlin	173.188	1982	Darrell Waltrip	168.157	1969	Richard Brickhouse	153.778
1994	Jimmy Spencer	163.217	1981	Ron Bouchard	156.737			

*From 1969 through 1988, the race was known as the Talladega 500. From 1989 through 2001, it was known as the Die Hard 500. In 2001, it was again called the Talladega 500. (Since 2002, the race has been called the Aaron's 499.)

NASCAR (cont.)

COCA-COLA 600 WINNERS

YEAR	DRIVER	M.P.H.	YEAR	DRIVER	M.P.H.	YEAR	DRIVER	M.P.H.
2006	Kasey Kahne	128.840	1990	Rusty Wallace	137.650	1974	David Pearson	135.720
2005	Jimmie Johnson	114.698	1989	Darrell Waltrip	144.077	1973	Buddy Baker	134.890
2004	Jimmie Johnson	142.763	1988	Darrell Waltrip	124.460	1972	Buddy Baker	142.255
2003	Jimmie Johnson	126.198	1987	Kyle Petty	131.483	1971	Bobby Allison	140.442
2002	Mark Martin	137.729	1986	Dale Earnhardt	140.406	1970	Donnie Allison	129.680
2001	Jeff Burton	138.107	1985	Darrell Waltrip	141.807	1969	Lee Roy Yarbrough	134.361
2000	Matt Kenseth	142.640	1984	Bobby Allison	129.233	1968	Buddy Baker	104.207
1999	Jeff Burton	151.367	1983	Neil Bonnett	140.707	1967	Jim Paschal	135.832
1998	Jeff Gordon	136.424	1982	Neil Bonnett	130.058	1966	Marvin Panch	135.042
1997	Jeff Gordon	136.745	1981	Bobby Allison	129.326	1965	Fred Lorenzen	121.772
1996	Dale Jarrett	147.581	1980	Benny Parsons	119.265	1964	Jim Paschal	125.772
1995	Bobby Labonte	151.952	1979	Darrell Waltrip	136.674	1963	Fred Lorenzen	132.418
1994	Jeff Gordon	139.445	1978	Darrell Waltrip	138.355	1962	Nelson Stacy	125.552
1993	Dale Earnhardt	145.504	1977	Richard Petty	137.676	1961	David Pearson	111.633
1992	Dale Earnhardt	132.980	1976	David Pearson	137.352	1960	Joe Lee Johnson	107.735
1991	Davey Allison	138.951	1975	Richard Petty	145.327			

BRICKYARD 400* WINNERS

YEAR	DRIVER	M.P.H.	YEAR	DRIVER	M.P.H.
2006	Jimmie Johnson	137.182	1999	Dale Jarrett	148.194
2005	Tony Stewart	118.782	1998	Jeff Gordon	126.772
2004	Jeff Gordon	115.037	1997	Ricky Rudd	130.814
2003	Kevin Harvick	134.554	1996	Dale Jarrett	139.508
2002	Bill Elliott	125.033	1995	Dale Earnhardt	155.206
2001	Jeff Gordon	130.790	1994	Jeff Gordon	131.977
2000	Bobby Labonte	155.912			

FAST FACT

Darrell Waltrip leads all drivers in wins (84) and pole positions won (59) since NASCAR's modern era began in 1972.

SOUTHERN 500** WINNERS

YEAR	DRIVER	M.P.H.
2006	Greg Biffle	135.127
2005	Greg Biffle	123.031
2004	Jimmie Johnson	125.044
2003	Terry Labonte	120.744
2002	Jeff Gordon	118.617
2001	Ward Burton	122.773
2000	Bobby Labonte	108.273
1999	Jeff Burton	107.816
1998	Jeff Gordon	139.031
1997	Jeff Gordon	121.149
1996	Jeff Gordon	135.757
1995	Jeff Gordon	121.231
1994	Bill Elliott	127.952
1993	Mark Martin	137.932
1992	Darrell Waltrip	129.114
1991	Harry Gant	133.508
1990	Dale Earnhardt	123.141
1989	Dale Earnhardt	135.462
1988	Bill Elliott	128.297
1987	Dale Earnhardt	115.520
1986	Tim Richmond	121.068
1985	Bill Elliott	121.254
1984	Harry Gant	128.270
1983	Bobby Allison	123.343
1982	Cale Yarborough	115.224
1981	Neil Bonnett	126.410
1980	Terry Labonte	115.210

Greg Biffle has 10 career wins, two in the Southern/Dodge Charger 500.

SAM SHARPE

*The race is now know as the Allstate 400 at the Brickyard.
**The race is now known as the Dodge Charger 500.

SOUTHERN 500 WINNERS (cont.)

YEAR	DRIVER	M.P.H.	YEAR	DRIVER	M.P.H.	YEAR	DRIVER	M.P.H.
1979	David Pearson	126.259	1969	Lee Roy Yarbrough	105.612	1959	Jim Reed	111.840
1978	Cale Yarborough	116.828	1968	Cale Yarborough	126.132	1958	Fireball Roberts	102.590
1977	David Pearson	106.797	1967	Richard Petty	130.423	1957	Speedy Thompson	100.094
1976	David Pearson	120.534	1966	Darel Dieringer	114.830	1956	Curtis Turner	95.067
1975	Bobby Allison	116.825	1965	Ned Jarrett	115.924	1955	Herb Thomas	93.281
1974	Cale Yarborough	111.075	1964	Buck Baker	117.757	1954	Herb Thomas	94.930
1973	Cale Yarborough	134.033	1963	Fireball Roberts	129.784	1953	Buck Baker	92.780
1972	Bobby Allison	128.124	1962	Larry Frank	117.965	1952	Fonty Flock	74.510
1971	Bobby Allison	131.398	1961	Nelson Stacy	117.787	1951	Herb Thomas	76.900
1970	Buddy Baker	128.817	1960	Buck Baker	105.901	1950	Johnny Mantz	76.260

TRIVIA CHALLENGE

Who is the youngest driver to win the Indianapolis 500?

Troy Ruttman. He was 22 years, 80 days old when he won the 36th Indianapolis 500 on May 30, 1952.

LEGENDS

Bobby Unser celebrates his third Indy 500 victory.

PAUL KENNEDY

■ **Bobby Unser,** b. February 20, 1934, Albuquerque, New Mexico. Unser is a member of one of racing's royal families. He was an inaugural inductee into the International Motorsports Hall of Fame in 1990. Unser is a three-time winner of the Indianapolis 500 (1968, 1975, 1981) and retired in 1982 with the third-most wins in IndyCar racing (35). He set speed records by being the first driver to reach 190 miles per hour at the Indianapolis 500 and the first to pass 170 miles per hour in a car powered by a piston engine.

■ **David Pearson,** b. December 22, 1934, Whitney, South Carolina. The "Silver Fox" is an inductee in two racing halls of fame — the International Motor Sports Hall of Fame and the Motorsports Hall of Fame of America. He ranks second all-time in NASCAR history in wins (105) and pole positions (113) and fourth in laps led (25,425). In 1976, Pearson won the Daytona 500. From 1972 to 1979 he averaged five wins per year. In 1969, he made history by becoming the first person to exceed 190 miles per hour at Daytona (190.029).

■ **Glenn "Fireball" Roberts,** b. January 20, 1931, Daytona Beach, Florida; d. July 2, 1964. In 14 years, Roberts won 24 races, including the 1962 Daytona 500. That year he also won the Firecracker 250, becoming the first driver to sweep both races at Daytona in the same season. He was a two-time winner of the Southern 500 (1958, 1963). In 1964, Roberts died of injuries suffered in a fiery crash at Charlotte. He was inducted into the International Motorsports Hall of Fame in 1990.

TENNIS

oger Federer of Switzerland still sits atop the men's tennis world. The world's Number 1 player won 81 of his 85 matches in 2005. He added two more Grand Slam titles — Wimbledon and the U.S. Open. And he started 2006 by winning the Australian Open, his third consecutive Grand Slam title and the seventh in his career.

But the road is getting rougher for Federer, because a new crop of young competitors is on the rise. Leading the way is Rafael Nadal. Nadal nearly beat Federer in one of the best matches of 2005, in the NASDAQ-100 Open final. Then, on his 19th birthday, Nadal beat Federer in the semifinals of the French Open. The young Spaniard went on to win the tournament, his first Grand Slam title. Finally, in June 2006, Nadal met Federer in the finals of the French Open and won in four sets. Federer, however, bounced back to defeat Nadal one month later at Wimbeldon.

The women's side featured a series of surprises and great comebacks. Venus Williams of the United States won Wimbledon, her first Grand Slam title since the 2001 U.S. Open. Williams' upset over fellow American Lindsay Davenport in the final was the longest women's championship match in tournament history (4–6, 7–6 [7–4], 9–7).

Kim Clijsters of Belgium had missed most of 2004 due to injuries. She finished the year ranked 22nd in the world. In 2005, she bounced back by winning her first Grand Slam — the U.S. Open — and finished the year ranked Number 2.

Fellow Belgian Justine Henin-Hardenne had her 2004 season ruined by a respiratory illness. But she came back strong in 2005. Henin-Hardenne won 24 straight matches in the clay court season, including the French

Roger Federer added two more Grand Slam titles in 2005.

Open singles title. She won the French Open title again in 2006.

Amelie Mauresmo of France won her first career Grand Slam title at the 2006 Australian Open. It was only her second Grand Slam final.

The upset of the year was in national team competition. Croatia became the first unseeded team to win the Davis Cup. In the other major national team event, Russia won the Federation Cup for the second year in a row.

GRAND SLAM TOURNAMENTS: ALL-TIME MEN'S CHAMPIONS

AUSTRALIAN CHAMPIONSHIPS

Year	Winner	Year	Winner	Year	Winner
2006	Roger Federer	1991	Boris Becker	1975	John Newcombe
2005	Marat Safin	1990	Ivan Lendl	1974	Jimmy Connors
2004	Roger Federer	1989	Ivan Lendl	1973	John Newcombe
2003	Andre Agassi	1988	Mats Wilander	1972	Ken Rosewall
2002	Thomas Johansson	1987	Stefan Edberg	1971	Ken Rosewall
2001	Andre Agassi	1986	no tournament	1970	Arthur Ashe
2000	Andre Agassi	1985	Stefan Edberg	*1969	Rod Laver
1999	Yevgeny Kafelnikov	1984	Mats Wilander	1968	Bill Bowrey
1998	Petr Korda	1983	Mats Wilander	1967	Roy Emerson
1997	Pete Sampras	1982	Johan Kriek	1966	Roy Emerson
1996	Boris Becker	1981	Johan Kriek	1965	Roy Emerson
1995	Andre Agassi	1980	Brian Teacher	1964	Roy Emerson
1994	Pete Sampras	1979	Guillermo Vilas	1963	Roy Emerson
1993	Jim Courier	1978	Guillermo Vilas	1962	Rod Laver
1992	Jim Courier	1977 (Dec.)	Vitas Gerulaitis	1961	Roy Emerson
		1977 (Jan.)	Roscoe Tanner	1960	Rod Laver
		1976	Mark Edmondson	1959	Alex Olmedo

* Became Open (amateur and professional) in 1969.
Note: Traditionally, the Australian Open was held in January. In 1977, it was moved to December, so there were two tournaments that year. It returned to January in 1987.

AUSTRALIAN CHAMPIONSHIPS (cont.)

Year	Winner
1958	Ashley Cooper
1957	Ashley Cooper
1956	Lew Hoad
1955	Ken Rosewall
1954	Mervyn Rose
1953	Ken Rosewall
1952	Ken McGregor
1951	Richard Savitt
1950	Frank Sedgman
1949	Frank Sedgman
1948	Adrian Quist
1947	Dinny Pails
1946	John Bromwich
1941-45	No tournament
1940	Adrian Quist
1939	John Bromwich
1938	Don Budge
1937	Vivian B. McGrath
1936	Adrian Quist
1935	Jack Crawford
1934	Fred Perry
1933	Jack Crawford
1932	Jack Crawford
1931	Jack Crawford
1930	Gar Moon
1929	John C. Gregory
1928	Jean Borotra
1927	Gerald Patterson
1926	John Hawkes
1925	James Anderson
1924	James Anderson
1923	Pat O'Hara Wood
1922	James Anderson
1921	Rhys H. Gemmell
1920	Pat O'Hara Wood
1919	A.R.F. Kingscote
1916-18	No tournament
1915	Francis G. Lowe
1914	Arthur Wood
1913	E. F. Parker
1912	J. Cecil Parke
1911	Norman Brookes
1910	Rodney Heath
1909	Tony Wilding
1908	Fred Alexander
1907	Horace M. Rice
1906	Tony Wilding
1905	Rodney Heath

FRENCH CHAMPIONSHIPS

Year	Winner
2006	Rafael Nadal
2005	Rafael Nadal
2004	Gaston Gaudio
2003	Juan Carlos Ferrero
2002	Albert Costa
2001	Gustavo Kuerten
2000	Gustavo Kuerten

Year	Winner
1999	Andre Agassi
1998	Carlos Moya
1997	Gustavo Kuerten
1996	Yevgeny Kafelnikov
1995	Thomas Muster
1994	Sergi Bruguera
1993	Sergi Bruguera
1992	Jim Courier
1991	Jim Courier
1990	Andres Gomez
1989	Michael Chang
1988	Mats Wilander
1987	Ivan Lendl
1986	Ivan Lendl
1985	Mats Wilander
1984	Ivan Lendl
1983	Yannick Noah
1982	Mats Wilander
1981	Bjorn Borg
1980	Bjorn Borg
1979	Bjorn Borg
1978	Bjorn Borg
1977	Guillermo Vilas
1976	Adriano Panatta
1975	Bjorn Borg
1974	Bjorn Borg
1973	Ilie Nastase
1972	Andres Gimeno
1971	Jan Kodes
1970	Jan Kodes
1969	Rod Laver
*1968	Ken Rosewall
1967	Roy Emerson
1966	Tony Roche
1965	Fred Stolle
1964	Manuel Santana
1963	Roy Emerson
1962	Rod Laver
1961	Manuel Santana
1960	Nicola Pietrangeli
1959	Nicola Pietrangeli
1958	Mervyn Rose
1957	Sven Davidson
1956	Lew Hoad
1955	Tony Trabert
1954	Tony Trabert
1953	Ken Rosewall
1952	Jaroslav Drobny
1951	Jaroslav Drobny
1950	Budge Patty
1949	Frank Parker
1948	Frank Parker
1947	Jozsef Asboth
1946	Marcel Bernard
1940-45	No tournament
1939	William McNeill
1938	Don Budge
1937	Henner Henkel
1936	Gottfried von Cramm
1935	Fred Perry

Year	Winner
1934	Gottfried von Cramm
1933	Jack Crawford
1932	Henri Cochet
1931	Jean Borotra
1930	Henri Cochet
1929	Rene Lacoste
1928	Henri Cochet
1927	Rene Lacoste
1926	Henri Cochet
†1925	Rene Lacoste

WIMBLEDON CHAMPIONSHIPS

Year	Winner
2006	Roger Federer
2005	Roger Federer
2004	Roger Federer
2003	Roger Federer
2002	Lleyton Hewitt
2001	Goran Ivanisevic
2000	Pete Sampras
1999	Pete Sampras
1998	Pete Sampras
1997	Pete Sampras
1996	Richard Krajicek
1995	Pete Sampras
1994	Pete Sampras
1993	Pete Sampras
1992	Andre Agassi
1991	Michael Stich
1990	Stefan Edberg
1989	Boris Becker
1988	Stefan Edberg
1987	Pat Cash
1986	Boris Becker
1985	Boris Becker
1984	John McEnroe
1983	John McEnroe
1982	Jimmy Connors
1981	John McEnroe
1980	Bjorn Borg
1979	Bjorn Borg
1978	Bjorn Borg
1977	Bjorn Borg
1976	Bjorn Borg
1975	Arthur Ashe
1974	Jimmy Connors
1973	Jan Kodes
1972	Stan Smith
1971	John Newcombe
1970	John Newcombe
1969	Rod Laver
*1968	Rod Laver
1967	John Newcombe
1966	Manuel Santana
1965	Roy Emerson
1964	Roy Emerson
1963	Chuck McKinley
1962	Rod Laver
1961	Rod Laver
1960	Neale Fraser
1959	Alex Olmedo
1958	Ashley Cooper

* Became Open (amateur and professional) in 1968.
† 1925 was the first year in which players from all countries were allowed to compete.

TODAY'S STARS

Rafael Nadal won the 2005 French Open.

■ **Rafael Nadal,** b. June 3, 1986, Manacor, Spain. The left-handed player has been the only man who can beat Roger Federer. Nadal won his first Grand Slam title at the 2005 French Open, defeating Federer in the semifinals. He won his second at the 2006 French Open, defeating Federer in the finals. Nadal's 11 singles titles in 2005 set the record for a teenager. His Number 2 ranking was also the highest ever for a Spaniard. In 2006, Nadal broke the record for consecutive wins on clay courts (53).

■ **Lleyton Hewitt,** b. February 24, 1981, Adelaide, Australia. Hewitt is one of the greatest Australian athletes of all-time. The son of an Australian Rules Football player, Hewitt is known for both his talent and his fiery attitude on the court. In 1998, he became the lowest-ranked player (550th) to win on the ATP tour when he won the Australian Men's Hardcourt Championships at age 16. He's also one of only five players to hold the world Number 1 ranking for an entire year (2002). Hewitt has won two Grand Slam titles: the U.S. Open in 2001 and Wimbledon in 2002.

■ **Nikolay Davydenko,** b. June 2, 1981, Severodonezk, Ukraine. Davydenko finished 2005 ranked Number 5 in the world, the first time he'd finished in the top 10. Davydenko won only one title in 2005, but he played in more tournaments than any top 10 player (30). Davydenko's best surface is clay: He won 25 of 35 matches on clay courts last season. He also made his best finish in a Grand Slam tournament in 2005 on clay, reaching the semifinals of the French Open.

GRAND SLAM TOURNAMENTS: ALL-TIME MEN'S CHAMPIONS (cont.)

WIMBLEDON CHAMPIONSHIPS (cont.)

Year	Winner	Year	Winner	Year	Winner
1957	Lew Hoad	1932	Ellsworth Vines	1907	Norman E. Brookes
1956	Lew Hoad	1931	Sidney B. Wood, Jr.	1906	H. Laurie Doherty
1955	Tony Trabert	1930	Bill Tilden	1905	H. Laurie Doherty
1954	Jaroslav Drobny	1929	Henri Cochet	1904	H. Laurie Doherty
1953	Vic Seixas	1928	Rene Lacoste	1903	H. Laurie Doherty
1952	Frank Sedgman	1927	Henri Cochet	1902	H. Laurie Doherty
1951	Dick Savitt	1926	Jean Borotra	1901	Arthur W. Gore
1950	Budge Patty	1925	Rene Lacoste	1900	Reggie F. Doherty
1949	Fred Schroeder, Jr.	1924	Jean Borotra	1899	Reggie F. Doherty
1948	Bob Falkenburg	1923	Bill Johnston	1898	Reggie F. Doherty
1947	Jack Kramer	1922	Gerald L. Patterson	1897	Reggie F. Doherty
1946	Yvon Petra	1921	Bill Tilden	1896	Harold S. Mahoney
1940-45	No tournament	1920	Bill Tilden	1895	Wilfred Baddeley
1939	Bobby Riggs	1919	Gerald L. Patterson	1894	Joshua Pim
1938	Don Budge	1915-18	No tournament	1893	Joshua Pim
1937	Don Budge	1914	Norman E. Brookes	1892	Wilfred Baddeley
1936	Fred Perry	1913	Anthony F. Wilding	1891	Wilfred Baddeley
1935	Fred Perry	1912	Anthony F. Wilding	1890	William J. Hamilton
1934	Fred Perry	1911	Anthony F. Wilding	1889	William Renshaw
1933	Jack Crawford	1910	Anthony F. Wilding	1888	Ernest Renshaw
		1909	Arthur W. Gore	1887	Herbert F. Lawford
		1908	Arthur W. Gore	1886	William Renshaw

WIMBLEDON CHAMPIONSHIPS (cont.)

Year	Winner
1885	William Renshaw
1884	William Renshaw
1883	William Renshaw
1882	William Renshaw
1881	William Renshaw
1880	John T. Hartley
1879	John T. Hartley
1878	P. Frank Hadow
1877	Spencer W. Gore

UNITED STATES CHAMPIONSHIPS

Year	Winner
2005	Roger Federer
2004	Roger Federer
2003	Andy Roddick
2002	Pete Sampras
2001	Lleyton Hewitt
2000	Marat Safin
1999	Andre Agassi

* Became Open (amateur and professional) in 1968.
** Separate amateur event held.

Year	Winner
1998	Patrick Rafter
1997	Patrick Rafter
1996	Pete Sampras
1995	Pete Sampras
1994	Andre Agassi
1993	Pete Sampras
1992	Stefan Edberg
1991	Stefan Edberg
1990	Pete Sampras
1989	Boris Becker
1988	Mats Wilander
1987	Ivan Lendl
1986	Ivan Lendl
1985	Ivan Lendl
1984	John McEnroe
1983	Jimmy Connors
1982	Jimmy Connors
1981	John McEnroe
1980	John McEnroe
1979	John McEnroe
1978	Jimmy Connors
1977	Guillermo Vilas
1976	Jimmy Connors
1975	Manuel Orantes
1974	Jimmy Connors

Year	Winner
1973	John Newcombe
1972	Ilie Nastase
1971	Stan Smith
1970	Ken Rosewall
**1969	Stan Smith
1969	Rod Laver
*1968	Arthur Ashe
**1968	Arthur Ashe
1967	John Newcombe
1966	Fred Stolle
1965	Manuel Santana
1964	Roy Emerson
1963	Rafael Osuna
1962	Rod Laver
1961	Roy Emerson
1960	Neale Fraser
1959	Neale Fraser
1958	Ashley Cooper
1957	Mal Anderson
1956	Ken Rosewall
1955	Tony Trabert
1954	Vic Seixas
1953	Tony Trabert
1952	Frank Sedgman

2005-06 MEN'S TIME LINE

■ **January 30, 2005:** Marat Safin of Russia defeats Lleyton Hewitt of Australia to win his first Australian Open title.

■ **June 5, 2005:** Rafael Nadal of Spain, age 19, defeats Mariano Puerta of Argentina to win the French Open, his first Grand Slam title.

■ **July 3, 2005:** Roger Federer defeats Andy Roddick of the United States to win his third Wimbledon title.

■ **July 31, 2005:** Andre Agassi wins his 60th career singles title. The 35-year-old American defeats Gilles Muller of Luxembourg to win the Mercedes Benz Cup.

■ **September 7, 2005:** In the match of the year, Andre Agassi defeats country-man James Blake in a fifth-set tiebreaker to win a U.S. Open quarterfinal match.

■ **September 11, 2005:** Roger Federer defeats Andre Agassi in four sets to win the U.S. Open.

■ **November 20, 2005:** David Nalbandian of Argentina upsets Roger Federer in the Tennis Masters Cup, snapping Federer's 35-match winning streak.

■ **January 29, 2006:** Roger Federer beats Marcos Baghdatis of Cyprus to win the Australian Open for the second time.

■ **June 11, 2006:** Rafael Nadal defeats Roger Federer to win the French Open. It is Nadal's 60th straight win on clay.

DID YOU KNOW?

In the first round of the 2004 French Open, Fabrice Santoro defeated Arnaud Clement in the longest match of the Open Era (six hours, 33 minutes).

GRAND SLAM TOURNAMENTS: ALL-TIME MEN'S CHAMPIONS (cont.)

UNITED STATES CHAMPIONSHIPS (cont.)

Year	Winner	Year	Winner	Year	Winner
		1928	Henri Cochet	1903	H. Laurie Doherty
1951	Frank Sedgman	1927	Rene Lacoste	1902	William A. Larned
1950	Arthur Larsen	1926	Rene Lacoste	1901	William A. Larned
1949	Pancho Gonzales	1925	Bill Tilden	1900	Malcolm D. Whitman
1948	Pancho Gonzales	1924	Bill Tilden	1899	Malcolm D. Whitman
1947	Jack Kramer	1923	Bill Tilden	1898	Malcolm D. Whitman
1946	Jack Kramer	1922	Bill Tilden	1897	Robert D. Wrenn
1945	Frank Parker	1921	Bill Tilden	1896	Robert D. Wrenn
1944	Frank Parker	1920	Bill Tilden	1895	Frederick H. Hovey
1943	Joseph R. Hunt	1919	Bill Johnston	1894	Robert D. Wrenn
1942	Fred R. Schroeder, Jr.	1918	R.L. Murray	1893	Robert D. Wrenn
1941	Bobby Riggs	1917	R.L. Murray	1892	Oliver S. Campbell
1940	Don McNeill	1916	Richard N. Williams	1891	Oliver S. Campbell
1939	Bobby Riggs	1915	Bill Johnston	1890	Oliver S. Campbell
1938	Don Budge	1914	Richard N. Williams	1889	H. W. Slocum, Jr.
1937	Don Budge	1913	Maurice E. McLoughlin	1888	H. W. Slocum, Jr.
1936	Fred Perry	1912	Maurice E. McLoughlin	1887	Richard D. Sears
1935	Wilmer L. Allison	1911	William A. Larned	1886	Richard D. Sears
1934	Fred Perry	1910	William A. Larned	1885	Richard D. Sears
1933	Fred Perry	1909	William A. Larned	1884	Richard D. Sears
1932	Ellsworth Vines	1908	William A. Larned	1883	Richard D. Sears
1931	Ellsworth Vines	1907	William A. Larned	1882	Richard D. Sears
1930	John H. Doeg	1906	William J. Clothier	1881	Richard D. Sears
1929	Bill Tilden	1905	Beals C. Wright		
		1904	Holcombe Ward		

LEGENDS

Yannick Noah was famous for his athletic play on the court.

STEVE POWELL

■ **Yannick Noah,** b. May 18, 1960, Sedan, France. Noah is one of the most popular athletes ever in France. He won the French Open in 1983, losing only one set during the entire tournament. He was also captain of the French team that won the Davis Cup in 1991, and led France to its first-ever Federation Cup title in 1997. Noah, the father of University of Florida basketball star Joakim Noah, is now a pop singer in Europe.

■ **Jim Courier,** b. August 17, 1970, Sanford, Florida. Courier dominated opponents with powerful groundstrokes during the early 1990's. He won back-to-back titles in both the French Open (1991 and 1992) and Australian Open (1992 and 1993). He also helped the United States team win Davis Cup titles in 1992 and 1995. Courier spent a total of 58 weeks as the Number 1 player in the world. He was inducted into the International Tennis Hall of Fame in 2005.

■ **Stefan Edberg,** b. January 19, 1966, Vastervik, Sweden. Edberg used his height (6'2") and strong serve to become one of the greatest serve-and-volley players of all-time. He won 41 singles titles in his career, including six Grand Slams (Wimbledon, the U.S. Open, and the Australian Open twice each). Edberg won the ATP Tour Sportsmanship Award five times in his career, more than any other player. In 1996, the ATP renamed the honor the Edberg Sportsmanship Award.

GRAND SLAM TOURNAMENTS: ALL-TIME WOMEN'S CHAMPIONS

AUSTRALIAN CHAMPIONSHIPS

Year	Winner
2006	Amelie Mauresmo
2005	Serena Williams
2004	Justine Henin-Hardenne
2003	Serena Williams
2002	Jennifer Capriati
2001	Jennifer Capriati
2000	Lindsay Davenport
1999	Martina Hingis
1998	Martina Hingis
1997	Martina Hingis
1996	Monica Seles
1995	Mary Pierce
1994	Steffi Graf
1993	Monica Seles
1992	Monica Seles
1991	Monica Seles
1990	Steffi Graf
1989	Steffi Graf
1988	Steffi Graf
1987 (Jan.)	Hana Mandlikova
1985 (Dec.)	Martina Navratilova
1984	Chris Evert Lloyd
1983	Martina Navratilova
1982	Chris Evert Lloyd
1981	Martina Navratilova
1980	Hana Mandlikova
1979	Barbara Jordan
1978	Chris O'Neil
1977 (Dec.)	Evonne Goolagong Cawley
1977 (Jan.)	Kerry Melville Reid
1976	Evonne Goolagong Cawley
1975	Evonne Goolagong Cawley
1974	Evonne Goolagong Cawley
1973	Margaret Smith Court
1972	Virginia Wade
1971	Margaret Smith Court
1970	Margaret Smith Court
*1969	Margaret Smith Court
1968	Billie Jean King
1967	Nancy Richey
1966	Margaret Smith Court
1965	Margaret Smith Court
1964	Margaret Smith Court
1963	Margaret Smith Court
1962	Margaret Smith Court
1961	Margaret Smith Court
1960	Margaret Smith Court
1959	Mary Carter-Reitano
1958	Angela Mortimer
1957	Shirley Fry
1956	Mary Carter
1955	Beryl Penrose
1954	Thelma Long
1953	Maureen Connolly
1952	Thelma Long
1951	Nancye Wynne Bolton
1950	Louise Brough
1949	Doris Hart
1948	Nancye Wynne Bolton
1947	Nancye Wynne Bolton
1946	Nancye Wynne Bolton
1941-45	No tournament
1940	Nancye Wynne Bolton
1939	Emily Westacott
1938	Dorothy Bundy
1937	Nancye Wynne Bolton
1936	Joan Hartigan
1935	Dorothy Round
1934	Joan Hartigan
1933	Joan Hartigan
1932	Coral Buttsworth
1931	Coral Buttsworth
1930	Daphne Akhurst
1929	Daphne Akhurst
1928	Daphne Akhurst
1927	Esna Boyd
1926	Daphne Akhurst
1925	Daphne Akhurst
1924	Sylvia Lance
1923	Margaret Molesworth
1922	Margaret Molesworth

FRENCH CHAMPIONSHIPS

Year	Winner
2006	Justine Henin-Hardenne
2005	Justine Henin-Hardenne
2004	Anastasia Myskina
2003	Justine Henin-Hardenne
2002	Serena Williams
2001	Jennifer Capriati
2000	Mary Pierce
1999	Steffi Graf
1998	Arantxa Sánchez-Vicario
1997	Iva Majoli
1996	Steffi Graf
1995	Steffi Graf
1994	Arantxa Sánchez-Vicario
1993	Steffi Graf
1992	Monica Seles
1991	Monica Seles
1990	Monica Seles
1989	Arantxa Sánchez-Vicario
1988	Steffi Graf
1987	Steffi Graf
1986	Chris Evert Lloyd
1985	Chris Evert Lloyd
1984	Martina Navratilova
1983	Chris Evert Lloyd
1982	Martina Navratilova
1981	Hana Mandlikova
1980	Chris Evert Lloyd
1979	Chris Evert Lloyd
1978	Virginia Ruzici
1977	Mima Jausovec
1976	Sue Barker
1975	Chris Evert Lloyd
1974	Chris Evert Lloyd
1973	Margaret Smith Court
1972	Billie Jean King
1971	Evonne Goolagong Cawley
1970	Margaret Smith Court
1969	Margaret Smith Court
**1968	Nancy Richey
1967	Francoise Durr
1966	Ann Jones
1965	Lesley Turner
1964	Margaret Smith Court
1963	Lesley Turner
1962	Margaret Smith Court
1961	Ann Haydon
1960	Darlene Hard
1959	Christine Truman
1958	Zsuzsi Kormoczy
1957	Shirley Bloomer
1956	Althea Gibson
1955	Angela Mortimer
1954	Maureen Connolly
1953	Maureen Connolly
1952	Doris Hart
1951	Shirley Fry
1950	Doris Hart
1949	Margaret Osborne duPont
1948	Nelly Landry
1947	Patricia Todd
1946	Margaret Osborne
1940-45	No tournament
1939	Simone Mathieu
1938	Simone Mathieu
1937	Hilde Sperling
1936	Hilde Sperling
1935	Hilde Sperling
1934	Margaret Scriven
1933	Margaret Scriven
1932	Helen Wills Moody
1931	Cilly Aussem
1930	Helen Wills Moody
1929	Helen Wills Moody
1928	Helen Wills Moody
1927	Kea Bouman
1926	Suzanne Lenglen
†1925	Suzanne Lenglen

WIMBLEDON CHAMPIONSHIPS

Year	Winner
2006	Amelie Mauresmo
2005	Venus Williams
2004	Maria Sharapova
2003	Serena Williams
2002	Serena Williams
2001	Venus Williams
2000	Venus Williams
1999	Lindsay Davenport
1998	Jana Novotna
1997	Martina Hingis
1996	Steffi Graf
1995	Steffi Graf
1994	Conchita Martinez
1993	Steffi Graf
1992	Steffi Graf
1991	Steffi Graf
1990	Martina Navratilova
1989	Steffi Graf
1988	Steffi Graf
1987	Martina Navratilova
1986	Martina Navratilova
1985	Martina Navratilova
1984	Martina Navratilova
1983	Martina Navratilova
1982	Martina Navratilova
1981	Chris Evert Lloyd

* Became Open (amateur and professional) in 1969.
** Became Open (amateur and professional) in 1968.
† 1925 was the first year in which players from all countries were allowed to compete.

TENNIS

TODAY'S STARS

Lindsay Davenport finished 2005 as the top-ranked player in the world.

■ **Lindsay Davenport,** b. June 8, 1976, Laguna Beach, California. Davenport won her first WTA Tour title at age 17 at the 1993 European Open. She has gone on to become one of nine players to win more than 50 titles on the tour (51). Davenport finished 2005 ranked Number 1 in the world and became the fourth player to complete a season ranked Number 1 four times. The French Open is the only Grand Slam tournament she has not won.

■ **Mary Pierce,** b. January 15, 1975, Montreal, Canada. Pierce was born in Montreal, Canada (while her mother was visiting the city), and grew up in Florida, where she still lives. But Pierce represents France in the tennis world. (She is considered a French citizen because her mother was born there.) Pierce had one of her best years in 2005, returning to the Top 5 in rankings for the first time since 2000. She won 29 of 33 matches during one stretch of the season, and made the finals of the U.S. Open and French Open. Since turning pro in 1989 at age 14, Pierce has won 18 WTA Tour singles tournaments through 2005, including French Open and Australian Open titles.

■ **Nadia Petrova,** b. June 8, 1982, Moscow, Russia. Petrova has great athletic genes. Her mother, Nadejda Ilina, won a bronze medal in the 400-meter relay at the 1976 Olympics. Her father, Victor, was one of Russia's top hammer throwers. In 2005, Petrova won the first title of her career at the Linz Open (Austria). She also finished a season ranked in the Top 10 (ninth) for the first time in her career. She advanced as far as the quarterfinals in four straight Grand Slam tournaments between the 2005 French Open and 2006 Australian Open.

GRAND SLAM TOURNAMENTS: ALL-TIME WOMEN'S CHAMPIONS (cont.)

WIMBLEDON CHAMPIONSHIPS (cont.)

Year	Winner	Year	Winner	Year	Winner
		1959	Maria Bueno	1931	Cilly Aussem
		1958	Althea Gibson	1930	Helen Wills Moody
1980	Evonne Goolagong Cawley	1957	Althea Gibson	1929	Helen Wills Moody
1979	Martina Navratilova	1956	Shirley Fry	1928	Helen Wills Moody
1978	Martina Navratilova	1955	Louise Brough	1927	Helen Wills Moody
1977	Virginia Wade	1954	Maureen Connolly	1926	Kathleen McKane Godfree
1976	Chris Evert Lloyd	1953	Maureen Connolly	1925	Suzanne Lenglen
1975	Billie Jean King	1952	Maureen Connolly	1924	Kathleen McKane
1974	Chris Evert Lloyd	1951	Doris Hart	1923	Suzanne Lenglen
1973	Billie Jean King	1950	Louise Brough	1922	Suzanne Lenglen
1972	Billie Jean King	1949	Louise Brough	1921	Suzanne Lenglen
1971	Evonne Goolagong Cawley	1948	Louise Brough	1920	Suzanne Lenglen
1970	Margaret Smith Court	1947	Margaret Osborne	1919	Suzanne Lenglen
1969	Ann Haydon Jones	1946	Pauline Betz	1915-18	No tournament
**1968	Billie Jean King	1940–45	No tournament	1914	Dorothea Lambert Chambers
1967	Billie Jean King	1939	Alice Marble	1913	Dorothea Lambert Chambers
1966	Billie Jean King	1938	Helen Wills Moody	1912	Ethel Larcombe
1965	Margaret Smith Court	1937	Dorothy Round	1911	Dorothea Lambert Chambers
1964	Maria Bueno	1936	Helen Jacobs	1910	Dorothea Lambert Chambers
1963	Margaret Smith Court	1935	Helen Wills Moody	1909	Dora Boothby
1962	Karen Hantze Susman	1934	Dorothy Round	1908	Charlotte Cooper Sterry
1961	Angela Mortimer	1933	Helen Wills Moody		
1960	Maria Bueno	1932	Helen Wills Moody		

**Became Open (amateur and professional) in 1968.

WIMBLEDON CHAMPIONSHIPS (cont.)

Year	Winner
1907	May Sutton
1906	Dorothea Douglass
1905	May Sutton
1904	Dorothea Douglass
1903	Dorothea Douglass
1902	Muriel Robb
1901	Charlotte Cooper Sterry
1900	Blanche Bingley Hillyard
1899	Blanche Bingley Hillyard
1898	Charlotte Cooper
1897	Blanche Bingley Hillyard
1896	Charlotte Cooper
1895	Charlotte Cooper
1894	Blanche Bingley Hillyard
1893	Charlotte Dod
1892	Charlotte Dod
1891	Charlotte Dod
1890	Lena Rice
1889	Blanche Bingley Hillyard
1888	Charlotte Dod
1887	Charlotte Dod
1886	Blanche Bingley
1885	Maud Watson
1884	Maud Watson

* Became Open (amateur and professional) in 1968.

UNITED STATES CHAMPIONSHIPS

Year	Winner
2005	Kim Clijsters
2004	Svetlana Kuznetsova
2003	Justine Henin-Hardenne
2002	Serena Williams
2001	Venus Williams
2000	Venus Williams
1999	Serena Williams
1998	Lindsay Davenport
1997	Martina Hingis
1996	Steffi Graf
1995	Steffi Graf
1994	Arantxa Sánchez-Vicario
1993	Steffi Graf
1992	Monica Seles
1991	Monica Seles
1990	Gabriela Sabatini
1989	Steffi Graf
1988	Steffi Graf
1987	Martina Navratilova
1986	Martina Navratilova
1985	Hana Mandlikova
1984	Martina Navratilova
1983	Martina Navratilova
1982	Chris Evert Lloyd
1981	Tracy Austin
1980	Chris Evert Lloyd

Year	Winner
1979	Tracy Austin
1978	Chris Evert Lloyd
1977	Chris Evert Lloyd
1976	Chris Evert Lloyd
1975	Chris Evert Lloyd
1974	Billie Jean King
1973	Margaret Smith Court
1972	Billie Jean King
1971	Billie Jean King
1970	Margaret Smith Court
1969	Margaret Smith Court
*1968	Virginia Wade
1967	Billie Jean King
1966	Maria Bueno
1965	Margaret Smith
1964	Maria Bueno
1963	Maria Bueno
1962	Margaret Smith
1961	Darlene Hard
1960	Darlene Hard
1959	Maria Bueno
1958	Althea Gibson
1957	Althea Gibson
1956	Shirley Fry
1955	Doris Hart
1954	Doris Hart
1953	Maureen Connolly
1952	Maureen Connolly

2005-06 WOMEN'S TIME LINE

■ **January 30, 2005:** After losing the first set, Serena Williams of the United States comes back to defeat country-woman Lindsay Davenport and win her second Australian Open.

■ **February 12, 2005:** Sania Mirza, age 18, becomes the first player from India to win a WTA Tour title. She defeats Alyona Bondarenko of the Ukraine to win the Hyderabad Open.

■ **June 4, 2005:** Justine Henin-Hardenne of Belgium wins her second French Open title, defeating Mary Pierce of France, 6-1, 6-1.

■ **July 2, 2005:** Venus Williams of the United States wins Wimbledon by defeating Lindsay Davenport, 9-7, in the third set. It's Williams's first Grand Slam title since the 2001 U.S. Open.

■ **September 4, 2005:** Venus Williams beats sister Serena in straight sets in the fourth round of the U.S. Open. It's Venus's second straight win over Serena.

■ **September 10, 2005:** Kim Clijsters of Belgium defeats Mary Pierce in the U.S. Open final to win her first Grand Slam title.

■ **November 13, 2005:** Amelie Mauresmo of France defeats Mary Pierce to win the WTA Tour Championships.

■ **December 3, 2005:** : Martina Hingis of Switzerland, the former Number 1 player in the world, announces she will come out of retirement and resume play in the 2006 Australian Open.

■ **January 28, 2006:** Amelie Mauresmo wins her first Grand Slam title — the Australian Open — when Justine Henin-Hardenne is forced to retire during the second set of tournament final.

GRAND SLAM TOURNAMENTS: ALL-TIME WOMEN'S CHAMPIONS (cont.)

UNITED STATES CHAMPIONSHIPS (cont.)		Year	Winner	Year	Winner
Year	Winner	1931	Helen Wills Moody	1911	Hazel Hotchkiss
		1930	Betty Nuthall	1910	Hazel Hotchkiss
1951	Maureen Connolly	1929	Helen Wills Moody	1909	Hazel Hotchkiss
1950	Margaret Osborne duPont	1928	Helen Wills Moody	1908	Maud Barger–Wallach
1949	Margaret Osborne duPont	1927	Helen Wills Moody	1907	Evelyn Sears
1948	Margaret Osborne duPont	1926	Molla Bjurstedt Mallory	1906	Helen Homans
1947	Louise Brough	1925	Helen Wills Moody	1905	Elisabeth Moore
1946	Pauline Betz	1924	Helen Wills Moody	1904	May Sutton
1945	Sarah Palfrey Cooke	1923	Helen Wills Moody	1903	Elisabeth Moore
1944	Pauline Betz	1922	Molla Bjurstedt Mallory	**1902	Marion Jones
1943	Pauline Betz	1921	Molla Bjurstedt Mallory	1901	Elisabeth Moore
1942	Pauline Betz	1920	Molla Bjurstedt Mallory	1900	Myrtle McAteer
1941	Sarah Palfrey Cooke	1919	Hazel Hotchkiss Wightman	1899	Marion Jones
1940	Alice Marble	1918	Molla Bjurstedt	1898	Juliette Atkinson
1939	Alice Marble	1917	Molla Bjurstedt	1897	Juliette Atkinson
1938	Alice Marble	1916	Molla Bjurstedt	1896	Elisabeth Moore
1937	Anita Lizane	1915	Molla Bjurstedt	1895	Juliette Atkinson
1936	Alice Marble	1914	Mary K. Browne	1894	Helen Hellwig
1935	Helen Jacobs	1913	Mary K. Browne	1893	Aline Terry
1934	Helen Jacobs	1912	Mary K. Browne	1892	Mabel Cahill
1933	Helen Jacobs			1891	Mabel Cahill
1932	Helen Jacobs			1890	Ellen C. Roosevelt
				1889	Bertha L. Townsend
				1888	Bertha L. Townsend
** Five-set final abolished.				1887	Ellen Hansell

DID YOU KNOW?

Steffi Graf was ranked No. 1 in the world longer than any player, female or male (377 weeks).

LEGENDS

Althea Gibson broke the color line in tennis.

■ **Althea Gibson,** b. August 25, 1927, Silver, South Carolina; d. September 28, 2003, East Orange, New Jersey. Gibson was a tall player (5'11") with a power game and a big serve. But most important, she was a pioneer. In 1950, she became the first African American to play in the U.S. Championships (now called the U.S. Open). In 1956, she became the first black player to win a major tournament — the French Open. She followed that with other firsts. In 1957, she became the first black player to win Wimbledon and the first to win the U.S. Open. She won Wimbledon again in 1958. Gibson finished her career with 11 major tournament victories in both singles and doubles.

■ **Pam Shriver,** b. July 4, 1962, Baltimore, Maryland. Shriver won 21 singles titles in her career, but her greatest accomplishments came in doubles play. She won 112 doubles titles — 22 of them coming in Grand Slam events. Shriver won most of those titles with fellow Hall of Famer Martina Navratilova. The twosome was named the WTA Tour Doubles Team of the Year nine consecutive times (1981–1989). Shriver is currently a commentator for ABC, CBS, ESPN, and the BBC.

■ **Margaret Smith Court,** b. July 16, 1942, Albury, Australia. No one — man or woman – won more Grand Slam tournaments than Smith Court. She won 62 major titles in singles, doubles, and mixed doubles between 1960 and 1975 (Martina Navratilova is second with 56). Her 24 Grand Slam singles titles are also the most of all-time (Steffi Graf is second with 21). Smith Court won the ladies singles championship in all four Grand Slam events in 1970. She won the Australian Open seven straight times between 1960 and 1966.

DAVID CALLOW

Former champion Martina Hingis came out of retirement at the 2006 Australian Open.

FAST FACT

Rod Laver is the only player to win all four Grand Slam singles tournaments (the Australian Open, French Open, Wimbledon, and the U.S. Open) in the same year twice (1962 and 1969).

ALL-TIME GRAND SLAM SINGLES CHAMPIONS

MEN					
PLAYER	AUS.	FR.	WIM.	U.S.	TOTAL
Pete Sampras	2	0	7	5	14
Roy Emerson	6	2	2	2	12
Bjorn Borg	0	6	5	0	11
Rod Laver	3	2	4	2	11
Bill Tilden	†	0	3	7	10
Andre Agassi	4	1	1	2	8
Jimmy Connors	1	0	2	5	8
*Roger Federer	2	0	4	2	8
Ivan Lendl	2	3	0	3	8
Fred Perry	1	1	3	3	8
Ken Rosewall	4	2	0	2	8
Henri Cochet	†	4	2	1	7
Rene Lacoste	†	3	2	2	7
Bill Larned	†	†	0	7	7
John McEnroe	0	0	3	4	7
John Newcombe	2	0	3	2	7
Willie Renshaw	†	†	7	†	7
Dick Sears	†	†	0	7	7
Mats Wilander	3	3	0	1	7

*Active player. †Did not compete.

WOMEN					
PLAYER	AUS.	FR.	WIM.	U.S.	TOTAL
Margaret Smith Court	11	5	3	5	24
Steffi Graf	4	6	7	5	22
Helen Wills Moody	†	4	8	7	19
Chris Evert Lloyd	2	7	3	6	18
Martina Navratilova	3	2	9	4	18
Billie Jean King	1	1	6	4	12
Maureen Connolly	1	2	3	3	9
*Monica Seles	4	3	0	2	9
Suzanne Lenglen	†	#2	6	0	8
Molla Bjurstedt Mallory	†	†	0	8	8
Maria Bueno	0	0	3	4	7
Evonne Goolagong	4	1	2	0	7
Dorothea L. Chambers	†	†	7	0	7
*Serena Williams	2	1	2	2	7
Nancye Wynne Bolton	6	0	0	0	6
Louise Brough	1	0	4	1	6
Margaret Osborne duPont	†	2	1	3	6
Doris Hart	1	2	1	2	6
Blanche Bingley Hillyard	†	†	6	†	6

*Active player. †Did not compete.
#Suzanne Lenglen also won four singles titles at the French Championships before 1925, when the tournament was first opened to players from all nations.

SIKIDS.COM

Visit our website for the latest stats and sports info.

TRIVIA CHALLENGE

How many times have either Venus or Serena Williams finished a year ranked No. 1 in the world?

Once (Serena in 2002).

SWIMMING

Aaron Piersol of the U.S. proved that he is the best backstroke swimmer in the world.

SIMON BRUTY

There were plenty of changes to the swimming record-book over the past year. Some familiar stars continued to flex their muscles, but several newcomers also made a big splash.

At the World Championships in July — the biggest international swimming event of the year — Americans broke three world records and won more overall medals (32) and gold medals (15) than any other country.

Aaron Peirsol continued to move forward while swimming backward, winning both backstroke events at the Worlds while breaking his own world record in the 200 meters. Peirsol had set the 100-meter record at the World Championships qualifying meet four months earlier.

Michael Phelps didn't make as many headlines in 2005 as he did at the 2004 Summer Olympics, but he still won two individual gold medals at the Worlds. Phelps won the 200-meter freestyle and 200-meter individual medley events. However, he was beaten in the 100-meter butterfly by friendly rival Ian Crocker, who set a world record in the event. Grant Hackett of Australia was the individual star of the meet. He became the first swimmer to win the 400-, 800-, and 1,500-meter freestyle at the same World Championships.

The Australians had the edge on the women's side, led by Leisel Jones's gold medals in the 100- and 200-meter breaststroke. But the United States team showed plenty of promise, thanks to three teenagers. Jessica Hardy, age 18, set a world record in the 100-meter breaststroke in the event's semifinals. Distance swimmer Kate Ziegler, age 17, won gold medals in the 800- and 1,500-meter freestyle.

The star of the United States women's side was 16-year-old Katie Hoff. Hoff won the 200- and 400-meter individual medley and appears to be well on her way to becoming the world's best all-around female swimmer.

Other international swimmers to watch made a splash at the European Short Course Championships held in December 2005. (Short course swimming is done in pools 25 meters or 25 yards long. Long course swimming is done in pools 50 meters or 50 yards long.) Laure Manaudou of France set short-course records in the 400- and 800-yard freestyle. Laszlo Cseh of Hungary, one of Phelps's top rivals, set short-course records in the 200- and 400-yard individual medley.

By the beginning of 2006, Phelps was back in dominating form. At the 2006 FINA World Cup, in February, he won three gold medals, breaking two U.S. records along the way. A month later at the U.S. Championships, eight new American records were set. Phelps set three of them. Still only 21 years old, Phelps is showing no signs of slowing down.

TRIVIA CHALLENGE

What is the order of the four strokes that make up the individual medley?

1. butterfly 2. backstroke 3. breaststroke 4. freestyle.

2005 MAJOR COMPETITIONS – MEN

WORLD CHAMPIONSHIPS
Montreal, Canada, July 17–31, 2005

EVENT	SWIMMER, TEAM	TIME
50-meter freestyle	Roland Schoeman, South Africa	21.69
100-meter freestyle	Filippo Magnini, Italy	48.12
200-meter freestyle	Michael Phelps, United States	1:45.20
400-meter freestyle	Grant Hackett, Australia	3:42.91
800-meter freestyle	Grant Hackett, Australia	7:38.65
1,500-meter freestyle	Grant Hackett, Australia	14:42.58
50-meter backstroke	Aristeidis Grigoriadis, Greece	24.95
100-meter backstroke	Aaron Peirsol, United States	53.62
200-meter backstroke	Aaron Peirsol, United States	1:54.66
50-meter breaststroke	Mark Warnecke, Germany	27.63
100-meter breaststroke	Brendan Hansen, United States	59.37
200-meter breaststroke	Brendan Hansen, United States	2:09.85
50-meter butterfly	Roland Schoeman, South Africa	22.96
100-meter butterfly	Ian Crocker, United States	50.40
200-meter butterfly	Pawel Korzeniowski, Poland	1:55.02
200-meter individual medley	Michael Phelps, United States	1:56.68
400-meter individual medley	Laszlo Cseh, Hungary	4:09.63
4x100-meter medley relay	United States (Aaron Peirsol, Brendan Hansen, Ian Crocker, Jason Lezak)	3:31.85
4x100-meter freestyle relay	United States (Michael Phelps, Neil Walker, Nate Dusing, Jason Lezak)	3:13.77
4x200-meter freestyle relay	United States (Michael Phelps, Ryan Lochte, Peter Vanderkaay, Klete Keller)	7:06.58

U.S. NATIONAL CHAMPIONSHIPS (SUMMER)
Irvine, California, August 3–7, 2005

EVENT	SWIMMER, TEAM	TIME
50-meter freestyle	Benjamin Wildman-Tobriner, Stanford Swimming (California)	22.13
100-meter freestyle	Roland Schoeman, Tucson Ford Dealers Aquatics (Arizona)	48.38
200-meter freestyle	Michael Phelps, Club Wolverine (Michigan)	1:46.40
400-meter freestyle	Klete Keller, Club Wolverine (Michigan)	3:46.20
800-meter freestyle	Klete Keller, Club Wolverine (Michigan)	7:56.66
1,500-meter freestyle	Charles Peterson, Carteret Current (North Carolina)	15:19.03
100-meter backstroke	Randall Bal, Stanford Swimming (Californnia)	54.09
200-meter backstroke	Christian Dejong, Club Wolverine (Michigan)	1:58.25
100-meter breaststroke	Matthew Lowe, Longhorn Aquatics (Texas)	1:01.64
200-meter breaststroke	Matthew Lowe, Longhorn Aquatics (Texas)	2:14.40
100-meter butterfly	Roland Schoeman, Tucson Ford Dealers Aquatics (Arizona)	53.08
200-meter butterfly	Michael Phelps, Club Wolverine (Michigan)	1:55.26
200-meter individual medley	Timothy Liebold, University of Wisconsin	2:01.75
400-meter individual medley	Robert Margalis, Saint Petersburg Aquatics (Florida)	4:18.66
4x100-meter medley relay	Tuscon Ford Dealers Aquatics A (Arizona)	3:42.23
4x100-meter freestyle relay	Club Wolverine A (Michigan)	3:19.38
4x200-meter freestyle relay	Club Wolverine A (Michigan)	7:12.35

2005 MAJOR COMPETITIONS – WOMEN

WORLD CHAMPIONSHIPS
Montreal, Canada, July 17–31, 2005

EVENT	SWIMMER, TEAM	TIME
50-meter freestyle	Lisbeth Lenton, Australia	24.59
100-meter freestyle	Jodie Henry, Australia	54.18
200-meter freestyle	Solenne Figues, France	1:58.60
400-meter freestyle	Laura Manaudou, France	4:06.44
800-meter freestyle	Kate Ziegler, United States	8:25.31
1,500-meter freestyle	Kate Ziegler, United States	16:00.41
50-meter backstroke	Giaan Rooney, Australia	28.63
100-meter backstroke	Kirsty Coventry, Zimbabwe	1:00.24
200-meter backstroke	Kirsty Coventry, Zimbabwe	2:08.52
50-meter breaststroke	Jade Edmistone, Australia	30.45
100-meter breaststroke	Leisel Jones, Australia	1:06.25
200-meter breaststroke	Leisel Jones, Australia	2:21.72
50-meter butterfly	Danni Miatke, Australia	26.11
100-meter butterfly	Jessicah Schipper, Australia	57.23
200-meter butterfly	Otylia Jedrzejczak, Poland	2:05.61
200-meter individual medley	Katie Hoff, United States	2:10.41
400-meter individual medley	Katie Hoff, United States	4:36.07
4x100-meter medley relay	Australia (Sophie Edington, Leisel Jones, Jessicah Schipper, Lisbeth Lenton)	3:57.47
4x100-meter freestyle relay	Australia (Jodie Henry, Alice Mills, Shayne Reese, Lisbeth Lenton)	3:37.32
4x200-meter freestyle relay	United States (Natalie Coughlin, Katie Hoff, Whitney Myers, Kaitlin Sandeno)	7:53.70

U.S. NATIONAL CHAMPIONSHIPS

Irvine, California, August 3–7, 2005

EVENT	SWIMMER, TEAM	TIME
50-meter freestyle	Amanda Weir, Swim Atlanta (Georgia)	25.45
100-meter freestyle	Amanda Weir, Swim Atlanta (Georgia)	54.47
200-meter freestyle	Brittany Reimer, Surrey Knights (Canada)	1:59.73
400-meter freestyle	Brittany Reimer, Surrey Knights (Canada)	4:10.13
800-meter freestyle	Kate Ziegler, The Fish (Virginia)	8:31.11
1,500-meter freestyle	Kate Ziegler, The Fish (Virginia)	16:14.52
100-meter backstroke	Helen Silver, California Aquatics	1:02.64
200-meter backstroke	Leah Retrum, Donner Swim Club (Indiana)	2:11.00
100-meter breaststroke	Jessica Hardy, Irvine Novaquatic (California)	1:07.45
200-meter breaststroke	Rebecca Soni, Scarlet Aquatic (New Jersey)	2:26.27
100-meter butterfly	Elaine Breeden, Wildcat Aquatics (Kentucky)	59.20
200-meter butterfly	Elaine Breeden, Wildcat Aquatics (Kentucky)	2:09.85
200-meter individual medley	Ariana Kukors, King Aquatic Club (Washington)	2:14.57
400-meter individual medley	Ariana Kukors, King Aquatic Club (Washington)	4:43.32
4x100-meter medley relay	Palo Alto Stanford Aquatics A (California)	4:10.00
4x100-meter freestyle relay	California Aquatics A, California Aquatics	3:44.99
4x200-meter freestyle relay	California Aquatics A, California Aquatics	8:13.29

2005-06 TIME LINE

■ **April 2, 2005:** Aaron Peirsol breaks his own world record in the 100-meter backstroke at the World Championships trials.

■ **May 25, 2005:** Janine Pietsch of Germany sets the world record in the 50-meter backstroke at the German Swimming Championships.

■ **July 16-31, 2005:** At the World Championships, the U.S. team sets three world records: Aaron Peirsol breaks the world record in the 200-meter backstroke, Ian Crocker in the 100-meter butterfly, and Jessica Hardy in the 100-meter breaststroke. Grant Hackett of Australia becomes the first freestyler to win the 400, 800, and 1,500 meters in one world championship, giving him a record 17 career world titles.

■ **August 5, 2005:** Michael Phelps wins the 200-meter freestyle at the U.S. Summer Nationals, his 27th national individual title. The win ties him for seventh among male and female swimmers on the all-time list.

■ **November 19, 2005:** Lisbeth Lenton of Australia breaks the world record in the 200-meter freestyle, her second record of the year. She broke the world record in the 100-meter freestyle in August.

■ **December 8-17, 2005:** At the European Championships, Laszlo Cseh of Hungary (200- and 400-meter individual medley) and Laure Manaudou of France (400- and 800-meter freestyle) each break two short-course world records.

■ **February 3-4, 2006:** At the FINA World Cup, Michael Phelps wins three gold medals and breaks two U.S. records (200-meter freestyle and 400-meter individual medley).

■ **March 2-4, 2006:** Eight American short-course records are broken at the American Short Course Championships. Michael Phelps breaks three (200- and 400-yard individual medley, 200-yard butterfly) and Tara Kirk breaks two (100- and 200-yard breaststroke).

■ **March 12, 2006:** Coach Mark Schubert of the University of Southern California is named USA Swimming National Team Head Coach and General Manager. The new position is the highest-ranking coaching spot in USA Swimming.

FREESTYLE

EVENT	TIME	RECORD HOLDER	DATE	SITE
50 meters	21.64	Alexander Popov, Russia (WR)	6-16-00	Moscow, Russia
	21.76	Gary Hall, Jr. (A)	8-15-00	Indianapolis, Indiana
100 meters	47.84	Pieter van den Hoogenband, Netherlands (WR)	9-19-00	Sydney, Australia
	48.17	Jason Lezak (A)	7-10-04	Long Beach, California
200 meters	1:44.06	Ian Thorpe, Australia (WR)	7-25-01	Fukuoka, Japan
	1:45.20	Michael Phelps (A)	7-26-05	Montreal, Canada
400 meters	3:40.08	Ian Thorpe, Australia (WR)	7-30-02	Manchester, England
	3:44.11	Klete Keller (A)	8-14-04	Athens, Greece
800 meters	7:38.65	Grant Hackett, Australia (WR)	7-27-05	Montreal, Canada
	7:45.63	Larsen Jensen (A)	7-27-05	Montreal, Canada
1,500 meters	14:34.56	Grant Hackett, Australia (WR)	7-29-01	Fukuoka, Japan
	14:45.29	Larsen Jensen (A)	8-21-04	Athens, Greece

BACKSTROKE

EVENT	TIME	RECORD HOLDER	DATE	SITE
50 meters	24.80	Thomas Rupprath, Germany (WR)	7-27-03	Barcelona, Spain
	24.99	Lenny Krayzelburg (A)	8-28-99	Sydney, Australia
100 meters	53.17	Aaron Peirsol (WR, A)	4-2-05	Indianapolis, Indiana
200 meters	1:54.66	Aaron Peirsol (WR, A)	7-29-05	Montreal, Canada

BREASTSTROKE

EVENT	TIME	RECORD HOLDER	DATE	SITE
50 meters	27.18	Oleg Lisogor, Ukraine (WR)	8-2-02	Berlin, Germany
	27.39	Ed Moses (A)	3-31-01	Austin, Texas
100 meters	59.30	Brendan Hansen (WR, A)	7-8-04	Long Beach, California
200 meters	2:09.04	Brendan Hansen (WR, A)	7-11-04	Long Beach, California

BUTTERFLY

EVENT	TIME	RECORD HOLDER	DATE	SITE
50 meters	22.96	Roland Schoeman, South Africa (WR)	7-25-05	Montreal, Canada
	23.21	Ian Crocker (A)	7-25-05	Montreal, Canada
100 meters	50.40	Ian Crocker (WR, A)	7-30-05	Montreal, Canada
200 meters	1:53.93	Michael Phelps (WR, A)	7-22-03	Barcelona, Spain

INDIVIDUAL MEDLEY

EVENT	TIME	RECORD HOLDER	DATE	SITE
200 meters	1:55.94	Michael Phelps (WR, A)	8-9-03	College Park, Maryland
400 meters	4:08.26	Michael Phelps (WR, A)	8-14-04	Athens, Greece

Michael Phelps, United States

RELAYS

EVENT	TIME	RECORD HOLDER	DATE	SITE
400-meter medley	3:30.68	United States (WR, A) (Aaron Peirsol, Brendan Hansen, Ian Crocker, Jason Lezak)	8-21-04	Athens, Greece
400-meter freestyle	3:13.17	South Africa (WR, A) (Lyndon Ferns, Ryk Neethling, Roland Schoeman, Darian Townsend)	8-14-04	Athens, Greece
	3:13.77	United States (A) (Michael Phelps, Neil Walker, Nate Dusing, Jason Lezak)	7-24-05	Montreal, Canada
800-meter freestyle	7:04.66	Australia (WR) (Grant Hackett, Michael Klim, Bill Kirby, Ian Thorpe)	7-27-01	Fukuoka, Japan
	7:06.58	United States (A) (Michael Phelps, Ryan Lochte, Peter Vanderkaay, Klete Keller)	7-29-05	Montreal, Canada

KEY (A)=American Record; (WR)=World Record

HEINZ KLUETMEIER

DID YOU KNOW?

In 2003, Aaron and Hayley Peirsol became the only siblings to win medals at the same World Championships.

SWIMMING

WORLD AND AMERICAN RECORDS — WOMEN

FREESTYLE

EVENT	TIME	RECORD HOLDER	DATE	SITE
50 meters	24.13	Inge de Bruijn, Netherlands (WR)	9-22-00	Sydney, Australia
	24.63	Dara Torres (A)	9-23-00	Sydney, Australia
100 meters	53.52	Jodie Henry, Australia (WR)	8-18-04	Athens, Greece
	53.99	Natalie Coughlin (A)	8-29-02	Yokohama, Japan
200 meters	1:56.64	Franziska van Almsick, Germany (WR)	8-3-02	Berlin, Germany
	1:57.41	Lindsay Benko (A)	7-24-03	Barcelona, Spain
400 meters	4:03.03	Laure Manaudou, France (WR)	5-12-06	Tours, France
	4:03.85	Janet Evans (A)	9-22-88	Seoul, South Korea
800 meters	8:16.22	Janet Evans (WR, A)	8-20-89	Tokyo, Japan
1,500 meters	15:52.10	Janet Evans (WR, A)	3-26-88	Orlando, Florida

BACKSTROKE

EVENT	TIME	RECORD HOLDER	DATE	SITE
50 meters	28.19	Janine Pietsch, Germany (WR)	5-25-05	Berlin, Germany
	28.49	Natalie Coughlin (A)	7-23-01	Fukuoka, Japan
100 meters	59.58	Natalie Coughlin (WR, A)	8-13-02	Fort Lauderdale, Florida
200 meters	2:06.62	Krisztina Egerszegi, Hungary (WR)	8-25-91	Athens, Greece
	2:08.53	Natalie Coughlin (A)	8-16-02	Fort Lauderdale, Florida

Natalie Coughlin, United States

HEINZ KLUETMEIER

BREASTSTROKE

EVENT	TIME	RECORD HOLDER	DATE	SITE
50 meters	30.45	Jade Edmistone, Australia (WR)	7-31-05	Montreal, Canada
	30.85	Jessica Hardy (A)	7-31-05	Montreal, Canada
100 meters	1:06.20	Jessica Hardy (WR, A)	7-25-05	Montreal, Canada
200 meters	2:21.72	Leisel Jones, Australia (WR)	7-29-05	Montreal, Canada
	2:22.44	Amanda Beard (A)	7-12-04	Long Beach, California

BUTTERFLY

EVENT	TIME	RECORD HOLDER	DATE	SITE
50 meters	25.57	Anna-Karin Kammerling, Sweden (WR)	7-30-02	Berlin, Germany
	26.00	Jenny Thompson (A)	7-26-03	Barcelona, Spain
100 meters	56.61	Inge de Bruijn, Netherlands (WR)	9-17-00	Sydney, Australia
	57.58	Dara Torres (A)	8-9-00	Indianapolis, Indiana
200 meters	2:05.61	Otylia Jedrejczak, Poland (WR)	7-28-05	Montreal, Canada
	2:05.88	Misty Hyman (A)	9-20-00	Sydney, Australia

INDIVIDUAL MEDLEY

EVENT	TIME	RECORD HOLDER	DATE	SITE
200 meters	2:09.72	Yanyan Wu, China (WR)	10-17-97	Shanghai, China
	2:10.41	Katie Hoff (A)	7-25-05	Montreal, Canada
400 meters	4:33.59	Yana Klochkova, Ukraine (WR)	9-16-00	Sydney, Australia
	4:34.95	Kaitlin Sandeno (A)	8-14-04	Athens, Greece

RELAYS

EVENT	TIME	RECORD HOLDER	DATE	SITE
400-meter medley	3:57.32	Australia (WR) (Giaan Rooney, Leisel Jones, Petria Thomas, Jodie Henry)	8-21-04	Athens, Greece
	3:58.30	United States (A) (B.J. Bedford, Megan Quann, Jenny Thompson, Dara Torres)	9-23-00	Sydney, Australia
400-meter freestyle	3:35.94	Australia (WR) (Jodie Henry, Lisbeth Lenton, Alice Mills, Petria Thomas)	8-14-04	Athens, Greece
	3:36.39	United States (A) (Natalie Coughlin, Kara Lynn Joyce, Jenny Thompson, Amanda Weir)	8-14-04	Athens, Greece
800-meter freestyle	7:53.42	United States (WR, A) (Natalie Coughlin, Carly Piper, Dana Vollmer, Kaitlin Sandeno)	8-18-04	Athens, Greece

LEGENDS

Before she became a TV commentator, Summer Sanders was a butterfly champion.

MANNY MILLAN

■ **Summer Sanders,** b. October 13, 1972, Roseville, California. Sanders is one of the greatest butterfly swimmers of all-time. She won four medals at the 1992 Summer Olympics: gold in the 200-meter butterfly and 400-meter medley relay, silver in the 200-meter individual medley, and bronze in the 400-meter individual medley. She won three medals — including gold in the 200-meter butterfly — at the 1991 World Championships. Sanders is now a commentator for Fox Sports, and hosts *NBA Inside Stuff.*

■ **Pablo Morales,** b. December 5, 1964, Chicago, Illinois. After failing to qualify for the 1988 Summer Olympics, Morales was so disappointed he went into a three-year temporary retirement. He returned for the 1992 Summer Olympics to go for his first individual Olympic gold medal. At age 27, the "Comeback Kid" became the oldest Olympic gold medalist in history when he won the 100-meter butterfly. He also won gold in the 400-meter medley relay that year. At the 1984 Summer Olympics, Morales won a gold medal in the 400-meter medley relay. He also took the silver medal in the 100-meter butterfly and the 200-meter individual medley.

■ **Donna deVarona,** b. April 26, 1947, San Diego, California. DeVarona was the biggest star in swimming in the 1960's. She made the U.S. team for the 1960 Olympics when she was just 13 years old. DeVarona would become one of the world's strongest and most versatile swimmers. At the 1964 Olympics she won gold in the 400-meter individual medley. That year, she was voted America's Most Outstanding Woman Athlete. In a career that lasted only about five years, deVarona won 37 national championship medals, including 18 gold medals.

ALL-TIME WORLD CHAMPIONSHIP RESULTS — MEN

50-METER FREESTYLE

1973-82	Event not held	
1986	Tom Jager, United States	22.49
1991	Tom Jager, United States	22.16
1994	Alexander Popov, Russia	22.17
1998	Bill Pilczuk, United States	22.29
2001	Anthony Ervin, United States	22.09
2003	Alexander Popov, Russia	21.92
2005	Roland Schoeman, South Africa	21.69

100-METER FREESTYLE

1973	Jim Montgomery, United States	51.70
1975	Andy Coan, United States	51.25
1978	David McCagg, United States	50.24
1982	Jorg Woithe, East Germany	50.18
1986	Matt Biondi, United States	48.94
1991	Matt Biondi, United States	49.18
1994	Alexander Popov, Russia	49.12
1998	Alexander Popov, Russia	48.93
2001	Anthony Ervin, United States	48.33
2003	Alexander Popov, Russia	48.42
2005	Filippo Magnini, Italy	48.12

200-METER FREESTYLE

1973	Jim Montgomery, United States	1:53.02
1975	Tim Shaw, United States	1:51.04
1978	Billy Forrester, United States	1:51.02
1982	Michael Gross, West Germany	1:49.84

200-METER FREESTYLE (CONT.)

1986	Michael Gross, West Germany	1:47.92
1991	Giorgio Lamberti, Italy	1:47.27
1994	Antti Kasvio, Finland	1:47.32
1998	Michael Klim, Australia	1:47.41
2001	Ian Thorpe, Australia	1:44.06
2003	Ian Thorpe, Australia	1:45.14
2005	Michael Phelps, USA	1:45.20

400-METER FREESTYLE

1973	Rick DeMont, United States	3:58.18
1975	Tim Shaw, United States	3:54.88
1978	Vladimir Salnikov, U.S.S.R.	3:51.94
1982	Vladimir Salnikov, U.S.S.R.	3:51.30
1986	Rainer Henkel, West Germany	3:50.05
1991	Joerg Hoffman, Germany	3:48.04
1994	Kieran Perkins, Australia	3:43.80
1998	Ian Thorpe, Australia	3:46.29
2001	Ian Thorpe, Australia	3:40.17
2003	Ian Thorpe, Australia	3:42.58
2005	Grant Hackett, Australia	3:42.91

800-METER FREESTYLE

1973-98	Event not held	
2001	Ian Thorpe, Australia	7:39.16
2003	Grant Hackett, Australia	7:43.82
2005	Grant Hackett, Australia	7:38.65

SWIMMING

ALL-TIME WORLD CHAMPIONSHIP RESULTS — MEN (cont.)

1,500-METER FREESTYLE
1973	Stephen Holland, Australia	15:31.85
1975	Tim Shaw, United States	15:28.92
1978	Vladimir Salnikov, U.S.S.R.	15:03.99
1982	Vladimir Salnikov, U.S.S.R.	15:01.77
1986	Rainer Henkel, West Germany	15:05.31
1991	Joerg Hoffman, Germany	14:50.36
1994	Kieran Perkins, Australia	14:50.52
1998	Grant Hackett, Australia	14:51.70
2001	Grant Hackett, Australia	14:34.56
2003	Grant Hackett, Australia	14:43.14
2005	Grant Hackett, Australia	14:42.58

50-METER BACKSTROKE
1973-98	Event not held	
2001	Randall Bal, United States	25.34
2003	Thomas Rupprath, Germany	24.80
2005	Aristeidis Grigoriadis, Greece	24.95

100-METER BACKSTROKE
1973	Roland Matthes, East Germany	57.47
1975	Roland Matthes, East Germany	58.15
1978	Bob Jackson, United States	56.36
1982	Dirk Richter, East Germany	55.95
1986	Igor Polianski, U.S.S.R.	55.58
1991	Jeff Rouse, United States	55.23
1994	Martin Zubero, Spain	55.17
1998	Lenny Krayzelburg, United States	55.00
2001	Matt Welsh, Australia	54.31
2003	Aaron Peirsol, United States	53.61
2005	Aaron Peirsol, United States	53.62

200-METER BACKSTROKE
1973	Roland Matthes, East Germany	2:01.87
1975	Zoltan Varraszto, Hungary	2:05.05
1978	Jesse Vassallo, United States	2:02.16
1982	Rick Carey, United States	2:00.82
1986	Igor Polianski, U.S.S.R.	1:58.78
1991	Martin Zubero, Spain	1:59.52
1994	Vladimir Selkov, Russia	1:57.42
1998	Lenny Krayzelburg, United States	1:58.84
2001	Aaron Peirsol, United States	1:57.13
2003	Aaron Peirsol, United States	1:55.92
2005	Aaron Peirsol, United States	1:54.66

50-METER BREASTSTROKE
1973-98	Event not held	
2001	Oleg Lisogor, Ukraine	27.52
2003	James Gibson, Great Britain	27.56
2005	Mark Warnecke, Germany	27.63

100-METER BREASTSTROKE
1973	John Hencken, United States	1:04.02
1975	David Wilkie, Great Britain	1:04.26
1978	Walter Kusch, West Germany	1:03.56
1982	Steve Lundquist, United States	1:02.75
1986	Victor Davis, Canada	1:02.71
1991	Norbert Rozsa, Hungary	1:01.45
1994	Norbert Rozsa, Hungary	1:01.24
1998	Frederik Deburghgraeve, Belgium	1:01.34
2001	Roman Sloudnov, Russia	1:00.16
2003	Kosuke Kitajima, Japan	59.78
2005	Brendan Hansen, United States	59.37

200-METER BREASTSTROKE
1973	David Wilkie, Great Britain	2:19.28
1975	David Wilkie, Great Britain	2:18.23
1978	Nick Nevid, United States	2:18.37
1982	Victor Davis, Canada	2:14.77
1986	Jozsef Szabo, Hungary	2:14.27
1991	Mike Barrowman, United States	2:11.23
1994	Norbert Rozsa, Hungary	2:12.81
1998	Kurt Grote, United States	2:13.40
2001	Brendan Hansen, United States	2:10.69
2003	Kosuke Kitajima, Japan	2:09.42
2005	Brendan Hansen, United States	2:09.85

50-METER BUTTERFLY
1973-98	Event not held	
2001	Geoff Huegill, Australia	23.50
2003	Matt Welsh, Australia	23.43
2005	Roland Schoeman, South Africa	22.96

100-METER BUTTERFLY
1973	Bruce Robertson, Canada	55.69
1975	Greg Jagenburg, United States	55.63
1978	Joe Bottom, United States	54.30
1982	Matt Gribble, United States	53.88
1986	Pablo Morales, United States	53.54
1991	Anthony Nesty, Suriname	53.29
1994	Rafal Szukala, Poland	53.51
1998	Michael Klim, Australia	52.25
2001	Lars Frolander, Sweden	52.10
2003	Ian Crocker, United States	50.98
2005	Ian Crocker, United States	50.40

200-METER BUTTERFLY
1973	Robin Backhaus, United States	2:03.32
1975	Bill Forrester, United States	2:01.95
1978	Mike Bruner, United States	1:59.38
1982	Michael Gross, West Germany	1:58.85
1986	Michael Gross, West Germany	1:56.53
1991	Melvin Stewart, United States	1:55.69
1994	Denis Pankratov, Russia	1:56.54
1998	Denys Sylantyev, Ukraine	1:56.61
2001	Michael Phelps, United States	1:54.58
2003	Michael Phelps, United States	1:54.35
2005	Pawel Korzeniowski, Poland	1:55.02

200-METER INDIVIDUAL MEDLEY
1973	Gunnar Larsson, Sweden	2:08.36
1975	Andras Hargitay, Hungary	2:07.72
1978	Graham Smith, Canada	2:03.65
1982	Aleksandr Sidorenko, U.S.S.R.	2:03.30
1986	Tamás Darnyi, Hungary	2:01.57
1991	Tamás Darnyi, Hungary	1:59.36
1994	Jani Sievin, Finland	1:58.16
1998	Marcel Wouda, Netherlands	2:01.18
2001	Massimiliano Rosolino, Italy	1:59.71
2003	Michael Phelps, United States	1:56.04
2005	Michael Phelps, United States	1:56.68

400-METER INDIVIDUAL MEDLEY
1973	Andras Hargitay, Hungary	4:31.11
1975	Andras Hargitay, Hungary	4:32.57
1978	Jesse Vassallo, United States	4:20.05
1982	Ricardo Prado, Brazil	4:19.78
1986	Tamás Darnyi, Hungary	4:18.98
1991	Tamás Darnyi, Hungary	4:12.36
1994	Tom Dolan, United States	4:12.30
1998	Tom Dolan, United States	4:14.95
2001	Alessio Boggiatto, Italy	4:13.15
2003	Michael Phelps, United States	4:09.09
2005	Laszlo Cseh, Hungary	4:09.63

400-METER MEDLEY RELAY
1973	United States (Mike Stamm, John Hencken, Joe Bottom, Jim Montgomery)	3:49.49
1975	United States (John Murphy, Rick Colella, Greg Jagenburg, Andy Coan)	3:49.00
1978	United States (Robert Jackson, Nick Nevid, Joe Bottom, David McCagg)	3:44.63
1982	United States (Rick Carey, Steve Lundquist, Matt Gribble, Rowdy Gaines)	3:40.84
1986	United States (Dan Veatch, David Lundberg, Pablo Morales, Matt Biondi)	3:41.25
1991	United States (Jeff Rouse, Eric Wunderlich, Mark Henderson, Matt Biondi)	3:39.66
1994	United States (Jeff Rouse, Eric Wunderlich, Mark Henderson, Gary Hall, Jr.)	3:37.74
1998	Australia (Matt Welsh, Phil Rogers, Michael Klim, Chris Fydler)	3:37.98
2001	Australia (Matt Welsh, Ian Thorpe, Geoff Huegill, Regan Harrison)	3:35.35
2003	United States (Aaron Peirsol, Brendan Hansen, Ian Crocker, Jason Lezak)	3:31.54
2005	United States (Aaron Peirsol, Brendan Hansen, Ian Crocker, Jason Lezak)	3:31.85

400-METER FREESTYLE RELAY

1973	United States (Mel Nash, Joe Bottom, Jim Montgomery, John Murphy)	3:27.18
1975	United States (Bruce Furniss, Jim Montgomery, Andy Coan, John Murphy)	3:24.85
1978	United States (Jack Babashoff, Rowdy Gaines, Jim Montgomery, David McCagg)	3:19.74
1982	United States (Chris Cavanaugh, Robin Leamy, David McCagg, Rowdy Gaines)	3:19.26
1986	United States (Tom Jager, Mike Heath, Paul Wallace, Matt Biondi)	3:19.59
1991	United States (Tom Jager, Brent Lang, Doug Gjertsen, Matt Biondi)	3:17.15
1994	United States (Jon Olsen, Josh Davis, Ugur Taner, Gary Hall)	3:16.90
1998	United States (Scott Tucker, Jon Olsen, Neil Walker, Gary Hall)	3:16.69
2001	Australia (Michael Klim, Ian Thorpe, Todd Pearson, Ashley Callus)	3:14.10
2003	Russia (Andrei Kapralov, Ivan Usov, Denis Pimankov, Alexander Popov)	3:14.06
2005	United States (Michael Phelps, Neil Walker, Nate Dusing, Jason Lezak)	3:13.77

800-METER FREESTYLE RELAY

1973	United States (Kurt Krumpholz, Robin Backhaus, Rick Klatt, Jim Montgomery)	7:33.22
1975	West Germany (Klaus Steinbach, Werner Lampe, Hans Joachim Geisler, Peter Nocke)	7:39.44
1978	United States (Bruce Furniss, Billy Forrester, Bobby Hackett, Rowdy Gaines)	7:20.82
1982	United States (Rich Saeger, Jeff Float, Kyle Miller, Rowdy Gaines)	7:21.09
1986	East Germany (Lars Hinneburg, Thomas Flemming, Dirk Richter, Sven Lodziewski)	7:15.91
1991	Germany (Peter Sitt, Steffen Zesner, Stefan Pfeiffer, Michael Gross)	7:13.50
1994	Sweden (Christer Waller, Tommy Werner, Lars Frolander, Anders Holmertz)	7:17.74
1998	Australia (Daniel Kowalski, Grant Hackett, Ian Thorpe, Michael Klim)	7:12.48
2001	Australia (Michael Klim, Ian Thorpe, William Kirby, Grant Hackett)	7:04.66
2003	Australia (Grant Hackett, Craig Stevens, Nicholas Sprenger, Ian Thorpe)	7:08.58
2005	United States (Michael Phelps, Ryan Lochte, Peter Vanderkaay, Klete Keller)	7:06.58

TODAY'S STARS

Katie Hoff was a three-time world champion in 2005.

■ **Katie Hoff,** b. June 3, 1989, Stanford, California. Hoff is well on her way to becoming one of the world's top all-around swimmers. At 15, she was the youngest athlete in any sport on the 2004 U.S. Olympic team. While Hoff didn't win a medal at the Athens Olympics, she had a breakout year in 2005. She won three gold medals at the World Championships: the 200- and 400-meter individual medley, and the 800-meter freestyle relay. Hoff set the American record in the 200-meter individual medley at that meet. She officially turned professional in October 2005, giving up her collegiate eligibility.

■ **Ian Crocker,** b. August 31, 1982, Portland, Maine. A butterfly specialist, Crocker won gold medals in the 400-meter medley relay at the 2000 and 2004 Olympics. He added a silver medal in the 100-meter butterfly at the 2004 Games. In the 2005 World Championships, Crocker won two gold medals (100-meter butterfly, 400-meter medley relay) and a silver (50-meter butterfly). Crocker was a 10-time NCAA champion while competing for the University of Texas. He's one of only three swimmers to win four consecutive NCAA 100-meter butterfly titles (along with Mark Spitz and Pablo Morales).

■ **Grant Hackett,** b. May 9, 1980, Mermaid Waters, Australia. Hackett had one of the greatest all-time performances at the 2005 World Championships. He became the first swimmer to ever win the 400-, 800-, and 1,500-meter freestyle at the same World Championships. He also became the first swimmer to win the 1,500 at the Worlds four consecutive times. The three wins in 2005 gave him 17 career titles at the World Championships, more than any swimmer in history. Hackett also won two Olympic gold medals in the 1,500 (in 2000 and 2004).

SWIMMING

ALL-TIME WORLD CHAMPIONSHIPS RESULTS – WOMEN

50-METER FREESTYLE

1973-82	Event not held	
1986	Tamara Costache, Romania	25.28
1991	Zhuang Yong, China	25.47
1994	Le Jingyi, China	24.51
1998	Amy Van Dyken, United States	25.15
2001	Inge de Bruijn, Netherlands	24.47
2003	Inge de Bruijn, Netherlands	24.47
2005	Lisbeth Lenton, Australia	24.59

100-METER FREESTYLE

1973	Kornelia Ender, East Germany	57.54
1975	Kornelia Ender, East Germany	56.50
1978	Barbara Krause, East Germany	55.68
1982	Birgit Meineke, East Germany	55.79
1986	Kristin Otto, East Germany	55.05
1991	Nicole Haislett, United States	55.17
1994	Le Jingyi, China	54.01
1998	Jenny Thompson, United States	54.95
2001	Inge de Bruijn, Netherlands	54.18
2003	Hanna-Maria Seppala, Finland	54.37
2005	Jodie Henry, Australia	54.18

200-METER FREESTYLE

1973	Keena Rothhammer, United States	2:04.99
1975	Shirley Babashoff, United States	2:02.50
1978	Cynthia Woodhead, United States	1:58.53
1982	Annemarie Verstappen, Netherlands	1:59.53
1986	Heike Friedrich, East Germany	1:58.26
1991	Hayley Lewis, Australia	2:00.48
1994	Franziska Van Almsick, Germany	1:56.78
1998	Claudia Poll, Costa Rica	1:58.90
2001	Giaan Rooney, Australia	1:58.57
2003	Alena Popchanka, Belarus	1:58.32
2005	Solenne Figues, France	1:58.60

400-METER FREESTYLE

1973	Heather Greenwood, United States	4:20.28
1975	Shirley Babashoff, United States	4:16.87
1978	Tracey Wickham, Australia	4:06.28
1982	Carmela Schmidt, East Germany	4:08.98
1986	Heike Friedrich, East Germany	4:07.45
1991	Janet Evans, United States	4:08.63
1994	Yang Aihua, China	4:09.64
1998	Chen Yan, China	4:06.72
2001	Yana Klochkova, Ukraine	4:07.30
2003	Hannah Stockbauer, Germany	4:06.75
2005	Laure Manaudou, France	4:06.44

800-METER FREESTYLE

1973	Novella Calligaris, Italy	8:52.97
1975	Jenny Turrall, Australia	8:44.75
1978	Tracey Wickham, Australia	8:24.94
1982	Kim Linehan, United States	8:27.48
1986	Astrid Strauss, East Germany	8:28.24
1991	Janet Evans, United States	8:24.05
1994	Janet Evans, United States	8:29.85
1998	Brooke Bennett, United States	8:28.71
2001	Hannah Stockbauer, Germany	8:24.66
2003	Hannah Stockbauer, Germany	8:23.66
2005	Kate Ziegler, United States	8:25.31

1,500-METER FREESTYLE

1973-98	Event not held	
2001	Hannah Stockbauer, Germany	16:01.02
2003	Hannah Stockbauer, Germany	16:00.18
2005	Kate Ziegler, United States	16:00.41

50-METER BACKSTROKE

1973-98	Event not held	
2001	Haley Cope, United States	28.51
2003	Nina Zhivanevskaya, Spain	28.48
2005	Giann Rooney, Australia	28.63

100-METER BACKSTROKE

1973	Ulrike Richter, East Germany	1:05.42
1975	Ulrike Richter, East Germany	1:03.30
1978	Linda Jezek, United States	1:02.55
1982	Kristin Otto, East Germany	1:01.30
1986	Betsy Mitchell, United States	1:01.74
1991	Krisztina Egerszegi, Hungary	1:01.78
1994	He Cihong, China	1:00.57
1998	Lea Maurer, United States	1:01.16
2001	Natalie Coughlin, United States	1:00.37
2003	Antje Buschschulte, Germany	1:00.50
2005	Kirsty Coventry, Zimbabwe	1:00.24

200-METER BACKSTROKE

1973	Melissa Belote, United States	2:20.52
1975	Birgit Treiber, East Germany	2:15.46
1978	Linda Jezek, United States	2:11.93
1982	Cornelia Sirch, East Germany	2:09.91
1986	Cornelia Sirch, East Germany	2:11.37
1991	Krisztina Egerszegi, Hungary	2:09.15
1994	He Cihong, China	2:07.40
1998	Roxanna Maracineanu, France	2:11.26
2001	Diana Mocanu, Romania	2:09.94
2003	Katy Sexton, Great Britain	2:08.74
2005	Kirsty Coventry, Zimbabwe	2:08.52

50-METER BREASTSTROKE

1973-98	Event not held	
2001	Xuejuan Luo, China	30.84
2003	Xuejuan Luo, China	30.67
2005	Jade Edmistone, Australia	30.45

100-METER BREASTSTROKE

1973	Renate Vogel, East Germany	1:13.74
1975	Hannalore Anke, East Germany	1:12.72
1978	Julia Bogdanova, U.S.S.R.	1:10.31
1982	Ute Geweniger, East Germany	1:09.14
1986	Sylvia Gerasch, East Germany	1:08.11
1991	Linley Frame, Australia	1:08.81
1994	Samantha Riley, Australia	1:07.96
1998	Kristy Kowal, United States	1:08.42
2001	Xuejuan Luo, China	1:07.18
2003	Xuejuan Luo, China	1:06.80
2005	Leisel Jones, Australia	1:06.25

200-METER BREASTSTROKE

1973	Renate Vogel, East Germany	2:40.01
1975	Hannalore Anke, East Germany	2:37.25
1978	Lina Kachushite, U.S.S.R.	2:31.42
1982	Svetlana Varganova, U.S.S.R.	2:28.82
1986	Silke Hoerner, East Germany	2:27.40
1991	Elena Volkova, U.S.S.R.	2:29.53
1994	Samantha Riley, Australia	2:26.87
1998	Agnes Kovacs, Hungary	2:25.45
2001	Agnes Kovacs, Hungary	2:24.90
2003	Amanda Beard, United States	2:22.99
2005	Leisel Jones, Australia	2:21.72

50-METER BUTTERFLY

1973-98	Event not held	
2001	Inge de Bruijn, Netherlands	25.90
2003	Inge de Bruijn, Netherlands	25.84
2005	Danni Miatke, Australia	26.11

100-METER BUTTERFLY

1973	Kornelia Ender, East Germany	1:02.53
1975	Kornelia Ender, East Germany	1:01.24
1978	Joan Pennington, United States	1:00.20
1982	Mary T. Meagher, United States	59.41
1986	Kornelia Gressler, East Germany	59.51
1991	Qian Hong, China	59.68
1994	Liu Limin, China	58.98
1998	Jenny Thompson, United States	58.46
2001	Petria Thomas, Australia	58.27
2003	Jenny Thompson, United States	57.96
2005	Jessica Schipper, Australia	57.23

200-METER BUTTERFLY

1973	Rosemarie Kother, East Germany	2:13.76
1975	Rosemarie Kother, East Germany	2:13.82
1978	Tracy Caulkins, United States	2:09.87
1982	Ines Geissler, East Germany	2:08.66
1986	Mary T. Meagher, United States	2:08.41
1991	Summer Sanders, United States	2:09.24
1994	Liu Limin, China	2:07.25
1998	Susie O'Neill, Australia	2:07.93
2001	Petria Thomas, Australia	2:06.73
2003	Otylia Jedrzejczak, Poland	2:07.56
2005	Otylia Jedrzejczak, Poland	2:05.61

200-METER INDIVIDUAL MEDLEY

1973	Andrea Huebner, East Germany	2:20.51
1975	Kathy Heddy, United States	2:19.80
1978	Tracy Caulkins, United States	2:14.07
1982	Petra Schneider, East Germany	2:11.79
1986	Kristin Otto, East Germany	2:15.56
1991	Li Lin, China	2:13.40
1994	Lu Bin, China	2:12.34
1998	Wu Yanyan, China	2:10.88
2001	Martha Bowen, United States	2:11.93
2003	Yana Klochkova, Ukraine	2:10.75
2005	Katie Hoff, United States	2:10.41

400-METER INDIVIDUAL MEDLEY

1973	Gudrun Wegner, East Germany	4:57.71
1975	Ulrike Tauber, East Germany	4:52.76
1978	Tracy Caulkins, United States	4:40.83
1982	Petra Schneider, East Germany	4:36.10
1986	Kathleen Nord, East Germany	4:43.75
1991	Li Lin, China	4:41.45
1994	Dai Guohong, China	4:39.14
1998	Chen Yan, China	4:36.66
2001	Yana Klochkova, Ukraine	4:36.98
2003	Yana Klochkova, Ukraine	4:36.74
2005	Katie Hoff, United States	4:36.07

400-METER MEDLEY RELAY

1973	East Germany (Ulrike Richter, Renate Vogel, Rosemarie Kother, Kornelia Ender)	4:16.84
1975	East Germany (Ulrike Richter, Hannelore Anke, Rosemarie Kother, Kornelia Ender)	4:14.74
1978	United States (Linda Jezek, Tracy Caulkins, Joan Pennington, Cynthia Woodhead)	4:08.21
1982	East Germany (Kristin Otto, Ute Gewinger, Ines Geissler, Birgit Meineke)	4:05.80
1986	East Germany (Kathrin Zimmermann, Sylvia Gerasch, Kornelia Gressler, Kristin Otto)	4:04.82
1991	United States (Janie Wagstaff, Tracey McFarlane, Crissy Ahmann-Leighton, Nicole Haislett)	4:06.51
1994	China (He Cihong, Dai Guohong, Liu Limin, Lu Bin)	4:01.67
1998	United States (Kristy Kowal, Lea Maurer, Jenny Thompson, Amy Van Dyken)	4:01.93
2001	Australia (Dyana Calub, Sarah Ryan, Petria Thomas, Leisel Jones)	4:01.50
2003	China (Shu Zhan, Xuejuan Luo, Yafei Zhou, Yu Yang)	3:59.89
2005	Australia (Sophie Edington, Leisel Jones, Jessicah Schipper, Lisbeth Lenton)	3:57.47

400-METER FREESTYLE RELAY

1973	East Germany (Kornelia Ender, Andrea Eife, Andrea Huebner, Sylvia Eichner)	3:52.45
1975	East Germany (Kornelia Ender, Barbara Krause, Claudia Hempel, Ute Bruckner)	3:49.37
1978	United States (Tracy Caulkins, Stephanie Elkins, Jill Sterkel, Cynthia Woodhead)	3:43.43
1982	East Germany (Birgit Meineke, Susanne Link, Kristin Otto, Caren Metschuk)	3:43.97
1986	East Germany (Kristin Otto, Manuela Stellmach, Sabine Schulze, Heike Friedrich)	3:40.57
1991	United States (Nicole Haislett, Julie Cooper, Whitney Hedgepeth, Jenny Thompson)	3:43.26
1994	China (Le Jingyi, Ying Shan, Le Ying, Lu Bin)	3:37.91
1998	United States (Catherine Fox, Lindsey Farella, Melanie Valerio, B.J. Bedford)	3:42.11
2001	Germany (Petra Dallman, Antje Buschschulter, Katrin Meissner, Sandra Volker)	3:39.58
2003	United States (Natalie Coughlin, Lindsay Benko, Rhi Jeffrey, Jenny Thompson)	3:38.09
2005	Australia (Jodie Henry, Alice Mills, Shayne Reese, Lisbeth Lenton)	3:37.32

800-METER FREESTYLE RELAY

1973–82	Event not held	
1986	East Germany (Manuela Stellmach, Astrid Strauss, Nadja Bergknecht, Heike Friedrich)	7:59.33
1991	Germany (Kerstin Kielgass, Manuela Stellmach, Dagmar Hase, Stephanie Ortwig)	8:02.56
1994	China (Le Ying, Yang Alhua, Zhou Guabin, Lu Bin)	7:57.96
1998	Germany (Silvia Szalai, Antje Buschschulte, Janina Goetz, Franziska Van Almsick)	8:01.46
2001*	Great Britain (Nicola Jackson, Janine Belton, Karen Legg, Karen Pickering) / United States (Natalie Coughlin, Cristina Teuscher, Julie Hardt, Diana Munz)*	7:56.53
2003	United States (Lindsay Benko, Rachel Komisarz, Rhi Jeffrey, Diana Munz)	7:55.70
2005	United States (Natalie Coughlin, Katie Hoff, Whitney Myers, Kaitlin Sandeno)	7:53.70

FAST FACT

In 1984, Americans Carrie Steinseifer and Nancy Hogshead had the first tie in Olympic gold-medal history, in the 100-meter freestyle. They were each awarded a gold medal.

*Because of timing malfunctions and an overturned disqualification of the United States, gold medals were awarded to Great Britain and the U.S.

TRACK and FIELD

BILL FRAKES

Justin Gatlin (center) **won the 100 and 200 meters at the World Championships.**

Athens, Greece. But he returned to the city in June 2005 for the Tsiklitiria Super Grand Prix and broke the world record in the 100 meters. He topped the old record of 9.78 seconds, held by American Tim Montgomery, by just 1/100th of a second.

Gatlin, who would tie the record in 2006, did not run in Athens. But he had beaten Powell in the 100 meters less than two weeks earlier at the Nike Prefontaine Classic. A month after Powell's record-setting run, Gatlin beat him again at the Norwich Union Grand Prix, when Powell suffered a groin injury. The injury kept Powell out of a re-match at the World Championships.

Many familiar faces from Team USA made headlines in the past year.

American sprinter Justin Gatlin staked his claim to the title of the "World's Fastest Man." Gatlin became the first man in 20 years to win the 100 and 200 meters at the U.S. National Championships. He repeated the feat at the International Association of Athletics Federations (IAAF) World Championships. Then, in May 2006, he tied the world record in the 100 meters (9.77 seconds) set by Asafa Powell of Jamaica less than a year earlier.

Americans won a meet-record 14 gold medals at the World Championships. Shotputter Adam Nelson won a gold medal in a major championship for the first time, and Bryan Clay claimed gold in the de-

cathlon. On the women's side, Lauryn Williams won the 100 meters, and little-known Tianna Madison pulled off an upset win in the long jump, which made her the second American woman to win the event at the Worlds (along with legend Jackie Joyner-Kersee).

American distance runners had a solid season, too. In September, Deena Kastor broke the 21-year-old American half-marathon record (1:07:53) at the Philadelphia Distance Run. Three weeks later, she became the first American woman in 11 years to win a major marathon by taking the Chicago Marathon.

Athletes around the world made their marks as well, beginning with Asafa Powell.

Powell, Gatlin's main rival, had finished a disappointing fifth at the 2004 Olympics in

Kenenisa Bekele of Ethiopia continued to leave his competition in the dust. He broke his own record in the 10,000 meters (26:17.53) at the Van Damme Memorial in Brussels, Belgium. Bekele is also the world record holder in the 5,000, which he set in 2004.

Haile Gebrselassie, also of Ethiopia, broke the world record in the half marathon (58:55) and 20 kilometers (55:48) in January. He then set the world mark in the 25 kilometers (1:11:37) in March.

Note: As this book went to press, Justin Gatlin was banned from competition for eight years for using performance-enhancing drugs. He also lost his share of the 100-meter world record.

Paul Tergat of Kenya won the closest race in the history of the New York Marathon. He beat Hendrick Ramaala of South Africa by just one second.

Pole vaulter Yelena Isinbayeva of Russia continued to compete in a class of her own. She raised her world records in both the outdoor (to 5.01 meters) and indoor (4.91 meters) events.

Along with Isinbayeva, sprinter Olesya Krasnomovets helped the Russian team reach the highest medal count (18) at the World Indoor Championships in Moscow, Russia, in March 2006. Krasnomovets won the 400 meters, then led the Russian 4x400 relay team to a gold medal.

YVES LOGGHE/AP

Yelena Isinbayeva is queen of the pole vault.

2005 WORLD TRACK AND FIELD CHAMPIONSHIPS

AUGUST 6–14, 2005,
HELSNIKI, FINLAND

Men's 100 Meters

ATHLETE	COUNTRY	TIME
Justin Gatlin	United States	9.88
Michael Frater	Jamaica	10.05
Kim Collins	St. Kitts & Nevis	10.05

Lauryn Williams, United States

BILL FRAKES

Women's 100 Meters

ATHLETE	COUNTRY	TIME
Lauryn Williams	United States	10.93
Veronica Campbell	Jamaica	10.95
Christine Arron	France	10.98

Men's 200 Meters

ATHLETE	COUNTRY	TIME
Justin Gatlin	United States	20.04
Wallace Spearmon	United States	20.20
John Capel	United States	20.31

Women's 200 Meters

ATHLETE	COUNTRY	TIME
Allyson Felix	United States	22.16
Rachelle Boone-Smith	United States	22.31
Christine Arron	France	22.31

Men's 400 Meters

ATHLETE	COUNTRY	TIME
Jeremy Wariner	United States	43.93
Andrew Rock	United States	44.35
Tyler Christopher	Canada	44.44

Women's 400 Meters

ATHLETE	COUNTRY	TIME
Tonique Williams-Darling	Bahamas	49.55
Sanya Richards	United States	49.74
Ana Guevara	Mexico	49.81

Men's 800 Meters

ATHLETE	COUNTRY	TIME
Rashid Ramzi	Bahrain	1:44.24
Yurly Borzakovskiy	Russia	1:44.51
William Yiampoy	Kenya	1:44.55

Women's 800 Meters

ATHLETE	COUNTRY	TIME
Zulia Calatayud	Cuba	1:58.82
Hasna Benhassi	Morocco	1:59.42
Tatyana Andrianova	Russia	1:59.60

Men's 1,500 Meters

ATHLETE	COUNTRY	TIME
Rashid Ramzi	Bahrain	3:37.88
Adil Kaouch	Morocco	3:38.00
Rui Ailva	Portugal	3:38.02

Women's 1,500 Meters

ATHLETE	COUNTRY	TIME
Tatyana Tomashova	Russia	4:00.35
Olga Yegorova	Russia	4:01.46
Bouchra Ghezielle	France	4:02.45

Men's 5,000 Meters

ATHLETE	COUNTRY	TIME
Benjamin Limo	Kenya	13:32.55
Sileshi Sihine	Ethiopia	13:32.81
Craig Mottram	Australia	13:32.96

Women's 5,000 Meters

ATHLETE	COUNTRY	TIME
Tirunesh Dibaba	Ethiopia	14:38.59
Meseret Defar	Ethiopia	14:39.54
Ejegayehu Dibaba	Ethiopia	14:42.47

TRACK and FIELD

2005 WORLD TRACK AND FIELD CHAMPIONSHIPS (cont.)

Men's 10,000 Meters

ATHLETE	COUNTRY	TIME
Kenenisa Bekele	Ethiopia	27:08.33
Sileshi Sihine	Ethiopia	27:08.87
Moses Mosop	Kenya	27:08.96

Women's 10,000 Meters

ATHLETE	COUNTRY	TIME
Tirunesh Dibaba	Ethiopia	30:24.02
Berhane Adere	Ethiopia	30:25.41
Ejegayehu Dibaba	Ethiopia	30:26.00

Men's 110-Meter Hurdles

ATHLETE	COUNTRY	TIME
Ladji Doucouré	France	13.07
Xiang Liu	China	13.08
Allen Johnson	United States	13.10

Women's 100-Meter Hurdles

ATHLETE	COUNTRY	TIME
Michelle Perry	United States	12.66
Delloreen Ennis-London	Jamaica	12.76
Brigitte Foster-Hylton	Jamaica	12.76

Bershawn Jackson, United States

Men's 400-Meter Hurdles

ATHLETE	COUNTRY	TIME
Bershawn Jackson	United States	47.30
James Carter	United States	47.43
Dai Tamesue	Japan	48.10

Women's 400-Meter Hurdles

ATHLETE	COUNTRY	TIME
Yuliya Pechonkina	Russia	52.90
Lashinda Demus	United States	53.27
Sandra Glover	United States	53.32

Men's 3,000-Meter Steeplechase

ATHLETE	COUNTRY	TIME
Saaeed Shaheen Saif	Qatar	8:13.31
Ezekiel Kemboi	Kenya	8:14.95
Brimin Kipruto	Kenya	8:15.30

Women's 3,000-Meter Steeplechase

ATHLETE	COUNTRY	TIME
Docus Inzikuru	Uganda	9:18.24
Yekatarina Volkova	Russia	9:20.49
Jeruto Kiptum	Kenya	9:26.95

Men's 20,000-Meter Race Walk

ATHLETE	COUNTRY	TIME
Jefferson Pérez	Ecuador	1:18.35
Javier Fernández Francisco	Spain	1:19.36
Juan Manuel Molina	Spain	1:19.44

Women's 20,000-Meter Race Walk

ATHLETE	COUNTRY	TIME
Olimpiada Ivanova	Russia	1:25.41
Ryta Turava	Belarus	1:27.05
Susana Feitor	Portugal	1:28.44

Men's High Jump

ATHLETE	COUNTRY	HEIGHT
Yuriy Krymarenko	Urkraine	2.32
Víctor Moya	Cuba	2.29
Yaroslav Rybakov	Russia	2.29

Kajsa Bergqvist, Sweden

Women's High Jump

ATHLETE	COUNTRY	HEIGHT
Kajsa Bergqvist	Sweden	2.02
Chaunte Howard	United States	2.00
Emma Green	Sweden	1.96

Men's Pole Vault

ATHLETE	COUNTRY	HEIGHT
Rens Blom	Netherlands	5.80
Brad Walker	United States	5.75
Pavel Gerasimov	Russia	5.65

Women's Pole Vault

ATHLETE	COUNTRY	HEIGHT
Yelena Isinbayeva	Russia	5.01
Monika Pyrek	Poland	4.60
Pavla Hamácková	Czech Republic	4.50

Men's Long Jump

ATHLETE	COUNTRY	DISTANCE
Dwight Phillips	United States	8.60
Ignisious Gaisah	Ghana	8.34
Tommi Evilä	Finland	8.25

Women's Long Jump

ATHLETE	COUNTRY	DISTANCE
Tianna Madison	United States	6.89
Tatyana Kotova	Russia	6.79
Eunice Barber	France	6.76

Men's Triple Jump

ATHLETE	COUNTRY	DISTANCE
Walter Davis	United States	17.57
Yoandri Betanzos	Cuba	17.42
Marian Oprea	Romania	17.40

Note: Height and distance measured in meters.

Women's Triple Jump

ATHLETE	COUNTRY	DISTANCE
Trecia Smith	Jamica	15.11
Yargelis Savigne	Cuba	14.82
Anna Pyatykh	Russia	14.78

**Adam Nelson,
United States**

RUBEN SPRICH/REUTERS

Men's Shot Put

ATHLETE	COUNTRY	DISTANCE
Adam Nelson	United States	21.73
Rutger Smith	Netherlands	21.29
Ralf Bartels	Germany	20.99

Women's Shot Put

ATHLETE	COUNTRY	DISTANCE
Nadzeya Ostapchuk	Belarus	20.51
Olga Ryabinkina	Russia	19.64
Valerie Vili	New Zealand	19.62

Men's Discus

ATHLETE	COUNTRY	DISTANCE
Virgilijus Alekna	Lithuania	70.17
Gerd Kanter	Estonia	68.57
Michael Möllenbeck	Germany	65.95

Women's Discus

ATHLETE	COUNTRY	DISTANCE
Franka Dietzsch	Germany	66.56
Natalya Sadova	Russia	64.33
Vera Popís´ilová-Cechlová	Czech Republic	63.19

Men's Hammer Throw

ATHLETE	COUNTRY	DISTANCE
Ivan Tikhon	Belarus	83.89
Vadim Devyatovskiy	Belarus	82.60
Szymon Ziółkowski	Poland	79.35

Women's Hammer Throw

ATHLETE	COUNTRY	DISTANCE
Olga Kuzenkova	Russia	75.10
Yipsi Moreno	Cuba	73.08
Tatyana Lysenko	Russia	72.46

Men's Decathlon

ATHLETE	COUNTRY	POINTS
Brian Clay	United States	8,732
Roman S˜ebrle	Czech Republic	8,521
Attila Zsivóczky	Hungary	8,385

Men's Javelin

ATHLETE	COUNTRY	DISTANCE
Andrus Värnik	Estonia	87.17
Andreas Thorkildsen	Norway	86.18
Sergey Makarov	Russia	83.54

Women's Javelin

ATHLETE	COUNTRY	DISTANCE
Osleidys Menéndez	Cuba	71.70
Christina Obergföll	Germany	70.03
Steffi Nerius	Germany	65.96

Women's Heptathlon

ATHLETE	COUNTRY	POINTS
Carolina Klüft	Sweden	6,887
Eunice Barber	France	6,824
Margaret Simpson	Ghana	6,375

Men's 50km Walk

ATHLETE	COUNTRY	TIME
Sergey Kirdyapkin	Russia	3:38.08
Aleksey Voyevodin	Russia	3:41.25
Alex Schwazer	Italy	3:41.54

Men's 4x100m Relay

TEAM	COUNTRY	TIME
Ladji Doucouré, Ronald Pognon, Eddy De Lépine, Lueyi Dovy	France	38.08
Kevon Pierre, Marc Burns, Jacey Harper, Darrel Brown	Trinidad and Tobago	38.10
Jason Gardener, Marlon Devonish, Christian Malcolm, Mark Lewis-Francis	Great Britain	38.27

Women's 4x100m Relay

TEAM	COUNTRY	TIME
Angela Daigle-Bowen, Muna Lee, Me'Lisa Barber, Lauryn Williams	United States	41.78
Daniele Browning, Sherone Simpson, Aleen Bailey, Veronica Campbell	Jamaica	41.99
Yuliya Nesterenko, Natallia Solohub, Alena Nevmerzhitskaya, Oksana Drahun	Belarus	42.56

Men's 4x400m Relay

TEAM	COUNTRY	TIME
Andrew Rock, Derrick Brew, Darold Williliamson, Jeremy Wariner	United States	2:56.91
Nathaniel McKinney, Avard Moncur, Andrae Williams, Christopher Brown	Bahamas	2:57.32
Sanjay Ayre, Brandon Simpson, Lanceford Spence, Davian Clarke	Jamaica	2:58.07

Women's 4x400m Relay

TEAM	COUNTRY	TIME
Yuliya Pechonkina, Natalya Antyukh, Olesya Krasnomovets, Svetlana Pospelova	Russia	3:20.95
Shericka Williams, Novlene Williams, Ronetta Smith, Lorraine Fenton	Jamaica	3:23.29
Lee McConnell, Donna Fraser, Nicola Sanders, Christine Ohuruogu	Great Britain	3:24.44

TRACK and FIELD

LEGENDS

Evelyn Ashford, won five Olympic gold medals.

■ **Evelyn Ashford, sprinter,** b. April 15, 1957, Shreveport, Louisiana. Despite being one of the greatest female sprinters of all-time, Ashford nearly missed her chance to win an individual Olympic gold medal. She finished fifth in the 100 meters as a 19-year-old in the 1976 Olympics. But then the U.S. team boycotted the 1980 Games. Ashford finally won her individual gold medals at the 1984 and 1988 Olympics. She also won Olympic 4x100 relay gold medals in '84, '88, and '92. Among her other accomplishments, Ashford won double gold — 100 and 200 meters — in the 1979 and 1981 World Cups. She also won 19 national titles.

■ **Bruce Jenner, decathlete,** b. October 28, 1949, Mount Kisco, New York. Jenner was a football player first — he earned a scholarship to Graceland University in Iowa — before a knee injury ended his career in that sport. He had little experience in the decathlon, but it didn't take him long to become the world's best. After finishing 10th at the 1972 Olympics, Jenner went on to set two world records in the event on his way to the 1976 Games. At the '76 Olympics, he broke his own world record again in winning the gold. Jenner earned the Sullivan Award that year as the top amateur athlete in the United States.

■ **Steve Prefontaine, distance runner,** b. January 25, 1951, Coos Bay, Oregon; d. May 30, 1975, Eugene, Oregon. "Pre" was considered the greatest United States distance runner of all-time before his death in a car accident at age 24. Pre finished fourth in the 5,000 meters at the 1972 Olympics. He then set every American record from the 2,000 to the 10,000 meters on the way to the 1976 Olympics but passed away before he could compete. At the University of Oregon, Pre won three NCAA Cross Country championships. He also won four NCAA track and field three-mile championships, becoming the first athlete to win four consecutive NCAA titles in the same event.

2006 U.S. INDOOR TRACK AND FIELD CHAMPIONSHIPS

FEBRUARY 24–26, 2006
BOSTON, MASSACHUSETTS

Women's 60 Meters

ATHLETE	TEAM	TIME
Me'Lisa Barber	Adidas	7.06
Lauryn Williams	Nike	7.11
Torri Edwards	Unattached	7.12

Men's 60 Meters

ATHLETE	TEAM	TIME
Leonard Scott	Nike	6.52
Terrence Trammell	Mizuno	6.53
Jason Smoots	Nike	6.55

Women's 400 Meters

ATHLETE	TEAM	TIME
Sanya Richards	Nike	51.28
Mary Danner	Unattached	52.69
Debbie Dunn	Unattached	53.17

Men's 400 Meters

ATHLETE	TEAM	TIME
Milton Campbell	Unattached	46.17
LaShawn Merritt	Nike	46.17
Tyree Washington	Nike	46.18

Women's 800 Meters

ATHLETE	TEAM	TIME
Alice Schmidt	Adidas	2:01.93
Frances Santin	Santa Monica	2:03.51
Krista Ferrara	Farm Team	2:04.51

Men's 800 Meters

ATHLETE	TEAM	TIME
Khadevis Robinson	Nike	1:46.98
David Krummenacker	Adidas	1:47.25
Samuel Burley	Asics	1:48.54

Women's 1,500 Meters

ATHLETE	TEAM	TIME
Treniere Clement	Nike	4:08.13
Tiffany McWilliams	Adidas	4:09.17
Jenelle Deatherage	Reebok	4:11.75

Men's 1,500 Meters

ATHLETE	TEAM	TIME
Christopher Lukezic	Reebok	3:41.84
Jason Lunn	Nike	3:41.98
Sean O'Brien	Farm Team	3:42.53

Women's 3,000 Meters

ATHLETE	TEAM	TIME
Carrie Tollefson	Adidas	9:05.80
Sara Hall	Asics	9:06.33
Sarah Schwald	Nike	9:08.28

Men's 3,000 Meters

ATHLETE	TEAM	TIME
Adam Goucher	Nike	7:49.78
Jonathon Riley	Nike	7:51.88
Luke Watson	Adidas	7:55.29

Women's 60-Meter Hurdles

ATHLETE	TEAM	TIME
Danielle Carruthers	Nike	7.93
Damu Cherry	Unattached	7.95
Lolo Jones	Nike	7.99

Men's 60-Meter Hurdles

ATHLETE	TEAM	TIME
Terrence Trammell	Mizuno	7.46
Dominique Arnold	Nike	7.51
Anwar Moore	Nike	7.52

Women's 3,000-Meter Race Walk

ATHLETE	TEAM	TIME
Joanne Dow	Adidas	12:45.05
Jolene Moore	New York AC	13:03.90
Amber Antonia	New York AC	13:13.24

Men's 5,000-Meter Race Walk

ATHLETE	TEAM	TIME
Tim Seaman	New York AC	19:15.88
Kevin Eastler	USAF	19:43.41
Benjamin Shorey	Wisc-Parkside	21:00.87

Women's High Jump

ATHLETE	TEAM	HEIGHT
Chaunte Howard	Nike	1.95m
Amy Acuff	Asics	1.89m
Gwen Wentland	Nike	1.86m

Men's High Jump

ATHLETE	TEAM	HEIGHT
Adam Shunk*	Nike	2.25m
Tora Harris	Shore AC	2.25m
Jesse Williams	USC	2.22m

Women's Pole Vault

ATHLETE	TEAM	HEIGHT
Kellie Suttle*	Nike	4.55m
Jillian Schwartz	Nike	4.55m
Jennifer Stuczynski	Adidas	4.50m

Men's Pole Vault

ATHLETE	TEAM	HEIGHT
Brad Walker	Nike	5.75m
Jeff Hartwig	Nike	5.70m
Toby Stevenson	Nike	5.60m

Women's Long Jump

ATHLETE	TEAM	DISTANCE
Akiba McKinney	Unattached	6.62m
Tianna Madison	Nike	6.59m
Grace Upshaw	Nike	6.49m

Men's Long Jump

ATHLETE	TEAM	DISTANCE
Brian Johnson	Nike	7.95m
Joe Allen	Unattached	7.82m
Bashir Ramzy	Unattached	7.79m

Women's Triple Jump

ATHLETE	TEAM	DISTANCE
Tiombe Hurd	Nike	13.89m
Shani Marks	Unattached	13.64m
Nicole Whitman	Unattached	13.42m

Men's Triple Jump

ATHLETE	TEAM	DISTANCE
Walter Davis	Nike	16.87m
Aarik Wilson	Unattached	16.60m
Joe Allen	Unattached	15.61m

Women's Shot Put

ATHLETE	TEAM	DISTANCE
Jillian Camarena	Unattached	19.26m
Kristin Heaston	Nike	18.24m
Jessica Cosby	Nike	17.19m

Men's Shot Put

ATHLETE	TEAM	DISTANCE
Reese Hoffa	New York AC	21.61m
Christian Cantwell	Nike	21.10m
John Godina	Adidas	20.50m

Women's Weight Throw

ATHLETE	TEAM	DISTANCE
Erin Gilreath	New York AC	22.95m
Amber Campbell	Unattached	22.66m
Loree Smith	New York AC	21.82m

Men's Weight Throw

ATHLETE	TEAM	DISTANCE
A.G. Kruger	Ashland Elite	23.74m
Kibwé Johnson	Unattached	23.72m
Thomas Freeman	New York AC	23.48m

*Won in jump-off.

TRACK and FIELD

TODAY'S STARS

Hurdler Allen Johnson has won two World Championship medals.

■ **Allen Johnson, hurdler,** b. March 1, 1971, Washington, D.C. Johnson has solidified his place as one of the greatest hurdlers of all-time. At the 2003 World Championships, he won his record fourth career world title in the 110-meter hurdles. He added a bronze medal at the 2005 World Championships. Johnson won an Olympic gold medal in that event at the 1996 Games, but has suffered from bad luck in the Olympics since then. In the 2000 Games, he injured his hamstring just prior to the Olympics and struggled to a fourth-place finish. In the 2004 Games, Johnson clipped a hurdle and fell, failing to qualify for the finals.

■ **Justin Gatlin, sprinter,** b. February 10, 1982, Brooklyn, New York. Gatlin burst onto the scene at the 2004 Olympics, where he won three medals, including a gold in the 100 meters. And he hasn't slowed down since. In 2005, Gatlin won gold in the 100 and 200 meters at the World Championships. He is the second man to win those events at the same Worlds. In 2006, he tied the world record in the 100 meters with a time of 9.77 seconds. Gatlin is also a talented artist. After high school, he almost gave up track to pursue a career in graphic design.

■ **Paula Radcliffe, marathoner,** b. December 17, 1973, Northwich, England. Radcliffe is the top woman marathoner in the world. She set the world record in the women's marathon (2:15:25) when she won the 2003 London Marathon. She also holds the 10- and 20-kilometer road world records. Radcliffe was crushed when she collapsed from exhaustion and had to drop out of the 2004 Olympic marathon. But she bounced back in 2005, winning gold in the marathon at the World Championships. She's also a three-time world champion in the half marathon, and won the New York City Marathon in 2004.

2006 WORLD CROSS-COUNTRY CHAMPIONSHIPS

APRIL 1–2, 2006
FUKUOKA, JAPAN

Long Race — Men

ATHLETE	COUNTRY	TIME
Kenenisa Bekele	Ethiopia	35:40
Sileshi Sihine	Ethiopia	35:43
Martin Irungu Mathathi	Kenya	35:44

Long Race — Women

ATHLETE	TEAM	TIME
Tirunesh Dibaba	Ethiopia	25:21
Lornah Kiplagat	Netherlands	25:26
Meselech Melkamu	Ethiopia	25:38

Short Race — Men

ATHLETE	TEAM	TIME
Kenenisa Bekele	Ethiopia	10:54
Isaac Kiprono Songok	Kenya	10:55
Adil Kaouch	Morocco	10:57

Short Race — Women

ATHLETE	TEAM	TIME
Gelete Burika Bati	Ethiopia	12:51
Priscah Jepleting Ngetich	Kenya	12:53
Meselech Melkamu	Ethiopia	12:54

FAST FACT

USA Track & Field Hall of Famer Jim Thorpe is also a member of the Pro Football Hall of Fame.

2005-06 MARATHONS

Chicago Marathon
OCTOBER 9, 2005

MEN	COUNTRY	TIME
Felix Limo	Kenya	02:07:02
Benjamin Maiyo	Kenya	02:07:09
Daniel Njenga	Kenya	02:07:14

WOMEN	COUNTRY	TIME
Deena Kastor	United States	02:21:25
Constantina Tomescu-Dita	Romania	02:21:30
Masako Chiba	Japan	02:26:00

New York City Marathon
NOVEMBER 5, 2005

MEN	COUNTRY	TIME
Paul Tergat	Kenya	2:09:30
Hendrick Ramaala	South Africa	2:09:31
Meb Keflezighi	United States	2:09:56

WOMEN	COUNTRY	TIME
Jelena Prokopcuka	Latvia	2:24:41
Susan Chepkemei	Kenya	2:24:55
Derartu Tulu	Ethiopia	2:25:21

Boston Marathon
APRIL 17, 2006

MEN	COUNTRY	TIME
Robert Cheruiyot	Kenya	2:07:14
Benjamin Maiyo	Kenya	2:08:21
Meb Keflezighi	United States	2:09:56

WOMEN	COUNTRY	TIME
Rita Jeptoo	Kenya	2:23:38
Jelena Prokopcuka	Latvia	2:23:48
Reiko Tosa	Japan	2:24:11

London Marathon
APRIL 23, 2006

MEN	COUNTRY	TIME
Felix Limo	Kenya	2:06:39
Martin Lel	Kenya	2:06:41
Hendrick Ramaala	South Africa	2:06:55

WOMEN	COUNTRY	TIME
Deena Kastor	United States	2:19:36*
Lyudmila Petrova	Russia	2:21:29
Susan Chepkemei	Kenya	2:21:46

*American record

WORLD RECORDS — MEN

EVENT	MARK	RECORD HOLDER	DATE	SITE
100 Meters	9.77*	Asafa Powell, Jamaica	6-14-05	Athens, Greece
		Justin Gatlin, United States	5-12-06	Doha, Qatar
200 Meters	19.32	Michael Johnson, United States	8-1-96	Atlanta, Georgia
400 Meters	43.18	Michael Johnson, United States	8-26-99	Seville, Spain
800 Meters	1:41.11	Wilson Kipketer, Denmark	8-24-97	Cologne, Germany
1,000 Meters	2:11.96	Noah Ngeny, Kenya	9-5-99	Rieti, Italy
1,500 Meters	3:26.00	Hicham El Guerrouj, Morocco	7-14-98	Rome, Italy
Mile	3:43.13	Hicham El Guerrouj, Morocco	7-7-99	Rome, Italy
2,000 Meters	4:44.79	Hicham El Guerrouj, Morocco	9-7-99	Berlin, Germany
3,000 Meters	7:20.67	Daniel Komen, Kenya	9-1-96	Rieti, Italy
Steeplechase	7:53.63	Saif Saaeed Shaheen, Qatar	9-3-04	Brussels, Belgium
5,000 Meters	12:37.35	Kenenisa Bekele, Ethiopia	5-31-04	Hengelo, Netherlands
10,000 Meters	26:17.53	Kenenisa Bekele, Ethiopia	8-26-05	Brussels, Belgium
20,000 Meters	56:55.6	Arturo Barrios, Mexico	3-30-91	La Flache, France
Hour	21,101 meters	Arturo Barrios, Mexico	3-30-91	La Flache, France
25,000 Meters	1:13:55.8	Toshihiko Seko, Japan	3-22-81	Christchurch, New Zealand
30,000 Meters	1:29:18.8	Toshihiko Seko, Japan	3-22-81	Christchurch, New Zealand
Marathon	2:04:55.0	Paul Tergat, Kenya	9-28-03	Berlin, Germany
110-Meter Hurdles	12.88*	Xiang Liu, China	7-11-06	Lausanne, Switzerland
400-Meter Hurdles	46.78	Kevin Young, United States	8-6-92	Barcelona, Spain
20-Kilometer Walk	1:17:21.0	Jefferson Perez, Ecuador	8-23-03	Paris, France
30-Kilometer Walk	2:01:44.1	Maurizio Damilano, Italy	10-3-92	Cuneo, Italy
50-Kilometer Walk	3:36:03	Robert Korzeniowski, Poland	8-27-03	Paris, France
4x100-Meter Relay	37.40*	United States (Mike Marsh, Leroy Burrell, Dennis Mitchell, Carl Lewis)	8-8-92	Barcelona, Spain
		United States (Jon Drummond, Andre Cason, Dennis Mitchell, Leroy Burrell)	8-21-93	Stuttgart, Germany

*Shared record

Michael
Johnson,
United
States

BOB MARTIN

DID YOU KNOW?

The distance of the Olympic marathon is 26 miles, 385 yards. That's because at the 1908 London Olympics, the 385 yards were added so that the race could start at Windsor Castle and end in front of the Royal Family's viewing box. Before the '08 Games, it was a 40-kilometer race (24.8 miles).

WORLD RECORDS — MEN (cont.)

EVENT	MARK	RECORD HOLDER	DATE	SITE
4x200-Meter Relay	1:18.68	Santa Monica TC (Mike Marsh, Leroy Burrell, Floyd Heard, Carl Lewis)	4-17-94	Walnut, California
4x400-Meter Relay	2:54.20	United States (Jerome Young, Antonio Pettigrew, Tyree Washington, Michael Johnson)	7-22-98	New York, New York
4x800-Meter Relay	7:03.89	Great Britain (Peter Elliott, Garry Cook, Steve Cram, Sebastian Coe)	8-30-82	London, England
4x1,500-Meter Relay	14:38.8	West Germany (Thomas Wessinghage, Harald Hudak, Michael Lederer, Karl Fleschen)	8-17-77	Cologne, Germany
High Jump	2.45 meters	Javier Sotomayor, Cuba	7-27-93	Salamanca, Spain
Pole Vault	6.14 meters	Sergei Bubka, Ukraine	7-31-94	Sestriere, Italy
Long Jump	8.95 meters	Mike Powell, United States	8-30-91	Tokyo, Japan
Triple Jump	18.29 meters	Jonathan Edwards, Great Britain	8-7-95	Goteborg, Sweden
Shot Put	23.12 meters	Randy Barnes, United States	5-20-90	Westwood, California
Discus Throw	74.08 meters	Jurgen Schult, East Germany	6-6-86	Neubrandenburg, Germany
Hammer Throw	86.74 meters	Yuri Syedikh, U.S.S.R.	8-30-86	Stuttgart, Germany
Javelin Throw	98.48 meters	Jan Zelezny, Czech Republic	5-25-96	Jena, Germany
Decathlon	9,026 points	Roman Sebrle, Czech Republic	5-27-01	Gotzis, Austria

Sergei Bubka, Ukraine

HEINZ KLUETMEIER

DID YOU KNOW?

In 1974, Herb Washington — the world-record holder in the 50- and 60-yard dashes — signed with the Oakland Athletics. He stole 30 bases in two seasons strictly as a pinch-runner.

WORLD RECORDS — WOMEN

EVENT	MARK	RECORD HOLDER	DATE	SITE
100 Meters	10.49	Florence Griffith Joyner, United States	7-16-88	Indianapolis, Indiana
200 Meters	21.34	Florence Griffith Joyner, United States	9-29-88	Seoul, Korea
400 Meters	47.60	Marita Koch, East Germany	10-6-85	Canberra, Australia
800 Meters	1:53.28	Jarmila Kratochvílová, Czechoslovakia	7-26-83	Munich, Germany
1,000 Meters	2:28.98	Svetlana Masterkova, Russia	8-23-96	Brussels, Belgium
1,500 Meters	3:50.46	Qu Yunxia, China	9-11-93	Beijing, China
Mile	4:12.56	Svetlana Masterkova, Russia	8-14-96	Zurich, Switzerland
2,000 Meters	5:25.36	Sonia O'Sullivan, Ireland	7-8-94	Edinburgh, Scotland
3,000 Meters	8:06.11	Wang Junxia, China	9-13-93	Beijing, China
Steeplechase	9:01.59	Gulnara Samitova, Russia	4-7-04	Iraklio, Greece
5,000 Meters	14:24.68	Elvan Abeylegesse, Turkey	6-11-04	Bergen, Norway
10,000 Meters	29:31.78	Wang Junxia, China	9-8-93	Beijing, China
Hour	18,340 meters	Tegla Loroupe, Kenya	8-8-98	Borgholzhausen, Germany
20,000 Meters	1:05:26.6	Tegla Loroupe, Kenya	9-3-00	Borgholzhausen, Germany
25,000 Meters	1:27:05.9	Tegla Loroupe, Kenya	9-21-02	Mengerskirchen, Germany
30,000 Meters	1:45:50.0	Tegla Loroupe, Kenya	6-6-03	Warstein, Germany
Marathon	2:15:25.0	Paula Radclifffe, Great Britain	4-13-03	London, England
100-Meter Hurdles	12.21	Yordanka Donkova, Bulgaria	8-20-88	Stara Zgora, Bulgaria
400-Meter Hurdles	52.34	Yuliya Pechenkina, Russia	8-8-03	Tula, Russia
5-Kilometer Walk	20:02.60	Gillian O'Sullivan, Ireland	7-13-02	Dublin, Ireland
10-Kilometer Walk	41:56.23	Nadezhda Ryashkina, Russia	7-24-90	Seattle, Washington
4x100-Meter Relay	41.37	East Germany (Silke Gladisch, Sabine Reiger, Ingrid Auerswald, Marlies Gohr)	10-6-85	Canberra, Australia

WORLD RECORDS — WOMEN (cont.)

EVENT	MARK	RECORD HOLDER	DATE	SITE
4x200-Meter Relay	1:27.46	United States (LaTasha Jenkins, LaTasha Colander-Richardson, Nanceen Perry, Marion Jones)	4-29-00	Philadelphia, Pennsylvania
4x400-Meter Relay	3:15.17	U.S.S.R. (Tatyana Ledovskaya, Olga Nazarova, Maria Pinigina, Olga Bryzgina)	10-1-88	Seoul, Korea
4x800-Meter Relay	7:50.17	U.S.S.R. (Nadezhda Olizarenko, Lyubov Gurina, Lyudmila Borisova, Irina Podyalovskaya)	8-5-84	Moscow, Russia
High Jump	2.09 meters	Stefka Kostadinova, Bulgaria	8-30-87	Rome, Italy

PETER READ MILLER

Jackie Joyner-Kersee, United States

TRIVIA CHALLENGE

Who was the first American woman to win three track and field gold medals in the same Olympics?

Wilma Rudolph at the 1960 Games.

Pole Vault	5.01 meters	Yelena Isinbayeva, Russia	8-12-05	Helsinki, Finland
Long Jump	7.52 meters	Galina Chistyakova, U.S.S.R.	6-11-88	Leningrad, Russia
Triple Jump	15.50 meters	Inessa Kravets, Ukraine	8-10-95	Goteborg, Sweden
Shot Put	22.63 meters	Natalya Lisovskaya, U.S.S.R.	6-7-87	Moscow, Russia
Discus Throw	76.80 meters	Gabriele Reinsch, East Germany	7-9-88	Neubrandenburg, Germany
Hammer Throw	76.81 meters	Tatyana Lysenko, Russia	7-15-05	Moscow, Russia
Javelin Throw	71.70 meters	Osleidys Menéndez, Cuba	8-14-05	Helsinki, Finland
Heptathlon	7,291 points	Jackie Joyner-Kersee, United States	9-23-88/9-24-88	Seoul, Korea

2005-06 TIME LINE

■ **June 14, 2005:** Asafa Powell of Jamaica sets a new world record in the 100-meter dash (9.77 seconds) at the Tsiklitiria Super Grand Prix in Athens, Greece.

■ **June 26, 2005:** A day after winning the 100 meters at the U.S. championships, Justin Gatlin wins the 200. He becomes the first man to win the 100 and 200 at the same U.S. championships since 1985.

■ **July 15, 2005:** Tatyana Lysenko of Russia breaks the women's world record in the hammer throw (77.06 meters) at the Vladimir Kuts Memorial meet in Moscow, Russia.

■ **August 10, 2005:** American Bryan Clay wins the decathlon at the World Championships by the biggest margin since 1995.

■ **August 12, 2005:** Yelena Isinbayeva of Russia raises her world record in the women's pole vault at the World Championships (5.01 meters). She later breaks her own indoor record on February 12, 2006, raising the bar to 4.91 meters.

■ **August 14, 2005:** The American 4x400 men's relay team wins gold at the World Championships, giving Team USA a World Championship-record 14 gold medals at the event. Osleidys Menéndez of Cuba breaks the women's world record in the javelin (71.54 meters) at the Worlds.

■ **August 26, 2005:** Kenenisa Bekele of Ethiopia breaks his own world record in the 10,000 meters (26:17.53) at the Van Damme Memorial meet in Brussels, Belgium.

■ **October 9, 2005:** Deena Kastor wins the Chicago Marathon, becoming the first American woman to win a major marathon since 1994.

■ **May 12, 2006:** Justin Gatlin of the United States wins the 100-meter sprint at the Qatar Grand Prix in 9.77 seconds. His time ties the world record set by Asafa Powell. Gatlin's actual time was 9.766 seconds, but IAAF rules require that times be rounded up to the nearest hundreth of a second.

SUMMER OLYMPICS

The XXIX Summer Olympics will be held in Beijing, China, from August 8-24, 2008.

Over 11,000 athletes from 203 countries are expected to participate in 28 sports. Athletes will compete in two disciplines for the first time: BMX racing and open-water swimming. One men's and one women's BMX race will replace two track cycling events. The women's and men's open-water race will be 10 kilometers (6.2 miles) long. This will be the longest swimming event at the Games.

The 2008 Games will also include baseball and softball competition for the last time. Both sports will be cut from the Olympics at the 2012 Games because there were not enough countries participating in the sports worldwide.

Whatever sports will be played in Beijing, the Games are predicted to be the most expensive ever. The Chinese government plans to spend $40 billion to build the venues and improve the transportation systems in Beijing. China hopes to get some of that money back in gold. China won 32 gold medals at the 2004 Summer Games, finishing second to the United States in total gold medals (35).

AP

The main Olympic stadium for the 2008 Games is being built in Beijing, China.

BEIJING 2008 SUMMER OLYMPICS SCHEDULE

AUGUST 6
- SOCCER

AUGUST 7
- SOCCER

AUGUST 8
- OPENING CEREMONIES

AUGUST 9
- ROWING
- BADMINTON
- BASKETBALL
- BOXING
- CYCLING
  Road – Finals
- EQUESTRIAN
  Eventing
- FENCING
  Finals
- SOCCER
- GYMNASTICS
  Artistic

- WEIGHTLIFTING
  Finals
- HANDBALL
- JUDO
  Finals
- SWIMMING
  Finals
- WATER POLO
- SHOOTING
  Finals
- ARCHERY
- SAILING
- VOLLEYBALL
- VOLLEYBALL
  Beach

AUGUST 10
- ROWING
- BADMINTON
- BASKETBALL
- BOXING

- CYCLING
  Road – Finals
- EQUESTRIAN
  Eventing
- FENCING
  Finals
- SOCCER
- GYMNASTICS
  Artistic
- WEIGHTLIFTING
  Finals
- HANDBALL
- HOCKEY
- JUDO
  Finals
- SWIMMING
  Finals
- WATER POLO
- TENNIS
- SHOOTING
  Finals

- ARCHERY
  Finals
- SAILING
- VOLLEYBALL
- VOLLEYBALL
  Beach

AUGUST 11

- ROWING
- BADMINTON
- BASKETBALL
- BOXING
- CANOE/KAYAK
  Slalom
- EQUESTRIAN
  Eventing
- FENCING
  Finals
- SOCCER
- GYMNASTICS
  Artistic – Finals
- WEIGHTLIFTING
  Finals
- HANDBALL
- HOCKEY
- JUDO
  Finals
- SWIMMING
  Finals
- WATER POLO
- TENNIS
- SHOOTING
  Finals
- ARCHERY
  Finals
- SAILING
- VOLLEYBALL
- VOLLEYBALL
  Beach

AUGUST 12

- ROWING
- BADMINTON
- BASKETBALL

- BOXING
- CANOE/KAYAK
  Slalom - Finals
- EQUESTRIAN
  Eventing - Finals
- FENCING
  Finals
- GYMNASTICS
  Artistic – Finals
- WEIGHTLIFTING
  Finals
- HANDBALL
- HOCKEY
- JUDO
  Finals
- WRESTLING
  Greco-Roman – Finals
- SWIMMING
  Finals
- WATER POLO
- SOFTBALL
- TENNIS
- SHOOTING
  Finals
- ARCHERY
- SAILING
- VOLLEYBALL
- VOLLEYBALL
  Beach

AUGUST 13

- ROWING
- BADMINTON
- BASEBALL
- BASKETBALL
- BOXING
- CANOE/KAYAK
  Slalom
- CYCLING
  Road – Finals
- EQUESTRIAN
  Dressage
- FENCING
  Finals

- SOCCER
- GYMNASTICS
  Artistic – Finals
- WEIGHTLIFTING
  Finals
- HANDBALL
- HOCKEY
- JUDO
  Finals
- WRESTLING
  Greco-Roman – Finals

In 2004, Manu Ginobili of the San Antonio Spurs led Argentina to the basketball gold medal.

- SWIMMING
  Finals
- WATER POLO
- SOFTBALL
- TENNIS
- SHOOTING
  Finals
- ARCHERY
- SAILING
- VOLLEYBALL
- VOLLEYBALL
  Beach

AUGUST 14

- ROWING
- BADMINTON
- BASEBALL
- BASKETBALL
- BOXING

JOHN W. MCDONOUGH

BEIJING 2008 SUMMER OLYMPICS SCHEDULE (cont.)

- **CANOE/KAYAK**
Finals
- **CYCLING**
Track
- **EQUESTRIAN**
Dressage – Finals
- **FENCING**
Finals
- **SOCCER**
- **GYMNASTICS**
Artistic – Finals
- **HANDBALL**
- **HOCKEY**
- **JUDO**
Finals
- **WRESTLING**
Greco-Roman – Finals
- **SWIMMING**
Finals
- **WATER POLO**
- **SOFTBALL**
- **TENNIS**
- **TABLE TENNIS**
- **SHOOTING**
Finals
- **ARCHERY**
Finals
- **SAILING**
- **VOLLEYBALL**
- **VOLLEYBALL**
Beach

AUGUST 15

- **TRACK AND FIELD**
Finals
- **ROWING**
- **BADMINTON**
Finals
- **BASEBALL**
- **BASKETBALL**
- **BOXING**
- **CYCLING**
Track – Finals
- **FENCING**
Finals

- **GYMNASTICS**
Trampoline – Finals
- **WEIGHTLIFTING**
Finals
- **HOCKEY**
- **HANDBALL**
- **JUDO**
Finals
- **SWIMMING**
Finals
- **WATER POLO**
- **SOFTBALL**
- **TENNIS**
- **TABLE TENNIS**
- **SHOOTING**
Finals
- **ARCHERY**
Finals
- **SAILING**
- **VOLLEYBALL**
- **VOLLEYBALL**
Beach

AUGUST 16

- **TRACK AND FIELD**
Finals
- **ROWING**
Finals
- **BADMINTON**
Finals
- **BASEBALL**
- **BASKETBALL**
- **BOXING**
- **CYCLING**
Track – Finals
- **EQUESTRIAN**
Jumping
- **FENCING**
Finals

- **SOCCER**
- **GYMNASTICS**
Trampoline – Finals
- **WEIGHTLIFTING**
Finals
- **HANDBALL**
- **HOCKEY**
- **WRESTLING**
Freestyle – Finals
- **SWIMMING**
Finals
- **WATER POLO**
- **SOFTBALL**
- **TENNIS**
Finals
- **TABLE TENNIS**
- **SHOOTING**
Finals
- **SAILING**
- **VOLLEYBALL**
- **VOLLEYBALL**
Beach

AUGUST 17

- **TRACK AND FIELD**
Finals
- **ROWING**
Finals
- **BADMINTON**
Finals
- **BASKETBALL**
- **BOXING**
- **CYCLING**
Track – Finals
- **EQUESTRIAN**
Dressage
- **FENCING**
Finals
- **SOCCER**

DID YOU KNOW?

At the 2004 Summer Olympics, the men's soccer team from Argentina won the gold medal without giving up a single goal in the tournament.

LEGENDS

Muhammad Ali (right), then known as Cassius Clay, won a gold medal at the 1960 Olympics.

UPI/BETTMANN/CORBIS

■ **Muhammad Ali, boxer,** b. January 17, 1942, Louisville, Kentucky. Ali is considered by many experts to be the greatest boxer of all time. At the 1960 Summer Olympics in Rome, Italy, he won the gold medal in the light-heavyweight division. He was then called Cassius Clay. He changed his name when he became a Muslim in 1964. Ali was the heavyweight champion of the world from 1964-1967, 1974-1978, and 1978-1979, the only boxer to hold that title three times. He was inducted in the U.S. Olympic Hall of Fame in 1983 and lit the Olympic cauldron to begin the 1996 Summer Games in Atlanta, Georgia.

■ **Kurt Angle, freestyle wrestler,** b. December 9, 1968, Mount Lebanon, Pennsylvania. Angle is now known as a professional wrestler performing for World Wresting Entertainment. But before turning pro, he won a gold medal in freestyle wrestling at the 1996 Summer Olympics in the 220-pound class. He broke his neck prior to the Olympic trials that year, but still went on to win the gold. Angle was inducted into the National Wrestling Hall of Fame in 2001.

■ **Olga Korbut, gymnast,** b. May 16, 1955, Grodno, Belarus. Korbut was known as a gymnast who took giant risks and performed extremely tough tricks. At the 1972 Summer Olympics in Munich, Germany, she won gold medals on the balance beam, in the floor exercise, and in the team all-around competition. She also won a silver medal on the uneven bars. At the 1976 Games, in Montreal, Canada, she won gold again in the team competition and also captured silver on the balance beam. Korbut was the first gymnast to perform a back somersault on the beam. She was inducted into the International Women's Sports Hall of Fame in 1982.

BEIJING 2008 SUMMER OLYMPICS SCHEDULE (cont.)

■ GYMNASTICS Artistic – Finals	■ WATER POLO	AUGUST 18
■ WEIGHTLIFTING Finals	■ SOFTBALL	■ TRACK AND FIELD Finals
■ HANDBALL	■ TENNIS Finals	■ BASEBALL
■ HOCKEY	■ TABLE TENNIS	■ BASKETBALL
■ WRESTLING Freestyle – Finals	■ SHOOTING Finals	■ BOXING
■ SYNCHRONIZED SWIMMING	■ SAILING	■ CANOE/KAYAK Flat Water
■ DIVING Finals	■ VOLLEYBALL	■ CYCLING Track – Finals
	■ VOLLEYBALL Beach	■ EQUESTRIAN Jumping

BEIJING 2008 SUMMER OLYMPICS SCHEDULE (cont.)

- SOCCER
- GYMNASTICS
  Artistic – Finals
- WEIGHTLIFTING
  Finals
- HANDBALL
- HOCKEY
- SYNCHRONIZED SWIMMING
- DIVING
  Finals
- WATER POLO
- SOFTBALL
- TABLE TENNIS
- TRIATHLON
  Finals
- SAILING
  Finals
- VOLLEYBALL
- VOLLEYBALL
  Beach

AUGUST 19

- TRACK AND FIELD
  Finals
- BASEBALL
- BASKETBALL
- BOXING
- CANOE/KAYAK
  Flat Water
- CYCLING
  Track – Finals
- EQUESTRIAN
  Jumping – Finals
- SOCCER
- WEIGHTLIFTING
  Finals
- HANDBALL
- HOCKEY
- WRESTLING
  Freestyle – Finals
- SYNCHRONIZED SWIMMING
  Finals
- DIVING
  Finals
- WATER POLO

- TABLE TENNIS
- TRIATHLON
  Finals
- SAILING
- VOLLEYBALL
- VOLLEYBALL
  Beach – Finals

Two of the five official Beijing 2008 mascots.

AUGUST 20

- TRACK AND FIELD
  Finals
- BASEBALL
- BASKETBALL
- BOXING
- CANOE/KAYAK
  Flat Water
- CYCLING
  BMX – Finals
- SOCCER
- GYMNASTICS
  Rhythmic
- HANDBALL
- HOCKEY
- WRESTLING
  Freestyle – Finals
- SWIMMING
  Finals
- DIVING
  Finals
- WATER POLO
  Finals
- SOFTBALL
- TAEKWONDO
  Finals

- TABLE TENNIS
  Finals
- SAILING
- VOLLEYBALL
- VOLLEYBALL
  Beach – Finals

AUGUST 21

- TRACK AND FIELD
  Finals
- BASKETBALL
- CANOE/KAYAK
  Flat Water
- CYCLING
  BMX – Finals
- EQUESTRIAN
  Dressage – Finals
- SOCCER
- GYMNASTICS
  Rhythmic
- HANDBALL
- HOCKEY
- WRESTLING
  Freestyle – Finals
- SWIMMING
  Finals
- SYNCHRONIZED SWIMMING
- DIVING
  Finals
- WATER POLO
- MODERN PENTATHLON
  Finals
- SOFTBALL
  Finals
- TAEKWONDO
  Finals
- TABLE TENNIS
  Finals
- SAILING
  Finals
- VOLLEYBALL

AUGUST 22

- TRACK AND FIELD
  Finals
- BASEBALL
- BASKETBALL

GREG BAKER/AP

■ BOXING

■ CANOE/KAYAK
Flat Water – Finals

■ CYCLING
Mountain Bike – Finals

The U.S. won gold in the 4x400-meter relay in 2004.

■ EQUESTRIAN
Jumping – Finals

■ SOCCER

■ GYMNASTICS
Rhythmic – Finals

■ HANDBALL

■ HOCKEY
Finals

■ SYNCHRONIZED SWIMMING
Finals

■ DIVING
Finals

■ MODERN PENTATHLON
Finals

■ TAEKWONDO
Finals

■ TABLE TENNIS
Finals

■ VOLLEYBALL

AUGUST 23

■ TRACK AND FIELD
Finals

■ BASEBALL
Finals

■ BASKETBALL
Finals

■ BOXING
Finals

■ CANOE/KAYAK
Flat Water – Finals

■ CYCLING
Mountain Bike – Finals

■ SOCCER
Finals

■ GYMNASTICS
Rhythmic – Finals

■ HANDBALL
Finals

■ HOCKEY
Finals

■ DIVING
Finals

■ WATER POLO
Finals

■ TAEKWONDO
Finals

■ TABLE TENNIS
Finals

■ VOLLEYBALL
Finals

AUGUST 24

■ TRACK AND FIELD
Finals

■ BASKETBALL
Finals

■ BOXING
Finals

■ SOCCER
Finals

■ HANDBALL
Finals

■ DIVING
Finals

■ VOLLEYBALL
Finals

■ CLOSING CEREMONIES

HEINZ KLUETMEIER

TRIVIA CHALLENGE

Since softball was added to the Olympic Games in 1996, how many different countries have won the gold medal?

One. The United States team won the gold medal in 1996, 2000, and 2004.

2005-06 TIME LINE

■ **July 13, 2001:** Beijing, China, is selected to host the 2008 Summer Olympics. Beijing beat out Toronto, Canada; Paris, France; Istanbul, Turkey; and Osaka, Japan, to become the host city.

■ **December 24, 2003:** Construction begins on Beijing National Stadium, where the Games' opening and closing ceremonies will take place.

■ **June 26, 2005:** The Beijing Olympic Committee announces the slogan for the 2008 Games: "One World, One Dream."

■ **June 30, 2005:** The International Olympic Committee announces BMX racing will be added to the 2008 Summer Games program.

■ **October 27, 2005:** The International Olympic Committee announces that the men's and women's 10-kilometer open-water swim race will be added to the 2008 Summer Games program.

■ **February 26, 2006:** The 2006 Winter Olympics in Turin, Italy, come to a close.

TODAY'S STARS

■ **Chellsie Memmel, gymnast,** b. July 23, 1988, Milwaukee, Wisconsin. At the 2005 World Championships, Memmel became the first U.S. woman to win the all-around title since Shannon Miller won it in 1994. She also won the silver medal on the uneven bars and the balance beam. Memmel was a finalist for the 2005 Sullivan Award, which is given to the nation's top amateur athlete each year. She was an alternate on the U.S. women's team that won a silver medal in the all-around competition at the 2004 Summer Olympics.

Chellsie Memmel is the defending all-around world champion.

JIM MCISAAC/GETTY IMAGES

■ **Kerron Clement, hurdler and sprinter,** b. October 31, 1985, Port of Spain, Trinidad. Clement competed for the University of Florida at the 2005 NCAA Indoor Track and Field Championships. At the meet, he broke former Olympic champion Michael Johnson's world record in the 400-meter sprint with a time of 44.57 seconds. (The old record was 44.63 seconds.) Clement also became the U.S. outdoor champion in the 400-meter hurdles in 2005. He finished with a personal best time of 47.24 seconds (the world record is 46.78, set by Kevin Young of the United States). Clement and his family immigrated to the United States in 1998.

■ **Steven Lopez, taekwondo,** b. September 11, 1978, New York, New York. Lopez is a two-time Olympic champion. He won gold medals in the lightweight class at the 2000 Games and as a welterweight in 2004. In 2005, Lopez won his third world championship in a row (2001, 2003, 2005). He was a finalist for the 2005 Sullivan Award, given each year to the nation's top amateur athlete.

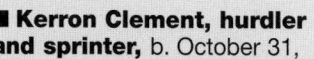

FAST FACT

At the first modern Olympic Games in 1896 in Athens, Greece, the winner of each event was awarded a silver medal and an olive branch. The full set of medals — gold, silver, and bronze for first-, second-, and third-place finishers — was introduced at the 1904 Games in St. Louis, Missouri.

DID YOU KNOW?

The 1916 Olympics were scheduled to be held in Berlin, Germany. They were canceled because of World War I. Berlin hosted the Games 20 years later, in 1936. The Olympics would be cancelled again in 1940 and 1944 because of World War II.

PAST SUMMER OLYMPIC HOSTS

YEAR		HOST	DATES	MEN	WOMEN	NATIONS
XXVIII	2004	ATHENS, GREECE	August 13-29	6,452	4,412	202
XXVII	2000	SYDNEY, AUSTRALIA	September 15-October 1	6,582	4,069	199
XXVI	1996	ATLANTA, GEORGIA, USA	July 19-August 4	6,806	3,512	197
XXV	1992	BARCELONA, SPAIN	July 25-August 9	6,652	2,704	169
XXIV	1988	SEOUL, KOREA	September 17-October 2	6,197	2,194	159
XXIII	1984	LOS ANGELES, CALIFORNIA, USA	July 28-August 12	5,263	1,566	140
XXII	1980	MOSCOW, U.S.S.R.	July 19-August 3	4,064	1,115	80
XXI	1976	MONTREAL, QUEBEC, CANADA	July 17-August 1	4,824	1,260	92
XX	1972	MUNICH, WEST GERMANY	August 26-September 11	6,075	1,059	121
XIX	1968	MEXICO CITY, MEXICO	October 12-27	4,735	781	112
XVIII	1964	TOKYO, JAPAN	October 10-24	4,473	678	93
XVII	1960	ROME, ITALY	August 25-September 11	4,727	611	83
XVI	1956	MELBOURNE, AUSTRALIA	November 22-December 8	2,938	376	72
XV	1952	HELSINKI, FINLAND	July 19-August 3	4,436	519	69
XIV	1948	LONDON, GREAT BRITAIN	July 29-August 14	3,714	390	59
XIII	1944	LONDON, GREAT BRITAIN	Canceled because of World War II			
XII	1940	TOKYO, JAPAN	Canceled because of World War II			
XI	1936	BERLIN, GERMANY	August 1-16	3,632	331	49
X	1932	LOS ANGELES, CALIFORNIA, USA	July 30-August 14	1,206	126	37
IX	1928	AMSTERDAM, THE NETHERLANDS	May 17-August 12	2,606	277	46
VIII	1924	PARIS, FRANCE	May 4-July 27	2,954	135	44
VII	1920	ANTWERP, BELGIUM	April 20-September 12	2,561	65	29
VI	1916	BERLIN, GERMANY	Canceled because of World War I			
V	1912	STOCKHOLM, SWEDEN	May 5-July 27	2,359	48	28
IV	1908	LONDON, GREAT BRITAIN	April 27-October 31	1,971	37	22
—	1906	ATHENS, GREECE	April 22-May 28	77	7	20
III	1904	ST. LOUIS, MISSOURI, USA	July 1-November 23	645	6	12
II	1900	PARIS, FRANCE	May 14-October 28	975	22	24
I	1896	ATHENS, GREECE	April 6-15	241	0	14

ALL-TIME SUMMER OLYMPIC MEDAL COUNT – NATION

NATION	GOLD	SILVER	BRONZE	TOTAL
UNITED STATES	907	697	615	2,219
SOVIET UNION (1952-88)	395	319	296	1,010
GREAT BRITAIN	189	242	237	668
FRANCE	199	202	230	631
ITALY	189	154	168	511
GERMANY (1896-1936, 1992-present)	151	154	178	483
SWEDEN	140	157	179	476
HUNGARY	158	141	161	460
EAST GERMANY (1956-88)	159	150	136	445
AUSTRALIA	119	126	154	399
JAPAN	113	106	114	333
WEST GERMANY (1952-88)	77	104	120	301
FINLAND	101	83	114	298
CHINA	112	96	78	286
ROMANIA	82	88	114	284
POLAND	59	74	118	251
RUSSIA	85	79	84	248
CANADA	54	87	101	242
THE NETHERLANDS	65	76	94	235

ALL-TIME SUMMER OLYMPIC MEDAL COUNT – MEN

ATHLETE, Nation	SPORT	GOLD	SILVER	BRONZE	TOTAL
NIKOLAI ANDRIANOV, U.S.S.R.	Gymnastics	7	5	3	15
BORIS SHAKHLIN, U.S.S.R.	Gymnastics	7	4	2	13
EDOARDO MANGIAROTTI, Italy	Fencing	6	5	2	13
TAKASHI ONO, Japan	Gymnastics	5	4	4	13
PAAVO NURMI, Finland	Track	9	3	0	12
SAWAO KATO, Japan	Gymnastics	8	3	1	12
ALEXEI NEMOV, Russia	Gymnastics	4	2	6	12
MARK SPITZ, United States	Swimming	9	1	1	11
MATT BIONDI, United States	Swimming	8	2	1	11
VIKTOR CHUKARIN, U.S.S.R.	Gymnastics	7	3	1	11
CARL OSBURN, United States	Shooting	5	4	2	11

Six tied with 10.

ALL-TIME SUMMER OLYMPIC MEDAL COUNT – WOMEN

ATHLETE, Nation	SPORT	GOLD	SILVER	BRONZE	TOTAL
LARISSA LATYNINA, U.S.S.R.	Gymnastics	9	5	4	18
BIRGIT FISCHER, Germany	Canoe/Kayak	8	4	0	12
JENNY THOMPSON, United States	Swimming	8	3	1	12
VERA CASLAVSKA, Czechoslovakia	Gymnastics	7	4	0	11
AGNES KELETI, Hungary	Gymnastics	5	3	2	10
POLINA ASTAKHOVA, U.S.S.R.	Gymnastics	5	2	3	10
NADIA COMANECI, Romania	Gymnastics	5	3	1	9
LYUDMILA TOURISCHEVA, U.S.S.R.	Gymnastics	4	3	2	9
DARA TORRES, United States	Swimming	4	1	4	9
KORNELIA ENDER, East Germany	Swimming	4	4	0	8
DAWN FRASER, Australia	Swimming	4	4	0	8
INGE DE BRUIJN, The Netherlands	Swimming	4	2	2	8
SHIRLEY BABASHOFF, United States	Swimming	2	6	0	8
SOFIA MURATOVA, U.S.S.R.	Gymnastics	2	2	4	8

Eight tied with 7.

ALL-TIME SUMMER OLYMPIC GOLD MEDALISTS

MEN

RAY EWRY, United States	10
PAAVO NURMI, Finland	9
CARL LEWIS, United States	9
MARK SPITZ, United States	9
SAWAO KATO, Japan	8
MATT BIONDI, United States	8
NIKOLAI ANDRIANOV, U.S.S.R.	7
BORIS SHAKHLIN, U.S.S.R.	7
VIKTOR CHUKARIN, U.S.S.R.	7
ALADAR GEREVICH, Hungary	7

WOMEN

LARISSA LATYNINA, U.S.S.R.	9
BIRGIT FISCHER, Germany	8
JENNY THOMPSON, United States	8
KRISTIN OTTO, East Germany	6
AGNES KELETI, Hungary	5
NADIA COMANECI, Romania	5
POLINA ASTAKHOVA, U.S.S.R.	5
KRISZTINA EGERSZEGI, Hungary	5
AMY VAN DYKEN, United States	5
KORNELIA ENDER, East Germany	4
DAWN FRASER, Australia	4
LARISSA LAZUTINA, United Team/Russia	4
LYUDMILA TOURISCHEVA, U.S.S.R.	4
EVELYN ASHFORD, United States	4
JANET EVANS, United States	4
FANNY BLANKERS-KOEN, The Netherlands	4
BETTY CUTHBERT, Australia	4
PAT MCCORMICK, United States	4
BARBEL ECKERT WOCKEL, East Germany	4
INGE DE BRUIJN, The Netherlands	4
YANA KLOCHKOVA, Ukraine	4
DARA TORRES, United States	4

TRIVIA CHALLENGE

Where will the 2012 Summer Games be held?

London, England

FAST FACT

Neroil Susan Fairhall of New Zealand was the first paraplegic to participate in the Olympic games. She competed in a wheelchair in archery at the 1984 Games in Los Angeles, California. Fairhall came in 35th place.

SIKIDS.com
Visit our website for the latest stats and sports info.

WINTER OLYMPICS

Ciao, Italia! The XX Winter Olympics were held from February 10–26, 2006, in Turin, Italy. More than 2,500 athletes from 85 countries competed in 15 sports: Alpine skiing, biathlon, bobsled, cross-country skiing, curling, figure skating, freestyle skiing, ice hockey, luge, Nordic combined, short-track speed skating, skeleton, ski jumping, snowboarding, and speed skating. The Germans finished first in the medal race (29), followed by the United States (25) and Canada (24). The United States medal total was the nation's best at an Olympics that was held on foreign soil.

The United States team had more highs and lows during the 16 days of competition than a roller coaster ride. In snowboarding, the American boarders won a total of seven medals: three gold, three silver, and one bronze. Shaun White, 19, who is nicknamed the "Flying Tomato" because of his bright red hair, captured gold in the men's halfpipe competition. Nineteen-year-old Hannah Teter won gold on the women's side. Lindsey Jacobellis, 20, won silver in women's snowboard-cross. Jacobellis was on course to win gold, but she showboated on the last jump of the course and fell. That allowed Tanja Frieden of Switzerland to board past her for the victory.

The U.S. long-track speed skating results were mixed. The women were shut out from the medal stand. But, the men captured seven medals, including three golds. Shani Davis won the 1,000 meters. He became the first black athlete to win an individual gold medal in Olympic Winter Games history. On the short-track side, American fan favorite Apolo Anton Ohno left these

BOB MARTIN

Hannah Teter of the United States won the gold medal in the women's Halfpipe event.

Games with three medals (one gold, two bronze).

One of the biggest disappointments in Turin was the performance of U.S. Alpine skier Bode Miller. Skiing experts in the media had predicted that Miller would win five medals at the Games. He didn't win any in his five races and failed to finish three of them.

Team Canada had one of its best showings ever in a Winter Olympics. Canada's haul of 24 medals was seven more than the country won at the 2002 Games in Salt Lake City, Utah. Canadian long-track speedskater Cindy Klassen won an Olympic-high five medals (one gold, two silver, two bronze). Perhaps the Canadians were just gearing up for the next Winter Games. They will be held in Vancouver, Canada, from February 12–28, 2010.

TURIN 2006 MEDAL COUNT – NATION

NATION	GOLD	SILVER	BRONZE	TOTAL	NATION	GOLD	SILVER	BRONZE	TOTAL
1. GERMANY	11	12	6	29	14. FINLAND	0	6	3	9
2. UNITED STATES	9	9	7	25	15. CZECH REPUBLIC	1	2	1	4
3. CANADA	7	10	7	24	16. ESTONIA	3	0	0	3
4. AUSTRIA	9	7	7	23	17. CROATIA	1	2	0	3
5. RUSSIA	8	6	8	22	18. AUSTRALIA	1	0	1	2
6. NORWAY	2	8	9	19	19. POLAND	0	1	1	2
7. SWEDEN	7	2	5	14	20. UKRAINE	0	0	2	2
8. SWITZERLAND	5	4	5	14	21. JAPAN	1	0	0	1
9. SOUTH KOREA	6	3	2	11	22. BELARUS	0	1	0	1
10. ITALY	5	0	6	11	23. BULGARIA	0	1	0	1
11. CHINA	2	4	5	11	24. GREAT BRITAIN	0	1	0	1
12. FRANCE	3	2	4	9	25. SLOVAKIA	0	1	0	1
13. NETHERLANDS	3	2	4	9	26. LATVIA	0	0	1	1

ALPINE SKIING

MEN

■ Downhill
GOLD – Antoine Deneriaz, France
SILVER – Michael Walchhofer, Austria
BRONZE – Bruno Kernen, Switzerland

■ Slalom
GOLD – Benjamin Raich, Austria
SILVER – Reinfried Herbst, Austria
BRONZE – Rainer Schoenfelder, Austria

■ Giant Slalom
GOLD – Benjamin Raich, Austria
SILVER – Joel Chenel, France
BRONZE – Hermann Maier, Austria

■ Super G
GOLD – Kjetil Andre Aamodt, Norway
SILVER – Hermann Maier, Austria
BRONZE – Ambrosi Hoffman, Switzerland

■ Combined
GOLD – Ted Ligety, USA
SILVER – Ivica Kostelic, Croatia
BRONZE – Rainer Schoenfelder, Austria

Ted Ligety, United States

WOMEN

■ Downhill
GOLD – Michaela Dorfmeister, Austria
SILVER – Martina Schild, Switzerland
BRONZE – Anja Paerson, Sweden

■ Slalom
GOLD – Anja Paerson, Sweden
SILVER – Nicole Hosp, Austria
BRONZE – Marlies Schild, Austria

■ Giant Slalom
GOLD – Julia Mancuso,USA
SILVER – Tanja Poutiainen, Finland
BRONZE – Anna Ottoson, Sweden

■ Super G
GOLD – Michaela Dorfmeister, Austria
SILVER – Janica Kostelic, Croatia
BRONZE – Alexandra Meissnitzer, Austria

■ Combined
GOLD – Janica Kostelic, Croatia
SILVER – Marlies Schild, Austria
BRONZE – Anja Paerson, Sweden

BIATHLON

MEN

■ 10km Sprint
GOLD – Sven Fischer, Germany
SILVER – Halvard Hanevold, Norway
BRONZE – Frode Andresen, Norway

■ 20km Individual
GOLD – Michael Greis, Germany
SILVER – Ole Einar Bjoerndalen, Norway
BRONZE – Halvard Hanevold, Norway

■ 4 x 7.5km Relay
GOLD – Ricco Gross, Michael Roesch, Sven Fischer, Michael Greis; Germany
SILVER – Ivan Tcherezov, Sergei Tchepikov, Pavel Rostovtsev, Nikolay Kruglov; Russia
BRONZE – Julien Robert, Vincent Defrasne, Ferreol Cannard, Raphael Poiree; France

■ 15km Mass Start
GOLD – Michael Greis, Germany
SILVER – Tomasz Sikora, Poland
BRONZE – Ole Einar Bjoerndalen, Norway

■ 12.5km Pursuit
GOLD – Vincent Defrasne, France
SILVER – Ole Einar Bjoerndalen, Norway
BRONZE – Sven Fischer, Germany

WOMEN

■ 7.5km Sprint
GOLD – Florence Baverel-Robert, France
SILVER – Anna Carin Olofsson, Sweden
BRONZE – Lilia Efremova, Ukraine

■ 15km Individual
GOLD – Svetlana Ishmouratova, Russia
SILVER – Martina Glagow, Germany
BRONZE – Albina Akhatova, Russia

■ 4 x 6km Relay
GOLD – Anna Bogaliy, Svetlana Ishmouratova, Olga Zaitseva, Albina Akhatova; Russia
SILVER – Martina Glagow, Andrea Henkel, Katrin Apel, Kati Wilhelm; Germany
BRONZE – Delphyne Peretto, Florence Baverel-Robert, Sylvie Becaert, Sandrine Bailly; France

■ 12.5km Mass Start
GOLD – Anna Carin Olofsson, Sweden
SILVER – Kati Wilhelm, Germany
BRONZE – Uschi Disl, Germany

■ 10km Pursuit
GOLD – Kati Wilhelm, Germany
SILVER – Martina Glagow, Germany
BRONZE – Albina Akhatova, Russia

BOBSLED

MEN

■ Two-Man
GOLD – Andre Lange, Kevin Kuske; Germany
SILVER – Pierre Lueders, Lascelles Brown; Canada
BRONZE – Martin Annen, Beat Hefti; Switzerland

DID YOU KNOW?

BRAIN ROBB

2006 SPORT-BY-SPORT RESULTS (cont.)

Four-Man
GOLD – Andre Lange, Rene Hoppe, Kevin Kuske, Martin Putze; Germany
SILVER – Aleksandr Zoubkov, Filipp Egorov, Alexej Seliverstov, Alexey Voevoda; Russia
BRONZE – Martin Annen, Thomas Lamparter, Beat Hefti, Cedric Grand; Switzerland

WOMEN
Two-Women
GOLD – Sandra Kiriasis, Anja Schneiderheinze; Germany
SILVER – Shauna Rohbock, Valerie Fleming; USA
BRONZE – Gerda Weissensteiner, Jennifer Isacco; Italy

CROSS COUNTRY SKIING
MEN
Sprint
GOLD – Bjoern Lind, Sweden
SILVER – Roddy Darragon, France
BRONZE – Thobias Fredriksson, Sweden

Team Sprint
GOLD – Thobias Fredriksson, Bjoern Lind; Sweden
SILVER – Jens Arne Svartedal, Tor Arne Hetland; Norway
BRONZE – Ivan Alypov, Vassili Rotchev; Russia

30km Pursuit
GOLD – Eugeni Dementiev, Russia
SILVER – Frode Estil, Norway
BRONZE – Pietro Piller Cottrer, Italy

4x10km Relay
GOLD – Fulvio Valbusa, Giorgio Di Centa, Pietro Piller Cottrer, Cristian Zorzi; Italy
SILVER – Andreas Schluetter, Jens Filbrich, Rene Sommerfeldt, Tobias Angerer; Germany
BRONZE – Mats Larsson, Johan Olsson, Anders Soedergren, Mathias Fredriksson; Sweden

15km Classical
GOLD – Andrus Veerpalu, Estonia
SILVER – Lukas Bauer, Czech Republic
BRONZE – Tobias Angerer, Germany

50km Freestyle
GOLD – Giorgio Di Centa, Italy
SILVER – Eugeni Dementiev, Russia
BRONZE – Mikhail Botwinov, Austria

WOMEN
Sprint
GOLD – Chandra Crawford, Canada
SILVER – Claudia Kuenzel, Germany
BRONZE – Alena Sidko, Russia

Team Sprint
GOLD – Anna Dahlberg, Lina Andersson; Sweden
SILVER – Sara Renner, Beckie Scott; Canada
BRONZE – Aino Kaisa Saarinen, Virpi Kuitunen; Finland

15km Pursuit
GOLD – Kristina Smigun, Estonia
SILVER – Katerina Neumannova, Czech Republic
BRONZE – Evgenia Medvedeva-Abruzova, Russia

4x5km Relay
GOLD – Natalia Baranova-Masolkina, Larisa Kurkina, Julija Tchepalova, Evgenia Medvedeva-Abruzova; Russia
SILVER – Stefanie Boehler, Viola Bauer, Evi Sachenbacher Stehle, Claudia Kuenzel; Germany
BRONZE – Arianna Follis, Gabriella Paruzzi, Antonella Confortola, Sabina Valbusa; Italy

10km Classical
GOLD – Kristina Smigun, Estonia
SILVER – Marit Bjorgen, Norway
BRONZE – Hilde G. Pedersen, Norway

30km Freestyle
GOLD – Katerina Neumannova, Czech Republic
SILVER – Julija Tchepalova, Russia
BRONZE – Justyna Kowalczyk, Poland

CURLING
MEN
GOLD – Canada
SILVER – Finland
BRONZE – USA

WOMEN
GOLD – Sweden
SILVER – Switzerland
BRONZE – Canada

Shizuka Arakawa, Japan

FIGURE SKATING
MEN
GOLD – Evgeni Plushenko, Russia
SILVER – Stephane Lambiel, Switzerland
BRONZE – Jeffrey Buttle, Canada

WOMEN
GOLD – Shizuka Arakawa, Japan
SILVER – Sasha Cohen, USA
BRONZE – Irina Slutskaya, Russia

Pairs
GOLD – Tatyana Totmiyanina, Maxim Marinin; Russia
SILVER – Dan Zhang, Hao Zhang; China
BRONZE – Xue Shen, Hongbo Zhao; China

Ice Dancing
GOLD – Tatyana Navka, Roman Kostomarov; Russia
SILVER – Tanith Belbin; Ben Agosto; USA
BRONZE – Yelena Grushina, Ruslan Goncharov; Ukraine

FREESTYLE SKIING
MEN
Aerials
GOLD – Xiaopeng Han, China
SILVER – Dmitry Dashinski, Belarus
BRONZE – Vladimir Lebedev, Russia

HEINZ KLUETMEIER

Moguls
GOLD – Dale Begg-Smith, Australia
SILVER – Mikko Ronkainen, Finland
BRONZE – Toby Dawson, USA

WOMEN
Aerials
GOLD – Evelyne Leu, Switzerland
SILVER – Nina Li, China
BRONZE – Alisa Camplin, Australia

Moguls
GOLD – Jennifer Heil, Canada
SILVER – Kari Traa, Norway
BRONZE – Sandra Laoura, France

HOCKEY
MEN
GOLD – Sweden
SILVER – Finland
BRONZE – Czech Republic

WOMEN
GOLD – Canada
SILVER – Sweden
BRONZE – USA

LUGE
MEN
Singles
GOLD – Armin Zoeggeler, Italy
SILVER – Albert Demtschenko, Russia
BRONZE – Martins Rubenis, Latvia

Doubles
GOLD – Andreas Linger, Wolfgang Linger; Austria
SILVER – Andre Florschuetz, Torsten Wustlich; Germany
BRONZE – Oswald Haselrieder, Gerhard Plankensteiner; Italy

WOMEN
Singles
GOLD – Sylke Otto, Germany
SILVER – Silke Kraushaar, Germany
BRONZE – Tatjana Huefner, Germany

NORDIC COMBINED
Sprint
GOLD – Felix Gottwald, Austria
SILVER – Magnus Moan, Norway
BRONZE – Georg Hettich, Germany

Individual
GOLD – Georg Hettich, Germany
SILVER – Felix Gottwald, Austria
BRONZE – Magnus Moan, Norway

Team
GOLD – Austria
SILVER – Germany
BRONZE – Finland

SHORT TRACK
MEN
500m
GOLD – Apolo Anton Ohno, USA
SILVER – Francois-Louis Tremblay, Canada
BRONZE – Hyun-Soo Ahn, South Korea

1,000m
GOLD – Hyun-Soo Ahn, South Korea
SILVER – Ho-Suk Lee, South Korea
BRONZE – Apolo Anton Ohno, USA

1,500m
GOLD – Hyun-Soo Ahn, South Korea
SILVER – Ho-Suk Lee, South Korea
BRONZE – Jiajun Li, China

Relay
GOLD – Hyun-Soo Ahn, Ho-Suk Lee, Se-Jong Oh, Ho-Jin Seo, Suk-Woo Song; South Korea
SILVER – Eric Bedard, Jonathan Guilmette, Charles Hamelin, Francois-LouisTremblay, Mathieu Turcotte; Canada
BRONZE – Alex Izykowski, J.P. Kepka, Anthony Lobello, Apolo Anton Ohno, Rusty Smith; USA

WOMEN
500m
GOLD – Meng Wang, China
SILVER – Evgenia Radanova, Bulgaria
BRONZE – Anouk Leblanc-Boucher, Canada

1,000m
GOLD – Sun-Yu Jin, South Korea
SILVER – Meng Wang, China
BRONZE – Yang Yang (A), China

1,500m
GOLD – Sun-Yu Jin, South Korea
SILVER – Eun-Kyung Choi, South Korea
BRONZE – Meng Wang, China

Relay
GOLD – Chun-Sa Byun, Eun-Kyung Choi, Dah-Ye Jeon, Sun-Yu Jin, Yun-Mi Kang; South Korea
SILVER – Alanna Kraus, Anouk Leblanc-Boucher, Amanda Overland, Kalyna Roberge, Tania Vicent; Canada
BRONZE – Marta Capurso, Arianna Fontana, Cecilia Maffei, Katia Zini, Mara Zini; Italy

SKELETON
MEN
GOLD – Duff Gibson, Canada
SILVER – Jeff Pain, Canada
BRONZE – Gregor Staehli, Switzerland

WOMEN
GOLD – Maya Pedersen, Switzerland
SILVER – Shelley Rudman, Great Britain
BRONZE – Mellisa Hollingsworth-Richards, Canada

Apolo Anton Ohno, United States

DAMIAN STROHMEYER

2006 SPORT-BY-SPORT RESULTS (cont.)

SKI JUMPING

MEN

■ **Normal Hill**
GOLD – Lars Bystoel, Norway
SILVER – Matti Hautamaeki, Finland
BRONZE – Roar Ljoekelsoey, Norway

■ **Large Hill**
GOLD – Thomas Morgenstern, Austria
SILVER – Andreas Kofler, Austria
BRONZE – Lars Bystoel, Norway

■ **Team**
GOLD – Andreas Widhoelzl, Andreas Kofler,
Martin Koch, Thomas Morgenstern; Austria
SILVER – Tami Kiuru, Janne Happonen,
Janne Ahonen, Matt Hautamaeki; Finland
BRONZE – Lars Bystoel, Bjoern Einar Romoeren,
Tommy Ingebrigtsen, Roar Ljoekelsoey; Norway

SNOW BOARDING

MEN

■ **Halfpipe**
GOLD – Shaun White, USA
SILVER – Danny Kass, USA
BRONZE – Markku Koski, Finland

■ **Parallel Giant Slalom**
GOLD – Philipp Schoch, Switzerland
SILVER – Simon Schoch, Switzerland
BRONZE – Siegfried Grabner, Austria

■ **Snowboard Cross**
GOLD – Seth Wescott, USA
SILVER – Radoslav Zidek, Slovakia
BRONZE – Paul-Henri Delerue,
France

WOMEN

■ **Halfpipe**
GOLD – Hannah Teter, USA
SILVER – Gretchen Bleiler, USA
BRONZE – Kjersti Buaas, Norway

■ **Parallel Giant Slalom**
GOLD – Daniela Meuli, Switzerland
SILVER – Amelie Kober, Germany
BRONZE – Rosey Fletcher, USA

■ **Snowboard Cross**
GOLD – Tanja Frieden, Switzerland
SILVER – Lindsey Jacobellis, USA
BRONZE – Dominique Maltais, Canada

SPEED SKATING

MEN

■ **500m**
GOLD – Joey Cheek, USA
SILVER – Dmitry Dorofeyev, Russia
BRONZE – Kang Seok Lee, South Korea

■ **1,000m**
GOLD – Shani Davis, USA
SILVER – Joey Cheek, USA
BRONZE – Erben Wennemars, Netherlands

Seth Wescott

■ **1,500m**
GOLD – Enrico Fabris, Italy
SILVER – Shani Davis, USA
BRONZE – Chad Hedrick, USA

■ **5,000m**
GOLD – Chad Hedrick, USA
SILVER – Sven Kramer, Netherlands
BRONZE – Enrico Fabris, Italy

■ **10,000m**
GOLD – Bob De Jong, Netherlands
SILVER – Chad Hedrick, USA
BRONZE – Carl Verheijen, Netherlands

■ **Team Pursuit**
GOLD – Matteo Anesi, Enrico Fabris,
Ippolito Sanfratello; Italy
SILVER – Arne Dankers, Steven Elm,
Justin Warsylewicz; Canada
BRONZE – Sven Kramer, Mark Tuitert, Carl Verheijen;
Netherlands

WOMEN

■ **500m**
GOLD – Svetlana Zhurova, Russia
SILVER – Manli Wang, China
BRONZE – Hui Ren, China

■ **1,000m**
GOLD – Marianne Timmer,
Netherlands
SILVER – Cindy Klassen, Canada
BRONZE – Anni Friesinger, Germany

■ **1,500m**
GOLD – Cindy Klassen, Canada
SILVER – Kristina Groves, Canada
BRONZE – Ireen Wust, Netherlands

■ **3,000m**
GOLD – Ireen Wust, Netherlands
SILVER – Renate Groenewold, Netherlands
BRONZE – Cindy Klassen, Canada

■ **5,000m**
GOLD – Clara Hughes, Canada
SILVER – Claudia Pechstein, Germany
BRONZE – Cindy Klassen, Canada

■ **Team Pursuit**
GOLD – Daniela Anschuetz Thoms, Anni Friesinger,
Claudia Pechstein; Germany
SILVER – Kristina Groves, Clara Hughes,
Christine Nesbitt; Canada
BRONZE – Yekaterina Abramova,
Yekaterina Lobysheva, Svetlana Vysokova; Russia

FAST FACT

The last time the Summer and Winter Games
were held the same year was 1992. Since then,
the Games have alternated every two years.

YEAR		HOST	DATES	MEN	WOMEN	NATIONS
XX	2006	TURIN, ITALY	February 10–16	1,611	996	84
XIX	2002	SALT LAKE CITY, USA	February 8–24	1,513	886	77
XVIII	1998	NAGANO, JAPAN	February 7–22	1,389	787	72
XVII	1994	LILLEHAMMER, NORWAY	February 12–27	1,215	522	67
XVI	1992	ALBERTVILLE, FRANCE	February 8–23	1,313	488	64
XV	1988	CALGARY, CANADA	February 13–28	1,122	301	57
XIV	1984	SARAJEVO, YUGOSLAVIA	February 8–19	998	274	49
XIII	1980	LAKE PLACID, USA	February 13–24	840	232	37
XII	1976	INNSBRUCK, AUSTRIA	February 4–15	892	231	37
XI	1972	SAPPORO, JAPAN	February 3–13	801	205	35
X	1968	GRENOBLE, FRANCE	February 6–18	947	211	37
IX	1964	INNSBRUCK, AUSTRIA	January 29–February 9	892	199	36
VIII	1960	SQUAW VALLEY, USA	February 18–28	521	144	30
VII	1956	CORTINA d'AMPEZZO, ITALY	January 26–February 5	687	134	32
VI	1952	OSLO, NORWAY	February 14–25	585	109	30
V	1948	ST. MORITZ, SWITZERLAND	January 30–February 8	592	77	28
--	1944	CORTINA d'AMPEZZO, ITALY	Canceled because of World War II			
--	1940	GARMISCH-PARTENKIRCHEN, GERMANY	Canceled because of World War II			
IV	1936	GARMISCH-PARTENKIRCHEN, GERMANY	February 6–16	566	80	28
III	1932	LAKE PLACID, USA	February 4–15	231	21	17
II	1928	ST. MORITZ, SWITZERLAND	February 11–19	438	26	25
I	1924	CHAMONIX, FRANCE	January 25–February 5	247	11	16

TRIVIA CHALLENGE

In 2006, speedskater Shani Davis was the first black athlete to win an individual gold medal at a Winter Games. Who was the first black athlete to win a team gold medal at the Winter Olympics?

U.S. bobsledder Vonetta Flowers, along with partner Jill Bakken, won a gold medal at the 2002 Winter Olympics in the two-person bobsled.

TODAY'S STARS

■ **Shani Davis, long-track speedskater,** b. August 13, 1982, Chicago, Illinois. Davis made history at the 2006 Winter Games. He won the 1,000 meters and became the first black athlete to win an individual gold medal in Winter Olympic history. He also won the silver medal in the 1,500 meters. Davis also competes in short-track skating. In 2002, he became the first African American to make the U.S. men's Olympic short-track team. He was an alternate and did not get a chance to compete at the Games.

■ **Hannah Teter, snowboarder,** b. January 27, 1987, Belmont, Vermont. Teter won the gold in the women's Halfpipe competition at the 2006 Winter Games. It was her first Olympics, but she had already received serious atten-

Shani Davis was a member of the both the United States long-track and short-track speedskating teams.

tion at many major competitions. She won bronze medals in Superpipe at the 2005 World Snowboard Championships and the 2005 Winter X Games. In 2002, Teter became the first woman boarder to land a 900 in a halfpipe competition.

■ **Yevgeny Plushenko, figure skater,** b. November 3, 1982, St. Petersburg, Russia. Plushenko is the world's best male figure skater. He easily won the short program and free skate at the Turin Games to become the fourth straight Russian skater to win Olympic gold in the men's event. He won a silver medal in 2002. Known for his technical skill and flair, Plushenko is a three-time world champion (2001, 2003, 2004).

FAST FACT

German luger Georg Hackl is the only Olympian to win a medal in the same event in five straight Games. He won the silver medal in the singles competition in 1988, the gold medal in 1992, 1994, 1998, and the silver medal again in 2002. He competed in the 2006 Games, but failed to win a medal.

ALL-TIME WINTER OLYMPIC MEDAL COUNT — NATION

NATION	GOLD	SILVER	BRONZE	TOTAL
NORWAY	98	98	84	280
UNITED STATES	79	79	58	216
SOVIET UNION (1956-88)	78	56	59	193
AUSTRIA	51	64	70	185
GERMANY	68	65	46	179
FINLAND	41	57	52	150
CANADA	38	38	43	119
SWEDEN	43	31	44	118
SWITZERLAND	37	37	43	117
EAST GERMANY (1956-88)	39	36	35	110

ALL-TIME WINTER OLYMPIC MEDAL COUNT — MEN

ATHLETE, Nation	SPORT	GOLD	SILVER	BRONZE	TOTAL
BJORN DAEHLIE, Norway	Nordic Skiing	8	4	0	12
OLE EINAR BJOERNDALEN, Norway	Biathlon	5	3	1	9
SIXTEN JERNBERG, Sweden	Nordic Skiing	4	3	2	9
RICCO GROSS, Germany	Biathlon	4	3	1	8
KJETIL ANDRE AAMODT, Norway	Alpine Skiing	4	2	2	8
A. CLAS THUNBERG, Finland	Speed Skating	5	1	1	7
IVAR BALLANGRUD, Norway	Speed Skating	4	2	1	7
VEIKKO HAKULINEN, Finland	Nordic Skiing	3	3	1	7
EERO MANTYRANTA, Finland	Nordic Skiing	3	2	2	7
BOGDAN MUSIOL, East Germany/Germany	Bobsled	1	5	1	7
THOMAS ALSGAARD, Norway	Nordic Skiing	4	2	0	6
GUNDE SVAN, Sweden	Nordic Skiing	4	1	1	6
VEGARD ULVANG, Norway	Nordic Skiing	3	2	1	6
JOHAN GROTTUMSBRATEN, Norway	Nordic Skiing	3	1	2	6
WOLFGANG HOPPE, East Germany/Germany	Bobsled	2	3	1	6
EUGENIO MONTI, Italy	Bobsled	2	2	2	6
VLADIMIR SMIRNOV, U.S.S.R./ United Team/Kazakhstan	Nordic Skiing	1	4	1	6
MIKA MYLLYLAE, Finland	Nordic Skiing	1	1	4	6
ROALD LARSEN, Norway	Speed Skating	0	2	4	6
HARRI KIRVESNIEMI, Finland	Nordic Skiing	0	0	6	6

ALL-TIME WINTER OLYMPIC MEDAL COUNT – WOMEN

ATHLETE, Nation	SPORT	GOLD	SILVER	BRONZE	TOTAL
RAISA SMETANINA, U.S.S.R./United Team	Nordic Skiing	4	5	1	10
LYUBOV EGOROVA, United Team/Russia	Nordic Skiing	6	3	0	9
LARISSA LAZUTINA, United Team/Russia	Nordic Skiing	5	3	1	9
STEFANIA BELMONDO, Italy	Nordic Skiing	2	3	4	9
CLAUDIA PECHSTEIN, Germany	Speed Skating	5	2	2	9
GALINA KULAKOVA, U.S.S.R.	Nordic Skiing	4	2	2	8
KARIN KANIA, East Germany	Speed Skating	3	4	1	8
GUNDA NEIMANN-STIRNEMANN, Germany	Speed Skating	3	4	1	8
URSULA DISL, Germany	Biathlon	2	4	2	8
MARJA-LIISA KIRVESNIEMI, Finland	Nordic Skiing	3	0	4	7
ELENA VALBE, United Team/Russia	Nordic Skiing	3	0	4	7
ANDREA EHRIG, East Germany	Speed Skating	1	5	1	7
LYDIA SKOBLIKOVA, U.S.S.R.	Speed Skating	6	0	0	6
BONNIE BLAIR, United States	Speed Skating	5	0	1	6
MANUELA DI CENTA, Italy	Nordic Skiing	2	2	2	6

Bonnie Blair

TOM LYNN

ALL-TIME INDIVIDUAL OLYMPIC GOLD MEDALISTS

MEN		WOMEN	
BJORN DAEHLIE, Norway	8	LYUBOV EGOROVA, United Team/Russia	6
OLE EINAR BJOERNDALEN, Norway	5	LYDIA SKOBLIKOVA, U.S.S.R.	6
ERIC HEIDEN, United States	5	BONNIE BLAIR, United States	5
A. CLAS THUNBERG, Finland	5	LARISSA LAZUTINA, United Team/Russia	5
		CLAUDIA PECHSTEIN, Germany	5

ATHLETES WITH WINTER AND SUMMER MEDALS

EDDIE EAGAN, United States — boxing gold medal (1920) and bobsled gold medal (1932)

JACOB TULLIN THAMS, Norway — ski jumping gold medal (1924) and yachting silver medal (1936)

CHRISTA LUDING-ROTHENBURGER, East Germany — speed skating gold medals (1984 and 1988), silver medal (1988), and bronze medal (1992), and cycling silver medal (1988)

CLARA HUGHES, Canada — two cycling bronze medals (1996) and speed skating gold (2006) and bronze medals (2002)

TRIVIA CHALLENGE

How many times has the United States hosted the Winter Olympics?

Four times. The Winter Games took place in Lake Placid, New York, in 1932 and 1980, Squaw Valley, California in 1960, and in Salt Lake City, Utah, in 2002.

LEGENDS

Picabo Street won skiing medals in back-to-back Winter Olympic Games.

CARL YARBROUGH

■ **Picabo Street, alpine skier,** b. April 3, 1971, Triumph, Idaho. Street is the best female downhill skier in United States history. She is a two-time Olympic medalist. She won a silver medal in the Downhill event at the 1994 Winter Games and a gold in the Super G in 1998. In 1995, Street became the first American skier to ever capture the World Cup title. She won the title again in 1996.

■ **Mike Eruzione, ice hockey player,** b. October 25, 1954, Winthrop, Massachusetts. Eruzione was the captain of the United States Olympic hockey team that won the gold medal in the 1980 Winter Games. Eruzione scored the winning goal in the semi-final game over the Russians. The U.S. victory was called "The Miracle On Ice" because the Russians were a huge favorite to win the gold medal. The U.S. then knocked off Finland in the final to win the gold medal.

■ **Elvis Stojko, figure skater,** b. March 22, 1972, Newmarket, Ontario, Canada. Stojko is the pride of Canadian figure skating. He won the World Figure Skating Championships in 1994, 1995, and 1997. He also won the Canadian Championships seven times (1994, 1996–2000, 2002). Stojko won the silver medal in the men's competition at the 1994 Winter Olympics. At the 1998 Games, despite battling a groin injury and a bout with the flu, he won the silver medal again.

DID YOU KNOW?

The oldest man to receive a Winter Olympics medal was 83-year-old Ander Haugen. The American ski jumper received his bronze 50 years after he competed in 1924 when a scoring error was discovered in 1974.

SIKIDS.com

Visit our website for the latest stats and sports info.

SPORTS DIRECTORY

Major League Baseball
245 Park Avenue
New York, NY 10167
(212) 931-7800

Arizona Diamondbacks
Chase Field
401 East Jefferson Street
Phoenix, AZ 85004
(602) 462-6500

Atlanta Braves
Turner Field
755 Hank Aaron Drive
Atlanta, GA 30315
(404) 522-7630

Baltimore Orioles
Oriole Park at Camden Yards
333 W. Camden Street
Baltimore, MD 21201
(410) 685-9800

Boston Red Sox
Fenway Park
4 Yawkey Way
Boston, MA 02215
(617) 267-9440

Chicago Cubs
Wrigley Field
1060 West Addison Street
Chicago, IL 60613
(773) 404-2827

Chicago White Sox
U.S. Cellular Field
333 West 35th Street
Chicago, IL 60616
(312) 674-1000

Cincinnati Reds
Great American Ball Park
100 Main Street
Cincinnati, OH 45202
(513) 765-7000

Cleveland Indians
Jacobs Field
2401 Ontario Street
Cleveland, OH 44115
(216) 420-4636

Colorado Rockies
Coors Field
2001 Blake Street
Denver, CO 80205
(303) 292-0200

Detroit Tigers
Comerica Park
2100 Woodward Avenue
Detroit, MI 48201
(313) 471-2000

Florida Marlins
Dolphins Stadium
2267 Dan Marino Boulevard
Miami, FL 33056
(305) 623-6100

Houston Astros
Minute Maid Park
501 Crawford Street
Suite 400
Houston, TX 77002
(713) 259-8000

Kansas City Royals
Kauffman Stadium
One Royal Way
Kansas City, MO 64129
(816) 921-8000

Los Angeles Angels of Anaheim
Angel Stadium of Anaheim
2000 Gene Autry Way
Anaheim, CA 92806
(714) 940-2000

Los Angeles Dodgers
Dodger Stadium
1000 Elysian Park Avenue
Los Angeles, CA 90012
(323) 224-1500

Milwaukee Brewers
Miller Park
One Brewers Way
Milwaukee, WI 53214
(414) 902-4400

Minnesota Twins
Metrodome
34 Kirby Puckett Place
Minneapolis, MN 55415
(612) 375-1366

New York Mets
Shea Stadium
123-01 Roosevelt Avenue
Flushing, NY 11368
(718) 507-6387

New York Yankees
Yankee Stadium
161st Street and River Avenue
Bronx, NY 10451
(718) 293-4300

Oakland Athletics
McAfee Coliseum
7000 Coliseum Way
Oakland, CA 94621
(510) 638-4900

Philadelphia Phillies
Citizens Bank Park
One Citizens Bank Way
Philadelphia, PA 19148
(215) 463-6000

Pittsburgh Pirates
PNC Park
115 Federal Street
Pittsburgh, PA 15212
(412) 323-5000

San Diego Padres
PETCO Park
100 Park Boulevard
San Diego, CA 92101
(619) 795-5000

San Francisco Giants
SBC Park
24 Willie Mays Plaza
San Francisco, CA 94107
(415) 972-2000

Seattle Mariners
Safeco Field
1250 First Avenue S.
Seattle, WA 98134
(206) 346-4000

St. Louis Cardinals
Busch Stadium
250 Stadium Plaza
St. Louis, MO 63102
(314) 421-3060

Tampa Bay Devil Rays
Tropicana Field
One Tropicana Drive
St. Petersburg, FL 33705
(727) 825-3137

Texas Rangers
Ameriquest Field in Arlington
1000 Ballpark Way
Arlington, TX 76011
(817) 273-5222

Toronto Blue Jays
Rogers Centre
1 Blue Jays Way
Suite 3200
Toronto, Ontario M5V 1J1
  Canada
(416) 341-1000

Washington Nationals
RFK Stadium
2400 E. Capitol Street, S.E.
Washington, D.C. 20003
(202) 675-6287

PRO FOOTBALL

National Football League
280 Park Avenue
New York, NY 10017
(212) 450-2000

Arizona Cardinals
8701 South Hardy Drive
Tempe, AZ 85284
(602) 379-0101

Atlanta Falcons
4400 Falcon Parkway
Flowery Branch, GA 30542
(770) 965-3115

Baltimore Ravens
1 Winning Drive
Owings Mills, MD 21117
(410) 701-4000

Buffalo Bills
One Bills Drive
Orchard Park, NY 14127
(716) 648-1800

Carolina Panthers
Bank of America Stadium
800 South Mint Street
Charlotte, NC 28202
(704) 358-7000

Chicago Bears
1000 Football Drive
Lake Forest, IL 60045
(847) 295-6600

Cincinnati Bengals
One Paul Brown Stadium
Cincinnati, OH 45202
(513) 621-3550

Cleveland Browns
76 Lou Groza Boulevard
Berea, OH 44017
(440) 891-5000

Dallas Cowboys
Cowboys Center
One Cowboys Parkway
Irving, TX 75063
(972) 556-9900

Denver Broncos
13655 Broncos Parkway
Englewood, CO 80112
(303) 649-9000

Detroit Lions
222 Republic Drive
Allen Park, MI 48101
(313) 216-4000

Green Bay Packers
Lambeau Field
1265 Lombardi Avenue
Green Bay, WI 54304
(920) 569-7500

Houston Texans
Reliant Stadium
Two Reliant Park
Houston, TX 77054
(832) 667-2000

Indianapolis Colts
7001 W. 56th Street
Indianapolis, IN 46254
(317) 297-2658

Jacksonville Jaguars
One ALLTEL Stadium Place
Jacksonville, FL 32202
(904) 633-6000

Kansas City Chiefs
One Arrowhead Drive
Kansas City, MO 64129
(816) 920-9300

Miami Dolphins
7500 S.W. 30th Street
Davie, FL 33314
(954) 452-7000

Minnesota Vikings
9520 Viking Drive
Eden Prairie, MN 55344
(952) 828-6500

New England Patriots
Gillette Stadium
One Patriot Place
Foxboro, MA 02035
(508) 543-8200

New Orleans Saints
5800 Airline Drive
Metairie, LA 70003
(504) 733-0255

New York Giants
Giants Stadium
East Rutherford, NJ 07073
(201) 935-8111

New York Jets
1000 Fulton Avenue
Hempstead, NY 11550
(516) 560-8100

Oakland Raiders
1220 Harbor Bay Parkway
Alameda, CA 94502
(510) 864-5000

Philadelphia Eagles
NovaCare Complex
One NovaCare Way
Philadelphia, PA 19145
(215) 463-2500

Pittsburgh Steelers
3400 South Water Street
Pittsburgh, PA 15203
(412) 432-7800

San Diego Chargers
Qualcomm Stadium
4020 Murphy Canyon Road
San Diego, CA 92123
(858) 874-4500

San Francisco 49ers
4949 Centennial Boulevard
Santa Clara, CA 95054
(408) 562-4949

Seattle Seahawks
11220 N.E. 53rd Street
Kirkland, WA 98033
(425) 827-9777

St. Louis Rams
One Rams Way
St. Louis, MO 63045
(314) 982-7267

Tampa Bay Buccaneers
One Buccaneer Place
Tampa, FL 33607
(813) 870-2700

Tennessee Titans
460 Great Circle Road
Nashville, TN 37228
(615) 565-4000

Washington Redskins
21300 Redskin Park Drive
Ashburn, VA 20147
(703) 726-7000

OTHER LEAGUES

Canadian Football League
50 Wellington Street, East
3rd Floor
Toronto, Ontario M5E 1C8
Canada
(416) 322-9650

NFL Europe
280 Park Avenue
New York, NY 10017
(212) 450-2000

PRO BASKETBALL

National Basketball Association
645 Fifth Avenue
New York, NY 10022
(212) 407-8000

Atlanta Hawks
Centennial Tower
101 Marietta Street, N.W.
Suite 1900
Atlanta, GA 30303
(404) 878-3800

Boston Celtics
226 Causeway Street, 4th Floor
Boston, MA 02114
(617) 854-8000

Charlotte Bobcats
129 West Trade Street
Suite 700
Charlotte, NC 28202
(704) 424-4120

Chicago Bulls
1901 W. Madison Street
Chicago, IL 60612
(312) 455-4000

Cleveland Cavaliers
One Center Court
Cleveland, OH 44115
(216) 420-2000

Dallas Mavericks
The Pavilion
2909 Taylor Street
Dallas, TX 75226
(214) 747-6287

Denver Nuggets
1000 Chopper Circle
Denver, CO 80204
(303) 405-1100

Detroit Pistons
Four Championship Drive
Auburn Hills, MI 48326
(248) 377-0100

Golden State Warriors
1011 Broadway
Oakland, CA 94607
(510) 986-2200

Houston Rockets
1510 Polk Street
Houston, TX 77002
(713) 758-7200

Indiana Pacers
125 South Pennsylvania Street
Indianapolis, IN 46204
(317) 917-2500

Los Angeles Clippers
1111 South Figueroa Street
Suite 1100
Los Angeles, CA 90015
(213) 742-7500

Los Angeles Lakers
555 North Nash Street
El Segundo, CA 90245
(310) 426-6000

Memphis Grizzlies
191 Beale Street
Memphis, TN 38103
(901) 205-1234

Miami Heat
601 Biscayne Boulevard
Miami, FL 33132
(786) 777-4328

Milwaukee Bucks
1001 North Fourth Street
Milwaukee, WI 53203
(414) 227-0500

Minnesota Timberwolves
600 First Avenue North
Minneapolis, MN 55403
(612) 673-1600

New Jersey Nets
390 Murray Hill Parkway
East Rutherford, NJ 07073
(201) 935-8888

New Orleans Hornets
Oklahoma Tower
210 Park Avenue
Suite 1850
Oklahoma City, OK 73102
(405) 208-4720
(Address for the 2006–2007 season)

New York Knicks
Two Pennsylvania Plaza
14th Floor
New York, NY 10121
(212) 465-6471

Orlando Magic
8701 Maitland Summit
  Boulevard
Orlando, FL 32810
(407) 916-2400

Philadelphia 76ers
3601 South Broad Street
Philadelphia, PA 19148
(215) 339-7600

Phoenix Suns
201 East Jefferson Street
Phoenix, AZ 85004
(602) 379-7900

Portland Trail Blazers
One Center Court
Suite 200
Portland, OR 97227
(503) 234-9291

Sacramento Kings
One Sports Parkway
Sacramento, CA 95834
(916) 928-0000

San Antonio Spurs
One SBC Center
San Antonio, TX 78219
(210) 444-5000

Seattle SuperSonics
351 Elliott Avenue West
Suite 500
Seattle, WA 98119
(206) 283-3865

Toronto Raptors
40 Bay Street
Suite 400
Toronto, Ontario M5J 2X2
Canada
(416) 815-5600

Utah Jazz
301 West South Temple
Salt Lake City, UT 84101
(801) 325-2500

Washington Wizards
601 F Street, N.W.
Washington, DC 20004
(202) 661-5000

WNBA
645 Fifth Avenue
New York, NY 10022
(212) 688-9622

Charlotte Sting
333 East Trade Street
Charlotte, NC 28202
(704) 688-8860

Chicago Sky
20 West Kinzie Street
Suite 1000
Chicago, IL 60610
(312) 828-9550

Connecticut Sun
1 Mohegan Sun Boulevard
Uncasville, CT 06382
(860) 862-4000

Detroit Shock
Four Championship Drive
Auburn Hills, MI 48326
(248) 377-0100

Houston Comets
1510 Polk Street
Houston, TX 77002
(713) 627-9622

Indiana Fever
125 S. Pennsylvania Street
Indianapolis, IN 46204
(317) 917-2500

Los Angeles Sparks
2151 East Grand Avenue
Suite 100
El Segundo, CA 90245
(310) 341-1000

Minnesota Lynx
600 First Avenue North
Minneapolis, MN 55403
(612) 673-1600

New York Liberty
Two Pennsylvania Plaza
New York, NY 10121
(212) 564-9622

Phoenix Mercury
201 East Jefferson Street
Phoenix, AZ 85004
(602) 514-8333

Sacramento Monarchs
One Sports Parkway
Sacramento, CA 95834
(916) 928-0000

San Antonio Silver Stars
One SBC Center
San Antonio, TX 78219
(210) 444-5050

Seattle Storm
351 Elliott Avenue West
Suite 500
Seattle, WA 98119
(206) 217-9622

Washington Mystics
MCI Center
401 9th Street, N.W.
Washington, DC 20004
(202) 266-2361

HOCKEY

National Hockey League
1251 Avenue of the Americas
47th Floor
New York, NY 10020
(212) 789-2000

Anaheim Ducks
Arrowhead Pond of Anaheim
2695 Katella Avenue
Anaheim, CA 92806
(714) 940-2900

Atlanta Thrashers
Centennial Tower
101 Marietta Street N.W.
Suite 1900
Atlanta, GA 30303
(404) 878-3300

Boston Bruins
TD Banknorth Garden
100 Legends Way
Boston, MA 02114
(617) 624-1900

Buffalo Sabres
HSBC Arena
One Seymour H. Knox III Plaza
Buffalo, NY 14203
(716) 855-4100

Calgary Flames
Pengrowth Saddledome
P.O. Box 1540
Station M
Calgary, Alberta T2P 3B9
Canada
(403) 777-4636

Carolina Hurricanes
RBC Center
1400 Edwards Mill Road
Raleigh, NC 27607
(919) 467-7825

Chicago Blackhawks
United Center
1901 W. Madison Street
Chicago, IL 60612
(312) 455-7000

Colorado Avalanche
Pepsi Center
1000 Chopper Circle
Denver, CO 80204
(303) 405-1100

Columbus Blue Jackets
Nationwide Arena
200 West Nationwide
  Boulevard
Columbus, OH 43215
(614) 246-4625

Dallas Stars
Dr Pepper StarCenter
2601 Avenue of the Stars
Frisco, TX 75034
(214) 387-5500

SPORTS DIRECTORY

Detroit Red Wings
Joe Louis Arena
600 Civic Center Drive
Detroit, MI 48226
(313) 983-6606

Edmonton Oilers
Rexall Place
11230-110th Street
Edmonton, Alberta T5G 3H7
 Canada
(780) 414-4000

Florida Panthers
BankAtlantic Center
One Panther Parkway
Sunrise, FL 33323
(954) 835-7000

Los Angeles Kings
1111 South Figueroa Street
Suite 3100
Los Angeles, CA 90015
(213) 742-7100

Minnesota Wild
317 Washington Street
St. Paul, MN 55102
(651) 602-6000

Montreal Canadiens
1275 St. Antoine Street West
Montreal, Quebec H3C 5L2
 Canada
(514) 932-2582

Nashville Predators
Gaylord Entertainment Center
501 Broadway
Nashville, TN 37203
(615) 770-7825

New Jersey Devils
50 Route 120 North
Continental Airlines Arena
East Rutherford, NJ 07073
(201) 935-6050

New York Islanders
1535 Old Country Road
Plainview, NY 11803
(516) 501-6700

New York Rangers
Madison Square Garden
Two Pennsylvania Plaza
14th Floor
New York, NY 10121
(212) 465-6000

Ottawa Senators
Scotiabank Place
1000 Palladium Drive
Kanata, Ontario K2V 1A5
 Canada
(613) 599-0250

Philadelphia Flyers
Wachovia Center
3601 South Broad Street
Philadelphia, PA 19148
(215) 465-4500

Phoenix Coyotes
5800 W. Glenn Drive
Suite 350
Glendale, AZ 85301
(623) 463-8800

Pittsburgh Penguins
Mellon Arena
66 Mario Lemieux Place
Pittsburgh, PA 15219
(412) 642-1300

San Jose Sharks
HP Pavilion at San Jose
525 West Santa Clara Street
San Jose, CA 95113
(408) 287-7070

St. Louis Blues
Savvis Center
1401 Clark Avenue
St. Louis, MO 63103
(314) 622-2500

Tampa Bay Lightning
St. Pete Times Forum
401 Channelside Drive
Tampa, FL 33602
(813) 301-6500

Toronto Maple Leafs
Air Canada Centre
40 Bay Street
Suite 400
Toronto, Ontario M5J 2X2
 Canada
(416) 815-5700

Vancouver Canucks
General Motors Place
800 Griffiths Way
Vancouver, British Columbia
 V6B 6G1
 Canada
(604) 899-4600

Washington Capitals
401 Ninth Street, N.W.
Suite 750
Washington, DC 20004
(202) 266-2200

COLLEGE SPORTS

**National Collegiate
Athletic Association
(NCAA)**
700 W. Washington Street
P.O. Box 6222
Indianapolis, IN 46206-6222
(317) 917-6222

**Atlantic Coast
Conference**
P.O. Drawer ACC
Greensboro, NC 27417-6724
(336) 854-8787

Big East Conference
222 Richmond Street
Suite 110
Providence, RI 02903
(401) 272-9108

Big Ten Conference
1500 West Higgins Road
Park Ridge, IL 60068-6300
(847) 696-1010

Big 12 Conference
2201 Stemmons Freeway
28th Floor
Dallas, TX 75207
(214) 742-1212

Big West Conference
2 Corporate Park
Irvine, CA 92606
(949) 261-2525

Conference USA
5201 North O'Connor Blvd.
Suite 300
Irving, TX 75039
(214) 774-1300

Ivy League
228 Alexander Street
2nd Floor
Princeton, NJ 08544
(609) 258-6426

Mid-American Conference
24 Public Square
15th Floor
Cleveland, OH 44113
(216) 566-4622

Pacific-10 Conference
800 South Broadway
Suite 400
Walnut Creek, CA 94596
(925) 932-4411

Southeastern Conference
2201 Richard Arrington
 Boulevard North
Birmingham, AL 35203
(205) 458-3000

Western Athletic Conference
9250 East Costilla Avenue
Suite 300
Englewood, CO 80112
(303) 799-9221

OTHER SPORTS

Association of Tennis Professionals Tour (ATP)
201 ATP Boulevard
Ponte Vedra Beach, FL 32082
(904) 285-8000

Championship Auto Racing Teams (CART)
5350 West Lakeview Parkway
South Drive
Indianapolis, IN 46268
(317) 715-4100

Indy Racing League
4565 West 16th Street
Indianapolis, IN 46222
(317) 484-6526

Ladies Professional Golf Association (LPGA)
100 International Golf Drive
Daytona Beach, FL 32124
(386) 274-6200

Major League Soccer (MLS)
110 East 42nd Street
10th Floor
New York, NY 10017
(212) 450-1200

National Association for Stock Car Auto Racing (NASCAR)
1801 W. International
 Speedway Boulevard
Daytona Beach, FL 32114
(386) 253-0611

PGA Tour
112 PGA Tour Boulevard
Ponte Vedra Beach, FL 32082
(904) 285-3700

United Soccer Leagues
14497 N. Dale Mabry
 Highway
Suite 201
Tampa, FL 33618
(813) 963-3909

United States Olympic Training Center
One Olympic Plaza
Colorado Springs, CO 80909
(719) 632-5551

USA Basketball
5465 Mark Dabling Boulevard
Colorado Springs, CO 80918
(719) 590-4800

USA Cycling
One Olympic Plaza
Colorado Springs, CO 80909
(719) 866-4581

USA Hockey
1775 Bob Johnson Drive
Colorado Springs, CO 80906
(719) 576-8724

USA Luge
57 Church Street
Lake Placid, NY 12946
(518) 523-2071

USA Swimming
One Olympic Plaza
Colorado Springs, CO 80909
(719) 866-4578

USA Track & Field
1 RCA Dome
Suite 140
Indianapolis, IN 46225
(317) 261-0500

USA Water Polo, Inc.
1631 Mesa Avenue
Suite A-1
Colorado Springs, CO 80906
(719) 634-0866

U.S. Bobsled and Skeleton Federation
196 Old Military Road
PO Box 828
Lake Placid, NY 12946
(518) 523-1842

U.S. Figure Skating Association
20 First Street
Colorado Springs, CO 80906
(719) 635-5200

U.S. Ski and Snowboard Association
Box 100
1500 Kearns Boulevard
Park City, UT 84060
(435) 649-9090

U.S. Soccer Federation
1801 South Prairie Avenue
Chicago, IL 60616
(312) 808-1300

U.S. Speedskating
P.O. Box 450639
Westlake, OH 44145
(440) 899-0128

Women's Tennis Association (WTA)
One Progress Plaza
Suite 1500
St. Petersburg, FL 33701
(727) 895-5000